ACKNOWLEDGMENTS

In the sixteen years it took to research and write this book, I received a great deal of support from those close to me, friends and family, particularly my wife Jaime, who lived with this project every day of her life for nearly fourteen of those years. I will be eternally grateful for her support. I would also like to thank everyone who assisted me by reading at least one full draft of this manuscript at some time during this process: Arthur Hawkeye "Skip" Baebler; John Bercaw; Dr. Eugene F. Diamond; Tim Diamond; Jim Dormuth; Dr. Ben Jagodzinski; Bethany Headley ("Peach Pit"); Joe Long; Alex McGimpsey; Bruce Metge; Myrna Neumann; Kelly Philips; Paul Reeves; Bob Sargus; Fred Weber; and Mike McNaughton (graphics). I would particularly like to thank Phil Foss, who read everything I ever sent him for all sixteen years, including manuscripts, sections, chapters, paragraphs and occasional random thoughts.

Finally, I want to acknowledge the assistance provided by Mr. James O'Shea Wade, whose editorial guidance was invaluable.

»» ««

This is dedicated to all who served . . . and kept the faith.

Table of Contents

Preface

[T]hose who rule the dominant institutions secure their power in large measure, directly and indirectly, by impressing their definition of the situation upon those they rule . . . and significantly limiting what is thought throughout society. . . . Hegemonic ideology enters into everything people do and think. . . . In every sphere of social activity, it meshes with "common sense" through which people make the world seem intelligible; it tries to become that common sense.[1]

Todd Gitlin

Unpopular ideas can be silenced, and inconvenient facts kept dark, without the need for any official ban. Anyone who has lived long in a foreign country will know of instances of sensational items of news—things which on their own merits would get the big headlines—being kept right out of the . . . press, not because the Government intervened but because of a general tacit agreement that 'it wouldn't do' to mention that particular fact. . . . At any given moment there is an orthodoxy, a body of ideas of which it is assumed that all right-thinking people will accept without question. It is not exactly forbidden to say this, that or the other, but it is 'not done' to say it, just as in mid-Victorian times it was 'not done' to mention trousers in the presence of a lady. Anyone who challenges the prevailing orthodoxy finds himself silenced with surprising effectiveness. A genuinely unfashionable opinion is almost never given a fair hearing, either in the popular press or in the high-brow periodicals.[2]

George Orwell

---

1 Todd Gitlin, *The Whole World is Watching: Mass Media in the Making and Unmaking of the New Left* (Berkeley: University of California Press, 1980), 10.

2 George Orwell, "The Freedom of the Press," Proposed Introduction to *Animal Farm*. http://theorwellprize.co.uk/george-orwell/by-orwell/essays-and-other-works/the-freedom-of-the-press, accessed May 10, 2012.

What follows is an examination of America's "long twilight struggle" against Communism and its transition through politics, history and popular culture from "first rough draft" to "hegemonic ideology." From America's Communist movement of the 1930s through the bitter foreign policy battles of the 1980s and our current mania for international socio-political engineering, this book is an exercise in identifying facts that have been hiding in plain sight—"elephants in the room" as they are commonly known—and saying things that, however clear and apparent within the historical literature, it is simply "not done to say." As a work of synthesis rather than original history, this work is necessarily based upon secondary sources, and it epitomizes Orwell's dictum that, "To see what is in front of one's nose needs a constant struggle."[3] Moreover, the historical facts I recount, particularly those that are surprising, disquieting and just "not done" to acknowledge, are accurate and easily checked. I quote liberally from others, moreover, for reasons outlined rather elegantly by Robert Conquest in *Reflections on a Ravaged Century:*

> Much of the knowledge and thought deployed here comes from a wide range of observers and thinkers, and these are given full credit. I have quoted them when, as Montaigne wrote, they do better "what I cannot so well express"; or when their authority gives weight to an argument (or, on the other hand, when a passage is a striking illustration of what I conceive to be an absurdity).[4]

Many people might not like much of what they read here, but I predict a paradigm shift in worldview for those who read with an open mind and consider carefully everything that follows.

---

3 George Orwell, "In Front of Your Nose," *Facing Unpleasant Facts: Narrative Essays (Complete Works of George Orwell)* (New York: Houghton Mifflin Harcourt, 2008), 213.
4 Robert Conquest, *Reflections on a Ravaged Century* (New York: W.W. Norton, 2000), xii-xiii.

Introduction: The Bad War

Vietnam is the shared crime that has turned our country into...a pact of blood. Now patriotism means the complicity of fellows in a crime; if we are all in it, no one is worse than the rest; we excuse each other; we keep the secret. That is why members of the pact had to re-elect a war criminal as their ruler. Senator George S. McGovern was hysterically feared because he was an accuser.

Members of the pact most fear the man who has not joined in their mystery of communal criminality. When ten men commit a crime, and the eleventh refuses, the ten will turn on him, fear him and suspect him. They resent him because he is free, his mouth is not gagged by the knowledge of his own guilt. [1]

Garry Wills

It was a "Bad War" fought for all the wrong reasons and in all the wrong ways...[2]

Peter Marin

What I seek is a reckoning...If healing what the war left behind is possible, I look for such healing in this therapy of honest self-examination and informed acceptance. I also find such a process the most fundamental form of respect. It obliges us to value one another's passing and refuse to spend lives without an accounting. So now, so much later, it is finally time to account.[3]

David Harris

---

1 Quoted in George S. McGovern, *Grassroots: The Autobiography of George McGovern* (New York: Random House, 1977), 245.

2 Peter Marin, "From Their Special Pain: What the Vietnam Vets Can Teach Us," *The Nation,* November 27, 1982, 545-562, 560.

3 David Harris, *Our War* (New York: Times Books, 1996), 3–6.

*W*ashington *Post* publisher Phil Graham once described journalism as the "first rough draft of history," and in 1972, historian Garry Wills, in the quote above, provided a perfect example of history's first rough draft of America's war in Vietnam. According to politicians, pundits, public intellectuals and celebrities from all walks of life, this country's attempt to enforce the Truman Doctrine in Southeast Asia "legitimized murder and expanded murder into genocide."[4] American conduct, we learned from history's first rough draft, included "a monstrous and intentionally genocidal air war";[5] "the day and night bombing of hamlets filled with women, children and the old....";[6] "dropping an enormous weight of explosives on purely civilian targets";[7] and "the massive use of cruel tactics directed indiscriminately against the civilian population in flagrant violation of the minimum rules of war."[8] Senator George McGovern, a decorated World War II veteran and public official with considerable credibility, accused this country of "the most immoral action this nation has ever committed in its national history"; "a policy of mass murder" in Vietnam.[9] Years after the war in Southeast Asia ended, Professor Peter L. Berger of Boston College condemned this country's conduct in Southeast Asia venomously, while admitting that Hanoi's victory was "a human catastrophe of monumental dimensions."[10]

Hand in hand with wholesale condemnation of this country, its armed forces and its allies, history's first rough draft included effusive praise for the Vietnamese Communists. After visiting North Vietnam, Susan Sontag described it as "a place which, in many

---

4 Daniel Berrigan, quoted in Guenter Lewy, *America in Vietnam* (New York: Oxford University Press, 1980), 299.

5 Ibid., 400.

6 Martha Gellhorn, "Suffer the Little Children . . ." *Ladies Home Journal,* January 1967. Reprinted in *Reporting Vietnam, Part One: American Journalism 1959-1969* (New York: Penguin Putnam Inc., 1998), 287, 293.

7 Harrison E. Salisbury, quoted in *Reporting Vietnam, Part One: American Journalism 1959–1969,* 327.

8 Professor Richard A. Falk, quoted in Lewy, *America in Vietnam,* 230.

9 Norman Podhoretz, *Why We Were in Vietnam* (New York: Simon & Schuster, 1982), 156.

10 Peter Berger, "Indochina and the American Conscience," *Commentary,* February 1980, 29-39, 30.

respects, *deserves* to be idealized,"[11] an "ethical society" that functioned "with genuine substantive democracy."[12] Author Mary McCarthy wrote of the Communists in a similar vein, as did Pulitzer Prize-winner Frances FitzGerald,[13] while George McGovern equated Ho Chi Minh with George Washington.[14]

In short, history's first rough draft presented "a 'Bad War' fought for all the wrong reasons and in all the wrong ways,"[15] and by the early 1980s, this represented a "hegemonic ideology" that had entered "into everything people do and think....In every sphere of social activity, it [meshed] with 'common sense' through which people make the world seem intelligible" and had "become that common sense."[16] With an entertainment industry that has "an uncanny ability to dissolve just about anything and incorporate it, transformed and repackaged, into the body politic,"[17] the Bad War, like the Good War before it, was soon part of America's national DNA. Television, the medium that so glorified the heroism of the so-called Greatest Generation in World War II, bombarded society in the post-Vietnam era with tales of drug-addicted, ragged, dysfunctional and homeless veterans. The same Hollywood that gave us movies like *Sands of Iwo Jima, Hell to Eternity,* and, more recently, *Saving Private Ryan* and *Memphis Belle*—which are monuments to the selflessness, courage and fundamental decency of Americans during World War II—produced movies like *Apocalypse Now* and *Platoon,* which consistently depict Americans in Southeast Asia as morons and misfits, psychopaths and sadists (who are invariably in positions of authority) and cowards who will never stand up to the psychopaths and sadists. None have any idea what they are doing or why they are doing it, and a frightful percentage of them just love to rape, pillage and kill.

As one would naturally expect, the real-life veterans, both

11 Podhoretz, *Why We Were in Vietnam,* 90.
12 Ibid., 91–92.
13 Ibid., 92–99.
14 Robert Sam Anson, *McGovern: A Biography* (New York: Holt, Rinehart & Winston, 1972), 180.
15 Marin, "What the Vietnam Vets Can Teach Us," 560.
16 Gitlin, *The Whole World is Watching,* 10.
17 Professor Robert Thompson, "Pop Culture Takes on Terrorism," *New York Times,* August 19, 2002.

during and after the war, paid greatly for history's first rough draft:

> In 1968, while on convalescent leave in Nashville, Tennessee, I witnessed one of the most egregious acts that I had ever seen before or witnessed since. In front of a packed auditorium at Vanderbilt University, the antiwar activist and Yale University chaplain Dr. William Sloane Coffin verbally dismembered a young veteran for voicing that he was proud to have fought for this country in Vietnam. The audience of intelligent Americans was on its feet, hooting and jeering the soldier. I thought they were going to lynch him. Then, I saw his legs. They were cut off at the thighs—blown off by a V.C. land mine.[18]

For those who think treatment like this was atypical, I recommend Bob Greene's *Homecoming*,[19] in which more than 120 veterans recount in their own words being spat upon, cursed, denounced as Fascists and baby killers and even physically assaulted for nothing more than wearing a uniform in public.

History's "first rough draft" was so powerful that, by the mid-1970s, the Truman Doctrine, which gave rise to this country's wars in Korea and Southeast Asia, was repudiated by Truman's own party, and mainstream liberals began embracing revisionist critiques of his presidency that posited moral equivalence between the Western and Communist worlds and blamed Truman for "starting" the Cold War.[20] This was all the rage in the 1970s, when American foreign policy took a left turn, and Jimmy Carter declared

---

18 Gil Dorland, *Legacy of Discord: Voices of the Vietnam Era* (Washington, D.C.: Brassey's, 2001), xi. Frederick Downs, who lost his left arm to a mine near Tam Ky in South Vietnam, was taking classes at the University of Denver in the fall of 1968. Pointing to the hook extending from his left sleeve, a man asked him if he'd gotten that in Vietnam. Downs told him that he had, and the man said, "Serves you right." Frederick Downs, *The Killing Zone: My Life in the Vietnam War* (New York: W.W. Norton & Company, 2007), Preface.

19 Bob Greene, *Homecoming: When the Soldiers Returned from Vietnam* (New York: G.P. Putnam, 1989).

20 See Robert James Maddox, *The New Left and the Origins of the Cold War* (Princeton: Princeton University Press, 1973).

the Cold War at an end. Twenty-five years after leaving office, Harry Truman and his doctrine seemed headed for the ash heap of history in a brave new world in which Henry Wallace, an ardent New Dealer who had been Franklin Roosevelt's vice-president, Truman's secretary of commerce and the Communist Party's choice in the 1948 presidential campaign, would be viewed as a visionary statesman.

But a funny thing happened to pop culture's Bad War on the road from first rough draft to established fact: the stunning collapse of Soviet Communism and all that came with it. This represented an American victory of staggering proportions that, as if rotating a kaleidoscope, created a whole new picture of American Cold War policy, which bears brief, introductory examination.

Beginning in 1947, the United States officially built its foreign policy around one goal: containment of the Soviet Empire and the system on which it was based. To this end, the American people spent trillions of dollars; trained millions of soldiers, airmen, sailors and marines (nearly 100,000 of whom were killed fighting to "contain" Communism); created vast international alliances; formed governments; installed governments; supported governments; opposed governments; overthrew governments; supported wars; opposed wars; fought wars; spied on everyone; and intervened diplomatically, politically, economically and militarily in the affairs of countries all over the world. It was, in terms of duration and cost, the greatest undertaking in this country's history, and despite various setbacks, including the collapse of the so-called anti-Communist consensus and one apparent break in the chain of causation under Jimmy Carter, American victory was total. And with victory came the inevitable conclusion that "the judgment of mid-century America was vindicated."[21]

First was the striking contrast between this country's handiwork and that of the Communists, which was there for everyone to see: stable and prosperous democracies in Western Europe such as France, Holland, West Germany and Italy; broken-down, bankrupt, authoritarian states to the east, such as Romania, East Germany

---

21 Lisle A. Rose, *The Cold War Comes to Main Street: America in 1950* (Lawrence: University Press of Kansas, 1999), 23.

and Yugoslavia, the last of which collapsed into years of near anarchy and genocide. Compare Greece to Albania, South Korea to North Korea, Thailand to what was left of Cambodia after its "cleansing" by the "narrow flame of revolution" so eagerly awaited by Frances FitzGerald.[22] Compare the United States to post-Communist Russia, which, absent nuclear weapons, was little more than a Third World country in 1991 and is not much different today. It was, as they say, a no-brainer. Communism was truly the god that failed and failed catastrophically.

Secondly, Western scholars acquired an all-too-brief glimpse into the Soviet archives at the end of the Cold War, which revealed not just that Stalin and his accomplices were every bit as evil and threatening as anyone imagined,[23] but that the Soviets were bent on initiating world-wide Communist revolution.[24] Last, but not least, there is the body count, both as it actually was and as it might have been.

As many as 100 million murders (not including wartime casualties, military or civilian) are attributable to totalitarian regimes during the twentieth century. Between twelve and fifteen million fell to Nazi violence between 1932 and 1945; the rest were murdered by Communists, who were responsible for "the most colossal case of political carnage in history."[25] "Communist regimes," writes historian Martin Malia, "did not just commit criminal acts (all states do on occasion); they were criminal enterprises in their very essence: on principle, so to speak, they all ruled lawlessly, by violence, and without regard to human life."[26]

So the Cold War has now become, like the Good War that preceded it, a splendid chapter in the American Century in which all Americans can take pride, and America's institutional memory has long been adjusting as needed to bring credit to as many as

---

22 Frances FitzGerald, *Fire in the Lake* (Boston: Little, Brown and Company, 1972), 442.

23 Rose, *The Cold War Comes to Main Street,* 23.

24 Jacob Heilbrunn, "Who Won the Cold War?" *The American Prospect,* September–October 1996, 87.

25 Martin Malia, foreword to *The Black Book of Communism: Crime, Terror Repression,* ed. Stephane Courtois (Cambridge: Harvard University Press, 1999), x.

26 Ibid., xvii.

possible, no matter what the historical record actually shows. Bill Clinton, for example, has told us that "a bipartisan foreign policy" was "one of the greatest sources of our strength throughout the Cold War." "Because our future was at stake," he said, "politics stopped at the water's edge."[27] Former Senator Bill Bradley makes a similar claim: "Until the fall of the Berlin Wall, we were sure about one thing: We knew where we stood on foreign policy."[28] "[T]he overwhelming majority of liberal Americans," wrote Anthony Lewis of the *New York Times,* "supported the West's staunch and successful resistance to Soviet Communism, and look back at that policy with pride."[29]

Now unless I miss my guess, this is the same Bill Clinton who would not serve in the Armed Forces when drafted because the Truman Doctrine's Southeast Asian campaign was a moral blot Americans could never erase. And this is the same Anthony Lewis who called air operations during that war "mass murder" and blasted Ronald Reagan's anti-Communist foreign policy as "simplistic," "sectarian," "terribly dangerous," "outrageous" and "primitive."[30] You would not, however, know any of this by examining popular culture today because America's Cold War victory brought many previously contested issues into sharp focus, and as Lawrence Kaplan noted in the *Wall Street Journal,* "We're all cold warriors now."[31] This revisionism conferred enormous ideological and political value on America's war in Korea, which was *the* pivotal moment in Cold War history in which Democrats, who have had political difficulty on defense and national security issues since the Vietnam era, made all the decisions that mattered. So the Forgotten War, as it was called, has now been resurrected, sanitized, remembered and embraced by the Vital Center Democrats as a fine, proud chapter in the American Century.[32]

---

27 Bill Clinton, 1997 State of the Union Address. http://clinton2.nara.gov/WH/SOU97/, accessed May 10, 2012.

28 "The Bradley Foreign Policy," *Washington Post,* December 1, 1999.

29 "Abroad at Home; Ghosts," *New York Times,* May 6, 2000.

30 "Abroad at Home; Onward Christian Soldiers," *New York Times,* March 10, 1983.

31 "We're All Cold Warriors Now," *Wall Street Journal,* January 18, 2000.

32 "Vital Center," which is a term I will use regularly, is taken from the title of Arthur M. Schlesinger's 1949 book, *The Vital Center: The Politics of Freedom* (New York: Da Capo Press, 1988).

Born-again cold warrior Bill Clinton praises American intervention in Korea because it "put the Free World on the road to victory in the Cold War...."[33] Korea, Clinton tells us, was the war that "kept the flame burning so that others across the world could share it."[34] "Righteousness," said Clinton of Truman's war in Korea, "overcomes all obstacles."[35]

Clinton was joined in his praise of this newly discovered "righteousness" by former governor, senator and Vietnam combat veteran Bob Kerrey. Although Kerrey told Don Imus on May 30, 2002, that he could not understand why it took Richard Nixon five years to abandon Southeast Asia to the Communists, which was clearly the right result in his view, he had this to say three months later about Korea:

> And then I'm sitting in a joint session of Congress, and I'm listening to Kim Dae-Jung of South Korea, and he says, "I'm alive because of America, and my people are free because of America," and I remember Oliver Waite, my first employer when I came home, and how bitter he was about the Korean War. He thought it was a waste of lives and blood. Well, it turns out it wasn't if you're one of the 44 million people living south of the 38th parallel.[36]

Just why, I wonder, are the forty-four million Koreans living south of the 38th parallel, like the people of Western Europe and Japan, entitled to America's protection from the well-documented ravages of Communism when millions of Vietnamese living south of the 17th parallel apparently are not? What makes Koreans so much higher and nobler a form of life? Kerrey, of course, provides no answers, and his myopia is widespread.

When reports surfaced in the fall of 1999 that American troops had killed a large number of Korean civilians in the summer of 1950

---

33 Charles J. Hanley, Sang-Hun Choe and Martha Mendoza, *The Bridge at No Gun Ri: A Hidden Nightmare from the Korean War* (New York: Henry Holt and Company, 2000), 239.

34 Ibid.

35 Ibid., 240.

36 "Two Questions for Bob Kerrey," *Esquire*, August 2002, 36.

at No Gun Ri, no one attempted to use this as an excuse to attack this country over its intervention in Korea. In fact, just the opposite occurred. The following from Charles Lane, writing in the *New Republic,* typifies the response of America's politicians, pundits and public intellectuals to the No Gun Ri affair:

> But let's hope that this won't turn into an occasion to besmirch the entire Korean War or to otherwise tilt the discussion of the U.S. role in the cold war. Horrible as it appears to have been, the No Gun Ri massacre does not invalidate the U.N.-sanctioned American effort to roll back a North Korean invasion, which, if successful, would have subjected the entire Korean peninsula to a long, dark night of official and economic deprivation.[37]

With this country's Cold War victory shining new light on Korea while bringing a vastly different perspective to many bitterly disputed issues, it was inevitable that the Bad War would make its own transition through America's institutional memories, and in time it did. Except for the ranting of a few die-hards,[38] tales of America's Bad War, which formed the bedrock of the antiwar movement, have almost disappeared from mainstream culture. Compare, for example, *In Country, Platoon,* and *Apocalypse Now* to the highly acclaimed 2002 cinematic blockbuster, *We Were Soldiers Once, and Young.* Everyone loved *We Were Soldiers* even though the movie contains not one instance of rape, murder or

---

37 Charles Lane, "Wounded," *New Republic,* October 25, 1999, 6. It should be noted that the precise nature of this incident was hotly disputed, and many of the facts included in the initial reports were quickly disproved. "The key player in the AP atrocity story, Ed Daily, was nowhere near the alleged site of No Gun Ri," noted the *Wall Street Journal* on June 5, 2000. In fact, Ed Daily served as a clerk and mechanic with the 27th Ordnance Maintenance Company and joined the Seventh Cavalry for but a short period some eight months after the incident at No Gun Ri. Daily cashed in on his claims, however, collecting some $2,300 per month in non-taxable disability payments from the Veterans Administration because of PTSD brought on by the horrors he supposedly witnessed in Korea. In April 2002, he pleaded guilty in federal court in Nashville, Tennessee, to defrauding the government of $412,839 in veteran's benefits and medical care after admitting to federal agents that his stories of the No Gun Ri affair were false.

38 See David Harris, *Our War* (New York: Times Books, 1996).

psychotic behavior by American personnel. Not a single officer is depicted as a moron or psychopath, and no one hates the Army, his country or the fact that he is fighting in Vietnam. In fact, the troops involved are depicted exactly like those in *Saving Private Ryan:* They are decent young men fighting and coping in a hard and brutal war. For those who know their history, *We Were Soldiers* is nothing short of amazing, and had I not lived to see it, I would never have believed it. Indeed, revisionism has reached the point where phonies claiming service in Southeast Asia are everywhere, being found among prominent people in all walks of life, including actors (Brian Dennehy[39]), politicians (Senator Tom Harkin;[40] Connecticut Senator Richard Blumenthal[41]) and renowned academics, like Pulitzer Prize-winning historian Professor Joseph Ellis.[42]

John Kerry's decorations, which he famously and publicly discarded in shame in 1971 while a national leader of Vietnam Veterans against the War, magically re-appeared and, in 2003, were prominently displayed in his senate office. Kerry proudly reminded Chris Matthews on *Hardball* that the men who fought in Vietnam never lost a battle. While running for the presidency, Kerry's official web site was filled with speeches in which he speaks with pride about his "fellow veterans." "There's a bond there which is hard to explain," he tells us. It is a "very, very special bond" between "a band of brothers." And he takes every opportunity to assure us that this country has never produced a finer group of "citizen soldiers" than those who served in Southeast Asia: "Make no mistake. American intentions were noble, and no soldiers have ever fought with more bravery or selflessness for their country."[43] "[T]he people who put on the uniform served with equal courage, equal commitment and

39 Burkett and Whitley, *Stolen Valor: How the Vietnam Generation was Robbed of Its Heroes and Its History* (Dallas: Verity Press, 1998), 164. See also Mark Holzer and Erica Holzer, *Fake Warriors: Identifying, Exposing and Punishing Those Who Falsify Their Military Service* (Bloomington: Xlibris, 2003).
40 Burkett and Whitley, *Stolen Valor,* 182.
41 "Candidate's Words Differ from His History," *New York Times,* May 18, 2010; "Vietnam Claims Grew in Time, Colleague Says," *New York Times,* May 19, 2010.
42 "Professor's Past in Doubt; Discrepancies Surface in Claim of Vietnam Duty," *Boston Globe,* June 18, 2001; "College Notes Regret on Falsities by Professor," *Boston Globe,* June 20, 2001.
43 World Affairs Council, Boston, Massachusetts, September 10, 2001.

an equal sense of contribution as anybody else in any other war and in any other time in American history."[44]

Now I find it somewhat strange that a man who appeared before a senate committee in 1971 and accused the veterans of rape, torture and murder "on a day-to-day basis with the full awareness of the officers at every level of command"[45] later praised those same veterans as fine, heroic men, and I find it even stranger that virtually no one ever seemed to notice this amazing transformation. But "in America," as the philosopher George Santayana once observed, "ideas are abandoned in virtue of a mere change of feeling, without any new evidence or new arguments. We do not nowadays refute our predecessors, we pleasantly bid them good-bye."[46] And in time, Americans bid goodbye to the Bad War in favor of viewing it as an "unwinnable" campaign that our leaders entered mistakenly but in good faith during a righteous Cold War. South Vietnam, David Halberstam told us nearly forty years ago, was involved in a revolutionary, anti-colonial struggle that did not lend itself to American meddling or military solutions: "This was a political war; one could not produce military answers."[47]

Over time, the "mistaken," "unwinnable," "political" war supplanted the Bad War and made the transition from hypothesis to orthodoxy. Robert Mann writes in *A Grand Delusion: America's Descent into Vietnam*, that the men who initiated this disaster were "well-meaning but misguided American leaders."[48] Ken Burns duly parrots this, telling us that the war "was begun in good faith by decent people."[49] Colonel Harry G. Summers states that "it was a violation of [the truths and principles of war], not evil or wicked leaders" that was the cause of our undoing," citing David

---

44 Keynote address, Congressional Black Caucus/Veterans Braintrust, September 22, 2002.

45 Congressional Record (92nd Congress, 1st Session), Thursday, April 22, 1971, pages 179-180.

46 George Santayana, *Character and Opinion in the United States* (New Haven: Yale University Press, 2009), 28.

47 David Halberstam, *The Best and the Brightest* (New York: Ballantine Books, 1992), 300.

48 Robert Mann, *A Grand Delusion: America's Descent into Vietnam* (New York: Basic Books, 2001), 4.

49 Ken Burns, *The Vietnam War: An Intimate History* (New York: Alfred A. Knopf, 2017), front matter.

Halberstam as authority.[50] Norman Hannah, a Foreign Service
Officer from 1947-1977, concluded, like Summers, that America's
war in Southeast Asia was winnable. Yet he assures us that Kennedy
and his "best and brightest" tried "to do the right thing."[51] Indeed,
many of those personally involved in the events Halberstam
chronicled advance this view. Clark Clifford, who was a top adviser
to both Harry Truman and John Kennedy and secretary of defense
under Johnson, described American intervention in Vietnam as
"not only tragic, [but] a cauldron in which good and able men of
high integrity, acting out of solid and well-reasoned motives, went
terribly wrong."[52] "Countries, like human beings, make mistakes.
We made an honest mistake. I feel no sense of shame. We felt what
we were doing was necessary. It proved to be unsound."[53]

Equally important today is the way this tragic mistake was
corrected through the efforts of equally good and able men of high
integrity—men like George McGovern, who praised the outcome of
the war in Southeast Asia as a "tribute" to American democracy:

> It is said by the supporters of the Vietnam War that
> the war was not lost in Vietnam but in the antiwar
> movement in America. *I hope that is a correct
> analysis.* It would be the highest tribute both to the
> antiwar movement and to American democracy if it
> could be firmly established that organized public
> opinion and political action were responsible for
> correcting the enormous blunders of the leaders who
> took us into the jungles of Vietnam.[54]

50 Col. Harry G. Summers, Jr., *On Strategy: A Critical Analysis of the Vietnam War* (Novato, California: Presidio Press, 1995), 181-182.

51 Norman Hannah, *The Key to Failure, Laos & the Vietnam War* (Lanham, Maryland: Madison Books, 1987),, xi.

52 Clark Clifford, *Counsel to the President* (New York: Random House, 1991), 403. See also Arthur M. Schlesinger, *The Bitter Harvest: Vietnam and the American Democracy, 1941–1966* (Boston: Houghton Mifflin, 1967), 31–32: It was unfair, said Schlesinger, "to seek out guilty men." The Vietnam conflict was "a tragedy without villains."

53 Stanley Karnow, *Vietnam: A History* (New York: The Viking Press, 1983), 20–21.

54 Adam Garfinkle, *Telltale Hearts: The Origins and Impact of the Vietnam Antiwar Movement* (New York: St. Martin's Press, 1995), 11 (emphasis in the original).

John Kerry shares McGovern's outlook, embracing defeat in Southeast Asia as a "triumph of the system"[55] that legitimizes his own conduct while providing the requisite silver lining to an otherwise dark cloud.

This, in its essence, forms the orthodox view, which critiques America's "mistake" in Southeast Asia without examining or challenging the long-term policies that gave rise to it because those very policies, in Bill Clinton's words, "put the Free World on the road to victory in the Cold War...."[56] This view is easy to propagate, is uniquely suited to providing the greatest comfort to the greatest number and leaves Americans reasonably satisfied with the last seventy years of the American Century. After all, they "saved the world" from 1941-1945, kept the flame of freedom burning brightly through their righteous, half-century Cold War that began in earnest with their "defense of democracy" in Korea and acted with both wisdom and courage to correct an honest mistake in Southeast Asia, ending the war on the Communists' terms because that gave rise to the historically and morally correct result. This makes Americans as wise, noble, selfless and courageous as any people who ever lived. *They are not perfect (the war in Vietnam proved that), but they are as good as it gets, and they have every reason to be proud.* This forms a perfect foundation for this country's national ideology, which can fairly be titled "American Exceptionalism."[57] And this is all very nice, if only it were true.

You see, I take my history non-fiction. I have an abiding respect for the historical record, rules of evidence and the power of reason, and I judge this country's wars by a single, reasonably objective set of standards that I apply to the conduct of enemies, allies and Americans. So I am unable to look back through history and find either the "Once-Forgotten-but-Recently Remembered-and-Now-Very-Righteous-and-Necessary War" or the "Once-Bad-but-Carefully Reconsidered-and-Now-Just-Mistaken War" within a

---

55 Dorland, *Legacy of Discord*, 115.

56 Hanley, Choe and Mendoza, *The Bridge at No Gun Ri,* 239.

57 "The body of ideas reflecting the social needs and aspirations of an individual, a group, a class or a culture." *The American Heritage Dictionary of the English Language* (Third Edition), Houghton Mifflin Company, 1992.

noble campaign to save the world from Communism in which Americans stood shoulder to shoulder under the leadership of, with a couple of exceptions, intelligent, courageous statesmen who acted in the national interest to the best of their abilities. I am also unable to find well-meaning but misguided American leaders—good and able men of high integrity—who mistakenly took this country into Southeast Asia while acting in good faith and trying to do the right thing in the national interest. *Such men are nowhere to be found.*

What I find instead is a grossly dysfunctional political system and a political class that, focused primarily on domestic politics, mostly stumbled, bumbled, lied and connived its way through the Cold War from one election cycle to the next, deceiving itself, its citizens and their allies and enemies alike. I find a "long twilight struggle" that ended as it did, when it did, due far more to dumb luck, unintended consequences and the relentless stupidity of our adversaries than any bi-partisan, long-term strategy. Where our "history" is concerned, I find an elaborate, disingenuous narrative in which Communism was bad, unless it was not. Communists were evil, except when they weren't. Communism had to be contained, even when millions had to die at American hands, except when it did not. Those who enforced the Truman Doctrine, like Harry Truman and Dean Acheson, were great statesmen, leaders and heroes standing tall for America—no matter where they intervened, no matter how corrupt and authoritarian their proxies and no matter how many laws they broke, bombs they dropped, countries they destroyed or non-combatants they slaughtered. Unless, of course, like Richard Nixon and Henry Kissinger, they were not.

Seen for the forest rather than the trees, little of the orthodox narrative makes any sense. Yet I find any attempt to discuss it largely pointless. Whether it be the propriety of intervention, the nature and quality of enemies or allies, American strategy and tactics or the casualties inflicted, I never get beyond the kind of mindless exchange recounted by Colonel Harry Summers in *On Strategy:*

> To many civilians it is axiomatic that the Vietnam
> War was the cruelest ever waged. To those of us who
> experienced war firsthand, this is hard to

understand. To the evidence of Vietnam cruelty portrayed by the horrible picture of the little girl running down the road seared with napalm, one asks about the tens of thousands of little girls incinerated in the fire bomb raids on Dresden and Tokyo in World War II only to be told, *"But that was different."* To the terrible picture of the Saigon police chief shooting the Viet Cong terrorist, one asks about the summary justice of the French Maquis or the Italian partisans and their photographs of Mussolini and his mistress strung up by their heels, only again to be told, *"That was different."* To those condemning the remark of the Army captain in the Delta that "we had to destroy the town in order to save it," one quotes the Continental Congress's orders, "If General Washington and his council of war should be of the opinion that a successful attack may be made on the [British] troops in Boston, he [may] do it in any manner he may think expedient, notwithstanding the town and the property in it may thereby be destroyed." Yet again the answer, *"That was different."*[58]

This kind of subrational thinking stems from an irreconcilable conflict between history and ideology, and as Hannah Arendt once noted, "Nothing so inoculates a person against reality than the hold of ideology."[59] Facts, no matter how clearly established, and arguments, no matter how principled or logical, that conflict with contemporary American ideology trigger deeply ingrained processes designed to "safeguard the infallibility of the [country]," which must "in all cases" be right.[60] *"[A]nd if the facts say otherwise, then the facts must be altered."*[61] Outlined by George

---

58 Summers, *On Strategy:,* xxxii37.

59 Quoted by John Howard Smith, faculty web pages, Texas A & M University. http://faculty.tamu-commerce.edu/jsmith/default.htm, accessed November 23, 2009.

60 George Orwell, *Nineteen Eighty-Four* (New York: Alfred A. Knopf, 1992), 221–222.

61 Orwell, *Nineteen Eighty-Four*, 222 (emphasis added).

Orwell more than half a century ago, these processes, with only slight modification, fit contemporary American society like a glove:

> The first and simplest stage in the discipline, which can be taught even to young children, is called, in Newspeak, *crimestop*. *Crimestop* means the faculty of stopping short, as though by instinct, at the threshold of any dangerous thought. It includes the power of not grasping analogies, of failing to perceive logical errors, of misunderstanding the simplest arguments if they are inimical to [American Exceptionalism], and of being bored and repelled by any train of thought which is capable of leading in a heretical direction. *Crimestop*, in short, means protective stupidity. But stupidity is not enough. On the contrary, orthodoxy in the full sense demands a control over one's own mental processes as complete as that of a contortionist over his body. [American] society rests ultimately on the belief that [American democracy] is omnipotent and that [the country] is infallible. But since in reality [American democracy] is not omnipotent and [the country] is not infallible, there is a need for an unwearying, moment-to-moment flexibility in the treatment of facts. The key word here is *blackwhite*. Like so many Newspeak words, this word has two mutually contradictory meanings. Applied to an opponent, it means the habit of imprudently claiming that black is white, in contradiction of the plain facts. Applied to a party member, it means a loyal willingness to say that black is white when Party discipline demands this. But it also means an ability to *believe* that black is white, and more, to *know* that black is white, and to forget that one has ever believed to the contrary. This demands a continuous alteration of the past, made possible by the system of thought which really embraces all the rest, and which is known in Newspeak as *Doublethink*....

> *Doublethink* means the power of holding two contradictory beliefs in one's mind simultaneously, and accepting them both....*Doublethink* lies at the very heart of [American Exceptionalism] since the essential act of [American society] is to use conscious deception while retaining the firmness of purpose that goes with complete honesty. To tell deliberate lies while genuinely believing in them, to forget any fact that has become inconvenient, and then, when it becomes necessary again, to draw it back from oblivion for just so long as it is needed, to deny the existence of objective reality and all the while to take account of the reality which one denies—all this is indispensably necessary.[62]

Though Americans have no official "Ministry of Truth" and no legal enforcement of orthodoxy, *crimestop, blackwhite, doublethink* and "readjustment of the past" are as essential to American society as they were to Orwell's fictional Oceania. This is why, in the words of David Halberstam, "Vietnam never goes away." As "the second American civil war...[,] [i]t's really against us."[63] And David Halberstam should know, as he virtually personified the problem, not the solution.

A highly acclaimed producer and purveyor of orthodoxy in all particulars, David Halberstam was very much a "party intellectual" in the Orwellian mode.[64] In his acclaimed work, *The Best and the Brightest,* which is still considered a must-read for anyone with an interest in the Vietnam War, Halberstam examined both Vietnamese and American society from every conceivable angle—historical, military and political—and simply demolished the assumptions and decision-making that drove American intervention. After reading history according to David Halberstam,

---

62 Ibid., 220–223.

63 David Halberstam quoted in *Time,* August 20, 2001, 48.

64 "The party intellectual knows in which direction his memories must be altered, therefore he knows that he is playing tricks with reality; but by the exercise of *doublethink,* he also satisfies himself that reality is not violated." Orwell, *Nineteen Eighty-Four,* 223.

one questions not only the judgment of those who mired this country in Vietnam but their very right to have intervened at all. And what, according to Halberstam, drove Americans to such folly? "McCarthyism," which, Halberstam tells us in the 1992 edition of *The Best and the Brightest,* played a far greater role in foreign policy that he previously believed. "[A]s I ponder the importance of the McCarthy era on both our domestic and foreign policy, I am convinced that this flaw in the society was even greater than I portrayed it, and if I were to do [*The Best and the Brightest*] over, I might expand the entire section." [65]

Over time, Halberstam exerted such influence over "an interwoven community of pundits, reporters, academics and foreign policy and military experts" [66]—"those who rule the dominant institutions"—that his basic analysis eventually transitioned to a form of "hegemonic ideology," "significantly limiting what is thought throughout society." [67] Daniel Ellsberg, for example, shared Halberstam's view regarding "the crucial relevance of McCarthy's career to our present position" in 1972, [68] and thirty years later, he continued to blame the Vietnam War on Joseph McCarthy: "In late 1949, with Communist victory in China—and with the rise of Senator Joseph McCarthy in early 1950, charging with others that it was Democratic malfeasance or worse that had led to the 'fall of China'—the U.S. administration suddenly saw preventing Communist control of Indochina as an American interest." [69]

Like many, there was a time when I accepted much of this. There is just no denying that McCarthy was a drunk, a fool and a liar who seemed to surround himself with others just like him, and where American intervention in Vietnam is concerned, the "received wisdom" of liberals, who maintained that his anti-Communist

---

65 Halberstam, *The Best and the Brightest,* xviii.

66 Gordon M. Goldstein, *Lessons in Disaster: McGeorge Bundy and the Path to War in* (New York: Times Books, 2008), 147.

67 Gitlin, *The Whole World is Watching,* 10.

68 Daniel Ellsberg, *Papers on the War* (New York: Simon and Schuster, 1972), 288–289.

69 Daniel Ellsberg, *Secrets: A Memoir of Vietnam and the Pentagon Papers* (New York: Viking Penguin, 2002), 253.

crusade created a momentum that ultimately led us into Vietnam, seemed infinitely plausible. But after years of studying the historical record, I realized that Halberstam's analysis is profoundly incomplete, factually inaccurate and intellectually dishonest, as exemplified by his treatment of a most crucial frame of reference, America's war in Korea. "Stopping short, as though by instinct, at the threshold of any dangerous thought," displaying a highly developed "power of not grasping analogies, of failing to perceive logical errors," Halberstam to his dying day pushed the official, United States government-sanctioned version of the Korean War like some bureaucrat in a Ministry of Truth, as evidenced by the following piece, which appeared in *AARP* in the summer of 2003:

> In 1945, when the Americans reclaimed the Korean peninsula from its Japanese invaders, they divided it at the 38th parallel. The land north of that line became a Communist country, under the influence and protection of the Soviet Union. South Korea came under the protection of the U.S. On June 25, 1950, for reasons that still remain somewhat unclear, the North Koreans attacked South Korea, and the world changed.... [70] Truman's original decision to respond to the North Korean invasion still seems to me to have been the right choice. The U.S. entered because a border had been crossed; the need to confront aggressors early had been an essential lesson of World War II. Although the war did not end in an outright victory, it did mark the last, as well as the first, time a Communist country openly crossed the border of a U.S. ally. In that sense, painful though it was, what the U.S. did in Korea worked. North Korea retrenched, and the South became an advertisement for how a once dictatorial, feudal society can evolve, in a relatively short time, into an infinitely more admirable

---

70 David Halberstam, "This is Korea, Fifty Years Later," *AARP,* July and August 2003, 48, 50.

society.[71]

For anyone familiar with the skepticism and highly developed analytical skills so prominently displayed by Halberstam in *The Best and the Brightest,* this statement is nothing short of amazing. Halberstam never analyzed or critiqued *anything* done in connection with American "success" in Korea as he did with American failure in Vietnam. "Americans," he told us, "*reclaimed the Korean peninsula*" from Japanese "invaders" as though Americans were not "invaders" because, apparently, Korea was somehow theirs to "reclaim." He accepted without question this country's right to divide Korea with the Soviet Union like Hitler and Stalin divided Poland and create an American protectorate in the South while avoiding any analysis of either the regime Truman imposed on South Korea ("essentially demagogues bent on autocratic rule," according to the CIA[72]) or the ruthless measures undertaken by America's proxies to facilitate American policy from 1946-1950 ("a cloud of terror...probably unparalleled in the world," according to *New York Times* reporter Walter Sullivan[73]). He labeled the other side "Communist," as if Kim Il Sung was somehow less a nationalist than Ho Chi Minh, and accused "North" Koreans of crossing a "border" as "aggressors" without explaining just how Koreans cross a "border" to invade Korea. And how, with fifty years for a historian of Halberstam's reputation to study the Korean War, which is crucial to his own analysis of this country's failure in Vietnam, could he tell us in 2003 that the reasons for the Korean War "still remain somewhat unclear" when he harbored no similar questions about Hanoi's war to unite Vietnam under its rule?

It also seems apparent that if the inflexible, all-consuming anti-Communism that drove this country into Southeast Asia is somehow attributable to Joseph McCarthy, the cornerstone of Cold War policy should be called not the Truman Doctrine but the McCarthy Doctrine. And since this doctrine, at least according to

---

71 Ibid., 86.

72 Jon Halliday and Bruce Cumings, *Korea: The Unknown War* (New York: Pantheon Books, 1988), 23.

73 Ibid., 45.

current orthodoxy, provided the ideological and political basis for the Marshall Plan, NATO, the Berlin Airlift and American intervention in Greece, China, Korea, the Philippines, Central America, the Middle East and Southeast Asia, Joseph McCarthy should receive as much credit for American success in the Cold War as he receives blame for the failure in Vietnam. Yet I have never heard David Halberstam or anyone else praise Joseph McCarthy for his splendid, brilliantly engineered victory over Soviet Communism.

As to the so-called McCarthy era that supposedly formed so crucial a role in American history, Halberstam advanced what he labeled a "revolutionary idea": "I believe from my research that the McCarthy period begins and gets a virus into the bloodstream of the society when the Republicans lose to Truman in '48."[74] That Halberstam considers "revolutionary" the idea that "McCarthyism" long pre-dated McCarthy is a sad commentary on the study of history in this country. Anyone who knows anything about American history knows that the politics of the Truman Era long pre-dated McCarthy, a fact George Kennan noted more than forty years ago: "What was involved here was a phenomenon that existed well before the prominent appearance of Senator Joseph McCarthy on the national scene....He was its creature, not its creator."[75]

What *is* revolutionary, however, was Halberstam's willingness to admit that McCarthy was not really responsible for "McCarthyism," which brings the real question into sharp focus: If McCarthy is not responsible for "McCarthyism," who was? Halberstam, of course, had the proper, ideologically correct answer: Republicans. (Now there is a big surprise!) *"They* lost four times to Roosevelt," Halberstam said. *"They* are chomping at the bit. *They* are already afraid that they are going to be a permanent minority party." So *they* "seize on another issue": "subversion in

74 Brian Lamb, interview of David Halberstam, *Booknotes,* July 11, 1993. Transcript available at http://www.booknotes.org/Transcript/index_print.asp?ProgramID=115, accessed October 26, 2009. Halberstam restated this analysis in March 2006 during his keynote address at a conference sponsored by the Presidential Libraries and the National Archives and Records Administration entitled "Vietnam and the Presidency."
75 George F. Kennan, *Memoirs: 1950–1963* (New York: Pantheon, 1972), 190.

government."[76] It was all just irresistible to a Vital Center liberal. After all, why should Joseph McCarthy bear all the blame when there is enough disinformation available to vilify and delegitimize an entire political order?

Well, as I stated earlier, I take my history non-fiction, which leads me to advance what is, but should not be, a *genuinely* revolutionary idea: 1948 is not year zero, and the "McCarthy era" was but one manifestation of a "virus" that entered "the bloodstream of the society" long before, as outlined by film and cultural critic Robert Warshow in a 1947 essay entitled "The Legacy of the '30s":

> For most American intellectuals, the Communist movement of the 1930s was a crucial experience....[It] was a time when virtually all intellectual vitality was derived in one way or another from the Communist Party. If you were not somewhere within the Party's wide orbit, then you were likely to be in the opposition, which meant that much of your thought and energy had to be devoted to maintaining yourself in opposition. In either case, it was the Communist party that ultimately determined what you were to think about and in what terms.[77]

The result was an age of "organized mass disingenuousness" and "a disastrous vulgarization of intellectual life in which the character of American liberalism and radicalism was decisively—and perhaps permanently—corrupted."[78] Nowhere do we find a better example of this corruption today than in the orthodox Cold War narrative, which begins shortly after World War II, when we are to believe that the course of history was set by two towering figures, Harry Truman and Joseph McCarthy, and their Manichean

---

76 Brian Lamb interview of David Halberstam on July 11, 1993 (emphasis added). *Booknotes.* http://www.booknotes.org/Transcript/?ProgramID=1157, accessed January, 15 2004.

77 Robert Warshow, *The Immediate Experience: Movies, Comics, Theatre and Other Aspects of American Culture* (Cambridge: Harvard University Press, 2001), 3.

78 Ibid., 3–4.

struggle for the soul of America. Truman, orthodoxy tells us, was a statesman and hero who withstood years of abuse and scurrilous attacks to emerge with "one of the most successful presidencies of the 20th Century,"[79] having set America on the road to Cold War victory while protecting American civil liberties.[80] His nemesis, Joseph McCarthy, was an unprincipled demagogue supported by others just like him who, representing the darkest forces in American society, orchestrated a vast, right-wing conspiracy against this country's righteous progressives that "transformed politics and society,"[81] doing enormous, long-term damage that drove this country into an unwinnable, neo-colonial war in Southeast Asia and that plagues us to this very day.

David Halberstam (among many others[82]) spent years spinning this yarn into an elaborate analysis of American foreign policy during two phases of the Cold War in which Democrats held all the reins of power, the Truman Era (1945-1953) and the Kennedy/Johnson era (1961-1968), devoting most of his efforts to the latter, which only makes sense. After all, for those who embrace this country's "long twilight struggle" as a proud and righteous chapter in the American experience as Halberstam did (at least once the final outcome was known), Truman's foreign policy requires little explanation or defense because: 1) Truman's actions appear consistent with his rhetoric and his immediate objectives; 2) there is virtually no historical record of indecision or self-doubt on his part; 3) the war in Korea, however ugly, is officially listed in the "win" column; and 4) this country's Cold War victory can be traced

---

79 "Reluctant but Ready," *Chicago Tribune,* May 6, 2008, sec. 1.

80 Lynne Joiner, *Honorable Survivor: Mao's China, McCarthy's America, and the Persecution of John S. Service* (Annapolis: Naval Institute Press, 2009), 216: "Truman was determined to eliminate real security risks while protecting the nation's civil rights."

81 David Aaronovitch, *Voodoo Histories: The Role of Conspiracy Theory in Shaping Modern History* (New York: Riverhead Books, 2010), 340.

82 The earliest example of the McCarthy-centric thesis I have found appeared in the April 1968 edition of the *Atlantic Monthly.* See "How Could Vietnam Happen? – An Autopsy," in which James C. Thomson, Jr., cited "*the legacy of the 1950s* – by which I mean the so-called 'loss of China,' the Korean War, and the Far East policy of Secretary of State Dulles," as a primary force driving the world view of JFK and his best and brightest.

http://www.theatlantic.com/past/docs/issues/68apr/vietnam.htm, accessed January 10, 2012.

in fact through a chain of events Truman initiated. In other words, the record, appropriately edited, can be read to support claims that Truman meant what he said, acted in conformance with his stated beliefs and achieved his stated objectives, which, given the Cold War's ultimate outcome, are viewed favorably today.

The war in Southeast Asia, however, is far more problematic for those who promote the orthodox version of Cold War history.

As with the Truman Era, all critical decisions during the Kennedy/Johnson era were made by liberal Democrats, but not one of those decisions was, on its alleged merits, even rational, much less defensible. We also have a rich historical record documenting both Kennedy's and Johnson's firmly held belief that this country had no interests in Southeast Asia sufficient to justify military intervention, leaving just one explanation for their conduct, as David Halberstam long acknowledged: "considerations of domestic politics, and [the] political fears of the consequences of looking weak in the forthcoming domestic election."[83] Given this inept, craven, illegal and supremely corrupt behavior and its bloody, humiliating result, the "Greatest Generation's" Democrats are uniquely beyond redemption absent some way to mitigate or shift blame for their actions. This is why the powerful, transcendent demonology of "McCarthyism" is indispensable, providing as it does the all-purpose tool by which the liberal Vital Center can lay claim to all the Cold War's perceived historical and political assets while assigning the bulk of its liabilities to the political Right and stifling debate whenever dissent rears its ugly head.

Yet however carefully designed to bring the greatest comfort to the greatest number while promoting the interests of "those who rule the dominant institutions," the orthodox, McCarthy-centric narrative floats on a sea of *doublethink*. Each and every factual and analytical point on which it depends—the dishonesty and bad faith underlying the Right's charges of Soviet espionage, the loyalty and integrity of those accused, the essential differences between Communists in Greece and Korea, on the one hand, and those in Vietnam on the other, the "well-meaning and intelligent"[84] nature

---

83 Halberstam, *The Best and the Brightest*, xviii.

84 Colonel Harry Summers cites David Halberstam as definitive authority in assuring us that

of Democrats who acted as best they could in the national interest—is crucial. Altering even one creates an entirely new picture, and the new picture appears with the now-undeniable fact that, in the words of American Communist Party member Alfred Bernstein, father of *Washington Post* reporter Carl Bernstein, "McCarthy was right":

> I think you do a disservice if you do this...You're muffing the problem; you're going to write about political oppression from the wrong perspective. *The premise people eventually accepted after the McCarthy period was that the victims weren't Communists. If you're going to write a book that says McCarthy was right, that a lot of us were Communists, you're going to write a dangerous book....*You're going to prove McCarthy right, because all he was saying was that the system was loaded with Communists. And he was right. You've got to take a big hard look at what you are doing, because the whole fight against him was that people weren't Communists.[85]

McCarthy was right! The phrase itself is practically an assault, and were the speaker not a card-carrying Communist and the chronicler not his own son—a sympathetic journalist with unimpeachable liberal credentials—it would be dismissed as the ranting of a disordered mind. But the truth eventually came to light, as columnist Nicholas Von Hoffman acknowledged in 1996: "Point by point Joe McCarthy got it all wrong, and yet he was still closer to the truth than those who ridiculed him."[86] For the collapse of the Soviet Union opened both Soviet and American intelligence archives to Western scholars, if only briefly, and we now know that McCarthy's charges were not, as we have been told for more than

---

America's war in Southeast Asia "was waged by well-meaning and intelligent men doing what they thought best." See Summers, *On Strategy,* 181–182.

85 Carl Bernstein, *Loyalties: A Son's Memoir* (New York: Simon and Schuster, 1989), 78–79 (emphasis added).

86 Nicholas Von Hoffman, "Was McCarthy Right about the Left?" *The Washington Post,* April 14, 1996.

half a century, baseless, groundless and irrational. The United States government *was* deeply and extensively penetrated by American citizens working for Soviet intelligence during the 1930s and 1940s, and many among this country's political and intellectual leadership knew it all along, as Daniel Patrick Moynihan noted in his 1998 book *Secrecy*.[87] So McCarthy's excesses notwithstanding, the "big lie" was not so much the accusation as the denial, which returns us to Robert Warshow, who did more in 1947 to identify the seminal cause of America's path through the Cold War with a fifteen-page essay than all the historical works, good and bad, produced in the last half-century. "[T]he center of the problem," he explained, "is in the political-intellectual movement of the 30s. The problem developed over many years and through many historical factors, but it happened in the 1930s. Thus it becomes our central intellectual task to evolve some method of assimilating the experience of those years if only to perfect our understanding of our cultural failure."[88]

Now "the problem" at the center of Robert Warshow's essay— "organized mass disingenuousness," "disastrous vulgarization of intellectual life" and corruption of American liberalism—was more cultural than political as he viewed it. He was, after all, a film and cultural critic, not a historian or a political scientist, and he died in 1955, long before anyone could have imagined the role "the Communist movement of the 1930s" would ultimately play in American politics, foreign policy and history. But he recognized Halberstam's "virus," his "flaw in the society," for what it actually was, thus taking the first step in a reckoning with history that cannot be dismissed with Garrison Keillor's glib admission and apparent desire to move on:

> Alger Hiss probably was a Soviet agent and the fact that Richard Nixon was his accuser doesn't change that. There was a Soviet espionage network in our government and the fact that Joseph McCarthy was a drunk, a bully and a cynical opportunist doesn't

87 Daniel Patrick Moynihan, *Secrecy* (New Haven: Yale University Press, 1998), 124.
88 Warshow, *The Immediate Experience,* 11.

change that. Along with a lot of other Democrats, I've wasted a lot of time on these issues that I was in fact, wrong about. I'm glad to be set straight.[89]

For the truth of Soviet espionage rotates history's kaleidoscope to produce an entirely new picture of this country's Cold War experience that reveals "the 'grey zone' of human affairs"—"that foggy universe of mixed motives, conflicting emotions, personal priorities, reluctant choices, opportunism and accommodation, all wedded, when convenient, into self-deception and denial."[90] Within the "grey zone of human affairs," this country's heroic statesmen are not nearly so heroic or statesmanlike, its villains not nearly so villainous, its people not nearly so exceptional or benign, its Cold War "victory" perhaps not much of a victory at all and its chroniclers neither honest nor disinterested.

This is not to suggest that the Cold War involved no objective right or wrong, good or bad, fact or fiction, truth or lies—all are present both in fact and in history as we know it. Rather, I wish to make three things essential to an honest reckoning with history abundantly clear: 1) war in any form, as the German military theorist Carl von Clausewitz famously recognized, is "not merely a political act, but also a political instrument, a continuation of political relations, a carrying out of the same by other means";[91] 2) gray indeed is all too often "the color of truth";[92] and 3) "in war, it is extraordinary how it all comes down to the character of one man."[93]

---

89 Garrison Keillor, "Remembering the Real Gene McCarthy," *Chicago Tribune,* December 14, 2005, sec. 1.

90 Erna Paris, *Long Shadows: Truth, Lies and History,* (New York: Bloomsbury, 2001), 313.

91 Quoted in "Foreigners in Russia: Carl Philipp Gottfried von Clausewitz." http://russiapedia.rt.com/foreigners/carl-philipp-gottfried-von-clausewitz/. See also Carl von Clausewitz entry in Conservapedia. http://www.conservapedia.com/Carl_von_Clausewitz, accessed May 10, 2012.

92 McGeorge Bundy, Epigraph to Kai Bird, *The Color of Truth* (New York: Touchstone, 1998).

93 General Creighton Abrahams, quoted in John A. Nagl, *Learning to Eat Soup with a Knife: Counterinsurgency Lessons from Malaya and Vietnam* (Chicago: The University of Chicago Press, 2005), 201.

PART ONE:
THE TRUMAN ERA

Chapter One:
The Legacy of the 1930s

The penetration of the American governmental services by members or agents of the American Communist Party in the late 1930s was not a figment of the imagination of the hysterical right-wingers of a later decade. Stimulated and facilitated by the effects of the Depression, particularly on the younger intelligentsia, it really existed; and it assumed proportions which, while never overwhelming, were also not trivial....

[B]y the end of the war, so far as I can judge from the evidence I have seen, the penetration was quite extensive—more so probably than at any time in the past, particularly in the hastily recruited wartime bureaucracies, the occupational establishments in Germany and Japan, and certain departments of the government normally concerned, for the most part, with domestic affairs and unaccustomed to dealing with matters of national security.[1]

George F. Kennan

There was scarcely a branch of the American government, including the War, Navy and Justice Departments, that did not have Soviet moles in high places, feeding Moscow information. Wild Bill Donovan's Office of Strategic Services, the forerunner of the CIA, had so many informers in its ranks that it was almost an

---

1 Kennan, *Memoirs, 1950–1963*, 191, 192.

arm of the KGB.[2]

Thomas Fleming

[N]o serious cold war historian now questions the penetration of Franklin Roosevelt's administration by Soviet spy rings...[3]

Thomas Powers

The Great Depression left nearly a third of all Americans unemployed, and when combined with the rise of Fascism in Europe, made it clear "to many intellectuals that the United States was drifting without plan, guidance, or goal. In their minds, salvation lay in two directions. The first was Roosevelt's New Deal, which revived interest in the Democratic Party as the rallying point for American progressives of all stripes. The other was Soviet Communism."[4]

In August 1919, two Communist parties were founded in the United States: the Communist Labor Party and the Communist Party of America. Both declared their intent to overthrow the American government through violence.[5] Controlled by the Soviet Union, they merged on the orders of Grigory Zinoviev, head of the Communist International ("Comintern"), which had been created in 1919 by Lenin to coordinate the activities of all Communist parties throughout the world.[6] "In all cases, the Comintern was the final arbiter of [American Communist] party feuds. The winner of each fight was always decided when disputing leaders went to Moscow for a Comintern ruling or when a Comintern representative

---

2 Thomas Fleming, *The New Dealers' War: F.D.R. and the War Within World War II* (New York: Basic Books, 2001), 319.

3 Thomas Powers, "The Fate of the Nation," *New York Times Book Review*, May 29, 2005.

4 Arthur Herman, *Joseph McCarthy: Reexamining the Life and Legacy of America's Most Hated Senator* (New York: The Free Press, 2000), 65.

5 Klehr, Haynes, Firsov, *The Secret World of American Communism* (New Haven: Yale University Press, 1995), 5.

6 Ibid., 6–7. See also Theodore Draper, *American Communism and Soviet Russia* (New York: The Viking Press, 1963), 24-28.

residing in America picked the winner on the spot."[7] The 1925 Constitution of the Communist Party of the United States ("CPUSA") proclaimed it "the American section of the Communist International," and the Party's membership card stated that "the undersigned declares his adherence to the program and the statutes of the Communist international and the Workers (Communist) Party and agrees to submit to the discipline of the Party and to engage actively in its work."[8] At the time of its founding, the Soviet government gave its American subsidiary several million dollars to further its efforts,[9] and over the next several decades, "millions and millions and millions of dollars" were poured into [CPUSA] coffers by Moscow.[10] William Z. Foster, the Communist Party candidate for president in 1928, declared the CPUSA's allegiance to Soviet Russia in plain terms: "No Communist, no matter how many votes he should secure in a national election, could, even if he would, become president of the present government. When a Communist heads a government in the United States—and that day will come just as surely as the sun rises—that government will not be a capitalist government but a Soviet government, and behind this government will stand the Red Army to enforce the Dictatorship of the Proletariat."[11] From its earliest days, the CPUSA was intimately involved in espionage,[12] and the FBI was aware by the late 1930s that the Soviet Union was funding its "espionage, sabotage [and] propaganda activities."[13]

In short, the CPUSA was a "subversive group...masquerading as

7 Klehr, Haynes, Firsov, *The Secret World of American Communism*, 7.

8 Draper, *American Communism and Soviet Russia*, 62.

9 Klehr, Haynes and Firsov, *The Soviet World of American Communism*, 24.

10 Harvey Klehr interviewed by David Hozel in *Life of the Party*. Sines & Cosines, http://www.mindspring.com/~dbholzel/klehr2.html, 1998, accessed February 9, 2004; Ted Morgan, *Reds, McCarthyism in Twentieth Century America* (New York: Random House, 2003) 115, 554, 567. The archives of the CPUSA are still located in Moscow, where one would expect to find the records of a Soviet government agency.

11 Herbert Romerstein and Eric Breidel, *The Venona Secrets* (Washington, D.C.: Regnery Publishing, 2000), 75.

12 Morgan, *Reds*, 114–115, 144.

13 Athan Theoharis, *Chasing Spies: How the FBI Failed in Counterintelligence but Promoted the Politics of McCarthyism in the Cold War Years* (Chicago: Ivan R. Dee, 2002), 57.

a political party,"[14] and its members were dedicated to Marxist dictatorship, an idea with which far too many American liberals were quite comfortable, as Roger Baldwin, director of the American Civil Liberties Union, made clear in 1934:

> *The class struggle is the central conflict of the world; all others are incidental. When that power of the working class is once achieved, I am for maintaining it by any means whatsoever.* Dictatorship is the obvious means in a world of enemies at home and abroad....The rigid suppression of any opposition to the program of socialism is a measure of the difficulties and in part of the sense of insecurity in a world of enemies....[If] American champions of civil liberties could all think in terms of economic freedom, as the goal of their labors, they too would accept "workers' democracy" *as far superior to what the capitalist world offers to any but a small minority. Yes, and they would accept—regretfully, of course—the necessity of dictatorship while the job of reorganizing society on a socialist basis is being done.*[15]

Franklin Roosevelt's New Deal attracted many of the day's best and the brightest to Washington, and no one paid any attention to who they were or what they believed. Disloyalty among this country's best and brightest was just unthinkable, and "American counterintelligence was virtually nonexistent in the 1930s."[16] Although most of liberalism's best and brightest were committed to American democracy and FDR's New Deal, some favored the road taken by the Soviets.[17] In fact, many of these bright young liberals

---

14 Morgan, *Reds*, 514.

15 Roger Baldwin, "Freedom in the U.S.A. and the U.S.S.R.," *Soviet Russia Today*, 1934 (emphasis in the original).

16 Allen Weinstein, "The Early Days of Soviet Espionage," *Booknotes*, ed. Brian Lamb (New York: PublicAffairs, 2001), 246.

17 Allen Weinstein and Alexander Vassiliev, *The Haunted Wood: Soviet Espionage in America—The Stalin Era* (New York: Random House, 1999), 3–4.

and their political and academic supporters saw no real difference, as incredible as that might sound today, between Soviet Communism and New Deal liberalism:

> In the minds of many American progressives, Communists were just "liberals in a hurry," much as Earl Browder of the Communist Party of the United States (CPUSA) and his subordinates claimed. Communist goals for the Soviet Union seemed to be pretty much the same as those of New Dealers for America....The plain truth—that Stalin was a mass murderer who governed through compulsory labor, prison camps, and the systematic murder of his own supporters—was ignored, explained or shrugged away.[18]

As they traveled through the Soviet Union at the height of the terror and the purges, American "progressives" saw nothing but freedom, democracy, economic success and satisfied citizens: "I have been over into the future," said Lincoln Steffens, "and it works."[19] Harry Ward, professor of Christian Ethics at Union Theological Seminary in New York City and chairman of the Soviet-controlled League for Peace and Democracy, stated that "the Soviet system was the fulfilment of the teachings of Christ."[20] The credulity of American liberals extended even to the bizarre Moscow show trials, complete with their fantastic "confessions" and endless death sentences: "'We see no reason,' wrote editors of the *New Republic* in September 1936, 'to take the trial at other than its face value.'"[21] Assessing Stalin's 1937-38 purges in which nearly 700,000 people were liquidated, scholar Owen Lattimore, who would later be the subject of an attack by Joseph McCarthy, said, "That sounds like democracy to me."[22] Liberals found little reason to dislike or distrust American Communists, who were, in their minds,

---

18 Herman, *Joseph McCarthy*, 61, 65–66.
19 Ibid., 65.
20 Ibid., 68.
21 Ibid., 69.
22 Ibid.

"fundamentally on the side of justice."[23] And these same liberals welcomed American Communists and their sympathizers into almost all agencies of the United States government.

In fact, hundreds of Americans working for the Soviet Union were active within the federal government during the New Deal and throughout the Second World War, as Army intelligence officers eventually determined by deciphering some three thousand telegraphic cables between Soviet agents in the United States and their superiors in Moscow. Code named Venona, this operation was a closely-guarded secret until declassification in 1996.[24] When these intercepts were combined with information acquired from Soviet archives after the collapse of the USSR, they revealed not only a massive penetration of American government, science and industry by Soviet spies but an American Communist Party that had assisted in these efforts, serving as an arm of Soviet intelligence.[25]

As of 1998, Venona had revealed 349 Americans working for Soviet intelligence services during the 1930s and 1940s—171 of whom have been positively identified while 178 remain known only by their Soviet code names—and the Western scholars who have had access to the former Soviet archives have seen only a *fraction* of what is contained in the KGB and GRU intelligence files.[26]

> America's World War II intelligence agency, the Office of Strategic Services, was home to between fifteen and twenty Soviet spies. Four other wartime agencies—the War Production Board, the Board of Economic Warfare, the Office of the Coordinator of Inter-American Affairs, and the Office of War Information—included at least a half a dozen Soviet sources among their employees....At least six sources worked in the State Department....Thanks to the influence of Assistant Secretary Harry D. White, the

---

23 Ibid., 61.

24 John Earl Haynes and Harvey Klehr, *Venona, Decoding Soviet Espionage in America* (New Haven: Yale University Press, 1999), 1.

25 Ibid., 21.

26 Ibid., 9.

Treasury Department was a congenial home to Soviet agents. Six of the eight known Soviet sources in the Department were connected with the Department of Monetary Research, headed first by White and then by a second Soviet source, Frank Coe, after White moved farther up in the Treasury hierarchy.[27]

"Taken together, all this added up to a massive and intractable security problem."[28] In other words (quoting American Communist Party member Alfred Bernstein), "McCarthy was right." "The system was loaded with Communists," and their efforts were noted at the time by men of unimpeachable integrity.

By 1937, the State Department's Division of Eastern European Affairs had amassed the finest library on the Soviet Union ever assembled. Soviet Minister of Foreign Affairs Maxim Litvinov noted in the early 1930s that the Division of Eastern European Affairs had better records on the Soviet diplomacy than the Soviet Foreign Office.[29] But in mid-1937, Robert Kellery, head of the Division of Eastern European Affairs, was informed by his superiors that the Division was to be abolished immediately and its library turned over to the Library of Congress. "Special" files were to be destroyed.[30] According to George Kennan, "There is strong evidence that pressure was brought to bear from the White House. I was surprised, in later years, that the McCarthyites and other right-wingers of the early fifties never got hold of the incident and made capital of it; for here, if ever, was a point at which there was indeed the smell of Soviet influence, or strongly pro-Soviet influence, somewhere within the higher reaches of government."[31]

27 Ibid., 331. See also Michael D. Gordin, *Red Cloud at Dawn: Truman, Stalin and the End of the Atomic Monopoly* (New York: Farrar, Straus and Giroux, 2009), 81: "[T]he OSS was so riddled by Soviet agents by the end of the war that it is unlikely that it would have served very effectively against [the Soviet Union.]"

28 Herman, *Joseph McCarthy*, 107. See also Fleming, *The New Dealers' War*, 318–322.

29 George F. Kennan, *Memoirs: 1925–1950* (Boston: Atlantic Little, Brown, 1967), 83–84.

30 Ibid., 84.

31 Ibid., 84–85. The Russian Defense Ministry newspaper *Red Star* reported in May 2006 that the Soviet intelligence services "obtained information from nearly 70 American ministries, departments,

Most importantly, Stalin's penetration of the United States government was no deep, dark secret. Daniel Patrick Moynihan (no right-wing demagogue and likely the finest public servant of the twentieth century) noted that the presence within government of Communists and their sympathizers was "common knowledge within the political and intellectual circles...of the 1930s,"[32] and the evidence certainly bears him out. In 1939, the House Un-American Activities Committee ("HUAC"), then led by Congressman Martin Dies of Texas, seized the records of the American League for Peace and Democracy, which CPUSA chief Earl Browder had freely admitted was "from the beginning led by our party quite openly."[33] Upon examination, the Committee discovered that 563 members of this Communist Party front group were employed within the United States government. Dies noted that the documents "reveal a systematic effort to penetrate the government by an organization which is under the control of Communists."[34] Yet Franklin Roosevelt did nothing but denounce Dies and his committee for publicizing this scandalous state of affairs, calling it a "sordid procedure."[35]

In fact, Franklin Roosevelt was advised *repeatedly* that the Soviet government had placed agents within the highest levels of his own administration but refused to do anything about it. Assistant Secretary of State Adolph Berle advised Roosevelt in 1939 that Whittaker Chambers, who (we now know) spoke truthfully regarding his own experiences as a Soviet agent, had reported an extensive espionage network within the Roosevelt administration, identifying both Alger and Donald Hiss as Soviet spies. Incredibly, Roosevelt made it clear that he was not interested.[36] Columnist Walter Winchell also went directly to Roosevelt with Chambers'

---

directorates, committees, and subcommittees in the governmental structure of the USA." See Christina Shelton, *Alger Hiss: Why He Chose Treason* (New York: Threshold Editions, 2012), 84.

32 Moynihan, *Secrecy*, 124.

33 Morgan, *Reds*, 207.

34 Ibid., 208.

35 Ibid., 209.

36 Herman, *Joseph McCarthy*, 61; Allen Weinstein, *Perjury, The Hiss-Chambers Case* (New York: Alfred A. Knopf, 1978), 330n.; Moynihan, Secrecy, 119–120.

accusations and was told "I don't want to hear another thing about it. It isn't true."[37] French authorities warned American Ambassador William C. Bullitt in 1940 that Alger and Donald Hiss were Soviet agents.[38] Even Lord Halifax, the British ambassador to the United States, warned Roosevelt of Soviet espionage to no avail: "Mr. President, there is a highly placed Russian agent in your organization." "Who?" FDR asked. "Henry Dexter White," Halifax responded. "Why," Roosevelt replied, "I've known Harry White for a long time. He's impossible. Now, what did you come to see me about?"[39] Future secretary of state Dean Acheson was equally irresponsible. When Adolph Berle informed Acheson that Donald Hiss had been identified as a Soviet agent, Acheson ordered Hiss into his office and asked Hiss directly if he was a Communist. Hiss denied it, and this was good enough for Acheson and Berle, who eventually invited Hiss, who like his brother was in fact a Soviet spy, to join his security staff.[40]

By the end of World War II, Soviet penetration of the American government was such common knowledge within "political and intellectual" circles that Arthur Schlesinger, Jr., who spent World War II with a low-level job in the Office of War Information, wrote the following in *Life* magazine (July 1946): "Underground cells under party direction became active in Washington in the 30s: some of their members are still well-placed in the administration. Ex-party members name several Congressmen as reliable from the party's point of view, and well-known Communist sympathizers are on the staffs of some senators and Congressional committees."[41]

The information passed to the Soviets by American

37 Sam Tanenhaus, Whittaker Chambers, A Biography (New York: Random House, 1997), 203–204.

38 Verne C. Newton, *The Cambridge Spies* (Lanham, Maryland: Madison Books, 1991), 128.

39 Curt Gentry, *J. Edgar Hoover, The Man and the Secrets* (New York: W.W. Norton & Co., 1991,) 344.

40 Herman, *Joseph McCarthy*, 61.

41 Arthur M. Schlesinger, Jr., "The U.S. Communist Party," Life, July 29, 1946, 84, 88. See also Arthur M. Schlesinger, Jr., *A Life in the Twentieth Century: Innocent Beginnings*, 1917–1950 (Boston: Houghton Mifflin 2000), 280: "As Communists secreted in the government held their regular cell meetings, so Pat [Jackson] convened dinners at regular intervals for what might be called an anticommunist cell." These were undertaken during World War II to facilitate "an exchange of information about the latest CP machinations inside the government."

Communists and their sympathizers—political, diplomatic, scientific, industrial and military—was extensive and historically unprecedented.[42] Even worse, Soviet agents like Henry Dexter White not only spied for the Soviets but helped formulate American policy, at the highest levels, in a manner that favored Soviet interests.[43]

This, then, was the "problem," the "virus," the "flaw in the society." It entered from the left, not from the right, and its legacy, the "Legacy of the '30s," would haunt American history and politics for decades. You see, "governing with public approval" in this country "requires a continuing political campaign," as Pat Caddell famously advised Jimmy Carter in December 1976:

> In devising a strategy for the Administration, it is important to recognize that we cannot successfully separate politics from government....Occasionally the result of "apolitical government" is positive, but most times it leads to disappointing the voters and eventual political disaster. When politics is divorced from government, it often happens that the talented, well-meaning people who staff the administration act without understanding the reasons "they all" were elected and instead pursue policies which run contrary to public expectations and desires....Essentially, it is my thesis that governing with public approval requires a continuing political campaign.[44]

Dubbed the "Permanent Campaign" by Sidney Blumenthal,[45] this was distilled to its very essence by Bill Clinton—"Don't look past the next election, or you might not get past the next election"[46]— and this is not a recent development. It was in full swing by the late-1940s, leaving no time for sober reflection or long-term analysis

42 Morgan, *Reds*, 225

43 Romerstein and Breindel, *The Venona Secrets*, 29.

44 Pat Caddell quoted in Sidney Blumenthal, *The Permanent Campaign* (New York: Touchstone, 1982), 56.

45 Ibid.

46 Wolf Blitzer, interview with Bill Clinton, August 11, 2005.

with Democrats running from years of folly and Republicans smelling blood. Few if any of the government officials, party bosses, cooperative pundits and public intellectuals involved on this side of the Cold War—particularly those responsible for the Democratic Party's decades-long journey through the world of doctrinaire anti-Communism—had any idea where their choices would ultimately lead as they maneuvered to avoid answering for years of folly and deceit. In short, when the "Legacy of the '30s" met the Permanent Campaign, the Truman Era was born, and it is "our central intellectual task" to understand that Joseph McCarthy, to paraphrase George Kennan, was the era's creature, not its creator.[47]

---

47 Kennan, *Memoirs: 1950–1963*, 190.

Chapter Two:
Harry Truman

I

What the Left was not saying was that they were in truth dedicated to replacing capitalism with a society based on Marxist principles, and this could well mean the suppression of non-Marxists for the good of mankind. Instead, they were simply espousing constitutional protections against self-incrimination. Thus the fresh wind of a debate of any real content was not blowing through these hearings or these terrible years.[1]

Arthur Miller

Communists lied to and deceived the New Dealers with whom they were allied. Those liberals who believed the denials then denounced as mudslingers those anti-Communists who complained of concealed Communist activity. Furious at denials of what they knew to be true, anti-Communists then suspected that those who denied the Communist presence were themselves dishonest. The Communists' duplicity poisoned normal political relationships and contributed to the harshness of the anti-Communist reaction of the late 1940s and 1950s.[2]

Harvey Klehr, John Earl Haynes and Fridrikh Igorevich Firsov

---

1 Arthur Miller, *Echoes Down the Corridor* (New York: Viking, 2000), 285–286.
2 Klehr, Haynes and Firsov, *The Secret World of American Communism*, 106.

The buck stops here.[3]

Ⅰn an attempt to determine how a secret government report appeared in the January 1945 issue of *Amerasia* magazine, which was published by Phillip Jaffe, who was long affiliated with the American Communist Party,[4] OSS agents (Office of Strategic Services) entered *Amerasia's* New York offices on the night of March 11, 1945, where they uncovered a major penetration of the US government. Among the trove of materials ultimately seized by federal agents were documents from the War Department, the State Department, the OSS, the Office of Postal and Telegraph Censorship and the Office of Naval Intelligence ("ONI"), among others.[5] Much of the material was relatively innocuous, but much was "highly sensitive," some was "Top Secret," and all of it had been purloined from government agencies.[6]

Within days, one of J. Edgar Hoover's top assistants, Myron Gurnea, ordered wiretaps on phones at the *Amerasia* offices and twenty-four-hour surveillance on Jaffe and Kate Mitchell, *Amerasia's* assistant editor.[7] On March 14, FBI agents conducted their own search of the *Amerasia* offices, photographing many of the classified documents scattered about. As the case progressed, FBI agents entered the *Amerasia* offices several more times while placing wiretaps on several of the suspects, including Jaffe, Mitchell, Mark Gayn (a journalist who wrote for many different mainstream publications such as *Colliers* and *Time*), Emmanuel Larson (who worked at the Office of Naval Intelligence) and Andrew Roth (a naval officer involved in the theft of documents). The taps provided a wealth of incriminating information. For example, Jaffe

---

3 Patterson, *Grand Expectations: The United States, 1945–1974* (New York: Oxford University Press, 1997), 95.

4 Bertram Wolfe, introduction to Philip Jaffe, *The Rise and Fall of American Communism* (Pittsburgh: Horizon Press, 1975), 3.

5 Harvey Klehr and Ronald Radosh, *The Amerasia Spy Case: Prelude to McCarthyism* (Chapel Hill: University of North Carolina Press, 1996), 6.

6 Ibid., 30–31; 105; 144–145.

7 Ibid., 32.

was overheard telling Roth that Joe Bernstein, a longtime fellow traveler and former *Amerasia* employee, had admitted to Jaffe that he had been a Soviet agent for many years and asked Jaffe to provide him with State Department material on China. "I'd be willing to do anything," Jaffe said.[8]

Six of those involved were ultimately arrested: Philip Jaffe, Mark Gayn, Kate Mitchell, Andrew Roth, Emmanual Larson and John Stewart Service. A career foreign service officer, Service was one of the State Department's "China Hands" who became enamored of Mao and the Communists when he visited their headquarters in Yenan. David Halberstam tells us that Service was a man of "rare excellence" with "a brilliant career" ahead of him before he was destroyed by McCarthyites for reporting the "truth" about the civil war in China between the Nationalists and the Communists.[9] The Nationalists, Service wrote, were "the enthronement of reaction," "fascist," "feudal," "Gestapo-like," "undemocratic,"[10] guilty of "corruption, unprecedented in scale and openness," "normally traitorous [in their] relations with the enemy" and guilty of "sabotage of the war effort."[11] When evaluating the Communists, however, "the hard-nosed reporter turned into a swooning groupie": They were "progressive," "straightforward and frank."[12] They displayed "impressive personal qualities," "incorruptibility," "realism and practicality."[13] "The Communist political program," according to Service, "is simple democracy...much more American than Russian in form and spirit." "They have a real desire for democracy in China...without the need of violent social upheaval and revolution."[14] The "so-called Communists," he said, supported "agrarian reform, civil rights [and] the establishment of democratic institutions."[15] (One would

---

8 Ibid., 62.

9 Ibid., 111.

10 M. Stanton Evans, *Blacklisted by History, The Untold Story of Senator Joseph McCarthy and His Fight against America's Enemies* (New York: Crown Forum, 2007), 102.

11 Ibid., 102.

12 Ibid., 103.

13 Ibid.

14 Ibid.

15 Klehr and Radosh, *The Amerasia Spy Case*, 19.

reasonably assume that with our current knowledge of history—including the tens of millions pitilessly slaughtered in one manner or another during the Chinese Communists' consolidation of power, the "Great Leap Forward," and the "Cultural Revolution," not to mention Mao's personal depravity, corruption, megalomania and sadism (all extensively documented in acclaimed works[16])—Service's judgment and reputation for "excellence" and "brilliance" would have suffered at least a little. But this has not happened. *Service remains beyond orthodox critique.*)

His unmistakably pro-Communist views placed Service at odds with powerful political appointees like Ambassador Patrick Hurley, and he was recalled and assigned to a meaningless position after Hurley read a lengthy memo from Service to Stilwell in which Service urged American support for the Chinese Communists.[17] Determined to make his views known, Service—with encouragement and direction from, among others, presidential adviser Lauchlin Currie (a Soviet agent code named "Page" by his Soviet controllers[18])—began delivering classified documents and other "very secret" information to Philip Jaffe, whose CPUSA connections were known to Service, as wiretapped conversations demonstrated.[19]

The guilt of the *Amerasia* defendants was beyond question, yet no real prosecution ever occurred. It is often suggested that failure to acquire warrants for wiretaps or entries by government officials, both OSS and FBI, somehow compromised the *Amerasia* prosecution, but this is simply not true. Hoover's surveillance of Soviet agents, including the CPUSA and its members, was authorized by both Roosevelt and Truman under the president's constitutional authority to gather intelligence from foreign powers,

---

16 Jung Chang and Jon Halliday, *Mao: The Unknown Story* (New York: Alfred A. Knopf, 2005); Li Zhi-Sui, *The Private Life of Chairman Mao* (New York: Random House, 1994); R.J. Rummel, *Death by Government* (New Brunswick: Transaction Publishers, 2000); *The Black Book of Communism: Crime, Terror Repression*, ed. Stephane Courtois (Cambridge: Harvard University Press, 1999).

17 Klehr and Radosh, *The Amerasia Spy Case*, 23–24.

18 Weinstein and Vassiliev *The Haunted Wood*, 106, 157, 161, 163n; Hynes and Klehr, Venona, 145–149; Tanenhaus, *Whittaker Chambers*, 162.

19 Evans, *Blacklisted by History*, 115; Klehr and Radosh, The Amerasia Spy Case, 61.

known as the foreign intelligence exception to the Fourth Amendment. Although wiretapping had been outlawed by Congress in the Communications Act of 1934, Franklin Roosevelt ordered Secretary of State Cordell Hull to authorize J. Edgar Hoover to conduct surveillance of Communist, Fascist and subversive organizations, rationalizing that the statute precluded the interception *and* "disclosure" of telephonic communications. As long as the information was not disclosed, by introducing it into evidence at a trial, for example, the government was free to gather whatever intelligence the executive branch deemed necessary.[20] The Supreme Court, however, rejected this claim in no uncertain terms in *Nardone v. United States,* 308 U.S. 338 (1939), ruling that the statute prohibited warrantless wiretapping, whatever use was made of the information. Roosevelt, however, "did not accept the view that the statute prohibited the wiretapping itself, since he discounted the possibility that any dictum in *Nardone* was intended 'to apply to grave matters involving the defense of the nation.'"[21] Accordingly, he issued an Executive Order authorizing the attorney general to employ "listening devices" at his discretion whenever he determined that "grave matters involving the defense of the nation" warranted their use.[22] This order remained in effect for twenty-five

---

20 Tim Weiner, *Enemies: A History of the FBI* (New York: Random House, 2012), 74–77.

21 *Zweibon v. Mitchell,* 516 F.2d 594, 617 (D.C. Cir. 1975).

22 See *Zweibon v. Mitchell,* 516 F.2d 594 at Appendix A:

THE WHITE HOUSE WASHINGTON

CONFIDENTIAL

May 21, 1940

MEMORANDUM FOR THE ATTORNEY GENERAL

I have agreed with the broad purpose of the Supreme Court decision relating to wire-tapping in investigations. The Court is undoubtedly sound both in regard to the use of evidence secured over tapped wires in the prosecution of citizens in criminal cases; and is also right in its opinion that under ordinary and normal circumstances wire-tapping by Government agents should not be carried on for the excellent reason that it is almost bound to lead to abuse of civil rights.

However, I am convinced that the Supreme Court never intended any dictum in the particular case which it decided to apply to grave matters involving the defense of the nation.

It is of course, well known that certain other nations have been engaged in the organization of propaganda of so-called "fifth columns" in other countries and in preparation for sabotage, as well as in actual sabotage.

years, providing authorization for 6,769 wiretaps and 1,806 bugging devices.[23]

Harry Truman followed suit, issuing his own Executive Order expanding the authority for warrantless wiretapping to "cases vitally affecting the domestic security, or where human life is in jeopardy."[24] When the federal courts eventually reviewed these orders, they affirmed the validity of the foreign intelligence exception to the Fourth Amendment but limited it to intelligence gathering from anyone who is "the agent of or acting in collaboration with a foreign power."[25] Congress formally codified the foreign intelligence exception in Title III of the Omnibus Crime Control and Safe Streets Act of 1968, as noted by the Supreme Court in *Mitchell v. Forsyth,* 472 U.S. 511, 540 (1985):

> Nothing contained in this chapter or in section 605 of the Communications Act of 1934 (48 Stat. 1143; 47 U.S.C. 605) shall limit the constitutional power of the President to take such measures as he deems necessary to protect the Nation against actual or potential attack or other hostile acts of a foreign power, to obtain foreign intelligence information deemed essential to the security of the United States, or to protect national security information against foreign intelligence activities. Nor shall anything contained in this chapter be deemed to limit the

---

It is too late to do anything about it after sabotage, assassinations and "fifth column" activities are completed.

You are, therefore, authorized and directed in such cases as you may approve, after investigation of the need in each case, to authorize the necessary investigation agents that they are at liberty to secure information by listening devices direct(ed) to the conversation or other communications of persons suspected of subversive activities against the Government of the United States, including suspected spies. You are requested furthermore to limit these investigations so conducted to a minimum and to limit them insofar as possible to aliens./s/ F. D. R.

23 Tim Weiner, *Enemies,* 88.

24 *Zweibon v. Mitchell,* 516 F.2d 594 at Appendix A.

25 *Zweibon v. Mitchell,* 516 F.2d at 614. See also 516 F.2d at 616: "Admittedly, Presidents since Franklin Roosevelt have authorized their Attorneys General to approve investigations 'to secure information by listening devices directed to the conversation or other communications of persons suspected of subversive activities against the Government of the United States.'"

constitutional power of the President to take such measures as he deems necessary to protect the United States against the overthrow of the Government by force or other unlawful means, or against any other clear and present danger to the structure or existence of the Government. The contents of any wire or oral communication intercepted by authority of the President in the exercise of the foregoing powers may be received in evidence in any trial hearing, or other proceeding only where such interception was reasonable, and shall not be otherwise used or disclosed except as is necessary to implement that power" (footnote omitted).[26]

Once lawfully invoked, the foreign intelligence exception allowed wiretapping without a warrant until the government's focus shifted from intelligence gathering to criminal prosecution of those involved. At that point, a warrant was required for further surveillance, as the Fourth Circuit ruled in *United States v. Truong Dinh Hung,* 629 F.2d 908 (4th Cir. 1980).

While there was undoubtedly some point during the *Amerasia* investigation at which a warrant would have been required, it is most likely that sufficient evidence had been gathered under the foreign intelligence exception to facilitate a successful prosecution. However, no one within the Truman administration was willing to fight these battles in court for one simple reason: Powerful people were opposed to prosecution, none more so than White House adviser (and Soviet agent) Lauchlin Currie, who initiated a campaign to ensure that Service would not be indicted. He contacted Tommy Corcoran, a New Deal insider and influential Washington attorney who was an officer of China Defense Supplies (a company that funneled American aid to the Nationalist Chinese) to solicit his assistance, and "Tommy the Cork" agreed to help. Unknown to Corcoran, Harry Truman, who suspected that

---

26 This provision was repealed in 1978 by § 201(c) of the Foreign Intelligence Surveillance Act, *Pub.L. 95-511*, 92 Stat. 1797.

Corcoran and other Roosevelt loyalists were somehow undermining his administration, had ordered illegal wiretaps on Corcoran's phones to gather political intelligence. (Wiretaps like these were felonies under federal law and, it bears noting, exactly what the Watergate burglars were doing for Richard Nixon in 1972.) These wiretaps, which remained in place for five full years, ultimately revealed a great deal of information on the *Amerasia* cover up.[27]

Corcoran began by calling Attorney General designate Tom Clark and assuring him that he was helping behind the scenes to ensure that Clark's nomination would not be opposed in the Senate. An FBI memo summarized the conversation as follows: "It is obvious that Corcoran is making every effort to develop Tom Clark and by inference has taken credit for having Tom Clark's nomination approved by the Senate committee."[28] In the meantime, Philip Jaffe and Kate Mitchell retained Arthur Scheinberg, whose law partner was a powerful Brooklyn congressman, Emmanuel Celler.[29] The political maneuvering appears to have succeeded. Clark appointed Robert Hitchcock, a federal prosecutor from New York, to handle the government's case, although Assistant United States Attorney Hugh Fulton from Washington had been the first choice. Hitchcock presented evidence to the grand jury on June 21, including testimony from eighteen witnesses—fourteen from the FBI, two from the State Department and one from the ONI—and he was confident that all six defendants would be indicted for theft of government property, with more serious charges awaiting the expected cooperation from those among the defendants who would seek favorable treatment in return for testimony. Things had gone exactly as planned, but the indictments returned by the grand jury (its term expired on June 30) were never filed by Tom Clark ("a highly unusual, if not unethical, action"[30]), a "deal" of some kind having already been made, as revealed by transcripts of conversations between Kate Mitchell (whose phone had been

---

27 Klehr and Radosh, *The Amerasia Spy Case*, 112; Theoharis, *Chasing Spies*, 100–102; Evans, *Blacklisted by History*, 119.

28 Klehr and Radosh, *The Amerasia Spy Case*, 115.

29 Ibid.

30 Ibid., 117.

tapped) and her attorney, Lowell Wadmon.[31]

Facilitating the "deal," Assistant US Attorney Hitchcock assured Service personally that he had nothing to fear from the currently sitting grand jury, while Assistant US Attorney James McInerney told Corcoran that questioning of Service would be perfunctory and guaranteed that the Justice Department would not acquire an indictment.[32] Corcoran was satisfied enough that he called Service on July 30, and, in a taped conversation, told Service that "[t]his is double riveted from top to bottom." "I also have a deal that you are not going to be used as a witness."[33] Then Hitchcock, in another highly unusual action, agreed to let the defendants see all of the government's grand jury evidence despite the fact that not one had agreed to cooperate. J. Edgar Hoover smelled a rat: "I don't like all this manipulation," he wrote.[34]

In the end, Robert Hitchcock presented a carefully prepared John Service to a second grand jury, which, of course, knew nothing of the evidence presented to the first grand jury or the indictments already returned, and Service, who had provided classified information to Soviet agents in violation of US law, was exonerated as promised on August 10, 1945—hardly a surprise. He was then reinstated and eventually promoted. Hitchcock left government service some four months later to take a job with a New York law firm in which James McCormick Mitchell, *Amerasia* suspect Kate Mitchell's uncle, was a partner. Mitchell had taken an active role in negotiating on behalf of his niece during the *Amerasia* affair. Like Service, she was cleared by Hitchcock's presentation to the second grand jury. J. Edgar Hoover, who was critical throughout the Justice Department's handling of the *Amerasia* affair, commented with considerable understatement that "certain aspects of this matter smell."[35] But it all worked out just fine for Harry Truman, who "successfully averted the political embarrassment that Service's indictment would bring....Conservative suspicions of a

---

31 Ibid., 118; Evans, *Blacklisted by History*, 119–122.
32 Ibid., 122.
33 Ibid.
34 Ibid., 119.
35 Ibid., 128.

high-level fix were correct."[36]

The *Amerasia* scandal was not yet over, however, and both perjury and obstruction would derail all further efforts to examine the matter. On June 22, 1950, John Service was subpoenaed to appear before the Tydings Committee, which was created by the Democratic-controlled Senate to investigate charges of Communists in government. When asked directly by committee counsel Robert Morris whether he had received any assurances, prior to his grand jury testimony, that he would be cleared of all charges, Service perjured himself, stating, "[O]f course not. None whatsoever."[37] Former Assistant United States Attorney James McGranery, who was deeply involved in the *Amerasia* affair, gave a similar performance when testifying in support of his own nomination as Attorney General in 1952. When questioned regarding his involvement, he lied, stating that any allegations that he had helped engineer a whitewash were "entirely without foundation."[38] "I had no connection with the *Amerasia* case during its investigation, its preparation or its prosecution."[39] His entire role in connection with *Amerasia*, he testified, was a two-minute conversation with Assistant United States Attorney James McInerney.[40] J. Edgar Hoover moved quickly, showing McGranery evidence that could convict him of perjury, specifically a memorandum "reflecting verbatim conversations had by you and Mr. Thomas Corcoran concerning this case."[41] Ironically, "The cover-up that began with one attorney general trying to clear away obstacles to his own confirmation thus ended with another lying to a congressional committee during his confirmation hearings and then being threatened with exposure by the director of the FBI."[42]

As history now reveals, *Amerasia* was just the tip of the iceberg,

---

36 Richard M. Fried, *Nightmare in Red* (New York: Oxford University Press, 1990), 61. See also Klehr and Radosh, *The Amerasia Spy Case*, 218–219.

37 Ibid., 196.

38 Transcripts reflecting McGranery's direct involvement in this "high-level fix" are quoted in Evans, *Blacklisted by History*, 121–122.

39 Klehr and Radosh, *The Amerasia Spy Case*, 205.

40 Ibid., 205.

41 Ibid., 206.

42 Ibid., 206.

and maneuvering to avoid the fallout from Soviet espionage, a "Legacy of the '30s," would drive foreign and domestic policy as much as any other factor for the next two decades as Truman's opponents continued amassing evidence of widespread Soviet espionage on the Democrats' watch, and Democrats fought back with all the power they could muster.

II

Two "major [Soviet] intelligence organizations are engaged in large-scale espionage in this country" that, through "membership in the Communist Party," have installed "thousands of invaluable sources of information in various industrial establishments as well as in the departments of the Government."[43]

Clark Clifford

On June 5, 1945, Brigadier General Carter C. Clarke, head of Army Signals Intelligence Special Branch, met with Harry Truman at the White House and advised him that "large scale Soviet intelligence operations in the United States" were indicated by early readings of Soviet cable traffic.[44] Truman refused to believe it, saying that it all sounded "like a fairy story."[45]

Oliver Kirby, a cryptanalyst working on Venona, was sent by General Clarke to inform officials at the State Department that it had been penetrated by Soviet agents, and his report was "rejected outright":

> The State Department kicked me out. Nobody was interested in the information. I'd say, "Look what I've got" and they would say, "That doesn't happen to be anything my boss has a priority on. The Russians are our friends and you'd better stop talking that way young man or we are going to have

---

43 Clark Clifford, "American Relations with the Soviet Union: A Report to the President by the Special Counsel to the President, September 24, 1946," 65–69.
44 Jerrold and Leona Schecter, *Sacred Secrets: How Soviet Intelligence Operations Changed American History* (Washington, D.C.: Brassey's, Inc., 2002), 111.
45 Ibid., 111.

your scalp tied to the flagpole. So you and your little known agency had better not come around here talking about that kind of thing." I was referred first to the director of the State Department Bureau of Intelligence and Research. I started talking about what we had recovered and was told, "None of that stuff around here. You pack yourself out of here."[46]

In September 1945, Igor Gouzenko, a code clerk at the Soviet Embassy in Ottawa, defected, bringing with him more than one hundred Soviet military intelligence documents outlining extensive Soviet espionage efforts in North America. He was thoroughly debriefed by both Canadian authorities and the FBI, and he advised them that America's nuclear program was the object of a concerted Soviet espionage effort. He also told his interrogators that a Lieutenant Kulakov, who worked for the Soviet military attaché, had advised him that Soviet Military Intelligence had an agent who was an assistant to Truman's secretary of state, Edward Stettinius. Once this information was compared to statements by other informants, it was clear to everyone—including the FBI and security officers at the State Department—that Alger Hiss was a Soviet agent.[47]

Hoover so advised Truman and Acheson in November 1945.[48] By the spring of 1946, nearly everyone on the State Department's security staff thought that Hiss was engaged in espionage.[49] Elizabeth Bentley and Whitaker Chambers, both former Soviet agents who had severed ties with the American Communist Party, came forward with allegations of widespread Soviet penetration of the United States government—Chambers in 1939 and Bentley in 1945.[50] Both were thoroughly debriefed by the FBI, and the appropriate officials, including President Truman, were notified in 1945 and 1946.

46 Ibid., 135.
47 Weinstein, *Perjury*, 356. See also Shelton, *Alger Hiss: Why He Chose Treason*, 120-125.
48 Herman, *Joseph McCarthy*, 438.
49 Weinstein, *Perjury*, 21–22, 365.
50 Hynes and Klehr, *Venona*, 89–92; 150.

J. Edgar Hoover sent Truman a memo on November 8, 1945, identifying the following—all but one a government official or employee—as Soviet agents: Dr. Nathan Gregory Silvermaster (Department of Agriculture); Henry Dexter White (Department of the Treasury); George Silverman (Railroad Retirement Board, War Department); Lauchlin Currie (aide to Franklin Roosevelt); Victor Perlo (War Production Board and Foreign Economic Administration); Donald Wheeler, Julius Joseph, Helen Tenney, and Maurice Halperin (Office of Strategic Services); Charles Kramer (National Labor Relations Board, Senate Subcommittee on War Mobilization, Office of Price Administration); Captain William Ullman (US Army Air Corps); Lt. Col. John Reynolds (US Army); and Mary Price (secretary to Walter Lippmann).[51] We now know from the declassification of Venona and our brief glimpse into the Soviet archives that each and every one had ties to Soviet intelligence, and many have been confirmed as Soviet agents.[52] In other words, the much-vilified J. Edgar Hoover was right on the money, and this was just one of many attempts by Hoover in 1945 and 1946 to interest Truman in this "massive and intractable security problem." Truman, however, remained indifferent.[53]

According to received wisdom, Truman consistently refused to act on Hoover's warnings because he feared overreaction and was determined to protect civil liberties.[54] Yet Truman's alleged concern for civil liberties did not stop him from placing wiretaps on the phones of Tommy Corcoran and columnist Drew Pearson, and Clifford himself told Truman in 1946 that the Soviets had long been

---

51 Jerrold and Leona Schecter, *Sacred Secrets*, 115.

52 Hynes and Klehr, *Venona*, Appendix A.

53 Weinstein, *Perjury*, 4; Hynes and Klehr, *Venona*, 13. See also Herbert Hoover, *Freedom Betrayed* (Stanford: Hoover Institution Press, 2011), 30–53. It is notable that Herbert Hoover's analysis of the Soviet espionage assault on this country, which includes detailed identification of numerous high-ranking Americans working for Soviet intelligence, was written decades before Venona was declassified.

54 Richard Hack, *Puppetmaster: The Secret Life if J. Edgar Hoover* (Beverly Hills: New Millennium Press, 2004), 248–249; David McCullough, *Truman* (New York: Simon & Schuster; Touchstone, 1992), 550–551; Clifford, *Counsel to the President*, 177.

engaged in "large-scale espionage in this country."[55] In fact, Truman's actual view of espionage can be judged from a statement Truman made to Arthur Krock shortly after the start of the Korean War:

> Our chief concern, or at least one of them, is the "Trojan horse Commies" in the United States. There is great fear of sabotage. We have no machinery adequate to police or check our strategic air bases, where we have the big bombers that would carry the bomb; and many of the "fifty thousand Communists in the U.S.A.," in contact with Russian agents are bent on sabotage, which would prevent many of our planes from leaving the ground.[56]

Whatever the accuracy of this particular statement, the fact is that Truman knew all along that Soviet penetration of this government represented "a real problem, not a witch hunter's fantasy."[57] But he knew that any genuine, public inquiry into the problem would lead to a political disaster, as Attorney General Tom Clark warned him in July 1946,[58] and he had no intention of traveling that road. When informed by none other than General

---

55 Clark Clifford, *American Relations with the Soviet Union: A Report to the President by the Special Counsel to the President, September 24, 1946*, 65, 67. Although he briefed Truman in 1946 on two "major [Soviet] intelligence organizations" engaged in "large-scale espionage in this country" that, through "membership in the Communist Party," had installed "thousands of invaluable sources of information in various industrial establishments as well as in the departments of the Government," Clark Clifford always insisted when writing for public consumption that no real problem existed. Compare Clark Clifford, *American Relations with the Soviet Union: A Report to the President by the Special Counsel to the President, September 24, 1946, 65–69*, to Clifford, quoted in Bernstein, Loyalties, 197–200: "My own feeling was that there was not a serious problem. I felt the whole thing was being manufactured. We never had a serious discussion about a loyalty problem." It was not a "substantive problem" but rather a "political problem." Truman, according to Clifford, enacted Order 9835 in response to political pressure from the Right: "He had to recognize the political realities of life. He'd gotten a terrible clobbering in 1946 in the Congressional elections."
56 Arthur Krock, *Memoirs* (New York: Funk & Wagnalls, 1968), 260.
57 Herman, *Joseph McCarthy*, 112.
58 Athan Theoharis, *Seeds of Repression, Harry S. Truman and the Origins of McCarthyism* (Chicago: Quadrangle Books, 1971), 127.

Omar Bradley that Henry Dexter White and Alger Hiss had been positively identified as Soviet agents by Venona decryptions, Truman cursed not White and Hiss but Venona: "That God damned stuff. Every time it bumps into us it gets bigger and bigger. *It's likely to take us down.*"[59]

The turning point came in 1947, after Republicans swept the 1946 congressional elections, gaining thirteen seats in the Senate, fifty-five in the House and returning to Washington in control of both chambers. Now they would chair the committees, set the agenda and have their first opportunity in sixteen years to do something about the Soviet espionage that, as "common knowledge" in Washington, had infuriated them since it began in earnest in 1933. Liberal Democrats viewed this as nothing but a right-wing attack on the domestic and foreign policies of the Roosevelt and Truman administrations,[60] and they were in part correct. Republicans desired not just the elimination of spies from government but repudiation of twenty years of liberal domestic and foreign policy.[61] And they would not have been "fair" about anything. Republicans intended to use the espionage issue to inflict as much collateral damage as possible on Democrats just as Democrats would use such an issue against them.

Liberals, however, did not intend to allow their long, comfortable relationship with American Communists to inure to Republican benefit. Meeting in January 1947 at the Willard Hotel in Washington, D.C., they formed the Americans for Democratic Action ("ADA"), which boasted among its founding members Democratic luminaries Reinhold Niebuhr, Walter Reuther, Arthur Schlesinger, Jr., and Eleanor Roosevelt. It was now time, according to Arthur Schlesinger, Jr., to "liberate the democratic left from Communist manipulation."[62] Communism had not changed, of course, and liberal Democrats did not know anything about Communism in 1947 that they had not known in 1937. But the political ground had shifted dramatically, and liberals would shift

---

59 Jerrold and Leona Schecter, *Sacred Secrets*, 149 (emphasis added).

60 Weinstein, *Perjury*, xviii.

61 Stephen E. Ambrose, *Eisenhower, The President* (New York: Simon and Schuster, 1984) 43.

62 Schlesinger, *A Life in the Twentieth Century*, 410.

with it. ADA publicly rejected "any association with Communism or sympathizers with Communism as completely as we rejected any association with fascists or their sympathizers."[63] And for the next twenty years, no one would be harder on Communists around the world than the Vital Center Democrats. Fighting to save Roosevelt's legacy and their own political lives, they would be the last ones to challenge anything done abroad in the name of anti-Communism while simultaneously obstructing all attempts to expose Soviet espionage at home and attacking anyone trying to uncover or report the truth. In the words of Clark Clifford, a political "counterattack" was necessary, and a counterattack it would be, on every front available, foreign and domestic. All "patriotic" Democrats were expected to toe the line; dissent in the ranks was not tolerated.[64] Thus began the so-called McCarthy era, and it long pre-dated McCarthy.

Determined to rid his administration of Communists and political radicals (due to both the security and political threats they represented), Truman issued Executive Order 9835 in March 1947, which established a Federal Employee Loyalty and Security Program that was placed under Justice Department and FBI jurisdiction in May.[65] Being administrative in nature, the Loyalty Program provided none of the protections afforded criminal defendants. Those suspected of disloyalty, which required nothing more than an allegation or some past affiliation with radical politics, were allowed neither to determine the source of adverse information nor to confront those who provided it. This was crucial since a great deal of the evidence used in the Loyalty Program had been acquired illegally—break-ins, wiretaps, bugs and mail covers directed at political radicals whose connection to a foreign government could not be demonstrated—and even more of it was hearsay and rumor that would never qualify for admission as

---

63 Ibid., 413.

64 Lynn Boyd Hinds and Theodore Otto Windt, Jr., *The Cold War as Rhetoric* (New York: Praeger Publishers, 1991), 159.

65 Athan Theoharis, "The Escalation of the Loyalty Program," *Politics and Policies of the Truman Administration*, ed. Barton J. Bernstein (Chicago: Quadrangel Books, 1970), 247–248.

evidence in court.[66] Truman then closed the administrative process, issuing an Executive Order sealing all federal employee loyalty files in March 1948.[67] Only Truman himself was allowed to approve congressional requests for loyalty files.[68] This meant that "anyone who wanted to learn more about possible Communist infiltration in the State Department or any other executive agency had to rely on the word of the sitting officials themselves—not a very trustworthy source..."[69] By the time Truman left office, some 1,200 federal employees had been dismissed by his loyalty boards while another 6,000 had resigned.[70] Yet well-connected Soviet agents like Philip and Mary continued to flourish.[71]

Philip Keeney had been fired from a teaching position at the University of Montana for his Communist affiliation, yet he moved easily into a sensitive government position with the OSS and then on to General MacArthur's staff in Japan. In the meantime, his wife, Mary, also a Soviet spy, went to work for the Allied Staff on Reparations in Germany and the Federal Economic Administration, which became part of the State Department in 1946.[72] Even after Mary was caught—FBI agents photographed her diary, in which she recorded all meetings with her KGB handlers— neither Philip nor Mary was prosecuted.[73] They simply moved on to the United Nations, where they continued their espionage careers, having been approved for UN employment by the Office of Special Political Affairs, which was headed by none other than Alger Hiss. Mary Keeney was not even fired by the State Department until March 1951, and then only because Joseph McCarthy, who allegedly never exposed a single genuine Soviet agent, exposed this affair.[74] Other powerful, politically connected spies like Alger and Donald

66 Theoharis, *Chasing Spies*, 56–61, 62–81, 84, 164–165, 249.

67 Theoharis, *Seeds of Repression*, 22.

68 Ibid., 110–111.

69 Herman, *Joseph McCarthy*, 96.

70 David Caute, *The Great Fear: The Anti-Communist Purge under Truman and Eisenhower* (New York: Simon and Schuster, 1978), 274–275.

71 Theoharis, *Chasing Spies*, 198–234; Hynes and Klehr, *Venona*, 354.

72 Herman, *Joseph McCarthy*, 109.

73 Ibid., 110.

74 Ibid., 109–110; Hynes and Klehr, *Venona*, 178–180.

Hiss, Dr. Nathan Gregory Silvermaster, Henry Dexter White and Lauchlin Currie, to name but a few, had little to fear from background checks and loyalty boards. When accused, they simply played their brazen game, which required them to appear before congressional committees and either: 1) deny the charges in righteous outrage and denounce their accusers; or 2) invoke the Fifth Amendment (in righteous outrage) and (of course) denounce their accusers. They could then wait, free from real investigation or prosecution, until the fallout could be handled by mainstream Democrats and their allies, who had no intention whatsoever of allowing a politically devastating scandal to unfold.

So it was Truman—and no one else—who established a Loyalty Program that forced thousands of government employees from their jobs without due process to protect himself and his party,[75] while taking no meaningful action at all against prominent, highly placed spies. This fact alone demolishes orthodoxy's image of Truman as a courageous liberal who "was determined to eliminate real security risks while protecting the nation's civil rights."[76]

III

After establishment of [a] Bolshevist regime, Marxist dogma, rendered even more truculent and intolerant by Lenin's interpretation, became a perfect vehicle for [the] sense of insecurity with which Bolsheviks, even more than previous Russian rulers, were afflicted. In this dogma, with its basic altruism of purpose, they found justification for their instinctive fear of [the] outside world, for the dictatorship without which they did not know how to rule, for cruelties they did not dare not to inflict, for sacrifice they felt bound to demand. In the name of

---

75 Liberal intellectuals have long maintained that a great deal of political calculation went into the design of the Loyalty Program. See Caute, *The Great Fear*, 27: "[I]t was largely to steal the Republicans' thunder that Truman signed Executive Order 9835, which launched a purge of the federal civil service and inspired similar purges at every level of American life." See also Bernstein, *Loyalties*, 195–205; McCullough, *Truman*, 552–553.

76 Joiner, *Honorable Survivor*, 216. See also David Oshinsky, "In the Heart of the Conspiracy," *New York Times Book Review*, January 27, 2008.

Marxism they sacrificed every single ethical value in their methods and tactics.[77]

George Kennan

By the winter of 1946, wartime illusions of cooperation between the Western Allies and the Soviet Union in creating a peaceful, stable world order had crumbled in the face of unrelenting Soviet belligerence on every issue imaginable. On February 9, Stalin publicly warned that the incompatibility between capitalism and Communism could lead to another war.[78] Stalin's "warning" was viewed with particular alarm in Washington. Unable to fathom Soviet policy and alarmed over its increasingly hostile tenor, the State Department solicited "an interpretive analysis" of Soviet behavior from George Kennan, who was the *chargé d'affaires* at the United States Embassy in Moscow.

Kennan was a career foreign service officer who had served from 1932 to 1933 in the Russian Section of the American legation in the Baltic city of Riga. He accompanied William C. Bullitt to Russia when Bullitt presented his credentials as the first US ambassador to the Soviet Union. In his *Memoirs,* Kennan noted that "[t]he years immediately following the establishment of relations between the United States and the Soviet Union I spent mostly in Russia." In 1941, he wrote that Russia—"widely feared and detested throughout this part of the world"—was not a fit "associate in defense of democracy,"[79] and by the end of the war, he favored "a full-fledged, and realistic showdown with the Soviet Union" over Eastern Europe.[80] If not, "the only thing to do was partition Germany, divide the continent into spheres and determine 'the line beyond which we cannot afford to permit the Russians to exercise unchallenged

---

77 Telegram, George Kennan to George Marshall ("Long Telegram"), February 22, 1946. Harry S. Truman Administration File, Elsey Papers [Bracketed Material Added]. http://www.trumanlibrary.org/whistlestop/study_collections/coldwar/documents/pdf/6-6.pdf, accessed May 10, 2012.

78 Walter Isaacson and Evan Thomas, *The Wise Men: Six Friends and the World They Made* (New York: Touchstone, 1988), 349–350.

79 Daniel Yergin, *Shattered Peace: The Origins of the Cold War* (New York: Penguin Books, 1990), 40.

80 Ibid., 75.

power or to take purely unilateral action.'"[81] Roosevelt and his advisers, however, "saw the Soviet Union behaving like a traditional Great Power within the international system" rather than a "world revolutionary state" trying to overthrow it.[82] So George Kennan jumped at the opportunity to outline his views, responding to the State Department's 1946 inquiry with what has become known as the Long Telegram: "They had asked for it. Now, by God, they would have it."[83]

Kennan cabled Washington that, contrary to what had become conventional wisdom, the Soviets' fundamentally neurotic and aggressive conduct did not result from American policy and was not amenable to change through American assurances of good faith, even when our conduct was, by any objective measure, consistent with those assurances. He advised American policy makers to purge themselves of the illusion that the Soviets were reacting in some rational, objectively defensible manner to *our* actions and that modification of our policies would somehow quell Soviet belligerence. According to Kennan, Soviet intransigence resulted from historic Russian insecurity and twentieth century totalitarian dogma, which had combined to form an aggressive, imperial power that was uncompromisingly hostile and would undertake "a patient but deadly struggle for total destruction of [a] rival power, never in compacts or compromises with it."[84] "We have here a political force committed fanatically to the belief that with the U.S. there can be no permanent *modus vivendi,* that it is desirable and necessary that the internal harmony of our society be disrupted, our traditional way of life destroyed, the international authority of our state be broken if Soviet power is to be secure."[85] This would be a long struggle, said Kennan, since the goals and philosophies of the United States and of the Soviet Union were "irreconcilable."[86] Averell Harriman, American ambassador to the Soviet Union,

---

81 Ibid.

82 Ibid., 11.

83 Kennan, *Memoirs: 1925–1950,* 293.

84 Yergin, *Shattered Peace,* 169.

85 Ibid.

86 Henry Kissinger, *Diplomacy* (New York: Simon and Schuster, 1994), 449.

believed that "there is no settlement with Russia and that this is a continuous thing." We were, according to Harriman, in for "a long, slow scrape ahead."[87] Kennan recognized, however, that "Soviet Power," although "impervious to the logic of reason...is highly sensitive to the logic of force."[88] Therefore, he said, we had to formulate a long-term policy "designed to confront the Russians with unalterable counter-force at every point where they show signs of encroaching upon the interests of a peaceful and stable world."

Reaction to Kennan's Long Telegram was "nothing less than sensational."[89] US diplomatic missions around the world, General Eisenhower, Secretary of War Robert Patterson and the top Pentagon officials all received copies. Navy Secretary James Forrestal had hundreds of copies made for distribution and, according to White House aide George Elsey, "sent it all over town."[90] Yet Truman remained unconvinced, disavowing Winston Churchill's famous "Iron Curtain" speech in March 1946. "Astonishing as it may seem to those who get their history from movies and TV, the American president invited Josef Stalin to come to Fulton and give a speech presenting his side of the story [and] actually offered to send the battleship Missouri to fetch the Soviet tyrant."[91]

Shortly thereafter, in July 1946, presidential adviser Clark Clifford and his assistant George Elsey co-authored a paper entitled "American Relations with the Soviet Union." The Clifford-Elsey Report, which drew heavily on the "Long Telegram" and other State Department materials, provided President Truman with a grim assessment of the new world order that was far more alarming than Kennan's Long Telegram.[92] According to Clifford, Soviet leaders had embarked "on a course of aggrandizement designed to lead to eventual world domination by the U.S.S.R." They were developing

---

87 Isaacson and Thomas, *The Wise Men,* 348.

88 Ibid., 353.

89 Kennan, *Memoirs: 1925–1950,* 295.

90 Yergin, *Shattered Peace,* 170–171.

91 Nicholas von Hoffmann, "Was McCarthy Right about the Left?", *Washington Post,* April 14, 1996, Outlook Section, C1. See also McCullough, *Truman,* 488–490.

92 McCullough, *Truman,* 543.

"atomic weapons, guided missiles, materials for biological warfare, a strategic air force, submarines of great cruising range, naval mines and minecraft, to name the most important," and employing "two major intelligence organizations" to engage in "large-scale espionage" within the United States. Clifford warned that the United States must be prepared "to wage atomic and biological warfare" while supporting and assisting "all democratic countries which are in any way menaced or endangered by the U.S.S.R." And this country would in time be prepared to do just that.

IV

I believe that it must be the policy of the United States to support free peoples who are resisting attempted subjugation by armed minorities or by outside pressures. I believe that we must assist free peoples to work out their own destinies their own way. I believe that our help should be primarily through economic and financial aid which is essential to economic stability and orderly political processes.[93]

Harry Truman

The Soviets had been particularly active in the Eastern Mediterranean since the end of World War II, and by the summer of 1946, they saw "the entire Middle East as ripe for the picking."[94] "In our opinion," Dean Acheson told Harry Truman on August 15, 1946, "establishment by the Soviet Union of bases in the Dardanelles or the introduction of Soviet armed forces into Turkey on some other pretext would [result] in Greece and the whole Near and Middle East, including the Eastern Mediterranean, falling under Soviet control and in those areas being cut off from the Western world."[95]

Greece was then involved in a civil war pitting Greek Communists against the British-backed Royalist government, and

---

93 President Harry S. Truman's Address before a Joint Session of Congress, March 12, 1947. http://avalon.law.yale.edu/20th_century/trudoc.asp, accessed May 10, 2012.
94 Isaacson and Thomas, *The Wise Men,* 369–370.
95 Ibid., 370–371.

in February 1947, the British informed the Truman administration that Great Britain intended to withdraw its 40,000 troops and halt all economic aid by the end of March. Dean Acheson believed that "the complete disintegration of Greece was only weeks away"[96] and outlined his fears in terms that would in later years be called the "domino theory,"[97] which is generally attributed to Dwight Eisenhower: "Like apples in a barrel infected by one rotten one, the corruption of Greece would infect Iran and all to the East. It would also carry the infection to Africa through Asia Minor and Egypt, and to Europe through Italy and France, already threatened by the strongest domestic Communist parties in Western Europe."[98] Although Acheson knew that "the Greek government was corrupt, oppressive, and incompetent,"[99] he advised Truman to step in on its behalf. Truman concurred and appeared before Congress on March 12, 1947, to outline what has become known as the Truman Doctrine:

> I believe that it must be the policy of the United States to support free peoples who are resisting attempted subjugation by armed minorities or by outside pressures. I believe that we must assist free peoples to work out their own destinies their own way. I believe that our help should be primarily through economic and financial aid which is essential to economic stability and orderly political processes....

> Should we fail to aid Greece and Turkey in this fateful hour, the effect will be far reaching to the West as well as to the East. We must take immediate and resolute action.

With support from both houses of Congress, Truman's "doctrine" became national policy in April 1947, when a $400

---

96 McCullough, *Truman*, 545.

97 Ibid., 542.

98 Hinds and Windt, *The Cold War as Rhetoric*, 138.

99 Isaacson and Thomas, *The Wise Men*, 388.

million aid package for Greece and Turkey passed with more than two-to-one margins in the House and Senate. *And so it began.*

The ease with which this occurred is primarily attributable to American memories of Munich, where in 1938 the French and British, confronted with Hitler's plan to dismember Czechoslovakia, acquiesced to ensure, in the words of British Prime Minister Neville Chamberlain, "peace in our time." Some sixty-five million would die before peace was achieved, and it need not have happened that way: "All the generals close to Hitler who survived the war agree that had it not been for Munich, Hitler would have attacked Czechoslovakia on October 1, 1938, and they presume that, whatever momentary hesitations there might have been in London, Paris and Moscow, in the end, Britain, France and Russia would have been drawn into the war. And—what is most important to history at this point—the German generals agree that Germany would have lost that war, and in short order."[100] This was the lesson of Munich, and by 1947, this particular lesson had become part of America's national DNA. "No more Munichs," writes James T. Patterson, "was virtually a battle cry to alarmed and anxious Americans throughout the postwar era of conflict with the Soviet Union."[101]

The problem with using the "lesson of Munich" as a blueprint for the Truman Doctrine should be readily apparent: Stopping the Nazis at Munich meant confronting a surrounded, virtually landlocked, industrialized state in the heart of Europe with diplomatic and overwhelming military power. (The Tripartite Pact between Germany, Italy and Japan was not signed until September 1940.) Any such move against Soviet Communism would have to have been undertaken in Russia before 1921. By 1947, it was far too late. *The short, easy war at the heart of the Munich counterfactual was never an option for dealing with the Soviets after World War II.* So the "lesson of Munich," badly misapplied in this case, would

---

100 William L. Shirer, *The Rise and Fall of the Third Reich: A History of Nazi Germany* (New York: Simon & Schuster, 1960), 423.

101 Patterson, *Grand Expectations*, 88. See also David Halberstam, "This is Korea, Fifty Years Later," AARP, July and August, 2003, 86: "[T]he need to confront aggressors early had been an essential lesson of World War II."

help launch the American people, determined as always to avoid the last war, through half a century of conflicts and intrigues all over the globe.

Truman was not without his critics, however, who were, to say the least, prescient. After reading George Kennan's famous *Foreign Affairs* article entitled "The Sources of Soviet Conduct," Walter Lippmann published a series of columns in the *New York Herald Tribune* attacking "containment" as a "strategic monstrosity" that would require Americans to "stake our own security and the peace of the world upon satellites, puppets, clients, agents about whom we can know very little."[102] "The U.S. would face the Soviets, Lippmann feared, with 'dispersed American power in the service of a heterogeneous collection of unstable governments.'"[103] "Frequently they will act for their own reasons and on their own judgments," he wrote, "presenting us with accomplished facts that we did not intend, and with crises for which we are unready. The 'unassailable barriers' will present us with an unending series of insoluble dilemmas. We shall either have to disown our puppets, which would be tantamount to appeasement and defeat and the loss of face, or must support them at an incalculable cost or an unintended, unforeseen and perhaps undesirable issue."[104]

George Kennan, however, was much closer in outlook to Lippmann than Lippmann realized. When shown beforehand a draft of Truman's March 12, 1947, speech to Congress, "he was appalled." Focusing on the open-ended commitment to "free peoples" everywhere, he told Acheson, "This is going too far."[105] There was, after all, a substantial and very reasonable middle ground between Truman's sweeping declaration that this country must undertake an open-ended commitment to help "free peoples" everywhere (which meant non-Communist governments, no matter how corrupt or inept) and a balanced policy designed to contain the

102 D. Steven Blum, *Walter Lippmann: Cosmopolitan in the Century of Total War* (Ithaca: Cornell University Press, 1984), 138. Lippmann's articles from the *New York Herald Tribune* were published in book form as *The Cold War: A Study in U.S. Foreign Policy* (New York: Harper & Brothers, 1947).
103 Isaacson and Thomas, *The Wise Men*, 401.
104 Blum, *Walter Lippmann*, 139.
105 Isaacson and Thomas, *The Wise Men*, 396.

Soviet Empire within the limits of American power, as Kennan advised at the time: "Repeatedly I expressed in talks and lectures the view that there were only five regions in the world—the United States, the United Kingdom, the Rhine Valley with adjacent industrial areas, the Soviet Union, and Japan—where the sinews of modern military strength could be produced in quantity; I pointed out that only one of these was under Communist control; and I defined the main task of containment, accordingly, as one of seeing to it that none of the remaining ones fell under such control."[106]

Robert A. Taft, leader of the Republican Old Guard, who is often derided today for his association with isolationism and McCarthyism, was also disturbed by the sweep of the Truman Doctrine, as outlined by his biographer James T. Patterson:

> Taft and others had raised some delicate questions that deserved more careful attention than they got in 1947. Were not the guerillas more independent of the Soviet Union than the administration claimed? Was it not in America's national interest to disengage itself from autocratic governments such as existed in Greece? Would not such a policy promote the Cold War, which Americans were so quick to blame on the Communists? In short, was not the Truman Doctrine a sign of the administration's exaggerated hostility toward the Soviet Union—and of the often irrational anticommunism—which was subsequently to distort the vision of makers of American foreign policy? The answer later given by many scholars to all these questions was "yes."[107]

William Fulbright, a first-term senator from Arkansas, was also concerned with the world-wide crusade on which Truman had

---

106 Kennan, Memoirs, 1925–1950, 359. See also Nicholas Thompson, *The Hawk and the Dove: Paul Nitze, George Kennan, and the History of the Cold War* (New York: Henry Holt and Company, 2009), 71–72, 77.

107 James T. Patterson, Mr. Republican, A Biography of Robert A. Taft (Boston: Houghton Mifflin Company, 1972), 371.

embarked. Fulbright agreed with Kennan on the need to balance ends and means and to distinguish between Communism as an ideology, on the one hand, and Soviet or Chinese imperialism on the other:

> We are not fighting Communists as a political party but we are actually fighting the Chinese and the Russians. The Russians have adopted the Communist doctrine as an instrument to be used in their effort to dominate their fellowman. They use this doctrine in the same way they might use airplanes or guns and have done so very effectively. In other words, if Communists in a country have no connections with the Russians in their efforts to dominate the world, then they can be considered much like any other political party with which one violently disagrees.[108]

No one, however, seemed to be listening, and Truman's doctrine was on its way, its first test in Greece an unqualified success. America's clients shouldered most of the burden, American losses were virtually nil and the expense involved relatively minor. No one seemed to notice the all-important conditions that favored Truman's effort, the most important being the lack of outside support for the Greek Communists, toward whom Stalin alternated between indifference and hostility,[109] having determined at the outset that the effort was doomed: "No, they have no prospect of success at all. What do you think, that Great Britain and the United States—the United States, the most powerful state in the world—will permit you to break their line of communication to the Mediterranean Sea! Nonsense."[110] The death knell for the Communist cause in Greece was sounded when Tito broke with Stalin, initiating a schism in the Communist camp. When the Greek

---

108 Randall Bennett Woods, *Fulbright: A Biography* (New York: Cambridge University Press, 1995), 165.

109 Yergin, *Shattered Peace*, 289.

110 Milovan Djilas, *Conversations with Stalin* (New York: Harcourt, Brace & World, Inc., 1962), 183.

Communists remained loyal to Moscow, Tito closed the border between Yugoslavia and Greece, ending what little outside support the Greek Communists had received and assuring victory for Truman's corrupt, authoritarian clients.[111] "The engagement eerily foreshadowed Vietnam, except in its outcome. American 'advisers,' trained in counterinsurgency, bolstered a corrupt right-wing government against Communist rebels. Napalm bombs were extensively used for the first time."[112] Casualties among Greeks were high: Some eighty thousand were killed, tens of thousands more were wounded, and 700,000 had become refugees. Regardless, Truman's doctrine was intended to check the spread of Communism by whatever means were required, and Truman had accomplished that goal. Greece was just the beginning, however, and it would be only a small taste of things to come, as Truman's critics warned at the time.

V

There is considerable political advantage to the Administration in its battle with the Kremlin. The best guess today is that our poor relations with Russia will intensify. The nation is already united behind the President on this issue. The worse matters get, up to a fairly certain point—real danger of imminent war—the more there is a sense of crisis. In times of crisis the American citizen tends to back up his President.[113]

Clark Clifford

Nineteen forty-eight was another banner year in the evolving Cold War. In February, Communists in Czechoslovakia staged a coup, murdering Jan Masaryk, the foreign minister and son of the country's first president, and bringing the country under Soviet

---

111 Yergin, *Shattered Peace*, 294.

112 Isaacson and Thomas, *The Wise Men*, 401.

113 Memo, Clark Clifford to Harry S. Truman, November 19, 1947, "The Politics of 1948," 15. http://www.trumanlibrary.org/whistlestop/study_collections/1948campaign/large/docs/documents/index.php?documentdate=1947-11-19&documentid=1-1&studycollectionid=Election&pagenumber=1, accessed May 5, 2012.

control. Eastern Europe's only democracy was gone. Walter Lippmann told his readers that the coup in Prague represented "strategical actions planned by military men in anticipation of war" and urged this country to "go on war footing with immediate mobilization, the draft, lend-lease, war powers over industry, and the declaration of national emergency."[114] A genuine war scare swept this country.[115]

Knowing that Truman faced a tough reelection campaign, Clark Clifford, a smooth, cold, cynical opportunist *par excellence*, urged him to make the most of it. "In times of crisis," Clifford said, "the American citizen tends to back up his President."[116] So Truman appeared before Congress on March 17 and warned Americans that the Soviets had a "clear design" to extend their domination to the "remaining free nations of Europe."[117] Things went just as Clifford intended. Two days later, the foreign aid bill sought by Truman rolled right through the Congress, with staunch support from Republican isolationists who had never before supported a foreign-aid bill.[118]

In June, Stalin attempted to force the Western Allies out of their occupation zones in the German capital by closing all road and rail links to the city. Truman responded with the Berlin Airlift, which kept West Berlin continuously supplied with the necessities of life. We were "eyeball to eyeball." Stalin would be forced either to capitulate or escalate, but without nuclear weapons, he was hamstrung: "The Soviet leadership, a Red Army general recalled many years later, had not been prepared to commit suicide over Berlin."[119] The airlift was successful, and this country injected itself more and more into European affairs while the Soviets called upon their loyal minions in Western Europe to oppose American foreign

---

114 Ronald Steel, *Walter Lippmann and the American Century* (Boston: Little, Brown & Company, 1980), 450–451.

115 Isaacson and Thomas, *The Wise Men*, 440.

116 Clifford, "The Politics of 1948," 15.

117 Isaacson and Thomas, *The Wise Men*, 441.

118 Ibid.

119 John Lewis Gaddis, *We Now Know: Rethinking Cold War History* (Oxford: Clarendon Press, 1997), 48.

policy through strikes, demonstrations and disorder in France and Italy during the winter of 1947-48.[120]

Unchallenged, the impact of Soviet-induced disorder in Western Europe might have been considerable. But Truman's newly created national security state swung into action, initiating a course of intervention that would become standard operating procedure for every administration until Jimmy Carter renounced Truman's doctrine in 1977.[121] This included propaganda, disinformation, secret payments to those opposing the Communists, threats to deny US aid if Communists won the election and aid to the Italian armed forces.[122] *Truman was prepared to go as far as necessary.* From the State Department, George Kennan advised US embassies in Europe that "Italy is obviously [the] key point. If Communists win [the] election there, our whole position in [the] Mediterranean, as possibly in Europe as well, would probably be undermined." If the Communists should win the election, Kennan recommended US military intervention.[123]

In the summer of 1948, Elizabeth Bentley, Louis Budenz (who had once been executive director of the Communist newspaper *The Daily Worker*) and Whittaker Chambers testified before the House Un-American Activities Committee at the request of Truman's Republican opponents, providing the Congress and the people with all the information they had previously provided the Truman administration, which had thus far done nothing with it. Bentley, Budenz and Chambers detailed their own careers in espionage and identified as Soviet agents a number of prominent people, many of them government officials who had also been identified by J. Edgar Hoover, including Lauchlin Currie, Victor Perlo, John Abt, J. Peters, Nathan Gregory Silvermaster, Alger and Donald Hiss and Henry Dexter White. Although Truman denounced Bentley and Chambers as "a crook and a louse,"[124] each and every one of the

120 Martin Walker, *The Cold War: A History* (New York: Henry Holt and Company, 1995), 54.
121 Ibid., 55.
122 Ibid.
123 Ibid.
124 Moynihan, *Secrecy*, 124n.

people they named was in fact a Soviet agent.[125] Bentley, Budenz and Chambers also described in great detail the means by which the Soviets had managed to assemble their massive North American espionage network.[126] Their testimony, as stated in Patrick Moynihan's book *Secrecy,* was "accurate in substance and detail."[127] Despite Truman's best efforts, the truth was finally out, and Democrats knew they were in trouble. House Speaker Sam Rayburn told a reporter off the record that "[t]here is political dynamite in this Communist investigation. Don't doubt that."[128] In the fall of 1948, George Elsey sent Clark Clifford a note "calling domestic Communism 'the Administration's most vulnerable point'" and warning that "our hopes this issue will die are ill-founded." Said Elsey, "There is paydirt here."[129]

Alger Hiss appeared before HUAC after Bentley and Chambers had testified and denied that he believed in Communism, denied that he ever "followed the Communist Party line, directly or indirectly," denied that he had ever "adhered to the tenets of the Communist Party" and denied that he had ever "been a member of any Communist-front organization."[130] After recounting his own career in government service, he stated categorically that the allegations made against him by Whittaker Chambers were "complete fabrications."[131] It was a virtuoso performance, with Hiss emerging unscathed.[132] It was clear to *everyone* that either Chambers or Hiss had committed perjury, and Mary Spargo of the *Washington Post* told Richard Nixon, "This case is going to kill the Committee unless you can prove Chambers' story."[133] Deeply disturbed by this, John Peurifoy, assistant secretary of state for security affairs, approached HUAC member Karl Mundt with some crucial information:

---

125 Hynes and Klehr, *Venona*, Appendix A, Appendix B.

126 Tanenhaus, *Whitaker Chambers*, 204.

127 Moynihan, *Secrecy*, 53.

128 McCullough, *Truman*, 652.

129 Clifford, *Counsel to the President*, 230.

130 Weinstein, *Perjury*, 11.

131 Ibid.

132 Ibid., 15.

133 Ibid.

Karl, I don't know what to do. I'm torn between loyalty and duty....Frankly, all I am, I owe, in this town, to Dean Acheson...and I don't want to do him a disservice. And still, I'm a good American. And I know that what you are saying about Alger Hiss is true, because I have access to Hiss's security files at the State Department....Would it be helpful to you if you could see those security files?[134]

In direct violation of Truman's Executive Orders sealing all such files, Peurifoy delivered the State Department's files on Hiss to Mundt in the middle of the night, and it became painfully clear that Hiss was a liar. "The evidence was there," said Mundt. "Hiss was involved with those Communist activities and Communist agents."[135] Truman knew full well what he was doing when he issued executive orders sealing these files, and he certainly knew, as did Dean Acheson and many others, that Hiss had perjured himself repeatedly while testifying. Yet the Truman administration turned immediately on Chambers. In a memo dated August 16, 1948, Truman aide George Elsey outlined a strategy to defend Hiss and discredit Chambers while directing the Justice Department to "make every effort to ascertain if Whittaker Chambers is guilty of perjury."[136] "If the Justice Department could keep the [Hiss-Chambers] case bottled up until January, when the Democrats reclaimed control of Congress (and of HUAC), the inquiry would end and the controversy fade with minimal damage sustained by the administration."[137] Truman, for his part, turned his guns on the messenger and, "In rousing stump speeches...promised to end the spy hearings and abolish HUAC."[138] At the same time, however, domestic politics demanded relentless anti-Communism from Democrats, who were scrambling madly to disprove Professor Frederick Schuman's proud claim that, "Underneath their skin,

---

134 Ibid., 21.
135 Ibid., 22.
136 Evans, *Blacklisted by History*, 323.
137 Tanenhaus, *Whittaker Chambers*, 296–297.
138 Ibid., 287.

Communism and liberalism are blood brothers."[139]

Hubert Humphrey, whose entire public life would epitomize the relationship between liberal Democrats and the Cold War (particularly the failed campaign in Vietnam), fought a desperate campaign to save himself and his party from the repercussions of a longstanding, cozy relationship with Communists. For Humphrey had long been "a Popular Front man" who spent years working quite comfortably with Communists and fellow travelers in Minnesota's Democratic-Farm-Labor Party.[140] By 1947, however, Humphrey knew that removal of his party's far-left state leadership was "a life or death matter" for him.[141] So he led a bitter and ultimately successful fight to gain control of the Democratic-Farm-Labor Party, purge it of Communists and sympathizers and throw its support behind Truman in the 1948 election. His reversal was so complete that he would eventually sponsor the 1954 Communist Control Act,[142] in which Congress defined the Communist Party as a "clear, present and continuing danger to the security of the United States" and outlawed it in no uncertain terms.[143]

Lyndon Johnson, in the meantime, began his own crusade against Communists in government in a manner that Joseph McCarthy would later emulate, slandering his opponent in the senate primary, former governor Coke Stevenson, with outlandish allegations of Communist sympathies and ultimately stealing the election, engaging in criminal conspiracy, vote fraud, bribery and perjury to acquire an eighty-seven-vote margin of victory out of

---

139 Herman, *Joseph McCarthy*, 66. Schuman was a professor of history at Williams College.

140 Carl Solberg, *Hubert Humphrey: A Biography* (New York: W.W. Norton & Company, 1984), 111–112.

141 Solberg, *Hubert Humphrey*, 116.

142 Patterson, *Grand Expectations*, 263.

143 "The Communist Party of the United States, or any successors of such party regardless of the assumed name, whose object or purpose is to overthrow the Government of the United States, or the government of any State, Territory, District, or possession thereof, or the government of any political subdivision therein by force and violence, are not entitled to any of the rights, privileges, and immunities attendant upon legal bodies created under the jurisdiction of the laws of the United States or any political subdivision thereof; and whatever rights, privileges, and immunities which have heretofore been granted to said party or any subsidiary organization by reason of the laws of the United States or any political subdivision thereof, are hereby terminated."

nearly 1,000,000 votes cast. [144] "What had been demonstrated before was now underlined in the strongest terms: in the context of the politics that was his life, Lyndon Johnson would do whatever was necessary to win. Even in terms of a most elastic political morality—the political morality of 1940s Texas—his methods were amoral."[145] In the words of Johnson supporter and future Texas governor John Connally, "It was the dawn of a whole new era in politics."[146] And then there was Henry Wallace, whose third-party campaign for president would prove a godsend for those with a need to be hard on Communism in 1948.

Wallace was an ultra-liberal and an ardent New Dealer who had been vice president during Franklin Roosevelt's third term and Truman's secretary of commerce. He was a popular political figure with powerful credentials who dissented early and vigorously from Truman's anti-Communist foreign policy. By 1948, he publicly opposed virtually everything done in the name of containment, including American aid to Greece and Turkey, the Marshall Plan and the Berlin Airlift.[147] So determined was Wallace to assist Stalin that he actually offered to act as an "agent of influence" for Stalin in his relations with Truman.[148] Democrats, who knew this was going to be a close election, feared his ability to take votes from Democrats while providing Republicans with a perfect means to taint the Democratic Party. At the same time, however, Wallace's third-party run for the presidency provided the Democrats with a heaven-sent opportunity. For Wallace was an irresistible target for anyone in need of a cheap and easy means to prove he was tough on Communism, and Democrats would be first in line, following Clark Clifford's advice, which was outlined in his forty-three-page memorandum entitled "The Politics of 1948." "Whenever the moment is psychologically correct," wrote Clifford, "the

144 Robert A. Caro, *The Years of Lyndon Johnson: Means of Ascent* (New York: Alfred A. Knopf, 1990), 303–384.
145 Ibid., 398.
146 Ibid., 193.
147 Herman, *Joseph McCarthy*, 79-80.
148 Weinstein and Vassiliev, *The Haunted Wood*, 284–285. See also Thompson, *The Hawk and the Dove*, 61.

administration must persuade prominent liberals and progressives—*and no one else*—to move publicly into the fray. They must point out that the core of the Wallace backing is made up of Communists and fellow travelers."[149] At the same time, Clifford crafted an analysis by which Truman could argue that nothing would serve Communist interests better than a Republican victory:

> Moscow is sufficiently aware of American politics to perceive that a Republican administration would be rigid and reactionary, and would fail to take those governmental steps necessary to bolster the capitalist economy in time of crisis. It is also convinced there is no longer any hope that the Truman Administration will submit to the Russian program of world conquest and expansion. From the Communist long-range point of view, there is nothing to lose and much to gain if a Republican becomes the next president. The best way it can achieve that result and hasten the disintegration of the American economy, is to split the independent and labor union vote between the President and Wallace—and thus insure the Republican candidate's election.[150]

Truman, who knew good political strategy when he saw it, followed Clifford's advice to the letter. He publicly spurned any help from "Henry Wallace and his Communists" and equated all his opponents—Communists, Progressives and Republicans. "The first, he argued, backed the second to elect the third; Communists 'wanted a Republican victory' to trigger the isolationism and depression best suited to their aims. Americans for Democratic Action issued pamphlets identifying Communist influences around Wallace. The Democratic National Committee hired several veteran anti-Communist liberals to keep watch on the Wallace

149 Clifford, "The Politics of 1948," 22-23.
150 Ibid., 4.

campaign."[151] Also following Clifford's advice and Truman's lead, well known liberals from all walks of life attacked Wallace relentlessly. Prominent newspaper columnist Dorothy Thompson said on national radio that "the Communist Party—let's tell the truth—initiated the movement for Wallace. No other group called for it."[152] Shortly thereafter, Alfred Friendly wrote an article for the *Washington Post* headlined "Reds Picked Wallace to Run, May Quit Him."[153] In a statement signed by Hubert H. Humphrey, Franklin D. Roosevelt, Jr., Leon Henderson and others, the ADA said, "Irrespective of Mr. Wallace's intentions, the goals of his sponsors are clear. They hope to divide progressives, create national confusion and insure the triumph of reactionary isolationism in 1948. They believe the achievement of these aims will serve the world interests of the international Communist movement."[154]

Even the *New York Times* joined in the redbaiting: "We have a new standard for measuring just how valuable a contribution Mr. Wallace's presidential candidacy is now making to the ideology of International Communism."[155]

In contrast to Truman, Republican Thomas E. Dewey was, in the words of David Halberstam, "an honest cop with the mind of an honest cop"[156] who refused to play the Communist card against Democrats as they played it against everyone else. According to Halberstam, Dewey refused as a matter of honor to attack Truman on the Communists-in-government issue.[157] So the Republican nominee took the high road to defeat while the Democrats rode a carefully crafted, anti-Communist whirlwind to an upset victory, which makes it rather clear, at least to those who prefer history to ideology, that the so-called McCarthy era began with the Democrats' defeat in 1946, not Dewey's defeat in 1948, as even

---

151 Fried, *Nightmare in Red*, 82.

152 John C. Culver and John Hyde, *American Dreamer: A Life of Henry A. Wallace* (New York: W.W. Norton & Company, 2000), 465–66.

153 Ibid., 465.

154 Ibid.

155 Ibid., 474.

156 David Halberstam, *The Fifties* (New York: Villard Books, 1993), 7 (quoting William Allen White).

157 Ibid.

David Halberstam unwittingly admitted: "The Communist issue would be fair game in the near future. *It was the only way [Republicans] knew how to fight back.*"[158]

VI

Our relationship with China since the end of the Second World War has been a tragic one, and it is of the utmost importance that we search out and spotlight those who must bear the responsibility for our present predicament. It was clearly enunciated on November 26, 1941, that the independence of China and the stability of the National Government was the fundamental object of our Far Eastern policy....During the postwar period began the great split in the minds of our diplomats over whether to support the Government of Chiang Kai-shek or force Chiang Kai-shek as the price of our assistance to bring Chinese Communists into his government to form a coalition. Our policy in China has reaped the whirlwind. The continued insistence that aid would not be forthcoming unless a coalition government was formed was a crippling blow to the National Government. So concerned were our diplomats and their advisers...with the imperfections of the democratic system in China after twenty years of war, and the tales of corruption in higher places, that they lost sight of our tremendous stake in a non-Communist China. This is the tragic story of China whose freedom we once fought to preserve. What our young men had saved, our diplomats and our President have frittered away.[159]

John F. Kennedy, January 25, 1945

In August 1949, the Soviets successfully tested their first nuclear weapon, a feat achieved at that time largely through the efforts of spies like George Koval, code-named "Delmar," who was decorated by Vladimir Putin on November 2, 2007, for helping Stalin get the bomb. According to the Kremlin, Koval "helped speed up

---

158 Ibid., 9 (emphasis added).
159 See also Patterson, *Grand Expectations*, 171–172, where Kennedy attributes the loss of China to "pinks" in the State Department.

considerably the time it took for the Soviet Union to develop an atomic bomb on its own."[160] The *New York Times* reports that Koval, who was trained in the Soviet Union as an agent, found himself within the Manhattan Program "by chance," where he was assigned to "health and safety," which gave him unusual access to Oak Ridge and other top-secret complexes. (Reading this article, it is clear that the *New York Times* believes that a trained Soviet intelligence agent was given unusual access to the Manhattan Project through sheer coincidence.)

Nuclear espionage saved the Soviets several years and enormous expense in producing their first atomic bomb.[161] Experts have estimated that this targeted espionage, which began as early as 1943, was responsible for fifty percent of Soviet efforts to develop nuclear weapons, which turned a twelve-year effort into a six-year effort. It was through espionage that Soviet scientists learned of centrifuging for separation of isotopes, which came as a complete surprise to them, and how to mix uranium oxide and heavy water, which Soviet scientists did not believe possible.[162] "'It was a very good intelligence operation by our Chekists,' Molotov recalled years later. 'They neatly stole just what we needed.'"[163]

On October 1, Americans were appalled by news that China, the world's most populous nation, had fallen to the Communists. The Nationalist forces escaped to Taiwan, where they subjugated the native Taiwanese, some 20,000 of whom they massacred.[164] Communist designs on Taiwan ended when Truman sent the United States Seventh Fleet to defend the island after war began in Korea.[165] Once again, the United States had intervened in another country's civil war and would be involved for the next several decades in supporting a corrupt, thoroughly non-democratic

---

160 "A Spy's Path: Iowa to A-Bomb to Kremlin Honor," *New York Times,* November 12, 2007.

161 Hynes and Klehr, *Venona,* 10.

162 Ronald Radosh and Eric Breindel, "Bombshell," *New Republic,* June 10, 1991, 12.

163 Gaddis, *We Now Know,* 94.

164 John F. Copper, *Taiwan, Nation-State or Province?* 3rd ed. (Boulder: Westview Press, 1999), 35–36.

165 Dean Acheson, *The Korean War* (New York: W.W. Norton & Company, 1971), 23; Geoffrey Perret, *Commander in Chief: How Truman, Johnson, and Bush Turned a Presidential Power into a Threat to America's Future* (New York: Farrar, Straus and Giroux, 2007), 137.

government in the name of Truman's doctrine, and dissent was (once again) virtually non-existent. Politicians were far too busy proving how tough they were on Communism to question whom this country supported or what was done in the name of containment. In fact, Truman and his advisers would be accused of "losing" China to the Communists, as much through treachery as ineptitude, and everyone with something to gain, mainstream Vital Center Democrats included, would repeat these charges. John F. Kennedy was one of the accusers.[166] "The responsibility for the failure of our foreign policy in the Far East," said Kennedy, "rests squarely with the White House and the Department of State....This House must now assume the responsibility of preventing the onrushing tide of communism from engulfing all of Asia."[167]

Soon enough, the Congress would "assume the responsibility of preventing the onrushing tide of communism," as exemplified by the Honorable Lyndon Johnson's destruction of Federal Power Commissioner Leland Olds. A longtime New Deal liberal, Olds was first appointed to the Power Commission by Franklin D. Roosevelt in 1940 and nominated by Harry Truman to chair the Commission in 1949. Chairing the subcommittee formed to examine Olds' re-nomination, Johnson ensured that all seven senators on the subcommittee were Communist haters and presented witness after witness who told the committee that Olds "commends Lenin"; supports "Marxian doctrine"; "praises the Russian system as the coming world order and as a model for the United States"; "preaches class war; echoes the Communist doctrine of class struggle, surplus value, exploitation, downfall of capitalism, and international action by workers, as proclaimed by Karl Marx in his *Communist Manifesto* and *Das Kapital*."[168] These claims were supported with statements from articles written by Olds over the course of years,[169] many of which had been published in the *Daily*

---

166 Richard Reeves, *President Kennedy: Profile of Power* (New York: Touchstone, 1994), 604.

167 James MacGregor Burns, *John Kennedy, A Political Profile* (New York: Harcourt, Brace & Company, 1959), 88–89.

168 Robert A. Caro, *The Years of Lyndon Johnson: Master of the Senate* (New York: Vintage Books, 2003), 248, 253–254, 257.

169 Ibid., 257–260.

Worker, "official organ of the Communist Party."[170] Newspapers across the country led their reports on the hearings with Senator Clyde Reed's proclamation that Leland Olds was "a first class, full-fledged Communist." "SENATOR REED HITS OLDS AS A COMMUNIST," headlined the *New York Times*. The *Houston Post* reported "LELAND OLDS LABELED CRACKPOT AND TRAITOR," while the *Chicago Tribune* noted that Olds had been "Denounced as a traitor to his country."[171]

"I do not charge that Mr. Olds is a Communist," said Johnson on the floor of the Senate. "No member of the subcommittee made any such accusation." Yet Leland Olds, said Johnson, chose "to travel with those who proposed the Marxian answer. His choice was not dictated by necessity; the company he chose, he chose of his own free will. He spoke from the same platforms [as] Earl Browder. He accepted subsidy from the so-called Garland Fund, a fund created and expended to keep alive Marxist organs and Marxist groups....There can be no question about the environment, the trend of thought, the bent of mind of Leland Olds." Johnson ended with a devastating flourish: "Shall we have a commissioner or a commissar?"[172]

Leland Olds stood not a chance. His nomination was rejected by a vote of 53-15. And Joseph McCarthy, it should be noted, had nothing to do with it.

VII

The s.o.b....is guilty as hell.[173]

Harry Truman on Alger Hiss

On the last occasion on which I saw [Alger Hiss], the dinner table was a convention of all that is noblest in New York left-wing tradition. (I do not name names.) As coffee time drew near, I

---

170 Ibid., 257.

171 Ibid., 278–279.

172 Ibid., 294–295.

173 Tanenhaus, *Whitaker Chambers*, 438. Like Clark Clifford, Truman lied shamelessly to the public when discussing the subject of espionage. Asked during a television interview in 1956 whether he thought Hiss was a Communist spy, Truman said, "No I do not." Evans, *Blacklisted by History*, 324.

52

whispered sarcastically to the hostess: "Why don't we secure the doors and say: 'Look, Alger, it's just us. Come on. You're among friends. Tell us why you really did it.'" She gave me a look, and a pinch, which eloquently conveyed the words Don't Even Think About It. And it's true that this has long been, for many people, a loyalty oath of its own. If Hiss was wrong, then Nixon and McCarthy were right. And that could not be.[174]

Christopher Hitchens

For those who do not believe in fairies, the Hiss affair is now closed.[175]

Tony Judt

In January 1950, Alger Hiss, the career state department officer who had famously denied under oath Whittaker Chambers' allegations that he had engaged in espionage, was convicted of perjury. Well-deserved (Hiss was a long-time, decorated Soviet agent[176]), the conviction was due in no small part to the efforts of Richard Nixon, who appeared before the grand jury convened to indict Chambers and attacked both Hiss and the Truman administration, outlining his belief in Hiss's guilt and lecturing the grand jurors on their duty to "reach the decision that will be in the best interests of the country."[177] Hiss being ground zero in the Communists-in-government issue,[178] Republicans were ecstatic over the conviction. Within two weeks, Klaus Fuchs was arrested in England and charged with passing nuclear secrets to the Soviets while working as a physicist on the Manhattan Project. He confessed and identified American Harry Gold as a co-conspirator. Gold, in turn, confessed to the FBI as quickly as had Fuchs and identified David Greenglass as a co-conspirator. Greenglass then

---

174 Christopher Hitchens, *The Quotable Hitchens* (Cambridge: Da Capo Press, 2011), 129.

175 Tony Judt, *Reappraisals: Reflections on the Forgotten Twentieth Century* (New York: Penguin Group, 2008), 299.

176 Weinstein and Vassiliev, *The Haunted Wood*, 268–269; Tanenhaus, *Whitaker Chambers*, 518–520.

177 Theoharis, *Chasing Spies*, 125–126.

178 Fried, *Nightmare in Red*, 17.

gave the FBI Julius and Ethel Rosenberg, his sister and brother-in-law. These espionage charges made headlines in every newspaper in this country, proving to the American public as nothing else could that Soviet penetration of this government was "a real problem, not a witch hunter's fantasy."[179]

Republicans did well in the 1950 elections, which forced Truman to act, just as he acted in 1947 with Executive Order 9835. But once again, politics, not security, was the order of the day. Truman attempted to create a presidential commission to defend *his* loyalty program.[180] In an effort to make the commission appear non-partisan, Truman asked former president Herbert Hoover (who described Communism as "the most disastrous plague that has come to free men"[181]) to chair the inquiry. Hoover, however, was as aware as anyone of "the clandestine activities" of American Communists that were "common knowledge" in Washington and had no intention of being used in this manner.[182] So he refused, explaining that far more than a review of current loyalty procedures was needed and informing Truman that Congress, as an independent body, should investigate not just existing procedures but the backgrounds and activities of federal employees.[183] This, he told Truman, would require congressional access to all loyalty files—files that Truman had refused to provide congressional investigators for years. Truman, of course, had no more intention of committing political suicide than did Richard Nixon during the Watergate affair, so he rejected Hoover's recommendations and continued his refusal to provide Congress with the materials needed to investigate this country's "massive and intractable security

---

179 Herman, *Joseph McCarthy*, 112. As with Hiss, the Left spent decades portraying the Rosenbergs as innocent victims of anti-Communist hysteria. We now know, however, that Julius Rosenberg, like Hiss, was guilty as charged. "57 Years Later, Figure in Rosenberg Case Says He Spied for Soviets," *New York Times*, September 12, 2008; "Father Was a Spy, Sons Conclude With Regret," *New York Times*, September 18, 2008; "A Rosenberg Co-Conspirator Reveals More about His Role," *New York Times*, March 21, 2011.
180 Theoharis, *Seeds of Repression*, 168.
181 Hoover, *Freedom Betrayed*, 13.
182 Ibid., 30–53.
183 Theoharis, *Seeds of Repression*, 169.

problem."[184] Congress made another attempt to investigate internal security matters in 1952, and Truman again refused to provide requested information, citing separation of powers, executive privilege and national security.[185]

Interestingly, this is exactly what both Richard Nixon and Donald Trump did in response to congressional investigations of their administrations, as a brief review of the charges against them reveals.

Article III of Nixon's Articles of Impeachment reads as follows:

> In his conduct of the office of President of the United States, Richard M. Nixon, contrary to his oath faithfully to execute the office of President of the United States and, to the best of his ability, preserve, protect, and defend the Constitution of the United States, and in violation of his constitutional duty to take care that the laws be faithfully executed, has failed without lawful cause or excuse to produce papers and things as directed by duly authorized subpoenas issued by the Committee on the Judiciary of the House of Representatives on April 11, 1974, May 15, 1974, May 30, 1974, and June 24, 1974, and willfully disobeyed such subpoenas.

Likewise, Article II of Donald Trump's Impeachment charged that, "without lawful cause or excuse, President Trump directed Executive Branch agencies, offices, and officials not to comply with [congressional] subpoenas," exactly as Truman had. On October 10, 2019, seventeen former Watergate prosecutors signed a letter published in the *Washington Post* declaring that "Trump should be impeached" because he had "obstructed lawful congressional investigations by systematically withholding evidence and by directing government agencies and employees to refuse to cooperate with legitimate oversight by Congress." This conduct involved "multiple acts of obstruction of justice in violation of

184 Herman, *Joseph McCarthy*, 107.
185 Theoharis, *Seeds of Repression*, 179.

federal criminal statutes and his oath of office to "take care that the laws be faithfully executed."[186]

There are only two differences between Truman's "[obstruction of] lawful congressional investigations" and that undertaken by Nixon and Trump: 1) Truman's involved matters exponentially more substantial than those involving Nixon and Trump; 2) Truman got away with it, and to this very day, no one seems to notice or care.

And yet, despite a level of ineptitude, dishonesty and partisanship that can only be described as staggering, the espionage networks it had taken the Soviets years to construct were crippled by 1950 due to: 1) the congressional testimony of Whittaker Chambers and Elizabeth Bentley, who exposed and thereby neutralized scores of Soviet agents and their contacts working within this government; 2) Truman's Loyalty Program, which drove thousands of Communist Party members and their supporters and sympathizers out of government; 3) the virtual destruction of the CPUSA through Smith Act prosecutions; and 4) an atmosphere so intensely anti-Communist that it became virtually impossible for the Soviets to recruit agents to replace those who had been exposed or otherwise driven from government.[187] (Soviet agent Rudolph Abel, who would be exchanged in 1962 for U-2 pilot Francis Gary Powers, arrived here in 1948, and in eight years recruited not a single American for Soviet intelligence.[188]) In addition, the Soviets were made aware of Venona through the efforts of both William Weisband, a Soviet agent working within the Army Security Agency, and British master spy Kim Philby, which also caused a curtailing of espionage activities.[189] Precious few of those whose treachery was so damaging to this country were ever prosecuted, however, and many of the most dangerous Soviet agents would continue their

---

186 "We Investigated the Watergate Scandal. We Believe Trump Should be Impeached. *Washington Post,* October 10, 2019.

187 Morgan, *Reds*, 374–376.

188 Ibid., 375.

189 Weinstein and Vassiliev, *Venona*, 47–52; Weinstein and Vassiliev, *The Haunted Wood*, 291; Katherine A.S. Sibley, *Red Spies in America: Stolen Secrets and the Dawn of the Cold War* (Lawrence: University Press of Kansas, 2004), 191.

efforts right through the Korean War, doing enormous damage to this country in the process.[190]

VIII

The design, therefore, calls for the complete subversion or forcible destruction of the machinery of government and structure of society in the countries of the non-Soviet world and their replacement by an apparatus and structure subservient to and controlled from the Kremlin. To that end Soviet efforts are now directed toward the domination of the Eurasian land mass. The United States, as the principal center of power in the non-Soviet world and the bulwark of opposition to Soviet expansion, is the principal enemy whose integrity and vitality must be subverted or destroyed by one means or another if the Kremlin is to achieve its fundamental design.[191]

NSC-68

In April 1950, the National Security Council completed and presented to President Truman the Strategic Reassessment of 1950 (NSC-68), which was probably the most important single document of the early Cold War era. "The purpose of NSC-68," said Dean Acheson, "was to so bludgeon the mass mind of 'top government' that not only could the President make a decision but the decision

---

190 That high-level espionage continued as long as it did is particularly inexcusable given that, of the large number of Americans serving Soviet interests throughout the New Deal and the early years of the Truman Era—to include those who provided Stalin inside information and nuclear technology that led directly to the war in Korea—many (if not most) were fools and dilettantes who confessed when apprehended and cooperated fully, like Julian Wadleigh, a Soviet spy who had worked with Whittaker Chambers during the 1930s, and the atomic spies Klaus Fuchs, Harry Gold and David Greenglass. In fact, the Soviet-funded and controlled CPUSA, along with the espionage networks it facilitated, could have been demolished as early as 1940, when Whittaker Chambers and Elizabeth Bentley first came forward, had its leadership been prosecuted relentlessly yet lawfully under 18 U.S.C. §951 for failing to register as the agents of a foreign government that they were, in law and in fact. See Theoharis, *Chasing Spies*, 56-57. See also *United States v. Duran*, 563 F.3d 1283 (11th Cir. 2010); *United States v. Khaled Abdul-Latif* 424 F.3d 566 (7th Cir. 2003).

191 NSC 68: "United States Objectives and Programs for National Security," April 14, 1950 ("NSC-68"). http://www.mtholyoke.edu/acad/intrel/nsc-68/nsc68-1.htm, accessed May 10, 2012.

could be carried out."[192] NSC-68 began by outlining fundamental differences between aims and purposes of the United States and the USSR: Americans wanted "to create conditions under which our free and democratic system can live and prosper" while "the fundamental design of those who control the Soviet Union and the international Communist movement is to retain and solidify their absolute power, first in the Soviet Union and second in the areas now under their control." NSC-68 analyzed the military needs of the United States in terms of a serious, long-term military and political threat that would require attention and planning long into the foreseeable future. The contrast between the potential obligations of and threats to the United States in the spring of 1950 on the one hand, and American military strength, which was described as "dangerously inadequate," on the other, was articulated forcefully. The issue was not whether this country had the capability to deter or if necessary confront directly an attack on it, but whether this government intended to maintain, in the long term, the military forces necessary to deter Communist adventurism wherever and whenever it manifested. In other words, did America have the means to support the ends outlined by Harry Truman in 1947? The answer was a resounding "No." "For example, it is clear that our present weakness would prevent us from offering effective resistance at any of several vital pressure points. The only deterrent we can present to the Kremlin is the evidence we give that we may make any of the critical points which we cannot hold the occasion for a global war of annihilation."[193] NSC-68 predicted "aggressive action against all or most soft spots on [the Soviet Empire's] periphery" and recommended the *tripling* of US defense expenditures in response.

As he had when Truman outlined his doctrine, George Kennan dissented, noting in later years that "with the preparation of NSC-68 I had nothing to do."[194] "I was disgusted," he would later write,

---

192 Dean Acheson, *Present at the Creation: My Years in the State Department* (New York: W.W. Norton & Co., 1969), 374.
193 NSC 68.
194 Thompson, *The Hawk and the Dove*, 113.

"about the assumptions regarding Soviet intentions."[195] Truman seemed to agree with Kennan, there being little evidence that he actually believed any of his own rhetoric regarding the force and scope of his famous doctrine.[196] But congressional elections loomed. Democrats were desperate for a way to prove their anti-Communist mettle while Republicans, embracing the Permanent Campaign with equal fervor, abandoned their previously conservative approach to foreign policy and became the Democrats' mirror image. It was not, in other words, bi-partisan consensus, shared core values, long-term vision and "brilliant" American leadership that forged American policy during the Cold War's early years but rather a perfect storm of self-interest, partisanship and unique circumstances, domestic and foreign. By 1950, the United States was primed for war. The only question was where. Korea would have that most unlucky honor.

IX

But it all seems so useless and stupid. To "liberate" South Korea we're destroying it and its people in the course of war more than we are the North Koreans. All Koreans hate us. Everyone here is an enemy. We can't trust anyone.[197]

Colonel Paul Freeman
Naktong, South Korea
September 1950

---

195 Ibid.

196 After studying the apocalyptic, anti-Communist report prepared by Clark Clifford and George Elsey in 1946, Truman ordered Clifford to provide all twenty copies to him. Clifford did so, and they disappeared, never to be seen again. But for the fact that Clifford kept one complete draft, the Clifford-Elsey Report would have been lost to history. See also McCullough, *Truman*, 772: When the National Security Council delivered NSC-68 in the spring of 1950 (which resembled Clifford-Elsey in tone and content), Truman locked it away.

197 David Halberstam, *The Coldest Winter: America and the Korean War* (New York: Hyperion, 2007), 286.

I've always believed that the Korean War could not stand the light of day.[198]

Professor Bruce Cumings

In 1945, Korea was a small, poverty-stricken country that had been annexed by Japan in 1910 and remained under Japanese control until the end of World War II. The Japanese were as exploitative and brutal in Korea as they were in every other country they seized, and the Korean people hated them, along with their own indigenous upper class, which, as in any country long colonized, acquired success and position through collaboration. By the end of World War II, the situation was ripe for the acquisition of power by indigenous Communists, who were described by the CIA as a "grassroots independence movement which found expression in the establishment of the people's committees throughout Korea in August 1945."[199] In other words, Korean society was in the midst of a revolutionary, post-colonial upheaval, and left to its own devices, Korea would undoubtedly have become a non-aligned Communist country of its own accord, just like Yugoslavia, in the wake of World War II.

But the great powers had other ideas. Korea was divided along the 38th parallel by the United States and the Soviets, with each occupying power sponsoring a Korean government of its choosing within its zone of occupation. *The Korean people had no say in the matter.* The Soviets gave their support to Kim Il Sung, whose credentials as both a revolutionary nationalist and an experienced guerilla fighter appeared unimpeachable. The United States, on the other hand, supported Syngman Rhee, an American-educated nationalist and fierce anti-Communist, who formed his government (described by the CIA as "essentially demagogues bent on autocratic rule"[200]) under American auspices.

---

198 Hanley, Choe and Mendoza, *The Bridge at No Gun Ri*, 232–233.

199 Bruce Cumings, *Korea's Place in the Sun: A Modern History* (New York: W.W. Norton & Company, 1997), 202.

200 Halliday and Cumings, *Korea: The Unknown War*, 23.

Unlike their Communist opponents, who had acquired legitimacy and moral authority among Koreans as a result of their long-standing resistance to the Japanese, the Rhee government was comprised of upper-class collaborators and led by an expatriate who had lived in the United States for forty years. As of September 1945, Americans on the scene harbored no illusions about where they stood:

> Southern Korea can best be described as a powder keg ready to explode at the application of a spark. There is great disappointment that immediate independence and sweeping out of the Japanese did not eventuate. [Those Koreans who] achieved high rank under the Japanese are considered pro-Japanese and are hated almost as much as their masters....The most encouraging single factor in the political situation is the presence in Seoul of *several hundred conservatives* among the older and better educated Koreans. Although many of them have served the Japanese, that stigma ought eventually to disappear. Such persons favor the return of the "Provisional Government" and although they may not constitute a majority, they are probably the largest single group.[201]

The quoted passages are accurate with one important exception: "The historical documentation could not be clearer: the United States intervened on behalf of the smallest group in Korea, not [the] 'largest single group,' and helped perpetuate its privileges thereafter."[202]

America's client was easily portrayed by the Communists as a collaborationist regime willing to exchange one set of foreign masters for another. General John R. Hodge, who commanded the US occupation forces in Korea, wrote in early 1946 that "[t]he word

---

201 H. Merrell Benninghoff, political adviser to General Hodge, quoted in Cumings, *Korea's Place in the Sun,* 192–193 (emphasis added by Professor Cumings).
202 Cumings, *Korea's Place in the Sun,* 193–194.

pro-American is being added to pro-Jap, national traitor, and collaborator."[203] In other words, the Korean Communists argued with considerable success exactly what the Vietnamese Communists and the antiwar Left would assert twenty years later with regard to Vietnam: The United States had stepped into the shoes of the recently vanquished colonial occupier. The effect was predictable: massive opposition from the South Korean people; suppression of people's committees in the provinces; a major rebellion in the fall of 1946; and guerilla warfare by 1948.[204]

Rhee eventually mounted a full-scale campaign to bring his rebellious subjects to heel. It was a war of exceptional brutality on the part of all participants. Although there was little public scrutiny in the West, this campaign was a subject of considerable interest in Washington. Colonel Preston Goodfellow told Rhee in 1948 that he had "many opportunities to talk with [Acheson] about Korea" and that guerillas must be "cleaned out quickly...everyone is watching how Korea handles the Communist threat." Eliminate this threat, and "Korea will be held in high esteem."[205] By the time Rhee's campaign was over in 1950, more than 100,000 South Koreans had been killed,[206] tens of thousands more had been tortured and imprisoned, thousands of villages had been razed to the ground and hundreds of thousands of people had been made homeless.

Many of Rhee's senior officers had held commissions in the Japanese Army during Japan's colonization of Korea. They simply exchanged their Japanese uniforms for American uniforms and went to work for Truman. For example, Chae Pyong-dok, chief of staff of the South Korean Army, had served as an officer in the Imperial Japanese Army. Kim Paek-il, who was a top commander during Rhee's suppression campaign, also learned his trade in Japanese service. Chong Il-gwon, who served the Japanese in the

---

203 Ibid., 198.

204 Ibid., 192.

205 Bruce Cumings, *The Origins of the Korean War*, vol. 2, *The Roaring of the Cataract* (Princeton: Princeton University Press, 1990), 285.

206 Bruce Cumings, *The Origins of the Korean War*, vol. 1, *Liberation and the Emergence of Separate Regimes 1945–1947* (Princeton: Princeton University Press, 1989), xxi; Patterson, *Grand Expectations*, 208.

Kwantung Army, became chief of staff of the South Korean Constabulary in 1947 and eventually prime minister.[207]

In May 1948, elections were held in South Korea as they were in all US protectorates during the Cold War. Rhee and his party won, as certified by a United Nations commission. (An Australian delegate noted that the elections were under "the control of a single party"[208] and drafted a resolution that would have eliminated any UN sanctioning of the outcome. The resolution, of course, was not adopted.) Thus was born America's ally, the Republic of Korea. "The problem was that Korean society had no base for either a liberal or a democratic party as Americans understood it; it had a population the vast majority of which consisted of poor peasants, and a tiny minority of which held most of the wealth: landowners, who formed the real base of the [American-supported Korean Democratic Party]."[209] So this country's entire Korean enterprise depended, in the long run, on its ability to form a viable, stable government in South Korea based upon, at least at its inception, a military and civilian cadre having no legitimacy among a large percentage of their own people.

Given this country's involvement in Korea, Truman's efforts to create a viable government allied to the United States seem reasonable. But first-order questions must be addressed: Why were Americans there at all? Once the Japanese had been disarmed and repatriated, the reason for America's entry into Korea was at an end, and American leaders, both military and civilian, had determined that Korea was a strategic liability, not an asset. George Kennan, hailed by David Halberstam as "the most brilliant American strategist of the era," considered America's position in Korea to be useless: "Since the territory is not of decisive strategic importance to us, our main task is to extricate ourselves without too much loss of prestige."[210] General Eisenhower and the Joint Chiefs of Staff were equally forceful: "The United States has little strategic interest

---

207 Cumings, *The Origins of the Korean War*, vol. 2, 234, 287. See also "Korea's Tricky Task: Digging Up Past Treachery," *New York Times*, January 5, 2005.

208 Cumings, *Korea's Place in the Sun*, 211.

209 Ibid., 193.

210 Halberstam, *The Fifties*, 64.

in maintaining the present troops and bases in Korea." In 1948, the Joint Chiefs concluded that the United States should accept the "probability" that Korea would in time be dominated by the USSR.[211] Truman concurred, declaring that military action in Korea "would not constitute a casus belli for the United States."[212] And in January 1950, Dean Acheson appeared at the National Press Club and outlined an American defense perimeter that did not include Korea.[213] No one, it seems, believed on the merits that Korea was of any real interest to this country, and they made this clear to everyone.

X

If the Soviets know where the holdline is drawn they will move on what isn't protected like any predatory animal.[214]

Donald Maclean

By 1950, Kim Il Sung felt that the time was right to unite Korea under his rule. In fact, he likely realized that it was now or never. For Truman, with great brutality and little if any scrutiny, had accomplished in South Korea what his successors would fight so hard to accomplish in South Vietnam: the suppression of a Communist-nationalist revolt by what would eventually become a viable, American-created government. Kim Il Sung understood that without overt military intervention by the North, South Korea was here to stay. But North Korea was militarily superior to South Korea, and Kim assumed, quite reasonably, that the United States would not intervene if he attacked. Truman had not, after all, introduced American forces into Greece or China but had acted largely through surrogates, as he had thus far in Korea. When they were successful (Greece), Truman accepted the benefits; when they were defeated (China), he accepted the loss. Mao Tse-tung,

---

211 James Chace, *Acheson: The Secretary of State Who Created the American World* (New York: Simon & Schuster, 1998), 269.

212 William Manchester, *American Caesar* (Boston: Little Brown & Company, 1978), 540.

213 H.W. Crocker, III, *Don't Tread on Me: A 400-Year History of America at War, from Indian Fighting to Terrorist Hunting* (New York: Crown Forum, 2006), 341.

214 Newton, *The Cambridge Spies*, 187.

moreover, was spoiling for a fight with the West and supported Kim, who skillfully played his Mao card and made this known to Stalin. Stalin, for his part, gave this operation his blessing for a number of reasons, not the least of which was the information provided him by his spies.[215]

Donald Maclean, who was recruited by the Soviets while a student at Cambridge, was one of Stalin's top agents. A career British diplomat, Maclean served in Washington, where he acted "as both saboteur to the West and adviser to the East."[216] "As a saboteur he operated behind enemy lines, fouling the machinery of Western foreign policy and sowing distrust among Anglo-American diplomats. As an adviser he could tell Stalin which cards the West held and how they intended to play them during the high-stakes geostrategic poker game that took place in the immediate postwar years."[217] Maclean attended both the secret meetings that led to the formation of the North Atlantic Treaty Organization ("NATO") and the American National Security Council sessions that formulated American policy in Asia,[218] and he provided Stalin with every bit of information that came into his hands, including Truman's official exclusion of the Asian mainland from the US defense perimeter.[219]

Although previously refusing to sanction Kim's assault on South Korea, Stalin authorized the operation in April 1950, citing: 1) the changed international environment (the Communists had defeated the Nationalists in China); 2) Soviet acquisition of nuclear weapons; and 3) "information coming from the United States."[220] Stalin did

215 Gaddis, *We Now Know*, 72–75.

216 Newton, *The Cambridge Spies*, 97.

217 Ibid.

218 Gaddis, *We Now Know*, 72.

219 Katheryn Weathersby, "The Soviet Role in the Korean War" in *The Korean War in World History*, ed. William Stueck (Lexington: University Press of Kentucky, 2004). See also Thompson, *The Hawk and the Dove*, 117.

220 Kathryn Weathersby, *"Should We Fear This?" Stalin and the Danger of War with America*, Woodrow Wilson International Center for Scholars, Working Paper No. 39, July 2002: "The Soviet Role in the Korean War." By March 1943, Stalin's spies had already provided enough information to accelerate Stalin's bomb by two full years. And this was just the start; nuclear espionage continued almost without interruption until 1949. See Richard Rhodes, *Dark Sun: The Making of the Hydrogen*

not need "press briefings" by Dean Acheson or anyone else to know that Truman did not intend to defend South Korea, and, half a century of conventional wisdom notwithstanding, it is foolish to suggest otherwise.[221] According to Professor Cumings, the very idea that Stalin "of all people" would launch a war as the result of a Press Club speech is "stupefyingly improbable," particularly when "Stalin was reading top secret American documents with his breakfast, courtesy of the British spies—Philby, McLean, Burgess, Blake, and that lot."[222]

Stalin warned Kim, however, that he would not involve the Soviet Union in any direct confrontation with the United States and made absolutely clear to Kim that he and Mao would have to stand on their own if the United States unexpectedly resisted.[223] With Mao's agreement in May, everything was in place. If Kim succeeded, of course, his victory would be Stalin's victory. If the United States resisted, huge reserves of Chinese manpower were available to fight in Communism's name, turning America's effort into a bloody nightmare that Stalin might well exploit elsewhere, perhaps even in Europe.[224] For Stalin, this was the best of all worlds, and on June 25, 1950, the second half of the twentieth century exploded into being as some 90,000 troops of the Korean People's Army swarmed into South Korea.[225] With the rise of global military power, American domestic politics would dictate world events as America's

---

Bomb (New York: Simon & Schuster, 1995), 74. The Soviets' first nuclear bomb, moreover, was a virtual carbon copy of the weapon dropped on Hiroshima. Ibid., 364.

221 See Newton, *The Cambridge Spies*, 136: "Stalin fervently believed that the Western media were a mirror of his own, a government-controlled propaganda tool. Certainly, any Soviet intelligence officer who stood before him and recommended action based on an item in *The Times* of London or *The New York Times* would quickly find himself bundled off to Lubyanka prison or Siberia's gulags."

222 Cumings, *The Origins of the Korean War*, vol. 2, 410. See also Thompson, *The Hawk and the Dove,* 117: "Stalin, fearing a clash with the United States, hesitated. Finally, after a top spy assured [Stalin] that the United States would not respond [to an attack on South Korea], he relented."

223 Gaddis, *We Now Know*, 74; Chang and Halliday, *Mao, The Unknown Story*, 361; Perret, *Commander in Chief*, 142.

224 Chang and Halliday, *Mao, The Unknown Story*, 359.

225 Manchester, *American Caesar*, 545.

problems became everyone's problems.[226]

Truman's efforts in Korea were hampered at the outset because the United States Army was in appalling shape,[227] and as with Stalin's acquisition of both high-level strategic planning and nuclear weapons through espionage, Truman had only himself to blame. In June 1950, the Army numbered only 591,000 men, and these numbers were "egregiously misleading."[228] Its ten "tactical" divisions had been crippled by budget cuts to which the Army responded by deactivating one battalion of three in each infantry regiment and one firing battery out of three in each of the divisional artillery battalions. "Inasmuch as Army doctrine and training were rigidly based on the concept of three-battalion regiments, and no substitute doctrine had been (or could be) promulgated, the deactivation greatly impaired—even crippled—the combat capability and 'readiness' of the divisions."[229] Moreover, "the 1948, 1949, and 1950 'peacetime' drafts, which provided a total of 300,000 men, had filled the army with all too many disgruntled, indifferent or even hostile soldiers. (For the affluent the draft was not difficult to evade.)"[230] Stockpiles of World War II equipment were deteriorating, and many of these weapons were outdated and of little use even if functional. "By June 25, 1950, Harry Truman and [Secretary of Defense] Louis Johnson had all but wrecked the conventional military forces of the United States."[231]

As Truman struggled with the undermanned, ill-trained and badly organized army he had worked so hard to create, his Republic of Korea collapsed like a house of cards. Not only would the South Koreans not fight, they ran away "like turpentined rats," beginning

---

226 As for the UN authorization that has always been cited to provide both legal and moral authority for Truman's war in Korea, it was certainly helpful but in no way essential. According to Dean Acheson, Truman was going to fight in Korea with or without UN approval. Merle Miller, *Plain Speaking*, (New York: Berkley Publishing, 1973), 276–278. See also Cumings, *Korea's Place in the Sun*, 264–265.

227 Clay Blair, *The Forgotten War: America in Korea, 1950–1953* (New York: Times Books, 1987), 27.

228 Ibid., 28.

229 Ibid.

230 Ibid.

231 Ibid., 29 [bracketed material added].

with the president and the senior military leadership.[232] By 1951, the South Korean Army had abandoned ten divisions worth of equipment on the battlefield.[233] In August 1950, George Kennan recommended that this country just leave South Korea to the Communists, stating, "It is beyond our capabilities to keep Korea permanently out of the Soviet orbit."[234] And yet Truman stayed, doing whatever was necessary to defend the line he had drawn. The massive defense expenditures outlined in NSC-68 were undertaken, with $48.2 billion—triple the defense budget for the prior year—appropriated for fiscal 1950-51 and $60 billion for fiscal 1951-52.[235] *Seldom in history has anyone so badly miscalculated as had Kim Il Sung and Stalin.*

Quickly driven into a defensive perimeter around the port of Pusan at the southeastern tip of the peninsula, American and South Korean forces, their backs to the sea, could retreat no further. Douglas MacArthur took charge of the American-led UN effort, and his first move was an amphibious landing at Inchon on September 15, nearly 200 miles behind the Communist forces besieging Pusan. It was a masterstroke that, in one move, saved the forces trapped at Pusan and, if properly exploited, would have bagged virtually the entire North Korean Army. But MacArthur erred grievously after Inchon. He lost much valuable time due to an ill-advised landing at Wonsan, where it took weeks to clear the harbor of mines, and large numbers of North Korean troops—most likely some 40,000—were able to escape.[236] Nevertheless, it was clear that by October 1950, the war for South Korea was over. Seoul, the capital, had been retaken and virtually destroyed in September. ("Few people have suffered so terrible a liberation," said British reporter Reginald Thompson.[237]) However, the war in fact had barely started, and "the Legacy of the '30s" would continue to play a commanding role.

K.M. Panikkar, India's ambassador to Beijing, was summoned

---

232 Bruce Cumings, *North Korea: Another Country* (New York: The New Press, 2004), 10.

233 Ibid.

234 Michael Lind, *Vietnam: The Necessary War* (New York: The Free Press, 1999), 68.

235 McCullough, *Truman*, 792.

236 Blair, *The Forgotten War*, 319.

237 Halberstam, *The Coldest Winter*, 311.

by Zhou Enlai and told bluntly that if the Americans crossed the thirty-eighth parallel, China would intervene in Korea.[238] Word of this reached Truman in short order (as intended), but he paid no heed.[239] "Occasional warnings from [George] Kennan and Paul Nitze, among others, could not dampen the enthusiasm of Dean Rusk, assistant secretary of state for Far Eastern affairs; and, most important, Dean Acheson and Harry Truman."[240] According to Professor Cumings, the historical record leaves no room for doubt: It was Truman in Washington, not MacArthur in Tokyo, who decided on the drive to the Yalu River, which formed the northern border between China and Korea.[241] Although a number of factors contributed to the decision, even Truman's great admirer David Halberstam admitted the overwhelming influence of domestic politics.[242] That Truman and his advisers "were more afraid of [MacArthur] than they wanted to admit was always the great secret of the Korean War. They were afraid of him in defeat and they were even more afraid of him in victory."[243] Orders were issued by Secretary of Defense George Marshall on September 27, 1950, telling MacArthur that he was free "to proceed north of the 38th parallel."[244]

Driving north to the Yalu, MacArthur violated one of the most basic principles of warfare by splitting his forces, with Eighth Army in the west, Tenth Corps in the east and a considerable gap between them. He also ignored a vast amount of solid intelligence from reliable sources warning that the Chinese had entered Korea in force. Not only had American and South Korean units repeatedly captured Chinese prisoners who were quite forthcoming about the scope of Chinese intervention, but former Nationalist officers whose units had been incorporated into Mao's forces provided a

---

238 Blair, *The Forgotten War*, 336. See also Halberstam, *The Coldest Winter*, 334–336.

239 Manchester, *American Caesar*, 586.

240 *The Truman Presidency*, ed. Michael J. Lacy (New York: Cambridge University Press, 1991), 428.

241 Bruce Cumings, *The Korean War* (New York: The Modern Library, 2010), 22.

242 Halberstam, *The Coldest Winter*, 330; Blair, *The Forgotten War*, 326.

243 Halberstam, *The Coldest Winter*, 331.

244 Thompson, *The Hawk and the Dove*, 123.

constant flow of information on their movements and whereabouts to their former comrades on Taiwan.[245] MacArthur, however, convinced himself that the Chinese would never enter the war, and his inept, sycophantic intelligence chief, Major General Charles Willoughby, saw to it that all information corresponded with MacArthur's desires. Said Lieutenant Colonel John Chiles, "MacArthur did not *want* the Chinese to enter the war in Korea," and "anything MacArthur wanted, Willoughby produced intelligence for....In this case, Willoughby falsified intelligence reports....He should have gone to jail."[246] Regardless, "There is no stopping MacArthur now," said Dean Acheson.[247] But stopped MacArthur would be, and a government "loaded with Communists"[248] on the Democrats' watch would play a crucial role.

XI

That there was some leak in intelligence was evident to everyone. [General Walton] Walker continually complained to me that his operations were known to the enemy in advance through sources in Washington.[249]

Douglas MacArthur

More than thirty years ago, William Manchester wrote in *American Caesar* that Douglas MacArthur believed in the autumn of 1950 that his strategic plans were being leaked to the Communists. MacArthur was not alone: "I have no doubt whatever," said General James Gavin, "that the Chinese moved confidently and skillfully into North Korea, and, in fact, I believe that they were able to do this because they were well-informed not only of the moves Walker would make but of the limitations on what he might do."[250] Manchester, as moderate and Vital Center a

---

245 Blair, *The Forgotten War*, 377; Halberstam, *The Coldest Winter*, 379–380.

246 Blair, *The Forgotten War*, 377 (emphasis in the original).

247 Halberstam, *The Coldest Winter*, 331–332.

248 Bernstein, *Loyalties*, 79.

249 Manchester, *American Caesar*, 596.

250 Ibid., 597.

Democrat as ever lived, concurred: "Almost certainly the enemy was now being provided with MacArthur's battle plans."[251]

We now know, of course, that MacArthur and Gavin were correct. Donald Maclean, head of the American Department at the British Embassy in Washington, provided Stalin with all of the policy and operational decisions coming from London, Washington and Tokyo.[252] Also involved in this espionage were Kim Philby, liaison officer between the CIA and the British Secret Intelligence Service, and Guy Burgess, who, among other duties, was assigned to the top secret Inter-Allied Board. According to Rebecca West, called "the world's best reporter" by none other than Harry Truman, "Every secret they learned during their official lives was certainly transmitted to the Soviet Union."[253] Also involved in espionage was George Blake, who was chief of British intelligence in Seoul in 1950.[254] Peking and Moscow knew everything UN Forces considered, accepted, rejected, intended and planned, and they used their knowledge to maximum effect.[255]

On the night of November 25, 1950, nearly 300,000 Chinese troops executed a powerful attack against MacArthur's forces, which were badly deployed and dangerously thin, as the Chinese general staff knew, courtesy of the Soviet agents who, according to orthodoxy, were the figments of fevered, right-wing imaginations. Within weeks, American forces, taking heavy casualties, were driven south of the 38th parallel, and Seoul was retaken by Communist forces on January 4, 1951. Chinese General Lin Pao later wrote: "I would never have made the attack and risked my men and military reputation if I had not been assured that Washington would restrain General MacArthur from taking adequate retaliatory

---

251 Ibid., 604.

252 Newton, *The Cambridge Spies*, 295–296.

253 Manchester, *American Caesar*, 597.

254 Cumings, *The Origins of the Korean War*, vol. 2, 410.

255 Not even the Inchon landing was the surprise that orthodoxy would have us believe. With his 98,000-man force (1/3 of them now raw replacements) completely tied up at Pusan fighting UN forces totaling 140,000 by September 1950, there was simply nothing Kim could do about Inchon. He could only hope to break through and destroy the forces at Pusan, then turn to face MacArthur coming down the peninsula. But the Pusan perimeter held, and caught between two forces, the predator quickly became prey. Cumings, *Korea's Place in the Sun*, 275–276.

measures against my lines of supply and communication."[256] (It seems rather clear from this that, however badly MacArthur conducted military operations after Inchon—and he conducted them very badly—the primary cause of the disaster inflicted by Chinese forces in December 1950 was, like the war in Korea itself, Truman's fecklessness on internal security, which orthodoxy simply does not acknowledge.) For example, MacArthur was instructed "NOT repeat NOT to destroy the Suiho dam,"[257] which spanned the Yalu River between China and Korea and, as the world's fourth largest electrical generating plant, supplied electricity throughout North Korea. The effect of this order, once transmitted to the Communists, was predictable: Chinese forces, now immune from air attack, massed and attacked south of the dam.[258]

As the war dragged on and casualties mounted, MacArthur, chafing under the restrictions imposed by Washington, pushed for authority to widen the war. He criticized the Truman administration, publicly and repeatedly, violating a directive issued by Truman in December 1950 prohibiting all such communiqués without prior approval. Time and again, MacArthur issued thinly veiled slaps at Truman, criticizing Truman's "wholly unrealistic and illusory" notions of "positional warfare" that would "insure the destruction of our forces piecemeal"; "abnormal military limitations"; "existing limitations on our freedom of counter-offensive action"; "obscurities which now becloud unsolved problems"; and "military stalemate" ("die for a tie" this one was dubbed).[259] In March 1951, MacArthur responded to a letter from Congressman Joseph Martin of Massachusetts in which Martin proposed the use of Nationalist Chinese troops in Korea and agreed wholeheartedly, knowing that: 1) this was an extremely provocative move that Truman had refused to sanction; and 2) the letter and his response would be published.[260] "There is no substitute for victory" he wrote. (Just what kind of "victory" he thought a war with China

---

256 Manchester, *American Caesar*, 597.
257 Newton, *The Cambridge Spies*, 296.
258 Ibid.
259 Blair, *The Forgotten War*, 684–685; 720, 744.
260 Ibid., 759–760.

would bring remains unclear.) Yet Truman did nothing until MacArthur issued an ultimatum to the Chinese on March 24, 1951, threatening a wider war if they did not relent and offering to "confer in the field with the Commander-in-Chief of the enemy forces in an earnest effort to find any military means whereby the realization of the political objectives of the United Nations in Korea, to which no nation may justly take exceptions, might be accomplished without further bloodshed."[261] He had no authority whatsoever to do this and knew, in fact, that he was effectively destroying a diplomatic initiative formulated by Truman.[262] Truman was furious, and he dismissed MacArthur on April 11, 1951, creating a political firestorm. "It is doubtful if there has ever been in this country so violent and spontaneous a discharge of political passion as that provoked by the President's dismissal of the General....Certainly there has been nothing to match it since the Civil War."[263] Tens of thousands of letters and telegrams poured into the White House mail room, expressing support for MacArthur at a rate of 20:1.[264] Smelling blood, Republicans began a furious assault on Truman and the Democrats. Senator William Jenner called for Truman's impeachment, stating that "this country today is in the hands of the secret inner coterie which is directed by agents of the Soviet Union.[265] In the meantime, the slaughter in Korea continued.

American tactics were consistent with those used during World War II, with artillery and airpower lavishly employed. By late August 1950, B-29s were dropping 800 tons of ordnance a day on North Korea, mostly pure napalm. Between June and late October, they had dropped more than 850,000 gallons.[266] P'yongyang, the North Korean capital, was deliberately reduced to a cinder by firebombing in this manner three times. The dams near P'yongyang, which supplied the water for irrigation systems producing three quarters of the country's rice crop, were targeted

---

261 Ibid., 768.

262 Manchester, *American Caesar*, 633–635.

263 Richard H. Rovere and Arthur M. Schlesinger, Jr., quoted in Manchester, *American Caesar*, 648.

264 Ibid.

265 Herman, *Joseph McCarthy*, 155.

266 Cumings, *North Korea, Another Country*, 19.

and destroyed. The flash flooding that resulted "scooped clean 27 miles of valley below....Flood conditions extended as far downstream as P'yongyang, causing considerable damage to the capital city."[267] Bomb tonnage dropped in Korea exceeded by more than 130,000 tons the total bomb tonnage dropped in the Pacific theater during World War II.[268] Communist guerilas had infiltrated into the whole of South Korea, and, as outlined in January 1951 by General Edward Almond, "Air strikes with napalm against those guerilla bands wherever found is the most effective way to destroy not only the bands themselves, but the huts and villages in the areas they retire to."[269] The results of such policies were predictable:

> The inhabitants throughout the village and in the fields were caught and killed and kept the exact postures they held when the napalm struck—a man about to get on his bicycle, fifty boys and girls playing in an orphanage, a housewife strangely unmarked, holding in her hand a page torn from a Sears-Roebuck catalogue crayoned at mail order No. 3,811,294 for a $2.98 "bewitching bed jacket—coral."[270]

By 1952 northern and central Korea had been flattened.[271]

Although consistent with Roosevelt's bombing campaign during World War II, Truman's use of airpower in Korea was undertaken in almost certain violation of international standards and norms that were precisely delineated in Article 6(b) of the Charter of the International Military Tribunal that assembled in Nuremberg for the trial of Nazi war criminals. This included under its definition of "WAR CRIMES" the "wanton destruction of cities, towns or villages, or devastation not justified by military necessity."

---

267 Halliday and Cumings, *Korea, The Unknown War*, 195.
268 Patterson, *Grand Expectations*, 216.
269 Cumings, *The Origins of the Korean War*, vol. 2, 753.
270 *New York Times* reporter George Barrett, quoted in Cumings, *The Origins of the Korean War*, vol. 2, 755.
271 Cumings, *The Origins of the Korean War*, vol. 2, 755.

The land war was marked by incredible brutality as well. Retreating American troops practiced scorched earth as a matter of policy.[272] And as in any other war, American troops on the field sometimes acted with the ruthlessness that manifests itself among terrified adolescents determined to survive:

> War correspondents found the campaign for the South "strangely disturbing," [Reginald Thompson] wrote, different from World War II in its guerilla and popular aspect. "There were few who dared to write the truth of things as they saw them." G.I.s "never spoke of the enemy as though they were people, but as one might speak of apes." Even among correspondents, "every man's dearest wish was to kill a Korean. 'Today'...'I'll get me a gook.'"... "[F]ear of infiltrators led to the slaughter of hundreds of South Korean civilians, women as well as men, by some U.S. troops and police of the Republic."...Keyes Beech wrote in the *Newark Star-Ledger,* "It is not time to be a Korean, for the Yankees are shooting them all...nervous American troops are ready to fire at any Korean."[273]

Massacres of leftists and their sympathizers were commonplace throughout South Korea as the American-backed Rhee regime redoubled its efforts to wipe out any and all opposition.[274] This is not to say, however, that excesses were unique to the American side. For the Communists gave as much as they received.[275]

---

272 Patterson, *Grand Expectations*, 216.

273 Cumings, *The Origins of the Korean War*, vol. 2, 705.

274 "Buried Truth of Killings Exposed; Korean War Records Show U.S. Ambivalent During 'Brutal Chapter,'" *Chicago Tribune*, July 7, 2008. See also "Unearthing War's Horrors Years Later in South Korea," *New York Times*, December 3, 2007; "Time Presses on Koreans Digging up a Dark Past," *New York Times*, September 4, 2009; "South Korea Commission Details Civilian Massacres Early in 1950s War," *New York Times*, November 27, 2009.

275 *The Black Book of Communism*, 547–564; Cumings, *Korea's Place in the Sun*, 270–275; Andrew Nahm, *Historical Dictionary of the Republic of Korea* (The Scarecrow Press: Metuchen, N.J., 1993), 129; Associated Press, October 13, 1999: "Thousands Perished In North Korean Outrages During War." http://www.pulitzer.org/archives/6355, accessed May 10, 2012.

Judged dispassionately, there is no avoiding the conclusion that Truman employed what Ivan Arreguin-Toft labeled the strategy of "barbarism" (there being just no kind or gentle way to describe it): "Barbarism is the systematic violation of the laws of war in pursuit of a military or political objective....Unlike other strategies, barbarism has been used to destroy an adversary's will and capacity to fight. When will is the target in a strategic bombing campaign, for example, the strong actor seeks to coerce its weaker opponent into changing its behavior by inflicting pain (destroying its values)."[276] By the summer of 1952, Korea was a wasteland. "There was nothing left to bomb," said Assistant Secretary of State Dean Rusk,[277] and Korean casualties had reached catastrophic levels, with some one-third of all adult males killed on the Communist side.[278] Kim Il Sung, desperate to end the war, was practically begging Mao to accept some compromise that would end the fighting.[279] But Mao, determined from the start to kill as many Americans as possible for as long as possible, had nothing to gain by compromise.[280] Stalin, for his part, was more than happy to watch Americans die by the thousands for South Korea while he manipulated the conflict with almost no cost to himself. So Truman's war in Korea continued, to the disgust of America's electorate and its fighting men, as exemplified by a sign posted in "Massacre Valley" by US Marines who recovered the bodies of hundreds of US and Dutch Army personnel overrun by the Chinese: "MASSACRE VALLEY/SCENE OF HARRY TRUMAN'S POLICE ACTION/NICE GOING HARRY."[281]

Clearly, Americans were very displeased with their president and their new world order in the summer 1952, and they had every reason to be. For Truman's war in Korea—a "certifiable disaster" that would lead them straight into Southeast Asia[282]—resulted

276 Ivan Arreguin-Toft, "How the Weak Win Wars," *International Security,* Summer 2001, 93–128.
277 Chang and Jon Halliday, Mao: *The Unknown Story*, 368.
278 Ibid.
279 Ibid.
280 Ibid., 360.
281 Halberstam, *The Coldest Winter*, 552.
282 Richard Rovere, *Final Report: Personal Reflections on Politics and History in Our Time* (Middletown, Connecticut: Wesleyan University Press, 1984), 204–207.

directly from his partisanship, his fecklessness on internal security and his schizophrenic foreign policy, making it rather difficult to accept the received wisdom that credits him with "one of the most successful presidencies of the 20th Century,"[283] as even brief critical analysis reveals.

By late 1947, George Kennan, the Joint Chiefs of Staff (led by General Eisenhower) and Dean Acheson had all agreed that this country had little strategic interest in Korea and that, in the Pentagon's words, "the United States should accept as a 'probability' the 'eventual domination of Korea by the U.S.S.R.' after American troop withdrawal."[284] As late as 1948, Truman concurred, declaring (as previously noted) that military action in Korea "would not constitute a casus belli for the United States."[285] He therefore continued withdrawing American forces from Korea and locked away NSC-68 as he had the Clifford-Elsey Report. Rhetoric notwithstanding, Truman had no intention of increasing defense budgets or fighting over small countries on the Soviet periphery, and Stalin, who almost daily "[read] top secret American documents with his breakfast,"[286] knew it. (Although it cost thousands of Americans their jobs, Truman's Loyalty Program did not eliminate the flow of high-level classified information to the Soviets.) Why then did Truman suddenly change his mind and plunge this country into a bloody, inconclusive conflict that haunts us all to this day?

With Eastern Europe, the USSR (a nuclear power as of 1949) and mainland China, which together represented some four-fifths of the Eurasian landmass and nearly a billion people, firmly in Communist hands by January 1950, did Truman actually believe that adding to the Communist world a small piece of Asian real estate called South Korea represented such "an extremely serious political and military threat" to Japan and "to U.S. interests in the Far East"[287] that some three to four million people had to die to

283 "Reluctant but Ready," *Chicago Tribune*, May 6, 2008, sec. 1.
284 Chace, *Acheson*, 269.
285 Manchester, *American Caesar*, 540.
286 Cumings, *The Origins of the Korean War*, vol. 2, 410.
287 Ibid., 268 (quoting a State Department report approved by Acheson).

prevent this? Did he really believe that Korea, if united under Communist control, would provide, *as if by magic,* the resources, wealth and technology needed to boost "Monolithic International Communism" (a now-universally ridiculed concept he firmly embraced) to victory in the Cold War? In other words, just what made South Korea, in Dean Acheson's words, "an area of great importance to the security of American occupied Japan"?[288] I have never seen plausible counterfactual analysis offered by anyone to substantiate this assertion, but I consistently note historians' recognition of the role played by domestic politics: "In the existing domestic political climate," noted Clay Blair, "the loss of South Korea to Communism would have been politically catastrophic for Truman and the Democratic Party."[289] Robert Mann agrees: "Had Truman wavered or refused to assist South Korea in the critical days following the invasion, it would have effectively ended his presidency and spelled an end to Democratic control of Congress."[290]

And if "American occupied Japan" was the real prize here, just what kind of threat did Kim Il Sung really represent? He launched his assault on South Korea after a long and careful build up with some 90,000 men,[291] virtually no navy and no air force. He required in short order *hundreds of thousands* of Chinese "volunteers" to save his regime from an under-equipped and ill-trained United States Army. This being the case, how did Kim threaten Japan? From what magic lantern was he going to conjure the millions of troops, thousands of airplanes, millions of tons of food, fuel, and

---

288 Acheson, *The Korean War,* 20. The same is true for Truman's handling of Taiwan. He declared in early 1950 that this country had no interest in China's civil war and that he would provide no more aid to Chiang Kai-shek's government, while Dean Acheson assured American diplomats that Taiwan's imminent fall would not greatly damage American security. See Joiner, *Honorable Survivor,* 228–229. Yet Truman intervened on Chiang's behalf after Kim Il Sung's attack on South Korea, an action that plagues this country to this very day. *Why?* Did Truman actually believe that, with the Chinese mainland already in Communist hands, the "loss" of Chiang's corrupt, ineffectual regime on a small island off the Chinese coast represented a tangible, quantifiable threat to American security? If so, how? Just what evidence and reasoning supports this?

289 Blair, *The Forgotten War,* 67.

290 Mann, *A Grand Delusion,* 36.

291 Manchester, *American Caesar,* 545.

ammunition and thousands of ships that the United States and its allies were assembling for their invasion of Japan in 1945?[292] No military buildup of this magnitude was noted in 1950, and of course, there is the obvious question: Assuming such power was available to Kim, why was it not brought to bear in South Korea, from which his relatively meager forces were driven almost effortlessly following MacArthur's landing at Inchon?

Finally, if keeping the southern half of the Korean peninsula out of the Communist orbit was so crucial to American security, why did Truman not act accordingly from the start, and why does orthodoxy impose no blame on him as a result? It was, after all, his first duty as president to ensure this country's security. Yet he "all but wrecked the conventional military forces of the United States" by 1950 and initiated an American withdrawal from South Korea while allowing, just for good measure, top-secret nuclear-, defense- and foreign policy-related information that was causal in the Communist attack to flow unhindered into Soviet hands despite repeated warnings.[293]

Having been warned, moreover, that China would enter the war if UN forces crossed the 38th parallel, Truman ordered MacArthur north and then—aware of both MacArthur's movements and the inept, perilous deployment of his troops in the face of "powerful, fully equipped, competent" Chinese forces that assaulted the Eighth Army in October[294]—he and his Wise Men (including George C. Marshall and the Joint Chiefs) sat around watching "like paralyzed rabbits," in Dean Acheson's words, for an entire month as the disaster unfolded because "the president and secretary of state were

---

292 Richard B. Frank, *Downfall: The End of the Imperial Japanese Empire* (New York: Random House, 1999), 117–122; D.M. Giangreco, *Hell to Pay: Operation Downfall and the Invasion of Japan, 1945–1947* (Annapolis: Naval Institute Press, 2009), 126.

293 Romerstein and Breindel, *The Venona Secrets*, xv: "Documents recently released in the former USSR…demonstrate that, absent an atomic bomb, Stalin would not have unleashed Pyongyang's army to conquer the entire Korean peninsula." With Stalin dead in the spring of 1953 and his successors ending the Korean War as soon as they could, espionage that turned perhaps a twelve-year effort (1943–1955) into a six-year effort (1943–1949) makes all the difference. See also John Earl Haynes, Harvey Klehr and Alexander Vassiliev, *Spies: The Rise and Fall of the KGB in America* (New Haven: Yale University Press, 2009), 545.

294 Acheson, *The Korean War*, 68–69.

far too unpopular to challenge the iconic general."[295] The overwhelming majority of casualties in Korea were inflicted during the two years and nine months *after* Truman, fearful of being called an appeaser shortly before national elections, ordered MacArthur to unite the country, and the war ended in the summer of 1953 almost precisely where American forces were in September 1950. *Under Truman's leadership, millions died for no measurable gain, and no one—but no one—was more responsible than Harry Truman.*

The facts alone are sufficient to dispel any notions of Truman's brilliant leadership or successful presidency, but if you remain unconvinced, consider the recent Bush administration's war in Iraq, which provides an excellent, contemporary frame of reference.

From the manipulation of intelligence and the inadequate number of troops employed to the decision to disband Iraq's government and army, America's war in Iraq was a fiasco from the start, and George W. Bush was ultimately held responsible—quite properly so—by both the media and the electorate, as evidenced by twenty-two percent poll ratings at the close of his administration. I have seen no attempt by any of this country's politicians, pundits or public intellectuals, from the Left or the Right, to assign blame for this train wreck to his political opponents and subordinates while insisting that Bush was a great commander in chief and a successful president. Yet not even this provides an appropriate frame of reference. To compare Truman to Bush, we must further imagine that Bush, having ignored an unequivocal warning that Russia would respond with force to an attack on Iraq, ended his presidency with millions of casualties and a war with Russia raging in the Middle East—a war in which Russian espionage kept our enemies apprised, in real time, of every plan formulated and every move intended. How would you judge George W. Bush then, and why should Truman be judged differently?

In summary, "to govern," as Charles de Gaulle once said, "is to choose," and from 1945 through 1953, an enormous number of choices were made by real people holding real power, here and

---

295 Thompson, *The Hawk and the Dove*, 123. "Wise Men" is taken from *The Wise Men: Six Friends and the World They Made*, by Walter Isaacson and Evan Thomas.

abroad. These choices gave history an espionage campaign without historical precedent; an ineffective, partisan response with a toxic backlash; Communist enslavement of Eastern Europe; the Truman Doctrine; a Communist coup in Czechoslovakia; the Berlin blockade; Communist victory in China; Soviet acquisition of nuclear weapons through espionage in 1949; American armed forces stripped to the bone; a Communist attack on South Korea; Truman's order to cross the 38th parallel; China's entry into the war; American military disaster; and an inconclusive stalemate that haunts Americans to this very day. America's side of this chain of events, which led directly into Southeast Asia, was shaped largely by "the Legacy of the '30s," and Harry S. Truman either made or was responsible for virtually every choice on the American side. *Had Joseph McCarthy been killed during World War II, nothing would have changed except the time and effort required by "those who rule the dominant institutions" to shield Truman from the effects of his choices while maneuvering to protect himself and his party from decades of ineptitude, dishonesty and folly.*[296]

This being what history reveals, orthodoxy's assignment of responsibility for these events and their poisonous, long-term effects to a junior senator from Wisconsin and a phantasm that bears his name cannot be taken seriously. It is like blaming all the human disasters associated with Soviet collectivization—bad choices made by real people holding real power—on "Zinovievism," "Bukharinism" and "Trotskyism" while insisting that "International Jewry" was responsible for the start of World War II.[297] And as George Orwell once noted, "One has to belong to the intelligentsia

---

296 McCarthy reminds me of Jane Fonda in later years. Like McCarthy, she was responsible for exactly nothing. However much attention she garnered with her childish, contemptible antics, she did not get this country into Southeast Asia, and she did not get this country out. Had she been killed in a traffic accident as a teenager, *nothing* would have changed.

297 Having "enormous ambition and considerable ability," Joseph McCarthy was "like a huge electric plant which by some oddity produces neither heat nor power, and feels bitterly hurt because it is not recognized as a valuable public utility." He was attracted to the espionage investigations by "the sort of demonstrative affection that a wet dog will often feel for a man in white-flannel trousers." Rebecca West, "As a Briton Looks at McCarthyism," *U.S. News and World Report*, May 22, 1963, 60.

to believe things like that; no ordinary man could be such a fool."[298] So it is time to purge the very word "McCarthyism" from our lexicon, since it provides, in the words of William Fulbright, "a perfect formula for the evasion of reality."[299]

XII

[W]e could have fought in Indo-China. We could have won, if we had been willing to pay the tremendous cost in men and money that such intervention would have required—a cost that in my opinion would have eventually been as great as, or greater than, what we paid in Korea.[300]

General Mathew Ridgway

Much like Korea, Vietnam was a small, Asian country that had been colonized for decades prior to the outbreak of World War II, first by the French (1870-1940) and then by the Japanese, who assumed control with French defeat in 1940. Driven by the demands of World War II, the Japanese, like the French before them, exploited Vietnam brutally. They exported millions of tons of rice and requisitioned large quantities for storage and use by their own troops while forcing the Vietnamese peasants to plant industrial crops like peanuts and jute. Floods aggravated the situation, and by 1945, fully one-fifth of Northern Vietnam's population of 10,000,000 had died of starvation.[301]

As in Korea, a large percentage of the mandarin class, the scholar-bureaucracy that historically administered the country for the Emperor, had been corrupted by the French and became agents of the colonial administration. As in Korea, the citizenry hated the occupiers, both French and Japanese, and had engaged in decades of resistance and guerilla warfare. And as in Korea, the

---

298 George Orwell, *The Sayings of George Orwell*, ed. Robert Pierce (London: Gerald Duckworth & Company, Ltd., 1994), 27.
299 Coffin, *Senator Fulbright*, 127–128.
300 Summers, *On Strategy*, 99.
301 Karnow, *Vietnam: A History*, 144.

Communists, then led by Ho Chi Minh, were the largest, most successful and most popular of the resistance groups. In the summer of 1945, they formed a National Liberation Committee, with Ho Chi Minh as president, to coordinate the seizure of power from the Japanese and greet the Allies as a functioning provisional government at the end of the war. On August 25, the puppet emperor Bao Dai, who had served both the French and the Japanese, handed over "sovereign power" to the Viet Minh. On September 2, with Viet Minh control established throughout the country, Ho Chi Minh proclaimed the establishment of the "Democratic Republic of Vietnam," quoting from the American Declaration of Independence as he did so in an effort to impress the Allies and win support for his government. So, was this nationalism or Communism, and how did post-war Vietnam differ, if at all, from post-war Korea? Let the record speak for itself.

Ho Chi Minh was born in 1890 and left Vietnam in 1912 to live, work and study in the United States, England, France and finally the Soviet Union. He did not return to Vietnam for nearly thirty years. While in Paris, Ho Chi Minh read Lenin's *Thesis on the National and Colonial Questions* and became convinced that Marxism-Leninism was "the path to our liberation."[302] "At first patriotism, not yet Communism, led me to have confidence in Lenin, in the Third International. Step by step, along the struggle, by studying Marxism-Leninism parallel with participation in practical activities, I gradually came up with the fact that only Socialism and Communism can liberate the oppressed nations and the working people throughout the world from slavery."[303] His conversion was total. He became a delegate to the Comintern in Moscow and spent 1924 studying Marxism-Leninism at the University of the Toilers of the East. He was eventually sent by the Soviet government, as a member of the Comintern's Asian Bureau, to form the Vietnamese Communist movement, which he led for the next forty-five years.

Ho clearly understood and appreciated the fundamental

---

302 James P. Harrison, *The Endless War: Fifty Years of Struggle in Vietnam* (New York: The Free Press, 1982), 39.

303 Ibid.

principles of democracy, civil society and civil liberties that he used as needed to manipulate Western liberals. In speeches and public pronouncements, he always invoked Western political tradition and values and paid homage to the French and American Revolutions.[304] When addressing the French Socialist Party in December 1920, Ho articulated the grievances of the Vietnamese people in terms of classic, Western values. "We have neither freedom of the press nor freedom of speech. Even freedom of assembly and freedom of association do not exist. We have no right to live in other countries or to go abroad as tourists."[305] Yet he was present in the Soviet Union as *millions* were systematically murdered during the worst of the purges in the 1930s, and upon his return to Vietnam in the 1930s, Ho emulated Josef Stalin,[306] annihilating all Vietnamese who were not loyal to Moscow, Communist and non-Communist alike. While attending the funeral service of a Vietnamese nationalist who had been murdered by the Communists for ideological deviation (he was a Trotskyist), Ho said, "He was a great patriot and we mourn him." *"All those who do not follow the line which I have laid down will be broken."*[307] Although evidence indicates that some 5,000 nationalist rivals were executed by the Communists and another 25,000 imprisoned at this time, Troung Chinh, one-time secretary-general and leading theoretician of the Vietnamese Communist Party, believed that the Party should have eliminated even more "enemies of the revolution."[308]

The French, of course, were no more inclined in 1945 to allow indigenous Communists to seize Vietnam, Laos and Cambodia than the Americans were inclined to allow indigenous Communists to seize Korea, and they were no less entitled to place and support a government in Vietnam as Truman was to place and support a government in Korea. The French attempted to use the old colonial

---

304 David Halberstam, *Ho* (New York: Alfred A. Knopf, 1971) 23.

305 Halberstam, *Ho,* 33

306 As Bernard Fall noted, "Ho probably was then unconditionally loyal to Stalin and Stalin knew it." (*Ho*, 58). "He had seen the crimes of Stalin and never flinched." (*Ho*, 71.)

307 Halberstam, *Ho*, 71.

308 Harrison, *The Endless War*, 103–104.

administration, just as Truman had used it in Korea. They enlisted the aid of anti-Communists from the collaborationist upper classes, just as Truman had in Korea. They fought a brutal war (but a war far less brutal than the war Truman had fought in Korea) to stop Vietnam's Communist nationalists as Truman had stopped Communist nationalists in Korea. In fact, they did virtually everything Truman did in Korea except maintain their position in the disputed territory. There were no real differences between the war in Korea and the war in Vietnam, but there were distinctions, and the distinctions made all the difference.

First, Korea was a peninsula that had been divided with Soviet acquiescence in 1945, which provided the South with a single, defensible border. The United States and its Korean allies had free reign within the South (as the Communists were given in the North) to crush their opponents and consolidate their rule, using whatever means were necessary, with minimal resistance and no public scrutiny whatsoever. Truman's Japanese-trained Korean allies were ruthless and efficient, and by 1950, the insurgency was over. South Korea was here to stay.

Second, American politicians throughout this period were engaged in a constant struggle to see who could be tougher on Communism. No one within the political or cultural mainstream questioned anything done in Korea. Nobody asked what right Truman had to divide and occupy Korea. No one questioned either the legitimacy of our allied "government" or the means by which it acquired or consolidated its power. No one asked how Koreans "invading" Korea could constitute "outside aggression" justifying massive international intervention. And to this day, no one asks why Communist nationalists in Korea (not to mention Greece, China or anywhere else in the world) should be any less entitled than Communist nationalists in Vietnam to employ military force to unite their country under their rule.

Finally, once the "invasion" of "South" Korea began, Americans faced a conventional rather than a guerilla war, fought over open territory with hundreds of thousands of troops, infantry, armor, artillery and airpower, which was the kind of fighting at which the United States excelled.

The French, on the other hand, faced a Soviet-backed insurrection in three contiguous countries (Vietnam, Laos and Cambodia) that covered a vast area with no defensible borders, making it impossible for them to "consolidate" anything, anywhere. They were not served, as Americans in Korea had been served, by ruthless, efficient, Japanese-trained surrogates, and the Vietnamese Communists, as we would soon learn, were led by people who were far more intelligent and sophisticated than the crude, stupid leadership in North Korea. By 1950, the French were stalemated.

But the evolving Cold War breathed new life into the French effort. "'All of a sudden,' as *U.S. News and World Report* observed in February 1950, 'Indo-China is out in front in the power struggle between Russia on the one hand and the Western world on the other.'"[309] The National Security Council determined that a loss of Southeast Asia to Communism would represent "a major political rout the repercussions of which will be felt throughout the rest of the world."[310] The State Department agreed:

> The choice confronting the United States is to support the French in Indochina or face the extension of Communism over the remainder of the continental area of Southeast Asia and, possibly, farther westward. We then would be obligated to make staggering investments in those areas and in that part of Southeast Asia remaining outside Communist domination or withdraw to a much-contracted Pacific line. It would seem a case of "Penny wise, Pound foolish" to deny support to the French in Indochina."[311]

The *New York Times* concurred, editorializing in May of 1950 that "Indochina is critical—if it falls, all of Southeast Asia will be in mortal peril."[312]

---

309 Mann, *A Grand Delusion*, 72.
310 Ibid.
311 Ibid., 73.
312 Halberstam, *The Best and the Brightest*, 338.

On the domestic front, Truman remained very much on the defensive. With even Democrats like John F. Kennedy accusing him of "losing" China as much through treachery as ineptitude, Truman and Acheson knew that another Communist victory in Asia would be politically disastrous.[313] So they began the process that would end ignobly twenty-five years later.

In May 1950, Truman agreed to provide $10 million in assistance to counties resisting Chinese Communism.[314] Weary of defending themselves for the "loss" of China, Democrats jumped at the chance to fight Communism in Asia.[315] For Truman, of course, the outbreak of war in Korea settled all doubts, and on December 30, 1950, he approved NSC 48/2, by which "the course of U.S. policy was set to block further Communist expansion in Asia...with particular attention...to the problem of French Indochina."[316] Former Popular Front man Hubert Humphrey, reiterating Acheson's domino theory, announced his support for the French effort in Vietnam, saying that a Communist victory there would lead to "the loss of Malaya, the loss of Burma and Thailand and ultimately the conquest of all the south and southeast Asiatic area."[317]

Moscow and Peking recognized Ho Chi Minh's government in January 1951, and Truman recognized the French proxy Bao Dai in February. Nine days later, Dean Acheson told Truman that "the choice confronting the U.S. is to support the legal governments in Indochina [and Bao Dai was just as "legal" as Syngman Rhee and Chiang Kai-shek] or to face the extension of Communism over the reminder of the continental area of Southeast Asia and probably westward."[318] Knowing that neither he nor his party would survive the "loss" of another Asian country to Communism, Truman would pour some $600 million into the French effort by the end of his

313 Mann, *A Grand Delusion*, 72.

314 Ibid., 73, 74.

315 Ibid., 74.

316 Neil Sheehan, Hedrick Smith, E.W. Kenworthy and Fox Butterfield, *The Pentagon Papers* (New York: Quadrangle Books, 1971), 10.

317 Mann, *A Grand Delusion*, 84.

318 Sheehan, Smith, Kenworthy and Butterfield, *The Pentagon Papers*, 10.

presidency.[319] "Having put our hand to the plow," said Acheson, "we would not look back."[320] And when our politicians, pundits and public intellectuals eventually did, they seem to have substituted a great deal of ideology for history in evaluating Truman, his Wise Men and both the quality and the long-term effects of their decisions.

For the Soviet Union's collapse ensured that "those who rule the dominant institutions,"[321] instinctively realizing the enormous amount of political capital at stake in so momentous an occurrence, would abandon the post-Vietnam, anti-anti-Communist revisionism and rehabilitate Truman by: 1) cherry picking facts; 2) ignoring both Truman's Nixonesque criminality (wiretapping for political intelligence, the attempted Hiss cover up, obstructing Congress) and his manifest failures (gutted armed forces, rampant high-level espionage); 3) blaming others for what cannot be ignored (China's entry into Korea, the politically toxic environment throughout his presidency); and 4) bestowing credit upon Truman for the ultimate effects of not just later decisions made by others but future events he could not possibly have foreseen or intended. It reminds me of nothing so much as the "Texas sharpshooter fallacy," in which a mythical Texan, after firing several shots at the sides of barns and outbuildings, paints targets centered on the hits and claims to be a sharpshooter.

---

319 Mann, *A Grand Delusion*, 89–90.

320 James Chase, *Acheson: The Secretary of State Who Created the American World* (New York: Simon & Schuster, 1998), 267.

321 Gitlin, *The Whole World is Watching*, 10.

Chapter Three:
Dwight Eisenhower

I

And it is essential to understand this: that a prince, and especially a new prince, cannot observe all those things for which men are considered good, for in order to maintain the state he is often obliged to act against his promise, against charity, against humanity, and against religion. And therefore, it is necessary that he have a mind ready to turn itself according to the way the winds of fortune and the changeability of affairs require him; and, as I said above, as long as it is possible, he should not stray from the good, but he should know how to enter into evil when necessity commands.

Niccolo Machiavelli

It is now clear that we are facing an implacable enemy whose avowed objective is world domination by whatever means and at whatever cost. There are no rules in such a game. Hitherto acceptable forms of human conduct do not apply. If the United States is to survive, long-standing American concepts of "fair play" must be reconsidered. We must develop effective espionage and counterespionage services and must learn to subvert, sabotage and destroy our enemies by more clever, more sophisticated and more effective methods than those used against us. It may become necessary that the American people be made acquainted with, understand and support this fundamentally repugnant philosophy.[1]

General James H. Doolittle

The so-called anti-Communist consensus was little more than a shabby façade, cobbled together by political enemies with little in common but the desire for power, and by 1952, stress fractures were apparent as Democratic disaster became Republican opportunity. With the bloody stalemate in Korea having driven Truman's approval ratings down to twenty-two percent, Republicans suddenly became the peace party, promising to end the war and "bring the boys home." The minority [Republican] report of the Joint Session of the Senate Committees on Armed Services and Foreign Relations criticized Truman's conduct of the war exactly as Democrats in later years would attack American policy in Vietnam:

> The policy of the United States in Korea, as outlined in the testimony of the Secretary of State and the Secretary of Defense and others, is that of destroying the effective core of the Communist Chinese armies by killing that government's trained soldiers, in the hopes that someone will negotiate. We hold that such a policy is essentially immoral, not likely to produce either victory in Korea or an end to aggression. At the same time such a policy tends to destroy the moral stature of the United States as a leader in the family of nations.[2]

It was enough, said columnist Ted Stokes, "to turn a stomach hardened to political extravagance."[3] Regardless, Truman's presidency had done so much damage to Democrats that highlighting Republican opportunism availed them nothing. Adlai

---

1 General James H. Doolittle, Introduction to "Report on the Covert Activities of the Central Intelligence Agency, September 30, 1954," pages 2-3.

2 Summers, *On Strategy*, 37–38.

3 Tristram Coffin, *Senator Fulbright, Portrait of a Public Philosopher* (New York: E.P. Dutton & Company, 1966), 119.

Stevenson carried only seven states of the Deep South, Kentucky and West Virginia, and Dwight Eisenhower was elected president. Unlike Truman, Ike was lucky. When Stalin died in March 1953, his successors moved quickly to end the fighting in June 1953, by which time the casualty figures included two million North Korean civilians (some twenty percent of the pre-war population) and 500,000 military personnel dead. Chinese dead have been estimated as high as three million.[4] Another million South Korean civilians were killed, and South Korea would remain a military dictatorship for the next four decades.

II

In November of 1952, Republicans took control of both the House and the Senate. With Eisenhower as president, the time to lance the boil of espionage had finally arrived. Eisenhower was "deeply shaken" by "the depth of the [national security] mess that Truman and the Democrats had left behind."[5] Among other things, he discovered that Henry Dexter White had in fact been a Soviet agent and that, although J. Robert Oppenheimer himself, who was at the very center of the Manhattan Project, had been identified for good reason as a major security risk, nothing had been done about it. Eisenhower's Special Assistant C.D. Jackson, wrote that "the foolishness and/or knavery of past Administration . . . unbelievable."[6] However, "one word defined the outlook of the Eisenhower team: moderate."[7] The turnout for the 1952 election had been the largest in American history, and the margin of victory had been narrow. Eisenhower could claim no mandate, and his advisors wanted desperately to end the partisan bickering that had become a staple of government:

---

4 Cumings, *The Origins of the Korean War*, vol. 2, 770; Halliday and Cumings, *Korea: The Unknown War,* 200. As always, these figures are problematic. Jon Halliday states in his later biography of Mao that Chinese sources put Chinese dead in Korea at 400,000 while official Russian sources list Chinese dead at 1 million. *Mao: The Unknown Story*, 378.

5 Herman, *Joseph McCarthy,* 245.

6 *Ibid.,* 245-246.

7 *Ibid.,* 213.

The modern Republican's catchwords were *consensus* and *convergence*. As Arthur Larsen explained in modern Republicanism's manifesto, *A Republican Looks at His Party*, the important split in American politics was no longer between Democrat and Republican, or conservative and liberal. It was between the center and the opposition, whether emanating from the left (meaning socialists and Communists) or the right (meaning Taftites and McCarthy). The center was where the action was, was the implication, and Ike and his troops were determined to occupy it.[8]

Moreover, Joseph McCarthy had alienated Eisenhower and the entire Republican establishment with his attacks on George Marshall and his crude, stupid behavior. With every passing day, he gave investigation into subversion and espionage a bad name. Eventually he turned on the Eisenhower administration, ending any chance that Executive Brach records would be available to Congress. In the end, Truman would avoid answering for years of folly and obstruction, and "those who rule the dominant institutions" would craft the narrative by which he became a statesman and champion of civil liberties.

III

Iran's downhill course toward Communist-supported dictatorship was picking up momentum.[9]

Dwight Eisenhower

"Viscerally" anti-Communist, according to his biographer Geoffrey Perret, Dwight Eisenhower was a devout believer in Dean Acheson's "rotten apple" theory, which is generally attributed to Eisenhower as the much-ridiculed "domino theory." Eisenhower

---

8 Ibid., 215.
9 Stephen Ambrose, *Eisenhower the President* (New York: Simon & Schuster, 1984), 109.

would stay the course plotted by Truman, whose policies had been supported by the British, the French, the United Nations, the *New York Times*, the *Wall Street Journal,* Thomas E. Dewey and Hubert Humphrey, who claimed that Truman's stand in Korea "may be the biggest blow for peace in the twentieth century."[10] With Korea as the frame of reference, there were virtually no moral or legal constraints on the foreign policy of anti-Communism by 1952 (excepting perhaps first use of nuclear weapons), and Dwight Eisenhower, a cold warrior *par excellence*, would act accordingly throughout his presidency, beginning with Iran.

In 1952, nationalist Prime Minister Mohamed Mossadegh, backed by, among others, the Iranian Communist Party (the Tudeh), seized the oil fields and refineries of the Anglo-Persian Oil Company. The British threatened legal action against any purchaser of Iranian oil, rendering it worthless on the world market, and by 1953, Iran was bankrupt and in a state of political turmoil. The shah fled in early August, and the Soviet Union began negotiating financial aid to Mossadegh's regime.

CIA Director Allen Dulles, who feared a Soviet takeover in Iran, viewed the combination of chaos and Communist influence in Mossadegh's government with alarm.[11] Although his view was not without merit, the situation in Iran was far more complex. Secular nationalists, Communists, royalists, socialists and powerful clerics were all jockeying for power and influence, and it is by no means certain that Iran was destined for a Communist takeover.[12] Eisenhower, however, saw nothing but Communism in Iran, which, with its vast oil reserves, was a genuine Cold War prize. So Eisenhower decided to mount a coup against Mossadegh, directed by Kermit Roosevelt (Teddy's grandson, FDR's cousin), to restore the shah to power.[13] The coup was successful, and the shah returned on August 22, 1953. Eisenhower had ordered the Mossadegh

10 Solberg, *Hubert Humphrey*, 145.

11 Ambrose, *Eisenhower the President*, 109.

12 Sandra Mackey, *The Iranians: Persia, Islam and the Soul of a Nation* (New York: Penguin Books, USA, 1996), 187–210.

13 Ibid., 111.

government overthrown and had succeeded.[14] Any and all Soviet designs on the Iranian oilfields had been foiled (at least for now), the shah wiped out the Iranian Communists just as Syngman Rhee wiped out South Korea's Communists, and Iran's vast oil reserves were secured for the West, with relatively little bloodshed, no loss of American life and no adverse publicity. Immensely pleased with his Iranian operation, Eisenhower personally presented Kermit Roosevelt with the National Security Medal in a closed-door ceremony as the Truman Doctrine marched on. Its next conquest would be Guatemala.

Jacobo Arbenz had been elected president of Guatemala in Guatemala's first legitimate democratic election in decades.[15] He was drawn to Marxist ideas,[16] and his wife was "a passionate leftist."[17] He surrounded himself with left-wing advisers (some undoubtedly Communists[18]) and began a land reform program that involved nationalization of large estates for redistribution to the peasants, taking some 400,000 acres of land between 1952 and 1954, much of it from the United Fruit Company, which owned nearly one-fifth of the country's arable land.[19] United Fruit's public relations man, Edward Bernays, visited *New York Times* publisher Arthur Sulzberger, inducing him to run several articles portraying Guatemala as a victim of Communism.[20] Francis Cardinal Spellman of New York was recruited to bring the Guatemalan clergy into line, and he moved with alacrity, helping to ensure that they circulated pastoral letters warning the faithful against Communism and encouraging them to rise up against "this enemy of God and country."[21] Future Speaker of the House John McCormick (D. Massachusetts) continuously warned that Arbenz and his

14 Ibid., 130.

15 Geoffrey Perret, *Eisenhower* (New York: Random House, 1999), 480.

16 Steven Kinzer, *Overthrow: America's Century of Regime Change, from Hawaii to Iraq* (New York: Times Books, 2006), 135.

17 Ibid., 132.

18 Perret, *Eisenhower*, 480; Kinzer, *Overthrow*, 135.

19 Stephen Rabe, *Eisenhower and Latin America: The Foreign Policy of Anti-Communism*, (Chapel Hill: University of North Carolina Press, 1988), 46–47; Kinzer, *Overthrow*, 132.

20 Kinzer, *Overthrow*, 134.

21 Ibid., 138.

government, "subservient to the Kremlin's design for world conquest," were turning Guatemala into "a Soviet beachhead."[22] Walter Bedell Smith told Eisenhower that "the Guatemalan government has abundantly proved its Communist sympathies."[23] Milton Eisenhower, the president's brother, returned from a fact-finding trip to Central America and informed the president that "the Guatemalan government has succumbed to Communist infiltration."[24]

Like any devotee of the Truman Doctrine, Eisenhower knew where this would lead. "My God," Eisenhower told his cabinet, "just think what it would mean if Mexico went Communist."[25] To paraphrase Dean Acheson, Eisenhower saw Guatemala as the rotten apple that would infect the entire Central American barrel. Under Truman's doctrine, of course, there was but one way to handle the problem: intervene. So Eisenhower launched operation "Pb success," which, like the coup against Mossadegh, was intended to replace Arbenz with someone acceptable to Eisenhower.[26]

Events came to a head on May 15, 1954, when a Swedish merchant vessel docked in Guatemala with a load of small arms and artillery from Czechoslovakia. Congress was immediately in an uproar. Senator Alexander Wiley, chairman of the Foreign Relations Committee, denounced this as "part of the master plan of world Communism."[27] John McCormick railed that this was "like an atom bomb in the rear of our backyard."[28] Democratic Senator Mike Mansfield stated that "there is no question of Communist control, there has been contact between Guatemalan leaders and Moscow."[29] Eisenhower imposed a naval blockade on Guatemala and shipped fifty tons of weapons and ammunition to America's proxies in Honduras,[30] who were led by Lt. Col. Carlos Castillo

---

22 Ibid., 135.

23 Ambrose, *Eisenhower the President*, 192.

24 Perret, *Eisenhower*, 480; Ambrose, *Eisenhower the President*, 192.

25 Perret, *Eisenhower*, 480.

26 Ambrose, *Eisenhower the President*, 192.

27 Ibid., 192.

28 Kinzer, *Overthrow*, 140.

29 Rabe, *Eisenhower and Latin America*, 57–58.

30 Ambrose, *Eisenhower the President*, 193.

Armas, whose entire force consisted of some 200 US-trained troops. Their "invasion" began on June 18, 1954, and they would have been crushed had the Guatemalan Army opposed them. But the Guatemalan Army remained in its barracks while American-piloted bombers and fighters engaged in strafing and bombing runs on airports, barracks and fuel supplies across the country.[31] Arbenz resigned, fled and was replaced by a military dictatorship.[32] Eisenhower, for his part, proudly told Americans that "[t]he people of Guatemala, in a magnificent effort, have liberated themselves from the shackles of international Communist direction. They have reclaimed their right to self-determination."[33]

Following Truman's lead, Eisenhower had once again intervened in the internal affairs of another country on behalf of a non-democratic government that this country would support for decades, just as in Greece, China and Korea. And once again, there was no criticism to be heard. Even William Fulbright, who would later become a leading critic of the Truman Doctrine's application in Vietnam, approved Eisenhower's assault on Guatemala's lawfully elected government.[34]

Eisenhower also launched a covert action against Patrice Lumumba in Congo, where Belgium, although granting "independence" to Congo in 1960, retained control of the civil service, the economic infrastructure and the army, allowing it to retain the benefits of a colony while avoiding the responsibility.[35] As Congo's first lawfully elected prime minister, Lumumba sought an end to colonialism in fact as well as law, denouncing Congo's pseudo-independence in fiery speeches heard throughout the Third World. When Congolese troops rebelled, the Belgian government sent in paratroopers while government-backed Belgian mining interests encouraged secessionists in Katanga, Congo's richest province. Determined to expel the Belgians and regain Katanga but unable to acquire support from the United States, Lumumba turned

31 Kinzer, *Overthrow*, 142.
32 Ambrose, *Eisenhower the President*, 193.
33 Perret, *Eisenhower*, 482.
34 Ibid., 58.
35 John Ranelagh, *The Agency: The Rise and Decline of the CIA* (New York: Touchstone, 1986), 339.

96

to the Soviets, who, given Katanga's immense copper and uranium deposits, were more than happy to help.[36]

On August 18, 1960, Larry Devlin, CIA chief of station in Congo, cabled Washington: "CONGO EXPERIENCING CLASSIC COMMUNIST EFFORT TAKEOVER....WHETHER OR NOT LUMUMBA ACTUAL COMMIE OR PLAYING COMMIE GAME...THERE MAY BE LITTLE TIME LEFT IN WHICH TO TAKE ACTION TO AVOID ANOTHER CUBA."[37] This message was delivered to Eisenhower at a National Security Council meeting that very day. According to testimony provided by Robert Johnson, who took the CIA's official notes of the meeting, Eisenhower told Allen Dulles that Lumumba should be "eliminated."[38] Said CIA operations chief Richard Bissell, "The President would have vastly preferred to have him taken care of some way other than by assassination, but he regarded Lumumba as I did and a lot of other people did: as a mad dog...and he wanted the problem dealt with."[39] To this end, Allen Dulles trained assassins and dispatched Sidney Gottlieb, head of the CIA medical division, to Congo with a supply of undetectable poisons.[40] In the end, however, poisons and hired assassins would prove unnecessary. For in Congolese Army Chief of Staff Joseph Mobutu, "the only man in Congo able to act with firmness," according to Allen Dulles,[41] the Eisenhower administration had the perfect ally. In November, Mobutu, who was paid and supplied by the United States and Belgian mining interests, seized Lumumba and flew him to Katanga, where he was savagely beaten, tortured and shot in January 1961.[42] Mobutu would go on to serve as one of Africa's longest-lasting, most corrupt dictators, receiving more than $1 billion in American and European aid while acquiring a personal fortune estimated at $4 billion before being ousted in 1997.[43]

---

36 Ibid., 342; Adam Hochschild, *King Leopold's Ghost: A Story of Greed, Terror and Heroism in Colonial Africa* (New York: Houghton Mifflin Company, 1998), 302.

37 Tom Weiner, *Legacy of Ashes: The History of the CIA* (New York: Doubleday, 2007), 162.

38 Ibid.

39 Hochschild, *King Leopold's Ghost*, 302.

40 Ibid; Ranelagh, *The Agency*, 343.

41 Weiner, *Legacy of Ashes*, 163.

42 Ludo De Witte, *The Assassination of Lumumba* (New York: Verso, 2001), 116–124.

43 Hochschild, *King Leopold's Ghost*, 303.

Eisenhower's enforcement of Truman's doctrine had gone rather well to this point, but the means, as with Truman's war in Korea, deserve far more scrutiny than they have ever been given.

Although Eisenhower's overthrows of Mossadegh and Arbenz were executed under NSC Directive 10/2 and its enabling legislation, the National Security Act of 1947,[44] federal courts have ruled for more than two hundred years that the Neutrality Act, which prohibits American citizens from waging war on foreign governments using private paramilitary or mercenary forces, makes no exception for the president.[45] The only way an operation unlawful under the Neutrality Act can be legalized by the subsequently enacted NSA is through the concept of "implied repeal," which cannot apply "unless the later statute 'expressly contradict[s] the original act,'" or such a construction "'is absolutely necessary [to give the later statute's words] any meaning at all.'"[46] The relevant section of the NSA was 102(d)(5), known as "the Fifth Function," which authorized the director of Central Intelligence to "perform such other functions and duties related to intelligence affecting the national security as the National Security Council may

---

44 National Security Act of 1947, Pub. L. No. 80-253, 61 Stat. 495, (codified as amended at 50 U.S.C. 403 (2000)).

45 18 U.S.C. §960 (2000): "Whoever, within the United States, knowingly begins or sets on foot or provides or prepares a means for or furnishes the money for, or takes part in, any military or naval expedition or enterprise to be carried on from thence against the territory or dominion of any foreign prince or state, or of any colony, district, or people with whom the United States is at peace, shall be fined under this title or imprisoned not more than three years, or both." *See United States v. Smith*, 27 F.Cas. 1192 (C.C.N.Y. 1807); *Dellums v. Smith*, 577 F.Supp. 1449, 1453–54 (N.D. Cal. 1984) (aid to Contras by Reagan administration a violation of the Neutrality Act). Although *Dellums v. Smith* was reversed because the plaintiffs lacked standing, its legal analysis, which is principled and consistent with both the language of the statute and long-standing case law, clearly prohibits Eisenhower's actions in Iran and Guatemala. But in *United States v. Jack Terrell*, 731 F.Supp. 473 (S.D. Fla. 1989), the court found no violation of the Neutrality Act by private defendants acting in support of the Contras because, although no formal state of war existed between the United States and Marxist Nicaragua, the history of relations between these governments made clear that "by no stretch of the imagination can the United States be said to have been 'at peace' with Nicaragua" during the relevant time period. *United States v. Terrell* would seem to legalize anything the president did in assaulting a foreign government, his actions themselves establishing that the countries were not "at peace." Clearly, this is an unsettled area of law, and the case authority provides little guidance.

46 *Traynor v. Turnage*, 485 U.S. 535, 548, (1988).

from time to time direct." Legislative history on the Fifth Function, being virtually non-existent, provides no affirmative guidance on its intended scope, but Lawrence Houston, the CIA's general counsel, advised shortly after the NSA was enacted that the legislative history included no basis to claim congressional authorization for covert action in foreign countries.[47] Houston's analysis is supported by the plain language of section 102(d)(5), which clearly limits its grant of authority to matters "related to intelligence affecting the national security." As such, many of the operations purportedly authorized by that section, such as "preventive direct action, including sabotage...demolition...[and] subversion against hostile states," clearly exceed the NSA's operational grant.[48] Needless to say, the overthrow of another country's government is simply beyond the pale, being unlawful under not just the Neutrality Act but the UN Charter as well, which guarantees "the principle of the sovereign equality of all its Members," prohibits "the threat or use of force against the territorial integrity or political independence of any state" and, as an international treaty, represents "the supreme law of the land" under Article VI of the United States Constitution.

Moreover, Eisenhower's assault on Guatemala's lawful government was illegal under not just the Neutrality Act and the UN Charter but, given the bombing attacks, 18 U.S.C. 956(b), which prohibits Americans from conspiring "to injure or destroy specific property situated within a foreign country and belonging to a foreign government or to any political subdivision thereof with which the United States is at peace . . ."[49]

Finally, Eisenhower's plot to murder Patrice Lumumba was a clear violation of 18 U.S.C. 956(a), which criminalizes conspiracies to commit any act "that would constitute the offense of murder, kidnapping, or maiming if committed in the special maritime and

---

47 William C. Banks and Peter Raven-Hansen, "Targeted Killing and Assassination: The U.S. Legal Framework," 37 University of Richmond Law Review, 667, 697 (2003). See also Peter Grose, *Gentleman Spy: The Life of Allen Dulles* (New York: Houghton Mifflin Company, 1994), 282.

48 This was no mistake or misunderstanding regarding the CIA's lawful role. CIA recruit Joseph B. Smith was told on his arrival that he had joined "the cold war arm of the U.S. government. We're not in the intelligence business in this office." Ranelagh, *The Agency*, 353.

49 The current version of 18 U.S.C. 956 (b) imposes a penalty of up to twenty-five years in prison.

territorial jurisdiction of the United States." This section provides for penalties including life imprisonment if the violation includes conspiracy to commit murder.

Although covert activities under Directive 10/2 were never subjected to rigorous legal analysis in an American court, Operation Condor, a program initiated during the mid-1970s by anti-Communist governments in South America to eliminate leftist opposition throughout the region, provides an excellent analogy. Among Operation Condor's victims were Orlando Letelier and Ronni Moffit, who were assassinated with a car bomb in Washington, D.C., on September 21, 1976, by agents of the Chilean government. When actions were filed against the Republic of Chile for damages, the United States District Court in Washington rejected any and all claims that, as a sovereign government, the Republic of Chile was entitled to immunity from suit for this conduct:

> As it has been recognized, there is no discretion to commit, or to have one's officers or agents commit, an illegal act. Whatever policy options may exist for a foreign country, it has no "discretion" to perpetrate conduct designed to result in the assassination of an individual or individuals, action that is clearly contrary to the precepts of humanity as recognized in both national and international law.[50]

The principles applied in *Letelier v. Republic of Chile* represent customary international law, which arose over the course of centuries and, as applied in American courts, exists separate and apart from treaty obligations and codes. It is neither suspended nor superseded by national sovereignty or domestic statutes (a proposition outlined in Articles 6, 7 and 8 of the Nuremberg Charter), and as the *Letelier* court ruled, it is binding on all

---

[50] *Letelier v. Republic of Chile*, 488 F.Supp. 665, 673 (D.C. Cir. 1980) (citations omitted).

members of the world community.[51] Similar rulings are found in *Liu
v. Republic of China* (Republic of China has no sovereign discretion
to commit mayhem or murder within the United States)[52] and *Doe
v. Qi* (conduct in violation of controlling domestic law, covertly
sanctioned but publicly disclaimed by a sovereign government,
remains unlawful and actionable).[53]

In summary, the only covert operations authorized by the NSA
involved intelligence gathering; "preventive direct action, including
sabotage...demolition...[and] subversion against hostile states," not
to mention conspiracy to commit murder, were clearly beyond its
scope and undertaken in violation of any pre-existing statutes
prohibiting such conduct, such as 18 U.S.C. 956 and 960. Moreover,
the NSA could not have authorized Eisenhower's "preventive direct
action," "sabotage," "demolition," "subversion against hostile
states" and conspiracy to commit murder even had Congress so
intended, such conduct violating "pre-existing universally
recognized rights under federal common law and international law"
that American courts consistently enforce against other sovereign
states regardless of domestic laws, policy or government
authorization. In other words, General Doolittle's dictum regarding
the need to disregard rules and "hitherto acceptable forms of
human conduct" while proceeding with a "fundamentally
repugnant philosophy" had been institutionalized but not legalized.

This being said, a word on legality and moral quality is in order
here given the partisan, Manichean lens through which Americans
still view the Cold War.

Acknowledging the historical truth of American Cold War
policy, including consistent disregard of controlling law, is much
like honest, critical analysis of the Allied bombing campaign during
World War II. It implies neither support for the other side nor
moral equivalence between the antagonists. (Although this is a
simple proposition, I find it uniquely difficult for even reasonable

---

51 See *Flatow v. Islamic Republic of Iran*, 999 F. Supp. 1, 13 (D.C. 1998) (ruling that customary
international law prohibits state-sponsored murder and mayhem in foreign countries regardless of
statutory enactments or principles of sovereign immunity).

52 892 F.2d 1419 (9th Cir. 1989).

53 349 F.Supp.2d 1258 (N.D. Cal., 2004).

people to grasp.) I have *never* lost sight of the fact that "Communist regimes," in the words of Martin Malia, "were criminal enterprises in their very essence: on principle, so to speak,"[54] and I am well aware that it was *they* who launched a hostile, unprovoked assault on the existing international order in 1919 with the founding of the Comintern, established, in their own words, with "the goal of fighting, *by every means,* even by force of arms, for the overthrow of the international bourgeoisie and the creation of an international Soviet republic."[55] It was *they* who declared that "the ends justify the means" and rejected, as a matter of policy, longstanding norms and principles of international law. They were relentless and remarkably successful in injecting themselves into the internal affairs of other countries through, among other means, citizens of the very states whose destruction they sought (another historically unprecedented phenomenon of which international law takes no cognizance to this day), and their primary target, we must always remember, was the United States.[56] Under these circumstances, self-defense and "necessity," which are concepts deeply embedded in both morality and law, were as applicable to American conduct as they were during World War II. [57] "We must face the fact that modern warfare as conducted in the Nazi manner is a dirty

---

54 *The Black Book of Communism*, xvii.

55 Christopher Andrew and Vasili Mitrokhin, *The World Was Going Our Way: The KGB and the Battle for the Third World* (Cambridge, Massachusetts, 2005), 1. I am nothing less than astonished when I read the revisionist tracts that were in such vogue during and after the Vietnam era in which leftist historians assign blame for the Cold War to the West and defend Stalin's brutal enslavement of Eastern Europe as facilitating one of many "legitimate" Soviet interests that Americans just did not understand. See Maddox, *The New Left and the Origins of the Cold War*; Richard Pipes, "1917 and the Revisionists" in *The Strange Death of Soviet Communism*: A Postscript, ed. Nikolas K. Gvosdev (New Brunswick: Transaction Publishers, 2008).

56 "[I]t must be recognized," wrote William C. Bullitt, American ambassador to the Soviet Union from 1933–1936, that "communists are agents of a foreign power whose aim is not only to destroy the institutions and liberties of our country, but also to kill millions of Americans." John Lewis Gaddis, *George Kennan: An American Life* (New York: The Penguin Press, 2011), 96.

57 See Illinois Criminal Code, 720 ILCS 5/7-1 (justifiable use of force) and 720 ILCS 5/7-13 (necessity): "Conduct which would otherwise be an offense is justifiable by reason of necessity if the accused was without blame in occasioning or developing the situation and reasonably believed such conduct was necessary to avoid a public or private injury greater than the injury which might reasonably result from his own conduct."

business," said Franklin Roosevelt, foreshadowing General Doolittle. "We don't like it—we didn't want to get in it—but we are in it and we're going to fight it with everything we've got."[58]

This is not to say by any means that "self-defense" and "necessity" trump all other considerations, only to note that the Cold War launched by Soviet Communists in 1919 was an inevitably dirty business and that any evaluation of American conduct, if it is to be treated seriously, must take this into account. Left, Right or Vital Center, "You are entitled to your own opinion," as Daniel Patrick Moynihan once said, "but you are not entitled to your own facts."[59]

Less than one year after the end of Truman's war in Korea, the French effort in Southeast Asia, which Truman and Acheson had declared an essential part of the Western World's campaign to contain Communism, was in complete shambles. Their troops were besieged at Dien Bien Phu, and pressure was mounting for some commitment by the United States to save the garrison. Some influential military men, such as Admiral Arthur Radford, chairman of the Joint Chiefs of Staff, were strongly in favor of employing American airpower, as were some powerful Republicans like Senator William Knowland and Richard Nixon. Army Chief of Staff General Matthew Ridgway, on the other hand, opposed any US military involvement in Southeast Asia, as did the American people and their elected representatives. When Eisenhower dispatched forty B-26 bombers and 200 American technicians to support the French in Vietnam in February 1954, "the Congressional reaction was swift and ferocious," and they were withdrawn by June.[60]

Ridgway was a thoughtful military professional who saw Vietnam as a morass that Americans might easily enter to their

---

58 Rhodes, *The Making of the Atomic Bomb*, 520.

59 Timothy Penny, "Facts are Facts," *National Review Online* June 11, 2010. http://www.nationalreview.com/articles/207925/facts-are-facts/timothy-j-penny, accessed May 10, 2012.

60 Halberstam, *The Best and the Brightest*, 139.

eternal regret. So he sent survey teams consisting of engineers, signalmen, logistics experts and others to Vietnam to examine roads, ports, railways and climate and to provide him the basis for a detailed analysis. Two questions were paramount: How much would be required, and how long would it take? The answers were sobering. Communication and transportation facilities were virtually non-existent in South Vietnam, so the Army would have to build everything—ports, railroads, highways, communications facilities. This would require at least five divisions and as many as ten, along with fifty-five engineering battalions, which would total between 500,000 and 1,000,000 troops. An undertaking of this magnitude would require draft calls of 100,000 per month, and the costs were staggering.[61] Most importantly, American intervention would likely require at least a ten-year commitment. *This country's ability to prevail was never at issue; the price to be paid and the people's willingness to pay it were.*

Eisenhower appreciated the accuracy and quality of everything Ridgway presented, noting that "war in Indochina would absorb our troops by divisions."[62] So Eisenhower imposed strict conditions on direct American involvement in Indochina:

1. A clear grant of independence to Indochina by the French;
2. British participation in any venture;
3. Participation by other nations in Southeast Asia;
4. Full and clear authorization by the United States Congress;
5. Participation by French troops under American command;
6. A French guarantee that they were not asking Americans to cover a fighting withdrawal.[63]

These conditions were based on the simple premise that

---

61 Ibid., 143.
62 Ambrose, *Eisenhower the President*, 176.
63 Ibid., 177.

Eisenhower would not commit this country to war without expecting to win, as he explained in connection with his actions in Guatemala: "If you at any time take the route of violence or support of violence...then you commit yourself to carry it through, and it's too late to have second thoughts, not having faced up to the possible consequences, when you're midway through an operation."[64] Needless to say, Eisenhower's conditions were never met. So there would be no American military involvement in Vietnam under Eisenhower, and the fate of French Indochina was sealed.

On May 7, 1954, the Communists overran the last French position at Dien Bien Phu. The very next morning, nine delegations representing the principal antagonists in Southeast Asia, their backers and other interested parties met in Geneva to seek a negotiated end to the conflict. What transpired would color the North Vietnamese worldview forever and shape the course of events for the next twenty years.

Having fought the French for nine years and crushed them at Dien Bien Phu, the Vietnamese Communists intended to "negotiate" nothing in Geneva. Expecting the full support of his Soviet and Chinese patrons, Pham Van Dong, Hanoi's minister of foreign affairs, came to impose terms, beginning with a total withdrawal from Vietnam by the French as the first order of business. The Communists demanded settlement of the political issue that had been central to nine years of war before so much as a cease-fire had been addressed. He also demanded French recognition of the Laotian and Cambodian Communists, whom the Vietminh had been supporting. But the French had come to Geneva to negotiate a mutually agreeable settlement, not tender their unconditional surrender, and they rejected these terms, deadlocking the conference.

Zhou Enlai, for his part, came to Geneva to secure China's

---

64 Rabe, *Eisenhower and Latin America*, 60.

interests, not Ho Chi Minh's.[65] Having just sustained millions of casualties in Korea, China's first aim was to preclude American involvement in Southeast Asia. Its second was to curb Vietminh designs on the rest of Indochina. As historic rivals of Vietnam, they much preferred a weakened, divided Vietnam to a powerful, unified state. China, in other words, wanted to "contain" Vietnam, and Zhou personally warned Ho Chi Minh that economic aid would depend upon Vietnamese flexibility in Geneva. Zhou then met secretly with French Prime Minister Pierre Mendes-France, who had sworn to end the war in four weeks or resign, and assured him that the Chinese preferred to settle the military issues first, with a cease-fire and separation of the combatants. Political issues, he said, could await resolution through political and diplomatic processes, suggesting that a divided Vietnam might serve everyone's interests. Mendes-France agreed, and the Vietnamese Communists were forced—by their allies in Geneva, not by their enemies on the battlefield—to accept the 1954 Geneva Accords, which mandated an immediate cease-fire and division of Vietnam along the 17th parallel. The Vietminh would govern in the North, the French in the South, and each party was required to remove its troops from the other's territory. Countrywide elections were to be held two years thereafter.

The French had succeeded beyond any reasonable expectation, while the Vietnamese Communists had "negotiated" themselves out of their victory, a fact that they would never forget.[66] Zhou Enlai "has double crossed us," said Pham Van Dong. They were confident, however, that they would win the scheduled elections,[67] and with this in mind, they began to build their Stalinist paradise with the ruthlessness of true revolutionaries.

The first order of business was "land reform," which required liquidation of those identified as "landlords," who made up two percent of the population. "The idea," as Stanley Karnow noted, "was insane," and land reform "touched off atrocities throughout

---

65 Karnow, *Vietnam: A History*, 201.

66 Larry Berman, *No Peace, No Honor: Nixon, Kissinger and Betrayal in Vietnam* (New York: The Free Press, 2001), 17; Karnow, *Vietnam: A History*, 625.

67 Karnow, *Vietnam: A History*, 204.

the country":

> Anxious to avoid indictment, peasants trumped up charges against their neighbors, while others accused rivals of imaginary crimes. Anybody suspected of having worked for the French was executed as a "traitor," and other victims included those who had shown insufficient ardor toward the Vietminh. The cadres, under pressure, singled out alleged culprits on no pretext at all. One group of cadres, reporting that it could discover only two "landlords" in a certain village, was ordered back to find six more, which it did by selecting a half dozen peasants at random.[68]

Eventually, peasants in Ho's native province, Nghe An, revolted, and Ho, like the French before him, sent troops, who suppressed the uprising, killing or deporting some six thousand peasants. The world, then as now, paid no attention.[69] Exact casualty figures during the "land reform" campaign are, as always, difficult to ascertain, but the *Black Book of Communism* estimates 50,000 executions in the countryside, excluding combat deaths.[70] More than a million Vietnamese (mostly Catholics) left their homes in the North to resettle in South Vietnam before the Communists began "reforming" society, and the Communists let them go. After all, the elections mandated by the Geneva Accords would return control of South Vietnam to them, and retribution against Vietnam's Catholics would follow in due time. The elections, however, would never take place. America's mandarin, Ngo Dinh Diem, would not allow them, and Dwight Eisenhower, with the full support of the Congress of the United States, Democrat and Republican, would back Diem under the Truman Doctrine, exactly as this country had backed non-

---

68 Ibid., 225.

69 Ibid., 226.

70 *The Black Book of Communism*, 569–570. Other sources place the land reform casualties far higher. See Rummel, *Death by Government*, 241–253 (from 1953–1956, Ho Chi Minh's government killed nearly 400,000 of its own people for various reasons, including land reform, political repression purges, and rebellion).

Communist authoritarians in Greece, China, Korea, Iran, Guatemala and dozens of other countries.

Ngo Dinh Diem was born into a Catholic family in central Vietnam in 1901. He attended the French-run School of Law and Administration, and after graduation, rose rapidly in the ranks of the colonial administration, becoming a provincial governor at the age of twenty-five. An ardent patriot, he resigned from the service of the French puppet emperor Bao Dai because he could not "act against the interests of my country."[71] Although harassed and threatened by the French for his anti-colonialism, he refused to join with the Vietnamese Communists, whom he opposed with equal fervor. After being imprisoned by the Communists, who murdered his brother and his brother's son, Diem told Ho Chi Minh to his face in 1946, "You are a criminal who has burned and destroyed the country."[72] The Communists sentenced Diem to death and made an attempt on his life. "Brave but not foolhardy," according to Stanley Karnow,[73] Diem left Vietnam and traveled to New York, where, as a genuine patriot who opposed both the Communists and the French, he earned the staunch support of powerful Americans such as Francis Cardinal Spellman and Senators John F. Kennedy and Mike Mansfield. After the Geneva Accords went into effect, Bao Dai (returned to power by the French) appointed him prime minister of South Vietnam. Diem understood the precariousness of his position, saying years before, with no inkling of his own future role, that "[t]he Communists will defeat us, not by virtue of their strength, but because of our weakness. They will win by default."[74] Whatever his early fears, Diem, once in power, had no intention of facilitating this default by allowing the Communists or anyone else to build any kind of political base in South Vietnam.

His first challenge came from the Binh Xuyen, a criminal organization numbering some 40,000. Rich from gambling, prostitution and drugs and supported by the French, the Binh Xuyen defied Diem in Saigon, openly challenging his authority and

---

71 Karnow, *Vietnam: A History*, 215.

72 Ibid. 215.

73 Ibid. 217.

74 Ibid., 216.

deploying its own troops. On April 27, 1955, Diem's forces attacked (against American advice), and after nearly a month of hard and bloody fighting, the Binh Xuyen forces were crushed.[75] Diem then turned on the Vietminh in the countryside, where he was ruthless and effective. By 1956, ninety percent of the Vietminh cells in the Mekong Delta had been smashed.[76] "[T]he Southern Communist movement," reports Stanley Karnow, "was nearly extinguished."[77] Although ruthless, Diem never inflicted the kind of carnage inflicted by the Communists in Hanoi.[78]

As for the Geneva Accords, they represented an agreement between the French and the Communists. Neither the United States nor South Vietnam was a signatory. As prime minister, Diem was not about to submit to an "election" that, in the totalitarian North, would be no more free or fair than a plebiscite under the Nazis. He was supported without reservation by Eisenhower and American political leaders from both sides of the aisle, who believed in the Truman Doctrine and shared an almost pathological fear of "losing" another country to Communism. Said Senator John F. Kennedy, "Neither the United States nor Free Vietnam is ever going to be a party to an election obviously stacked and subverted in advance, urged upon us by those who have already broken their own pledges under the agreement they now seek to enforce."[79] Senator Mike Mansfield, an outspoken anti-Communist and strong supporter of Diem, went along as well, as did the British.[80] The Chinese, of course, who desired a weakened, divided Vietnam and better relations with the West, did nothing to force compliance with the Geneva Accords, and neither did the Soviets, for similar reasons.[81]

And just what was it that American leaders were doing with Vietnam after 1954? *They were applying Truman's doctrine and*

---

75 Ibid., 222–223; A.J. Langguth, *Our Vietnam: The War*, 1954–1975 (New York: Simon & Schuster, 2000), 92–94.

76 Karnow, *Vietnam: A History*, 227.

77 Ibid., 659.

78 Derek Leebaert, *The Fifty-Year Wound: How America's Cold War Victory Has Shaped Our World* (Boston: Little, Brown and Company, 2002), 309.

79 Langguth, *Our Vietnam*, 96.

80 Ambrose, *Eisenhower the President*, 314–315.

81 William J. Duiker, *Ho Chi Minh* (New York: Hyperion, 2000), 467–473.

doing just what Truman had done in Korea without any of the work or the bloodshed. The French had fought the Communists in Vietnam just as Americans had fought them in Korea, and they had acquired an ostensibly similar settlement, with a Communist zone in the North and a non-Communist zone in the South. Of course, there would be elections in two years (there were always "elections"), but these could be handled just as easily as they had been in Korea. After all, we had East and West Germany along with North and South Korea, and the Soviets and Chinese had so far been quite accommodating on Vietnam, joining forces to impose the 1954 settlement on their client. There was just no reason to imagine then that a permanent, Korean type settlement could not be negotiated in time. Truman, after all, had provided the blueprint:

> [Eisenhower and General Lawton] Collins had a model in mind. Before Collins' departure for Saigon, they met (November 3) in the oval office. There they agreed that Collins should follow the pattern that had been so successful in Greece and Korea, building an indigenous army that could defend the country by itself, with American arms. Eisenhower had often complained that the French wanted American equipment but not American advice; Diem, he hoped, would be more cooperative, as the leaders in Greece and Korea had been. To that end, the President agreed to "build up" the American military mission in Saigon, shift a $400 million aid package intended for the French to the South Vietnamese, and put the whole program under the command of a career soldier.[82]

Diem, for his part, proved a loyal and competent ally who did *exactly* what was expected of him under Truman's doctrine, just as Rhee, another loyal ally, had done in South Korea from 1946-1950. Diem's policies were "devastatingly successful" and left the

---

82 Ambrose, *Eisenhower the President*, 215.

Communists in the South "facing extinction."[83] By 1958, he had eliminated ninety percent of the Communist Party's members and cadres, some 55,000 out of 60,000 lost in Cochinchina alone.[84] By 1960, he had, as recounted in a captured document that was duly authenticated, "truly and efficiently destroyed" the Communist Party in South Vietnam.[85] This was, according to the Communists in Hanoi, their "darkest hour."[86] Like America's proxies in Greece, Taiwan, South Korea, the Philippines, Guatemala and Iran, to name a few, Diem was in effective control, and Americans, most notably the editors of the *New York Times,* were singing Diem's praises. "A five-year miracle, not a 'plan,' has been carried out. Vietnam is free and is becoming stronger in defense of its freedom and of ours. There is reason today to salute President Ngo Dinh Diem," they wrote on July 7, 1959.[87]

Like South Korea in 1950, South Vietnam, absent military conquest, was here to stay. The Vietnamese Communists knew this and acted accordingly.

In May 1959, Hanoi created the 559th Transportation Group to enlarge its infiltration route into South Vietnam and placed it under the command of General Vo Bam.[88] By the end of the year, thirty-one tons of supplies, including nearly 3,000 weapons (all of non-Communist manufacture to conceal their source), 100,000 rounds of ammunition and 188 kilograms of TNT had been delivered to Communist forces in the South.[89] Tens of thousands of North Vietnamese troops would soon be moving down this trail to wage war on South Vietnam.

---

83 George Herring, *America's Longest War: The United States and Vietnam* 1950–1975, 2nd ed. (New York: McGraw-Hill, 1986), 67.

84 Mark Moyar, *Triumph Forsaken: The Vietnam War*, 1945–1965 (New York: Cambridge University Press, 2006), 81.

85 King C. Chen, "Hanoi's Three Decisions and the Escalation of the Vietnam War," *Political Science Quarterly* 90, no. 2 (Summer 1975): 244.

86 Howard Jones, *Death of a Generation: How the Assassinations of Diem and JFK Prolonged the Vietnam War* (New York: Oxford University Press, 2008), 14.

87 Moyar, *Triumph Forsaken*, 81.

88 Norman Hannah, *The Key to Failure, Laos & the Vietnam War* (Lanham, Maryland: Madison Books, 1987), 5.

89 Moyar, *Triumph Forsaken*, 85.

And so began, as the Vietnamese call it, the "American War." Americans entered the 1960s supporting in South Vietnam just what they were supporting in Greece, Taiwan, South Korea, the Philippines, Guatemala, Iran and a host of other places around the world: a functional, reasonably stable, non-democratic but far from totalitarian regime that ran the country, under American auspices, for the primary if not sole purpose of keeping it out of Communist hands. In other words, American policy in Southeast Asia was defined and driven by Truman's venerable doctrine, not McCarthy's "ism," and the legacy of Korea would provide the paradigm within which all decision making in connection with Southeast Asia would be made, as outlined by Daniel Ellsberg in 1972:

> We have already seen one Presidential ruling at work both in 1950 and 1961: *This is a bad year for me to lose Vietnam to Communism....*

> Starting in early 1950, the first Administration to learn painfully this "lesson of China" began to undertake—as in a game of Old Maid—to pass that contingency on to its successor. And each Administration since has found itself caught in the same game.

> Rule 1 of that game is: *Do not lose the rest of Vietnam to Communist control before the next election.*

> But the rules do not end with Rule 1. There is also— ever since late 1950, when Chinese Communists entered Korea—Rule 2, which asserts among other things: *Do not commit U.S. ground troops to a land war in Asia, either.*[90]

What Ellsberg recognizes here is that the "American War" was fought, from beginning to end, as "a continuation of political relations" between Democrats and Republicans "by other means."

---

90 Ellsberg, *Papers on the War*, 101–102 (emphasis in the original).

As such, Ellsberg's Rules embodied both strategy (what is the goal; what do you intend to achieve?) and tactics (how do you intend to achieve this?) Strategically, the goal was to hold political power in Washington, and this required future administrations to avoid the "loss of Vietnam to Communist control before the next election," which was, of course, a never-ending proposition. Tactically, this required enough military power to hold the line but prohibited commitment of sufficient force to defeat Hanoi's designs, lest the electorate become alarmed by "a land war in Asia."

Clearly, all was *not* well in the land of Truman's doctrine, where the soaring rhetoric of 1947 had crashed head-on into the reality of Korea, a wind-swept, alien land where America's sons had died by the tens of thousands while this country's political system tore itself apart. The effect was so profound that, although Truman was given, almost without dissent, hundreds of thousands of troops and billions of dollars to impose his doctrine on Korea in a bloody crusade that continued through 1953, Eisenhower found it politically impossible, the very next year, to keep forty airplanes and 200 American technicians in Southeast Asia to "contain" Communism. Appearances notwithstanding, the electorate was quite fed up, at least for now, with Truman's world-wide crusade, and fear of another land war in Asia was a major factor that complicated greatly the already complicated "Legacy of the '30s," which continued, like a retrovirus, adapting as necessary to dominate the American landscape.

Eisenhower, you see, was far more lucky than good. Korea and Vietnam remained largely dormant on his watch, and he was able to intervene quickly, easily and almost bloodlessly, with no direct American involvement, to create or sustain friendly, non-Communist regimes—Iran, Guatemala and even South Vietnam among them—that were every bit as legal and viable in 1960 as South Korea. To paraphrase Daniel Ellsberg, American financing, proxies, technicians and firepower had been sufficient on Eisenhower's watch,[91] and his policies, which appeared carefully measured and successful, restored Americans' faith in the Truman

---

91 Ellsberg, *Secrets*, 255.

Doctrine, leading them to believe that *everything* was attainable—security from Communist expansion *anywhere* on the globe without large-scale commitment or the risk of war. The political class, of course, became addicted to this theme rather easily, and by 1960, no sensible, reasonable, Vital Center politician would dare suggest otherwise, adding one more absurd idea to the already absurd politics of the Truman Era. The problem here was simple: Vietnam was like Korea, not Guatemala, and even under the best of circumstances, American financing, proxies, technicians and firepower would not be enough. Pilots and troops by the hundreds of thousands would in time be required, as General Ridgway warned in 1954. So there was a choice to be made: Prepare for another land war in Asia—prepare for what the electorate might well perceive as another Korea—or "lose" the region to Communism. It was just that simple. What Americans required now was a genuine profile in courage, the kind of man willing to say what was needed and, in John F. Kennedy's words, "take the hard and unpopular decisions necessary for our survival."[92] What they got instead was John F. Kennedy, the self-proclaimed "total politician."

---

92 John F. Kennedy, *Profiles in Courage* (New York: Harper & Brothers, 1955), 19.

PART TWO:
THE VIETNAM
ERA

Chapter Four:
John Kennedy

I

This is a young and capable man; it is necessary to give him his due. But he can neither stand up to the American public, nor can he lead them.[1]

Nikita Khrushchev

All who wrote of Alexander [the Great] preferred the marvelous to the true.

Strabo

The "torch was passed" to the Greatest Generation on January 20, 1961, when John Fitzgerald Kennedy was inaugurated. Born into wealth and privilege, he had served with distinction during the Second World War and was decorated for heroism in the South Pacific. First elected to the House of Representatives in 1946, he became a senator in 1952 and the youngest man ever elected president in 1960. In 1955, he was awarded the Pulitzer Prize for *Profiles in Courage.*[2] ("Kennedy conceived the book and supervised its production but did little of the research and writing. If you or I were discovered doing the same for a sophomore term paper in

---

1 "Word for Word/Khrushchev Unplugged; From the Middle East to Cuba, The Fine Art of Political Bluster," *New York Times*, September 14, 2003, sec. 4.
2 John F. Kennedy, *Profiles in Courage* (New York: Harper & Brothers, 1955).

sociology, we'd get an F.")[3]

Written shortly after the worst excesses of the so-called McCarthy era, *Profiles in Courage* was intended to refute Walter Lippmann's claim "that the Senate can no longer boast of men of courage." "[S]uccessful democratic politicians," wrote Lippmann,

> are insecure and intimidated men. They advance politically only as they placate, appease, bribe, seduce, bamboozle, or otherwise manage to manipulate the demanding threatening elements in their constituencies. The decisive consideration is not whether the proposition is good but whether it is popular—not whether it will work well and prove itself, but whether the active-talking constituents like it immediately.[4]

Kennedy thought this view unjustified and so produced a tribute to public officials who had the integrity to avoid conflating the public interest with their own and the courage to act accordingly, like Senator Edmund G. Ross, whose vote against impeachment saved Andrew Johnson's presidency at the cost of his own political career. Kennedy's clear purpose, of course, was to assure Americans that he was a man of integrity and courage, who, "in the days ahead...will be able to take the hard and unpopular decisions necessary for our survival in the struggle with a powerful enemy— an enemy with leaders who need give little thought to the popularity of their course, who need pay little tribute to the public opinion they themselves manipulate, and who may force, without fear of

---

3 *Profiles in Courage* was written almost entirely by Ted Sorenson. "Kennedy sent Sorensen a steady stream of notes and dictation, requested books, asked that memos be prepared, and so on. Sorensen worked virtually full-time on the project for six months, sometimes 12 hours a day. He coordinated the work and drafted many chapters. Others also made contributions, most importantly Georgetown University history professor Jules Davids." Cecil B. Adams, *The Straight Dope,* http://www.straightdope.com/columns/read/2478/did-john-f-kennedy-really-write-profiles-in-courage/, November 7, 2003. See also Herbert S. Parmet, *Jack: The Struggles of John F. Kennedy* (Norwalk: The Easton Press, 1980), 330–333.

4 Kennedy, *Profiles in Courage*, 3, quoting Walter Lippmann, *The Public Philosophy* (Boston: Little, Brown & Company, 1955), 27.

retaliation at the polls, their citizens to sacrifice present laughter for future glory."[5] Coming from a man well known in Washington for his deliberate avoidance of the Senate's vote to censure Joseph McCarthy (Kennedy was the *only* Senate Democrat who did not appear for the vote to censure McCarthy [6]), this tribute to "political courage" was an act of supreme hypocrisy, but just what one would expect from a man dedicated to becoming, in his own words, "the total politician."[7]

Nothing better exemplifies Kennedy's status as the "total politician" than his presidential campaign in 1960, in which he alleged a "missile gap" that left Americans dangerously exposed to Soviet attack despite officially acquired knowledge that the United States had several times the Soviets' nuclear capability.[8] Eisenhower could not respond to Kennedy's "missile gap" assertions without compromising national security, as Kennedy well knew, and he considered Kennedy not just aggressive, but dishonest.[9] Due in no small part to the supposed missile gap, Dwight Eisenhower initiated the deployment of Jupiter medium-range missiles, thirty in Italy and fifteen in Turkey,[10] which he knew was reckless and senseless. Khrushchev, he said, was "absolutely right in accusing the United States of provocations," noting that if the Soviets put intermediate-range missiles in Cuba or Mexico as we had placed them in Turkey, the United States would have taken military action.[11] The Jupiters, moreover, added nothing to

---

5 Kennedy, *Profiles in Courage*, 19.

6 Robert Dallek, *An Unfinished Life: John F. Kennedy*, 1917–1963 (Boston: Little Brown and Company, 2003), 199. See also Thomas C. Reeves, *A Question of Character: A Life of John F. Kennedy* (Roseville, California: Prima Publishing, 1997), 120–124; Parmet, *Jack: The Struggles of John F. Kennedy*, 307–311.

7 Richard Reeves, *President Kennedy: Profile of Power* (New York: Simon & Schuster, First Touchstone Edition, 1994), 15: "You don't get far in public life unless you become the total politician," said Kennedy after losing the 1956 Democratic vice-presidential nomination. "That means you've got to deal, not just with the voters, but with the party leaders, too. From now on, I'm going to become the total politician."

8 Ibid., 37.

9 Perret, *Eisenhower*, 603.

10 Reeves, *President Kennedy: Profile of Power*, 350.

11 Ibid., 350–351.

American security. They "took hours to fuel and launch, were wildly inaccurate, and could be ruined by a sniper firing a rifle from a public highway."[12]

Shortly after the election, Secretary of Defense Robert McNamara told several Pentagon correspondents that there was no missile gap.[13] There was a huge flap over this, and John Kennedy responded like a real "profile in courage." He lied, issuing a press release denying McNamara's assessment.[14] McNamara, of course, realized his error and told Kennedy that, despite this country's overwhelming nuclear superiority, "he would be 'politically murdered' if he built less than a thousand missiles."[15] So Kennedy rejected a proposal to negotiate a reasonable ceiling on nuclear weapons with the Soviets and instead initiated a major contribution to the arms race while taking the world into the most dangerous confrontation in history.

II

Fidel Castro had come to power on Eisenhower's watch, and John Kennedy, who stood on the floor of the House of Representatives to blame Truman for "losing China," attacked Richard Nixon relentlessly during the 1960 presidential campaign for "losing" Cuba: "Mr. Nixon hasn't mentioned Cuba very prominently in this campaign," said Kennedy. "The transformation of Cuba into a Communist base of operations a few minutes from our coast—by jet plane, missile, or submarine—is an incredibly dangerous development to have been permitted by our Republican policymakers."[16]

Kennedy had his first opportunity to deal with this "incredibly dangerous development" shortly after his election, through an operation in which some 1,500 American-trained and equipped

---

12 Ibid., 405.

13 Ibid., 58. See also Bird, *The Color of Truth*, 215–216.

14 Reeves, *President Kennedy: Profile of Power*, 57–58.

15 Kai Bird, *The Color of Truth*, 215–216. See also Gregg Herken, *Counsels of War* (New York: Oxford University Press, 1987), 155.

16 Reeves, *President Kennedy: Profile of Power*, 388–389.

Cuban exiles were to land in Cuba and, it was hoped, start an uprising that would end with Castro dead or in exile.[17] Our Cubans would fight their Cubans just as our Greeks fought their Greeks, our Chinese fought their Chinese, our Koreans fought their Koreans, and our Guatemalans fought their Guatemalans. Allen Dulles, who had briefed Kennedy prior to his election on plans for the use of anti-Castro military forces,[18] assured Kennedy that the prospects for success at the Bay of Pigs were even better than they had been in Guatemala, where Arbenz had been defeated in a similar but smaller operation without a fight. Kennedy had serious reservations but decided to proceed, against the advice of Dean Acheson (who was incredulous when told by Kennedy that he planned to land 1,500 Cubans to face an opposing force estimated to number some 25,000[19]), Dean Rusk (who thought the plan had no chance of success) and William Fulbright (who was bitterly opposed[20]).

Elected United States Senator from Arkansas in 1944, Fulbright was not a New Dealer, he was not a liberal, and, untainted by espionage scandals and Popular Front politics, he had been a consistent, principled opponent of Truman's doctrine.[21] When Dwight Eisenhower appeared before Congress in January 1957 requesting not just $200 million in discretionary funds to preserve "the independence and integrity of the nations of the Middle East" but authorization to deploy American troops to support any Middle Eastern state facing "overt armed aggression from any country controlled by international Communism," Fulbright went on the offensive, calling "improvident and unwise" "a grant of authority to disburse large sums of public money, without restrictions of any kind, for objectives which are vague and unspecified...by people who have disproved their foresight, wisdom, and effectiveness in

17 This would represent a violation of the Neutrality Act under *United States v. Smith*, 27 F.Cas. 1192 (C.C.N.Y. 1807), but not under *United States v. Terrell*, 731 F.Supp. 473 (S.D. Fla. 1989), and was most likely a violation of 18 U.S.C. 956 (a) and (b), not to mention various treaty obligations and principles of customary international law as applied by American courts.
18 Reeves, *A Question of Character*, 199–200.
19 "It doesn't take Price-Waterhouse," said Acheson, "to figure out that fifteen hundred Cubans aren't as good as twenty-five thousand." Reeves, *President Kennedy: Profile of Power*, 77.
20 Ibid., 80–81.
21 Coffin, *Senator Fulbright, Portrait of a Public Philosopher*, 167.

the field of foreign affairs."[22] The very next year, Eisenhower sent Marines to Lebanon after a pro-Western government was overthrown in Iraq. Fulbright again attacked, challenging the very foundation of Truman's doctrine: "Let something go wrong, whether in China or Nigeria—and we have a ready answer: The Soviet Union is behind it. What a perfect formula for the evasion of reality. I suggest that some of the blame belongs closer to home. In the fear of the deviltry of Communism, we have cast ourselves indiscriminately in the role of the defender of the status quo throughout the world."[23]

When briefed on the Bay of Pigs operation, Fulbright advised Kennedy to end his obsession with Cuba and abandon this operation, stating quite sensibly that Cuba, although "a thorn in the flesh," was not "a dagger in the heart."[24] But Kennedy, having attacked the Republicans as "soft on Communism" and made eradication of Castro's regime central to his presidential campaign, was a prisoner of his own rhetoric and could not now be swayed. A refusal at this point would be, in the words of Kennedy's adviser Ted Sorensen, "a show of weakness inconsistent with his general stance."[25]

In the weeks prior to the landings, Kennedy was warned repeatedly that the operation had been compromised. In fact, Kennedy was told that the planned assault was common knowledge in Latin America and at the U.N.[26] Both CBS news and radio Moscow reported on the invasion preparations.[27] The *New York Times* headlined "U.S. HELPS TRAIN AN ANTI-CASTRO FORCE AT SECRET GUATEMALAN BASE" while the *New York Daily News* informed its readers that 35,000 saboteurs were ready to strike from within while 6,000 Cuban patriots prepared to land.[28]

---

22 Ibid., 126.

23 Ibid., 127–128.

24 Patterson, *Grand Expectations*, 493.

25 Garry Wills, *The Kennedy Imprisonment: A Mediation on Power* (Boston: Houghton Mifflin Company, 2002), 234. See also Dallek, *An Unfinished Life*, 358.

26 Reeves, President Kennedy: *Profile of Power*, 82–83.

27 Ibid., 84.

28 Goldstein, *Lessons in Disaster*, 37.

Kennedy himself said that "Castro doesn't need agents over here. All he has to do is read our papers. It's all laid out for him."[29] Yet the operation proceeded, and it was an unmitigated disaster. The exile force was hit immediately by some 20,000 Cuban troops. *Their* Cubans had air cover. *Our* Cubans did not. Although the carrier *Essex* was only 50 miles off the coast, Kennedy insisted that there would be no "obvious" American involvement. Within three days, all 1,300 men in the landing force were either killed or captured.

The plan was doomed from the start. Former Joint Chiefs Chairman Maxwell Taylor was incredulous.[30] He would have used at least a division of regular troops, some 15,000 men, to hold such a beachhead.[31] Supportive in public, Eisenhower was very critical in private. When told by Kennedy that "[keeping] our hands from showing in this affair" rather than success was of primary concern to the operational design, Eisenhower, like Taylor, could not believe what he heard. "Mr. President, how could you expect the world to believe that we had nothing to do with it? Where did these people get the ships to go from Central America to Cuba? Where did they get the weapons? Where did they get all the communications and all the other things that they would need? How could you possibly have kept from the world any knowledge that the United States had been involved? I believe there is only one thing to do when you go into this kind of thing, it must be a success."[32]

Kennedy, of course, had been humiliated, in public and in private, and he was furious. Most of his advisers, military and civilian, knew all along that the operation as planned would never succeed. But they believed that, when faced with loss of the landing force, Kennedy would lift his self-imposed restriction and commit US forces. "We felt that when the chips were down—when the crisis arose in reality, any action required for success would be authorized rather than permit the enterprise to fail," said CIA Director Allen

---

29 Reeves, *President Kennedy: Profile of Power*, 84.

30 Ibid., 102.

31 Ibid.

32 Ibid., 103.

Dulles.[33] "Those sons of bitches with all the fruit salad just sat there nodding, saying it would work....How could I have been so stupid," Kennedy said when he realized the extent of their duplicity.[34]

It had certainly been an ugly little affair, but it might have been a blessing in disguise. Four months later, at a meeting in Uruguay, Che Guevara told White House aide Richard Goodwin that Castro desired a *modus vivendi* with the United States. Specifically, Castro would agree not to enter a political alliance with the Soviets. He would also accept curbs on his own activist foreign policy and would agree to pay for American property expropriated by the Cuban government. *Castro was scared and ready to compromise.* Goodwin sent a detailed memorandum of this meeting to Kennedy, but Kennedy never responded to Castro's offer.[35] A better man might have grabbed this opportunity, but Kennedy acquired little from his Bay of Pigs fiasco but an intense hatred of Castro and an increased desire to prove himself tough on Communism. From this point forward, Cuba became "an obsession." "We were hysterical about Castro," said McNamara.[36] So John Kennedy ordered the employment of "our available assets to overthrow Castro."[37] "Thus was born operation Mongoose,"[38] which was, quite simply, "a U.S. financed and directed terrorist operation" directed by Attorney General Robert Kennedy.[39]

"My idea," wrote Bobby in November 1961, "is to stir things up on the island with espionage, sabotage [and] general disorder..."[40] Bobby called Richard Helms, future head of the CIA, into his office and told him that eliminating Castro was "the top priority of the U.S. government. All else is secondary. No time, money, effort or

33 Ranelagh, *The Agency*, 372. See also Bird, *The Color of Truth*, 198, 199; Goldstein, *Lessons in Disaster*, 38–39; Dallek, *An Unfinished Life*, 360–361.

34 Reeves, *President Kennedy: Profile of Power*, 103.

35 Bird, *The Color of Truth*, 201. See also David Talbot, *Brothers: The Hidden History of the Kennedy Years* (New York: Free Press, 2007), 57–61.

36 Bird, *The Color of Truth*, 199.

37 Ronald Steel, *In Love with Night: The American Romance with Robert Kennedy* (New York: Simon & Schuster, 2000), 79.

38 Bird, *The Color of Truth*, 201.

39 Steel, *In Love with Night*, 79.

40 Patterson, *Grand Expectations*, 499; Steel, *In Love with Night*, 79.

manpower is to be spared."[41] For the next eighteen months, John and Bobby Kennedy waged an unlawful, undeclared war on Cuba.[42] "Bobby Kennedy wanted things blown up. So we blew things up," said CIA executive officer Sam Halpern.[43] On October 4, 1962, Robert Kennedy chaired a meeting of the Special Group Augmented ("SGA"), an interagency group including personnel from both the CIA and the Departments of State and Defense that had been formed for the sole purpose of destroying the Castro regime. He expressed concern about "progress on the MONGOOSE program" and advised the members that "more priority should be given to sabotage operations."[44] In addition to paramilitary attacks on Cuba's infrastructure, the Kennedys ordered Castro's assassination. According to Richard Helms, "Robert Kennedy ran with it, those operations, and I dealt with him almost every day. . . . Robert Kennedy personally managed the operation on the assassination of Fidel Castro."[45] Later claims that the CIA was a rogue operation acting on its own in this regard are just nonsense, as Helms made

41 Steel, *In Love with Night*, 78. The quoted language is taken from an "EYES ONLY" Memo from Richard Helms to Director CIA dated January 19, 1962, reporting on a meeting chaired by Robert Kennedy that day.
http://www.gwu.edu/~nsarchiv/nsa/cuba_mis_cri/620119%20Meeting%20with%20the%20Attorney%20Gen..pdf, accessed May 10, 2012
42 Bird, *The Color of Truth*, 201. To appreciate the truly idiotic, almost childish nature of Mongoose operations, I recommend Bradley Ayers, *The War that Never Was* (New York: The Bobbs Merrill Company, Inc., 1976).
43"The American Experience, RFK."
http://www.pbs.org/wgbh/amex/rfk/sfeature/sf_enemies_02.html, accessed June 2008.
44 Meeting Minutes, Special Group Augmented, October 4, 1962.
http://www.gwu.edu/~nsarchiv/nsa/cuba_mis_cri/621004%20Minutes%20of%20Meeting%20of%20Special.pdf, accessed May 10, 2012.
45 Steel, *In Love with Night*, 92, 94. On May 10, 1962, Bobby Kennedy informed J. Edgar Hoover that CIA personnel had offered mobster Sam Giancana $150,000 to "hire some gunmen to go into Cuba and kill Castro." Bobby Kennedy was disturbed by this, not because the US government was plotting a murder but because, in Hoover's words, "a man of Giancana's background" should not be used "for such a project. The Attorney General shared the same views." J. Edgar Hoover, memorandum of conversation with Attorney General Robert Kennedy, May 10, 1962. JFK Lancer Productions and Publications, http://www.jfklancer.com/cuba/links/Hoover%3ARFK.pdf, accessed May 12, 2012. See also Jones, *Death of a Generation*, 365–367; Thomas C. Reeves, *A Question of Character*, 259: "Kennedy, it is now all but certain, both knew and approved of the conspiracy to murder Castro."

clear years later to presidential historian Michael Beschloss: "There are two things you have to understand. Kennedy wanted to get rid of Castro, and the Agency was not about to undertake anything like that on its own."[46] Robert McNamara agreed, saying that the CIA was "a highly disciplined organization, fully under the control of senior officials of the government."[47] In fact, Robert Kennedy actually forced CIA officials into conduct they had previously resisted.[48] *"The evidence that the Kennedys directly ordered Castro's death is circumstantial but convincing."*[49]

Operation Mongoose was to culminate on October 20, 1962, at which time the Armed Forces were to be fully prepared for a full-scale invasion of the island.[50]

Like Eisenhower's overthrows of Mossadegh in Iran, Arbenz in Nicaragua and Lumumba in Congo, Operation Mongoose was undertaken by the Kennedy administration in violation of domestic law (18 U.S.C. 956, 960) and clear violation of international law, including the UN and Organization of American States ("OAS") Charters (which as treaties represent "the supreme law of the land"). And whatever can be said of Eisenhower, Kennedy was fully aware of this, having publicly disclaimed any intention of waging war on Castro during the 1960 election campaign in the following terms: "I have never advocated and do not advocate intervention in Cuba in violation of our treaty obligations."[51] When asked at a news conference shortly after the Bay of Pigs whether the Neutrality Act or the OAS Treaty barred Kennedy from giving aid to anti-Castro Cubans within the United States, Kennedy dodged the question.[52] Being entirely unlawful, all public funds employed for Operation

---

46 Michael R. Beschloss, *The Crisis Years: Kennedy and Khrushchev*, 1960–1963 (New York: Edward Burlingame Books, 1991), 139.

47 Ibid., 138.

48 Wills, *The Kennedy Imprisonment*, 252.

49 Ibid (emphasis added).

50 Bird, *The Color of Truth*, 243. See also Memorandum for the Secretary of Defense from the Joint Chiefs of Staff, "Justification for US Military Intervention in Cuba," March 13, 1962. http://www.gwu.edu/~nsarchiv/news/20010430/doc1.pdf, accessed May 10, 2012.

51 Reeves, *A Question of Character*, 200.

52 Ibid., 267.

Mongoose, which totaled more than $100 million dollars,[53] represent money misappropriated from the United States Treasury by the Kennedy administration (in other words, stolen).[54] And all those participating were guilty of conspiracy as well as all principal offenses in which they took part.[55] A similar operation (minus assassination attempts) by Ronald Reagan against Marxist Nicaragua some twenty years later would be denounced by Democrats as a criminal enterprise, adjudged a violation of federal law by a United States District Court[56] and ruled a violation of both customary international law and various treaties by which the United States was bound by the International Court of Justice at The Hague.[57] *The crimes for which Richard Nixon was driven from office pale when compared to Operation Mongoose.*

In July, Edward Lansdale reported to McGeorge Bundy and the SGA that the Joint Chiefs had "fully met its responsibility under the March [1961] guidelines" for "planning and initiating a decisive U.S. intervention in Cuba."[58] Everyone, it seemed, was in favor: "The

---

53 Evan Thomas, *Robert F. Kennedy: His Life* (New York: Simon & Schuster, 200), 151.

54 See 18 U.S.C.A. § 641:

> Whoever embezzles, steals, purloins, or knowingly converts to his use or the use of another, or without authority, sells, conveys or disposes of any record, voucher, money, or thing of value of the United States or of any department or agency thereof, or any property made or being made under contract for the United States or any department or agency thereof; or

> Whoever receives, conceals, or retains the same with intent to convert it to his use or gain, knowing it to have been embezzled, stolen, purloined or converted—

> Shall be fined under this title or imprisoned not more than ten years, or both; but if the value of such property in the aggregate, combining amounts from all the counts for which the defendant is convicted in a single case, does not exceed the sum of $1,000, he shall be fined under this title or imprisoned not more than one year, or both.

See also US Constitution, Article I, Section 9, Clause 7: "No money shall be drawn from the treasury, but in consequence of appropriations made by law; and a regular statement and account of receipts and expenditures of all public money shall be published from time to time."

55 *United States v. Elliott*, 266 F.Supp 318 (S.D.N.Y. 1967).

56 *Dellums v. Smith*, 577 F.Supp. 1449, 1453–54 (N.D. Cal. 1984).

57 "World Court Supports Nicaragua after U.S. Rejected Judges' Role," *New York Times*, June 27, 1986, sec. 1.

58 Bird, *The Color of Truth*, 199.

U.S.," insisted *Time* on September 14, 1962, "simply cannot afford to let Cuba survive indefinitely as a Soviet fortress just off its shores and a cancer throughout the hemisphere." It was time to "just get it over with."[59] John Kennedy apparently intended to do just that, having approved in August plans formulated by CIA Director John McCone "to deliberately seek to provoke a full-scale revolt against Castro that might require U.S. intervention to succeed." These plans would provide for "the instantaneous commitment of sufficient [U.S.] armed forces to occupy and control the country [and] destroy the regime...."[60]

On October 1, Robert McNamara ordered Admiral Robert Denison, commander of the Atlantic Fleet, "to be prepared to institute a blockade of Cuba."[61] Three days later, Bobby Kennedy told CIA Director John McCone that President Kennedy wanted more sabotage in Cuba. He wanted "massive activity," including mining harbors and kidnapping Cuban soldiers for interrogation.[62] The available evidence, from long-range planning to blockade orders and troop movements, suggests that "the Kennedy administration was hatching an 'October surprise,' an invasion of Cuba just weeks before a hard fought mid-term Congressional election."[63]

The Soviets, of course, were neither blind nor entirely stupid. Soviet spies, after all, operated within the United States throughout the Cold War, from the Rosenbergs and Alger Hiss during the early Cold War through John Walker, Aldrich Ames and Robert Hansen at the very end, and the Soviets were certainly aware of Operation Mongoose, if not of all of its details. According to Alexei Adzhubei, Khrushchev's son-in-law, Kennedy told him at a White House luncheon on January 30, 1962, that Soviet influence in Cuba was "intolerable" and reminded him that when the Soviets invaded

59 Eric Alterman, *When Presidents Lie: A History of Official Deception and its Consequences* (New York: Viking, 2004), 123.
60 Bird, *The Color of Truth*, 243.
61 Ibid., 244.
62 Ton Weiner, *Legacy of Ashes*, 196.
63 Bird, *The Color of Truth*, 244.

Hungary, the United States had not interfered.[64] What exactly Kennedy said or meant is the subject of some controversy, but Castro, who read Adzhubei's report on the conversation, firmly believed that Kennedy was hinting that an attack on Cuba was in the works.[65] "It was the copy of that report that started everything," he later said.[66] Khrushchev agreed, so he shipped nuclear missiles to Cuba and prepared launch sites, all of which went undiscovered until October 15, 1962, which—and this is a crucial point—was two weeks *after* McNamara had ordered Admiral Denison to prepare for a blockade. Khrushchev's fears of an invasion were perfectly reasonable.[67]

The Executive Committee ("ExComm") formed to handle the famous "missile crisis" included the president, McGeorge (Mac) Bundy, Robert McNamara, General Maxwell Taylor, Lyndon Johnson and Bobby Kennedy. These ExComm sessions were secretly taped by John Kennedy, who, like Harry Truman, thought nothing of law, privacy or civil liberties when it came to *his* interests. Not only did he secretly install a taping system in the Oval Office, but he also had illegal wiretaps placed on the phones of newspaper correspondents, including Hanson Baldwin of the *New York Times* and Lloyd Norman of *Newsweek,* various government employees, his brother Bobby and his wife Jacqueline.[68] Much of the surveillance was conducted at Kennedy's request by the CIA, which, in addition to being illegal under the Communications Act, was a violation of the CIA's charter, which expressly forbids the CIA from operating within the United States and spying on American citizens.[69] Bobby Kennedy, for his part, conducted domestic surveillance through warrantless FBI wiretaps on congressmen, their staff, private attorneys and lobbyists, not to mention Martin

---

64 Beschloss, *The Crisis Years*, 361–362.

65 Ibid., 361–362

66 Ibid., 362.

67 Bird, *The Color of Truth*, 242.

68 Beschloss, *The Crisis Years*, 346–347.

69 "J.F.K. Turns to the C.I.A. to Plug a Leak," *New York Times*, July 1, 2007, sec. X. See also J. Edgar Hoover, memorandum of conversation with Attorney General Robert Kennedy, May 10, 1962 (discussing CIA wiretaps on mobster Sam Giancana). JFK Lancer Productions and Publications, http://www.jfklancer.com/cuba/links/Hoover%3ARFK.pdf, accessed May 12, 2012.

Luther King and his associates.[70] More than 1,300 warrantless FBI wiretaps and bugs were authorized by the Kennedy administration.[71] (When it was revealed years later that Richard Nixon had taped people without their knowledge, former members of the Kennedy administration said that it was "inconceivable" that Kennedy would have done such a thing."[72] Ben Bradlee of the *Washington Post*, on the other hand, said of the Kennedys, "My God, they wiretapped practically everybody else in this town."[73] And it bears noting here, once again, that warrantless wiretapping—a criminal violation of federal law—is exactly what the Watergate burglars were attempting for Richard Nixon in 1972.) Whatever its ethical or legal ramifications, the taping system created a priceless record of the real reason why the world came so close to nuclear war in 1962: domestic politics.[74]

Kennedy was mystified by Khrushchev's, in his words, "provocation," saying of the missiles in Cuba that "[i]t's just as if we suddenly began to put a major number of MRBMs [medium range ballistic missiles] in Turkey. Now that'd be goddamn dangerous, I would think."[75] *Mac Bundy immediately reminded him that we just had.*

Bundy then asked McNamara directly what effect Soviet missiles in Cuba would have on the strategic balance. McNamara replied, "My personal view is, not at all." He was right. The United States had some 5,000 deliverable nuclear warheads by October of 1962 while the Soviets had approximately 300, leaving this country with a 17:1 advantage in nuclear arms.[76] Aware of the strategic balance, John Kennedy knew that he faced nothing but a political

---

70 Weiner, *Enemies*, 224, 230–233.

71 Ibid., 224

72 Beschloss, *The Crisis Years*, 346n.

73 Ibid., 347.

74 There are still 100 hours of tape-recorded White House conversations "under lock and key" that would undoubtedly provide some insight on the reality of Kennedy's plans toward Cuba. But the Kennedy family will not allow us to hear them. "The frontier of Kennedy scholarship," said historian Robert Dallek in 2002, "is still in the archives." "Kennedy Agonistes," *New York Times*, November 18, 2002.

75 Reeves, *President Kennedy: Profile of Power*, 376.

76 Ibid., 375–376.

problem of his own making: "Last month I should have said we're—that we don't care. But when we said we're not going to, and then they go ahead and do it, and then we do nothing, then..."[77] *Then what?* The answer was provided by Secretary of the Treasury Douglas Dillon on October 18, when he wrote the following note to Ted Sorensen: "Have you considered the very real possibility that if we allow Cuba to complete installation...of the missile bases, the next House of Representatives is likely to have a Republican majority?"[78]

Later that same day, McNamara stated again that, in his view, Soviet missiles in Cuba represented nothing but a political problem for the Kennedy administration: "...I'll be quite frank. I don't think there is a military problem here." Mac Bundy replied, "That's my honest judgment." McNamara: "...I've gone through this today, and I asked myself, Well, what is it then if it is not a military problem? Well, it's just exactly this problem, that if Cuba should possess a capacity to carry out offensive actions against the U.S., the U.S. would act....This is a domestic political problem...we said we'd act...well how will we act?" Bundy agreed.[79] Right up to the final decision to blockade, John Kennedy was considering his actions in terms of domestic politics: "Well, we've made our decision now. Quite frankly, I think it'll be an unpopular decision. I think we will lose votes."

After considering many alternatives, Kennedy imposed a naval blockade on Cuba, which prompted the Soviets, hopelessly outgunned in such a confrontation, to propose a deal: their missiles in Cuba for our missiles in Turkey along with a bi-lateral pledge to respect the territorial integrity of both countries. This was an infinitely reasonable proposition, and Kennedy knew it, stating that,

> From many points of view the removal of missiles from Turkey and Cuba to the accompaniment of guarantees of the integrity of the two countries had

77 Bird, *The Color of Truth*, 229.
78 Alterman, *When Presidents Lie*, 127.
79 Bird, *The Color of Truth*, 229–230.

considerable merit. . . . In the first place, we last year tried to get the missiles out of there, because they're not militarily useful, number 1. Number 2, it's going to—to any man at the United Nations or any other rational man—it will look like a very fair trade....We can't very well invade Cuba, with all its toil, when we could have gotten them out by making a deal on the missiles in Turkey. If that's part of the record, I don't see how we'll have a very good war....*Let's not kid ourselves. They've got a very good proposal.*"[80]

But the ever-present demands of domestic politics would not allow "a very fair trade," because, as Roger Hilsman later wrote, "President Kennedy and his administration were peculiarly vulnerable on Cuba. He had used it in his own campaign against Nixon to great effect, asking over and over why a Communist regime had been permitted to come to power just ninety miles off our coast. Then came the Bay of Pigs, and now the Soviets were turning Cuba into an offensive military base..."[81] John Kenneth Galbraith concurred: "Once [the missiles] were there the political needs of the Kennedy administration urged it to take almost any risk to get them out."[82] McGeorge Bundy later wrote that removal of the Soviet missiles was essential because they were politically intolerable for the Kennedy administration, not because they represented a genuine, useable Soviet asset.[83] "Having fooled the people in order to lead them," noted Gary Wills, "Kennedy was forced to serve the folly he had induced."[84]

In the end, Khrushchev agreed to remove the missiles in return for two assurances from Kennedy: 1) an American pledge not to invade Cuba, which was given in public as Kennedy's end of the

---

80 Alterman, *When Presidents Lie*, 116–117 (emphasis added).

81 Roger Hilsman, *To Move a Nation: The Politics of Foreign Policy During the Administration of John F. Kennedy* (New York: Dell Publishing, 1967), 196.

82 Ibid., 122.

83 Bird, *The Color of Truth*, 246, quoting McGeorge Bundy, *Danger and Survival: Choices about the Bomb in the First Fifty Years* (New York: Random, House, 1988), 453.

84 Wills, *The Kennedy Imprisonment*, 263.

deal; and 2) Kennedy's assurance that the Jupiter missiles in Turkey would be withdrawn, which was given in secret to facilitate the "organized mass disingenuousness" of the Kennedy machine, which kicked into high gear immediately.[85] On October 29, the *New York Times* headlined "Turkey Relieved at U.S. Firmness: Gratified That Bases Were Not Bargained Away."[86] *Time* declared on November 2 that "[g]enerations to come may well count John Kennedy's resolve as one of the decisive moments of the 20th century. For Kennedy was determined to move forward at whatever risk. And when faced by that determination, the bellicose Premier of the Soviet Union first wavered, then weaseled, and finally backed down."[87] But within six months, the Jupiter missiles in Turkey had been dismantled and demolished, as Kennedy promised. When suspicions were raised in Congress that there had been a trade, both Dean Rusk and Robert McNamara lied to the Senate Foreign Relations Committee, insisting that no deal had been made.[88] Particularly egregious was John Kennedy's attack on Adlai Stevenson. Stevenson had advocated during the ExComm meetings the kind of trade Kennedy ultimately made, missiles in Turkey for missiles in Cuba, and in time, Kennedy dispatched Michael Forrestal to provide "background" to the *Saturday Evening Post,* stating that, according to "a non-admiring official," "Adlai wanted a Munich." The non-admiring official was none other than John Kennedy, who specifically approved the "Adlai wanted a Munich" terminology to "destroy the integrity and perceived respectability of the suggestion of a Cuba-for-Turkey missile trade."[89]

---

85 Robert Kennedy lied about the trade in his book *Thirteen Days*, as Ted Sorensen admitted in 1989: "I was the editor of Robert Kennedy's book. . . .[H]is diary was very explicit that [the trade of missiles in Turkey for missiles in Cuba] was part of the deal; but at the time it was still secret...So I took it upon myself to edit that out of the diaries." Bird, *The Color of Truth*, 238-239.

86 Alterman, *When Presidents Lie*, 96.

87 Ibid., 93.

88 Ibid., 97; Eric Alterman, "Presidential Lies," *New York Times Book Review*, November 14, 2004.

89 Alterman, *When Presidents Lie*, 94–95, 118–119. See also Thomas, *Robert F. Kennedy: His Life*, 231–232. John Kennedy's attack on Stevenson was vintage John Kennedy, whose conniving behavior was on par with Richard Nixon's throughout his public life, whether his opponent of the moment was Republican or Democrat. See Caro, *The Years of Lyndon Johnson*, 85-86 (John and Bobby's contrived attack on Hubert Humphrey as a draft dodger during the 1960 primary in West Virginia).

»» ««

One can only conclude that our nation was extremely fortunate to have had John F. Kennedy as president in October 1962.[90]

Richard Holbrooke

I have changed my mind on a number of things since, including almost everything to do with Cuba, but the idea that we should be grateful for having been spared, and should shower our gratitude upon the supposed Galahad of Camelot for his gracious lenience in not opting to commit genocide and suicide, seemed a bit creepy. When Kennedy was shot the following year, I knew myself somewhat apart from this supposedly generational trauma in that I felt no particular loss at the passing of such a high-risk narcissist.[91]

Christopher Hitchens

Illustrating the vast gap between history and ideology, the Missile Crisis has been presented for decades in terms of naked Soviet aggression resisted heroically by America's wise and righteous young president who, innocent of aggressive designs of his own, saved us all by his "combination of toughness and restraint, of will, nerve and wisdom, so brilliantly controlled, so matchlessly calibrated."[92] I spent some forty years believing every bit of this. But there are a few things Americans have overlooked when evaluating the Missile Crisis, the most important being that "Kennedy had effectively created his own dilemma in Cuba."[93] As Gary Wills wrote in 1981, "To the American public, [installation of missiles] looked unprovoked, mysteriously aggressive, threatening because it added resources to a side that had a strong will already."[94] But the American public "did not know...that thousands of agents

90 Richard Holbrooke, "Real WMDs," *New York Times Book Review*, June 22, 2008.

91 Christopher Hitchens, *Hitch-22: A Memoir* (New York: Hatchett Book Group, 2010), 65–66.

92 Schlesinger, *A Thousand Days: John F. Kennedy in the White House* (New York: Mariner Books, 2002), 841

93 Alterman, *When Presidents Lie*, 124.

94 Wills, *The Kennedy Imprisonment*, 259.

were plotting [Castro's] death, the destruction of his government's economy, the sabotaging of his mines and mills, the crippling of his sugar and copper industries."[95] "[T]he Kennedys looked like brave resisters of aggression, though they had actually been the cause of it."[96] McNamara himself admitted that "if I had been a Cuban leader at the time, I might well have concluded that there was a great risk of U.S. invasion....If I had been a Soviet leader at the time, I might have come to the same conclusion."[97] *If anyone's conduct represented "swashbuckling attacks on peace and security"—as Soviet behavior was described in the aftermath of the crisis—it was more Kennedy's than Khrushchev's.*[98]

We now know, moreover, that Kennedy's game of nuclear chicken brought the world far closer to the brink than anyone then realized. Many of Kennedy's ExComm advisers, including Dean Acheson, Paul Nitze and the Joint Chiefs, had pushed for a military solution, starting with air strikes on the missile sites, which seemed to represent a reasonable option at the time. In the early 1990s, however, we learned that the Soviets had not 10,000 but some 41,000 troops in Cuba, and at least ninety-eight *tactical* nuclear warheads that the local commander had discretionary authority to use in the event of a US attack.[99] These warheads had already been dispersed to combat units and would undoubtedly have been used had Kennedy ordered the invasion urged by many of his advisers. *Soviet commanders would never have allowed American forces to overrun 41,000 Soviet troops, seize their nuclear weapons and eliminate Castro without using the tactical weapons they had stockpiled for just this eventuality.*[100]

Moreover, Soviet Foxtrot-Class diesel-electric submarines were present in the Western Atlantic during the blockade. These were outdated, relatively noisy vessels that were set upon quickly by the US Navy. Forced to remain submerged, they suffered numerous

---

95 Ibid.

96 Ibid.

97 Steel, *In Love with Night*, 80.

98 Alterman, *When Presidents Lie*, 98, quoting Henry M. Pachter.

99 Bird, *The Color of Truth*, 245.

100 Ibid., 245.

breakdowns from faulty equipment as American destroyers pummelled them with grenade-sized explosives intended to force them to the surface. Unknown to the US, each Soviet submarine was carrying a nuclear-armed torpedo. After two days of pursuit and harassment, Captain Valentin Savitsky had reached the end of his tether. His submarine, B-59, was plagued with mechanical breakdowns, including the ventilation system, the diesel coolers and electrical compressors. Temperatures ran between 110 and 140 degrees, and carbon dioxide levels had reached critical levels, with crewmen "falling like dominoes."[101] Vadim Orlov, chief of the signals intelligence unit on B-59, witnessed his captain's near-disastrous loss of control:

> The Americans hit us with something stronger than a grenade, apparently some kind of practice depth charge. We thought "that's it, that's the end." After this attack, a totally exhausted Savitsky became furious. In addition to everything else, he had been unable to establish communications with the General Staff. He summoned the officer who was in charge of the nuclear torpedo and ordered him to make it combat ready. "Maybe the war has already started up there while we are doing somersaults down here," shouted [Savitsky] emotionally, justifying his order. "We're going to blast them now! We will perish ourselves, but we will sink them all. We will not disgrace our Navy!"[102]

Luckily, the submarine flotilla commander, Captain Vasili Arkhipov, was aboard the B-59, and use of a nuclear weapon required his authorization. This he refused, and he convinced Savitsky to surface, establish communications, report the situation and request instructions. Savitsky did so, and an hour later, B-59 was ordered to "throw off your pursuers" and move closer to

---

101 Michael Dobbs, *One Minute to Midnight: Kennedy, Khrushchev, and Castro on the Brink of Nuclear War*, (New York: Alfred A. Knopf, 2008), 302.
102 Ibid., 303.

Bermuda, which ended the immediate threat of nuclear war.[103] *But for Vasili Arkhipov, the chain of events the Kennedy brothers initiated might well have resulted in nuclear war.*

The Missile Crisis was the most dangerous confrontation of the entire Cold War,[104] and shamefully, it was Khrushchev, in the end, who acted most sensibly, accepting the enormous humiliation of a secret deal that allowed Kennedy to claim a total victory he had not achieved. And it might well have been Khrushchev who, through a "combination of toughness and restraint," was in some ways the real victor. He wanted, primarily, two things: an end to Kennedy's war on Cuba and withdrawal of the Jupiter missiles in Europe, and he achieved both objectives (at least for the moment) with no loss of life on his side.

Finally, we should note that forty-two missiles in Cuba affected the strategic balance only to the extent that they served to neutralize this country's ability to undertake a first strike against Soviet Russia with impunity. With missiles in Cuba, there would be disastrous consequences to such an action. But since no American administration ever seriously considered a first strike, the missiles in Cuba meant nothing but a domestic political problem for the Kennedys, who, it is clear from the ExComm tapes, knew it.[105]

So the only threat that ever arose from Castro's Cuba was John F. Kennedy's missile crisis, and the biggest problem for Americans would stem not from the missiles in Cuba but the Soviet response to Kennedy's "victory" over Khrushchev, which brings us to the most important question of all: Just what did Americans gain from their brush with nuclear holocaust in October of 1962?

Soviet diplomat Vasily Kuznetsov, who helped negotiate an end to the Missile Crisis, told his American counterpart John J. McCloy, "Well Mr. McCloy, we will honor this agreement. But I want to tell

---

103 Ibid.

104 Bird, *The Color of Truth*, 201.

105 Robert Kennedy later admitted that "[the missiles in Cuba] weren't posing any threat, really. I don't see what the problem was." "Totally missing the point," *Chicago Tribune*, October 17, 2002, sec. 1.

you something. You will never do this to us again."[106] "Humiliation on Cuba galvanized the Soviets into action," giving rise to "the largest military buildup in history…"[107] Within five short years, Soviet Yankee-class missile submarines, each with sixteen one-megaton warheads, were deployed along the US coastline, and by 1972, the Soviets possessed a modern ICBM force of 1,500 missiles to America's 1054.[108] *America's 17:1 nuclear advantage had vanished.* It was "in retrospect…a heavy price to pay for an ephemeral victory."[109]

III

We had to stop the aggression through Laos or we had to stop defending South Vietnam. Either way—and I hoped it would be the first—the Gordian knot would be cut and our position rectified. Either way, we couldn't go on this way much longer. We couldn't have it both ways.

I was wrong. We went on trying to have it both ways for years, throwing in our wealth, our power, our prestige, to fill the gap.[110]

Norman Hannah

An outspoken supporter of Truman's doctrine, Kennedy backed Diem's refusal to hold the elections mandated by the 1954 Geneva Accords, charging that they would be "obviously stacked and subverted in advance."[111] Speaking in June of 1956, Kennedy famously stated that South Vietnam represented "the cornerstone

106 Richard Rhodes, *Arsenals of Folly: The Making of the Nuclear Arms Race* (New York: Alfred A. Knopf, 2007) 94; Beschloss, *The Crisis Years*, 563.
107 Robert M. Gates, *From the Shadows, The Ultimate Insider's Story of Five Presidents and How they Won the Cold War* (New York: Simon & Schuster Paperbacks, 1996), 29.
108 Rhodes, *Arsenals of Folly*, 95. See also Norman Polmar and John D. Gresham, *Defcon-2, Standing on the Brink of Nuclear War during the Cuban Missile Crisis* (Hoboken: John Wiley & Sons, Inc., 2006), 282–287.
109 Bird, *The Color of Truth*, 247.
110 Hannah, *The Key to Failure*, 82.
111 George W. Ball, *The Past Has Another Pattern* (New York: W. W. Norton & Company, 1982), 364.

of the Free World in Southeast Asia, the keystone to the arch, the finger in the dike. Burma, Thailand, India, Japan, the Philippines and obviously Laos and Cambodia are among those whose security would be threatened if the red tide of Communism overflowed into Vietnam."[112] Evidence indicates, however, that Kennedy never really believed any of this, having stated in the House of Representatives in January 1952 that "I am frankly of the belief that no amount of American military assistance in Indochina can conquer an enemy which is everywhere and at the same time nowhere....The forces of nationalism are rewriting the geopolitical map of the world."[113] Yet Kennedy's anti-Communist rhetoric was politically and ideologically correct, being *exactly* what Truman said about Korea. ("Our homes, our Nation...are in great danger."[114]) It was just as true (or false) with regard to Vietnam, and virtually everyone seemed to believe it right up through the early 1960s, when John Kennedy told the world that Americans were prepared to "pay any price" and "bear any burden."

Yet the very same Americans who sacrificed tens of thousands of their sons defending an authoritarian proxy regime on a tiny peninsula halfway around the world stood by and watched, a mere six years later, as an insurgent force small enough to be crushed with a tiny fraction of their military power seized Cuba and transformed it into a Communist outpost just ninety miles off their own coast. *America's days of effective, decisive interference with Communist designs on the Third World using any means necessary were over, and its Cold War enemies took note.* "A war took place [in Cuba] too," said Nikita Khrushchev in January 1961. "[I]t...started as an uprising against the internal tyrannical regime supported by U.S. imperialism...However, the United States did not interfere in that war directly with its armed forces. The Cuban people, under the leadership of Fidel Castro, have won."[115] Sensing that it was time to shift strategy, Khrushchev renounced Stalin's

---

112 Lewy, *America in Vietnam*, 12–13.

113 *Congressional Record*, January 8, 1952, HR 5879, cited in Reeves, *President Kennedy: Profile of Power*, 254. See also Dallek, *An Unfinished Life*, 185–187.

114 Chang and Halliday, *Mao: The Untold Story*, 365.

115 Gaddis, *We Now Know*, 183. See also Kissinger, *Diplomacy*, 644.

belief in the inevitability of world war and declared that it would henceforth be Soviet policy to fight the West on "political, social and psychological" grounds while supporting Communist revolutionaries in the Third World, where "national liberation wars...are not only admissible but inevitable."[116]

This was nothing short of a *modus vivendi* that might well serve everyone's interests, and John Kennedy was intrigued, telling his top aides to "read, mark, learn and inwardly digest" every aspect of Khrushchev's speech.[117] "This is our clue to the Soviet Union," he said.[118] He would soon accept not just Khrushchev's offer but Khrushchev's ground rules as well, which, along with Ellsberg's Rules, would provide the basic framework for the conduct of America's war in Southeast Asia from 1961-1975.

Laos, which straddles Thailand, Cambodia and Vietnam, was the gateway to Southeast Asia.[119] Dwight Eisenhower warned John Kennedy the day before his inauguration that a Communist Laos "would be fatal to American interests in all of Asia."[120] "We must not permit a Communist takeover," he said, adding that, "Unilateral intervention would be our last, desperate hope if we cannot get others to go in with us."[121] Eisenhower would repeat this warning in the spring of 1962, telling Robert McNamara on May 13 that, "If Laos is lost, South Vietnam and Thailand will ultimately go because they will be outflanked. All Southeast Asia will be lost..."[122] So he advised Kennedy to send American combat troops into Laos.[123] His reasons were simple: 1) he was a true believer in Truman's doctrine;

116 Gaddis, *We Now Know*, 183. See also Andrew and Mitrokhin, *The World Was Going Our Way*, 9; Hannah, *The Key to Failure* 36; Beschloss, *The Crisis Years*, 60.

117 Beschloss, *The Crisis Years*, 61.

118 Ibid.

119 John Prados, *The Blood Road: The Ho Chi Minh Trail and the Vietnam War* (New York: John Wiley & Sons, Inc., 1999), 20.

120 Clifford, *Counsel to the President*, 343. See also Reeves, *President Kennedy: Profile of Power*, 31.

121 Clifford, *Counsel to the President*, 343. See also Arthur M. Schlesinger, Jr., *Robert Kennedy and His Times* (Boston: Houghton Mifflin Co., 1978), 702.

122 Moyar, *Triumph Forsaken*, 163.

123 John M. Newman, *J.F.K. and Vietnam: Deception, Intrigue and the Struggle for Power* (New York: Warner Books, 1992), 267–268

and 2) he was a competent, experienced military commander who saw the former French Indochina (Vietnam, Laos and Cambodia) as a single, unified theatre of operations that would stand or fall as one unit. And it was Laos, he knew, that provided the North Vietnamese with the supply and reinforcement routes necessary to sustain their efforts. Kennedy's Joint Chiefs, it should be noted, agreed with Eisenhower.[124]

Douglas MacArthur, on the other hand, told Kennedy in the spring of 1961 to stay out of Southeast Asia entirely, as Kennedy noted in his own hand: "[MacArthur] believes it would be a mistake to fight in Laos."[125] *This country's two most senior military commanders—honest, competent and (in this case) non-partisan— provided Kennedy a clear and simple choice: get in or get out.*

In February 1961, Communist forces in Laos (almost entirely North Vietnamese), supported by a Soviet airlift that was, according to Soviet Deputy Foreign Minister Georgiy Pushkin, "apart from the Second World War, the highest priority Soviet supply operation since the Revolution,"[126] inflicted a major defeat on America's allies. By April, Communist forces were positioned to march on Vientiane and the Mekong Valley that led to South Vietnam.[127] Absent American military intervention, Laos would fall to the Communists in weeks, and it would only be a matter of time until Saigon followed, leaving Kennedy confronting the same problem in Vietnam that Truman confronted in Korea a decade earlier: military conquest of the non-Communist South (not to mention Laos and Cambodia) by the Communist North. Having laid the "loss" of China at Truman's door and the "loss" of Cuba at Eisenhower's while calling South Vietnam "the cornerstone of the Free World in Southeast Asia, the keystone to the arch, the finger in the dike" of American national security, Kennedy could not afford to "lose" Southeast Asia. But his options were disagreeable at best.

Kennedy's Laos Task Force recommended Operation Millpond, which would begin with military advisers and culminate with a

---

124 Jones, *Death of a Generation*, 286. See also Dallek, *An Unfinished Life*, 305.
125 Reeves, *President Kennedy: Profile of Power*, 110; Manchester, *American Caesar*, 696.
126 Hannah, *The Key to Failure*, 38.
127 Newman, *J.F.K. and Vietnam*, 9–11.

massive deployment.[128] The State Department, on the other hand, offered a plan to insert 26,000 troops, including 13,000 Americans, "merely to hold certain key centers for diplomatic bargaining purposes, not to conquer the country. They [were to] shoot only if shot at."[129] The Joint Chiefs, while not opposed to intervention, opposed all such half-measures, advising Kennedy to go into Laos with at least 60,000 troops with air cover or stay out.[130] In case of Chinese intervention, the Chiefs recommended seizure of Hainan Island, then occupied by *three* Chinese Divisions (40-50,000 men), and deployment of 250,000 American troops to South Vietnam, for whose protection nuclear weapons would be used if necessary.[131] Kennedy was told directly that without nuclear weapons, American forces attacked by the Chinese in Laos would have to retreat or surrender.[132]

Kennedy rejected all advice to insert American troops, telling Arthur Schlesinger, "If it hadn't been for Cuba, we might be about to intervene in Laos. I might have taken this advice seriously."[133] A good decision for the moment perhaps, but one that provided no long-term solution, and as the situation continued to deteriorate, Kennedy was briefed in October 1961 on the "Concept for Intervention in Vietnam" that called for deployment of 22,800 SEATO ground combat troops (Southeast Asian Treaty Organization[134]), of whom 11,000 were to be American, in an area north of Pleiku.[135] Still resisting the military's call to send in American ground troops, Kennedy sent General Maxwell Taylor on a tour of South Vietnam to provide him with a first-hand report on the situation.

In November, Taylor returned from South Vietnam and recommended deployment of 8,000 US ground troops under the

---

128 Ibid., 12.

129 Ibid., 13.

130 Ibid., 14.

131 Ibid., 17; Jones, *Death of a Generation*, 86.

132 Newman, *J.F.K. and Vietnam*, 52–53.

133 Ibid., 55.

134 An international defense organization including the United States, Britain, France, Australia, New Zealand, Pakistan, the Philippines and Thailand that was founded in Manila in 1954.

135 Newman, *J.F.K. and Vietnam*, 127.

guise of "flood relief." These troops would conduct combat operations deemed necessary for self-defense, provide support when needed for the Army of the Republic of Vietnam ("ARVN"; pronounced Arvin) and act as an advance party for additional US forces.[136] Two days later, the National Security Council objected. If Americans were to succeed in Southeast Asia, the Council advised, a "Berlin-type" commitment had to be made.[137] On November 8, 1961, Robert McNamara reported that 205,000 American troops would be required to cut the Ho Chi Minh Trail and secure South Vietnam's border.[138] Kennedy, however, continued insisting that South Vietnam's problems were social and political rather than military in nature, so he increased the number of "advisers" and initiated myriad "civil action" programs—building schools, wells, latrines, dispensaries and of course, the famous, peasantry-alienating strategic hamlets. America's military establishment, led by soldier-intellectuals like Maxwell Taylor who knew the drill, went right along with this folly with nary a word of protest as Kennedy's civilian advisers began discussing, in the fall of 1961, the need to remove Diem from power.[139]

On the merits, Kennedy faced a simple choice, as McNamara had noted on November 8: 1) "lose" to Communism a vast, populous territory that for years he had claimed was crucial to American security, thereby violating Ellsberg's Rule 1, and pay the price ("another Munich," an "Asian Bay of Pigs," Republicans would howl); or 2) deploy the forces necessary to enforce Truman's doctrine in Southeast Asia as Truman had enforced it in Korea with all the attendant costs and risks, thereby violating Ellsberg's Rule 2, and (of course) pay whatever price events ultimately exacted, as Truman and the Democrats had paid for Korea.[140] It was a pivotal

136 Ibid., 134.
137 Ibid., 137.
138 Sheehan, Smith, Kenworthy and Butterfield, *The Pentagon Papers*, document # 30, 154–156. See also James G. Blight, janet M. Lang, David A. Welch, and Fredrik Logevall, *Vietnam if Kennedy Had Lived: Virtual JFK* (Lanham, Maryland: Rowman & Littlefield Publishers, Inc., 2009), 127; Prados, The Blood Road, 33–38.
139 Jones, *Death of a Generation*, 109; 132–134.
140 Hilsman, *To Move a Nation*, 128–130.

moment, and for the supposed author of *Profiles in Courage,* the role of a lifetime. But he was entirely unsuited to the role, so when Nikita Khrushchev, with his own plans for Southeast Asia, offered America's "total politician" a politician's way out—a plan for "neutralization" of Laos that was perfectly suited to *both* of their immediate interests—Kennedy was quick to accept. "Why take risks over Laos?" Khrushchev told Averell Harriman in Moscow. "It will fall into our laps like a ripe apple."[141]

Harriman assured Kennedy in May that he had "Khrushchev's word that he will work to establish Laos as a neutral similar to Austria."[142] ("Khrushchev's word"—now there's a gold standard for you.) Harriman, every inch the politician, believed, as could be expected, exactly what he wanted to believe: "Regardless of other considerations I continue to feel that the South Vietnamese problem can best be solved in *South Vietnam* rather than by trying to find the solution by military means in Laos. I fear that if SEATO forces are introduced into Laos it will be difficult to prevent an extremely dangerous escalation and at best will have forces bogged down indefinitely."[143]

Secretaries Rusk and McNamara, exquisitely attuned as well to the president's political needs, soon followed suit, advising Kennedy that "after a Laotian settlement, the introduction of United States forces into Vietnam could...stabilize the position both in Laos and Vietnam."[144] So John Kennedy, determined, in Bobby Kennedy's words, "to avoid a Korea"[145] and handle Southeast Asia as "something other than a war,"[146] rejected Eisenhower's professional, non-partisan warning that Laos, not South Vietnam, was "the present key to the entire area"[147] and MacArthur's professional, non-partisan warning to stay out of Southeast Asia

---

141 Hannah, *The Key to Failure*, 36.

142 Ibid., 37.

143 Ibid., 39 (emphasis in the original).

144 Ibid., 40.

145 Robert Kennedy, *Robert Kennedy in His Own Words*, ed. Edwin O. Guthman and Jeffrey Shulman (New York: Bantam Books, 1988), 395.

146 Hilsman, *To Move a Nation*, 536.

147 Schlesinger, *Robert Kennedy and His Times*, 702.

entirely. Instead, he accepted Khrushchev's proposal for "neutralization" because *political* advisers like Averell Harriman, the former governor of New York, told him that fighting a guerilla war in South Vietnam presented the best option.

The fourteen-nation "neutralization" conference began in Geneva in May 1961 and ended in July 1962 with an agreement that required withdrawal of all foreign military forces from Laos (ninety percent of whom were North Vietnamese) by October 7, 1962, and created an international commission (the "ICC") with members from India, Canada and Poland to monitor their departure.[148] *Had the 1962 Geneva Accords been effectuated, the "Vietnam War" of history would never have occurred.* But as Averell Harriman noted years later, "The North Vietnamese did not keep the Laos Agreement of 1962 for a single day."[149] The Communist Pathet Lao declared that their side had no foreign troops to be evacuated and refused to designate departure checkpoints for some 9,000 North Vietnamese personnel (who in fact controlled fully one-third of the country) or allow ICC inspection in their area.[150] Secretary of State Rusk formally protested to the Soviets (Khrushchev had, after all, given "his word"), but Soviet Deputy Foreign Minister Georgiy Pushkin brushed aside the Accords' legal technicalities and said that "the Vietminh would just melt into the jungle."[151] Like Eisenhower, the Communists knew that Laos was the key to Southeast Asia and had no intention of relinquishing it.

America's Laotian allies protested angrily. Royalist General Phoumi declared the Accords worthless and said that if the withdrawal provisions could not be implemented, the entire charade should be abandoned and fighting should resume.[152] But this would put Kennedy right back to square one, forcing him to choose between "losing Laos" or employing the force necessary to enforce Truman's doctrine as Truman had in Korea, and the self-proclaimed "total politician" was *not* going down that road. So the

---

148 Hannah, *The Key to Failure*, 46.
149 Ibid., 49.
150 Ibid., 50–53.
151 Ibid., 55.
152 Ibid., 53.

best and the brightest would do what was politically expedient, understanding fully the actual effect of a "neutralization accord" the Communists had no intention of keeping, as Roger Hilsman, who served John Kennedy as director of the State Department's Bureau of Intelligence and Research and later as assistant secretary of state for Far Eastern affairs, explained. It was clear, Hilsman wrote, that the Kennedy administration and the North Vietnamese "had arrived at a tacit agreement—not on the settlement of the Laos problem, but on its temporary postponement":

> The Communist North Vietnamese could easily put enough troops into Laos to take it over within two to four weeks, if they were willing to take the risk of American intervention. But they were not willing to take that risk, mainly because the United States made sure that the risk was real. By using the more ambiguous guerilla techniques they were applying to Vietnam, they could probably have taken over Laos on a longer time scale with even less risk. But they were unwilling to take even that level of risk over Laos, apparently because they felt the main arena was Vietnam. For this very reason, however, the Communists wanted to keep using the infiltration routes through Laos into South Vietnam. But they were apparently willing to keep their use of the routes at guerilla warfare levels; that is, to keep the use of the routes down to a level that was less than fully provocative. Until the matter of Vietnam was settled . . . the Communists would keep some token representation in Souvanna's government at Vientiane and thus avoid scuttling the Geneva agreements openly and irrevocably. Then, if the guerilla struggle in Vietnam went *against* the Communists, Laos would quickly become the model for a truly neutral country in which the Communists participated in a coalition government without attempting to subvert it—at least for a while. But if the Communists won in Vietnam—they seemed to be

saying—then they would regard Laos as part of the prize.[153]

As hard as this is to believe, General Maxwell Taylor, another of Kennedy's closest advisers, explained the Kennedy administration's thinking in nearly identical terms:

> The Geneva Accords did not result in the withdrawal of the North Vietnamese troops supporting the Pathet Lao or the cessation of the use of the Ho Chi Minh trails to supply the war in South Vietnam. Fighting on the ground continued around the Plaine des Jarres, ebbing and flowing with the monsoon changes of the weather. However, the dividing line between Pathet-Lao [read "North Vietnamese"] held territory and that under government or neutralist control did not change in any important way from 1962 for the next seven years. There seemed to be a tacit understanding on both sides that the fate of Laos would be resolved in Vietnam. For that reason the Pathet Lao took as a primary objective the protection of the supply lines in the Laotian panhandle, and maintained a de facto partition of the country on a north-south line which prevented any effective military action from the Mekong valley against their communications.[154]

There is one thing—and one thing only—driving this bizarre "agreement": Truman's war in Korea. The Communists in Hanoi would have loved to send their army across the DMZ to eliminate South Vietnam just as Kim Il Sung attempted to eliminate South Korea, and without the threat of American intervention, they would have done just that. But they knew that a conventional assault on South Vietnam, "the finger in the dike" of American security, would force Kennedy's hand just as Kim had forced Truman's in Korea,

---

153 Hilsman, To Move a Nation, 154.
154 Maxwell Taylor, *Swords and Plowshares* (New York: W.W. Norton & Company, Inc., 1972), 218–219.

and they had no intention of watching Kennedy do to their hopes of reunification, not to mention their country, what Truman had done to Kim's. Kennedy, on the other hand, knew that his forces could crush North Vietnam's just as Truman's had crushed North Korea's but also feared that this would bring in the Chinese, which would end his presidency just as it had ended Truman's. *Mirror images, both Hanoi and Washington were determined to avoid another Korean War.* Hence, the 1962 Geneva Accords, by which John Kennedy, unwilling to pay the price required to enforce Truman's doctrine in Southeast Asia but equally unwilling to bear the burden of withdrawal, *agreed,* after careful deliberation, to settle Southeast Asia's fate through a guerilla war in South Vietnam. As part of the agreement, Kennedy ceded crucial terrain and gave the enemy every conceivable advantage. In return, by allowing the fiction of a neutralist government in Laos, the North Vietnamese agreed to help Kennedy keep the truth—that Laos had "fallen" to the Communists on Kennedy's watch—from the American people, whose sons would ultimately be sacrificed by the tens of thousands in the "guerilla war" that would grow exponentially under Kennedy's "tacit agreement." *The North Vietnamese, who needed above all to avoid a major, potentially effective deployment of American power as in Korea, would get their very best shot at South Vietnam so that Kennedy, who needed above all the appearance of containment through November 1964 without the risk of another Korean War, would get his very best shot at another term of office.*

IV

I suppose it is tempting, if the only tool you have is a hammer, to treat everything as if it were a nail.[155]

Abraham Harold Maslow

If ever a doctrine without serious analytical foundations appeared in the annals of military history, it was the U.S. doctrine of

---

155 Abraham Harold Maslow, *The Psychology of Science: A Reconnaissance* (New York: Harper & Row, 1996), 15–16.

147

counterinsurgency which made its appearance at the onset of the New Frontier.[156]

Paul M. Kattenburg

With Southeastern Laos and several hundred miles of South Vietnam's western border firmly in North Vietnamese hands under Kennedy's 1962 agreement with Hanoi, some 13,000 Communist troops entered South Vietnam effectively unopposed during 1962 to wage the agreed-upon "insurgency,"[157] and by October, the North Vietnamese were fielding large military units in the South and engaging in large-scale attacks.[158] These were not ragtag, pajama-clad, bolt-action-rifle-toting indigenous insurgents rebelling against America's client government, but well-trained, well-equipped, regular North Vietnamese Army ("NVA") formations sent by Hanoi. Yet Kennedy, unwilling to deploy American forces in sufficient numbers to stop the infiltration lest he go the way of Truman, remained determined "to treat the problem of Vietnam as something other than war"[159] and kept telling himself that the problem facing this country's South Vietnamese allies was essentially *political* in nature. His best and brightest "fully agreed...that Vietnam was a political problem of winning the allegiance of the people rather than a military problem of killing Vietcong."[160] Facing in South Vietnam what Truman faced in South Korea—a military invasion undertaken by Communist forces encouraged and supplied by their great-power patrons (only the overt "border crossing" aspect was missing, and this was form rather than substance)—Kennedy was determined to handle the situation, given Ellsberg's Rules, as if it were Greece. In Greece, however, the Communists were indigenous to the territory in dispute, received little outside support from a great power ally and none whatsoever after Tito closed the border.

156 Paul M. Kattenburg, *The Vietnam Trauma in American Foreign Policy*, 1945–75 (New Brunswick: Transaction, Inc., 1984), 110.
157 Hannah, *The Key to Failure*, 91.
158 Newman, *J.F.K. and Vietnam*, 126.
159 Hilsman, *To Move a Nation*, 536.
160 Ibid., 525. See also Hannah, *The Key to Failure*, 27.

Mistrustful of his Joint Chiefs and confident in his own judgment, Kennedy had no reason to ask the Army for a genuine analysis and just demanded development of policies designed to fit his needs. Thus was born the doctrine of "counterinsurgency." Had the officer corps as a whole been honest and competent, Kennedy would have been informed, officially and in short order, that his goal (hold South Vietnam despite the "tacit agreement" without deploying large combat formations) was simply unattainable and that pursuing it—in any manner—would be criminal folly. *From Kennedy's earliest days in office, his military advisers and many of his civilian advisers recognized that closing South Vietnam's border was crucial to the survival of South Vietnam, and history shows that they were right on this point.*[161]

The United States Army, however, is a hierarchical organization that does not, by its very nature, lend itself to the longevity, much less the active promotion, of those who demonstrate even the slightest unwillingness or inability to complete their assigned tasks, which gives rise to a threat familiar to anyone who has ever served as an officer: "Lieutenant (or Captain or Major), if you cannot get this done [whatever "this" might be, from running a supply room to improving scores on the rifle range or drafting the plan for a regimental assault], I will find someone who can." Being relieved for a failure to perform, even once, is career ending, and the system functions the same way from top to bottom; majors, colonels and even generals will suffer the same fate as lieutenants or captains if either they or their subordinates, for whom they are responsible, fail to perform. So those who make it to the top are well skilled at avoiding conflict with superiors who require particular policies, especially in a peacetime setting. Civilian control, moreover, is holy writ that, while essential to the proper functioning of the armed forces within a democracy, is often in actual practice almost totally corrupting. What the President of the United States wants, by God, the President of the United States will get. If he and his top advisers are inept and corrupt, the officer corps will invariably follow their lead, embracing *doublethink* and *crimestop* as naturally and easily

---

161 Jones, *Death of a Generation*, 43, 46, 86, 100, 111, 112, 136, 179, 186, 195, 211, 218, 222, 230, 245, 282. See also Hannah, *The Key to Failure*, 82.

as any politician in Washington, as the history of the military's ever-changing views on Southeast Asia reveals.

When in 1947 Truman outlined the doctrine on which his party had decided to stake its future, there was no dissent from the Army. General George C. Marshall, recently appointed secretary of state by Truman, provided the military's point of view in May:

> We cannot conceive setbacks to long range interests of France which would not also be setbacks [to] our own. . . . In our view, southern Asia [is] in [a] critical phase [of] its history with seven new nations in [the] process [of] achieving or struggling [for] independence or autonomy. These nations include [a] quarter [of the] inhabitants [of the] world and their future course, owing [to the] sheer weight [of their] populations, resources they command, and strategic location, will be [a] momentous factor [in] world stability.[162]

Yet in May 1954, the Joint Chiefs, disgusted and bitter over this country's "die for a tie" in Korea—and now led by a president of the same mind—reversed course completely, advising the secretary of defense that *"Indochina is devoid of decisive military objectives and the allocation of more than token U.S. armed forces in Indochina would be a serious diversion of limited U. S. capabilities."*[163] But then came John "keystone-to-the-arch, finger-in-the-dike" Kennedy, who placed enormous pressure on the military for a solution tailored to fit his needs—counterinsurgency—with his demands striking the Army "with a force it is difficult to

162 May 1947 cable from George C. Marshall to the American Embassy in France, quoted in Robert McMahon, ed., *Major Problems in the History of the Vietnam War: Documents and Essays* (Lexington: D.C. Heath and Company, 1990), 71.

163 Sheehan, Smith, Kenworthy and Butterfield, *The Pentagon Papers*, 45 (emphasis in the original). See also *Vietnam: The Definitive Documentation of Human Decisions*, ed. Gareth Porter, Ph. D., vol. 1 (Stanfordville, New York: 1979), 593.

appreciate twenty years later."[164]

> He pushed his concerns in every imaginable form—in his second National Security Action Memorandum (and in others to follow, especially numbers 52, 56, 124, 162, and 182), in a May 1961 "Special Message to Congress on Urgent National Needs," in sessions with the JCS, in letters to Secretary of Defense McNamara, through key officials in the White House and the departments, in a graduation address at West Point, in "hiring and firing" of military officers, through an introduction to a collection of articles on counter-guerilla warfare, and even through personal involvement in the selection of equipment to be used by Special Forces units.

> Some appreciation for the impact of the Kennedy administration's emphasis on counterinsurgency warfare capabilities may be gained by reviewing such journals as *Army* magazine, which devoted the March 1962 issue to, in the words of its editor, "spreading the gospel" of counterinsurgency. As Colonel Harry Summers recently observed, "Reading it today sounds more like the description of a new liturgy than a discussion of strategic doctrine."[165]

To ensure the unwavering allegiance (read "total corruption") of the officer corps, Kennedy fired Generals George Decker (Army chief of staff) and Lyman Lemnitzer (chairman of the JCS) for resisting his emphasis on "counterinsurgency" and made clear that promotion would depend on an officer's adoption of the party line, making counterinsurgency more dogma than doctrine.[166] And never

---

164 Petraeus, David H., "The American Military and the Lessons of Vietnam: A Study of Military Influence and the Use of Force in the Post-Vietnam Era," Ph. D. diss., Princeton University, 1987, 94.

165 Ibid., 94–95.

166 Summers, *On Strategy*, 73.

in the course of American history would more time, money, effort, and intellect be brought to bear on pounding so square a peg into so round a hole.

"Counterinsurgency" stemmed primarily from the British experience in Malaya, where, applying techniques developed specifically for the situation in Malaya by army officers on the scene, the British were able to quell an indigenous Communist insurgency over a period of some twelve years. Yet, however attractive "counterinsurgency" appeared to someone operating within the confines of Ellsberg's Rules, the British experience in Malaya was hopelessly misapplied in Vietnam for several reasons:

- The Malay Peninsula shared no border with a Communist-controlled territory, which, as Malayan Communist Party chief Chin Peng noted in his memoirs, was crucial to a successful insurgency.[167] So the British—with a "colossal" manpower advantage of as much as 35:1[168]—faced a genuine, indigenous insurgency that received very little outside support.

- The Malayan Communists were almost all from the country's ethnic Chinese minority, which had a long, difficult relationship with native Malayans, whom they regarded contemptuously.[169] This provided the British with sharp ethnic divisions that served them well and made it nearly impossible for the Malayan Communists to claim the mantle of Malayan nationalism.

- Those most subject to Communist exploitation and influence were poor ethnic Chinese "squatters" who worked in mines and plantations. They had no historic ties to land and villages and lived on the fringes of Malayan society.[170] This allowed for their successful relocation into "New Villages," complete with schools, dispensaries, community

---

167 Chin Peng, *My Side of History* (Singapore: Media Masters, 2003), 433.

168 Fredrik Logevall, *Embers of War: The Fall of an Empire and the Making of America's Vietnam* (New York: Random House, 2012), 708.

169 John A. Nagl, *Learning to Eat Soup with a Knife: Counterinsurgency Lessons from Malaya and Vietnam* (Chicago: University of Chicago Press, 2002), 60.

170 Ibid., 60–61.

centers, cooperatives and Boy Scout troops, all provided by the government. By 1951, some 400,000 former "squatters" had been resettled in communities where their lives improved dramatically, which served to separate those most vulnerable from the guerillas who sought to exploit them while giving them a stake in the existing order, two classic goals of counterinsurgency.[171]

• Being Malayan nationals, whether an ethnic minority or not, the insurgents were subject to government blandishment and amnesty, which in the end the vast majority accepted, ending the conflict.

South Vietnam, in contrast, was being invaded by regular armed forces whose personnel were dedicated and loyal to an established government outside of the territory they were assaulting. Although switching between guerilla and conventional warfare when it suited them, North Vietnamese troops were no more "insurgents" indigenous to South Vietnam and subject to their enemy's enticement than were Americans in Europe during World War II. Unlike in Malaya, the invading forces were in fact Vietnamese who were able to claim the mantle of Vietnamese nationalism. South Vietnam, moreover, shared hundreds of miles of border with territories that, thanks to Kennedy's agreement with Hanoi, were controlled entirely by hostile forces, allowing for limitless re-supply and reinforcement. The only way to separate the people from the invaders under these circumstances was to uproot them without their consent from their ancestral lands and herd them into "strategic hamlets," which was entirely different from the situation that allowed the British to resettle landless, poverty-stricken squatters in Malaya.

Finally, winning the "allegiance of the people," which forms the ultimate goal of counterinsurgency, was impossible in the face of Communist terror that was widespread and methodical throughout South Vietnam. As General Maxwell Taylor noted, "The record shows that the disintegration of the political situation in South

---

171 Ibid., 74–75.

Vietnam since 1959 is primarily due to the government's inability to protect its citizens and to conduct the war effectively."[172] In 1959, some 1,200 South Vietnamese government officials were assassinated. The number increased steadily; 4,000 were killed in 1961.[173] Government officials, including policeman, teachers and civil servants of all types, were not the only regular victims of North Vietnamese terror. Ordinary civilians were expected to give unwavering allegiance to the Communist cause as well, and they were slaughtered by the thousands for any offense against "the revolution," whether real or imagined:

> A couple of nights later, the Viet Cong came back in force and arrested everyone who had been on watch. They went through the village shouting "Come to a meeting!" and paraded your mother and four other women, hands tied, to a clearing outside Bai Gian. They even tied my hands so I could not interfere and told your uncle Luc to come along as a witness. When we got there, the leader accused each woman of collaborating with the enemy. When he got to your mother, she replied that she had given a warning, but had simply shouted too late. The leader slapped her again and said she should have given her life to save the [Viet Cong] fighters.
>
> So the cadre leader pronounced them all guilty and lined them up on their knees in front of the crowd. One by one, he walked down the line and blew their brains out with his pistol. Your mother was the last in line. When he got to her and put the barrel behind her ear, I closed my eyes and started praying. But your uncle Luc jumped out and told the cadre leader to stop. He asked how a woman who sent her eldest son to Hanoi could even think of betraying her country. He said, "Huyen has six nephews and two

---

172 Moyar, *Triumph Forsaken*, 136. See also Lewy, *America in Vietnam*, 272.
173 Karnow, *Vietnam: A History*, 238

sons-in-law right now fighting the enemy—how dare you accuse her of treason!" You have to remember, Bay Ly, Uncle Luc is well known to the cadre. He's supported them for years and helped the saboteurs at Danang. His appeal gave the cadre leader time to realize what he was doing. He had just killed four of the five village mothers he had arrested and killing them all, without showing any mercy, might have turned the people against him. So he eased the hammer down and told your mother to get up. He said that for her, the revolution would be lenient and he paroled her back to uncle Luc. He said she had to stay within a hundred paces of our house and not associate with our neighbors.[174]

"Allegiance" for South Vietnam's rural population had nothing to do with nationalism, reform, democracy, social values, political theory or any other abstract nonsense on which so many focus their critiques of American policy. "Allegiance" was a matter of day-to-day survival. ("It is absurd to suggest," John Updike once noted, "that a village in the grip of guerillas has freely chosen..."[175]) With the Government of South Vietnam ("GVN") unable to secure and protect its population, "allegiance" was too often given to a North Vietnamese military administration that was immensely more powerful than the insurgents in Malaya and formed a shadow government with representatives and informants (whether volunteer or coerced) in every village. Acting with a ruthlessness easily rivaling that of the Nazis, this shadow government was assured a constant stream of men and arms courtesy of Kennedy's "tacit agreement" with Hanoi.

Simply put, the British experience in Malaya applied far more by distinction than analogy, and less than three months after

---

174 Le Ly Hayslip, *When Heaven and Earth Changed Places* (New York: Penguin Group, 2003), 111. See also Jones, *Death of a Generation*, 102–103. Guenter Lewy noted that the Communists assassinated more than 36,000 South Vietnamese between 1957 and 1972, eighty percent of whom were ordinary civilians. Lewy, *America in Vietnam*, 272.

175 John Updike, *Self-Consciousness* (New York: Knopf. 1989), 113.

Kennedy's "neutralization" of Laos, with "counterinsurgency" having failed completely, Diem requested US combat troops.[176] In the meantime, members of the Fourth Estate, most famous among them David Halberstam, began their own efforts to solve America's problems in Southeast Asia and help win the war.

»» ««

Naïve and inexperienced, David Halberstam arrived in September 1962 as a true-believing Cold War liberal who expected to find this country holding the line against Communism while bringing "democracy" and liberal society to South Vietnam as he believed this country had brought "democracy" and liberal society to South Korea.[177] What he found instead was the plain, unvarnished truth of Truman's doctrine, complete with the authoritarianism and corruption that typified America's Third World allies. *He found just what he would have found had he visited South Korea during the late 1940s.* He also found a regime under siege and an American mission determined to hide *everything* from *everyone* while lying about whatever could not be hidden as the only alternative to the truth, which was summarized succinctly for UPI's Neil Sheehan by Homer Bigart of the *New York Times*: "It doesn't work. That's the story kid. It doesn't work."[178] Although the lies were often easy to spot, spotting lies and uncovering the truth are entirely different matters, and neither Halberstam nor any of his allies in the Saigon press corps ever got it right, having relied for almost everything they wrote on what Halberstam described as "a small but first-rate intelligence network"[179] that combined Communist agents of influence with dissident American officers to create for Halberstam a parallel universe in which Ngo Dinh Diem and his brother Ngo Dinh Nhu

---

176 Newman, *J.F.K. and Vietnam*, 125–126.

177 William Prochnau, *Once Upon a Distant War* (New York: Vintage Books, 1996), 90, 140–141, 193–194, 294.

178 Ibid., 54.

179 David Halberstam, *The Making of a Quagmire: America and Vietnam During the Kennedy Era*, rev. ed., ed. Daniel J. Singal (Boston: McGraw-Hill, 1988), 125.

became nothing less than devils incarnate and the cause of all America's problems in Southeast Asia.

Pham Xuan An, the "Dean of the Vietnamese Press Corps," worked for Reuters, the *New York Herald Tribune*, the *Christian Science Monitor* and finally, *Time*. During his entire career in journalism, he was a Communist agent who would in time be promoted to the rank of general by the Hanoi regime for his services. Throughout this most crucial period, An worked closely with David Halberstam, Neil Sheehan and Stanley Karnow.[180] "We would huddle together in the Brodard or the Givral, his favorite cafes, as he chain-smoked and patiently deciphered the puzzles of Vietnam for me," wrote Karnow.[181] Muoi Huong, who recruited Pham Xuan An for the Communists, said later that An's job was manipulating foreign journalists, "'the fourth power' whose voice was of great influence."[182] Another of our crusading journalists' favorite sources was Pham Ngoc Thao, a colonel in the South Vietnamese Army who was also a Communist agent.[183]

Consider this carefully. Communist agents, recruited to influence foreign journalists, "deciphered the puzzles of Vietnam" for leading members of our Fourth Estate, who in turn reported the deciphered puzzles as the "truth" and would later write acclaimed histories of the war based on that "truth," including their own roles in these events. *It would seem rather obvious to any reasonable person that our wellspring is polluted with disinformation and self-interest.* One cannot help but wonder how differently things might have gone in Korea had skilled Communist agents been on hand to influence and "decipher the puzzles of Korea" for credulous journalists who were there to report on the state of "democracy" and liberal society under Rhee from 1946-1950.

On the American side, Halberstam found his muse in John Paul Vann. As a field adviser who was determined to see this country succeed in Vietnam, nothing angered Lt. Col. Vann more than the

---

180 Moyar, *Triumph Forsaken*, 215; Thomas A. Bass, "The Spy Who Loved Us," New Yorker, May 23, 2005, 56.

181 Stanley Karnow, *Vietnam: A History* (New York: Penguin Books, 1997), 39.

182 Moyar, *Triumph Forsaken*, 215.

183 Ibid., 214; Prochnau, *Once Upon a Distant War*, 461–462n.

manifest shortcomings of both the Saigon regime and its American patrons, shortcomings with which he dealt daily. The South Vietnamese officer corps was built more on political reliability than competence, and good military units remained in Saigon to keep casualties at a minimum while protecting Diem from coups. This left only second-rate units in the field against North Vietnamese forces whose numbers, power and terrorist attacks increased daily as a result of Kennedy's 1962 agreement on Laos, while civil action and "nation building" programs flooded the countryside with weapons, materials, and above all, money. In other words, Kennedy's policies created a culture of ineptitude, fear and corruption that was crippling to American interests. But no one in authority would listen when Vann and others tried to report the reality they saw daily. The official line was that America was succeeding, the Diem regime was doing well, and the Communists were being defeated. And nothing was to interfere with the official line, as exemplified by the fiasco at Ap Bac.

On January 2, 1963, a South Vietnamese force equipped with artillery, armored personnel carriers and American-crewed helicopters assaulted a Communist force approximately one quarter its size. It should have been a rout, yet it ended in disaster, due largely to the cowardice and incompetence of the South Vietnamese officers in command, who bungled the attack, refused to commit reserves and allowed almost the entire Communist force to escape after losing several American helicopters and more than eighty dead, including three Americans.[184] The Communists suffered only eighteen killed.[185] Vann, who helped plan and then observed the operation, was furious, calling it "a miserable damn performance, just like always."[186] He was not the only American officer who viewed Ap Bac in this light.[187] David Halberstam, among others, arrived in time to photograph the wreckage while the bodies of the fallen remained on the field and reported the entire fiasco in the *New York Times*. Yet General Paul Harkins, the American

---

184 Prochnau, *Once Upon a Distant War*, 228.
185 Ibid., 228, 241.
186 Ibid., 234.
187 Ibid., 236–237.

commander in Vietnam, and Admiral Felt, commander in chief, Pacific, insisted a week later that the fight was a South Vietnamese victory.[188]

In Halberstam's pantheon of incompetents, General Harkins, who stood at the gateway of American dissembling both up and down the line, ranked right up with Ngo Dinh Diem and his brother Nhu. (Halberstam called him "a man of compelling mediocrity"[189] and once said that Harkins "should be court-martialed and shot."[190]) Although Harkins might actually have been as stupid as Halberstam claimed (we really have no way to know), it is more likely that Harkins was simply a life-long player within the intrinsically corrupt system John Kennedy manipulated so well. (This does not exonerate him for his role in this disaster but merely explains who he was and what he did.) He was appointed commander of American forces in Vietnam neither to ascertain the situation nor to formulate policy like a military version of George Kennan; those roles were reserved for John Kennedy and his best and brightest. Harkins' task was threefold: 1) hold the line in South Vietnam within the confines of Kennedy's "tacit agreement" (no attempt to control South Vietnam's border; no interdiction of the Ho Chi Minh Trail); 2) execute this policy entirely through the doctrine of "counterinsurgency" (never request or suggest the need for American ground troops); and 3) never report or imply that things are not going well. (Everyone in the Kennedy administration knew that Washington was a sieve and that any criticism, setbacks, dissent or controversy would make the front page of the *New York Times* in short order, as David Halberstam demonstrated on a regular basis.) *"If you cannot get this done, General Harkins, we will find someone who can."*

Paul Harkins knew the rules, understood what was expected of him and did his job. Because John Kennedy's policies simply did not work in the field, this demanded disingenuous nonsense, like the "victory" at Ap Bac, on an almost daily basis and suppression of *anything* that ran counter to the Kennedy administration's policies,

188 Ibid., 216–244.
189 Halberstam, *The Best and the Brightest*, 153.
190 Prochnau, *Once Upon a Distant War*, 168.

like the truth on Communist infiltration through Laos, which Harkins later admitted "was bad" when he got there and "got worse and worse" as time went on.[191] It all drove John Vann to distraction. Unable to sway his superiors, Vann turned to the press, and he could not have done more damage to American interests if damage had been his purpose.

Vann met Halberstam in the fall of 1962 and knew immediately that Halberstam was the man he needed. Within twenty-four hours of their first meeting, Vann provided Halberstam with an all-night monologue on just why, in Homer Bigart's words, "It doesn't work." He would eventually convey his views to his superiors in a September 1965 paper entitled "Harnessing the Revolution,"[192] from which much of the following is taken.

America's problems, according to Vann, stemmed from a "social revolution underway in South Vietnam,"[193] an uprising by indigenous peasants willing to risk their lives "to secure a better government."[194] The Diem regime, based as it was on a small number of educated, urban anti-Communists associated with the former colonial administration, did not understand "the aspirations of the rural population"[195] and thus failed to "exploit the potential of this revolutionary movement,"[196] forcing "many patriotic and non-Communist Vietnamese" "to ally themselves with a Communist-dominated movement in the belief that this is their only chance to secure a better government."[197] The South Vietnamese armed forces were not effectively utilized, and the firepower employed to make up for a lack of tactical skill and courage was enormously counterproductive. The Communists' objectives, Vann noted, were "in conflict with those of the

---

191 Newman, *JFK and Vietnam*, 269–274.

192 John Paul Vann, "Harnessing the Revolution," September 10, 1965, Neil Sheehan Papers, Manuscript Division, Library of Congress, Box 48. See also http://smallwarsjournal.com/documents/bobandrews1.pdf, accessed May 10, 2012.

193 Vann, *Harnessing the Revolution*, 2

194 Ibid., 4

195 Ibid.

196 Ibid.

197 Ibid.

revolution,"[198] but the Communists displayed "political astuteness by moving to the fore of the revolution and assuming control of its direction."[199] To reverse these trends, Vann recommended a virtual takeover and complete restructuring of the Saigon regime by the United States, as had occurred in Germany and Japan in the wake of World War II. He phrased this as overt involvement "in the internal affairs of governing"[200] and advised that this country should undertake such overt involvement "to the extent necessary to insure the emergence of a government responsive to a majority of its people."[201] Coining a phrase that would in time become dogma to the antiwar Left, he told Halberstam: "This is a political war."[202]

Coming from a field-grade officer with Vann's experience, this all sounds very impressive. Halberstam and his colleagues in Saigon bought it hook, line and sinker—particularly, it is well worth noting, Vann's carefully contrived masquerade as "the one authentic hero of this shameful period . . . the David who had stood up to the Goliath of lies and institutional corruption."[203] Vann, you see, had worked diligently to ensure that the correspondents he had befriended viewed him as a rising star of such uncompromising integrity that, when he left the Army shortly after his tour ended, they would tell the world that he renounced a promising career to protest the ineptitude and dishonesty on which American policy was foundering. Halberstam, who took everything Vann said as gospel, wrote a glowing article that appeared in the November 1965 edition of *Esquire,* in which he told the world that Vann had been "clearly on his way to a colonelcy and with a very good chance for a promotion to a general star." "Clearly," wrote Halberstam, Vann was "a man about to take off in his career." But it was all a lie. Vann was not a rising star, and there was no career to throw away. Like Pham Xuan An, Vann saw Halberstam for what he was and played

---

198 Ibid., 5.

199 Ibid.

200 Ibid., 3.

201 Ibid.

202 Prochnau, *Once Upon a Distant War*, 162.

203 Neil Sheehan, *A Bright and Shining Lie: John Paul Vann and America in Vietnam* (New York: Random House, 1988), 384.

him like a violin.

In fact, Vann was an utterly amoral, sexually compulsive man who focused a great deal of his attention on underage girls, beginning in post-war Japan, where his family's sixteen- to eighteen-year-old Japanese maids, who needed their jobs desperately, were always available to him.[204] In Germany, Vann's wife Mary Jane was confronted by a German girl in her late teens who told Mary Jane of her affair with Vann, who, she said, had sworn he would divorce his wife and marry her. Mary Jane, long aware of Vann's chronic unfaithfulness, felt sorry for the girl and advised her there would be no divorce. When confronted, Vann admitted the affair and told Mary Jane that "he knew how to handle himself."[205] His sexual escapades had no effect on his professional life or career until his luck ran out in 1959.

While attending postgraduate study in Syracuse, New York, Vann was informed by an agent from the Army's Criminal Investigation Division ("CID") that he was under investigation for the statutory rape of a fifteen year-old girl at Ft. Leavenworth, where Vann was stationed while attending the Command and General Staff College. He was, as Harry Truman would say, "as guilty as hell." Knowing the stakes (the charge was a felony that could land him in jail for fifteen years and would end his career even if he was shown leniency), he enlisted the help of his wife, who, also knowing the stakes, agreed to perjure herself by corroborating events he fabricated as part of his defense during an Article 132 investigation (the Army's equivalent to a preliminary hearing). Vann then studied polygraphy and acquired tranquilizers that would help him lower blood pressure and control his reactions before submitting to a lie detector test conducted by the Army CID. He beat the lie detector, and the Army dropped the charges.[206] But the investigation was still part of his file, and no one with an accusation like that would ever become a general officer, as Vann well knew. So a masquerade was all he had for the Saigon press corps, and he played it, with consummate skill, for all it was worth.

---

204 Ibid., 474.

205 Ibid., 484–485.

206 Ibid., 489–492.

When Vann left Saigon, Halberstam told him that the correspondents to whom he furnished so much information had always worried about his career and now hoped that, after all his difficulties standing up to the system in Vietnam, he would succeed professionally. Vann, who knew the truth, assured Halberstam, "You never hurt me any more than I wanted to be hurt."[207] More than twenty years later, Neil Sheehan would admit that Vann had deceived him, Halberstam and all of his admirers.[208] Vann was, in short, a manipulative, deeply dishonest man whose character and judgment were as flawed as his analysis of the situation in Vietnam, which does not withstand critical review.

First, the rural population provided no real opposition to Diem from 1954-1961 as he crushed the Binh Xuyen gangsters, brought the sects to heel and practically destroyed the genuine, indigenous Communists in the countryside. Yet Vann provided no reason why the peasants would spontaneously rise in bloody rebellion against a government that was no worse than scores of others across the Third World and far less cruel and repressive than its counterpart in the North. Vann failed to mention, moreover, even in passing, Kennedy's Geneva Accords of 1962, by which the North Vietnamese were granted freedom of movement, un-interdicted supply lines and control over several hundred miles of South Vietnam's border. By 1963, infiltration of North Vietnamese troops had reached 1,500 per month, and tens of thousands of weapons came with them— some 165,000 since 1961.[209] By the end of 1963, 40,000 NVA troops had entered South Vietnam through Laos.[210] As Neil Sheehan later noted, there were only 23,000 North Vietnamese troops in South Vietnam in January 1963, comprising twenty-five battalions of 150-300 men each. By that summer, Hanoi was moving 600-man battalions into South Vietnam, and by December 1964, Hanoi was fielding a force of 56,000 troops, comprising seventy-three full battalions of 600-700 men each, along with six heavy weapons and

---

207 Ibid., 333.

208 Ibid., 486–494.

209 Moyar, *Triumph Forsaken*, 211.

210 John Prados, *Vietnam: The History of an Unwinnable War*, 1945–1975 (Lawrence: University Press of Kansas, 2009), 115.

antiaircraft machine-gun battalions.[211] The battalions were being formed into fully equipped, complete regiments and the regiments were being formed into divisions.[212] This was not a peasant revolt but an invasion by a powerful military force already two-thirds the size of the force employed by Kim Il Sung to sweep America's Korean proxies from the field almost effortlessly, and these troops were tearing the fabric of South Vietnamese government and society to pieces.

Some 50,000 more entered South Vietnam in 1965,[213] giving the North Vietnamese a force considerably larger than the force employed by Kim Il Sung in the summer of 1950, and "by early summer [1965], they were annihilating ARVN battalions like a blast furnace consumes coke,"[214] which is just the way Kim's army consumed Syngman Rhee's before the Americans arrived in force.[215] It is inconceivable that Vann was unaware of the infiltration, the means by which it was undertaken or its effect on a conflict in South Vietnam that was virtually non-existent prior to its start. Yet in "Harnessing the Revolution" (September 1965), Vann focused exclusively on the shortcomings of the Saigon regime and continued insisting that South Vietnam's problems were essentially political in nature.

Even more striking than Vann's inability to distinguish between cause and effect is the extent to which his analysis coincides with the views and political needs of the Kennedy administration, remaining both in harmony with John Kennedy's stated views (the problems in South Vietnam were essentially "political" in nature) and within Harkins' mandate to hold the line in South Vietnam

---

211 Sheehan, *A Bright and Shining Lie*, 381.

212 Ibid., 381–382.

213 Prados, *The Blood Road*, 157. See also Prados, "A Window on the Enemy: Keeping an Eye on the Ho Chi Minh Trail," *The VVA Veteran*, March/April 2003.

214 Sheehan, *A Bright and Shining Lie*, 536.

215 And yet, like Halberstam, Sheehan toes the party line like some clerk in a Ministry of Truth, blaming "Diem and the Americans" for all this while saying nothing about the Ho Chi Minh trail or the "tacit agreement" that allowed these massive new units to pass unmolested through hundreds of miles of jungle, referring at all times to the officers as "Viet Cong" rather than North Vietnamese while describing the units themselves as "guerilla regiments," as if they had all materialized like magic from the ranks of a disgruntled peasantry.

within the confines of Kennedy's 1962 agreement with Hanoi using only indigenous forces backed by American advisers. Vann, it would seem, was very skilled at cherry picking evidence and tailoring his analysis to follow the party line and provide a reasonable critique of existing tactics without challenging either the commitment itself or overall strategy, and he did everything possible after his return to present his views to the Joint Chiefs of Staff, leaving the Army only when it became clear that his desired audience with the Chiefs would never occur. Had he impressed the Chiefs as he no doubt imagined he would, he might have salvaged his career.[216] His analysis was as much a part of his self-promotion as anything else he did in Vietnam.

This is not to say that those observations he chose to convey were inaccurate. The cronyism, corruption and incompetence of the Saigon regime—its ineffective, badly led armed forces and the systemic shortcomings Vann listed—were certainly present and damaging to American interests. But these problems, like the collapse of Syngman Rhee's government in the summer of 1950, were the *results* of a military invasion on a society that had barely begun reconstructing itself following decades of politically destructive colonial exploitation and war. If Vann actually believed that the situation could be salvaged if this country would only involve itself "in the internal affairs of governing" South Vietnam, as it had in post-World War II Germany, while at the same time denying South Vietnam the military protection and border control it had provided Germany (or Korea for that matter), "he was, there is no kinder or gentler a word for it, a fool."[217] If he actually believed in September 1965 (when "Harnessing the Revolution" was completed) that some 120,000 recently infiltrated, fully armed, properly supported troops (with thousands more coming every month)—organized not just into battalions and regiments but divisions complete with communications, engineers and combat support units—represented "a social revolution underway in South

---

216 Sheehan, *A Bright and Shining Lie*, 336–342.

217 Halberstam, *The Best and the Brightest*, 250. Although this was Halberstam's description of Robert MacNamara, the description applies to far more of those involved than MacNamara.

Vietnam,"[218] a "political problem" to be countered with "reforms," civil action programs and American advisers, he was a fool. If he actually believed that a delicate sprig like the Republic of Vietnam would survive a determined assault by hundreds of thousands of North Vietnamese troops over an undefended border several hundred miles in length for the time needed to create a viable, popularly supported, democratic nation-state allied to the West, no matter who governed the country or how honestly it was run, he was a fool. *When similarly assaulted, South Korea collapsed like a house of cards. Why would anyone expect South Vietnam to do any better?* Yet Vann's analysis would ultimately find a vast and receptive audience, providing the basic analytical and intellectual prism through which David Halberstam, for one, would view the Vietnam War until the day he died. Even worse, that prism would eventually become institutionalized and would do enormous damage to American interests in the process. In the meantime, Vann, through Halberstam, became a valued resource in Pham Xuan An's "intelligence network."

Author William Prochnau describes Vann's all-night session with Halberstam as "the opening ploy in the use-and-be-used game and both men were world-class players, each of them far better than the other understood that night."[219] But in fact, the only "world class" player here was Pham Xuan An. For Vann, like an American captain befriended by Neal Sheehan, was now a full-fledged if unwitting member of An's "intelligence network," providing An with inside information on the workings of the Saigon regime and its American patrons from the perspective of an American officer who understood their plans, their purposes and their shortcomings. Sheehan's captain would call him and say, "Get cracking." Sheehan would then go to the captain's office, where a "friendly Vietnamese colonel" provided Sheehan with reports, often marked "Top Secret," that Sheehan would read, sharing the information with Halberstam and other journalists, who in turn shared their information with Halberstam and Sheehan: "It was very shrewd," noted Keyes Beech of the *Chicago Daily News*. "They had everybody working for

218 Vann, *Harnessing the Revolution*, 2.
219 Prochnau, *Once Upon a Distant War*, 162.

them."[220] But they in turn were working, however unwittingly, for An, providing crucial, up-to-date, classified information to the North Vietnamese on a regular basis. An, you see, was "the reporters' favorite."[221] An "went everywhere with the gang—with Sheehan on his first helicopter mission, to the disaster at AP Bac, on raids deep into Camau."[222] Everything Halberstam and Sheehan knew, An knew as well, and nothing underscores Vann's lack of judgment more than his relationship with the Saigon press corps. "I may be a commissioned officer in the United States Army who's sworn to safeguard classified information," he once told Halberstam, "but I'm also an American citizen with a duty to my country. Now listen carefully."[223] *Vann's career should have ended in Leavenworth.* Although General Harkins infuriated the Saigon press corps by telling them that "he viewed them as a channel to the Vietcong,"[224] he had this one right, however wrong he might have been on almost everything else:

> An's writing was so lively and detailed that General
> Giap and Ho Chi Minh are said to have rubbed their
> hands with glee on getting these reports from Tran
> Van Trung—An's code name. "We are now in the
> United States' war room!" they exclaimed, according
> to members of the Vietnamese politburo.[225]

I cannot help but wonder how much Halberstam and Sheehan contributed to the outcome at Ap Bac by providing Pham Xuan An with information that allowed the Communists to "surprise the surprisers."[226] And this was but one small operation. How many more did they compromise, and how much blood is on their

---

220 Ibid., 275.
221 Ibid., 462n.
222 Ibid.
223 Sheehan, *A Bright and Shining Lie*, 328.
224 Ibid., 168. See also Jones, *Death of a Generation*, 22.
225 Thomas A. Bass, *The Spy Who Loved Us: The Vietnam War and Pham Xuan An's Dangerous Game* (New York: PublicAffairs, 2009), 2.
226 Prochnau, *Once Upon a Distant War*, 162.

hands?[227]

By February 1963, Halberstam and Sheehan were fed up with the incompetence and dishonesty of both the Diem regime and the American mission in Saigon, but they remained true-believing cold warriors who questioned neither this country's right nor its need to save Southeast Asia from the onrushing tide of Communism. "I was convinced," Sheehan wrote in 1991, "that this was the right war in the right place."[228] Halberstam maintained as late as 1965 that South Vietnam was "a strategic country in a key area...perhaps one of five or six nations that is truly vital to U.S. interests."[229] (So embarrassed was Halberstam by this pronouncement that, like a commissar in some Ministry of Truth, he airbrushed his own historical record, removing the quoted statement from his 1988 edition of *The Making of a Quagmire* as if it had never been written.) Sheehan, for his part, agreed with Halberstam, later admitting that this "was what produced all the anger. You've got to understand, we thought these people were losing the war."[230] Little did he realize that first and foremost among "these people" was John Kennedy, who, "never in any deep sense a believer"[231] in America's cause in Vietnam, was only buying time to ensure his reelection. "We don't have a prayer of staying in Vietnam. We don't have a prayer of prevailing there," Kennedy told his friend Charles Bartlett in April 1963. "But I can't give up a piece of territory like that to the Communists and get the American people to re-elect me."[232] He made his clearest statement of purpose and intent to

---

227 This is one of the largest of our elephants in the room.

228 Neil Sheehan, *After the War Was Over: Hanoi and Saigon* (New York: Random House, 1991), 58.

229 David Halberstam, *The Making of a Quagmire* (New York: Random House, 1965), 319.

230 Prochnau, *Once Upon a Distant War*, 294.

231 Halberstam, *The Best and the Brightest*, 212.

232 Patterson, *Grand Expectations,* 516; *Record, The Wrong War,* 8; Frederick Logevall, *Choosing War: The Lost Chance for Peace and the Escalation of War in Vietnam,* (Berkeley: University of California Press, 2001), 38–39: "Those people hate us," said Kennedy. "They are going to throw our asses out of there at almost any point." See also Blight, Lang and Welch, *Vietnam if Kennedy Had Lived: Virtual JFK,* 137: "Charles Bartlett, who was a close friend of Kennedy, says that in any political conversation he had with him during the thousand days of his presidency, Kennedy would always talk about reelection. It was an absolute."

Senator Mike Mansfield:

> In the spring of 1963, [Senator] Mike Mansfield again criticized our military involvement in the Vietnam War, this time in front of the Congressional leadership at a White House breakfast, much to the President's annoyance and embarrassment. Later the President asked me to invite Mansfield to his office for a private talk on the problem. I sat in on part of the discussion. The President told Mansfield that he had been having serious second thoughts about Mansfield's argument and that he now agreed with the Senator's thinking on the need for a complete military withdrawal from Vietnam.
>
> "But I can't do it until 1965—after I'm re-elected," Kennedy told Mansfield.
>
> President Kennedy explained, and Mansfield agreed with him, that if he announced a withdrawal of American military personnel from Vietnam before the 1964 election, there would be a wild conservative outcry against returning him to the Presidency for a second term.
>
> After Mansfield left the office, the President said to me, "in 1965, I'll be one of the most unpopular Presidents in history. I'll be damned everywhere as a Communist appeaser. But I don't care. If I tried to pull out completely from Vietnam now, we would have another Joe McCarthy red scare on our hands, but I can do it after I'm re-elected. So we had better make damned sure that I am re-elected."[233]

---

233 Kenneth P. O'Donnell and David F. Powers with Joe McCarthy, *"Johnny, We Hardly Knew Ye"* (Boston: Little Brown and Company, 1972), 18. Mike Mansfield later confirmed in writing that Kennedy informed him in "early 1963" that "he did plan to begin the withdrawal of some troops from Vietnam following the next election." Letter from Mike Mansfield to Francis X. Winters, October 24, 1989, cited in Francis Winters, *The Year of the Hare* (Athens, Georgia: University of Georgia Press, 1997, 3, n. 4. See also Mann, *A Grand Delusion*, 282; Don Oberdorfer, *Senator Mansfield: The*

Kennedy's plan to withdraw from Vietnam soon after his reelection is holy writ among liberals today,[234] who fail to note that continuing a war and escalating American involvement to serve the needs of his party in an upcoming election constitutes impeachable conduct, including abuse of power, conspiracy, misleading Congress (which had to appropriate the public funds required) and gross misappropriation of this country's foreign policy, armed forces, funds and citizenry for non-public purposes. Kennedy's "secret plan,"[235] in other words, is not a defense but an indictment, and it gives rise to a question that historians, particularly Kennedy's hagiographers, have always avoided: Just how many lives can a president sacrifice to secure his reelection before his conduct becomes criminal? From 1961-1963, 120 American and more than 14,000 South Vietnamese troops were killed. During 1964, with Johnson continuing to hold the line in Vietnam as required to secure the 1964 election, 147 American and 7,457 South Vietnamese were killed (these figures do not include civilian deaths).[236] If you find more than 21,000 people killed for partisan advantage in an upcoming election acceptable, how many would be required before it became unacceptable? Would 25,000 be too many? Do you draw your line at 50,000? Or do the numbers, if not the entire enterprise, depend upon the president's party affiliation? Consider, for example, how you would view these policies if they were pursued by, not John Kennedy, but his political opponents. Imagine a

---

Extraordinary Life of a Great American Statesman and Diplomat (Washington: Smithsonian Books, 2003), 195–196; Newman, *JFK and Vietnam*, 324.

234 Talbot, *Brothers: The Hidden History of the Kennedy Years*, 215. Talbot cites to an alleged "conclusive body of evidence" indicating "that JFK formally decided to withdraw from Vietnam, a process he planned to begin by bringing home 1,000 military personnel in December 1963 and finish in 1965, after his reelection gave him political cover to complete what he knew would be a controversial action." See also Ted Sorensen, *Counselor: A Life at the Edge of History* (New York: HarperCollins, 2008), 357; Jones, *Death of a Generation*, 1–12.

235 It is interesting to note the proliferation of authors claiming to have discovered Kennedy's "secret plan" to withdraw from Vietnam in view of the sarcastic references that have always been made to Nixon's alleged "secret plan," which was itself a media fabrication, Nixon never having claimed a secret plan to end the war. See David Brinkley, *Tour of Duty: John Kerry and the Vietnam War* (New York: HarperCollins, 2004), 130n.

236 Vietnam War U.S. Military Fatal Casualty Statistics | National Archives; Clarke, Jeffrey J., *United States Army in Vietnam: Advice and Support: The Final Years, 1965-1973* (Washington D.C., Center of Military History, United States Army, 1988), 275.

historical record that provided the following exchange between a barely elected President Richard Nixon and Senator Barry Goldwater in 1963, as recorded for history by a top White House aide:

> In the spring of 1963, [Senator] Mike Mansfield again criticized our military involvement in the Vietnam War, this time in front of the Congressional leadership at a White House breakfast, much to [President Nixon's] annoyance and embarrassment. Later the President asked me to invite [Senator Goldwater] to his office for a private talk on the problem. I sat in on part of the discussion. The President told [Goldwater, who had to agree with any decision of this magnitude,] that he had been having serious second thoughts about Mansfield's argument and that he now agreed with [Mansfield's] thinking on the need for a complete military withdrawal from Vietnam.
>
> "But I can't do it until 1965—after I'm re-elected," Nixon told [Goldwater].
>
> President [Nixon] explained, and [Goldwater] agreed with him, that [with Cuba still in Communist hands,] if he announced a withdrawal of American military personnel from Vietnam before the 1964 election, [Democrats would lead a wild] outcry against returning him to the Presidency for a second term. ["If I remove 'the finger in the dike' of American security," he said, "Kennedy will just destroy me in '64."]
>
> After [Goldwater] left the office, the President said to me, "If I tried to pull out completely from Vietnam now, we would have [the same damn bunch who gave us Alger Hiss, the Rosenbergs and that mess in Korea right back in the White House, and I cannot allow that to happen.] [B]ut I can [get out of

Vietnam] after I'm re-elected. So we had better make
damned sure that I am re-elected."

Think carefully about this counterfactual before judging
Kennedy, his advisers, his policies, and his biographers. Better yet,
consider some recent frames of reference as they apply to John
Kennedy's policies in Southeast Asia.

Donald Trump was impeached in 2020 by House Democrats
over allegations that he requested Ukrainian authorities to
investigate his opponent, Joe Biden, for the purpose of gaining an
advantage in the 2020 election. This was labeled "Abuse of Power,"
and the controlling moral and legal frames of reference were quickly
drawn: "A president's use of his power for his own political gain, at
the expense of the public interest, is the quintessence of an
impeachable offense. It was, in fact, one of the examples the
Constitution's framers deployed to explain what would constitute
'high crimes and misdemeanors,' the standard for
impeachment."[237] Stated Representative Adam Schiff: "The Ukraine
call was one piece of a larger operation to redirect US foreign policy
to benefit Trump's personal interests, not the national interest."[238]
"It is a core *premise* of our liberal democracy," wrote Andrew
Sullivan, "that the powers of the presidency are merely on loan, and
that using them to advance a personal interest is a definition of an
abuse of power."[239]

Whatever can be said of Donald Trump's phone call to Ukraine's
president, no troops were deployed, no bombs were dropped, no
napalm was spread, no herbicides were sprayed, nobody was
injured, nobody was killed, and in the end, his impeachment was
the only result. This pales when compared to Kennedy's "use of his
power for his own political gain, at the expense of the public
interest," which included all of the horrors outlined above, killed
and maimed thousands from 1961 through 1963 and left this
country and Southeast Asia with a war that would ultimately kill

---

237 "Why the Trump Impeachment Inquiry is the Only Option," *New York Times*, September 9, 2019.

238 Adam Schiff, "Trump Betrayed America. Soon the Public Will Hear from the Patriots Who Defended It." *USA Today*, November 6, 2019.

239 Andrew Sullivan, "This is No Ordinary Impeachment," *New York Magazine,* November 8, 2019 (emphasis in the original).

millions—a war that Kennedy knew would have ended if he had just left well enough alone. *If Kennedy's Permanent-Campaign-based war in Southeast Asia was not "the quintessence of an impeachable offense," nothing is.*

<h1 style="text-align:center">V</h1>

I couldn't figure out what the Kennedy administration's goal was. You had a group of people who pursued personal and political ambitions. It was like the Mafia.[240]

Tran Van Dinh

Whoever has the Americans as allies does not need any enemies.[241]

Madame Nhu

By 1963, John Kennedy wanted out of Vietnam. "We've reached the peak," he said. "From now on, we're going to cut advisers back. If the Vietnamese win it, okay, great. But if they don't, we're going to go to Geneva and do what we did with Laos."[242] The best way to facilitate his designs, he told his top advisers, would be to "put a government in there that would ask us to leave."[243] Bobby Kennedy would later describe this option as "a Laotian type solution, some form of coalition government with people who would ask us to leave."[244] In May 1963, Diem's brother Nhu (sarcastically referred to as "Bobby" by both Americans and Vietnamese[245]) began that process, publicly calling for a major reduction in US forces, whose presence, he said, fueled Communist propaganda.[246] Having already authorized Averell Harriman to initiate a dialogue with North Vietnamese representatives in Geneva with an eye toward

---

240 Diem's *charge' d' affaires* in Washington, quoted in Hersh, *The Dark Side of Camelot*, 434.

241 Jones, *Death of a Generation*, 407. Madame Nhu was Diem's sister-in-law. His brother Ngo Dinh Nhu and she are often described within the source material as "the Nhus." Ibid.

242 Ibid., 267.

243 Goldstein, *Lessons in Disaster*, 238.

244 Schlesinger, *Robert Kennedy and His Times*, 717

245 Jones, *Death of a Generation*, 306, 424.

246 Ibid., 256.

some type of "neutralization,"[247] this was just what Kennedy needed. When questioned about Nhu's statements at a press conference on May 23, 1963, Kennedy said, "We would withdraw the troops, any number of troops, any time the Government of South Vietnam would request it. . . . [If] requested to [withdraw troops], we will do it immediately."[248] Yet with swift and angry congressional and press reaction to Nhu's statements, Roger Hilsman in Washington directed Ambassador Frederick Nolting in Saigon to protest Nhu's statements using the "strongest possible language"[249] while plans to facilitate Diem's removal, which had been a subject of continuous discussion within the Kennedy administration since the fall of 1961, began in earnest.[250]

Consider that carefully: Plans to facilitate Diem's removal began in earnest with Kennedy's belief that Diem was going to end American involvement in Vietnam.

Kennedy was trapped between the interests of his country ("We don't have a prayer of staying in Vietnam. We don't have a prayer of prevailing there.") and those of his party ("But I can't give up a piece of territory like that to the Communists and get the American people to re-elect me."). His policies—from his "neutralization" of Laos and his calls to reform and democratize the GVN ("exactly what could bring it down"[251]) to "strategic hamlets" and plots to overthrow America's longtime ally—had by now made the transition from ill-advised and self-defeating to incoherent and schizophrenic. Yet it all makes sense if you understand that Kennedy viewed the fate of Southeast Asia just like Abraham Lincoln viewed emancipation—as a collateral matter to be advanced or impeded depending on its perceived effect upon the "paramount object" of his endeavor. This is easily demonstrated by replacing Abraham Lincoln's references to his "paramount object" (saving the Union) and its collateral matter (slavery) with Kennedy's "paramount object" (his reelection) and its collateral matter, the

---

247 Ibid., 310.
248 Ibid., 257-258.
249 Ibid., 257.
250 Ibid., 258.
251 Ibid., 29.

fate of Southeast Asia:[252]

> My paramount object in this struggle is to [win the next election] and is not either to save or to destroy [South Vietnam, Laos or Cambodia]. If I could [win the next election] without [saving South Vietnam, Laos and Cambodia] I would do it, and if I could [win the next election], by [saving South Vietnam, Laos and Cambodia] I would do it; and if I could [win the next election] by [saving South Vietnam] and leaving [Laos and Cambodia to the Communists] I would also do that. What I do about [Southeast Asia] I do because I believe it helps to [secure my reelection]; and what I forbear, I forbear because I do not believe it would help to [secure my reelection].[253]

Halberstam and Sheehan (the Robert McNamara and McGeorge Bundy of the Fourth Estate) were determined for their part to ensure American victory in Southeast Asia because they knew, in their infinite, twenty-something wisdom, "that this was the right war in the right place"[254] (Sheehan) and that South Vietnam was "a strategic country in a key area...perhaps one of five or six nations that is truly vital to U.S. interests"[255] (Halberstam). So they embarked on "a large and controversial agenda [that] would mean getting rid of a foreign government and changing an American foreign policy as well as sending an ambassador, a four-star general and a CIA head of station home in disgrace."[256] Diem's next crisis—described by author William Prochnau with uncanny accuracy as "the bizarre Buddhist uprising that would soon blindside

---

252 "My paramount object in this struggle," Lincoln wrote to Horace Greely on August 22, 1862, "is to save the Union, and is not either to save or to destroy slavery. If I could save the Union without freeing any slave I would do it, and if I could save it by freeing all the slaves I would do it; and if I could save it by freeing some and leaving others alone I would also do that. What I do about slavery, and the colored race, I do because I believe it helps to save the Union; and what I forbear, I forbear because I do not believe it would help to save the Union."

253 Abraham Lincoln letter to Horace Greeley, August 22, 1862; bracketed material added.

254 Sheehan, *After the War Was Over*, 58.

255 David Halberstam, *The Making of a Quagmire* (New York: Random House, 1965), 319.

256 Prochnau, *Once Upon a Distant War*, 274.

everyone"—provided their opportunity.

»» ««

Orthodoxy tells us that in May 1963, Buddhists in Hue felt slighted when they were prohibited from flying their flag as part of Buddha's birthday celebration although Vatican flags had been flown when Diem (a Catholic) visited Hue several days earlier. Tri Quang, described by the CIA as "an ambitious, skillful, ruthless political manipulator and born demagogue,"[257] was the Buddhists' most militant anti-Diem agitator. Leading a demonstration on May 7, he said, "Now is the time to fight."[258] When civil authorities attempted to break up the demonstration, shots were fired and grenades or some other explosives were thrown into the crowd, killing nine.[259] Although this is precisely the kind of terrorist provocation typical of Communists, there is to this day no reliable evidence regarding who fired what or who fired first. The entire episode came as a shock to everyone. "Who are these people," asked John Kennedy. "Why didn't we know about them before?"[260] A good question with a simple answer: "These people" were Communists, using the Buddhists as they used everything else, as stated in a Communist communiqué dated July 27, 1963: "[Communists] have pushed the political struggle movement by initiating the demonstrations against the terrorization of Buddhism at the province and districts."[261] With some 14,000 Communist agents in South Vietnam,[262] it should come as no surprise that the so-called Buddhist movement was manipulated endlessly, if not actually controlled, by Hanoi, as noted at the time by the CIA.[263] Noted one Communist history: "Revolutionary agents among the Buddhists and students, laborers and *petit bourgeoisie* from the Dong Ba

257 Jones, *Death of a Generation*, 249.

258 Moyar, *Triumph Forsaken*, 212; Jones, *Death of a Generation*, 249.

259 Moyar, *Triumph Forsaken*, 213.

260 Prochnau, *Once Upon a Distant War*, 304; Reeves, *President Kennedy: Profile of Power*, 490.

261 Moyar, Triumph Forsaken, 217.

262 Bass, "The Spy Who Loved Us," 63.

263 Jones, *Death of a Generation*, 353.

Market called upon the people to struggle to demand justice for those who had been killed."[264]

Tri Quang's brother, a senior official in North Vietnam's Ministry of the Interior, was responsible for coordinating subversion in South Vietnam, and the evidence available indicates that Tri Quang was himself a Communist operative.[265] Tri Quang consistently refused to accept any concessions made by Diem and stated openly that he would not stop protesting until Diem fell from power.[266] David Halberstam said almost everything there was to be said on this issue when he noted that the young Buddhist priests agitating for Diem's overthrow "were highly skilled in politics and...had a keen insight about the psychology of their people. . . . They could discuss the populace, the war, the family and American foreign policy skillfully and with originality."[267]

Averell Harriman (one of Truman's "Wise Men") and Roger Hilsman (one of Kennedy's "best and brightest"), two of the geniuses behind Kennedy's 1962 agreement to host a guerilla war in South Vietnam, pressured Diem to act like an American politician and be conciliatory toward those determined to destroy him. "I cannot seem to convince the [American] embassy that this is Vietnam—not the United States of America," Diem told Marguerite Higgins of the *New York Herald Tribune*. "It is impossible—a delusion—to think that a solution for Asia consists in blindly copying Western methods. . . . Your press and radio mock the idea of discipline and respect for authority and glorify so-called civil liberties and the right to criticize and the need for political opposition, but this country is in a life or death struggle. Even the Western democracies suspend civil liberties during emergencies."[268] Yet Diem had little choice given the bent and leverage of his patrons, so he offered concession after concession to the Buddhists, which damaged him greatly in the eyes of the Vietnamese.

---

264 Moyar, *Triumph Forsaken*, 217.
265 Moyar, *Triumph Forsaken*, 218.
266 Ibid.; Jones, *Death of a Generation*, 286.
267 Halberstam, *The Making of a Quagmire*, 115–116.
268 Moyar, *Triumph Forsaken*, 229–230.

In June, Quang Duc famously immolated himself on a Saigon street. AP correspondent Malcolm Browne, notified at Tri Quang's request to appear for the spectacle, took the photograph that would turn Vietnam into a major crisis for the Kennedy administration.[269] When Tri Quang met Marguerite Higgins, who was awarded a Pulitzer Prize for her reporting from Korea, he told her that there would be "many more immolations" and urged her to warn President Kennedy that "[t]hese events would blacken his reputation...."[270] On July 3, David Halberstam, no doubt repeating what he had been fed by An and his "intelligence network," reported that "some Vietnamese military officers are reported ready to act but give the impression that they would like the Americans to make a public statement calling for a change" and further claimed that "the Americans" wanted a new government.[271] The *New York Times* called for a change in policy or regime change in Saigon.[272] Two weeks later, the *Washington Post* openly recommended that the United States government engineer Diem's overthrow due to his alleged persecution of the Buddhists.[273] And on August 20, 1963, Secretary of State Dean Rusk decided that "removal of [the] Nhus is the center of the problem."[274] (Like Aaron Altman, played by Albert Brooks in *Broadcast News*, An must have marveled at his almost magical power: "I say it here; it comes out there.")

Ambassador Frederick Nolting, on the other hand, was one of the few Americans on the scene who understood what was happening. He believed that the Buddhist movement had fallen into the hands of militants who intended to bring down Diem, which was exactly what the Communists wanted,[275] and further believed that "hotheaded instructions from Washington, burned into action by the American press, [telling Diem] to apologize and eat crow and do things he couldn't possibly afford to do as president of the country"

269 Ibid., 221.
270 Prochnau, *Once Upon a Distant War*, 438.
271 Moyar, *Triumph Forsaken*, 226.
272 Jones, *Death of a Generation*, 302.
273 Moyar, *Triumph Forsaken*, 226, n 84.
274 Jones, *Death of a Generation*, 296.
275 Ibid., 278, 289.

were counterproductive.[276] Nolting stated publicly that after two
and one-half years in Vietnam, he had no evidence of religious
persecution,[277] and a number of experienced journalists took issue
with Halberstam *et al.* Marguerite Higgins, who understood the
enemy, the allies, South Vietnamese society and the nature of the
fight at issue, openly critiqued Halberstam's coverage of the
Buddhist crisis in the *New York Herald Tribune,* noting egregious
errors in both his reporting and his analysis.[278] But in the end, of
course, the victors always write the history. And as victors,
Halberstam and his Saigon cronies would have the last word.

When Diem began losing his grip on South Vietnam, Kennedy
had one final chance to extricate this country from a war in which,
in his mind, it did not belong. In August, the South Vietnamese
General Staff urged Diem to raid the pagodas and end the Buddhist
agitation, noting that similar forceful action had ended the crisis
with the sects in 1955. General Don, a Buddhist, advised Diem that
"[c]ontinued disorders cannot be tolerated. . . . [They] deeply
undermine the people's faith in the power of the government to
keep the situation under control. The ring leaders of the disorders
have to be rounded up. . . .The pagodas cannot be privileged
sanctuaries for subversion."[279] Diem agreed, and the raids took
place on August 21, 1963. Hundreds of monks were arrested, the
vast majority of whom were unharmed and released shortly.[280]

David Halberstam, attuned as always to the truth, the whole
truth and nothing but the truth through the good offices of An and
his "intelligence network," reported that, according to "highly
reliable sources," the raids were instituted by Diem's brother Ngo
Dinh Nhu rather than the Army.[281] He also reported that monks
were bayoneted, clubbed and hurled down stairs and that there had
been mass defections from the ranks of the South Vietnamese Army
and open warfare between Catholic and Buddhist troops in

---

276 Ibid., 278.
277 Ibid., 291.
278 Moyar, *Triumph Forsaken*, 239.
279 Ibid., 231–232.
280 Ibid., 232.
281 Halberstam, *The Making of a Quagmire*, 126–132.

Mytho.[282] All of this was nonsense.[283] "POWER SHIFT TO NHU SEEN IN VIET-NAM" headlined the *Washington Post* over a story by Halberstam's comrade Neil Sheehan.[284] Stanley Karnow, as in thrall to Communist agents as Halberstam and Sheehan, reported that high-ranking civil servants and military officers, including some close to Diem, spoke of Diem's forthcoming assassination.[285]

Averell Harriman, Roger Hilsman, Michael Forrestal and George Ball advised John Kennedy that "[i]t is now quite certain that Brother Nhu is the mastermind behind this whole operation against the Buddhists and is calling the shots."[286] *This was nonsense.* They drafted a memorandum to newly arrived Ambassador Henry Cabot Lodge in Saigon instructing Lodge to tell South Vietnam's generals that if Diem did not remove his brother from power and make further concessions to the Buddhists, "we must face the possibility that Diem himself cannot be preserved." "We must...tell key military leaders that [the] US would find it impossible to continue to support GVN militarily and economically unless [concessions to the Buddhists] are [made] immediately which we recognize requires removal of the Nhus from the scene."[287]

Although Lodge was instructed to "examine all possible alternative leadership and make detailed plans for how we might bring about Diem's replacement if this should become necessary," he was also told that "Diem must be given a chance to rid himself of Nhu and his coterie and replace them with the best military and political personalities available."[288] John Kennedy, who was in Cape Cod, said he would approve the cable *if* both the Departments of State and Defense agreed. George Ball, Roger Hilsman and Averell Harriman now acted like children playing a game. When they

---

282 Moyar, *Triumph Forsaken*, 233–234.
283 Ibid., 234.
284 Reeves, *President Kennedy: Profile of Power*, 560.
285 Ibid., 561.
286 Ibid.
287 Cable to Ambassador Lodge, August 24, 1963, quoted in Reeves, *President Kennedy: Profile of Power*, 562.
288 Reeves, *President Kennedy: Profile of Power*, 562–563.

contacted Secretary of State Rusk, who was attending a baseball game, they told him that Kennedy had approved the message, so he concurred. Roswell Gilpatrick, who was standing in for Robert McNamara, was then contacted by Michael Forrestal and told that both Kennedy and Rusk had already agreed, so he concurred as well. The cable was sent to Lodge in Saigon on Saturday, August 24, 1963. *Despite Kennedy's direction, neither Secretary of Defense McNamara nor Secretary of State Rusk had seen or approved the cable.*

Lodge, for his part, spent a great deal of time with Halberstam, Sheehan and Malcolm Brown, whom he treated as equals and who in turn shared with him the insights they gained from their Communist-run "intelligence network." Said Major General John Dunn, Lodge's chief of staff: "They weren't sitting out there as neutral observers. They were players. I think it's fair to say that Ambassador Lodge depended upon them very heavily as sources of information, not just from what they were sending home in dispatches, but from what they told him in private."[289] *Pham Xuan An had succeeded beyond his wildest dreams.*

When he received the August 24 cable, Lodge, who arrived in Vietnam determined to facilitate Diem's overthrow,[290] responded that "chances of Diem meeting our demands are virtually nil," and he suggested bypassing Diem entirely and allowing the South Vietnamese generals to remove Nhu immediately and decide for themselves whether to keep Diem. George Ball (the number two man at the State Department and a long-time critic of Diem), Averell Harriman and Roger Hilsman "[agreed] to [the] modification proposed" without consulting their superiors and, on Sunday morning, authorized Lodge to proceed.[291] What had started as a warning to Diem based on false information had ended with authorization to instigate the overthrow of an allied government, a move that neither Kennedy nor McNamara nor Rusk had approved.

Upon receipt, Lodge advised a select group of South Vietnamese generals to remove Nhu and keep Diem if they chose, and on Roger

289 Moyar, *Triumph Forsaken*, 238.
290 Jones, *Death of a Generation*, 305.
291 Reeves, *President Kennedy: Profile of Power*, 563.

Hilsman's authorization, the Voice of America announced that "Washington officials say the [pagoda] raids were made by police under the control of President Diem's brother, Ngo Dinh Nhu. They say that America may cut its aid to Vietnam if President Diem does not get rid of the police officials responsible."[292] General Khiem, the South Vietnamese Army chief of staff, now believed that they had to overthrow Diem "to please the United States. We thought that was what the Kennedy administration wanted. . . . If the United States was so angry with Diem that that it would cut off aid, it was even possible that the United States would pull out of the war." And this "would have been the end of everything."[293]

When word of these astonishing developments reached Washington on Monday, Kennedy, McNamara, Maxwell Taylor and CIA Director John McCone, who realized they had all been either conned or deliberately bypassed, were furious. Taylor's anger was "blood-curdling to behold."[294] Kennedy lashed out at those responsible and noted that they all seemed to be inspired by David Halberstam's reporting. Halberstam, he said, was "wholly unobjective" and "actually running a political campaign." "It is essential," he said, "that we not permit Halberstam unduly to influence our actions." "Diem and his brother," he continued, "however repugnant in some respects, have done a great deal along the lines that we desire and, when we move to eliminate this government, it should not be as a result of *New York Times* pressure."[295] America's best and brightest, however, decided not to reverse course as this might harm American credibility. (Instigating the overthrow and murder of an allied head of state, apparently, would not.) George Ball, virtually canonized within orthodoxy for

---

292 Moyar, *Triumph Forsaken*, 239.

293 Ibid., 240.

294 Ibid.

295 Ibid., 241; Prochnau, *Once Upon a Distant War*, 403. See also Memorandum of Conversation ("Memcon"), "*Vietnam*," August 26, 1963, Noon. JFKL: Roger Hilsman Papers, Country Series, box 4, folder: Vietnam: White House Meetings 8/26/63–8/29/63, State Memcons: "The President wanted assurances that we were not being influenced by the *New York Times*; specifically, the Halberstam article. He said that Halberstam was a 28-year old kid and he wanted assurances that we were not giving him serious consideration in our decision; that this reminded him of Matthews on Cuba." http://www.gwu.edu/~nsarchiv/NSAEBB/NSAEBB101/index.htm, accessed November 24, 2009.

his supposedly steadfast opposition to America's escalation of the war, was particularly forceful during an August 28 meeting with President Kennedy, insisting that "we can't win the war against the Communists with Diem in control" and that "we must decide now to go through with a successful overthrow of Diem."[296] Averell Harriman agreed with Ball, noting that if the coup fails or does not go forward, "We [will] have lost the fight in Vietnam and must withdraw...."[297] *The coup was initiated to prolong a war that would soon end if events were allowed to take their course, as CIA analysts in Saigon noted at the time.*[298]

Rumors eventually reached Washington that Diem himself, aware that his position grew more precarious by the day, sought a negotiated settlement with Hanoi through the good offices of the French ambassador in Saigon,[299] a move that had been anticipated in Washington,[300] and the evidence available indicates rather strongly that this intelligence was accurate. In August, General Nguyen Khanh informed the Saigon CIA station chief John Richardson that Nhu was seeking a compromise with Hanoi, and Frederick Nolting admits that he knew of regular contact between Nhu and the Communists. Mieczyslaw Maneli, a Polish member of the International Control Commission formed to supervise the 1954 Geneva Accords, was deeply involved in these intrigues, which he outlined in an essay published in the *New York Times* on January 27, 1975. Hanoi's only unshakeable demand was that the Americans

296 Memcon, *"Vietnam,"* August 28, 1963, Noon. JFKL: Roger Hilsman Papers, Country Series, box 4, folder: Vietnam: White House Meetings 8/26/63–8/29/63, State Department Memcons. http://www.gwu.edu/~nsarchiv/NSAEBB/NSAEBB101/index.htm, accessed November 24, 2009.
297 Ibid.
298 See Dallek, *An Unfinished Life,* 673–674: "The CIA analysts in Saigon warned that if Diem and the Nhus continued in power, 'they and Vietnam [would] stagger on to final defeat at the hands of their own people and the VC' and 'American public opinion and Congress, as well as world opinion, would force withdrawal or reduction of American support for VN.'"
299 Mann, *A Grand Delusion,* 285; Karnow, *Vietnam: A History,* 291–292.
300 Memorandum of Conversation, *"Vietnam,"* August 29, 1963, 12:00 Noon. JFKL: Roger Hilsman Papers: Country Series, box 4, folder: Vietnam: White House Meetings 8/26/63–8/29/63, State Department Memcons. http://www.gwu.edu/~nsarchiv/NSAEBB/NSAEBB101/index.htm, accessed November 24, 2009.

must leave; everything else was negotiable.[301]

> I was secretly asked by President Ngo Dinh Diem
> and his brother...through Roger Lalouette to
> approach the Government in Hanoi in order to
> explore the possibilities for a peaceful resolution of
> the struggle. During the subsequent months, I had
> many wide-ranging discussions with the highest
> North Vietnamese officials, including President Ho
> Chi Minh and Premier Pham Van Dong....The North
> Vietnamese leaders were slowly developing plans,
> which I discussed with a group of Western
> ambassadors....They were willing to accept a
> negotiated agreement whose result would not have
> been worse for the West than the one in 1973:
> Vietnam would have been divided into two parts,
> with free commercial and cultural
> intercommunication between them. [302]

Several former American officials corroborate Maneli, including Richard Smyser, a state department officer who worked closely with Ambassador Lodge in Saigon; Allen Whiting, a China scholar and intelligence officer;[303] and Thomas Hughes, director of intelligence and research at the State Department. Hughes wrote that Nhu, who had "an overriding, immutable influence over Diem," wanted to reduce American involvement because it threatened South Vietnam's independence and intended to negotiate a settlement with Hanoi.[304] The French made several attempts to facilitate a settlement between North and South Vietnam and an American exit

---

301 Jones, *Death of a Generation*, 310–312.

302 Quoted in Hersh, *The Dark Side of Camelot*, 421–422. See also Jones, *Death of a Generation*, 310–311.

303 Hersh, *The Dark Side of Camelot*, 420–423.

304 Goldstein, *Lessons in Disaster*, 80; See also King C. Chen, "Hanoi's Three Decisions and the Escalation of the Vietnam War." *Political Science Quarterly* 90, no. 2 (Summer 1975): 254–256; Jones, *Death of a Generation*, 362–363.

and advised Lodge against instigating a coup.[305] Ambassador Lodge informed Kennedy that "the government the United States was officially supporting and financing and fighting for might be dealing secretly with the Communists—and might ask the Americans to leave."[306]

For a man who wanted to end American involvement and told his top advisers that the best way to end American involvement would be to "put a government in there that would ask us to leave"[307]—a man who during the previous year had sent Averell Harriman to initiate contact with the North Vietnamese with an eye toward the "neutralization" of South Vietnam—this was a heaven-sent opportunity. "[T]he French president was offering the perfect vehicle for a graceful and honorable withdrawal."[308] All Kennedy had to do was leave well enough alone, as Paul Kattenburg, staff director to the Interdepartmental Task Force on Vietnam, told Kennedy in the presence of Dean Rusk, Robert McNamara, Robert Kennedy and Lyndon Johnson on August 28, 1963.[309]

John Kennedy and his advisers, however, reacted to this state of affairs (for which they, their policies and their decision making were largely responsible) just as Truman and those around him reacted to the reality of widespread espionage by Democratic officeholders and government employees. They rejected it out of hand: "That's just your speculation," said Dean Rusk. "We will not pull out of Vietnam until the war is won. . . . And we will not run a coup." McNamara agreed and said, "We are winning this war."[310] *Kattenburg was abruptly transferred to Guyana.*[311]

So Kennedy crossed his Rubicon. Assurances were given to South Vietnam's generals that the Kennedy administration would neither oppose a coup nor terminate its support of the South Vietnamese regime if the coup succeeded. That same day, the

305 Jones, *Death of a Generation*, 341–342.

306 Reeves, *President Kennedy: Profile of Power*, 577.

307 Goldstein, *Lessons in Disaster*, 238; Schlesinger, *Robert Kennedy and His Times*, 717.

308 Bird, *The Color of Truth*, 256.

309 Reeves, *President Kennedy: Profile of Power*, 576–577.

310 Ibid., 577.

311 Jones, *Death of a Generation*, 343; Reeves, *President Kennedy: Profile of Power*, 577.

embassy and military mission in Saigon, along with the Departments of State and Defense and the CIA, received orders from the White House to destroy all cables related to the planned coup as John Kennedy, who could have quashed this coup anytime he chose, initiated a series of deeply disgraceful, dishonorable events that would end on November 2, 1963 with an allied head of state overthrown and then shot and stabbed to death in the back of an armored personnel carrier after being promised safe conduct.[312] (Although orthodoxy maintains that Kennedy had no idea that Diem would be murdered, Kennedy sent Congressman Torbert Macdonald to Diem in the fall of 1963 with an explicit warning: "They're going to kill you," Torbert told Diem. "You've got to get out of here temporarily to seek sanctuary in the American Embassy and you must get rid of your sister-in-law and your brother." Upon his return, Macdonald told Kennedy, "He just won't do it. He's too stubborn; just refuses to."[313])

Kennedy had acted in gross violation of American and international law to prolong the war and deepen this country's involvement, knowing full well what he was doing and why he was doing it: "If the coup fails," noted Bobby Kennedy four days before Diem's assassination, "Diem will throw us out."[314] John Kennedy agreed: Failure of the coup "could in one blow defeat our whole effort in Vietnam. . . . If we miscalculated, we could lose our entire position in Southeast Asia overnight."[315]

Reading American press response to the coup, which took place on November 1-2, one would never imagine that a loyal ally had been undermined, conned, betrayed and murdered by the United

---

312 Jones, *Death of a Generation*, 431; Reeves, *President Kennedy: Profile of Power*, 649.

313 James W. Douglass, *JFK and the Unspeakable: Why He Died and Why It Matters* (New York: Simon & Schuster, 2008), 167–168. See also Herbert S. Parmet, *JFK: The Presidency of John F. Kennedy* (Norwalk: The Easton Press, 1983), 335; Hersh, *The Dark Side of Camelot*, 432. Although NSC 48/2 explicitly stated that "covert operations" were to be "so planned and executed that any US Government responsibility for them is not evident to unauthorized persons and that if uncovered the US Government can plausibly disclaim any responsibility for them," John and Bobby Kennedy appear to be history's only real beneficiaries of this policy.

314 Jones, *Death of a Generation*, 403.

315 Ibid., 404. See also Francis Fitzgerald, quoted in *Virtual JFK*, 137: "Without a coup, Saigon would have fallen; things were that bad."

States government. The *New York Times* called this disgraceful affair "highly desirable" while the *Washington Post* ran an editorial entitled "Hope in Saigon."[316] Ambassador Lodge, who had lied and schemed to destroy Diem from the moment he arrived in Saigon, was arrogant and unrepentant. John Kenneth Galbraith advised Averell Harriman that "the South Vietnam coup is another feather in your cap."[317] The Vietnamese Communists, on the other hand, had an entirely different, and as events would prove, far more accurate perspective. NLF leader Nguyen Huu Tho called the coup "a gift from heaven for us."[318] When told of Diem's assassination, Ho Chi Minh was nothing less than amazed: "I can scarcely believe," he said, "that the Americans would be so stupid."[319] The Politburo in Hanoi agreed:

> The consequences of the 1 November coup d'état will be contrary to the calculations of the U.S. imperialists....Diem was one of the strongest individuals resisting the people and Communism. Everything that could be done in an attempt to crush the revolution was carried out by Diem. Diem was one of the most competent lackeys of the U.S. imperialists....Among the anti-Communists in South Vietnam or exiled in other countries, no one has sufficient political assets and abilities to cause the others to obey. Therefore, the lackey administration cannot be stabilized. The coup d'état on 1 November 1963 will not be the last.[320]

Wilfred Burchett, a pro-Communist Australian journalist, visited Vietnamese Communist leaders after Diem's overthrow and reported that they considered Diem's overthrow a "gift," telling him that "the Americans have done something that we haven't been able

---

316 Moyar, *Triumph Forsaken*, 275.
317 Ibid., 276.
318 Jones, *Death of a Generation*, 419–420.
319 Moyar, *Triumph Forsaken*, 286.
320 Ibid.

to do for nine years and that was get rid of Diem."[321] Always happy to see an American setback, Burchett was pleased as well: "We never believed the Americans would let Diem go, much less aid and abet his departure. Diem was a national leader, and you will never be able to replace him—never."[322]

As history demonstrates, the North Vietnamese perspective was accurate. By 1959, Diem had virtually destroyed the Communist infrastructure and established a viable government in South Vietnam, just as Rhee had in South Korea between 1945 and 1950. This prompted Hanoi's military assault, which in turn gave rise to political problems for John Kennedy. Fearing the "loss" of Vietnam as much as he feared another Korean War, Kennedy unilaterally changed the rules of Truman's doctrine by insisting on "reforms" as a condition of support (Truman forced no such "reforms" on Rhee in South Korea), ceding vast tracts of crucial terrain (Truman ceded *nothing* to the Communists in Korea) and *agreeing* to host an "insurgency" in South Vietnam (conduct unthinkable to Truman in Korea), which then gave rise to a coordinated assault on the GVN by Hanoi's army, a Saigon press corps played by Hanoi like a violin and a large contingent of high-level American officials who were themselves dishonest, inept and thoroughly manipulated by the press corps. Had Syngman Rhee faced a similar assault as he strived to create a viable regime in South Korea from 1946-1950, he would have failed as well. *No Third World leader on America's side of the Cold War could have survived this American-engineered maelstrom, and to the extent that a "corrupt," "incompetent" government prevented enforcement of the Truman Doctrine in Southeast Asia, that government was Kennedy's, not Diem's.*

And if ever there was a Bright and Shining Lie, it is the reputation of David Halberstam, Neil Sheehan and their like-minded colleagues in the Saigon press corps, who were as responsible for this unfolding disaster as anyone in Washington. More pawns than players, they were very much among the "best and brightest" they so despised, with all the hubris that "best and brightest" implies. They entered into a world of politics, history and

---

321 Ibid.
322 Ibid.

intrigue—both American and Vietnamese—that they did not understand, took matters into their own hands because Kennedy and Diem "were losing the war"[323] (a war in which victory, as they in their infinite, twenty-something wisdom *knew,* was *crucial* to American security interests) and in concert with their counterparts in Washington, eliminated any chance of acquiring either a viable non-Communist regime or a reasonable, Diem- or French-engineered American exit in 1963 or 1964. It is supremely ironic that, of all the principal actors in this drama, the only ones *not* interested in ending America's involvement in Southeast Asia were John Kennedy and his advisers in Washington and their Fourth Estate counterparts in Saigon, whose contribution to this disastrous affair is an "elephant in the room" we have too long ignored. We pretend that—like Charles Tatum, the manipulative reporter played by Kirk Douglas in Billy Wilder's 1951 classic, *Ace in the Hole—* Halberstam *et al* didn't make things happen; all they did was write about them. This is not to say, by any means, that the Saigon press corps "lost" the war. It would take far more than a handful of fools like Halberstam and Sheehan to accomplish that. But they could not have done more long-term damage to this country's interests as they viewed them at the time if damage had been their intended purpose. *And the long-dead Joseph McCarthy had nothing to do with it.*[324]

VI

Many historians share my conviction that the world would have been a better place had [John] Kennedy lived. The Vietnam War would not have been escalated. The cold war would not have long

---

323 Prochnau, *Once Upon a Distant War*, 294.

324 It is impossible to imagine how history would have played out had Halberstam, Sheehan and their like-minded colleagues in the Saigon press corps avoided their disastrous involvement with Pham Xuan An, or had the Saigon press corps been staffed entirely by ethical, experienced correspondents like Marguerite Higgins, Robert Elegant, Keyes Beach and Richard Tregaskis. These were members of the Saigon press corps who were never ensnared by the Communists and remained critics of Halberstam and his colleagues for years after the end of the war. See for example Harrison E. Salisbury, ed., *Vietnam Reconsidered: Lessons from a War* (New York: Harper & Row, 1984), 144-152. Let it suffice to say that this was a kaleidoscopic episode in the history of that war that changed everything thereafter.

continued. He would have set the world on a course of peaceful multilateralism much as FDR did. LBJ's Great Society, Civil Rights and other domestic programs, largely based on JFK's 1963 initiatives, would have been enacted in time."[325]

Ted Sorensen

The heart of the Kennedy legend is what might have been. [326]

James Reston

Let us suppose, then, that JFK had been hit by a bullet [in late March 1961]. Let us further suppose that Lyndon Johnson, finding the plans [for the Bay of Pigs invasion] already in place, had authorised the invasion of Cuba. There would now be a herd of revisionist historians and propagandists, all assuring us that if he had lived, "Jack" would never have allowed the CIA and the Joint Chiefs to do anything so barbarous and stupid. Why, just the night before he fell to an assassin, he was "wryly" reconsidering. . .[327]

Christopher Hitchens

It is impossible to evaluate John Kennedy without addressing the question so often asked and so passionately answered by his hagiographers: How would history have differed had Kennedy lived? This is the magic "what might have been" that forms the very "heart of the Kennedy legend,"[328] and it provides some of the finest, real-world examples of *crimestop, blackwhite* and *doublethink* in existence, beginning with the ever-popular claim that Kennedy's every move in Southeast Asia was part of a carefully balanced "secret plan" to withdraw that was, of course, formulated in the national interest by "good and able men of high integrity, acting out of solid and well-reasoned motives."[329]

Tales of the "secret plan" all begin with National Security Action

---

325 Sorensen, *Counselor*, 373.

326 O'Donnell and Powers, *"Johnny, We Hardly Knew Ye,"* 413–414.

327 Christopher Hitchens, "Brief Shining Moments: Christopher Hitchens on Donkey Business in the White House," *London Review of Books* 20, no. 4 (February 1998), 3-7.

328 O'Donnell and Powers, *"Johnny, We Hardly Knew Ye,"* 414.

329 Clark Clifford, *Counsel to the President*, 403.

Memorandum 263, a three-sentence document dated October 11, 1963 and signed by McGeorge Bundy:

> At a meeting on October 5, 1963, the President considered the recommendations contained in the report of Secretary McNamara and General Taylor on their mission to South Vietnam.
>
> The President approved the military recommendations contained in Section I B (1-3) of the report, but directed that no formal announcement be made of the implementation of plans to withdraw 1,000 U.S. military personnel by the end of 1963.
>
> After discussion of the remaining recommendations of the report, the President approved the instruction to Ambassador Lodge which is set forth in State Department telegram No. 534 to Saigon.

This memo, of course, means nothing without "the report of Secretary McNamara and General Taylor," and in this report, McNamara and Taylor assured Kennedy that things were going well in Southeast Asia and that "the military campaigns in the Northern and Central areas of [South Vietnam]" could be completed "by the end of 1964, and in the Delta by the end of 1965." By that time, Vietnamese could be trained to replace the Americans and, being no longer needed, "the bulk of U.S. personnel" could be withdrawn.[330] The problem with citing this as proof of a viable plan to withdraw should be apparent: The program depends on the success of military and counterinsurgency campaigns throughout Vietnam and the creation of a reliable South Vietnamese Army, which is just what Johnson and Nixon attempted without success until 1973 (it was called "Vietnamization").[331] It is fatuous to imagine that such a program would, for some magical reason, have

---

330 Robert S. McNamara, *In Retrospect: The Tragedy and Lessons of Vietnam* (New York: Times Books, 1995), 78–79. See also Goldstein, *Lessons in Disaster*, 82.
331 Newman, *JFK and Vietnam*, 409–410.

succeeded under Kennedy in a two-year period.

Moreover, Kennedy's "secret plan" to withdraw from Southeast Asia did not appear until 1970, by which point it was politically and ideologically essential to disassociate the sainted, martyred John Kennedy from the war, and its proponents are consistently contradicted by accounts from those actually involved. Dean Rusk, Kennedy's secretary of state, said, "I had hundreds of talks with John F. Kennedy about Vietnam, and never once did he say anything [about withdrawal].[332] Leslie Gelb is president emeritus and board senior fellow of the Council on Foreign Relations. As director of policy planning and arms control for international security affairs at the Department of Defense from 1967 to 1969, Gelb directed the Pentagon Papers project, and he agrees with Rusk. Where assertions that John Kennedy intended to withdraw from Vietnam are concerned, Gelb is adamant: "I don't believe that for a minute, I mean, not for a minute. . . . Everything that you can lay your hands on, other than a remark thrown off to Senator Mansfield, another remark to Kenny O'Donnell, everything else pointed in the direction of his being prepared to do whatever was necessary not to lose."[333] (Note carefully Gelb's terminology. While Kennedy was determined "not to lose," he had formed no plan designed to secure South Vietnam as Truman secured South Korea.) Wrote Gelb:

> There's just a startling difference between the early memoirs written by those who were close to him and the later memoirs. If you look at what Arthur Schlesinger and Ted Sorensen wrote about Kennedy and Vietnam right after they left government, they all said Kennedy was committed to sticking it out. They all quoted these interviews JFK gave to Cronkite and Brinkley as symbolic of the president's views at the end of his life. But by the end of the

---

332 Patterson, *Grand Expectations*, 516. See also William J. Rust, *Kennedy in Vietnam* (New York: Scribners, 1985), x: "I had talked with him hundreds of times about Vietnam, and on no single occasion did he ever whisper any such thing."
333 C. David Heymann, RFK: *A Candid Biography* (New York: Dutton, 1998), 437.

sixties, early seventies, they rewrote it themselves. I trust the earlier accounts.[334]

No one corroborates Gelb more than Bobby Kennedy. Interviewed by John Bartlow Martin in 1964, Bobby denied adamantly that his brother had any intention of withdrawing this country from Vietnam: "The President felt that he had a strong, overwhelming reason for being in Vietnam and that we should win the war in Vietnam."[335] *"There was never,"* he agreed, *"any consideration given to pulling out."*[336] In the speech Kennedy planned to give in Dallas on November 22, 1963, John Kennedy himself intended to warn the American people that "[w]e dare not weary of the task" in Vietnam.[337]

Nothing, however, more serves to deconstruct the claims of Kennedy hagiographers than critical analysis of their work, which is epitomized by a well-researched, well-written chronicle of Kennedy's effort in Southeast Asia entitled *Death of a Generation: How the Assassinations of Diem and Kennedy Prolonged the Vietnam War,* published in 2003 by Professor Howard Jones. No aspect of Kennedy's half-hearted, politically driven attempt to enforce Truman's doctrine in Southeast Asia escaped Jones' notice, and he acknowledged several times that, at every crucial juncture, Kennedy acted to prolong and deepen a commitment that was against his better judgment and that "worsened almost in direct proportion to America's growing involvement."[338] As recounted by Jones, Kennedy's policies were dishonest, inept, contradictory and almost incoherent. Yet it was all, Professor Jones repeatedly assures us, part of a carefully conceived plan to facilitate an "unconditional" withdrawal from Southeast Asia designed, of course, in the

---

334 Ibid. For a perfect example of earlier versus later memoirs, see Ted Sorensen, Kennedy, 660–661 (first published in 1965, Sorensen wrote that John Kennedy was going to stay the course) and Ted Sorensen, Counselor: *A Life at the Edge of History* (New York: HarperCollins, 2008), 357, 373 (Kennedy would have withdrawn). See also Robert Kennedy, *Robert Kennedy in His Own Words* (New York: Bantam Books, 1989), 395; Jones, *Death of a Generation*, 452, n.27.

335 Robert Kennedy, *Robert Kennedy in His Own Words*, 395.

336 Ibid. (emphasis added).

337 Patterson, *Grand Expectations*, 516.

338 Jones, *Death of a Generation*, 392.

country's best interests:

- "The White House had to resolve a host of problems in Vietnam before scaling back its involvement."
- "The secret war escalated as the Kennedy administration steered toward a major disengagement."
- "The only feasible way out of Vietnam, it seemed, was to wade in further."
- "The premise was clear: A major reduction in the U.S. involvement in Vietnam depended on a greatly enhanced program of U.S. military assistance."
- "And so the war's escalation continued, even as the White House worked toward a major disengagement."
- "The most prudent U.S. action was a major disengagement but the prerequisite was a victory in the field that could afford a graceful exit."
- "America's prestige rested on maintaining at least the semblance of success. Only then could the White House implement its withdrawal plan."[339]

Being not among those who prefer the marvelous to the true, I have but one word in response to each of these statements: Nonsense. The way to get out was to get out, and Kennedy could have gotten out anytime he was willing to accept the political fallout from, in his own words, a "hard and unpopular decision" that he worked assiduously to bring upon himself. Anytime he wanted to emulate those "Profiles in Courage" whose virtues he extolled and implicitly claimed for himself by doing, in his own words, "what [was] right, rather than what [was] expedient,"[340] the war in Southeast Asia would have ended, then and there. It was just that simple. *This point cannot be overstressed or too often restated: For the supposed author of Profiles in Courage, it was history's perfect moment.* "Solving problems," "escalating," "wading in further," a "victory in the field" and a "semblance of success" were needed not

339 Jones, *Death of a Generation*, 174, 200, 201, 204, 220, 231, 292.

340 Homepage, John F. Kennedy Profile in Courage Award, John F. Kennedy Library Foundation. http://www.jfklibrary.org/Events-and-Awards/Profile-in-Courage-Award.aspx.

for this country but for the Permanent Campaign—specifically Kennedy's interests in the 1964 elections. The only way to turn this sow's ear into a silk purse is by insisting, as Professor Jones does, that where the 1964 elections were concerned, Kennedy's interests were perfectly aligned with those of the country: "The president must first win reelection in 1964 before implementing his phased withdrawal plan. Otherwise, the public outcry over the loss of Vietnam could cost him a second term and bring in a hard-line advocate of military victory."[341] Kennedy aide and loyalist Ted Sorensen agrees: John Kennedy, he writes, "saw no merit in a withdrawal plan that would so antagonize the political right in this country that he would be replaced as president in 1964 by someone who would make matters worse by sending in more troops."[342]

However reasonable this appears, it is meaningless without an answer to the following question: Just what would a "hard-line advocate of military victory," assuming office on January 20, 1965, have done in Southeast Asia after Kennedy's "loss of Vietnam"? The answer should be as apparent as it is simple: Nothing.

The Saigon regime teetered on the brink of collapse by the fall of 1962, when Diem officially requested American combat troops, and it would have either collapsed or "negotiated" its own liquidation (a process that was actually in the works when the Kennedys moved against Diem) within weeks (months at most) of an American withdrawal, which leads to an inescapable conclusion: Had Kennedy pulled the plug between January 1961 and November 1963 (or simply allowed events to take their natural course), the Truman Doctrine's Southeast Asian campaign would have been long over when the dreaded "hard-line advocate of military victory" entered the White House on January 20, 1965. There would have been no ally to support, no enemy to fight, no more need for troops and no conflict to escalate with no "military victory" for the "hard-liner" to advocate. The alternative requires one to believe that Republicans, who, despite years of overheated partisan rhetoric,

---

341 Jones, *Death of a Generation*, 377.

342 Sorensen, *Counselor*, 357. See also Schlesinger, *Robert Kennedy and His Times*, 745: "In any event, would it have been better to have lost in 1964 to a presidential candidate who agreed with General Curtis LeMay that North Vietnam should be bombed back to the stone age?"

had never once initiated a major armed conflict using American forces to facilitate "rollback" of Communist gains anywhere in the world, would have based their 1964 election campaign on a promise to place this country on a full war footing, raise the several million-man force now required to cross the Pacific and storm the beaches at Vung Tau and Danang to "liberate" the now "lost" former French Indochina. (Imagine the Normandy landings and march across France in all aspects multiplied by a factor of ten.) Or perhaps this "liberation" would have been accomplished with a titanic ground assault launched through the rainforest from staging areas in Thailand. (Imagine the Guadalcanal Campaign in all aspects multiplied by a factor of fifty.) An operation like this would have required at minimum several hundred thousand American troops just to initiate (remember Operation Desert Storm, which involved neither rainforest nor mountains) and given American airlift and sealift capability at the time, a year or more to prepare. Whatever the plan, this would have been an operation that would have dwarfed any previous such venture and launched a land war in Asia that would have made Truman's war in Korea pale by comparison—all of which would have been clear to any reasonable person. We must further believe that, with this as a major plank in the 1964 Republican platform, the American people would have swarmed to the Republican side because another Korean War—one guaranteed to be much larger, costlier and bloodier than the last one—was just what they wanted. And this, to put it mildly, is just preposterous.

Republicans would certainly have used the "loss" of Indochina against the Democrats throughout the 1964 campaign just as they used the Korean War and the "loss" of China against Truman; just as Kennedy used the mythical "missile gap" and the "loss" of Cuba against them in 1960. Dispositional behavior does not change.[343] Given the closeness of the 1960 election and what would have been viewed as a rather dismal foreign policy record (the Berlin Wall was

---

[343] "Social psychologists make a useful distinction between what they call 'dispositional behavior' and 'situational behavior' in interpreting the actions of individuals. Dispositional behavior reflects deeply rooted personal characteristics which remain much the same regardless of the circumstances in which people find themselves. One responds inflexibly—and therefore predictably—to whatever happens." Gaddis, *We Now Know*, 20.

constructed without resistance on Kennedy's watch; the Bay of Pigs was a disaster), Democratic concerns over the "loss" of Indochina were, from a political standpoint, more than justified. But there was a vast gap between the rhetoric and the reality of anti-Communism, and Republican concern over the "loss" of Indochina would have been just like their concern over the "negative, futile and immoral policy of 'containment,'" which Republicans proposed to abandon in favor of a policy designed to "roll the communists back"[344] during the 1952 campaign: all show and no go. Republicans no more believed that a major land war in Asia was in the country's interest than Democrats, and even if they did, they were politically astute enough to know that any attempt to lead the electorate into such folly would be both futile and politically suicidal, the one sure way to snatch defeat from the jaws of victory in 1964. Indeed, the "loss" of Indochina by a Democratic administration led by the man who proclaimed it "the keystone to the arch, the finger in the dike" of American security would have provided Republicans, at absolutely no cost, with a weapon they would have wielded effectively for a generation or more. And no electable Republican in 1964—Barry Goldwater included—would have squandered so priceless a gift by re-igniting a war the Democrats had long since "lost," thereby paving his way into the White House while simultaneously eliminating the most intractable political issue he could ever have faced. Simply put, Republicans were dishonest and manipulative but neither irrational nor suicidal, and being well acquainted with Ellsberg's Rules, they would *never* have retied and then placed their own necks into the very noose they had just used to hang the Kennedy administration—and counterfactuals suggesting that they would have cannot be taken seriously.[345]

---

344 Thompson, *The Hawk and the Dove*, 150.

345 For another perfect, real-world example of *blackwhite* and *doublethink*, see *Brothers: The Hidden History of the Kennedy Years*, 216. In this paean to John and Bobby masquerading as history, David Talbot admits that John Kennedy was "operating on 'multiple levels of deception' in his Vietnam decision making" but concludes that it was really "a brilliant shadow dance that succeeded in keeping America out of the war as long as Kennedy was president." Exactly how increasing American troop strength in Vietnam from 500 to more than 16,000 and then overthrowing a regime that, on the brink of collapse, was preparing to conclude its own peace with Hanoi kept America "out of the war" is

In summary, history reveals that John Kennedy *knowingly* and *deliberately* continued the war in Southeast Asia and deepened American involvement at every crucial juncture with his eye on Republicans in Washington, not Communists in Hanoi. His policy in Southeast Asia was designed around his stake in the upcoming election, and there would always be an upcoming election, for Bobby if not for John.[346] There was no "secret plan" to end American involvement, and claims to the contrary represent mythology, not history, as do claims that Kennedy would have brought an early end to the Cold War he worked so hard to inflame.

Nikita Khrushchev, to put it mildly, was no white knight who came in peace and good faith. He was neither democratic nor liberal, and like many Nazi functionaries condemned to the gallows after World War II, he was himself guilty of mass murder and large-scale crimes against humanity, both in the service of Comrade Stalin and on his own watch.[347] He ran a totalitarian empire through the continuous use of state terror on a small scale (try passing out Christian pamphlets in Moscow in 1961 and see what you get) and occasional state terror on a large scale (Hungary in 1956[348]), a fact well known to his foreign and domestic subjects. He was, moreover, bellicose and belligerent, claiming that the USSR was turning out heavy ICBM's like "sausages" and would "bury" the United States. But he blustered from a position of weakness, as he well knew, and he was in fact among the relative moderates on the Communist side, having denounced Stalin's crimes, implemented limited reform within the Communist orbit and struggled with his own hard-liners regularly in an effort to reduce tension and military expenditures,

---

anyone's guess, particularly when one considers the fact that all Kennedy had to do was end the commitment.

346 That Bobby intended to succeed his brother in the White House was no great secret. See Robert A. Caro, *The Years of Lyndon Johnson: The Passage of Power* (New York: Alfred A. Knopf, 2012), xii-xiii.

347 William Taubman, *Khrushchev: The Man and His Era* (New York: W.W. Norton & Company, 2003), xi, xix, 74–75, 99–108, 116, 194–197. See also Melvyn P. Leffler, *For the Soul of Mankind: The United States, the Soviet Union and the Cold War* (New York: Hill and Wang, 2007), 173, 299.

348 Leffler, *For the Soul of Mankind*, 299. Twenty thousand Hungarians were slaughtered by Soviet troops when Khrushchev suppressed Hungary's 1956 revolution.

which he understood were strangling the Soviet economy.[349] He was, as the late Christopher Hitchens noted, "a man with whom business could be done."[350]

Enter John Kennedy, who knew that the only "missile gap" in existence overwhelmingly favored the United States and that Khrushchev's rhetoric was driven by weakness rather than strength. *If ever there was a time to initiate an early end to the arms race and perhaps the Cold War, the moment had arrived.*

From the day of his inauguration, however, Kennedy was the Soviet hard-liners' dream come true. A prisoner of both domestic politics and his own disposition and rhetoric (Republicans were appeasers, Cuba was "dangerous," a "missile gap" threatened this country's very existence), he governed as he campaigned, starting with his program to construct 1,000 *additional* ICBMs that were, by any objective measure, far in excess of legitimate defense needs and needlessly provocative. He then proceeded with his foolish, unlawful Bay of Pigs fiasco, which gave this country a humiliating defeat, and followed this with an unlawful, eighteen-month terrorist campaign against Cuba (initiated by Kennedy *after* Castro had attempted to settle all outstanding issues on American terms). The result was Soviet missiles in Cuba.[351] Finally, it bears noting that, his agreement ending the Missile Crisis notwithstanding, Kennedy kept Cuban invasion plans at the ready, noting that "the time will probably come when we will have to act again on Cuba."[352] And act again he did.

In early December 1962, McGeorge Bundy circulated a memorandum that noted, "Our ultimate objective with respect to

---

349 Martin Malia, *The Soviet Tragedy: A History of Socialism in Russia* (New York: The Free Press, 1994), 328, 331–334. See also Leffler, *For the Soul of Mankind*, 165–166.

350 Hitchens, *The Quotable Hitchens*, 165. See also: George F. Kennan. *The Nuclear Delusion: Soviet-American Relations in the Nuclear Age* (New York: Pantheon Books, 1976), 37-41. Kennan recognized that Khrushchev, who provided the best opportunity this country ever had to reduce tension and perhaps end the Cold War, was destroyed in no small part by Kennedy's aggressive anti-Communism.

351 Eisenhower launched 170 covert operations in eight years as president; JFK was far more aggressive, launching 163 in less than three years. See Weiner, *Legacy of Ashes*, 180.

352 Stephen Rabe, "After the Missiles of October: John F. Kennedy and Cuba, November 1962 to November 1963," *Presidential Studies Quarterly* 30, no. 4, (2000): 714–26, 719.

Cuba remains the overthrow of the Castro regime and its replacement by one sharing the aims of the Free World."[353] Bobby Kennedy met with Cuban exiles shortly after the end of the Missile Crisis and insisted that anti-Castro training operations, for which an additional $6 to $9 million had been provided, be moved outside the United States where American laws, well known to the Kennedys but generally observed only in their breach, would not apply.[354] On April 9, 1963, John Kennedy personally approved sabotage of Cuban ships and cargoes along with harassment of and attacks on Soviet military personnel in Cuba "provided every precaution is taken to prevent attribution."[355] In June he launched another round of military operations against Castro[356] that included assassination plots so open and notorious in administration circles that Joseph Califano (a life-long Democratic insider who worked for John Kennedy and Lyndon Johnson and later became secretary of health education and welfare in the Carter administration) and his boss, Cyrus Vance (Jimmy Carter's secretary of state), were appalled.[357] Both believed that John and Bobby wanted Castro assassinated.[358] According to Califano, Robert Kennedy "bombed railroads, bridges, piers, warehouses, power plants and transformers" and "continued to infiltrate radio equipment, arms, and supplies to resistance forces on the island."[359] "The morality of operation Mongoose had not bothered them earlier, and their consciences did not appear to cry out in mid-1963."[360]

The Soviets, fully aware of these activities, protested bitterly given the agreement ending the Missile Crisis, but to no avail. "It is not the United States," Kennedy told Khrushchev in September 1963, "but the behavior of the Castro regime that is to blame for the

---

353 Ibid. Robert McNamara considered the "the elimination of Castro" as "a requirement" in the spring of 1963.

354 Gus Russo and Stephen Molton, *Brothers in Arms: The Kennedys, the Castros and the Politics of Murder* (New York: Bloomsbury, 2008), 245.

355 Rabe, "After the Missiles of October," 720.

356 Reeves, *A Question of Character*, 393; Parmet, *JFK: The Presidency of John F. Kennedy*, 299.

357 Joseph Califano, Jr., *Inside: A Public and Private Life* (New York: PublicAffairs, 2004), 124.

358 Ibid.

359 Ibid.

360 Reeves, *A Question of Character*, 393.

difficulties in the Caribbean area."[361] Humiliated by Kennedy in the Missile Crisis and powerless to enforce compliance with the agreement ending it, Khrushchev was deposed within two years and replaced by Leonid Brezhnev. (This is not to suggest that the Missile Crisis or Kennedy's continued aggressions in its aftermath were the only reasons for Khrushchev's ouster, but the Soviets' loss of face and fears of further humiliation were particularly important factors.)

A hard-liner himself, Brezhnev was installed by hard-liners who were determined to succeed where Khrushchev had failed and, as history demonstrates, had little interest in ending the Cold War. With nuclear parity and nothing to fear thirteen years later, Brezhnev would reject Jimmy Carter's sincere peace overtures and, assuming John Kennedy's role, launch a round of proxy wars and attacks on American clients throughout the Third World while deploying a new generation of offensive missiles against Western Europe, threatening the very foundation of the Atlantic Alliance. With Brezhnev unwilling to accept peace overtures from Jimmy Carter in the mid-1970s, it is ridiculous to suggest that he, of all people, would have accepted peace overtures during the 1960s from, of all people, the Kennedy brothers, whose aggressive anti-Communism had contributed so much to Khrushchev's downfall.

In summary, the die was cast by November 22, 1963. "We had purchased submission at the price of later intransigence, which is often the case after gratuitous humiliation."[362] Some twenty years would pass before Russia's Old Bolsheviks would be gone, making it possible to reduce tension and end the arms race. And no one bears more responsibility for this than John Kennedy, who initiated a major round in the arms race before bringing us the Bay of Pigs, Operation Mongoose, the Missile Crisis, an enormous increase in the size and power of the Soviet arsenal and a twenty-year deep freeze in relations between the superpowers rather than the continuous process of outreach and accommodation that provides a basis for imagining an end to the arms race if not the Cold War as we knew it by the late 1960s. *The policies needed to facilitate an*

---

361 Ibid.
362 Wills, *The Kennedy Imprisonment*, 271.

early end to the Cold War through "peaceful multilateralism"
during the 1960s depended entirely upon a John Kennedy who
never existed, the same John Kennedy whose "secret plan" would
have ended the Vietnam War peacefully and quickly.

So what might have been, as James Reston noted, is indeed an appropriate measure of John Kennedy, provided "what might have been" is considered in light of fact and not myth, history rather than ideology. "What might have been" must be measured from January 20, 1961, through November 22, 1963, when John Kennedy, his eyes on the 1964 election, stoked the fires of Cold War confrontation at every opportunity while escalating and prolonging the war in Southeast Asia because he feared the political consequences of ending it. Having spent half his life fighting to lead this country, he simply refused to lead. For John Fitzgerald Kennedy was no profile in courage, and as Nikita Khrushchev noted, he was just not up to the job.

Chapter Five:
Lyndon Johnson

I

His morality was the morality of the ballot box, a morality in which nothing matters but victory and any maneuver that leads to victory is justified, a morality that was amorality.[1]

Robert Caro

Lyndon Johnson was in on the ground floor of the so-called McCarthy era and rode the anti-Communist bandwagon for all it was worth, as when he accused Coke Stevenson of having Communist sympathies in 1948 and ended the public career of Leland Olds, whom he labeled a "commissar" in 1949. During a speech in Texas, Johnson railed that "a final showdown with the Reds" was "inevitable." "It is foolish to talk of avoiding war," he said. "We are already in a war—a major war. The war in Korea is the war of Soviet Russia."[2] Speaking at a luncheon of civic leaders in Dallas, Johnson stated that Americans must prepare to take the fight to Soviets: "We are tired of fighting your stooges....The next aggression will be the last. We will strike back not at your satellites—but you...and it will be a crushing blow."[3]

---

1 Robert Caro, *The Years of Lyndon Johnson: Means of Ascent* (New York: Alfred A. Knopf, 1990), 287.

2 Dallek, *Lone Star Rising*, 396–397.

3 Ibid.

But Johnson's public statements and his actual beliefs were often at odds. Johnson realized, for example, that a negotiated end to the Korean War was essential and did not join the hard-liners attacking Eisenhower over the armistice talks in 1953. Yet when the armistice agreement was signed, he attacked the agreement. Charging that Eisenhower was simply releasing Communist armies for aggression elsewhere, he proposed retaliation against Moscow for any aggression by a Soviet satellite.[4] The same was true regarding Vietnam. When the French garrison was besieged at Dien Bien Phu, Eisenhower was reluctant to intervene but knew that Democrats, who were mirror images of Republicans when it came to the use of anti-Communism for partisan purposes, would use any excuse to attack him for being "soft on Communism." "The damn Republicans blamed us for losing China and now we can blame them for losing Southeast Asia," said Congressman Franklin Roosevelt, Jr.[5] So Eisenhower arranged a meeting between key Democrats and Secretary of State John Foster Dulles in April 1954 to allow Dulles to make his case for enforcing Truman's doctrine in Vietnam as Truman had enforced it in Korea. Both Johnson and his mentor, Richard Russell of Georgia, were opposed, and Johnson himself led the inquiry that exposed the weakness of Dulles' arguments. Yet Johnson turned immediately on Eisenhower, charging the very next month that "American foreign policy has never in all its history suffered such a stunning reversal....Our friends and allies [who Johnson knew had refused to support intervention] are frightened and wondering, as we do, where we are headed. We stand in clear danger of being left naked and alone in a hostile world."[6]

The difference between the public and the private Lyndon Johnson was easily explained by David Halberstam: "Nothing existed for him but politics....He was the totally political man, living and breathing for the political act."[7] For such a man, the war in

---

4 Ibid., 435.

5 Halberstam, *The Fifties*, 405.

6 Dallek, *Lone Star Rising*, 444.

7 Halberstam, *The Best and The Brightest*, 439. Johnson was also, it should be noted, deeply and personally corrupt. Although he had been on the public payroll almost his entire adult life, he had

Korea meant nothing apart from its politics, meaning Johnson's analysis of what he could gain from it. And in later years, his "morality of the ballot box" would manifest at a staggering price.

II

I am not going to lose Vietnam....I am not going to be the President who saw Southeast Asia go the way of China.[8]

Lyndon Johnson

[T]wo aspects of the early decisions on Vietnam . . . that Johnson took during that Christmas vacation on the ranch, are clear: first, whatever steps he took during that vacation, he took as well steps to conceal them, to keep them secret from Congress and the American people; and, second, the steps he took had, as their unifying principle, an objective dictated largely by domestic— indeed, personal—political concerns.[9]

Robert A. Caro

Like John Kennedy before him, Lyndon Johnson was a prisoner of Ellsberg's Rules, which came to us as part of "the Legacy of the '30s." Like Kennedy before him, Johnson constructed his policy in Southeast Asia around the 1964 election and focused on Republicans in Washington rather than Communists in Asia: "But we're [in Vietnam] now, and there's one of three things you can do. One is run and let the dominoes start falling over. *And God Almighty, what [the Republicans] said about us leaving China would just be warming up, compared to what they'd say now. I see Nixon is raising hell about it today. Goldwater too.*"[10] Like

amassed a several-million-dollar fortune by the fall of 1963. Only John Kennedy's assassination prevented *Life* magazine from revealing what it had learned of Johnson's fortune in November 1963. See Robert A. Caro, *The Years of Lyndon Johnson: The Passage of Power* (New York: Alfred A. Knopf, 2012), 284-287, 296-299, 308, 318.

8 Halberstam, *The Best and The Brightest*, 298.

9 Caro, *The Years of Lyndon Johnson*, 534.

10 Michael R. Beschloss, *Taking Charge: The Johnson White House Tapes, 1963–1964* (New York: Simon and Schuster, 1997), 213 (emphasis added). See also pages 266–267, 363–370: "The

Kennedy before him, he feared "another Korea"[11] and avoided major escalation since "a Korean operation" might alarm the electorate.[12] Like Kennedy before him, Johnson allowed the Communists a free hand in southeastern Laos, through which some 40,000 NVA troops had passed on their way into South Vietnam by the time Johnson took office. And like Kennedy before him, Johnson revealed in private just how little he believed Southeast Asia meant to this country: "I don't see what we can ever hope to get out of there with, once we're committed. I believe that the Chinese Communists are coming into it. I don't think we can fight them ten thousand miles away from home....I don't think it's worth fighting for and I don't think that we can get out. It's just the biggest damned mess I ever saw."[13]

On May 27, 1964, Senator Richard Russell told Johnson that Vietnam "isn't important a damn bit." Russell called Southeast Asia "the damn worse mess I ever saw,"[14] . . . a "rathole," and he described American involvement as an "impossible situation."[15] He told Johnson in no uncertain terms that Johnson "can make a tremendous case for moving out"[16] and warned him the next month that enforcing Truman's doctrine in Southeast Asia would "take a half a million men [who would] be bogged down in there for ten years."[17] And Russell did not know the half of it. McNamara had informed Johnson only two months earlier that "the situation [in

---

Republicans are going to make a political issue out of it, every one of them, even Dirksen." Johnson was trying his best to "get by till November," "but these politicians ["Nixon and Rockefeller and Goldwater"] got to raising hell." "[O]utside of Morse, everybody I talk to says you got to go in, including Hickenlooper, including all the Republicans....And I don't know how in the hell you're gonna get out unless [the Republicans] tell you to get out."

11 Ibid., 370.

12 Ibid., 266–267. In late 1963, Mike Mansfield recognized the driving force of Ellsberg's Rules when he advised Lyndon Johnson that, "As you remarked to [Valeo] on the telephone, we do not want another China in Vietnam," but "neither do we want another Korea." Caro, *The Years of Lyndon Johnson*, 533.

13 Beschloss, *Taking Charge*, 370 (conversation between Johnson and presidential adviser McGeorge Bundy, Wednesday, May 27, 1964).

14 Ibid., 363.

15 Ibid., 366–367. See also (generally) 363-373.

16 Ibid., 368.

17 Ibid., 402.

Vietnam] has unquestionably been growing worse."[18] He reported
at that time that forty percent of the countryside was under Viet
Cong control; a large percentage of the population was showing
signs of apathy and indifference; South Vietnamese Army desertion
rates were high and increasing, as was "North Vietnamese support."
He reported further that the South Vietnamese government was
noticeably weakening as "the political control structure extending
from Saigon down into the hamlets [had] disappeared following the
November coup."[19] Most importantly, McNamara acknowledged
the root cause at the time. "In Laos, we are still working largely
within the framework of the 1962 Geneva Accords. . . As a
consequence . . . we and the GVN have had to condone the extensive
use of Cambodian and Laotian territory by the Viet Cong, both as a
sanctuary and as infiltration routes."[20]

Having been informed by pollster Lou Harris that Vietnam was
an issue working in Goldwater's favor, Johnson was looking for an
excuse to demonstrate his mettle, and he got his chance on August
2, 1964, when the USS *Maddox* was attacked by North Vietnamese
torpedo boats in retaliation for OPLAN 34-A raids. Authorized by
Johnson in early 1964, these raids were launched against North
Vietnamese port facilities by American-supported South
Vietnamese commandos.[21] Although McNamara told Johnson that
the attack was a direct result of the 34-A raids,[22] Johnson lied,
claiming that the attack had been "unprovoked."[23] Two days later,
when McNamara received a report that a second attack had
occurred, Johnson ordered air strikes on torpedo boats, bases and
other military targets.[24] As strike preparations were undertaken on

18 Sheehan, Smith, Kenworthy and Butterfield, *The Pentagon Papers*, 287.

19 Ibid.

20 Ibid., 286.

21 Beschloss, *Taking Charge*, 493, 499.

22 Ibid., 494–495. See also Goldstein, *Lessons in Disaster*, 125; John Prados, *Vietnam: The History of an Unwinnable War*, 95–97.

23 H.R. McMaster, *Dereliction of Duty: Lyndon Johnson, Robert McNamara, The Joint Chiefs of Staff and the Lies that Led to Vietnam* (New York: HarperCollins, 1997), 118–124. Sheehan, Smith, Kenworthy and Butterfield, *The Pentagon Papers*, 271.

24 Robert Dallek, *Flawed Giant: Lyndon Johnson and His Times*, 1961–1973 (New York: Oxford University Press, 1998) 147–156.

the aircraft carriers in the South China Sea, however, the commander of the *Maddox* destroyer task force, Captain John Herrick, reported serious doubts that the August 4th attack had actually occurred and recommended a "complete evaluation before any further action taken."[25]

Johnson, however, was far more interested in politics than reality. Determined to make his announcement of the strikes prior to the final deadline for inclusion into the morning papers and the 11:00 p.m. national news broadcast, he telephoned McNamara repeatedly. "Bob, I'm exposed here! I've got to make a speech right now."[26] Johnson knew full well that advance notice of the attack was a betrayal of his own military personnel: "I'd sure as hell hate to have some mother say, 'you announced it and my boy got killed.'"[27] Yet Johnson announced the strike at 11:36 p.m., Eastern Standard Time, *which was one hour and thirty minutes before the planes reached their targets!*[28] Two aircraft were shot down. Lt. Richard Sather was killed, and Lt. Everett Alvarez, Jr., was taken prisoner, spending more than eight years in the hell of a North Vietnamese prison before his release in 1973, all to ensure that Lyndon Johnson would receive the news coverage he needed. It was but a small taste of things to come.

On August 6, 1964, Robert McNamara, Dean Rusk and General Earl Wheeler, chairman of the Joint Chiefs of Staff, appeared before a joint session of the Senate Foreign Relations and Armed Services Committees during consideration of the Gulf of Tonkin Resolution, which authorized the president to employ whatever force he deemed necessary "to repel any armed attack against the forces of the United States and to prevent further aggression."[29] In other words, it represented congressional authorization for Johnson to do in Vietnam *exactly* what Truman had done in Korea. Oregon

---

25 Dallek, *Flawed Giant*, 151.

26 McMaster, *Dereliction of Duty*, 132.

27 Beschloss, *Taking Charge*, 503.

28 McMaster, *Dereliction of Duty*, 133; Robert David Johnson, *All the Way with LBJ: The 1964 Presidential Election* (New York: Cambridge University Press, 2009), 154.

29 See The Avalon Project: Documents in law, History and Diplomacy, Yale Law School, Lillian Goldman Law Library. http://avalon.law.yale.edu/20th_century/tonkin-g.asp, accessed May 10, 2012.

Senator Wayne Morse, who had received a tip that the North Vietnamese attack had *not* been unprovoked, asked McNamara what our ships were doing at the time of the attacks. In response, McNamara lied repeatedly, stating that the "U.S. Navy played absolutely no part in, was not associated with, was not aware of any South Vietnamese actions, if there were any. I want to make that very clear."[30] General Wheeler knew that McNamara was lying, yet he went along, lending both his credibility and that of the Armed Forces to McNamara's dissembling. Maxwell Taylor also lied to Congress about 34-A raids.[31]

Clearly, there were no "mistakes" being made here by "good and able men of high integrity."[32] Like Kennedy before him, Johnson, who knew exactly what he was doing, formulated policy around Republicans in Washington rather than Communists in Asia without regard for truth, law or long-term consequences. There are simple, harsh, yet appropriate words to describe his conduct, words like conspiracy, obstruction, abuse of power and perjury—precisely the type of criminal offenses that ended Richard Nixon's presidency. Any genuine inquiry into the Gulf of Tonkin incident would undoubtedly have worked wonders. But Democrats controlled both houses of Congress, and they would no sooner question the integrity of their own president three months before an election than they would prosecute their friends and allies for espionage in the post-war years. Besides, Johnson made clear that the Gulf of Tonkin Resolution was a partisan measure aimed at Republicans, so everyone got on board.[33] William Fulbright did Johnson's bidding and ensured that the resolution passed smoothly, without debate or amendment.[34] George McGovern, who would in time become a fierce critic of the war, was as partisan, dishonest and manipulative as anyone in Washington:

---

30 McMaster, *Dereliction of Duty*, 134; Sheehan, Smith, Kenworthy and Butterfield, *The Pentagon Papers*, 273.

31 McMaster, *Dereliction of Duty*, 152–153. See also Sheehan, Smith, Kenworthy and Butterfield, *The Pentagon Papers*, 273–275.

32 Clifford, *Counsel to the President*, 403.

33 Halberstam, *The Best and the Brightest*, 418–420.

34 Herring, *America's Longest War*, 122.

[Fulbright] said [the Resolution] wouldn't mean a lot one way or the other. He said we had to get the whole Congress behind the President on this thing. He said if we didn't that Goldwater was going to hammer [Johnson] over the head for doing nothing. I certainly didn't want to help Goldwater, and what Fulbright was saying made sense. So I voted yes.[35]

"In a single stroke," wrote pollster Lou Harris, "Mr. Johnson has, at least temporarily, turned his greatest political vulnerability in foreign policy into one of his strongest assets."[36] And for the rest of the election campaign, Barry Goldwater would serve Johnson as the perfect foil.

For Goldwater was clear on Southeast Asia: "I would turn to my Joint Chiefs of Staff and say, 'Fellows, we made the decision to win, now it's your problem.'"[37] Lyndon Johnson, of course, played this like a violin and positioned himself as "the reasonable, moderate 'peace' candidate, emphasizing domestic issues, while painting [Goldwater] as a dangerous, unbalanced extremist, eager to escalate to full-scale war in Vietnam."[38] One campaign ad after another associated Goldwater with the threat of nuclear war. Democrats even linked Goldwater, whose father was Jewish, to the Ku Klux Klan.[39] The Democrats' smear campaign worked like a charm. Polls showed that sixty-four percent of women and forty-five percent of men believed that *Goldwater* would take this country to war if he were elected, even as *Johnson* finalized plans for US bombing of North Vietnam to begin as soon as the election was over.[40]

---

35 Anson, *McGovern: A Biography*, 153. See also *All the Way with LBJ*, 155.

36 Halberstam, *The Best and The Brightest*, 422.

37 Rick Perlstein, *Before the Storm: Barry Goldwater and the Unmaking of the American Consensus* (New York: Hill and Wang, 2001), 373.

38 Ellsberg, *Secrets*, 49.

39 Perlstein, *Before the Storm*, 432–433.

40 Ibid., 424. See also Patterson. *Grand Expectations*, 558–559.

»» ««

Immediately after Johnson's landslide victory, his top civilian advisers formed a working group, including John McNaughton, William and McGeorge Bundy, Daniel Ellsberg, Dean Rusk and Robert McNamara, to create a plan of action for the United States in Vietnam. Although they outlined several potential courses of action, including "forceful measures and military moves,"[41] some already believed that enforcing Truman's doctrine in Southeast Asia would be impossible within the limits set by Johnson's pursuit of domestic goals.[42] Their fears were confirmed in late November, when Maxwell Taylor returned to Washington from Saigon and reported that the strength and resilience of the North Vietnamese were amazing while the Army and Government of South Vietnam were on the verge of collapse as Buddhist agitation under Thich Tri Quang (which was never about religious persecution) continued.[43] Yet the charade went on.

On the first day after his inauguration, Johnson and McNamara had a meeting with key Democratic and Republican leaders at which they provided an assessment that was as spurious as it was optimistic.[44] McNamara reviewed 34-A operations and air attacks in Laos, depicting them as successful, knowing they were not. He advised that the South Vietnamese Army was improving in effectiveness, knowing it was not. He did not disclose the plans for reprisal bombing of the North and stated that no US troops would be needed. Johnson agreed with all of this and assured the leaders of Congress that no more US troops would be needed. *Within days of this briefing, McNamara concluded that South Vietnam "was on the brink of total collapse" and brought this belief directly to Johnson.*[45]

Of course, the major impediment to stability in South Vietnam were Kennedy's 1962 Geneva Accords, which Johnson continued to

---

41 McMaster, *Dereliction of Duty*, 181.

42 Ibid., 180–185.

43 Logevall, *Choosing War*, 239–242; 311–312.

44 Ibid., 211.

45 Ibid., 210–212.

honor, and the Communist forces that freely entered South Vietnam as a result.[46] The North Vietnamese sent hundreds of trucks down the Ho Chi Minh Trail every month during 1964, carrying supplies to fuel their "insurgency" (tonnage *quadrupled* that year) along with 9,000 troops. The whole situation was absurd, and the solution was as clear and simple under Johnson as it had been under Kennedy: Either withdraw from Southeast Asia or scrap Kennedy's phony "neutralization" accord and cut the Ho Chi Minh trail, as General James Gavin wrote in 1966: "If our objective is to secure all of South Vietnam, then forces should be deployed on the 17th parallel and along the Cambodian border adequate to do this. In view of the nature of the terrain, it might be necessary to extend our defenses on the 17th parallel to the Mekong River and across part of Thailand."[47] (The distance between the South China Sea and the Thai border was only some 160 miles, which is no longer than the fortified DMZ in Korea.) Such a plan was proposed in 1965 by both South Vietnamese General Cao Van Vien and the Joint Chiefs:

> [Cao Van Vien's] plan entailed fortifying a zone along the 17th parallel from the Dong Ha in Vietnam to Savannakhet on the Lao-Thai border. He further proposed to follow this up with a landing operation at Vinh or Ha Tinh in North Vietnam "to cut off the north's front from its rear." The DMZ portion of General Vien's plan paralleled a concept proposed by the Joint Chiefs of Staff in August 1965. Their plan would deny North Vietnam "the physical capacity to move men and supplies through the Lao corridor down the coastline, across the DMZ and through Cambodia."[48]

Eisenhower weighed in to support an attack on the Ho Chi Minh Trail through Laos on July 2, 1965: "You've got to go along with your military advisers because otherwise you are just going to continue

---

46 Prados, "A Window on the Enemy."

47 Summers, *On Strategy*, 100; Prados, *The Blood Road*, 100–101.

48 Summers, *On Strategy*, 119.

to have these casualties indefinitely. . . . My advice is, do what you have to do. I'm sorry that you have to go to the Congress . . . but I guess you would be calling up the Reserves. . . . I would go ahead and . . . do it as quickly as I could."[49]

According to North Vietnamese Colonel Bui Tin, a political and military insider who served from 1945 until well after North Vietnam's conquest of the South (it was he who accepted the South Vietnamese surrender in April 1975), an assault such as this on the Ho Chi Minh trail would have made all the difference: "If Johnson had granted General Westmoreland's request to enter Laos and block the Ho Chi Minh Trail, Hanoi could not have won the war."[50] "If the American side had occupied just a chunk of the trail— between 30 and 50 kilometers (20-30 miles), not all 800 kilometers (500 miles)—it could have upset our logistics for several months! The attack could have been carried out by as few as three thousand GIs—one-tenth of the number used in the Junction City or Cedar Falls operations!"[51] This would have been a very small effort compared to the several division-size Laotian offensives being urged by Generals Vien, Gavin, and the Joint Chiefs, which were designed not just to cut the Trail but to create permanent, defensible borders for America's allies. But Johnson refused to consider it. Like Kennedy before him, Johnson wanted no part of what might be seen as another Korea, which, while successful in terms of containment, had destroyed Truman's administration, as he told Bobby Kennedy on June 9, 1964: "We had the United Nations behind us but we had a very divided country . . . and we finally really lost—the Democrats did—on the Korea thing."[52]

Johnson continued his disingenuous little dance throughout the winter and spring of 1965, and his advisers, both civilian and military, gave him their support. "Johnson hated criticism or any

---

49 Beschloss, *Reaching for Glory*, 383–384. Westmoreland was proposing a movement into Laos in the summer of 1965. Lewis Sorley, *Westmoreland: The General Who Lost Vietnam* (Boston: Houghton Mifflin Harcourt, 2011), 91-92.

50 Richard H. Schultz, Jr., *The Secret War against Hanoi* (New York: HarperCollins, 1999) 205.

51 Bui Tin, *From Enemy to Friend: A North Vietnamese Perspective on the War* (Annapolis: Naval Institute Press, 2002), 76.

52 Beschloss, *Taking Charge*, 390.

challenge to his authority. Everyone who worked for him was expected to be 100 percent a Johnson man, a loyalist who, whatever his inner thoughts, would subordinate his views and ambitions to Johnson's....'I want people around me,' Johnson said repeatedly, 'who would kiss my ass on a hot summer day and tell me it smells like roses.'"[53] When considering General John P. McConnell for Air Force chief of staff in February 1965, Johnson asked him directly if he would support policies inconsistent with his professional military opinion. General McConnell assured the president that he would, and that is how Johnson fought his war.[54] *The contrast between the Joint Chiefs' professional opinions and their public pronouncements is stunning.*

In June of 1965, for example, Johnson asked General Earl Wheeler, chairman of the Joint Chiefs of Staff, "Bus, what do you think it will take to do the job?" Wheeler's answer was militarily sound: Victory will require "seven hundred, eight hundred thousand, a million men and about seven years."[55] Wheeler also said that even after "victory" with this number of men, this country would have to keep a major force in Southeast Asia for twenty or thirty years.[56] Army Chief of Staff Harold K. Johnson believed that 600,000-700,000 men and five years of fighting would be necessary, which was consistent with Marine Corps Commandant Wallace Greene's estimate.[57] The Chiefs also estimated that troop deployments needed just to hold the line consistent with Johnson's strategy (defined by Kennedy's "tacit agreement" and Ellsberg's

---

53 Dallek, *Flawed Giant*, 160. See also Halberstam, *The Best and The Brightest*, 433–434. "I don't want loyalty. I want *loyalty*. I want him to kiss my ass in Macy's window at high noon and tell me it smells like roses. I want his pecker in my pocket."

54 McMaster, *Dereliction of Duty*, 223–224.

55 Halberstam, *The Best and The Brightest*, 596.

56 Ibid., 596–597.

57 McMaster, *Dereliction of Duty*, 304. In 1966, William Westmoreland directed a "study group" at MACV Headquarters in Saigon to calculate the requirements to "win" in Vietnam. The answer? A million and a half men and ten years. Westmoreland was furious and refused to forward the estimate to Washington, saying (correctly) that "it was politically unacceptable." Sorley, *Westmoreland*, 156–157.

Rules) would cost \$12.7 billion.[58] Most importantly, McNamara advised Lyndon Johnson in July that 235,000 reservists would have to be called up by the Congress for two years of active duty if the forces recommended for intervention in Vietnam were to be assembled.[59] Johnson, however, was determined to avoid any increase in troop strength that might threaten his domestic legislative program.[60] He feared above all that activating the reserves would end his Great Society legislation.[61]

His Joint Chiefs knew the agenda, so when they met with members of the House Armed Services Committee in July 1965, they lied about everything. When asked if a reserve call-up would be needed, Army Chief of Staff Harold K. Johnson said he "didn't really know." He lied further by stating that about 250,000 men would be required in Vietnam, in sharp contrast to the 600,000-700,000 he actually thought were necessary. Air Force Chief of Staff McConnell refused to estimate the number of personnel needed by the Air Force in Vietnam. Admiral McDonald did not address the reserve activation issue. When questioned specifically on their advice regarding the mining of North Vietnamese harbors, the Chiefs lied again. The only one among them who responded honestly was Marine Corps Commandant Wallace Greene, who estimated, as he did in private, that 500,000 men would be needed. In fact, Greene was so disturbed by the others' dissembling that he called John Blandford, the committee's chief counsel, shortly after this meeting and provided him the honest assessment that the Chiefs had not. Greene told Blandford that this country was on the verge of a major war that would require half a million troops, take at least five years and cost this country a large number of casualties.[62] No one, apparently, followed up on this.

Johnson and McNamara then met with the leaders of Congress,

58 Ibid., 316. McNamara believed that the figure would equal "roughly \$10 billion" through the end of 1966. McNamara, *In Retrospect*, 205.

59 John K. Singlaub, *Hazardous Duty, An American Soldier in the Twentieth Century* (New York: Summit Books, 1991), 276–277; Halberstam, *The Best and the Brightest*, 593.

60 McMaster, Dereliction of Duty, 308; Dallek, *Flawed Giant*, 274.

61 Halberstam, The Best and the Brightest, 594.

62 McMaster, *Dereliction of Duty*, 309–312.

both Democratic and Republican, and lied about Westmoreland's troop requests, cutting in half the 100,000 requested for deployment by the end of the year. They lied about mobilizing the reserves, which both McNamara and the Chiefs thought necessary, calling it an inefficient use of a "perishable asset." They lied about the $10-12 billion that even the earliest stages of their little adventure were expected to cost, with Johnson claiming that "we have the money" when he knew full well that he did not. In fact, Senate Minority Leader Everett Dirksen told Johnson that if he needed the money, he should ask for it. But Johnson declined, stating that the Great Society programs should come first.[63] According to presidential aide Jack Valenti, "[T]he last thing that Lyndon Johnson wanted was to make public his strategy about the Great Society and the war. He wasn't going to do it. There's no question that he wanted to *sotto-voce* the whole thing."[64] And everyone in the Johnson administration knew that the American people were being conned, as Robert McNamara noted: "The greatest contribution Vietnam is making—right or wrong is beside the point—is that it is developing an ability in the United States to fight a limited war, to go to war without the necessity of arousing public ire."[65]

By the end of 1965, the North Vietnamese had so improved their supply routes in "neutralized" Laos that their troops could make the entire journey by truck, and 50,000 entered South Vietnam to continue the agreed-upon "insurgency" that year.[66] American forces climbed from 125,000 in the summer of 1965 to 200,000 by the end of the year, but these numbers remained inadequate to the task at hand, as virtually all reasonable people—military and civilian—had warned since Ridgway's report to Eisenhower in 1954.[67] With an inadequate number of troops facing a determined enemy allowed limitless reinforcement and re-supply, there was one sure way to stave off defeat and protect American personnel: firepower.

---

63 Ibid., 319–320.

64 Ibid., 313.

65 Summers, *On Strategy*, 18.

66 Prados, *The Blood Road*, 157. See also Prados, "A Window on the Enemy."

67 McNamara, *In Retrospect*, 213.

Americans had it in spades and used it accordingly. The death, destruction and population displacement added to North Vietnamese recruiting efforts, requiring greater numbers of Americans with ever-increasing firepower and predictable consequences. Aggravating the situation geometrically was America's commander, General William Westmoreland. Intellectually dishonest and pathologically inept, his response to the ever-deteriorating situation was to employ conventional American forces in larger and larger formations, not along the border where they might have been of some use, but on "search and destroy" operations through the rain forest, where the Communists held the initiative and could almost always avoid contact.[68] *Everything this country's so-called leaders did worked in favor of the Communists.* Yet all reasonable advice was rejected out of hand, as when Clark Clifford, perpetual counselor to Democratic presidents and master manipulator, reacted with "colorful" and "pithy" language when advised by Ambassador to South Vietnam Gram Martin in the fall of 1966 that operations in Laos were essential to our efforts in South Vietnam.[69] During 1966, another 60,000 North Vietnamese troops had entered the war through "neutralized" Laos, half of them coming in regimental-size units, as American troop strength in South Vietnam reached 470,000.[70]

Having ceded the initiative to Hanoi while violating, just for good measure, every strategic principle imaginable, Johnson paid the price and blamed everyone else, particularly the Joint Chiefs, whom he abused mercilessly for providing advice he did not want to hear. In November 1965, General Earl Wheeler advised Johnson that the Chiefs were concerned about his handling of the war. Unwilling "to be piling up American boys like cordwood fighting endless Asian troops," they recommended mining Haiphong Harbor, blockading the Vietnamese coast and employing B-52s against North Vietnam.[71] Johnson asked the assembled Joint Chiefs

---

68 Sorley, *Westmoreland: The General Who Lost Vietnam*, 156–157.

69 Prados, *The Blood Road*, 231–32.

70 Ibid., 181.

71 Christian Appy, *Patriots: The Vietnam War Remembered from All Sides* (New York: Viking, 2003), 122.

if they agreed with Wheeler. When they did, he exploded:

> "You goddamn fucking assholes. You're trying to get
> me to start World War III with your idiotic bullshit—
> your military 'wisdom.'"[72] He screamed obscenities,
> he cursed them personally, he ridiculed them for
> coming to his office with their "military advice."
> Noting that it was he who was carrying the weight of
> the free world on his shoulders, he called them filthy
> names—shitheads, dumbshits, pompous assholes—
> and used "the F-word" as an adjective more freely
> than a Marine at boot camp would use it....It was
> unnerving, degrading.[73]

Yet none of them had the guts to stand up to Johnson. Army Chief of Staff General Harold K. Johnson considered resigning in protest over Lyndon Johnson's conduct of the war, but when it came time to act, he failed miserably, rationalizing, as his ilk always do, that he could be of more use by staying within the system than by resigning. "And now," he said years later, "I will go to my grave with that lapse of moral courage."[74] As David Halberstam noted in *The Coldest Winter,* there are often "two very different kinds of courage in military men—bravery in battle, and independence or bravery within the institution—and they do not often reside side by side."[75] John Krakauer, author of *Where Men Win Glory: The Odyssey of Pat Tillman,*[76] is even more to the point: "There are a lot of officers who will risk their lives for the country, but damn few who will risk their careers."[77]

---

72 Ibid.

73 Cooper, Charles, *Cheers and Tears: A Marine's Story of Combat in Peace and War* (Reno: Wesley Press, 2002), 4.

74 Singlaub, *Hazardous Duty,* 283.

75 Halberstam, *The Coldest Winter,* 478.

76 John Krakauer, *Where Men Win Glory: The Odyssey of Pat Tillman* (New York: Doubleday 2009).

77 "Author Talks of Deceit Where Honor is Taught," *New York Times,* September 17, 2009. It is tragic that this country's so-called military leaders were unfamiliar with one of Napoleon's most compelling statements about duty and honor: "A commander in chief cannot take as an excuse for his mistakes in warfare an order given by his sovereign or minister, when the person giving the order is absent from

Democrats knew that enforcing Truman's doctrine in Southeast Asia was going to hurt them at the polls in 1966: "If the war drags on," Mike Mansfield told Johnson, "the Party will suffer badly."[78] (It's all about the party, isn't it Mike?) And suffer it did, due in no small part to the unflagging efforts of its old nemesis, Richard Nixon, who knew opportunity when he saw it.

Nixon had spent years attempting to rejuvenate the Republican Party and re-claim his role as leader after Goldwater's defeat in 1964, and Johnson's half-hearted attempt to enforce Truman's doctrine provided him with an excellent way to continue "political relations" with Democrats "by other means." "We are losing the war in Vietnam," he said in January 1965. Americans, he said, had to "get out, surrender on the installment plan through neutralization...or...find a way to win."[79] He criticized Johnson for never doing enough, never sending enough troops, never dropping enough bombs, and he condemned Johnson for indicating a willingness to negotiate, calling it "a sign of weakness that has actually prolonged the war."[80]

Nixon's positions kept him well in tune with the electorate, most of whom remained hawks, viewing the war as "part of our worldwide commitment to stop Communism."[81] In February 1965, sixty-seven percent of Americans responding to a Gallup poll favored continued bombing in North Vietnam while only twenty-four percent disapproved.[82] Pollster Lou Harris observed that "the dominant middle-ground opinion is now convinced that intensified military activity, including the bombing of North Vietnam, represents the best chance to bring the Communists to the

---

the field of operations and is imperfectly or wholly unaware of the latest state of affairs. It follows that any commander in chief who undertakes to carry out a plan which he considers defective is at fault; he must put forward his reasons, insist on the plan being changed, and finally tender his resignation rather than be the instrument of his army's downfall." Quoted in Summers, *On Strategy*, 120.

78 Mann, *A Grand Delusion*, 518.

79 Stephen E. Ambrose, *Richard Nixon: The Triumph of a Politician*, 1962-1972 (New York: Simon and Schuster, 1989), 61.

80 Ibid.

81 Dallek, *Flawed Giant*, 340.

82 Mann, *A Grand Delusion*, 531.

negotiating table."[83]

In July 1966, Nixon called for a massive troop increase, from 287,000 to 500,000, and advocated heavier and more frequent air attacks against targets in the North, calling Johnson's bombing campaign a case of "too little and too late."[84] When Johnson, after meeting in September with the leaders of Australia, Korea, New Zealand, the Philippines and Thailand, issued a joint communiqué offering an Allied troop withdrawal from South Vietnam within six months of a North Vietnamese troop withdrawal and an end to logistical support for the Vietcong, Nixon went on the offensive, saying that "the effect of this mutual withdrawal would be to leave the fate of South Vietnam to the Vietcong and the South Vietnamese Army....The South Vietnamese Army could not prevail for any length of time over the Communist guerillas without American advisers, air support, and logistical backing. Communist victory would most certainly be the result of 'mutual withdrawal' if the North Vietnamese continued their own logistical support of the Communist guerillas...."[85] Yet in mid-September, he urged caution when rumors of an increase in American troop levels to 750,000 began circulating, saying that we risked at that level turning South Vietnam into an American dependency, which was "the wrong way to handle it. . . . We must not get in the position of fighting their war for them."[86] (Just what Nixon thought we had been doing since 1961 is anyone's guess.)

Nixon's carefully balanced efforts bore fruit. In November, the Republicans gained forty-seven seats in the House, three in the Senate, eight governorships and 540 seats in state legislatures, leaving Nixon poised to begin his own comeback.[87]

Johnson responded to the 1966 elections by increasing military efforts in Southeast Asia from *every* perspective. In February 1967, he ordered the largest infantry assault of the war, a 25,000 man sweep of the Cambodian border in search of North Vietnam's

---

83 Ibid.

84 Ambrose, *Nixon: The Triumph of a Politician*, 1962-1972, 85, 88.

85 Richard Nixon, *The Memoirs of Richard Nixon* (New York: Grosset & Dunlap, 1978), 274.

86 Ambrose, *Nixon: The Triumph of a Politician*, 1962-1972, 91.

87 Ibid., 100.

Central Office for South Vietnam (COSVN). That same month, US Navy planes began mining rivers in North Vietnam, and downtown Hanoi came under air assault in May. General William Westmoreland asked for 100,000 more troops in July, and Johnson promised to provide them. US troop strength climbed to over 500,000 as Westmoreland began another ground offensive in the South.[88] McNamara, however, had by now concluded that the air war against North Vietnam was pointless. "No amount of bombing," he decided, "can end the war."[89] And with the entire conflict still framed by Kennedy's agreement to enforce Truman's doctrine by hosting an "insurgency" in South Vietnam—a strategy dictated by Ellsberg's Rules—McNamara was correct. Nearly 80,000 North Vietnamese troops entered South Vietnam through Laos to feed the "insurgency" in 1967, some 44,000 during the four-month period from October 1967 through January 1968 alone.[90] For the first time, entire divisions were infiltrated through Laos,[91] and the Saigon regime was simply unable to cope, for obvious reasons.

As Professor George Herring noted more than two decades ago, the "fundamental problem [for American policy] was the absence of security" in South Vietnam.[92] This absence of security, which could not be affected by tactical air strikes in the North, had a devastating effect on American policy designed around "counterinsurgency" in the South—designed, in other words, around pacifying a mythical insurrection rather than stopping a large-scale military invasion. At Washington's behest, the Revolutionary Development Program was created. Imitating the Vietcong, fifty nine-man teams, trained in propaganda and social services, went into the villages to live with the people and, hopefully, build support for the government while subverting the Viet Cong.[93] It was all very nice, of course, and had American policy makers been facing a genuine insurrection by the South Vietnamese citizenry, Revolutionary Development and

---

88 Ibid., 103.
89 Karnow, *Vietnam: A History*, 498.
90 Prados, *The Blood Road*, 238.
91 Prados, *Vietnam: The History of an Unwinnable War*, 194.
92 Herring, *America's Longest War*, 158.
93 Ibid.

similar programs might have been successful. The "absence of security" resulting from the Geneva Accords of 1962 trumped all, however, and over a seven-month period in 1966, more than 3,000 Revolutionary Development personnel were either murdered or kidnapped.[94] Unless and until South Vietnam's territorial integrity was secured—a goal as far beyond Saigon's capabilities in 1967 as was securing South Korea's territorial integrity beyond Seoul's in 1950—"counterinsurgency" in the South was as pointless as tactical bombing in the North.

In August 1967, Johnson was forced to propose a ten percent surcharge on individual and corporate incomes. By October, more Americans than not believed that the war had been a mistake. Yet the overwhelming majority still favored a more aggressive approach.[95] As one housewife told a pollster, "I want to get out, but I don't want to give up."[96] Sensing Johnson's concern, Clark Clifford, the Democratic Party's master strategist who, as much as any single individual, engineered its entry into the world of doctrinaire anti-Communism, swung into action.

Clifford gathered a carefully selected group of senior political, diplomatic and military leaders to review the situation in Southeast Asia, including Dean Acheson, Omar Bradley, George Ball, McGeorge Bundy, Douglas Dillon, Abe Fortas, Averell Harriman, Henry Cabot Lodge and Maxwell Taylor. (Clifford called them the Wise Men.) Carefully orchestrated, upbeat and optimistic briefings were provided, and as expected, the group advised Johnson to stand firm, providing "a strong and unanimous negative" when asked if this country should withdraw.[97] Robert McNamara, however, had reconsidered the entire course of the war and provided Johnson with a confidential memorandum advising him to halt all bombing of North Vietnam and seek "negotiations," stressing that the "American public...does not give the appearance of having the will to persist."[98] Only a select few among the Wise Men were privy to

---

94 Ibid., 159.

95 Karnow, *Vietnam: A History*, 487–488.

96 Ibid., 488.

97 Clifford, *Counsel to the President*, 455.

98 McNamara, *In Retrospect*, 308.

this (Clifford among them), and most of those few rejected McNamara's view out of hand. Johnson, satisfied that "the most experienced leaders in their fields, men who had spent the past two decades dealing—successfully—with the challenges and perils of the Cold War"[99] (if you consider this country's war in Korea and its war in Southeast Asia through the fall of 1967 "successes"), decided to stay the course, the Wise Men having strengthened him at this critical moment.[100] Nothing, however, "strengthened" public opinion, "the essential domino,"[101] which had begun to topple. The Tet Offensive, a direct result of Kennedy's "neutralization" of Laos and his decision to enforce Truman's doctrine by hosting an "insurgency" within South Vietnam, would knock it flat.

The Tet Offensive began on January 30, 1968, the very day Clark Clifford was confirmed as secretary of defense by the Senate, when tens of thousands of North Vietnamese troops launched attacks against most of South Vietnam's major cities and towns. The most brazen of these was the assault on the US Embassy in Saigon, in which a small group of them managed to blast into the embassy compound, killing several Vietnamese and US military personnel before they were killed in the yard outside the building. The most brutal was the seizure of Hue, the old imperial capital, where North Vietnamese troops, after securing the city, sent out death squads that combed the city for the ideologically unacceptable— Communism's *untermenschen*—massacred thousands of them— teachers, bureaucrats, POWs, clergy and foreign medical personnel—and buried them in mass graves.[102]

Meanwhile, North Vietnamese forces surrounded the US Marine base at Khe Sanh in a siege that lasted seventy-seven days. High-profile media personalities, such as Walter Cronkite, engaged in endless, empty-headed blather in which they compared the situation at Khe Sanh to the French disaster at Dien Bien Phu: "The parallels are there for all to see," Cronkite informed a CBS radio

99 Ibid., 309.

100 Clifford, *Counsel to the President*, 455.

101 Leslie Gelb with Richard K. Betts, *The Irony of Vietnam: The System Worked* (Washington, D.C.: The Brookings Institution, 1979), 332.

102 Karnow, *Vietnam: A History*, 530.

audience in early February.[103] In fact, the Marines were never in any danger of being overrun, as anyone with even minimal knowledge and judgment would have known.[104] "The Dien Bien Phu analogy," noted Stanley Karnow, "was preposterous."[105] The American public, however, was simply stunned by the offensive. And Pham Xuan An, once again, was in the middle of everything, having selected targets for Communist forces in Saigon[106] and, most importantly, ensuring that the offensive was represented by Western correspondents as a devastating defeat for US and Allied forces.

> As time went on, the ruins of Hue, the refugees of Saigon, the wounded Marines at Khe Sanh were not only made to represent destruction and human suffering, but they were presented as symbolic evidence of a stunning 'defeat' (variously implied or defined) for allied forces, and hence *proof* of failure of the Administration's conduct of the war in Vietnam.[107]

In reality, however, the offensive was a military disaster for North Vietnam. The South Vietnamese Army was *not* routed, the South Vietnamese people did *not* rise up against their government and tens of thousands of North Vietnamese troops, who formed virtually the entire Southern Communist infrastructure—"the best of a generation of resistance fighters"—were lost "in a deadly rain of fire and steel within the cities."[108] Communist veterans, including senior commanders, have long since admitted both their mistakes and their enormous losses.[109] *American and allied forces had accomplished more in two months than in the previous two years.*

---

103 Ibid., 541.

104 Peter Braestrup, *The Big Story: How the American Press and Television Reported and Interpreted the Crisis of Tet 1968 in Vietnam and Washington* (Novato, California: Presidio Press, 1994), 262–267.

105 Karnow, *Vietnam: A History*, 540.

106 Thomas A. Bass, "The Spy Who Loved Us," the *New Yorker,* May 23, 2005.

107 Braestrup, *The Big Story*, 467 (emphasis in the original).

108 Don Oberdorfer, *Tet* (New York: Avon Books, 1972), 343.

109 Karnow, *Vietnam: A History*, 534, 544. See also Crocker, *Don't Tread on Me*, 371–374.

Yet this marked the beginning of the end of American involvement, and Robert McNamara tells us why: the "credibility gap."[110]

The American people had first been told that American boys would not be sent to fight a war that Asian boys should fight for themselves, which was repeated endlessly to ensure Americans that another Korea was not in the offing. Next, they were told that perhaps 100,000 American boys would be needed. Then they were told 200,000, then 300,000, and on and on until half a million American boys were fighting in Southeast Asia with some 500 being killed weekly. Americans had been told for years that they were winning the war, beating the guerillas, stabilizing the situation, that they had "turned the corner" and that there was "light at the end of the tunnel." They had been told by Johnson, Vice-President Humphrey and General Westmoreland in November of 1967 that all was going well and that we could begin to withdraw in as little as two years.[111] It was the same thing, year after year: "Trust us; we know what we are doing. With a little more time, a little more money and a few more men, it will all be over, and the boys will be coming home." They were told these things by government officials and professional military officers who knew all along that success in Vietnam, given the "neutralization" of Laos and the nature of the "guerilla war" this government had agreed to host in South Vietnam, would require a commitment of 500,000–700,000 men for ten years and knew as well that nowhere near that commitment had been made. *Johnson, his Joint Chiefs and his cabinet officers had lied so much about so many things to so many people so often and for so long that now even when telling the truth, no one believed them.* By the spring of 1968, the Johnson administration's foreign policy in Asia was in shambles even as the kind of smashing military victory for which the Joint Chiefs had long hoped had truly been attained. In the six weeks following the Tet attacks, Johnson's overall public approval dropped from forty-eight to thirty-six percent while approval for his war policies dropped from forty to twenty-six percent.[112]

---

110 McNamara, *In Retrospect*, 169.

111 Braestrup, *The Big Story*, 49–55.

112 Karnow, *Vietnam: A History*, 546.

The death knell of the Johnson administration was sounded in New Hampshire. In March, after word of a requested 200,000-man troop increase had leaked to the media ("the fatal leak," as Clark Clifford called it[113]), Senator Eugene McCarthy challenged Johnson in the New Hampshire primary, making Johnson's conduct of the war the central issue. Johnson won that primary on March 12 by only a seven percent margin (49-42 percent) out of 50,000 cast.[114] Four days later, Bobby Kennedy announced his candidacy for president. Under siege by his own party, Johnson's first reaction was to dig in his heels and defend his conduct of the war. On March 18, he told the National Farmers Union in Minneapolis that "the time has come when we ought to stand up and be counted, when we ought to support our leaders, our government, our men, and our allies until aggression is stopped wherever it had occurred."[115] He called for a "total national effort to win the war."[116] Politics, however, was all that really mattered, and politics, as always, would dictate Johnson's conduct.

With the Wisconsin primary two weeks away, Johnson faced a serious threat from both Bobby Kennedy and Eugene McCarthy. James L. Rowe, a well-connected party insider since the days of the New Deal, sent Johnson a no-nonsense memorandum advising him that Kennedy and McCarthy had become the peace candidates while he remained "the war candidate." "Hardly anyone today is interested in winning the war. Everyone wants to get out, and the only question is how," said Rowe.[117] Johnson telephoned Secretary of Defense Clifford the very next day and said, "I've got to get me a peace proposal."[118]

Lyndon Johnson, who had pushed Truman's doctrine in Southeast Asia against his own judgment until some 30,000 Americans and untold hundreds of thousands of Vietnamese and others were dead to best his Republican opponents at the national

---

113 Clifford, *Counsel to the President*, 499.
114 Dallek, *Flawed Giant*, 527.
115 Karnow, *Vietnam: A History*, 559.
116 Mann, *A Grand Delusion*, 595.
117 Karnow, *Vietnam: A History*, 559.
118 Ibid.

level, would now reverse course to overcome Democratic rivals in a state primary. *The "continuation of political relations" "by other means" had reached truly epic proportions.*

Clark Clifford knew by now that this war was destroying the Democratic Party, and the Party, of course, was what really mattered. So, he assembled the Wise Men again in March of 1968 to advise the president. The briefings this time around were far more candid—and pessimistic—than those given the previous fall. *Clifford, as always, knew just how to produce the desired result.* The Wise Men—including Dean Acheson, Arthur Goldberg, George Ball, McGeorge Bundy, Henry Cabot Lodge, Abe Fortas, Douglas Dillon, Dean Rusk, Walt Rostow and Generals Omar Bradley, Maxwell Taylor, Matthew Ridgway and Earl Wheeler—were told that, under current policy, Americans faced five to ten more years of fighting, exactly as Ridgway had reported to Eisenhower in 1954.[119] Stanley Karnow describes the group as "stupefied" by this, their first honest, no-nonsense assessment.[120] When they met the next day with Lyndon Johnson, Dean Acheson led the discussion. Recognizing political reality when he saw it, he advised Johnson that a military solution was unattainable "*in any time the American people will permit.*"[121] "Acheson did not think the American people would allow the war to go on for more than another year."[122]

Johnson bugged out on March 31, 1968, leaving the appalling mess he had created to others: "I shall not seek, and I will not accept, the nomination of my party for another term as president." He also advised that he was prepared to suspend all bombing of North Vietnam to induce the North Vietnamese to the conference table. On April 3, Hanoi indicated its willingness to begin discussions. On May 3, Johnson announced that American and North Vietnamese representatives would meet in Paris for "conversations" toward a peace process.[123] These "conversations," however, were meaningless from the start. Still remembering their

---

119 Ibid., 562.
120 Ibid.
121 Ibid. (emphasis added).
122 George Ball, *The Past Has Another Pattern*, 409.
123 Mann, *A Grand Delusion*, 604.

1954 betrayal in Geneva, the North Vietnamese intended at this stage to "negotiate" nothing, insisting that the Paris meetings were limited to acquiring an "unconditional cessation of the U.S. bombing raids and all other acts of war so that the talks may start."[124] Consider that carefully: talks would "start" when the United States had effectively abandoned the effort. In June, Robert Kennedy was assassinated, leaving Vice President Hubert Humphrey, who had entered the presidential race after Johnson's withdrawal, as the only viable Democratic candidate. The political landscape had changed dramatically since March 31. But one thing would remain unchanged: "Political relations" between Democrats and Republicans would continue to dictate this country's course of conduct in Southeast Asia.

III

[Vietnam] is our great adventure—and a wonderful one it is![125]

Hubert H. Humphrey
November 1967

There is no way to grasp what a shallow, contemptible and hopelessly dishonest old hack Hubert Humphrey is until you've followed him around for a while on the campaign trail.[126]

Hunter S. Thompson

Hubert Humphrey, whose political persona had run the gamut from Popular Front man to axiomatic anti-Communist, always doubted the wisdom of extending Truman's doctrine to Southeast Asia. As early as February 1965, he expressed serious misgivings about Johnson's decision to launch Rolling Thunder, which was the first sustained air campaign against North Vietnam.[127] Johnson, of course, never accepted dissent, and he was petty and abusive

---

124 Ibid., 605.

125 Mann, *A Grand Delusion*, 567.

126 Hunter S. Thompson, *Fear and Loathing on the Campaign Trail '72* (New York: Warner Books, 1973), 206, 209.

127 Logevall, *Choosing War*, 346–47; Blight, Lang, Welch and Logevall, *Virtual JFK*, 190–191.

towards anyone who challenged him.[128] For expressing his doubts, Humphrey became *persona non grata* to Johnson. For nearly a year, Humphrey was excluded from all high-level meetings involving Vietnam and generally abused by Johnson.[129] A fundamentally weak man, it was all too much for him to bear.[130] So he climbed on board. From early 1966 until his own political fortunes hung in the balance during the fall of 1968, Humphrey would bury his own doubts and become one of the Vietnam War's most ardent and public supporters, *even as his doubts were reaffirmed*. A trip to Vietnam in the fall of 1967 convinced Humphrey that American involvement in Southeast Asia had become worse than he had ever imagined. We were "throwing lives and money down a corrupt rat hole. . . . As of right now, I'm damn sure we're not doing the Vietnamese or ourselves any good. We're murdering civilians by the thousands and our boys are dying in rotten jungles—for what? A corrupt, selfish government that has no feeling and no morality. I'm going to tell Johnson exactly what I think, and I just hope and pray he'll take it like I give it."[131]

Yet when it came time to lie to the American people, Humphrey never hesitated, stating at a US Embassy press conference in Saigon during this same trip that he believed "that Vietnam will be marked as the place where the family of man has gained the time it needed to finally break through to a new era of hope and human development and justice."[132] At a National Security Council meeting on November 8, Humphrey lied again, providing "an upbeat assessment describing progress in the war and Saigon's advance toward political democracy."[133] In the end, Humphrey would regret it bitterly when he was forced to defend, during his run for the presidency, indefensible policies he had publicly endorsed but actually (and deeply) opposed. "Anyone who would repudiate a government and a policy of which he has been a part in order to gain

---

128 Halberstam, *The Best and the Brightest*, 532.

129 Ibid., 533–536; Logevall, *Choosing War*, 356.

130 Halberstam, *The Best and the Brightest*, 535.

131 Dallek, *Flawed Giant*, 496.

132 Mann, *A Grand Delusion*, 567.

133 Dallek, *Flawed Giant*, 497.

votes," he told Oklahoma Democrats in June 1968, "is not the kind of person you can trust to keep the promises he makes in a campaign and deliver on them in a general election."[134] He was, of course, just such a man, as Hunter S. Thompson outlined rather well.

In the meantime, Richard Nixon, as smooth and cynical as ever, played his cards carefully and well. He promised Johnson on July 24, 1968, that he would not advocate a bombing halt or criticize Johnson's Vietnam policies provided Johnson did not soften his stance, calling the bombing of North Vietnam "the one piece of leverage you have left."[135] Johnson, who always believed just what he wanted to believe, was immensely pleased by this. Secretary of Defense Clark Clifford, on the other hand, a cynical, sophisticated political operative who knew full well that Johnson's peace initiative was intended to stop not the war but the Republicans, understood immediately that Nixon's gambit was aimed not at Asian Communists but American Democrats. He was as appalled as Johnson was pleased when he heard this piece of news:

> If I were Nixon, the development that would worry me most would be an announcement that the bombing was being stopped in response to indications that progress was being made in Paris. Nixon's game plan is to offer us his support in return for inflexibility in our negotiating position, and thereby freeze poor Hubert out in the cold. Humphrey wants to change the policy, but the President won't let him say so. I think the President has been so anxious to take a hard and inflexible line that he thinks he actually achieved an advantage by getting Nixon to go along with him. In fact, Nixon has outmaneuvered the President again, digging him in more deeply. Nixon is trying to hang the war so tightly around the Democrats' neck that it can't be

134 Ibid., 610.
135 Langguth, *Our Vietnam*, 514.

loosened.[136]

When the Democratic convention opened in Chicago on August 25, 1968, Johnson's enforcement of Truman's doctrine in Southeast Asia was the dominant issue. Humphrey was determined to unite his party behind him with a platform that would be agreeable to both the liberal and conservative wings, and his proposal was exceedingly modest: He called for the transfer of more responsibility to the South Vietnamese and included a bombing halt that took account of both the risk to American troops and Hanoi's response.[137] Politically, it was perfect for Humphrey, who needed to separate himself somewhat from Johnson on the war while maintaining unity within the Democratic Party. Johnson, however, still firmly in control, considered it a personal affront and would have no part of it: "[T]his plank just undercuts our whole policy, and by God, the Democratic Party ought not to be doing that to me, and you ought not to be doing it. You've been a part of this policy."[138] Humphrey again capitulated to Johnson.

George McGovern, now leading the antiwar wing of the party, fought back intensely. He demanded a withdrawal of 300,000 American troops within sixty days, which was a proposal far more radical than anything previously advocated by any serious political leader.[139] When the platform committee voted by a two-to-one margin to support the Johnson plank, McGovern and Eugene McCarthy took their fight to the convention floor, demanding an immediate end to the bombing and a mutual withdrawal of all US and North Vietnamese forces from South Vietnam. *As far as McGovern was concerned, it was time to consign Truman's doctrine to history's dustbin.* But after hours of acrimonious debate, the full convention adopted the Johnson-Humphrey platform by a vote of 1,567 to 1,048.[140] This, Clark Clifford later

136 Clifford, *Counsel to the President*, 563.
137 Langguth, *Our Vietnam*, 514–515; Karnow, *Vietnam: A History*, 580.
138 Langguth, *Our Vietnam*, 515.
139 Mann, *A Grand Delusion*, 612.
140 Ibid., 613.

noted, "was a disaster for Humphrey."[141]

Disastrous as well for the Democrats was the chaos surrounding the convention. Thousands of antiwar demonstrators had come to Chicago to protest, and bedlam reigned on the streets as they clashed violently with police, who blocked their access to the convention hall and, after "provocation few men could tolerate,"[142] staged a counter-attack. Inside the hall, Senator Abraham Ribicoff railed against what he labeled "Gestapo tactics on the streets of Chicago" while Mayor Richard J. Daley shouted obscenities at him. In the end, Humphrey won the nomination without alienating the president whose support he felt he needed. But he began his campaign more than twenty points behind Nixon in the polls, and no amount of rhetoric could hide the massive rift in the Democratic Party or the chaos within its ranks.

To millions of Americans who had had enough of Truman's doctrine, Humphrey was now Public Enemy Number One, and he received a torrent of abuse. He was called "warmonger" by a woman in Vermont who spat in his face.[143] "Dump the Hump" became the favorite placard of hecklers who appeared everywhere he campaigned. By the third week of September, Humphrey, who still trailed Nixon in the polls by as many as fifteen points, was clearly going nowhere, and political adviser Larry O'Brien told him why. "You are not your own man. Unless you change direction on this Vietnam thing, and become your own man, you're finished."[144] O'Brien told Humphrey that he needed "a clean break [with Johnson] this week or never."[145] The break came on September 30. Humphrey spoke in Salt Lake City, Utah, and outlined his intention to stop the bombing of North Vietnam and negotiate with the Communists while reducing American involvement.[146] The effect on

---

141 Clifford, *Counsel to the President*, 564.

142 Edgar Berman, M.D., *Hubert: The Triumph and Tragedy of the Humphrey I Knew* (New York: G.P. Putnam's Sons, 1979), 187.

143 Langguth, *Our Vietnam*, 520.

144 Mann, *A Grand Delusion*, 618.

145 Ibid.

146 Hubert H. Humphrey, *The Education of a Public Man* (Minneapolis: University of Minnesota Press, 1991), 302, n. 11.

his campaign was both immediate and positive. William Connell, Humphrey's chief of staff, noted that, "Instead of students getting up and raising hell with him, people were cheering him. . . . He got cheering crowds the next day. And the press accepted it, didn't ask any more questions. Vietnam became a non-issue."[147] Humphrey was supported in this turnaround by prominent members of the Johnson administration such as McGeorge Bundy, who told an audience at DePauw University on October 12 that "[t]here is no prospect of military victory against North Vietnam by any level of U.S. military force which is acceptable or desirable."[148] Humphrey gained momentum and began to close the gap, but it was clear that he would need help. The North Vietnamese, exquisitely attuned to the American political system, would do their best to provide it.[149]

In late October, Hanoi made a major concession, advising Averell Harriman in Paris that they would now accept the GVN's participation in four-way peace talks (Washington, Hanoi, Saigon and the NLF) in return for a halt to the bombing.[150] This was just the breakthrough Humphrey needed. Johnson, realizing that the election hung in the balance, accepted the North Vietnamese proposal and announced on October 31 (five days before the election) that he would end all air, naval and artillery bombardment of North Vietnam the very next morning so that talks could begin in Paris on November 6 (the day *after* the election), "at which the representatives of the Government of South Vietnam are free to participate."[151] The South Vietnamese, however, understood the politics of this affair as well as anyone and had no intention of helping Humphrey win the election, believing that Nixon, the quintessential anti-Communist, represented for them a more reliable ally. The Nixon camp, moreover, had contacted South Vietnamese President Thieu through Anna Chennault, the widow of Flying Tiger commander General Claire Chennault, and urged the South Vietnamese to boycott the Paris talks, insisting that the GVN

---

147 Mann, *A Grand Delusion*, 619.

148 Langguth, *Our Vietnam*, 526.

149 Ibid., 519.

150 Mann, *A Grand Delusion*, 622.

151 Langguth, *Our Vietnam*, 527.

would get a better deal with Nixon in the White House.[152] Nixon's interactions with Thieu, of which Lyndon Johnson soon became aware, were likely felonies for which Nixon could have been prosecuted by under the Logan Act, 18 U.S.C. 953.[153] But Johnson became aware through the use of illegal wiretaps and was unwilling to make the information public.[154] Thieu announced his boycott of the talks on November 3, which ended the momentum Humphrey had acquired. Two days later, Richard Nixon was elected President of the United States by less than five hundred thousand out of some seventy million votes cast, and he could never have done it without the unflagging efforts of Lyndon Baines Johnson and hundreds of loyal Democrats in the Congress, who ushered Nixon into the White House over the bodies of well over a million Americans, Koreans, Australians, Vietnamese, Laotians and Cambodians killed primarily to keep him out. Yet Americans, although still getting just what they wanted when they wanted it, were no closer to a satisfactory solution than they were four years earlier, "peace talks" notwithstanding.

For the Tet Offensive had been a military disaster for the North Vietnamese, with losses so great that not even the long-sought coalition government (which the American side was not willing to accept in any event) would help them. So weak were they now in the South that such an arrangement in 1968 or 1969 "would be ruinous."[155] They needed time; they needed years to rebuild, regroup and reinforce their position in South Vietnam, and time is what the Paris talks would provide them. "There were several layers to Hanoi's strategy, but until the balance of power shifted dramatically in their favor, the Politburo had no intention of

---

152 Larry Berman, *No Peace, No Honor*, 32–36; Robert Dallek, *Nixon and Kissinger: Partners in Power* (New York: Harper Collins, 2007), 75–78; Karnow, *Vietnam: A History*, 585–586.

153 "Private correspondence with foreign governments. Any citizen of the United States, wherever he may be, who, without authority of the United States, directly or indirectly commences or carries on any correspondence or intercourse with any foreign government or any officer or agent thereof, with intent to influence the measures or conduct of any foreign government or of any officer or agent thereof, in relation to any disputes or controversies with the United States, or to defeat the measures of the United States, shall be fined under this title or imprisoned not more than three years, or both."

154 Mann, *A Grand Delusion*, 622; Weiner, *Enemies*, 276.

155 Langguth, *Our Vietnam*, 543–544.

negotiating, seeking only to frustrate Lyndon Johnson as peacemaker."[156]

So, from the day the "peace talks" began, Hanoi refused to separate the military and political issues as they had to their eternal regret in 1954. They refused to discuss a cease-fire in any form or a return of American prisoners of war until the United States had facilitated a political settlement that was entirely to their satisfaction. This required: 1) a total and *unconditional* withdrawal of US forces from South Vietnam; and 2) American removal of the existing regime in Saigon, which was to be replaced with a regime satisfactory to Hanoi.[157] Only then would they be willing to *discuss* the ultimate fate of still-unidentified American POWs, for whose return they intended to extort an enormous ransom.[158] These demands were absurd, and they knew it. No American president— *no American president*—would walk away from Southeast Asia without a return of the surviving POWs and some sort of accounting for those who had been killed in captivity. *No one publicly calling for anything less had an ice cube's chance in hell of being elected.* Yet Hanoi would insist upon these terms for the next four years, waiting until October 8, 1972, when they thought the time was right for them, to make their first concession. Time was what they needed, and time is what the "peace talks" would give them.

The American electorate of 1968, on the other hand, had been shaped by more than twenty years of strident, relentless anti-Communist rhetoric that had come from every point on the compass and from virtually every reasonable person in public life. *Everyone* preached anti-Communism, Democrats and Republicans, from Truman and Eisenhower to Kennedy, Johnson, Humphrey, Goldwater and Nixon, from the *New York Times* to the *Chicago Tribune*. Since 1947, to be labeled "soft on Communism"

156 Berman, *No Peace, No Honor*, 22.

157 Henry Kissinger, *The White House Years* (London: Weidenfield and Nicolson and Michael Joseph, 1979), 259; Mann, *A Grand Delusion*, 632; Berman, *No Peace, No Honor*, 43; Dallek, *Nixon and Kissinger*, 106; Karnow, *Vietnam: A History*, 595.

158 Berman, *No Peace, No Honor*, 86–88. See also Bill Hendon and Elizabeth A. Stewart, *An Enormous Crime: The Definitive Account of American POWs Abandoned in Southeast Asia* (New York: St. Martin's Press, 2008), 11–18.

was the kiss of death. So everyone within the Vital Center of this country's political system competed to be hardest on Communism, whenever and wherever it reared its ugly head, leaving Americans convinced, by people who intended to convince them and did their work well—people they trusted—that to give an inch to the Communists, any Communists anywhere, was to give a mile. Americans had sent hundreds of thousands of their sons to Korea, where nearly 40,000 of them had died, to keep the southern half of a tiny, impoverished peninsula out of Communist hands because they believed that its fall would represent a serious blow to their own security. Precious few politicians, pundits or public intellectuals had yet seriously challenged that view. Moreover, Americans knew from their experience in Korea that a negotiated settlement was both desirable and attainable, even if, as in Korea, two more years of fighting and negotiating would be needed. Although they had tired of carrying the burden of combat, Americans still desired an independent, non-Communist South Vietnam. *And virtually no one within the political class, no one with any real power or credibility with the electorate (at least yet), questioned seriously the desirability or attainability of this outcome.*

With few exceptions, this country's political leadership preached that it was time to change tactics, time to "negotiate" from a position of strength, not withdraw unconditionally. Sixteen antiwar senators, including William Fulbright (who was prepared to keep American troops in Vietnam "indefinitely"[159]), George McGovern, Frank Church, Wayne Morse, Gaylord Nelson and Robert Kennedy, said this explicitly in May 1967 when they signed a declaration entitled "A Plea for Realism," in which they informed Hanoi that, although supporting a peaceful settlement, they remained "steadfastly opposed to any unilateral withdrawal of American troops from Vietnam."[160]

Eugene McCarthy, who everyone today seems to think was the Democrats' "end-the-war-now" man, announced his candidacy in the following terms:

---

159 Mann, *A Grand Delusion*, 508.
160 Ibid., 544.

I intend to enter the Democratic presidential primaries in four states, Wisconsin, Oregon, California and Nevada. My decision to challenge the president's position and the administration's position has been strengthened by recent announcements of the administration, the evident intention to escalate and to intensify the war in Vietnam and on the other hand the absence of any positive indication or suggestion for a compromise. . . . I am not for peace at any price, but for an honorable, rational and political solution to this war."[161]

The operative words here are "honorable," "rational" and "political solution," which can be found within the rhetoric of *every* leading Democrat. George McGovern told Americans on August 10, 1968, that "[t]he next president of the United States, if he has the will to do so, can end this war on terms fully acceptable to the American people."[162] Fulbright and Mansfield both favored "negotiations" and international supervision to "guarantee the arrangements made by the belligerents" with an eye toward "a neutral Vietnam."[163] Edmund Muskie pushed for a "negotiated settlement."[164] Hubert Humphrey never implied, not even once, that he would abandon South Vietnam and the American POWs with it, counting upon the innate goodness of their captors for their return. He advocated "de-Americanizing"[165] the war, acquiring a cease fire and negotiating a mutually satisfactory settlement with the North Vietnamese while doing nothing that would, as he stated in September 1968, "weaken the overall allied defense posture" in South Vietnam. And there is no evidence that he secretly intended anything else. Bobby Kennedy, like every other Democratic

161 "The Quiet Man," *New York Times*, December 19, 2005.
162 Mann, *A Grand Delusion*, 610.
163 Ibid., 506.
164 Kissinger, *The White House Years*, 290.
165 Mann, *A Grand Delusion*, 611.

contender, called for "a negotiated 'settlement which will give the Vietcong a chance to participate in the political life of the country.'"[166]

In summary, the American people had reached a consensus by the end of 1968. They opposed unilateral withdrawal, desiring a negotiated settlement that guaranteed their ally's survival and the return of their prisoners, as in Korea. This is what they wanted, it was what they had been led to believe they could attain, and they would vote for the candidate who they felt could deliver this result, as the political class well knew. This was the "moderate," "reasonable" course needed to secure the Vital Center of the electorate, and this was the only course that would win the election, as evidenced by the fact that Wayne Morse and Ernest Gruening— the only two senators who opposed the Gulf of Tonkin Resolution and remained consistent, outspoken advocates of disengagement— were defeated in 1968.

In fact, anyone who thinks that there was a genuine "peace process" underway in Paris in 1968 need only review the state of these absurd "negotiations" at the end of Nixon's first year in office, which had to that point involved little more than proposals for the shape of the table (square, rectangular, "two opposite though not separated arcs of a circle; two opposite and separated semicircles; and two opposite semicircles, with a gap separating them"). "The United States would call the talks two-party; the Communists would call them four-party. The United States called them the Paris Peace Talks, Hanoi the Paris Talks. For months, nobody spoke the same language."[167]

In short, peace was *never* at hand in 1968, and claims to the contrary are just nonsense. Nothing short of total victory— including indeterminate imprisonment for hundreds of unidentified American POWs—would satisfy the North Vietnamese, and the American electorate was absolutely unwilling, at that time, to vote for anyone who would even consider such a thing, as the political class well knew. Johnson's conduct throughout 1968 was

---

166 Steel, *In Love with Night*, 145; Irwin Unger, *LBJ: A Life* (New York: John Wiley & Sons, Inc., 1999), 412.

167 Berman, *No Peace, No Honor*, 59–60.

vintage Johnson. If he actually believed he could achieve a "mutually satisfactory" peace through "negotiations," he was a fool. If not, he was undertaking another in his long line of cynical ploys to manipulate the electorate and nothing more. As for Nixon, if he contributed to Thieu's intransigence, he "sabotaged" nothing but the Democrats' attempt to win an election through manipulation of a disastrous war for which they were responsible. He was no guiltier of continuing "political relations" "by other means" than any other party involved, as noted by Stephen Ambrose: "Insofar that the charges imply that Nixon prevented peace in November 1968, they are false."[168] Johnson/Nixon biographer Robert Dallek agrees. Nixon's machinations, he writes, "made no difference": "[Thieu] didn't need Nixon to tell him that participation in the discussions would improve Humphrey's chances of winning, and Thieu clearly preferred a more hard-line Republican administration to one that was almost certain to make unpalatable concessions to the Communists in a peace settlement."[169]

Nixon's victory, however, would prove to be the war's crucial turning point, initiating both a precipitous collapse of the so-called anti-Communist consensus and a complete change in the political landscape.

With Johnson's resignation and Humphrey's defeat, the Party of Truman was effectively supplanted by the Party of McGovern, which was led by antiwar liberals of the "Greatest Generation," who were untainted by espionage scandals and Popular Front politics and, by 1968, oblivious to the label "soft on Communism." The very thought that a war they had deeply opposed (at least in private)—a war for which they held Richard Nixon and the political order he represented responsible—had destroyed their president and put Nixon, of all people, in the White House, was almost too much for them to bear. So, just as they had used support for the war as a shield, Democrats would now wield opposition to the war like a sword. Like Republicans of the late 1940s, who were genuinely determined to expose and stop Soviet espionage both as an end in itself and as a means of discrediting the New Deal and everything

---

168 Ambrose, *Nixon: The Triumph of a Politician*, 1962-1972, 215–216.
169 Dallek, *Nixon and Kissinger*, 77.

associated with it, antiwar Democrats genuinely desired an end to their war in Southeast Asia. But they also wanted to discredit anti-Communism as a political force and dismantle both Truman's doctrine and the foreign policy it spawned. For the so-called anti-Communist consensus, it bears restatement,[170] was never anything but a chimera, and by 1969, it was a spent force. *Richard Nixon, for all his sophistication and political skill, never understood this.* A "negotiated" settlement that would protect America's client and return American POWs, like the one that ended the war in Korea, was the very last thing antiwar Democrats wanted, as columnist John Roche, a former aide to Lyndon Johnson, outlined on December 18, 1969: "The Democratic Party has...a vested interest in a U.S. catastrophe in Vietnam"; "liberal Democrats," he noted, "are rooting for a U.S. defeat in South Asia . . ."[171] George McGovern, described by Martin Peretz (former editor in chief of the *New Republic*) as "a morally imperious isolationist with fellow-travelling habits,"[172] would eventually admit just that: "I didn't want us to win that war."[173]

Elected by a slender margin, Nixon knew that to withdraw from Vietnam as his opponents would soon demand—unilaterally and without so much as the identity, much less the return, of American POWs—would be political suicide. Tens of millions of those who voted for him because he represented the best chance for an acceptable compromise settlement, particularly his conservative base, would abandon him as a result of what they would undoubtedly view as a gross betrayal. On the other hand, he felt that any real escalation of the conflict would be equally damaging, knowing that millions of swing voters wanted a reduction of the violence and an end to the war. So this country would leave Southeast Asia just as it had entered, one step at a time, with each step measured by its anticipated effect on the electorate as the war

---

170 "[R]estatement of the obvious is the first duty of intelligent men." George Orwell, "Review of *Power: A New Social Analysis* by Bertrand Russell," *The Adelphi*, January 1939, reprinted in George Orwell, *Essays* (New York: Alfred A. Knopf, 2002), 107.
171 Richard Reeves, *President Nixon, Alone in the White House* (New York: Simon & Schuster, 2001), 155 (emphasis added).
172 "Martin Peretz is not sorry. About anything." *New York Times Magazine*, January 24, 2011.
173 Dorland, *Legacy of Discord*, 220.

remained the focus of "political relations" between Democrats and Republicans. And the American people would get exactly what they wanted, when they wanted it, every step of the way, through a political system that functioned as designed but not as intended.

Chapter Six:
Richard Nixon

I

I want to get out, but I don't want to give up.[1]

A Housewife, 1967

The president is aware of what is going on in Southeast Asia. That is not to say that there is anything going on in Southeast Asia.[2]

Ron Ziegler
Presidential Press Secretary
February 1971

You'll forget amidst this stupid sham, we're the ones who got you into 'Nam.

Lyrics to "Sgt. Shriver's Bleeding Heart's Club Band,
National Lampoon,
November 1972

L ike John Kennedy and Lyndon Johnson, Richard Nixon was a member of the so-called Greatest Generation. He had served during World War II in the South Pacific and was elected to Congress, along with John Kennedy and Joseph McCarthy, as a

---

1 Karnow, *Vietnam: A History,* 488.
2 "The Nondenial Denier," *New York Times,* February 16, 2003, sec. 4.

member of the class of 1946. He first came to prominence as a member of the House Un-American Activities Committee, making his name when, with single-minded determination, he succeeded in exposing Alger Hiss as a Soviet agent. In 1950, Nixon ran for the Senate against a liberal Democrat, Helen Gahagan Douglas. Her views on foreign policy were consistent with those of Henry Wallace. She claimed, for example, that the real obstacles to friendship and cooperation between the United States and Soviet Russia were "deliberately created by sinister and dangerous forces in this country who have never given up their allegiance to the ideas of Hitler."[3] She would not support Truman on aid to Greece and Turkey and opposed any form of security checks for federal employees. The American Communist Party newspaper, the *Daily Worker,* praised her as "one of the heroes of the Eightieth Congress."[4] Nixon, of course, capitalized on all this, dubbing her the "pink lady." In fact, Douglas was so far to the left that Nixon received wide, bipartisan support, including a $1,000 contribution from none other than Joseph P. Kennedy.[5] He defeated Douglas handily and entered the Senate, where he remained a hard-driving anti-Communist. Selected by Dwight Eisenhower as his running mate in 1952, Nixon served as vice president under Eisenhower and secured the Republican nomination in 1960.

Like many of his contemporaries, Nixon believed that Communism was the scourge of humanity and was determined to see this country put an end to it. He wanted victory over Communism and felt that coexistence was "another word for creeping surrender."[6] He joined John Kennedy in accusing Truman of "losing" China[7] and supported this country's war in Vietnam from the start. Through all the posturing and all of the politics, one thing was certain: Where anti-Communism was concerned, Nixon appeared to be the true believer Kennedy and Johnson never were:

---

3 Nixon, *The Memoirs of Richard Nixon*, 75–76.

4 Stephen Ambrose, *Nixon: The Education of a Politician*, 1913-1962 (New York: Simon and Schuster, 1987), 217.

5 Nixon, *The Memoirs of Richard Nixon*, 75.

6 Ambrose, *Nixon: The Triumph of a Politician*, 20.

7 Mann, *A Grand Delusion*, 96.

Nixon, for all his political convolutions over his long career, had been consistent on this one: for seventeen years, ever since the Communist victory in China, he had been the most prominent and persistent advocate of taking the offensive against Communism in Asia, Europe, or wherever it threatened freedom. At every critical moment—Korea, 1950-53; Dien Bien Phu, 1954; Hungary and Suez, 1956; Cuba, 1959; the Bay of Pigs, 1961; the Berlin Wall, 1961; the Cuban missile crisis, 1962; Vietnam, 1964-66—Nixon had scorned accommodation and negotiation to urge escalation.[8]

This represented a serious, substantive difference between Nixon and his predecessors. Kennedy was highly intelligent and certainly understood and disliked Communism. But where Southeast Asia was concerned, he was never a true believer,[9] and he viewed the "loss" of South Vietnam almost entirely through the lens of domestic politics. Johnson, for his part, thought very little of the domino theory and also viewed Southeast Asia through the lens of domestic politics.[10] This made Nixon the first genuine anti-Communist to direct American policy in Southeast Asia. Yet he would handle the issue almost exactly as Kennedy and Johnson had handled it before him, as the "continuation of political relations" with his opponents. And the results would speak for themselves.

»» ««

Nixon entered office with no intention of abandoning the Saigon regime after a "decent interval," crafting a long-term strategy involving two possible alternatives:

- A mutual withdrawal of US and North Vietnamese forces from South Vietnam. The United States would

8 Ambrose, *Nixon: The Triumph of a Politician*, 95.
9 Halberstam, *The Best and the Brightest*, 212.
10 Ibid., 355.

continue to provide financial and material support to the GVN along with air support to the ARVN. This agreement would be enforced by the threat of renewed US attacks on the North.

• "Vietnamization." American forces would be withdrawn over a period of several years while the South Vietnamese were built up to the levels necessary to defend the GVN. Without an agreement for mutual withdrawal, however, US forces in considerable numbers (at least 150,000 and probably more) would remain indefinitely.[11]

The first alternative was a pipe dream. North Vietnamese forces, infiltrated into South Vietnam at great difficulty through hundreds of miles of rainforest, were Hanoi's *only* means of carrying on the struggle against a GVN that they had not even come close to toppling during Tet despite the enormous losses they suffered. Withdrawal now would be tantamount to surrender. So "Vietnamization," a program first proposed by Robert McNamara in 1967,[12] was Nixon's only alternative. Its weak points—time and American casualties—were apparent, particularly to the North Vietnamese, who faced two interrelated tasks in January 1969 that would require several years to complete: 1) rebuild and replenish their shattered forces in South Vietnam; and 2) ensure that *all* US forces, which had not been and could never be defeated, were withdrawn from the battlefield. *For as long as the American people remained willing to guarantee South Vietnam's existence, military victory for Hanoi would remain unattainable, just as it remains unattainable to this day in Korea for the North Koreans.* So the Communists embarked on a "peace process" that, coupled with the unending war of attrition sustained and supplied through "neutralized" Laos pursuant to Kennedy's 1962 agreement with Hanoi (which was honored by Johnson and Nixon), would provide them with exactly what they needed. And they formulated their long-term strategy accordingly.

In February 1969, the North Vietnamese began an offensive

11 Ellsberg, *Secrets*, 258–259.
12 Prados, *Vietnam: The History of an Unwinnable War*, 213; 261.

involving artillery and ground attacks on over 500 separate targets, ultimately killing more than 1,100 Americans.[13] Nixon responded with an increase in air attacks that included Cambodia and Laos, from which as many as 300,000 North Vietnamese troops were now staging.[14] The Democrats, of course, lashed out at Nixon, with George McGovern attacking Nixon in a strident speech in the Senate in which he demanded "an immediate end to the killing."[15]

Although Nixon had accurately conveyed North Vietnam's conditions for an end to the fighting (unconditional American withdrawal and replacement of the Saigon regime with no discussion of American POWs until these conditions had been met), George McGovern traveled to Paris in May 1969 to meet with North Vietnamese representatives himself. The North Vietnamese confirmed Nixon's veracity (at least on this issue) but won McGovern over completely, and he returned endorsing Hanoi's every demand.[16] In September 1969, Senator Mike Mansfield appeared on ABC's *Issues and Answers*. "My patience began to wear thin with the start of this tragic, useless, barbaric war, some years ago," he said. *"I have never been in favor of it."*[17] (Of course, this was the same Mike Mansfield who went along with John Kennedy as Kennedy sent 16,000 men into Southeast Asia to secure victory for the Democrats in the 1964 elections and went along with Lyndon Johnson as he fought in Southeast Asia to secure his Great Society.) J. William Fulbright, using language that might well have emanated from Hanoi, now demanded an end to support for "the puppet government in Saigon."[18] McGovern began to vote against military appropriations, which he had refused to do while Johnson was in office, saying then that such conduct would be detrimental to the troops in the field.[19] In October, Hubert "Vietnam-is-our-great-adventure" Humphrey began publicly protesting the war.

13 Langguth, *Our Vietnam*, 544.
14 Kissinger, *The White House Years*, 240.
15 Mann, *A Grand Delusion*, 631–632.
16 Ibid., 632; Berman, *No Peace, No Honor*, 95.
17 Mann, A Grand Delusion, 636–637 (emphasis added).
18 Ibid., 637.
19 Ibid., 640.

Thus, with Nixon's election, the total delegitimizing of America's attempt to enforce Truman's doctrine in Southeast Asia moved from the margins to the Vital Center.

In the spring of 1969, Nixon ordered the secret bombing of North Vietnamese sanctuaries in Cambodia under the code name Operation Menu, which involved wholesale falsification of Air Force records and continued for some fourteen months.[20] Like the Kennedy brothers' $100 million-dollar war on Cuba, these raids were a clear violation of American law. In the meantime, 70,000 more North Vietnamese entered South Vietnam even as American troop withdrawals became inexorable.[21] According to Henry Kissinger, "We had come a long way: We had accepted total withdrawal, we had started out of Vietnam unilaterally, and we had de-escalated our military activities—all without the slightest response."[22] The balance of power in Southeast Asia was shifting exactly as Hanoi had planned.

Kissinger feared that this process would lead to defeat, warning Nixon that "a strategy entirely dependent on Vietnamization would not work."[23] So Nixon and Kissinger prepared a massive military assault on the North Vietnamese that was intended as a killing blow to be undertaken if the Paris talks remained deadlocked. Code named "Duck Hook," the plan included mining North Vietnamese and Cambodian ports, renewing air attacks on North Vietnam, destroying Red River dikes and invading North Vietnam itself across the DMZ.[24] In short, Nixon was going to act in Vietnam more like Truman had acted in Korea. The North Vietnamese were duly warned by Henry Kissinger that, without some progress in Paris, "measures of the greatest consequences" would commence on November 1. Wrote Kissinger: "I refuse to believe that a little fourth-rate power like North Vietnam does not have a breaking

20 Lewis Sorley, *A Better War: The Unexamined Victories and Final Tragedy of America's Last Years in Vietnam* (New York: Harcourt Brace & Company, 1999), 117–120; Reeves, *President Nixon: Alone in the White House*, 70.
21 Prados, *The Blood Road*, 312.
22 Kissinger, *The White House Years*, 283–284.
23 Ibid., 284.
24 Berman, *No Peace, No Honor*, 55.

point."[25]

Meanwhile, antiwar leaders were planning their October 15 Moratorium, which was a major, nationwide antiwar protest that was publicly backed by the North Vietnamese: "We are firmly confident that with the solidarity and bravery of the people of our two countries and with the approval and support of the peace-loving people in the world, the struggle of the Vietnamese People and the U.S. progressive people against U.S. aggression will certainly be crowned with total victory. May your fall offensive succeed splendidly."[26] Nixon had said repeatedly that he would not "allow government policy to be made in the streets" and dismissed the planned Moratorium as irrelevant. "[U]nder no circumstances will I be affected whatever by it."[27] But this was bold talk and nothing more. In fact, Nixon was unnerved by thousands of protestors, many of them middle class and middle aged, around the White House, and he cancelled Duck Hook.[28] For the North Vietnamese, the Moratorium had been a stunning success. For Nixon, it was a disaster of his own making. Having tendered an ultimatum to the North Vietnamese, he backed down under peaceful, domestic pressure that the North Vietnamese had solicited and encouraged, and which would only increase with time. If the North Vietnamese ever questioned their ability to manipulate the fire-breathing anti-Communist Richard Nixon as they had manipulated Lyndon Johnson, John Kennedy and the French before them, those doubts were being erased. They were in almost complete command, and they knew it.

Nixon took to the air on November 3, 1969. Speaking on national television, he outlined his plan to end this country's involvement in the ground war simply and clearly: He would strive for a just peace

through a negotiated settlement if possible or

---

25 Ibid.

26 Nixon, *Memoirs of Richard Nixon*, 402.

27 Ibid., 399; Mann, *A Grand Delusion,* 639.

28 Nixon, *Memoirs of Richard Nixon*, 402–403; Ambrose, *Nixon: The Triumph of a Politician,* 1962-1972, 303–304.

through continued implementation of our plan for Vietnamization if necessary—a plan in which we will withdraw all our forces from Vietnam on a schedule in accordance with our program, as the South Vietnamese become strong enough to defend their own freedom. I have chosen the second course. It is not the easy way. It is the right way.[29]

A Gallup poll taken immediately after the speech gave Nixon a seventy-seven percent approval rating, and soon the public favored Nixon's plan by more than a two-to-one margin.[30] Like Kennedy and Johnson before him, Nixon had gauged the American electorate and was crafting his strategy accordingly. But his long-term goal—successful application of Truman's doctrine in Southeast Asia—would require both time and the cooperation of his political opponents, with the former depending almost entirely on the latter. In the end, he would have neither.

Nothing, you see, would mollify the Democrats now that a Republican occupied the White House. Senators Mike Mansfield, Edward Kennedy, Albert Gore, William Fulbright and George McGovern denounced Nixon's plan, without offering any constructive or realistic alternative. McGovern typically demanded that we just end it now. Others kept insisting that "negotiation" provided the key to this country's salvation, although what any reasonable person believed was to be gained by negotiation is a mystery given the state of the absurd negotiations in Paris at the end of Nixon's first year in office.[31] "Not a meeting [in Paris] would pass in which [Le Duc] Tho did not offer his opinion on U.S. public opinion, dissent or Congressional actions aimed at curtailing the war effort. The antiwar movement was one of his strongest allies, and he knew it."[32]

In the meantime, tens of thousands of North Vietnamese troops continued moving through Laos and into South Vietnam, as noted

---

29 Mann, *A Grand Delusion*, 644.

30 Ibid., 652.

31 Mann, *A Grand Delusion*, 648, 651.

32 Berman, *No Peace, No Honor*, 67.

by C.L. Sulzberger in a remarkably cogent analysis that appeared in the *New York Times* on January 2, 1970, entitled "Foreign Affairs: The Key to All Trouble." "Had U.S. diplomacy plugged the Laotian sewer already being exploited by Communist guerillas ten years ago, the sordid drama that subsequently tortured external and internal U.S. relationships might have been avoided."[33] Noting Soviet responsibility for the offensive through which the North Vietnamese gained control of southeastern Laos in 1961, Sulzberger criticized the Kennedy administration for having accepted "a de facto partition of the worst sort, leaving in Communist hands the entire Ho Chi Minh Trail down which North Vietnamese warriors are still marching." The Kennedy administration's "settlement," wrote Sulzberger, was "precisely what its adversaries wanted."[34]

In April 1970, Nixon conferred with Admiral John S. McCain, Jr., who was commander of United States forces in the Pacific and whose own son, Lieutenant John S. McCain, III, was a prisoner of war in Hanoi. McCain warned Nixon that, according to Ambassador Ellsworth Bunker and General Creighton Abrams, commander of US forces in Vietnam, the Cambodian government was facing certain defeat by the North Vietnamese, who had invaded Cambodia from Laos, occupied large swatches of Cambodian territory, and were now, in conjunction with their Khmer Rouge allies, threatening Cambodia's very existence.[35] McCain warned Nixon that Vietnamization would never succeed if American troops were freely attacked from the Cambodian sanctuaries.[36] Abrams and McCain were not politicians. They were career officers whose advice in this case was both strategically sound and sincerely offered. *If Vietnamization were to succeed, something had to be done.* Although Nixon tells us in his memoirs that he decided to "go

---

33 C.L. Sulzberger, "Foreign Affairs: The Key to All the Trouble," *New York Times*, January 2, 1970.

34 Ibid. It is worth noting here that this is precisely the partition John Kennedy's Assistant Secretary of State for Far Eastern Affairs Rogers Hilsman acknowledged was knowingly created by the 1962 Geneva Accords on Laos. Hilsman, *To Move a Nation*, 154.

35 Karnow, *Vietnam: A History*, 606–607.

36 Reeves, *President Nixon, Alone in the White House*, 192. See also Karnow, *Vietnam: A History*, 607.

for broke,"[37] nothing (as usual) could be further from the truth. Once again, his actions, like those of Johnson and Kennedy before him, would be defined by his fear of his political opposition.

On the evening of April 30, 1970, Nixon went on national television to announce that American and South Vietnamese troops had crossed the Cambodian border to drive North Vietnamese troops from Cambodia and destroy the bases from which they had been launching attacks against American forces. Seeking to control the political backlash from his opponents, however, Nixon severely and publicly limited the incursion, advising that the penetration would be limited to twenty-one miles and was not expected to last beyond June 30. "Our purpose is not to occupy these areas. Once the enemy is driven out of these sanctuaries and once their military supplies are destroyed, we will withdraw."[38] The limitations, dictated by Nixon's fear of his political opponents, ensured that little would be accomplished on the ground. There was far too little time for an effective sweep of the territory involved while the geographical limits, clearly stated with domestic opposition in mind, told the Communists exactly how far to withdraw troops and supply caches to avoid American forces.[39]

On the domestic front, condemnation was ferocious. College campuses erupted. Four students were killed by National Guardsmen at Kent State in Ohio, two more at Jackson State in Mississippi. From the *New York Times* to the halls of Congress, Nixon's opponents charged that he was "extending" and "escalating" the war.[40] Senator Albert Gore called the Cambodian incursion "a sad and bloody day." William Fulbright claimed that this country was "sinking deeper into the morass."[41] Mike Mansfield, who had steadfastly and publicly opposed "unilateral withdrawal" while Johnson was in office, wrote now that "it is about

---

37 Nixon, *The Memoirs of Richard Nixon*, 450.

38 Mann, *A Grand Delusion*, 658.

39 Kissinger, *The White House Years*, 507. See also Langguth, *Our Vietnam*, 568: "Christ! It's so clear," said General Creighton Abrahams. "Don't let them pick up the pieces. Just like the Germans. You give them 36 hours and, goddam it, you've got to start the war all over again."

40 Kissinger, *The White House Years*, 509–517.

41 Mann, *A Grand Delusion*, 659.

time that we wrote off this mistaken war, this tragedy for our country, this penetration into an area in which we have no business and which is not tied to the security of this country."[42] Now that it was "Nixon's war,"[43] Mansfield declared that "he was prepared to give 'most serious consideration to a termination date after which no more funds will be appropriated for military operations in Indochina.'"[44]

In the Senate, John Cooper and Frank Church sponsored a bill to cut off funds for operations in Cambodia after June 20. A modified version of this bill would pass the Senate on June 30, which was the day the last troops were withdrawn. Another bill, authored by George McGovern and Mark Hatfield, went even further and included a provision that would end all funding for operations in Indochina six months thereafter. This battle would continue until the end of the year. McGovern-Hatfield as eventually amended would mandate an end to US involvement in Southeast Asia by December 31, 1971. The bill was defeated in the Senate by a vote of 55-39 as McGovern assailed the Senate itself, saying "this chamber reeks of blood."[45] The handwriting, however, was on the wall, as noted in *Time:* "The willingness of more than a third of the Senators to take the unprecedented step of handing the President a deadline for terminating a shooting war was a clear warning that senatorial patience was precariously thin."[46] The North Vietnamese, of course, knew this as well as anyone. "Throughout the negotiations, Hanoi would demonstrate a good grasp of American democratic politics. Throughout 1970, North Vietnamese followed the antiwar movement closely. They brought it up again

42 Ibid.

43 Brinkley, *Tour of Duty: John Kerry and the Vietnam War*, 359. Referring to the Truman Doctrine's Southeast Asian campaign as "Nixon's War" remains ever popular with the Left. See Paul Begala, "Anti-War Imagery and the Iconography of Hate," TPM Café, August 17, 2005. http://tpmcafe.talkingpointsmemo.com/2005/08/17antiwar_imagery_and_the_icon/#more, accessed fall 2005; "John Kerry v. Oliver North," Accuracy in Media, January 29, 2004. http://www.aim.org/media-monitor/john-kerry-versus-oliver-north/, accessed May 10, 2012.

44 Mann, *A Grand Delusion*, 659.

45 Ibid., 669–670.

46 Ibid., 670.

and again to a frustrated Kissinger"[47] as 103,000 more North Vietnamese troops entered South Vietnam through Laos.[48] *There was absolutely no reason for them to negotiate anything, not even a return of American POWs.*

Nixon, in the meantime, continued constructing his policy in Southeast Asia with an eye more toward political opponents in Washington than Communists in Southeast Asia. When Secretary of Defense Melvin Laird warned Nixon that the Republican Party's interest in the 1970 mid-term elections mandated troop withdrawals that were far in excess of anything Nixon considered prudent (60,000 by the end of 1970; 90,000 more by the end of 1971), Nixon acquiesced.[49] He then announced a new proposal to end the war in October. He dropped his heretofore "non-negotiable" demand for North Vietnamese withdrawal from South Vietnam and proposed for the first time a standstill cease-fire throughout Southeast Asia. This represented another unilateral concession with staggering implications, as Henry Kissinger acknowledged:

> The standstill cease-fire was put forward as being provisional. If achieved, it was to be followed by a diplomatic conference to settle the war, at which we would presumably continue to put forward the demand for the withdrawal of North Vietnamese forces. If rebuffed, we could then maintain a residual force in South Vietnam. *But nobody could take such a prospect seriously.* Even with a war going on, Congressional pressures for the unilateral withdrawal of our forces were mounting; not a month passed without some sort of legislated deadline being before one of the Houses of Congress. In such an atmosphere, it was inconceivable that Congress would permit us to keep troops in Indochina when a cease-fire had already been

---

47 Berman, *No Peace, No Honor*, 79.

48 Prados, *Vietnam: The History of an Unwinnable War*, 329.

49 Kissinger, *The White House Years*, 481–482.

achieved, no matter what Hanoi did about its forces. *The decision to propose a standstill cease-fire in 1970 thus implied the solution of 1972. That North Vietnamese forces would remain in the South was implicit in the standstill proposal; no negotiation would be able to remove them if we had not been able to expel them by force of arms.*[50]

At the end of Nixon's first two years in office, American policy in Southeast Asia was in shambles, just as it had been at the start. This country was retreating irreversibly, both militarily and diplomatically, while receiving nothing in return—not so much as a list identifying American POWs. Like Kennedy and Johnson before him, Nixon knew that his policy in Southeast Asia was ill-advised. Like Kennedy and Johnson before him, he was determined to hold the Vital Center, so his opponents controlled much of his policy. Even the trite little metaphors were similar. John Kennedy once said that sending troops into Vietnam would be "like taking a drink. The effect wears off and you have to take another."[51] Kissinger, on the other hand, said that troop withdrawals "would become like 'salted peanuts' to the American public; the more troops we withdrew, the more would be expected..."[52] Like Kennedy and Johnson before him, Nixon had the advice of brilliant intellectuals who lent substance and credibility to political decisions undertaken for political purposes, as White House Chief of Staff H. R. Haldeman recorded in his diary on December 15, 1970:

> [Kissinger] came in and the discussion covered some of the general thinking about Vietnam and [Nixon's] big peace plan for next year, which [Kissinger] later told me he does not favor. He thinks that any pullout next year would be a serious mistake because the adverse reaction to it could set in well before the '72 elections. He favors, instead, a continued winding

---

50 Ibid., 974 (emphasis added).

51 Halberstam, *The Best and the Brightest*, 175.

52 Kissinger, *The White House Years*, 284.

down and then a pullout right at the fall of '72 so that
if any bad results follow they will be too late to affect
the election. It seems to make sense.[53]

Nixon knew that Kissinger was right. "Whether or not we
survive is going to depend on whether we hold public opinion," he
said.[54] So the American political system was functioning just as it
had functioned all along, with Nixon a mirror image of his
predecessors. Assuming he genuinely believed that this country
could and should secure a non-Communist South Vietnam as it had
secured a non-Communist South Korea, he was withdrawing in his
own interests but contrary to the country's. Assuming, on the other
hand, that he believed the war was lost yet maintained the
commitment to secure his reelection in 1972, he was continuing the
war in his own interests but not the country's. In either case, Nixon
was doing *exactly* what Kennedy and Johnson had done before him,
and he always managed to convince himself that he would succeed
if he could just kick the can a bit further down the road. In so doing,
he badly misjudged his opponents, both foreign and domestic, but
he managed to hold the Vital Center. Americans were not yet ready
to let go of Truman's doctrine or the war in Southeast Asia that came
with it.

>>» «<

Nixon began 1971 by approving a South Vietnamese offensive
into Laos to cut the Ho Chi Minh Trail, code named Lam Son 719.
After nearly a decade of honoring Kennedy's "neutralization"
accord—an accord the North Vietnamese had not honored for a
single day—an American president was finally going to undertake
an operation fundamental to enforcing Truman's doctrine in
Southeast Asia, an operation so basic to America's stated purpose
that any competent ROTC cadet would have recommended it in
1961. Begun on February 8, the operation was, from start to finish,
a disaster, both on the field and in the Congress. American planners
estimated that four seasoned divisions—nearly 60,000 men—

---

53 Maureen Dowd, "Don't Pass the Salted Peanuts, Henry," *New York Times*, October 4, 2006.
54 Dallek, *Nixon and Kissinger: Partners in Power*, 263.

would be required for an operation such as this. Yet only twenty thousand South Vietnamese troops were used in the assault. To make matters worse, President Thieu ordered his commanders to end the operation when they had sustained 3,000 casualties. They duly complied, stalling their offensive while only halfway to the objective. By April, the South Vietnamese had lost half their men and were all but routed while US forces supporting the operation suffered 168 helicopters shot down and over 600 more damaged. Although Nixon tried to portray this operation as a success and complained about negative news coverage from biased reporters, reality was inescapable. Even Nixon's long-standing political allies began to break ranks. Republican Senator Hugh Scott warned Defense Secretary Laird that he was losing his ability to defeat the antiwar amendments being pushed by the doves. "The hawks are all ex-hawks. . . . We just can't hold the line any longer on numbers. . . . There's a feeling that the Senate ought to tell the President that we should get the hell out of the war."[55] "I come from the most hawkish state in the union," said Republican Senator Ted Stevens. "I ran in '70 as a hawk. I can't do it again in '72."[56] (It's all about you, isn't it Ted.)

Yet antiwar Democrats (and a few Republicans) remained frustrated. No matter what they did, no matter how determined their efforts or how strident their language, it seemed as though the American people would not let go of South Vietnam, and Nixon continued the Vietnamization process to widespread public support. So, in the spring of 1971, they shifted their focus from the war to the warriors, bringing a carefully constructed war crimes industry into the mainstream of public dialogue.[57]

---

55 Mann, *A Grand Delusion*, 678.

56 Ibid. Although senators are elected for six-year terms, Stevens was appointed by Alaska Governor Wally Hickel in December 1968 after Alaska Senator Bob Bartlett died. Stevens then won a special election to complete Bartlett's term in 1970 and won the seat in his own right in 1972.

57 The phrase "war crimes industry" was coined by Guenter Lewy. See Lewy, *America in Vietnam*, 311.

II

There is the related question about the special qualities of the group of men I have worked with. Almost all of them belong to the minority of Vietnam veterans who emerge with an articulable antiwar position . . . I made no attempt to gather data from a "representative" group of veterans.[58]

Robert Jay Lifton

The intellectual godfather of the war crimes industry was psychiatrist Robert Jay Lifton. A strident left-wing ideologue, Lifton theorized that the Vietnam War would create "a very large pool of young, embittered veterans. . . . Some are likely to seek continuing outlets for a pattern of violence to which they have become habituated, whether by indulging in antisocial or criminal behavior—almost in the fashion of mercenaries—offering their services to the highest bidder. . . . Disturbances may not be evident for five or eight or ten years." [59] It was clear at the outset, however, that Lifton's claims were political and not empirical in nature. His hypothesis was based entirely on "the minority of Vietnam veterans who emerge with an articulate antiwar position..."[60] Lifton had found the mother lode. Antiwar veterans, particularly those willing to, in Lifton's words, "publicly proclaim the endless series of criminal acts they have witnessed or participated in,"[61] no matter how small their numbers or unverifiable their claims, would soon wield enormous power and influence in politics and popular culture as everyone on the Left, from student radicals to United States Senators, rushed to embrace them. And as the war crimes industry made its transition from the margins to the mainstream, Lifton's focus and methodology became standard.

The first complete book dedicated to the war crimes industry was Mark Lane's *Conversations with Americans*. Published in

---

58 Robert Jay Lifton, *Home from the War, Vietnam Veterans: Neither Victims nor Executioners* (New York: Simon & Schuster, 1973), 19.

59 Burkett and Whitley, *Stolen Valor*, 143.

60 Lifton, *Home from the War*, 19.

61 Ibid., 31.

1970, it was based entirely on Lifton's methodology and advertised in the following terms: "A generation is being brutalized. Thirty-two Vietnam veterans give first-hand accounts of what is happening to our under 30s as they are trained in savagery, sadism, torture, terrorism and murder."[62] The book provided just what it promised: 247 pages of interviews with "Vietnam veterans" intended to demonstrate that "the Army and the Marine Corps consciously operate on a moral par with Hitler's SS."[63] It was all very powerful and very impressive, but Mark Lane was careless. Many of the stories he recounted were plainly absurd. For example, one antiwar veteran reported that his entire battalion had raped a Vietnamese girl (impossible when one considers that, as James Reston, Jr., noted in his review of the book, a battalion has nearly 1,000 men). Other claims were also easy to debunk, like one alleged veteran's claim that his father, who had been a senior officer in Hitler's SS during World War II, was the commanding officer of the 11th Armored Cavalry Regiment in Vietnam. As with most of Lane's claims, this was easy to check through public records. Neil Sheehan did just that, and was able to determine, time after time, that the men Lane interviewed were lying. They were clearly not who they said they were or had never been where they claimed to have been. Neither Mark Lane nor the book's publisher made any attempt to verify any of the stories recounted although the records were easily available. "It's not relevant," said Lane. Sheehan blasted him: "This kind of reasoning," wrote Sheehan, "amounts to a new McCarthyism, this time from the left. Any accusation, any innuendo, any rumor, is repeated and published as truth. The accused, whether an institution or an individual, has no right to reply because whatever the accused says will *ipso facto* be a lie."[64] Sheehan warned that "those on the left who cherish their integrity might do well to take a careful look at Mark Lane's methods."[65] By and large, "those on the left" would heed this warning, but only the

---

62 Quoted in Neil Sheehan's review of *Conversations with Americans, New York Times Book Review*, December 27, 1970.

63 Ibid.

64 Ibid.

65 Ibid.

methods would change. The message remained the same.

Shortly after Sheehan's scathing review of *Conversations with Americans,* Vietnam Veterans Against the War ("VVAW") made its first major appearance and would soon become a major force in antiwar activity for reasons that are easy to understand. The antiwar Left had done so much to alienate ordinary Americans by 1969 that many historians, like Adam Garfinkle, author of *Telltale Hearts,* have concluded that the antiwar movement actually helped prolong the war through the image it conveyed.[66] VVAW, complete with uniforms, wounds and medals to discard, helped blur if not eliminate for many the clear lines between those who served and sacrificed and antisocial radicals for whom the war represented more opportunity than tragedy. VVAW served to provide both the movement and the war crimes industry with respectability.

Antiwar activists were quick to grasp this, and VVAW was soon the darling of the movement, expanding from some 600 members in April 1970 to 8,000 in the spring of 1971. But VVAW never represented more than a tiny fraction of those who served in Southeast Asia. According to VVAW's own figures, membership increased from 8,000 in the spring of 1971 (0.00266% of those who served) to some 50,000 (.016%) by the summer of 1972 *only after membership was opened to non-veterans.*[67] Senator James Webb, while working as counsel to the House Veterans Committee, asked the legislative director of Vietnam Veterans Against the War if he could document that VVAW had more than 7,000 actual Vietnam veterans in it, and "he told me that he could not."[68]

Among VVAW leadership, Marx, Mao and revolution were very popular, a fact that even those sympathetic to VVAW accept. The Maoist Revolutionary Union, a "far left radical group, formed in California from both the Communist Party USA and SDS [Students for a Democratic Society]," had many of its members in "important

66 Garfinkle, *Telltale Hearts*, 1-2.

67 Richard Stacewicz, ed., *Winter Soldiers, An Oral History of the Vietnam Veterans against the War* (New York: Twayne Publishers, 1997), 430.

68 "Vietnam and Patriotism," National Public Radio interview with David Halberstam and James Webb, September 1, 2004. http://www.npr.org/templates/story/story.php?storyId=3883670, accessed May 10, 2012.

leadership positions in VVAW."[69] And dishonesty within VVAW's ranks was endemic.

Marxist radical Al Hubbard was one of VVAW's national leaders who appeared with John Kerry on *Meet the Press* in the spring of 1971 to denounce the war. He claimed to be an ex-captain who had been wounded and decorated while serving in Vietnam. According to the Air Force, however, "*there is no record of any service in Vietnam* [emphasis in the original], but since he was an aircrew member he could have been in Vietnam during brief periods during cargo loading, unloading operations, or for crew rest purposes. His highest grade held was staff sergeant E-5." Hubbard was a complete fraud.[70] Michael Harbert, another of VVAW's national leaders, was also a phony. He claimed that he had been a sergeant who had flown forty-seven combat missions over Vietnam.[71] Harbert's official records, however, show no Vietnam service. He was stationed at McClellan Air Force Base in California. A stay in Taiwan is as close as he ever got to the war zone. Another of VVAW's national leaders, Joe Urgo, was a self-proclaimed "revolutionary Communist"[72] who traveled to Hanoi on behalf of VVAW and there declared his allegiance to the Communist cause. "I will work with them on any level they want."[73] If you had served in Vietnam, he said in 1994, "You were nothing more than a murderer, a rapist, a baby killer."[74]

VVAW did more to legitimize the war crimes industry than any other group through its famous "Winter Soldier" hearings. Bankrolled by, among others, Jane Fonda and presented in Detroit with the advice and guidance of Mark Lane, these "hearings" featured scores of people who claimed to be veterans and told ghastly stories of rape, torture and murder that, according to them, represented the daily conduct of Americans in Vietnam.[75] But having learned well from Neil Sheehan's scathing review of Lane's

69 Gerald Nicosia, *Home to War* (New York: Crown Publishers, 2001), 227.
70 Burkett and Whitley, *Stolen Valor*, 136–137.
71 Ibid., 137.
72 Stacewicz, *Winter Soldiers*, 412.
73 Wells, *The War Within*, 525; Stacewicz, *Winter Soldiers* 290.
74 Wells, *The War Within*, 454.
75 Nicosia, *Home to War*, 73–93.

Conversations with Americans, Fonda, Lane and VVAW took steps to avoid the pitfalls inherent in this endeavor. Like Joseph McCarthy, they vetted their witnesses very carefully ahead of time to ensure that the stories they presented would be both believable and completely unverifiable. Those who "testified," moreover, refused to cooperate in any way with news organizations or military investigators, saying that non-cooperation had been mandated by the VVAW leadership. Those in leadership positions have confirmed this.[76] To this day, there is no record that any claim made by an alleged veteran in Detroit has been verified. Mainstream news organizations largely ignored VVAW until John Kerry, whose hands were clean, whose credentials were unimpeachable and whose political connections were as solid as his ambitions, entered to launder these accusations through the United States Senate.

After returning from an unusually short tour of duty in Vietnam (four months in country, three months in a combat unit), Kerry, running as a relative moderate in 1970, sought the Democratic nomination for a congressional seat from Massachusetts and was defeated. Realizing immediately that moderation was not in his interest, Kerry changed his tone completely, joined VVAW and began launching vitriolic attacks on this country and its veterans at every opportunity. During an antiwar rally on Wall Street, Kerry stated that, "Guilty as Lieutenant Calley may have been of the actual act of murder, the verdict does not single out the real criminal ... the United States of America."[77] Returning to his "Lt. Calley-R-Us" theme on *Meet the Press*, Kerry accused this country of "genocide" and declared that "thousands" of his fellow veterans committed war crimes that, according to Kerry, were "ordered as a matter of written

76 Stacewicz, *Winter Soldiers*, 240. See also Burkett and Whitley, *Stolen Valor*, 133; Deborah Nelson, *The War Behind Me: Vietnam Veterans Confront the Truth About U.S. War Crimes* (New York: Basic Books, 2008). In *The War Behind Me*, Appendix A, lists forty-two allegations made during VVAW's Winter Soldier Investigation, and in twenty-two of these, the complainant "declined to cooperate" while in four other cases, the complainant could not be located. Nelson also acknowledged (page 146) that the VVAW leadership insisted on non-cooperation.

77 Tom Bowman, "Kerry went from soldier to anti-war protester," *Baltimore Sun*, February 14, 2004, Telegraph Section, 1A. Lt. William Calley was convicted of murder by a US Army court martial in March 1971 for his role in the deliberate massacre of more than 300 Vietnamese civilians at My Lai in March 1968.

established policy by the government of the United States from the top down." As for officers in the chains of command and members of their staffs, "I think these men, by the letter of the law, the same letter of the law that tried Lieutenant Calley, are war criminals."[78] His big chance came in April 1971, when he appeared as a spokesman for VVAW before a senate committee chaired by William Fulbright. It was the opportunity of a lifetime, and Kerry played it for all it was worth.

Wearing combat decorations to emphasize both his character and his unique personal experience, Kerry provided a picture of Vietnam service that was consistent with the picture provided by Joe "murderer-rapist-baby killer" Urgo. Kerry solemnly told Americans that those who served in Vietnam had "personally raped, cut off ears, cut off heads, taped wires from portable telephones to human genitals and turned up the power, cut off limbs, blown up bodies, randomly shot at civilians, razed villages in a fashion reminiscent of Genghis Kahn, shot cattle and dogs for fun, poisoned food stocks, and generally ravaged the countryside of South Vietnam in addition to the normal range of war and the normal and very particular ravaging which is done by the applied bombing power of this country."[79] "These were not isolated incidents," he said, "but crimes committed on a day-to-day basis with the full awareness of officers at all levels of command."[80] Loyally parroting Robert Jay Lifton, Kerry warned Americans that in these "millions of men...taught to deal and trade in violence," this country had "created a monster."[81]

An indictment more damning you will never find. But a careful reading of Kerry's statement reveals that it was all form and no substance. Kerry never claimed personal knowledge of a single war crime. He provided no names, dates, places or unit identifications that would allow anything he said to be verified, and none of the

78 "Vietnam 30 Years Later: What John Kerry Said on Meet the Press," History News Network, George Mason University, February 13, 2004. http://hnn.us/articles/3552.html, accessed May 10, 2012.

79 Congressional Record (92nd Congress, 1st Session) for Thursday, April 22, 1971, page 180.

80 Ibid., 179.

81 Ibid., 180

elected officials he was addressing pressed him for details. For Kerry, as they all knew, was on very thin ice. If his statements were true, if rape, torture and murder were daily activities in the field, Kerry, whose special credibility was based on his status as a front-line fighting man, must have participated in or at least witnessed scores of such incidents. But sustaining his allegations through personal testimony would require implicating himself in either war crimes or cover-up. He was, after all, an officer, and he was at least obligated to stop and report such conduct. The records would be available. On the other hand, if Kerry personally witnessed no such thing, he would have been exposed as the posturing phony and liar that he was. It would have required about three minutes of cross-examination to uncover the truth, one way or the other.

The next step, had there been any honest, responsible public officials available, would have been to issue subpoenas on those who testified in Detroit. Each one of them could have been brought before Congress under oath to repeat their allegations and provide dates, places and the names of others who could be subpoenaed to provide corroboration. Immunity from prosecution would have undoubtedly been required and should have been provided liberally. American personnel committing war crimes "on a day-to-day basis with the full awareness of the officers at all levels of command," acting, in other words, like the Waffen SS or the Japanese at the Rape of Nanking, should be identified and prosecuted. But this was hyper-partisan political theatre—"McCarthyism" at its very best—not congressional fact-finding. None of the politicians who engineered this country's entry into Southeast Asia—such as J. William Fulbright, who rammed the Gulf of Tonkin Resolution through Congress for Johnson and later presided during Kerry's testimony—were going to conduct a real interrogation of the Left's newest fair-haired boy. So, an entire generation of veterans was demonized beyond measure of retribution so that antiwar politicians, most all of them liberals, could fabricate a case for withdrawal as they had previously fabricated the case for intervention. Meanwhile, Kerry moved into the national spotlight he craved. "By the time he was done with that appearance before the committee, those guys were all drooling over him to be a candidate. The moment he finished talking, there wasn't the slightest doubt about it. It was a real star turn..."[82] "I have a very high personal regard for [John Kerry]," said Senator Claiborne Pell, "and hope before his life ends he will be a colleague of ours in this body."[83]

With Democrats having now embraced this country's fringe radicals and *all* of the loathsome tactics historically attributable to Joseph McCarthy, it was only natural for George McGovern to reprise Nixon's machinations of 1968 in an effort to enhance his own election prospects by undermining Nixon as Nixon had allegedly undermined Johnson.

III

I don't know why I am negotiating with you. I have just spent six hours with Senator McGovern. Your anti-war movement will force you to give me what I want.[84]

Le Duc Tho

George McGovern wanted to be President of the United States, and he knew he would be strengthened politically if he made some progress with the POW issue.[85] On September 11, 1971, McGovern traveled to Paris for a meeting with Hanoi's "negotiators," who as yet had refused even to release a list identifying Americans who were being held as POWs without an unconditional US withdrawal and an overthrow of the Saigon government.[86] He met the same brick wall that American negotiators had faced for three long years. He was told repeatedly (as he had been told more than two years earlier) that there could be no separation of the military and political issues and that, even if the US would set a terminal date for

82 "Storied Past, Golden Resume, But Mixed Reviews for Kerry," *New York Times*, November 30, 2003.

83 Congressional Record (92nd Congress, 1st Session) for Thursday, April 22, 1971, page 191.

84 Berman, *No Peace, No Honor*, 101.

85 Ibid., 94.

86 These meetings, like Nixon's 1968 election-eve contact with the Thieu regime, were likely violations of the Logan Act, which seems to have been observed throughout the Vietnam War only in its breach.

unilateral withdrawal, Hanoi would only be willing to discuss, not identify or return, American prisoners.[87] Every attempt to reason with Hanoi's representatives resulted in endless doubletalk and criticism of American involvement in Southeast Asia.[88] The Communists then rubbed McGovern in Kissinger's face at every opportunity: "I don't know why I am negotiating with you," Le Duc Tho told Kissinger. "I have just spent six hours with Senator McGovern. Your anti-war movement will force you to give me what I want."[89] George McGovern and his antiwar colleagues intended to undermine Nixon at every turn, and they were succeeding beyond their dreams. McGovern, of course, returned from Paris and blamed everything on Nixon, concluding "that if President Nixon would set a date of December 31, 1971 as the terminal date for a withdrawal of all U.S. military forces and operations in Vietnam, then simultaneously there would be a release of U.S. prisoners."[90] If McGovern actually believed any of this, he was a fool.

Richard Nixon's next gambit occurred on January 25, 1972. On national television, Nixon revealed the secret talks that Kissinger had been conducting with the North Vietnamese in Paris and informed the American people that he had offered a peace initiative that included yet another major concession to Hanoi:

1. A cease fire.
2. A fixed withdrawal date for US and other foreign forces (not including North Vietnamese) from South Vietnam.
3. A return of POWs.
4. Elections five months after a settlement that would be supervised by a commission that would include Communists.
5. The resignation of President Thieu (who would then be entitled to run again for office) one month before

---

87 Berman, *No Peace, No Honor*, 86–87.

88 Ibid., 93.

89 Ibid., 101. By any objective measure, McGovern's conduct in undermining Nixon was just as foul and unlawful as Nixon's in undermining Johnson and Humphrey.

90 Ibid., 95.

the elections.

As with everything else that had been done in Southeast Asia for ten long years through three administrations, this initiative was aimed at the president's domestic opposition. Neither Nixon nor Kissinger actually believed that Hanoi would accept the proposal. But election year politics demanded it, and concessions, once made, could never be retracted. *Nixon had now agreed to help Hanoi replace Thieu.* Nixon's critics, from the *New York Times* to antiwar Democrats, praised the initiative. Senator Cooper, who had become an outspoken opponent of the war, called the plan "fair and just." Frank Church, a McGovern ally and one of the most strident critics of the war, praised Nixon's offer as "a starting point for serious negotiations" (acknowledging thereby that no "serious" negotiations had as yet taken place despite nearly four years of unilateral American concessions).[91] It was "a political masterstroke" but little else.[92] As expected, Hanoi rejected the proposal, sent nearly 150,000 more men into South Vietnam through Laos from January 1971 through March 1972 and launched a major offensive that began Easter weekend. Having been in Vietnam for slightly more than a month when some of the first shots were fired (at me, among others) near Firebase Sarge west of Quang Tri, I remember it well.

This offensive involved nearly 200,000 men spearheaded by armored formations equipped with Soviet-built main battle tanks. It represented North Vietnam's calculated response to four years of declining American resolve and end-the-war amendments that littered both houses of Congress and gained support every time they were revived or rewritten. Particularly important in Hanoi's mind was Nixon's October 1970 offer of a cease fire in place. With American combat troops all but gone, never to return, and a South Vietnamese Army of questionable reliability, the balance of forces, so adverse to them in 1969, now favored Hanoi. Hanoi's play for time had paid great dividends, and it was now time to collect. This massive escalation was intended to conquer as much South

---

91 Mann, *A Grand Delusion*, 693–694.
92 Ibid., 693.

Vietnamese territory as possible in preparation for the inevitable cease-fire in place, and Hanoi counted upon its allies in the United States Congress to support its move unconditionally when Nixon responded. As events would prove, their trust was not misplaced.

Nixon reacted to the invasion by unleashing massive air assaults on North Vietnamese forces and mining their harbors, including Haiphong. The North Vietnamese rejected all attempts by Kissinger to negotiate as Nixon's opponents in Congress attacked Nixon relentlessly. Mansfield, of course, accused Nixon (as always) of "expanding" the war. McGovern demanded immediate congressional action to force an American withdrawal. Fulbright attacked Nixon's recklessness while praising North Vietnam's backers, the Soviets, for their "restraint" in not canceling the summit scheduled for May.[93] In the Foreign Relations Committee, legislation was initiated to end American involvement in the war by August 31, 1972. As Senator Mansfield put it, "There are no preconditions. There are no ifs, ands or buts. Every last serviceman on the ground in Vietnam will be out by August 31, whether he plays a combat role or a supporting role."[94] These initiatives were eventually defeated, but just barely as antiwar forces grew stronger every day. On the political front, the North Vietnamese offensive was proving successful. Militarily, however, things were not going so well.

Nixon's massive aerial assault on North Vietnamese forces, infrastructure and supply lines took a fearsome toll. More than 100,000 tons of ordnance had been dropped by early June, and Hanoi's offensive stalled.[95] It was "the most successful use of airpower during the Vietnam War."[96] North Vietnam lost tens of thousands of men and returned to the conference table, while Nixon had again secured the Vital Center. Opinion polls revealed that Americans supported the bombing by considerable margins.[97] It was again clear that the American people were not yet ready to

---

93 Ibid., 701.

94 Ibid., 702.

95 Ibid., 702–703.

96 Berman, *No Peace, No Honor*, 132. See also Mann, *A Grand Delusion*, 702.

97 Berman, *No Peace, No Honor*, 133.

abandon South Vietnam. But the American electorate's real test would come in the fall, when they would choose between two men within the American political establishment whose worldviews were as diametrically opposed as any two men who held political power at the national level, Richard Nixon and George McGovern.

Like Richard Nixon, George McGovern was a true believer. But he was a true believer from the opposite end of the political and ideological spectrum. He was, long before the term had gained widespread use, a genuine anti-anti-Communist. From his earliest days in politics, he was a man of the Left, and much farther left then he would ever let people know during his career in public office.

Recall, for example, the 1948 presidential campaign of Henry Wallace, in which, as Arthur Schlesinger, Jr., writes, "Communist Party control was arrogant and shameless."[98] Wallace believed that the Soviets had as much moral right to occupy and communize any area they had conquered as Americans had to restore political rights, re-establish democracy and civil society and withdraw. Wallace opposed Marshall Aid to Europe, stating four days after the Marshall Plan was revealed that the United States was now "the center of world reaction" and that "at the present rate of progress it will be less than a decade before Americans start praising Hitler and Mussolini as heroes who prepared the way for us to fight Soviet Russia."[99] He opposed American intervention in Greece and aid to Turkey, and he opposed creation of the NATO Alliance. Wallace in fact opposed the whole concept of containment, which he claimed was an invention of the British, who were acting *deliberately* to facilitate World War III. He urged Truman to put the issue of Greece and Turkey before the United Nations, *where he knew the Soviets would exercise their veto.*[100] Had he not been replaced as vice president by Harry Truman in 1944, Henry Wallace would have become president upon the death of Franklin Roosevelt, and he would likely have appointed Lawrence Duggan secretary of state and Henry Dexter White secretary of the treasury.[101] Both men, as

---

98 Arthur M. Schlesinger, Jr., *The Vital Center* (New Brunswick: Transaction Publishers, 1998), 118.

99 Schlesinger, *A Life in the Twentieth Century*, 417.

100 Kissinger, *Diplomacy*, 469.

101 Herman, *Joseph McCarthy*, 86.

we now know, were Soviet agents.[102] Wallace garnered less than three percent of the vote nationwide in the 1948 presidential election.

In understanding George McGovern, it is important to understand that he was a *passionate* supporter of Henry Wallace in 1948. He was devoted to Wallace and his worldview.[103] As of 1972, George McGovern still admitted that he "liked what Wallace had to say about foreign policy. I still think he was essentially right."[104] In fact, McGovern never lost his admiration for the man who saw eye-to-eye with Josef Stalin on every foreign policy issue in the late 1940s, naming him as one of his "historical heroes" in the December 2002 issue of *Harper's*.[105] Yet he avoided any mention of his abiding admiration of Henry Wallace throughout his subsequent political career. As of 1972, Robert Sam Anson would write, "McGovern's own feelings about Wallace are one of the few things he does not readily volunteer about his past. One searches his official biography in vain for some mention of the man, or McGovern's regard for him....McGovern's campaign propaganda conveys the impression that his beliefs have never been anything except the most regular, Democratic kind."[106]

It is also important to understand that McGovern was a party man through and through, as he made clear when praising Chicago Mayor Richard J. Daley: "He and I were very different men. But I respected him for what he was—a nuts and bolts politician to whom party and personal loyalty took precedence over immediate issues."[107] In McGovern's world, the Party *always* came first, which made him a stealth candidate who had no intention of revealing to his constituents where he really stood. For he understood the need to hold the Vital Center, and so long as anti-Communism was in his

---

102 Hynes, Klehr and Vassiliev, Spies: *The Rise and Fall of the KGB in America*, 220–245 (Duggan); 258–262 (White).

103 Anson, *McGovern: A Biography*, 59.

104 Ibid., 60.

105 George McGovern, "The case for Liberalism: a defense of the future against the past," *Harper's*, December 2002, 37.

106 Anson, *McGovern: A Biography*, 59.

107 McGovern, *Grassroots*, 231.

interest and the interests of his party, he embraced anti-Communism, at least in public. He would eventually prove more willing to abandon the anti-Communist bandwagon than most, but not until he knew he could do so safely—after a brutal debacle he had helped create in Southeast Asia had shifted the Vital Center to the left.

McGovern was an early critic of this country's involvement in Vietnam (not surprising for a passionate admirer of Henry Wallace) and outlined his position in the Senate in September 1963, when he described the United States as "powerless to cope with a ragged band of illiterate guerillas fighting with homemade weapons." He criticized the government we supported in South Vietnam for "tyrannizing its citizens and throwing insults at our President when he objects." American policy, he said, was not "a policy of 'victory'; it is not even a policy of 'stalemate.' It is a policy of moral debacle and political defeat."[108] He sounds prescient, but as with so much of the rhetoric throughout the Vietnam War, it was, at least in the early stages when it really mattered, just rhetoric. For when it came time to stand behind either his beliefs or his president—when it was time to choose between his country and his party during the crucial vote on the Gulf of Tonkin Resolution—McGovern, a good and loyal Democrat "to whom party and personal loyalty took precedence over immediate issues," opted for his party, voting to approve the resolution because he was assured that it was aimed at Republicans in Washington rather than Communists in Asia.[109]

Despite his misgivings, McGovern supported Kennedy and Johnson in their half-hearted, half-baked "commitment" in Southeast Asia. On January 15, 1965, he outlined his own proposal for resolution of the conflict. Military power, McGovern believed, should be used in Vietnam "not [for] military victory, but [for] bringing Ho Chi Minh to the conference table,"[110] where this country could negotiate a five-point solution, providing for:

1. A "close association or federation between North

108 Anson, *McGovern: A Biography*, 150–151.
109 Ibid., 153.
110 Ibid., 155–156.

and South Vietnam, not under a unitary Communist government from the North, but with local autonomy for the South as well as the North."

2. Trade and rail links between the two Vietnams.
3. Cooperative planning between North and South to develop the Mekong River.
4. Neutralization of both North and South Vietnam, along with a withdrawal of American troops.
5. A UN presence in Southeast Asia, empowered to enter every country in the area to "guarantee national borders, to offer protection against external aggression, and insofar as possible to insure fair treatment of tribal and other minorities within the boundaries of a given state." [111]

"Until such time as negotiation is possible and settlement can be devised which will not surrender South Vietnam to Communism," he continued, "the United States would doubtless not find it feasible to withdraw. *If necessary, we can maintain our military position in Vietnam indefinitely*, since it is essentially a policy of holding the cities while taking whatever attrition is possible of the guerillas in the countryside." [112]

If McGovern actually believed that any of this nonsense represented a viable "solution," he was, like Robert McNamara, a fool.

Although occasionally critical of Johnson's efforts on behalf of Truman's doctrine in Southeast Asia, "for the most part, McGovern remained moderate." [113] What this means, of course, is that he toed the Democratic line. In October 1965, for example, he told an audience that "[w]e crossed the bridge long ago in Vietnam. It's too late to turn back now. Our nation has decided that we must stay and fight to stop the Communists from taking over. We have a commitment, and we must stay there until the dispute is

111 Ibid.
112 Ibid. (emphasis added).
113 Ibid., 160.

resolved."[114] As to antiwar demonstrators, he declared, "Recent protests staged serve no useful purpose. If these individuals would put their talents to work helping, the war effort would be greatly aided."[115] He reaffirmed his commitment to an independent, non-Communist South Vietnam in May of 1967, when he joined moderate, antiwar senators in a statement assuring Hanoi that they remained "steadfastly opposed to any unilateral withdrawal of American troops from Vietnam."[116] And he voted for all annual appropriations for the war, totaling more than $40 billion, through the end of Johnson's presidency, saying that it was necessary to provide the men in Vietnam with means to defend themselves. Public opinion shifted dramatically in 1968, however, and McGovern shifted as well.

It was McGovern who, along with Eugene McCarthy, led the antiwar wing of the Democratic Party at the 1968 Democratic National Convention and fought passionately against the compromise war plank that was eventually adopted, demanding an end to US air operations and a withdrawal of 300,000 US troops, with no preconditions, within sixty days. His plank was defeated, and so was his party's nominee. But with Nixon in the White House, McGovern moved steadily and rapidly left. Having learned for himself by 1972 that Hanoi was prepared to offer this country *nothing* but virtual surrender, he moved into the 1972 elections outlining his intentions in the following terms:

1. "All American bombing in Indochina would be immediately stopped—with no preconditions."
2. "All American ground forces would be withdrawn from Indochina within 90 days—with no preconditions."
3. "All military assistance to the Thieu regime would be immediately terminated—with no preconditions."
4. "Vigorous diplomatic efforts would be undertaken to achieve the release of U.S. prisoners of war."

---

114 Ibid., 161.
115 Ibid.
116 Mann, *A Grand Delusion*, 544.

    5.   Upon the release of American prisoners, American
        bases in Thailand would be closed and naval forces
        off the shores of Southeast Asia would be removed.[117]

George McGovern was unwilling even to bargain for, much less secure, the release of American POWs as a condition for American withdrawal. He would be satisfied, he said, to *beg* Hanoi for their release.[118] He called US air operations in Southeast Asia "the most barbaric action that any country has committed since Hitler's effort to exterminate Jews in Germany in the 1930s,"[119] and he made clear that, in his mind, all who served in Vietnam were Lieutenant William Calley's moral equivalent.[120] For McGovern, Vietnam was not a mistake or an error in judgment. "The root cause," as Theodore H. White noted, was "American criminality."[121] On national defense and the Cold War in general, he was equally extreme.

"The war against Communism is over; the challenge to the free world from Communism is no longer relevant. We're entering a new era, and the Kennedy challenge of 1960 is a pretty hollow one. Somehow, we have to settle down and learn to live with them...there has to be an easing off on our reliance on power; too much reliance on power weakens a society."[122] To ensure that we would not be "weakened" by too much power, McGovern proposed a thirty-seven percent cut in defense spending. Aircraft carriers would be reduced from fifteen to six; total military personnel would be cut to 1,750,000, and American strategic missiles would be cut without any attempt to secure corresponding cuts in the Soviet arsenal. Ideologically and politically, the contrast between these two candidates was probably greater than at any time in this country's history, and Nixon was far closer to the Vital Center. When given

---

117 Ibid., 705.

118 Langguth, *Our Vietnam*, 603.

119 Theodore H. White, *The Making of the President, 1972* (New York: Atheneum Publishers, 1973), 122.

120 Mann, *A Grand Delusion*, 749.

121 White, *The Making of the President, 1972*, 123.

122 Ibid., 122.

the opportunity, moreover, McGovern would prove to be ambitious and dishonest enough to damage himself further.

McGovern selected Senator Thomas Eagleton as his running mate and then, when records of Eagleton's psychiatric treatment surfaced, unceremoniously dumped him despite having initially assured the American public that, the disclosures notwithstanding, he remained "1000% behind his running mate."[123] McGovern stumbled again when he sent Pierre Salinger to Paris to meet with the North Vietnamese in an effort to trump Nixon. When word of this leaked, McGovern lied, denying that he had anything to do with Salinger's trip.[124] By the close of the Republican Convention in August, McGovern was twenty-three points behind Nixon in the polls.[125] Determined to close the gap, he sought the support of one of the chief architects of the Vietnam War as we know it: Lyndon Baines Johnson. This episode, as recounted by McGovern, tells us a great deal about both men.

On August 22, 1972, McGovern traveled to Johnson's ranch, where Johnson told him in no uncertain terms that, issues aside—particularly the war in Southeast Asia—"I'm a Democrat. . . . You're the nominee of the party and I'm backing you."[126] Clearly, his war policies had never been about containing Communism or protecting national security. They were designed solely to serve the interests of his party during the mid-1960s, when the label "soft on Communism" was as damaging as "another Korea." Times had changed due in no small part to Johnson's policies, and the interests of his party had changed with the times. Now that the antiwar wing had secured the nomination, the antiwar wing would get his unqualified support, the actual merits of a war costing millions of lives through his own actions be damned. (This is not to suggest that the war did or did not have any real merit—only to note that for Johnson, the merits never mattered.) For this, McGovern praised him as a "genuine old-fashioned, honest-to-God Democrat" who (astonishingly) "was not responsible for the intervention in

123 Ibid., 207–218.
124 Ibid., 225–226.
125 Ibid., 227.
126 McGovern, *Grassroots*, 229.

Vietnam as such."[127]

By the end of summer 1972, it was clear that McGovern was going nowhere. Exquisitely attuned as always to the American political system, the North Vietnamese, battered again into stalemate by overwhelming military power, exhibited a renewed desire to "negotiate" with the Nixon administration. On October 8, 1972, Le Duc Tho, North Vietnam's chief negotiator in Paris, made several major concessions.

Most importantly, Hanoi now agreed, *for the first time,* to separate the military and political issues, proposing as follows: 1) a cease-fire in place; 2) a withdrawal of American troops; 3) return of American prisoners; and 4) no requirement for replacement of the GVN, which would be allowed to remain in power. Political questions regarding the future of South Vietnam, including the fate of Viet Cong prisoners held in South Vietnam, would be settled later. Hanoi also scrapped its heretofore non-negotiable demand for a total end to military aid to the GVN. As Le Duc Tho admitted, it was they who, in October, were accepting Nixon's terms of May 1971. "[It] is your proposal, and we met it with great good will, in order to end the war."[128] Although peace was not "at hand" in October 1972, nothing could now stop Nixon's electoral juggernaut. He was re-elected in a landslide on November 7, 1972, taking 521 out of 538 electoral votes and winning every state except Massachusetts. The seventy-seven million who cast their ballots represented the largest number of voters in history, and Nixon's nearly eighteen-million-vote advantage represented the largest numerical margin ever recorded. The Vietnam War had, without question, been the pivotal issue, but it was not yet over. Just as Nixon had to sell the October 8 peace plan to America's South Vietnamese allies, the North Vietnamese had to sell the plan to their own. Both would meet with rejection.

Kissinger flew to Saigon on October 18, 1972, to brief Nugyen Van Thieu on the agreement negotiated in Paris. Thieu viewed the October 8 framework as little more than a sellout. Particularly

127 Ibid., 230.

128 Kissinger, *The White House Years*, 1344–1345. See also Mann, *A Grand Delusion*, 707; Berman, *No Peace, No Honor*, 155–157; Langguth, *Our Vietnam*, 607–608.

egregious in his view were the provisions allowing North Vietnamese troops to remain in the South, recognition of the NLF and the creation of the National Council of Reconciliation and Concord, which Thieu viewed as a coalition government. "If we accept the document as it stands, we will commit suicide—and I will be committing suicide," he said.[129] The South Vietnamese ultimately demanded sixty-nine changes to the agreement, including withdrawal of North Vietnamese forces from South Vietnam. These demands, as Kissinger viewed it, "verge on insanity."[130] For time had run out. Not only had the antiwar forces in Congress grown far more powerful in the last four years, but the October 8 agreement—calling for a return of POWs, a cease fire, a formula for Thieu to remain in power and elections to determine the future of South Vietnam—was considered acceptable even to the majority of Nixon's supporters in Congress. A refusal by Thieu to sign the agreement now would result in a separate peace between the United States and North Vietnam and an immediate termination of all US aid to the Saigon regime. Congress would tolerate no repeat of 1968.[131] Nevertheless, Kissinger duly returned to Paris to present Saigon's demands but with no real intention to press them. He was in for a surprise.

Not only did the North Vietnamese reject Saigon's counterproposals, but Le Duc Tho, giving in to pressure from the NLF in South Vietnam, reneged on the October 8 agreement and now linked the return of US POWs to the release of Viet Cong detainees in South Vietnam. He also demanded a withdrawal of all US civilian technicians working in South Vietnam along with US military personnel. This would make future maintenance of the South Vietnamese Air Force impossible. The Communists also demanded the grounding of the South Vietnamese Air Force and immobilization of South Vietnamese naval units as part of the cease-fire protocols. For days, Henry Kissinger met with Le Duc Tho in Paris to reach an agreement around the October 8 framework, but nothing worked. Every time an agreement was

---

129 Berman, *No Peace, No Honor*, 169.
130 Ibid., 170.
131 Ibid., 195–96, 200, 205.

seemingly reached, the North Vietnamese would return adding new demands. "There was no intractable substantive issue separating the two sides, but rather an apparent North Vietnamese determination *not to allow the agreement to be completed*. This was the insoluble problem over which we began the Christmas bombing five days later."[132]

In the words of Kissinger aide John Negroponte, Hanoi's conduct was not just "clumsy, blatant, and essentially contemptuous of the United States" but "tawdry, petty and at times transparently childish."[133] It eventually became clear to Kissinger that the October 8 agreement was dead. The reason was clear: The 93rd Congress, voted into office in November, was going to cut off funds for the war, giving the North Vietnamese what they wanted. Hanoi was aware of this and had no reason to give this country anything, not even its POWs. So, Nixon launched Operation Linebacker II. On December 18, 1972, Nixon dispatched the B-52s to Hanoi, telling Chairman of the Joint Chiefs Admiral Thomas Moorer, "I don't want any more of this crap about the fact that we couldn't hit this target or that one. This is your chance to use military power effectively to win this war, and if you don't, I'll consider you responsible."[134]

For twelve days, the B-52s pounded military and industrial targets in North Vietnam. As expected, Nixon's opponents at home and abroad accused the United States of "indiscriminate terror bombing" and crimes against humanity. In fact, the bombing paled next to the day-to-day conduct of air operations during World War II and Korea and inflicted only a tiny fraction of the number of casualties inflicted on a regular and deliberate basis by the likes of "Bomber pilot McGovern"[135] during the "Good War."[136] The bombing, however, had the intended effect on both the Hanoi

---

132 Kissinger, *The White House Years*, 1444 (emphasis in the original).

133 Ibid., 1443.

134 Mann, *A Grand Delusion*, 712.

135 McGovern complained during the 1972 presidential campaign that, although Congressman Pete McCloskey was always called "war hero Pete McCloskey," no one ever called him "Bomber pilot" McGovern. Anson, *McGovern: A Biography*, 274.

136 Lewy, *America in Vietnam*, 412–413.

regime and the South Vietnamese. "It was a classic case of cause and effect."[137] Kissinger and Tho next met in Paris on January 8, 1973, and completed an agreement within the October 8 framework. The United States withdrew its military forces and recovered its POWs. The GVN, at least for now, would live another day. The North Vietnamese Army remained in place and prepared for the eventual seizure of the entire country. Nixon called it "Peace with Honor." But there would never be a moment's peace, and if this were "honor," God help us. As it had been throughout this war, Vietnam's fate would be decided in Washington.

Richard Nixon remained a true believer to the end. Hanoi's 1972 offensive had demonstrated to him that, with continued political and economic support and the full might of US air power behind them, the South Vietnamese could stand up to the North Vietnamese. He believed that the American people would support the use of American air power to enforce the peace agreement when (not if) Hanoi violated its terms. "[W]hat really counts is not the agreement but my determination to take massive military action against North Vietnam in the event they break the agreement."[138] This, of course, was America's solution to the Korean War: no peace treaty, unending economic and political support to its ally, a permanent armed presence by the United States and a guarantee of massive American retaliation in the event America's client was attacked. Speaking to President Thieu's assistant Nguyen Phu Duc on November 29, 1972, Nixon made his position clear: "Why did Korea survive today? Partially because of U.S. aid, but primarily because North Korea knew that if they violated the DMZ a violent reaction would ensue. The situation was the same in Vietnam. If North Vietnam infiltrated again they would run a mortal risk."[139]

The Korean solution was stressed by Kissinger as well at a meeting with South Vietnamese leaders: "No one knows what the Korean Armistice Agreement says. But the people know they have achieved something and if the North Koreans violate it, the President can defend it....The major use of the agreement to you is

---

137 Berman, *No Peace, No Honor*, 219.
138 Ibid., 196.
139 Ibid., 200.

it links us legally to you on a long-term basis for an indefinite period."[140] But it was not to be, as Nixon destroyed himself with the Watergate scandal, and South Vietnam's opponents moved with alacrity to seal its fate.

In June 1973, Congress passed legislation cutting off all funds for American combat operations in Southeast Asia. Nixon vetoed this bill, but the handwriting was on the wall. In November, the War Powers Act was passed over Nixon's veto. From this point forward, Nixon said, "I had only words with which to threaten. *The Communists knew it too.*"[141] By the summer of 1974, Congress was scaling back aid to the South Vietnamese, providing less than half of what had been requested, and busily driving Nixon from office for his attempts to cover up a burglary at Democratic National Committee Headquarters, a relatively trivial matter given the "high crimes and misdemeanors" that had been a daily aspect of American foreign policy under every president since FDR. With Nixon's Watergate-related resignation in August, the South Vietnamese had lost their last hope. By the spring of 1975, America's abandonment of South Vietnam was clear for all to see:

> The ammunition supply rate (daily allowance) for rifles was set at 1.6 rounds per man (compared with 13 rounds authorized for U.S. forces when they were still in the war). Machine guns got 10.6 rounds (versus 165), mortars 1.3 rounds (instead of 16.9), and 105mm howitzer shells authorized per gun were 6.4 (not 36.5). Said Colonel Hoang Ngoc Lung, "Stories of RF and PF units in IV Corps buying grenades out of their pocket money were, though incredible, nevertheless true." The profligacy with which the enemy continued to expend ammunition pointed up the contrast. At just one location, the Tong Le Chon border camp, the Communists shelled the base 300 times over a period of sixteen weeks, expending more than 10,000 rounds in the

---

140 Ibid., 211.
141 Mann, *A Grand Delusion*, 717 (emphasis added).

process.[142]

Hanoi had stockpiled an enormous quantity of supplies of all types—food, fuel and ammunition—several times the amount that had been stockpiled for the 1972 offensive.[143] On January 6, 1975, North Vietnamese forces seized the province of Phuoc Long, which was a major defeat for the South Vietnamese. It was to some extent a test, and Hanoi was pleased with the result. Pham Van Dong noted that Gerald Ford, who did nothing but issue a diplomatic protest, was "the weakest president in U.S. history." "When Ford kept American B-52s in their hangars," said Bui Tin, "our leadership decided on a big offensive against South Vietnam."[144]

South Vietnam's collapse was now imminent, as South Korea's collapse would have been imminent had the United States removed all its military and economic support in 1955. Gerald Ford requested an emergency aid package that Congress refused in no uncertain terms. Jacob Javits told Ford, "I will give you large sums of money for evacuation but not one nickel for military aid."[145] Frank Church feared that even an evacuation of refugees would not be worth the cost, and Joseph Biden, advocating as callous a betrayal as possible, agreed: "I will vote for any amount for getting Americans out. *I don't want it mixed with getting Vietnamese out.*"[146]

On April 30, 1975, the last American helicopter lifted off from the roof of the United States Embassy in Saigon (carrying the final contingent of Marines, who provided security for the evacuation) with the following transmission: "All the Americans are out. Repeat out." That rooftop was a microcosm of America's war in Southeast Asia. For over 400 Vietnamese who had been promised that "no one will be left behind" were, of course, left behind, betrayed and abandoned by this country, its people and its venal, corrupt politicians, acting to advance their own interests, half a world away.

---

142 Sorley, *A Better War*, 370.

143 Ibid., 372.

144 Ibid., 374 (emphasis added).

145 Mann, *A Grand Delusion*, 721.

146 Ibid., 721 (emphasis added).

It was all summed up rather poignantly by Sirik Matak, a Cambodian government official who refused to abandon his country during America's evacuation of Phnom Penh and wrote the following letter to US Ambassador John Gunther Dean in the last hours of his life:

> Dear Excellency and Friend, I thank you very sincerely for your letter and your offer to transport me toward freedom. I cannot, alas, leave in such a cowardly fashion. As for you, and in particular for your great country, I never believed for a moment that you have this sentiment of abandoning a people, which has chosen liberty. You have refused us your protection, and we can do nothing about it. You leave, and it is my wish that you and your country will find happiness under this sky. But, mark it well, that if I die here on the spot and in my country that I love, it is too bad, because we are all born and must die one day. I have committed this mistake of believing in you, the Americans.[147]

"It was not," as Colonel Harry Summers noted with considerable understatement, "a proud day to be an American."[148]

---

147 Berman, *No Peace, No Honor*, 3.
148 Ibid., 272.

Chapter Seven:
Aftermath

The Americans might force the Vietnamese to accept the disorder for years, but behind the dam of American troops and American money the pressure is building towards one of those sudden historical shifts when "individualism" and its attendant corruption gives way to the discipline of the revolutionary community. When this shift takes place, the American officials will find it difficult to recognize their former protégés. They may well conclude the "hard-core Communists" have brainwashed and terrorized them into submission, but they will be wrong. It will simply mean that the moment has arrived for the narrow flame of revolution to cleanse the lake of Vietnamese society from the corruption and disorder of the American war. The effort will have to be greater than any other the Vietnamese have undertaken, but it will have to come, for it is the only way the Vietnamese of the south can restore their country and their history to themselves.[1]

Frances FitzGerald

1972

"Vietnam may even (in the long run) be better off for the Communists' victory. In power they discredited themselves in a way that never would have been possible if they'd remained a Philippine-like guerilla opposition." This is a worthwhile line of

---

[1] FitzGerald, *Fire in the Lake*, 442.

reasoning if only because it makes nonsense of Frances Fitzgerald's prophecies about the "cleansing effects" of the Vietnamese revolution. The only thing that the Vietnamese revolution cleansed, or should have cleansed, was the foolish idea that Third World revolutions are cleansing.[2]

Adam Garfinkle,

1995

M any Americans who claim the antiwar movement as their own romanticized Communist "liberation" of Southeast Asia and continue to do so, having convinced themselves that they were right all along, like Michael Blumenthal, who evaded the draft by inhaling canvas dust to "revive a childhood history of bronchial asthma" and tells us years later that, "What many of us 'believed,' largely out of fear and narcissism, we now believe out of conviction."[3] ("Convictions," as Friedrich Nietzsche once noted, "are more dangerous enemies of truth than lies."[4]) Malcolm Browne, one of David Halberstam's comrades in the Saigon press corps who served as an agent in Pham Xuan An's "intelligence network," proposed that perhaps "there were two sets of good guys, one led by John F. Kennedy and the other by Ho Chi Minh, who were equally convinced that the other side was the bad guy."[5] The first step in evaluating claims like these, which are central to America's reigning ideology, is through a brief review of history since the Communist victory—because the fall of Saigon was not a conclusion, but rather "a point of departure from which the validity of both sides' goals during the war could be measured."[6]

In April of 1975, the North Vietnamese swept into Saigon and united Vietnam under their control. At the time of their final

---

2 Garfinkle, *Telltale Hearts*, 270.

3 Myra MacPherson, *Long Time Passing: Vietnam and the Haunted Generation* (New York: Anchor Books, 1984), 155.

4 Friedrich Nietzsche, *The Anti-Christ* (New York: Tribeca Books, 2012), 71.

5 Bill McCloud, *What Should We Tell Our Children about Vietnam?* (Norman: University of Oklahoma Press, 1989), 19.

6 James Webb, introduction to Bui Tin, *From Enemy to Friend*, xi. See also James Webb, "History Proves the Vietnam Victors Wrong," *Wall Street Journal*, April 28, 2000.

victory, Saigon boasted twenty-seven daily newspapers, three television stations and more than twenty radio stations. These were *all* closed down immediately and replaced with two papers, two radio stations and one television station, all officially controlled outlets for government propaganda.[7] All bookstores and theatres were closed, and a vast number of books were confiscated or burned as the victors initiated a relentless campaign to indoctrinate the newly conquered with the idea that the "Soviet Union is a paradise of the Socialist world."[8]

Hundreds of thousands of people were herded into concentration camps to be re-educated through the same type of mind-numbing brutality that marked Nazi Germany and Stalinist Russia. Prime Minister Pham Van Dong admitted that 200,000 people had been "re-educated" in the South. The actual number, however, is estimated to be between 500,000 and 1,000,000.[9] Doan Van Toai, who opposed the Thieu regime and had worked as a Viet Cong agent during the war, resigned from his post as a member of the finance committee for the Provisional Revolutionary Government installed by Hanoi when he was directed to draft a plan for confiscating all private property in South Vietnam, which "had nothing to do with fulfilling the aspirations of the South Vietnamese, and . . . went against my conscience."[10] Arrested shortly thereafter, he described life as a political prisoner for the *New York Times* in March of 1981:

> I was thrown into a three-foot-by-six-foot cell with my left hand chained to my right foot and my right hand chained to my left foot. My food was rice mixed with sand...After two months in solitary confinement, I was transferred to a collective cell, a room 15 feet wide and 25 feet long, where at different times anywhere from 40 to 100 prisoners were crushed together. Here we had to take turns lying

---

7 Carl Gershman, "After the Dominoes Fell," *Commentary*, May 1978, 3-10, 5.

8 "A Lament for Vietnam," *New York Times Magazine*, March 29, 1981.

9 *The Black Book of Communism*, 572.

10 "A Lament for Vietnam."

down to sleep, and most of the younger, stronger prisoners slept sitting up. In the sweltering heat, we also took turns snatching a few breaths of fresh air in front of the narrow opening that was the cell's only window. Every day I watched my friends die at my feet.[11]

For these inmates, life became, in the words of Jean Lacouture, a French journalist who had once been an ardent supporter of the Communists in Southeast Asia, "a prefabricated hell."[12] We will likely never know how many hundreds of thousands died in these camps.

The North Vietnamese imposed a system of internal passports to eliminate freedom of travel, just like in the Soviet Union. Religious freedom came under immediate assault, just like in the Soviet Union. Oppression of religious leaders reached such a stage that *twelve* Buddhist priests and nuns burned themselves to death in protest on November 2, 1975, which of course went virtually unnoticed in the West. (The official government report stated, "Abbot Hue Hien killed eleven monks and nuns and then burned himself and the monastery."[13]) Freedom of association ceased to exist, and all political activity not government approved was simply outlawed, just like in the Soviet Union. Those who transgressed soon found themselves being re-educated in a forced labor camp for years on end, often being re-educated to death, just like in the Soviet Union.

In taking measure of the victors, we must also note the "vast tide of human misery in Southeast Asia" described by Tom Wicker in the *New York Times* on July 8, 1979, more than four years after the Communists had united the country: "hundreds of thousands of homeless persons in United Nations camps, perhaps as many more dead in flight, tens of thousands of the most pitiable forcibly repatriated to Cambodia, no one knows how many adrift on the high seas or wandering the roads." It was an event unprecedented in

11 Ibid.
12 Gershman, "After the Dominoes Fell," 4.
13 Ibid., 5.

Vietnamese history:

> Our people have a traditional attachment to their country. No Vietnamese would willingly leave home, homeland and ancestors' graves. During the most oppressive French colonial rule and Japanese domination no one escaped by boat at great risk to their lives. Yet you see that my countrymen by the thousands and from all walks of life, including a number of disillusioned Vietcongs [*sic*], continue to escape from Vietnam; six out of ten never make it, and for those who are fortunate enough to make it, they are not allowed to land.[14]

Truong Nhu Tang, former minister of justice in the Communist Provisional Revolutionary Government who fled as one of the Boat People in November of 1979, agreed: "Never has any previous regime brought such masses of people to such desperation. Not the military dictators, not the colonialists, not even the ancient Chinese overlords."[15]

In Cambodia, the victorious Khmer Rouge began a bloodletting as ghastly as any in recorded history. In the cities, people were given just twenty-four hours to leave their homes with whatever small number of possessions they could carry. Phnom Penh, with a population of between two and three million, was evacuated in just this manner. At least 10,000 (the old, the sick, the infirm) died or were killed outright during this evacuation. Millions of these forced evacuees were repeatedly "deported" within the country as "the regime...sought to rid itself of a maximum number of 'useless mouths.' Each successive evacuation—whether on foot, in carts, or in slow, badly overcrowded trains that sometimes took as long as a week to reach their destination—was an extremely demanding experience for severely undernourished people. In light of the

---

14 Nguyen Cong Hoan, who had been an opponent of the Thieu regime and served as a member of the National Assembly under the Communists before escaping in 1977, testifying before the Subcommittee on International Organizations of the House Committee on International Relations, July 26, 1977, 145–167, quoted in Gershman, "After the Dominoes Fell," 3-4.
15 Podhoretz, *Why We Were in Vietnam*, 198–199.

severe shortage of medical facilities, losses were high."[16] Purges and massacres began on a stupendous scale in 1976. By the time the "narrow flame of revolution" so eagerly anticipated by Frances FitzGerald had "cleansed the lake" of Cambodian society, by the time Cambodians had "[restored] their country and their history to themselves," between 1.5 and 2 million Cambodians had lost their lives to disease, starvation and execution.[17] *"No other country in the world seems to have suffered so much since 1945."*[18]

In the end, it was all summarized rather nicely by David Halberstam's North Vietnamese controller, NVA General Pham Xuan An, who tried twice to flee Vietnam for the West before his death in 2006: "All that talk about 'liberation' twenty, thirty, forty years ago, all the plotting, and all the bodies, produced this, this impoverished, broken down country led by a gang of cruel and paternalistic half-educated theorists."[19]

---

16 *The Black Book of Communism*, 585.

17 Ibid., 537–635.

18 Ibid., 590 (emphasis added).

19 Sorley, *A Better War*, 384.

PART THREE:
EVOLUTION AND
END GAME

Chapter Eight:
Jimmy Carter

Being confident of our own future, we are now free of that inordinate fear of Communism which once led us to embrace any dictator who joined us in our fear. For too many years we have been willing to adopt the flawed principles and tactics of our adversaries, sometimes abandoning our values for theirs. We fought fire with fire, never thinking that fire is better fought with water. This approach failed, with Vietnam the best example of its intellectual and moral poverty. But through failure we have found our way back to our own principles and values, and we have regained our lost confidence.[1]

Jimmy Carter

By the mid-1970s, Truman's doctrine ("this approach" as Jimmy Carter put it) was dead, rhetorically and effectively. Since 1950, nearly 100,000 Americans had died enforcing it, and very few Americans felt that they had much to show for the effort. They had Korea, an annihilative near disaster that had ended in stalemate. Their ally remained a military dictatorship, and nearly a million men, tens of thousands of them Americans (formally described as a "tripwire"), faced each other across the most heavily fortified border in the world. They also had Southeast Asia, which had been a complete debacle, with more than $130 billion expended

---

1 Notre Dame Commencement, May 22, 1977.

and more than 3 million dead (including 58,000 Americans), seemingly for nothing. And all around the world, from the Philippines to Central America to the Middle East, Americans had corrupt autocracies exchanging their "friendship" for American support lest they be next on the world's revolutionary agenda. *This was, after all, the essence of Truman's doctrine.*[2] Americans were quite sick of it all, and any illusions regarding their willingness to "pay any price" or "bear any burden" in the name of Truman's doctrine had vanished. The phony, politically driven "anti-Communist consensus" that had governed American foreign policy for more than twenty years had collapsed completely, and the split within the intellectual and political classes over Communism and how to deal with it, which had existed since the 1930s, now returned to the very forefront of public debate. For the first time in decades, liberals, both in and out of government, emboldened by the disaster in Vietnam and untainted by "the clandestine activities of the American Communist Party" during the 1930s and 1940s, began to critique not just Truman's doctrine but the Cold War itself, stepping forward to seize the moment and provide a new direction to American foreign policy.

Leading this effort from within the establishment was the Trilateral Commission. Founded by David Rockefeller, the Trilateral Commission assembled businessmen, investment bankers, multinational corporate directors and the liberal wing of the foreign policy establishment to assist in developing a new world order.[3] Senator Walter Mondale and future President Jimmy Carter were both charter members of this group. Many of the first Trilateralists had been members of the venerable Council on Foreign Relations, but the Council and its house publication,

---

2 The Truman Doctrine's last hurrah was the American-supported overthrow of Salvador Allende in Chile in September 1973. Although this incident is bitterly denounced by liberals to this very day, Nixon had just as much right to support "regime change" in Chile as Kennedy had to act against Diem, which was the same right Eisenhower had to install the shah and the same right Truman had to sustain Syngman Rhee with hundreds of thousands of American troops. (This is not a value judgment or a claim that any president has the "right" to act in this manner. I am merely recognizing that there is no qualitative difference in the conduct.)

3 Jerry W. Sanders, *Peddlers of Crisis: The Committee on the Present Danger and the Politics of Containment* (Cambridge: South End Press, 1983), 175.

Foreign Affairs, had become, in their minds, much too closely tied to the militaristic policies of the Cold War establishment to serve as an instrument of change. A clean break was necessary, symbolized in part by a new quarterly journal, *Foreign Policy,* first published in 1971 by the Carnegie Endowment for International Peace. *Foreign Policy* devoted its first issue to deconstructing Cold War orthodoxy, from its theoretical underpinnings to its application and practical effects in both the industrialized world and the Third World, beginning with a blunt repudiation of the Truman Doctrine that had shaped this country's relationship with the rest of the world for more than twenty years.

Jimmy Carter embraced this "antimilitarism manifesto" during his 1976 presidential campaign: "We must replace balance-of-power with world-order politics. It is likely in the near future that issues of war and peace will be more a function of economic and social problems than of the military-security problems which have dominated international relations since World War II."[4] Carter, who selected fellow Trilateralist Walter Mondale as his running-mate, was elected president in November 1976. The Trilateralists were determined to consign Truman's doctrine, if not the entire Cold War, to the dustbin of history, and from 1970-1976, everything had been moving their way. But they would not go unchallenged.

As early as December 1972, a small but powerful group of "Scoop Jackson Democrats" (to whom today's "neocons" trace their lineage) formed the Coalition for a Democratic Majority ("CDM"). They were appalled by George McGovern and the New Left, which they described as "a movement that derided America," whose members "cheered not for American soldiers but for Mao, Ho Chi Minh and the Vietcong," "praised the Arab Liberation Movement, criticized the Czech reformers for opening up contacts with western imperialism, and glorified the brave North Vietnamese infantryman heading off to battle."[5] In the minds of Scoop Jackson Democrats, they had not left the Democratic Party; the party had left them, and

4 Ibid., 235.
5 Jay Winik, *On the Brink: The Dramatic, Behind-the-Scenes Saga of the Reagan Era and the Men and Women Who Won the Cold War* (New York: Simon & Schuster, 1996), 78–79.

they were determined to bring it back where it belonged.[6]

On November 11, 1976, just days after Jimmy Carter's election, another opposition group, the Committee on the Present Danger ("CPD") was formed. The CPD had 141 members on its board of directors, including luminaries such as Nobel Laureate Saul Bellow, John Connally, C. Douglas Dillon, General Andrew Goodpaster, Lane Kirkland, Jeane Kirkpatrick, General Lyman Lemnitzer, Jay Lovestone, Claire Booth Luce, Paul Nitze (principal author of NSC-68), Norman and Midge Dector Podhoretz, General Matthew Ridgway, Eugene Rostow, Dean Rusk, General Maxwell Taylor, Edward Teller and Admiral Elmo Zumwalt. The CPD steadfastly adhered to the worldview outlined in NSC-68 and, like the CDM, intended to resist implementation of Carter's Trilateralist foreign policy, as outlined in its founding policy statement, "Common Sense and the Common Danger."

Intending to exert as much influence as possible, the CPD and the like-minded CDM submitted fifty-three names to the newly elected Carter administration for appointment in the fields of defense and foreign affairs. All were rejected as Carter selected Trilateralists for his administration, appointing twenty-five to key policy making positions.[7] Although the newly created counter-establishment was firmly in charge, its road would be a rough one indeed. "On Carter's appointments, my views are unprintable," said the CPD's Eugene Rostow, while CDM's chairman Ben Wattenberg said, "It is customary to wait one hundred days to see how the president is doing, but considering what Jimmy Carter has done by appointing a bunch of Johnny-one-notes to his foreign policy team, liberals who clapped for Jimmy Carter with one hand, I will wait only a hundred hours to make my pronouncement about his foreign policy."[8] When Carter nominated Paul Warnke, who ridiculed the anti-Communist world view in "Apes on a Treadmill," published by *Foreign Policy,* to head both the Arms Control and Disarmament Agency and the American delegation to the Strategic Arms Limitation Talks, the CPD marshaled its forces in opposition and

---

6 Ibid., 80–81.

7 Sanders, *Peddlers of Crisis*, 180–181.

8 Winik, *On the Brink*, 85.

went in swinging.[9] Testifying before the Senate, Paul Nitze blasted Warnke's views as "absolutely asinine," "screwball," "arbitrary" and "fictitious."[10] Warnke was eventually confirmed by the Senate, but Senator Henry Jackson, the CDM's honorary co-chairman, claimed victory, noting that Warnke's narrow margin of victory for the SALT leadership position (58–40) would signal to the world that any arms control treaty he negotiated would likely be dead on arrival in the Senate, where a two-thirds majority was required for ratification. The battle lines had been drawn in a fight that would continue throughout Carter's presidency as Carter sought to implement the Trilateral Commission's new world order while the Cold War establishment, now out of power for the first time in nearly three decades, fought him every step of the way.

Carter officially and very publicly renounced the Truman Doctrine during his commencement address at Notre Dame University in May 1977, when he declared Americans "free of that inordinate fear of Communism which once led us to embrace any dictator who joined us in our fear." Since nothing more symbolized the Truman Doctrine's "inordinate fear of Communism" than this country's commitment to South Korea (long an irritant to the American Left), this commitment was first on Carter's chopping block. He was supported in this by among others, George McGovern, who called South Korean President Park Chung Hee a "disreputable tyrant" and said that "totalitarian rule" in South Korea did not merit risk of US involvement in another Korean war.[11] Carter, however, found himself opposed by virtually everyone, including the Joint Chiefs and his own secretaries of state and defense. It was, in the words of Assistant Secretary of State for East Asian and Pacific Affairs Richard Holbrooke, "a full-scale rebellion against the president."[12] Carter persisted until his intended withdrawal from Korea was stopped by Congress after substantial

---

9 Sanders, *Peddlers of Crisis*, 170. See also Paul C. Warnke, "Apes on a Treadmill," *Foreign Policy*, No. 18 (Spring 1975), 12-29.

10 Ibid., 207.

11 "McGovern Asks U.S. to Leave Korea," *New York Times*, September 16, 1976. See also Chalmers Johnson, "Carter in Asia: McGovernism without McGovern," *Commentary*, January 1978, 36-39.

12 Don Oberdorfer, *The Two Koreas* (Reading, Massachusetts: Addison-Wesley, 1997), 89.

public debate. But this was one small setback for Carter and the Trilateralists, who continued to apply their new trade- and human rights-based foreign policy at every available opportunity, with unwavering support from politicians, pundits and public intellectuals from the Left and results that consistently strengthened Carter's opponents.

»» «»

Shortly after Carter, in his unprecedented act of goodwill, renounced Truman's doctrine and all but declared an end to the Cold War, Leonid Brezhnev slapped his face, deploying the SS-20, a new, highly accurate, intermediate-range missile with multiple nuclear warheads. Although insufficient in range to reach North America, the SS-20s were superior to anything this country had deployed in Europe and provided the Soviets with a considerable advantage: "We were immediately able to hold all of Europe hostage, said Andrian Danilevich, one of the Soviets' principal war planners."[13] Western European governments sought deployment of American missiles as a guarantee that the United States would indeed fight the Soviet Union, risking Chicago and New York to protect London and West Berlin. Without such a guarantee, the NATO Alliance would have been at risk, which was exactly what the Soviets wanted.[14]

This was the most serious move ever undertaken by the Soviets against American interests, and the Soviets opposed any attempt to counteract their SS-20 deployment, bullying, threatening and claiming that even a "single missile" deployed in response was "unacceptable."[15] The issue was clear enough, but as with all aspects of foreign policy during the last twenty years of the Cold War, there was no consensus. George Kennan, Robert McNamara and McGeorge Bundy argued that there was no need for deployment of

---

13 Thompson, *The Hawk and the Dove*, 284.

14 Peter Beinart, *The Good Fight: Why Liberals—and Only Liberals—Can Win the War on Terror and Make America Great Again* (New York: HarperCollins, 2006), 65. See also Dana H. Allin, *Cold War Illusions: America, Europe and Soviet Power*, 1969–1989: (New York: St. Martin's Press, 1994), 86–87.

15 Winik, *On the Brink*, 156.

American Pershing II missiles because a nuclear war in Europe would never occur without a full scale strategic exchange, and at the strategic level, each side could destroy the planet several times over. NATO's best course, they said, was in renouncing first use.[16]

In the meantime, leftist insurgents gained the upper hand in civil wars against non-Communist governments in the Middle East, Africa and Central America. A Cuban expeditionary force was dispatched, via a Soviet airlift, to intervene in Angola's civil war—conduct unthinkable only ten years before. With no American response, Communist victory was assured. Soviet-backed, Marxist Sandinistas seized power in Nicaragua after the Carter administration, declaring a "sharp break with the past," abandoned the Somoza regime, which had been "a faithful if distasteful ally of the West."[17] The Sandinistas began an immediate military buildup with Soviet and Cuban supplied equipment and began supporting longstanding insurgent campaigns against US allies in El Salvador, Guatemala and Honduras.[18] From 1974 to 1980, ten countries moved into the Communist orbit—South Vietnam, Laos, Cambodia, South Yemen, Angola, Ethiopia, Mozambique, Grenada, Nicaragua and Afghanistan—while the Soviets advanced toward the Persian Gulf. The kinder, gentler foreign policy of the Carter years culminated in the seizure of the US Embassy in Tehran in November 1979 and the Soviet invasion of Afghanistan in December.

Hard-pressed to believe that Carter's foreign policy did anything to advance the cause of human rights, contain the spread of totalitarianism or increase American security, Americans grew increasingly alarmed and disgusted with this course of events, so Jimmy Carter was born again as a cold warrior. On December 12, 1979, as NATO agreed to deploy a new generation of nuclear missiles in Europe (Pershing IIs), Carter announced a five percent increase in defense spending over five years. "In the dangerous and uncertain world of today," said Carter, "the keystone of our national

---

16 Thompson, *The Hawk and the Dove*, 282–283.

17 Paul Johnson, *Modern Times: The World from the Twenties to the Nineties* (New York: Perennial Classics Edition, 2001), 673.

18 Ibid., 673.

security is still military strength—strength that is clearly recognized by Americans, by our allies and by any potential adversary."[19] Reversing to some extent his stated position on fighting fire with water instead of fire, Carter offered a $400 million aid package to the repressive Zia regime in Pakistan and resumed shipments of fissionable material to Pakistan's rival, India.[20]

On January 23, 1980, with Soviet forces moving south through Afghanistan, Jimmy Carter announced what became known as the "Carter Doctrine." "Let our position be absolutely clear," he said. "An attempt by any outside force to gain control of the Persian Gulf will be regarded as an assault on the vital interests of the United States of America, and such an assault will be repelled by any means necessary, including military force."[21] "Any means necessary" underscored a return to Cold War policies previously repudiated by Carter, such as aid to the Zia regime in Pakistan and aid to the Islamic rebels in Afghanistan, who were as totalitarian as the Soviets and far more "distasteful" than Somoza had ever been. But this was no return to Truman's doctrine. Carter's policy was not designed to "contain" Communism as much as to protect this country's oil supply, an objectively identifiable vital interest. Under the Carter Doctrine, "threats" would not be analyzed through the lens of ideological anti-Communism but individually and objectively. This was much closer to what George Kennan had in mind when he first spoke of "containment" nearly thirty years before than was Truman's limitless ideological crusade that had led this country into Korea and Vietnam.

Coming as they did on the heels of American defeat in Southeast Asia, the Carter years, which did not appear very successful by any measure, served the unreconstructed cold warriors well, providing Americans with both a fine, first-class, unrestrained, long-overdue and very public debate over this country's relationship to the world—particularly the Communist world—and a clear frame of

---

19 Sanders, *Peddlers of Crisis*, 236.

20 Ibid.

21 "The Carter Doctrine," airforce-magazine.com, http://www.airforce-magazine.com/MagazineArchive/Pages/2010/April%202010/0410keeper.aspx, accessed May 10, 2012.

reference by which that relationship could be judged. Mainstream media publications carried the debate between the liberal establishment and the conservative and neo-conservative establishments on an almost daily basis, discussing everything from Soviet gains in the Third World to the intermediate-range nuclear missiles.[22] Every subject imaginable was being considered and reconsidered, such as the nature of Communism (was it a fundamentally legitimate form of government with shortcomings that would be corrected over time or was it just Nazism dyed red?); the validity of the recently renounced Truman Doctrine (was the Cold War necessary or did Americans overreact to "legitimate" Soviet security concerns in the wake of World War II?); and the practical effect of Carter's "human rights" based foreign policy (was a policy that undermined the shah in favor of the Ayatollah Khomeini or South Korea in favor of North Korea really very advisable as a means of advancing the cause of "human rights"?). In short, was the world better off now than when American foreign policy was built around anti-Communism?

One thing cannot be overstated: This was exactly the type of debate Americans would almost certainly have had during the late 1940s had the political system not been so poisoned by "the Communist movement of the 1930s" that Truman would create his rather questionable doctrine and impose it on the world with virtually no dissent from either the Left or the Right.

As events unfolded and the greatest debate of the so-called American Century continued, Carter's opponents gained the upper hand. By 1980, most Americans, rightly or wrongly, agreed on three things: 1) the Soviet Empire was and remained everything the anti-Communists had claimed since the earliest days of the Cold War; 2) "[i]ts inherent expansionist tendencies," as George Kennan had advised in 1947, would only be contained "by counter-pressure which makes it constantly evident that attempts to break through this containment would be detrimental to Soviet interests";[23] and 3)

---

22 Sydney Blumenthal, *The Rise of the Counter-Establishment: The Conservative Ascent to Political Power* (New York: Times Books, 1986), 141.

23 John Lewis Gaddis, "Containment: A Reassessment," *Foreign Affairs* 55, No. 4 (July 1977), 873–887, 877.

foreign policy that emphasized "human rights," "reform" and "democracy" over realism was not having the desired effect. The electorate now had a clear view of what happens when "they gave a war"[24] and your side doesn't come and turned to Ronald Reagan, who campaigned on a promise to return anti-Communism to the forefront of American foreign policy and begin an impressive defense buildup, emphasizing that nuclear terror need not be the status quo.

---

24 Charlotte Keyes, "Suppose They Gave a War and No One Came," McCall's, October 1966. http://www.genekeyes.com/CHET/Chet-1.html#Suppose, accessed May 10, 2012. This was one of the most popular phrases of the Vietnam era, appearing in posters, bumper stickers and songs.

Chapter Nine:
Ronald Reagan

The more he looked, the more he studied, the more he saw, the more he concluded that this was a regime that had to go.

We were really going to try and win the Cold War.[1]

Casper Weinberger

My idea of American policy toward the Soviet Union is simple, and some would say simplistic. It is this: We win and they lose.[2]

Ronald Reagan

In my view, the 40th President of the United States will go down in history for his rare perception.[3]

Mikhail Gorbachev

Unlike his predecessors, Ronald Reagan was determined to end both the Cold War *and* the Soviet Union. The goal of American foreign policy, in Reagan's view, was "not just the prevention of war but the expansion of freedom."[4] He rejected any notion of

---

1 Paul Kengor, *The Crusader: Ronald Reagan and the Fall of Communism* (New York: Regan, 2006), 42, 43.

2 Richard V. Allen, "The Man Who Won the Cold War," Hoover Digest, January 30, 2000. http://www.hoover.org/publications/hoover-digest/article/7398, accessed May 10, 2012.

3 Mikhail Gorbachev, *Memoirs* (New York: Doubleday, 1996), 457.

4 http://reagan2020.us/speeches/A_Future_That_Works.asp, accessed May 10, 2012.

moral equivalence between the superpowers, described the Soviet leadership as people willing "to commit any crime, to lie, to cheat" to further their cause,[5] called the Soviet Union an "evil empire and labeled the Cold War as "a struggle between right and wrong, good and evil."[6] Making a radical break with several decades of American foreign policy, Reagan rejected Carter's human rights-based strategy, Henry Kissinger's détente and George Kennan's containment in favor of pushing the Soviet Union toward complete dissolution through economic collapse. "The situation [within the USSR] was so bad," Reagan wrote in his diary, "that if Western countries cut off credits to it, we could bring it to its knees."[7] Reagan declared his intentions openly, stating in an interview published in the *New York Post* that it was important for the Western allies to "curtail" credit to the Soviets "because I think they've run out of hard cash and they economically are very vulnerable right at the moment."[8] He expressed similar sentiments during an address to members of the British Parliament on June 8, 1982, in which he outlined "a plan and a hope for the long term...which will leave Marxism-Leninism on the ash heap of history."[9] Dubbed the Reagan Doctrine, this was, as Henry Kissinger wrote, "a direct moral challenge from which all [Reagan's] predecessors would have recoiled."[10] No American president had ever spoken like this, and the Soviets were profoundly disturbed.[11] Soviet leaders would have been far more disturbed had they truly understood Reagan's insight and his determination to, as the *New York Times* noted at the time,

---

5 Presidential Press Conference, January 29, 1981.http://www.presidency.ucsb.edu/ws/index. php?pid=44101#axzz1ub40bKu5, accessed May 10, 2012.

6 Speech before the National Association of Evangelicals, Orlando Florida, March 8, 1983. http://www.presidentreagan.info/speeches/empire.cfm, accessed May 10, 2012.

7 Kengor, *The Crusader*, 119.

8 Ibid., 149.

9 Kiron K. Skinner, ed., *Turning Points in Ending the Cold War* (Palo Alto: Hoover Institution Press, 2008), 97.

10 Kissinger, *Diplomacy*, 767.

11 John Lewis Gaddis, *Strategies of Containment: A Critical Appraisal of American National Security during the Cold War* (Oxford University Press, 2005), 356.

"declare economic and technological war on the Soviet Union."[12]

"[H]ow the [Soviet] state kept alive," wrote David Remnick, "how it got from day to day, was a mystery. History was a fairy tale and the mechanisms of daily life a vast Rube Goldberg machine that somehow, just barely, kept moving. If not for the plundering of the Soviet oil fields and the worldwide energy crisis, the economy might have collapsed even before it did; and by the early 1980s, KGB reports declared that the cushion of oil profits was all but gone."[13] Long in the works, however, was a two-strand natural gas pipeline from Siberia's Urengoi gas field that would provide Western Europe with 1.37 trillion cubic feet of natural gas per year while providing Moscow as much as $30 billion annually in the Western hard currency that was its lifeblood.[14] This project alone would nearly double Moscow's annual hard currency earnings while leaving Western Europe vulnerable to Soviet blackmail, but it required vast amounts of Western credit and technology. The same was true of the Soviets' attempts to improve their ability to exploit their enormous oil reserves. They needed rotary drills and exploration technology on which American companies had a virtual monopoly, and until now, they were simply stealing or buying vast amounts of crucial Western technology through the Soviet Military Industrial Commission, which employed 100,000 people full time just translating technical documents acquired from the West.[15] Through these efforts, the Soviet aviation industry alone saved $800 million in research and development costs representing 100,000 man-hours of high-tech research.[16]

Early in his administration, Reagan initiated a concerted effort designed to kill the natural gas pipeline by preventing Western financial and technical participation in the project and to end Soviet

---

12 "Pentagon Draws Up First Strategy for Fighting A Long Nuclear War," *New York Times,* May 30, 1982.

13 David Remnick, *Lenin's Tomb: The Last Days of the Soviet Empire* (New York: Random House, 1993), 24.

14 Peter Schweitzer, *Victory: The Reagan Administration's Secret Strategy that Hastened the End of the Soviet Union* (New York: The Atlantic Monthly Press, 1994), 42.

15 Ibid., 46.

16 Ibid., 46–47.

acquisition of Western technology through an embargo authorized by section 6 of the Export Administration and Control Act, which gave the president the power to prohibit the export "of any goods, technology or other information subject to the jurisdiction of the United States or exported by a person subject to the jurisdiction of the United States."[17] This extended his reach to American overseas subsidiaries and foreign companies producing or using American technology or equipment under a licensing agreement.[18] As expected, Western Europeans objected to Reagan's embargo. French President Francois Mitterand declared that France would reject Reagan's efforts "to enlist Western Europe in a campaign of economic warfare against the Soviet Union."[19] Eventually, Reagan compromised at a G-7 economic summit in Williamsburg, Virginia, in May 1983, where, having succeeded in delaying the natural gas project for at least two full years, he agreed to a one-strand Soviet pipeline (rather than two) in exchange for agreements by the Western allies to limit their purchases of Soviet natural gas to no more than thirty percent of their needs and to tighten restrictions on technology exports and low-interest loans to the Soviet bloc.[20] Losing half of the greatly delayed natural gas project would cost the Soviets $10-15 billion annually—nearly half their hard-currency income—which was a massive blow from which the Soviet economy never recovered.[21] The Soviets were furious, and they laid the blame squarely on Reagan, where in fact it belonged.[22]

Reagan also initiated a policy of disinformation and sabotage that was very damaging to Soviet interests. Through various channels, the CIA and Pentagon began passing defective designs and technological information to Soviet agents along with defective hardware and software. This included oil rig designs, compressors, flawed mainframe computers, computer chips and satellites, which

---

17 Pub. L. No. 96-72, 93 Stat. 503 (effective October 1, 1979), codified as amended at 50 U.S.C. §§ 2401–20.

18 Schweitzer, *Victory*, 49.

19 Kengor, *The Crusader*, 150.

20 Ibid., 185. See also Schweitzer, *Victory*, 141.

21 Kengor, *The Crusader*, 185.

22 Ibid.

not only caused Soviet engineers to spend enormous amounts of time and effort on technological dead ends but resulted at one point in a pipeline explosion so powerful that it was recorded by US satellites.[23] Oleg Tikov, a specialist with the Soviet Oil Ministry, acknowledged the effect of Reagan's efforts in no uncertain terms: "It was not an excuse when we blamed American sanctions for the delay. It was the truth. Everything was chaotic. First we had no turbines, then we tried to make our own, then we could get them again. What chaos, what disruptions. Two years, and billions of dollars it cost us."[24]

In the meantime, Reagan resurrected the Truman Doctrine for enforcement in Central America, focusing his efforts on El Salvador, where Communist guerillas were attempting to seize power, and on Nicaragua, where they already had. There was, of course, considerable dissent from the Left. Not only did liberals bash Reagan exactly as Reagan and his supporters had bashed Carter ("simplistic," "sectarian," "terribly dangerous," "outrageous" and "primitive" were terms used by Anthony Lewis in the *New York Times* to describe Reagan's March 1983 "evil empire" speech[25]), but they unashamedly supported Communist regimes targeted by Reagan in a manner that would have been unthinkable during the first twenty years of the Cold War.

In December 1982, Congress passed the Boland Amendment. Named after Edward Boland, a liberal Democrat who headed the House Intelligence Committee, the Boland Amendment prohibited the use of any US funds to aid in the overthrow of the Marxist government in Nicaragua. This was eventually followed in the fall of 1984 by the much more stringent Boland II, which barred all military aid to the Contras, regardless of its stated purpose. In the meantime, the Sandinistas had received hundreds of millions of dollars in Soviet military aid, including 340 tanks, advanced Soviet artillery, MIG-25s and helicopter gunships. They now possessed ten times the military power of the Somoza regime and "openly boasted

23 Ibid., 155.
24 Schweitzer, *Victory*, 216.
25 "Abroad at Home; Onward, Christian Soldiers," *New York Times*, March 10, 1983.

that they had 'the largest military force in all of Central America.'"[26] Regardless, Democratic congressmen and senators openly collaborated with Sandinista envoys to undermine Reagan's policies in Central America.[27] Democratic Senator Tom Harkin actually traveled to Nicaragua where he urged Violetta Chamorro, owner of the independent newspaper *La Prensa,* to submit to Sandinista censorship.[28] *Commandante* Daniel Ortega himself visited Washington to lobby on behalf of his Communist government and make the rounds with friendly American senators and representatives. He traveled to New York, where he attended dinner parties in his honor, addressed church groups and appeared on the Phil Donahue show before heading off to Denver to address the National Bar Association.[29]

On March 23, 1983, Reagan launched the Strategic Defense Initiative or SDI, a program intended to make nuclear missiles obsolete. In theory, the system would be able to track and destroy incoming nuclear missiles using ground- and space-based laser and particle beam systems. The Soviets, of course, denounced SDI hysterically, calling the concept "insane" and "a bid to disarm the Soviet Union." Reagan's critics seized this as another opportunity to ridicule him: The *New York Times* editorialized SDI as "a farfetched quest, . . . a pipe dream, a projection of fantasy into policy."[30] The *Chicago Sun Times* labeled Reagan's speech "an appalling disservice," while Democrats in Congress had a field day. Ted Kennedy accused Reagan of "misleading Red-scare tactics and reckless Star Wars schemes."[31] Delighted at liberal criticism of Reagan, Soviet commentator Vitaly Kobysh informed the world that US politicians called SDI "the greatest deception of our time."[32] (If a program like this had been announced during the 1950s, the

26 Winik, *On the Brink,* 423.

27 Christopher Smith, *Resisting Reagan* (Chicago: University of Chicago Press, 1996), 231. See also Winik, *On the Brink,* 563.

28 Ibid.

29 "Sandinista Heads West after a 6-Day Wooing of New York," *New York Times,* August 1, 1986.

30 "Nuclear Facts, Science Fictions," *New York Times,* March 27, 1983, sec. 4.

31 Kengor, *The Crusader,* 181.

32 Ibid., 183.

administration would surely have been criticized by the opposition, but only for waiting too long and not requesting enough money to make the program operational sooner.)

On October 25, 1983, Reagan sent an expeditionary force of Marines and airborne units to seize the island of Grenada and expel its pro-Soviet government, which had signed a treaty giving the Soviet Union landing rights and was preparing its airport, with Cuban assistance, to handle heavy military aircraft. Grenada was, Reagan said, "a Soviet-Cuban base colony being readied for use as a major military bastion to export terror."[33] From the anti-Communist perspective, the operation was a complete success: "For the first time since the Bolshevik revolution, a Communist government in a sovereign state had been removed by an outside power's military force."[34] Reagan's opposition, of course, was apoplectic. The Soviets called it "state-inspired terrorism."[35] *New York Times* columnist Anthony Lewis compared Reagan's removal of Grenada's government to a Soviet invasion of Poland.[36] Writing in the *Washington Post* on October 30, 1983, Robert G. Kaiser called Reagan "myopic"; compared his actions in Grenada to the Soviet conquest and subjugation of Czechoslovakia, Poland and Afghanistan; and quoted George Ball, who said that Reagan was "[getting] away with murder."[37] Yet Reagan pressed on, oblivious to his critics, determined to see the end of Communism in his lifetime and largely unwilling to compromise on anything because compromise, in his view, would assist the Soviets in maintaining their empire. And the Soviets knew it. In early 1984, TASS economic writer Vladimir Pirogov noted that Reagan was trying to "exhaust" the Soviet Union while Soviet officer-scholars noted that Reagan's "schemes of economic warfare are closely interwoven with plans to achieve military superiority, since it is precisely the economy that is

33 Brian Crozier, *The Rise and Fall of the Soviet Empire* (Rocklin, California: Forum 1999), 373.
34 Ibid., 371.
35 Kengor, *The Crusader*, 196.
36 "Abroad At Home; President Pyrrhus," *New York Times*, October 27, 1983.
37 Given his involvement in Kennedy administration shenanigans, particularly the overthrow and murder of Ngo Dinh Diem—an episode in which he was a principal player—this is an astonishing level of hypocrisy, but one that is typical of Ball and his ilk.

the material basis of defense."[38] They were, of course, exactly right.

On November 21, 1983, the German Bundestag, despite crude threats and nuclear blackmail by the Soviets, voted 286-226 to approve the deployment the first Pershing II missiles in Western Europe to offset the Soviet SS-20s placed shortly after Jimmy Carter declared an end to the Cold War. The nuclear freeze movement, which was powerful and international in scope, had resisted every step of the way, having failed to notice that it was the Soviets who began this round of escalation and that Reagan had offered to halt deployment of the Pershings if the Soviets would remove their own SS-20s, an offer the Soviets rejected.[39] That very evening, ABC television aired what Massachusetts Democrat Edward Markey called "a $7 million advertising campaign" for the nuclear freeze resolution he sponsored in the House. Entitled *The Day After*, the movie was a shocking, depressing portrayal of the destruction of Lawrence, Kansas, in a nuclear exchange. No matter what ABC executives said, it was clear that the movie was made to convey the idea that deterrence was not a viable concept and that, as the *Washington Post* later editorialized, the deployment of American missiles rather than Soviet SS-20s represented the fatal provocation.[40] Senator Edward M. Kennedy, who believed that "Reagan's belligerence" was the source of difficulty in Soviet-American relations, even offered to assist the Soviets in presenting their case for SS-20s in Europe to the American people. Making a direct appeal to Yuri Andropov through his friend, former senator John V. Tunney, Kennedy offered to help Andropov secure interviews with Walter Cronkite and Barbara Walters as a means of offsetting what Kennedy considered to be distortion from the

---

38 Kengor, *The Crusader*, 203–204.

39 Mikhail Gorbachev would later acknowledge how grievous an error Soviet deployment of the SS-20s was. Although superior to the missiles it replaced, the SS-20 remained an intermediate-range weapon unable to reach the United States. The Pershing IIs with which Reagan responded, although an intermediate-range system like the SS-20s, placed, in Gorbachev's words, "the most populated part of the USSR" within five minutes of their launch. A land-based "intermediate-range" weapon for the Soviets was, in practical terms, an intercontinental system when placed in Western Europe by the United States, making SS-20 deployment, according to Gorbachev, an "unforgivable adventure." Gorbachev, Memoirs, 443–444.

40 Winik, *On the Brink*, 292.

Reagan administration.[41]

Meanwhile, this Soviet-initiated round in the arms race was taking its toll on the Soviets. By 1984, the Soviets were spending some $30 billion per year, thirty-two percent of their Gross Domestic Product ("GDP"), on arms. The United States, by comparison, spent more than eight times as much, some $250 billion per year, on its military. But this represented only six percent of the American GDP. That is, the United States was spending more than twice the entire Soviet GDP on its military with only six percent of its own GDP. Moreover, some eighty percent of the Soviets' lifeblood, hard currency from the West, came from oil and natural gas exports.[42] Having seriously dampened Soviet hopes for natural gas sales to Western Europe, Reagan now turned his attention to Soviet oil exports. He encouraged the Saudis, who were far more cooperative than America's allies in Western Europe, to increase oil production from less than two million barrels a day to nine million. Between the fall of 1985 and the spring of 1986, oil prices dropped from $30 per barrel to $10 per barrel.[43] For the Soviets, the effects were simply catastrophic. In just one year, they moved from a $700 million trade surplus with the West to a $1.4 billion deficit, which tripled during the following year.[44] Mikhail Gorbachev acknowledged Reagan's masterstroke in his memoirs, noting that the 1985 drop in oil prices cost the Soviets half their hard currency earnings.[45]

Gorbachev had become general secretary of the Communist Party of the Soviet Union in March 1985. More Communist true believer than liberal reformer, he intended to save, not destroy, the Soviet Union. ("I am not ashamed to say anywhere in public that I am a Communist and believe in the socialist idea. I will die believing in this and will pass into the next world believing this."[46]) In his 1987 book *Perestroika,* he wrote that Lenin was no authoritarian

41 Kengor, *The Crusader*, 205–210.

42 Ibid., 241.

43 Ibid., 251.

44 Ibid., 252–253.

45 Gorbachev, *Memoirs*, 468.

46 Kengor, *The Crusader*, 296.

but a man who believed in democracy.[47] The Soviet Union was, throughout its history, a land of "indisputable progress";[48] with "immense potentialities for resolving the most complex problems of social progress."[49] Accordingly, he was not going "to change Soviet power...or abandon its fundamental principles...."[50] Among its fundamental principles, of course, was the Brezhnev Doctrine, by which the Soviets declared that any challenge to Communism within a Soviet-bloc state would entitle the Soviets to intervene with armed force, as they intervened in Hungary in 1956, Czechoslovakia in 1968 and Afghanistan in 1979, where Ronald Reagan found a marvelous opportunity to turn the screws.

In an effort requiring several years, Reagan trumped formidable opposition from both the bureaucracy and his opponents in Congress and began delivering Stinger anti-aircraft missiles to the anti-Communist rebels in Afghanistan.[51] In September 1986, the destruction of the Soviet Air Force in Afghanistan began. The first eleven Stingers fired brought down ten Soviet helicopters, and for the next 200 days, one Soviet aircraft or helicopter would be destroyed each day. Six months earlier, Mikhail Gorbachev described the war in Afghanistan as "a running sore."[52]By the end of the year, it was exponentially worse, and something had to give, as Gorbachev told the politburo: "If we don't back down on some specific, maybe even important issues, if we won't budge from the positions we've held for a long time, we will lose in the end. We will be drawn into an arms race that we cannot manage. We will lose,

---

47 Mikhail Gorbachev, *Perestroika: New Thinking for Our Country and the World* (New York: Harper & Row, 1986), 32.

48 Ibid., 38.

49 Ibid., 44.

50 Ibid., 54. See also Victor Sebestyen, *Revolution 1989: The Fall of the Soviet Empire* (Pantheon Books, 2009), xix: "His overriding aim was to save communism in the Soviet Union. He believed the people of Eastern Europe would choose to stay allied to the Soviets in a socialist commonwealth. His miscalculations were staggering."

51 Under *United States v. Smith*, 27 F. Cas. 1192 (C.C.N.Y. 1807), arming the Afghan rebels might have violated the Neutrality Act. Under *United States v. Terrell*, 731 F.Supp. 473 (S.D. Fla. 1989), it would not. This might also have violated 18 U.S.C. 956 and involve several violations of international law.

52 Kengor, *The Crusader*, 260.

because right now we are already at the end of our tether."[53]

In the fall of 1986, it was revealed that in 1985, Reagan had authorized the sale of Hawk anti-aircraft missiles and TOW anti-tank weapons to Iran through Israel in part to obtain the release of Americans being held hostage by terrorists in Lebanon, which was contrary to Reagan's stated policy of never negotiating with terrorists. Lt. Col. Oliver North, an NSC staff member, began diverting profits from the sales in early 1986 to provide support to the Contra guerillas fighting the Sandinistas in Nicaragua, which, having been expressly forbidden by Congress, represented in its simplest terms a major violation of US law and accompanying theft of the diverted funds. Reagan was never tied to the diversion and survived the scandal, but it was now beyond question that the Reagan administration had joined in the long tradition of lawlessness that had been institutionalized under the National Security Act of 1947 and honored by every Cold War president except Jimmy Carter.

Even as Iran-Contra unfolded, SDI was reaching strategic fruition, ironically, despite technical infeasibility. No matter how much Reagan's domestic critics ridiculed what they labeled "Star Wars," the Soviets were just frantic over it. Soviet Ambassador Anatoly Dobrynin wrote in his memoirs that "[o]ur leadership was convinced that the great technical potential of the U.S. had scored again and treated Reagan's statement as a real threat."[54] *Isvestiya* denounced it as an attempt to impose upon the Soviet Union "an even more ruinous arms race." Andre Gromyko saw behind SDI "the clear calculation that the USSR will exhaust its material resources...and therefore will finally be forced to surrender."[55] Gromyko was right. Without nuclear weapons, the Soviet Union was little more than a Third World country. Nearly seventy years of Marxism, empire and most importantly, Cold War, had left it bankrupt and without the means to maintain its existing military

---

53 Thompson, *The Hawk and the Dove*, 307.

54 Anatoly Dobrynin, *In Confidence: Moscow's Ambassador to America's Six Cold War Presidents* (Seattle: University of Washington Press, 1995), 528.

55 Dinesh D'Souza, *Ronald Reagan: How an Ordinary Man Became an Extraordinary Leader* (New York: Touchstone, 1997), 179–180.

forces, much less compete with the United States in a high-tech arms race. Knowing that, "like a snake that had broken its jaw trying to swallow an elephant," the Soviet Union "was on the verge of collapse,"[56] Gorbachev did everything in his power to retard if not halt Reagan's plans for SDI.[57] The last great confrontation of the Cold War would be diplomatic, not military. It would be fought neither in Europe nor in the Third World but in Reykjavik, Iceland, and the court of public opinion.

On October 13, 1986, Gorbachev, proposed deep and unprecedented cuts in strategic nuclear arms along with a complete removal of both US and Soviet intermediate-range missiles from Europe, leaving French and British intermediate-range nuclear forces untouched. "'This,' Gorbachev told Reagan, was 'your own zero option.'"[58] Eventually, Gorbachev proposed a complete elimination of all nuclear weapons in ten years, provided that the SDI would be limited to the research laboratory. Neither side was to deploy a missile shield. To this, Reagan would not agree, and the summit ended in failure. Reagan, of course, was pounded by the press. "REAGAN-GORBACHEV SUMMIT TALKS COLLAPSE AS DEADLOCK ON SDI WIPES OUT OTHER GAINS," said the *Washington Post* in a banner headline on October 13, 1986. "No Deal: Star Wars Sinks the Summit" proclaimed *Time* magazine while *Newsweek* asked, "Is Star Wars Worth the Price"? The *Los Angeles Times* ran an article attacking Reagan's stance at Reykjavik as a "colossal mistake," a "fumble," a "debacle" and a "colossal failure of leadership."[59] Gorbachev himself declared that SDI was "a symbol of obstruction to the cause of peace" and "the epitome of military schemes."[60]

But Reagan would not budge. "The [Soviet] system was dying, and Reykjavik was one of the USSR's last chances to survive."[61]

---

56 Thompson, *The Hawk and the Dove*, 307.

57 D'Souza, *Ronald Reagan*, 183.

58 Lou Cannon, *President Reagan: The Role of a Lifetime* (New York: Public Affairs, 2000), 687.

59 John Tirman, "Fixated on the Technological Fix: SDI, a Colossal Blunder, Demonstrates Failure of Leadership," *Los Angeles Times*, October 15, 1986, Metro Section, 5.

60 "Quote of the Day," *New York Times*, October 15, 1986.

61 Thompson, *The Hawk and the Dove*, 307.

Reagan knew it, and Gorbachev knew it as well, bitterly denouncing Reagan's "immoral intention to bleed the Soviet Union white economically" while events were actually unfolding.[62] After seven decades of terror, repression, aggression and mass murder, the Soviets needed concessions to forestall their own impending collapse, and Reagan would have no part of it.

On December 7, 1988, Gorbachev addressed the United Nations in New York. After claiming that "the principle of freedom of choice is a must for all nations" (an apparent repudiation of the Brezhnev Doctrine), Gorbachev announced deep, unilateral cuts in the Soviet Armed Forces, including the demobilization of six tank divisions and virtually all units with offensive capability in Eastern Europe, which were to be withdrawn and disbanded. In total, Soviet power in the Western USSR and Eastern Europe was to be reduced by 500,000 men, 10,000 tanks, 8,500 artillery systems and 800 combat aircraft.[63]

This speech marked the beginning of the end. With the will to suppress their satellites exhausted and the means diminishing rapidly, it was only a matter of time before Soviet power in Eastern Europe unraveled.

In June of 1989, the Communist government of Poland held the first free elections in its history. The results were stunning: Solidarity, the democratic opposition party, swept the elections, winning 99 out of 100 seats in the upper house while thirty-three of thirty-five top Communist Party and government leaders lost their seats in the lower house, although they ran unopposed. More than half the voters simply crossed out their names on the ballots.[64] On August 24, 1989, the impossible happened: Solidarity member Tadeusz Mazowiecki was elected prime minister. Communists willingly relinquished power to non-Communists in a Warsaw Pact country, and the Soviet Union allowed it.[65]

Within hours, the Hungarian government decided to ignore a

---

62 Gorbachev, *Perestroika*, 219.

63 Don Oberdorfer, *From the Cold War to a New Era: The United States and the Soviet Union, 1983–1991* (Baltimore: The Johns Hopkins University Press, 1998), 217–218.

64 Ibid., 359.

65 Ibid., 361.

1968 treaty with East Germany that obligated Hungary to prevent the escape of East German citizens to the West. Within three days more than 13,000 East Germans had fled through Hungary despite strenuous objections by the East German government. In October, the Communist Party in Hungary officially renounced Leninism, renamed itself the Hungarian Socialist Party and declared Hungary a Western-style democratic republic. By November, East Germany was in the throes of popular, democratic revolution. With hundreds of thousands of demonstrators in the streets, Gorbachev suggested to East German leader Egon Krenz that he open the border to provide an escape valve. On November 9, Krenz complied. *The Wall was down.* Democratic revolution in Bulgaria and Czechoslovakia soon followed, and by the end of the year, Communist power had been effectively eliminated in five of six Warsaw Pact countries.

In early 1990, one of the Reagan administration's most bitterly contested campaigns came to fruition in Nicaragua, where, following in the footsteps of Dwight Eisenhower and John Kennedy, among others, Reagan had waged a years-long proxy war on Nicaragua's Marxist government using rebels known as the Contras. (This was adjudged a violation of international law by the World Court on June 27, 1986, and it was possibly a violation of US law as well, including 18 U.S.C. §§ 956 and 960.[66]) On February 27, Marxist Daniel Ortega was defeated in an internationally supervised presidential election by Violetta Chamorro. Both the United States and the Soviet Union had agreed in advance to respect the results, and Gorbachev kept his word. Although the Soviet Union would continue to limp along for another two years, the Soviet Empire was virtually dead but still unpredictable and dangerous, as the Baltic Republics, which had passed into Soviet hands as part of the 1939 Hitler-Stalin pact, soon learned.

In December 1989, the Lithuanian Communist Party seceded from the Soviet Communist Party and nullified Article 6 of the Soviet Constitution, which guaranteed the Communist Party's monopoly on power, giving independent parties the right to seek

---

66 "World Court Supports Nicaragua After U.S. Rejected Judges' Role," *New York Times*, June 27, 1986.

and hold office.[67] The Latvian Supreme Soviet followed suit in January 1990, as did the Estonians in February. In March, the Lithuanian Parliament nullified all Soviet military obligations, which Lithuanians labeled forced service in an occupation army.[68] Lithuanian Communists still loyal to the Soviet Union demanded the disbanding of Parliament and the introduction of presidential rule. Attempting to put the best face possible on the inevitable process of dissolution, Gorbachev had the Supreme Soviet enact a rather complex, five-year secession process, but it was far too late for legal charades by the occupying power. Protests against Soviet power in Azerbaijan were crushed, leaving scores dead as tension between the Baltic Republics and the Soviets mounted throughout the rest of the year. Early on the morning of January 13, 1991, the Soviets launched a last-ditch effort to halt the unraveling of their empire.

A column of Soviet tanks blasted through a crowd of civilians and a cordon of parked cars and seized the television broadcast center of Lithuania, killing at least eleven civilians and wounding 100 more.[69] Lithuanian Communists loyal to Moscow formed a "National Salvation Committee" and called for direct rule by Mikhail Gorbachev as similar "Committees" making similar requests arose in Latvia and Estonia.[70] On January 21, violence erupted in Latvia when Soviet Interior Ministry troops seized the Latvian Interior Ministry after a furious gun battle in which five people were killed. Although Gorbachev denied advance notice of the raid, he endorsed the assault.[71] As in Lithuania, an anonymous, self-appointed "All-Latvian Committee of National Salvation" claimed that it was dissolving the elected, pro-independence government and assuming power "for the time it takes to stabilize the situation" to avoid "bourgeois dictatorship" and "economic collapse." "Soviet Latvia," said the Committee, "must remain in a

---

67 Malia, *The Soviet Tragedy*, 464.

68 "Gorbachev Warns the Lithuanians to Halt Defiance," *New York Times*, January 11, 1991.

69 "Soviet Tanks Roll in Lithuania; 11 Dead," *New York Times*, January 13, 1991.

70 "Wider Soviet Crackdown Is Foreseen in the Baltics," *New York Times*, January 16, 1991.

71 "Soviet Crackdown: Latvia; Soviet Commandos Stage Latvia Raid; At Least 5 Killed," New York Times, January 21, 199.

renewed U.S.S.R."[72] On February 5, Gorbachev declared an upcoming plebiscite on Lithuanian independence to be "without legal foundation," but did not threaten action. On February 9, Lithuanians voted overwhelmingly for independence while Latvia and Estonia scheduled plebiscites.[73] Meanwhile, Russians prepared, for the first time in their history, to elect, by direct popular vote, the president of the Russian Republic. Gorbachev, who felt secure in his own power as general secretary of the Communist Party, did not run for the Russian presidency, which allowed his rival Boris Yeltsin to win handily. This was one of Gorbachev's greatest miscalculations. It created a legitimate opposition with a power base of its own while galvanizing the party apparatchiks, military officers and other denizens of the old regime who were bitterly opposed to the path charted by Gorbachev.

Through the summer of 1991, Gorbachev did his best to lead, reorganize and reform, but nothing could check the Soviet Union's decline. On August 18, hard-liners who believed that liberalization was responsible for the country's ills attempted a coup against Gorbachev, who had been isolated at his vacation home on the Black Sea. The plotters, who had formed what they dubbed the State Committee for the State of Emergency, sent emissaries to demand Gorbachev's resignation. He refused, dismissing them contemptuously as "adventurers and criminals."[74] The next morning, the Soviet media broadcast news that the Committee had taken over the government, reintroduced censorship and banned all political activity. It was much too little, however, and far too late. Independent radio stations remained on the air and foreign broadcasts beamed in. The truth was known to everyone. Russian President Boris Yeltsin defied the plotters and climbed on a tank to exhort crowds, numbering in the tens of thousands, to resist the Committee. Military commanders directed by the Committee to maintain order would not employ the kind of lethal force needed to disperse the crowds, and it was soon clear that the coup had failed.

---

72 Ibid.

73 "Lithuania Votes Overwhelmingly for Independence from Moscow," *New York Times*, February 10, 1991, sec. 1.

74 Oberdorfer, *From the Cold War to a New Era*, 459–460.

On August 22, Gorbachev returned to Moscow proclaiming himself "a different man" and swearing to make the Communist Party "a living force of *perestroika.*"[75] But he and his party had become virtually irrelevant. Having effectively defeated the Army, the KGB and the Interior Ministry, democratic forces were in control and wanted nothing to do with the Communists. Gorbachev, on the advice of his own aides, resigned as general secretary of the Communist Party, disbanded the Central Committee and transferred party property to the Parliament, which then banned all Communist Party activity, casting Soviet Communism into history's dustbin.

On December 1, 1991, Ukraine voted for independence. Seven days later, Yeltsin and the presidents of Ukraine and Belarus met in secret at a Belorussian hunting lodge, where they declared that "the Union of Soviet Socialist Republics is ceasing its existence as a subject of international law and a geopolitical reality" and drafted a blueprint for the Commonwealth of Independent States.[76] On December 21, the Commonwealth, comprised of Russia and ten former Soviet republics, was officially established, declaring within its founding documents that "the Union of Soviet Socialist Republics ceases to exist."[77]

Gorbachev officially resigned from the Soviet presidency on December 25, 1991, gave a farewell address and transferred the codes for the Soviet nuclear arsenal to Boris Yeltsin, president of the Russian Republic. The hammer and sickle of the Soviet Union was lowered, and the red, white and blue flag of Russia was raised in its stead. Communism, "the most colossal case of political carnage in history,"[78] was dead (at least for now). Both the Soviet Union (essentially the Russian Empire of 1914) and the Soviet Empire (which included Stalin's World War II conquests) were dead with it, ending the Cold War with as many questions as answers, beginning with perhaps the most important of all: What role if any did American policy from 1945-1991 play in the ultimate demise of the

---

75 Ibid., 464–465.

76 Ibid., 469.

77 Ibid., 471.

78 Martin Malia, Foreword to *The Black Book of Communism*, x.

Soviet Union as it actually occurred?

Chapter Ten:
Cause, Effect and the Legend of
George Kennan

[T]he soldiers who'd died in Korea and my friends and classmates who had been killed in Vietnam....It meant something now.[1]

P. J. O'Rourke

[I]t is easy to look back now and say it was dumb...but at the time, Communism was trying to take over the whole world, and [the men who died in Vietnam] didn't die for nothing. They really didn't....If they didn't do it, the whole world could be very different now.

Bill Maher

No country ever won a war as utterly and convincingly as the United States went on to win the Cold War.[2]

Christopher Hitchens

It requires no particular genius to understand that the Western democracies, led when not dragged by the United States, destroyed the Soviet Union, which was an aggressive, expansionist power that

---

1 P.J. O'Rourke, *Give War a Chance* (New York: Vintage Books, 1993), 12.
2 Christopher Hitchens, "America Counts Its Cold War Casualties," *Newsday*, June 18, 1992, Nassau ed., 70.

would have brought within its orbit, directly or through surrogates, any territory available, as a brief review of history reveals.

Stalin maintained a substantial Red Army presence in Iran (with vast oil reserves) in the immediate aftermath of World War II until the British and Americans *forced* him out. As Khrushchev noted, Stalin "would have liked...very much" to have moved into "the Near East . . . but he realistically realized that the balance of power wasn't in our favor and that Britain wouldn't have stood for our interference."[3] Stalin then attempted to force concessions from Turkey and acquire naval access to the Mediterranean—which would have represented a major shift in the balance of power in Europe—and once again, he was checked by American-led opposition. Communists tried to seize power in Greece, and they were stopped only because the United States threw its support to the Royalist dictatorship, which was known by Truman and Acheson to be "corrupt, repressive and incompetent,"[4] and steadfastly supported it for decades to come. Stalin next closed all road and rail links to Berlin to force the Western Allies out of the city. Unable to starve the city into submission and unwilling to raise the stakes by attacking allied relief aircraft, Stalin backed down. *American default at any of these points would have changed Cold War history considerably.*

Next came the Korean conflict, which militarized the Cold War to an extent unimaginable in January 1950, transforming the Clifford-Elsey analysis and NSC-68 from classified theory into public policy, triggering a stupendous increase in the defense budget and the size and power of both the military-industrial complex and the national security state while launching an arms race that, over the long-term, would destroy the Soviet economy. *Truman's multi-faceted response to Kim Il Sung's attack on this country's Korean allies ("proxies" if you prefer), which was the product of myriad factors more domestic than foreign, was probably the most important single link in a chain of causation that would end with the collapse of Soviet power some four decades later.*

---

3 Gaddis, *We Now Know*, 165.
4 Isaacson and Thomas, *The Wise Men*, 388.

Likewise, John Kennedy's policies were enormously damaging over the long term to Soviet interests. In Khrushchev, it bears restatement, Kennedy faced a man with whom business could be done. If any president had an opportunity to initiate policies designed to reduce tension, end the arms race and perhaps the Cold War itself, Kennedy was the one. But as a creature of domestic politics, he rejected the role of peacemaker in favor of an arms race coupled with an aggressive, unlawful war on Cuba that brought the world to the brink of nuclear disaster. By the time Kennedy's thousand days were over, a humiliated Khrushchev was on the way out in favor of hard-liners who, responding in kind to Kennedy's provocations, took the Soviet Union to the brink of economic collapse, as noted by Soviet Lieutenant General Nikolai Detinov:

> During the 1960s, the Soviet government mobilized the economy to the point that all industrial facilities were turned to military production. All factories were included....The rate of growth in our national economy went down in all branches. While before the Caribbean crisis we had a steady rate of production, after the Caribbean crisis all production started going down thanks to the fact that all factories were mobilized in the name of military technology. Turning the national economy around later was very hard.[5]

Soviet war planner Vitalii Tsygichko agreed: "The whole country worked with weapons. We just had to keep feeding the Machine. We couldn't stop it."[6]

Norman Polmar and John D. Gresham state explicitly what the historical record reveals: "The massive military buildup program began even before Leonid Brezhnev and Alexei Kosygin took power in 1964 [and took] the Soviet Union down the road to eventual bankruptcy and, ultimately, the breakup of the Soviet Union."[7]

---

5 Rhodes, *Arsenals of Folly*, 94.
6 Thompson, *The Hawk and the Dove*, 261.
7 Polmar and Gresham, *Defcon 2*, 282–283.

However idiotic and unlawful, Kennedy's policies played as important a role in the Soviet Union's demise as Truman's.

But what of America's war in Southeast Asia? The orthodox narrative tells us that it contributed nothing to the outcome of the "long twilight struggle": "One great irony of the Vietnam War, nearly forty years after it began and thirty years after it ended, is its essential lack of effect upon the Cold War."[8] Malcolm Browne, one of Halberstam's Saigon comrades who was a central figure in the events leading up to Diem's overthrow, said in 1988 that "Vietnam had no appreciable effect on history."[9] James Fallows, who famously chronicled his draft dodge in the May 1975 *Washington Monthly,* tells us that "Asian countries are over the Vietnam War because they realize how little difference it made."[10] This perspective is particularly attractive today since it allows born-again cold warriors (purveyors of orthodoxy *par excellence*) to repudiate the Truman Doctrine's Southeast Asian campaign while embracing both America's Cold War victory and the Truman Doctrine itself, which they well know was essential to that victory as history actually unfolded. But like most Cold War orthodoxy, it fails to withstand critical analysis.

Ho Chi Minh was a loyal, Moscow-trained Comintern functionary dedicated to "the overthrow of the international bourgeoisie and the creation of an international Soviet republic."[11] He founded Communist parties throughout Southeast Asia during the 1930s,[12] where Communists trained, supported and encouraged by the Soviets and Chinese were active and eager to initiate their own "wars of national liberation" when the time was right.[13] Absent

---

8 David Kaiser, *American Tragedy: Kennedy, Johnson and the Origins of the Vietnam War* (Cambridge: The Belknap Press of Harvard University Press, 2000), 493.

9 McCloud, *What Should We Tell Our Children about Vietnam*, 20.

10 James Fallows, "No Hard Feelings," *Atlantic Monthly*, December 1988, 71. http://0-go.galegroup.com.library.naperville-lib.org/ps/i.do?id=GALE%7CA6838610&v=2.1&u=napervillepl&it=r&p=GRGM&sw=w, accessed May 10, 2012.

11 Andrew and Mitrokhin, *The World Was Going Our Way*, 1.

12 Moyar, *Triumph Forsaken*, 138.

13 Peng, *My Side of History*, 428–430; Moyar, *Triumph Forsaken*, 140: "On Matters concerning all of Southeast Asia, [Southeast Asian Communist leaders] deferred to Mao."

the Truman Doctrine, the time would have been right by the mid-1950s at the latest. ("We do know now," noted Professor John Lewis Gaddis, "that Stalin, Mao, and Ho met in Moscow in 1950 to map out the strategy for an eventual takeover of Indochina."[14]) But the outbreak of war in Korea placed Truman squarely behind the French, and on December 30, 1950, "the course of U.S. policy was set to block further Communist expansion in Asia...with particular attention...to the problem of French Indochina."[15] Truman's support (some $600 million by 1953) delayed French defeat for several crucial years while his war in Korea left the Chinese brutally mauled, terrified of American intervention and anxious to facilitate a divided Vietnam, to the shock and dismay of Ho Chi Minh's representatives, who arrived in Geneva fully expecting their great power allies to support their demand for an unconditional surrender by the French, but found instead that the Soviets and Chinese had, in the words of a furious Pham Van Dong, "double crossed us."[16] *American policy had already altered the course of events considerably.*

The French had no cards to play by 1954, and had Eisenhower simply walked away, the Geneva Accords, assuming there were any Accords, would have looked vastly different. Vietnam would have been united under Communist rule rather quickly, with Cambodia and Laos, unsupported and powerless, following shortly thereafter. Even with the Geneva Accords as written, had Eisenhower supported the 1954 settlement, the countrywide elections of 1956 would have delivered Vietnam to the Communists, with Cambodia and Laos, once again, following shortly thereafter. This would have left Thailand sharing more than 1,000 miles of its border with three aggressive new Communist states, providing Thai Communists with the "common border with a national territory controlled by a fraternal party" that, as Malayan Communist Party chief Chin Peng noted in his memoirs, was crucial to a successful insurgency.[17] If

---

14 John Lewis Gaddis, "Were the Hawks Right about the Vietnam War?" *Atlantic Online* (April 2000). http://www.theatlantic.com/past/docs/issues/2000/04/gaddis.htm, accessed May 10, 2012.

15 See NSC 48/2, cited in Sheehan, Smith, Kenworthy and Butterfield, *The Pentagon Papers*, 10.

16 Karnow, *Vietnam: A History*, 200.

17 Chin Peng, *My Side of History*, 433.

South Vietnam could not survive a Moscow- and Beijing-supported invasion across a 700-mile border with as many as 500,000 American troops defending it, what chance would Thailand have had on its own bordering three states led by doctrinaire Communists who, not having been betrayed at Geneva, would have remained loyal to their great-power patrons? It is rather silly, after all, to imagine that, with everything going their way—proving the superiority of their system and the inevitability of their ultimate triumph—the Soviets and their Third World allies were going to abandon their pursuit of world revolution. And it is equally silly to imagine that American policy makers insightful enough to grasp the supposed futility of extending Truman's doctrine to French Indochina—and politically courageous enough to act on that belief—would remain determined to enforce the Truman Doctrine through "Vietnam Wars" in Thailand, Burma, Malaya, Indonesia or anywhere else. *If the Truman Doctrine's Southeast Asian campaign was going to end in the mid-1950s or early 1960s, it was going to end in its entirety, altering considerably the historical record thereafter.*

The Thais, being neither stupid nor suicidal, would have seen the writing on the wall and made whatever accommodation was necessary with the emerging regional powers, just as they did with the Japanese during World War II.[18] (Not that this would have saved them in the end from the inevitable demands for a "coalition" government.) And a Communist or at least an accommodating Thailand was the key in turn to the secure, cross-border sanctuaries and supply areas "desperately needed," in Chin Peng's words, by the Communists in Malaya and elsewhere. Like rotating a kaleidoscope, American withdrawal at any time would have created an entirely different picture and changed everything that followed. Even with American policy as it was through 1964, Pham Van Dong, Hanoi's minister of foreign affairs, advised a Canadian diplomat that a US defeat in South Vietnam would "in all probability start a chain reaction,"[19] which was exactly what Kenneth Young, the American

18 Moyar, *Triumph Forsaken*, 139.
19 Gelb, *The Irony of Vietnam*, 114.

ambassador to Thailand, warned in October 1961.[20]

As it was, there was no "chain reaction" because the Truman Doctrine's Southeast Asian campaign: 1) lasted some twenty-five years; 2) absorbed virtually *all* Soviet and Chinese effort in Asia, including considerable resources they could have and would have employed elsewhere; 3) left the Vietnamese Communists, although victorious in 1975, bankrupt and virtually exhausted; and 4) ensured that American-backed, non-Communist states stood between China and almost all of its Southeast Asian allies until 1975. This left Communist insurgencies throughout Southeast Asia to wither on the vine while giving the non-Communist states the support and time they needed to develop into stable, prosperous countries no longer vulnerable to leftist "insurgencies" whose time had long passed, as Lee Kuan Yew, prime minister of Singapore from 1959-1990, has noted time and again:

> Although America intervention failed in Vietnam, it bought time for the rest of Southeast Asia. In 1965, when the U.S. military moved massively into South Vietnam, Thailand, Malaya and the Philippines faced internal threats from armed communist insurgencies, and the communist underground was still active in Singapore. Indonesia, in the throes of a failed communist coup, was waging *konfrontasi*, an undeclared war against Malaya and Singapore....Standards of living were low and economic growth slow. America's action enabled noncommunist Southeast Asia to put their own houses in order. By 1975, they were in better shape to stand up to the communists. Had there been no U.S. intervention, the will of these countries to resist them would have melted and Southeast Asia would most likely have gone communist. The prosperous market economies of ASEAN were nurtured during

---

20 Moyar, *Triumph Forsaken*, 139.

the Vietnam War years.[21]

In summary, twenty-five years of American intervention and a fifteen-year proxy war between the superpowers permanently halted Communist expansion into an area of the world with a vast wealth of natural resources while consuming, just for good measure, an enormous amount of Communist money, effort and resources they could have and surely would have employed elsewhere. You cannot possibly eliminate an episode of this magnitude from history without altering the outcome of a superpower conflict that turned, in the end, more on economics than anything else, which brings us to the Soviet side of the Cold War equation, where chronic, systemic defects and rigid ideology produced both core economic dysfunction and policies that were invariably crude, brutal and too cunning by half.

The Cold War began not in 1947 but in March 1919, when the Soviet government founded the Comintern, with "the goal of fighting, by every means, even by force of arms, for the overthrow of the international bourgeoisie and the creation of an international Soviet republic."[22] Although consistently seeking and acquiring loyal followers and fellow travelers throughout the West, Stalin never really understood how powerful a hold the Soviet experiment had on Western liberals during the 1930s and 1940s and failed to exploit them properly. Thousands of Americans not actually disloyal—with hundreds well placed at every level of government, academia and the media—sympathized with the Soviet Union, thereby providing the Soviets with a priceless asset that, cultivated skillfully, could have yielded an army of Henry Wallaces, each of whom, in the long run, was worth ten like Alger Hiss.[23] It is impossible to imagine how history would read today had the Henry

---

21 Lee Kuan Yew, *From Third World to First: The Singapore Story*: 1965–2000 (New York: HarperCollins, 2000), 467.

22 Andrew and Mitrokhin, *The World Was Going Our Way*, 1.

23 Wallace claimed that the 1948 Soviet coup in Czechoslovakia—during which Jan Masaryk, Czech foreign minister and son of one of modern Czechoslovakia's founding fathers, was murdered—was a perfectly appropriate response to a right-wing plot against the government in which the American ambassador was complicit. This was all, of course, utter nonsense. See Culver and Hyde, *American Dreamer*, 472–474.

Wallace worldview been wholly legitimized during the immediate post-war years as it was during the 1970s and 1980s, when there was no foreign policy consensus, and Left and Right fought tooth and nail over this country's relationship with the Soviet Union. Nothing would have better served Soviet interests.

Instead, the Soviets neutralized their most reliable, formidable supporters and sympathizers, from Party members and Popular Front radicals to sympathetic New Dealers, through crude, brutal, stupid foreign policy and espionage that was, overall, so unprofessional, widespread and reckless that it became "common knowledge" in Washington. This eventually gave rise to a powerful anti-Communist backlash in American politics and culture even as the espionage, when effective, provided the Soviets with the nuclear weapons and inside information that led directly to the war in Korea. Although immensely pleased with the fruits of their efforts at the time, it was the Korean War, as previously noted, that transformed the Clifford-Elsey analysis and NSC-68 from classified theory into widely supported public policy, giving rise to a stupendous increase in the size and influence of the military-industrial complex, the national security state and the power of the "Imperial Presidency" while launching an arms race that would prove to be the most important single factor in the Soviet Union's demise some four decades later. Twenty crucial years would pass before anyone willing to suggest accommodation and détente in place of militarized confrontation would have any real voice in American politics, and by then, the die was effectively cast. *It was nothing less than a perfect storm of events to which no one, ironically, contributed more than the Soviets, proving the law of unintended consequences as nothing else could.*[24] It all might still have amounted to very little, however, without the Soviet leadership's crude, stupid response to Jimmy Carter's attempt to kill the Cold War with kindness and the resulting election of Ronald Reagan, whose arms race and economic warfare, pursued

---

24 "The law of unintended consequences, often cited but rarely defined, is that actions of people—and especially of government—always have effects that are unanticipated or 'unintended.'" Rob Norton, *The Concise Encyclopedia of Economics*, http://www.econlib.org/library/Enc/UnintendedConsequences.html, accessed May 10, 2012.

relentlessly throughout the 1980s, completed the process initiated (albeit unknowingly) by Truman.

By 1976, Americans were through with Truman's doctrine and ready for a new direction in foreign policy. Western Europeans, for their part, were governed at the time by parties of the moderate Left, worn out by Cold War tension, tired of living in what could at a moment's notice become the world's largest nuclear firing range and generally eager for trade and cooperation with their neighbors to the east. With the election of Jimmy Carter, the anti-anti-Communist Left had firm control of American foreign policy for the first time since the end of World War II, and President Carter, extending an olive branch, formally declared an end to the Cold War in the spring of 1977. If ever a chance to save the Soviet Union had arisen, this was it. But rather than embrace this priceless opportunity to co-opt long-time adversaries now led by people ready and willing to be co-opted and seek—through cooperation, commerce and a reduction of tension and arms—the savings and hard currency on which their very existence depended, the dogmatic old Bolsheviks slapped their Western friends and benefactors in the face, deploying SS-20s against Western Europe and moving aggressively everywhere they could, adding several states to the Communist bloc in a few short years. *No one worked harder to reinvigorate anti-Communism as a political force and bring Ronald Reagan to the White House than the crude, brutal, incredibly stupid Soviet gerontocracy, and the combination of Ronald Reagan and Mikhail Gorbachev made all the difference during what became the Soviet Union's final years.*

For the end of Communism, which Gorbachev knew was inevitable, need not have meant the end of the Soviet Union, which collapsed as it did, when it did, from a combination of: 1) decades of militarized Cold War and all that came with it; 2) Reagan's policies; and 3) Gorbachev's mistakes. Communism, after all, was no more synonymous with the Soviet Union or the Soviet Empire than it was with either China or Vietnam, both of which existed long before Communism and, having made successful transitions from Marxism to state-capitalist, market-based economies, are here today and will likely be here as rigid, one-party states for a long time to come.[25] Even the Cuban government, one of Communism's very last holdouts, is trying to adapt as needed to survive without relinquishing its monopoly on power: "We are updating our economic model," said Marino Murillo, Cuba's vice president of the Council of Ministers, "but we are not talking about political reform."[26] As with China and Vietnam, Cuba validates Adolph Hitler's dictum that Communists make *excellent* Fascists:

> It is not Germany that will turn Bolshevist, but Bolshevism that will become a sort of National Socialism. Besides, there is more that binds us to Bolshevism than separates us from it. There is, above all, genuine, revolutionary feeling, which is alive everywhere in Russia except where there are Jewish Marxists. I have always made allowance for this circumstance, and given orders that former Communists are to be admitted to the party at once. The *petit bourgeois* Social-Democrat and the trade-union boss will never make a National Socialist, but the Communist always will.[27]

Simply put, totalitarian systems can adapt without genuine reform, as China and Vietnam amply demonstrate, and it was the politically unreformed, state-capitalist system they represent that Gorbachev, who was no "democrat,"[28] had in mind for the Soviet Union, which he believed was in a "pre-crisis" stage when he assumed power. *He did not believe that the Soviet Union was*

---

25 "Power," as George Orwell noted, "is not a means; it is an end. One does not establish a dictatorship in order to safeguard a revolution; one makes the revolution in order to establish the dictatorship." *Nineteen Eighty-Four*, 276. This postulate's real-world application is found in Sebestyen, *Revolution 1989*, 16: "We did not seize power," said East Germany's Erich Honecker, "in order to give it up."
26 "Cuban Official Rules Out Reform Urged by Pope," *New York Times*, March 28, 2012.
27 Hermann Rauschning, *Hitler Speaks: A Series of Political Conversations with Adolph Hitler on His Real Aims* (London: Thornton Butterworth Ltd., 1939), 134.
28 As David Remnick noted, Gorbachev "was not Andrei Sakharov. He *was* not a moral prophet or an intellectual giant. He was not even a man of exceptional goodness. Gorbachev, above all, was a politician."

beyond salvation, [29] *and he was likely correct.* Unrestricted sales of natural gas and oil to the West at normal market prices throughout the 1980s would have combined rather nicely with major nuclear arms reduction agreements (which, given the nuclear stockpiles in existence, would not have changed the balance of power at all) to provide the Soviets enormous savings along with the hundreds of billions in hard currency they needed to facilitate a transition to a potentially functional economy, and to do so without demobilizing their enormous conventional formations and withdrawing from Eastern Europe (which were actions undertaken in an effort to avoid bankruptcy). The Russian people, chafing under decades of privation, would have experienced a considerably improved standard of living through a major influx of cash and consumer goods as the Western press hailed it all as a smashing example of constructive engagement and high-minded statesmanship, rendering Gorbachev's ultimately fatal embrace of political and social reform (a mistake not made by the regimes in Hanoi and Beijing) unnecessary.

In other words, had he faced the Carter administration or any American administration that was willing to end the arms race, reduce nuclear stockpiles and provide Gorbachev the kind of cooperation and assistance he required, the Soviet Union might well have survived just as China and Vietnam survived, with its government intact and the borders of its empire secure. The Cold War did not end that way primarily because the arms race, which China never entered to any extent, brought the Soviet economy to the brink of collapse just when a hard core of American conservatives won the White House, which gave them enormous influence and power through a decades-old collective security system still dominated at the time by the executive branch of the United States government. This allowed them to ratchet up the Cold War when the complete destruction of Soviet power was still attainable, and the laws of economics then took their course, leaving Gorbachev "dragged along by events and never...able to decide how to maneuver from one day to the next without losing

---

29 Seweryn Bialer, "The Death of Soviet Communism," *Foreign Affairs*, 70, No. 5 (Winter 1991-1992), 166-181.

himself entirely."[30] The Soviet Union's assets and efforts, particularly during what became its waning days, were inadequate not in some absolute sense but only as compared to the forces *actively* employed against it. *The Soviet Union was no more destined to collapse as it did, when it did, with or without the Cold War, than Imperial Russia was destined to collapse in 1917, with or without World War I.*

Yet nearly two years before Gorbachev's resignation, the battle for history was joined when *Time* published an essay by Strobe Talbot, president of the Brookings Institution and deputy secretary of state under Bill Clinton. Talbot asserted that the Soviet Union was dying of natural causes so manifest and crippling that it never really posed a genuine threat to the West, concluding that "the doves in the great debate of the past 40 years were right all along."[31]

> The Soviet system has gone into meltdown because of inadequacies and defects at its core, not because of anything the outside world has done or threatened to do....It is a solipsistic delusion to think the West could bring about the seismic events now seizing the U.S.S.R. and its "fraternal" neighbors. If the Soviet Union had ever been as strong as the threatmongers believed, it would not be undergoing its current upheavals. Those events are actually a repudiation of the hawkish conventional wisdom that has largely prevailed over the past 40 years, and a vindication of the Cassandra-like losers, including [George] Kennan.[32]

Like Kennan, Talbot condemned the militarization of foreign policy inherent in the Truman Doctrine and insisted that, "If Kennan's view and his recommendations had prevailed, the world would probably at least still be where it is today, beyond

---

30 Remnick, *Lenin's Tomb*, 503. Zbigniew Brzezinski labeled Gorbachev the "Grand Miscalculator." See Zbigniew Brzezinski, "The Cold War and Its Aftermath," *Foreign Affairs* 71, No. 4 (Fall 1992), 31-49, 46.

31 Strobe Talbot, "Rethinking the Red Menace," *Time*, January 1, 1990, 66-72, 69.

32 Ibid., 69-70.

containment, and perhaps it might have arrived there considerably sooner and at less expense."[33]

Wrong on almost everything else in his *Time* essay, Talbot here makes one excellent point that is contrary to received wisdom: Although George Kennan is often credited as the primary architect of American Cold War policy and hence, the Soviet Union's collapse in 1991,[34] nothing could be further from the truth. For it was not Kennan's "containment" that gave rise to history's Soviet collapse but Truman's "Doctrine" and all that came with it, including the war in Korea, the arms race, the NATO Alliance, Operation Mongoose, the war in Southeast Asia and Reagan's economic and political warfare during the 1980s, which completed the chain of events initiated by Truman. Kennan, it cannot be overstated, strenuously opposed it all.[35] "If, then, I was the author in 1947 of a 'doctrine' of containment," he wrote in 1967, "it was a doctrine that lost much of its rationale with the death of Stalin and with the development of the Soviet-Chinese conflict. I emphatically deny the paternity of any

---

33 Ibid., 70. See also Nicholas Thompson, "Nuclear Monopolist," *New York Times Book Review*, January 10, 2010. The arms race was "catastrophically unwise." "And one of the great debates for historians—as well as for those concerned with American national security—is whether anything could have been done between 1945 and 1949 to avoid all that."; Robert Dallek, *The Lost Peace: Leadership in a Time of Horror and Hope*, 1945-1953 (New York: HarperCollins, 2010). It is very easy, and very popular these days, to imagine a supposedly wonderful historical record in which "all that" had been avoided, but we must never lose sight of the fact that "all that" is what brought the Soviet Union to its knees. Absent "all that," there is no basis to imagine a peaceful, satisfactory end to Soviet power.

34 See Thompson, *The Hawk and the Dove*, 309–311. See also John Lewis Gaddis, *George F. Kennan* (New York: The Penguin Press, 2011), 672, quoting journalist Peter Jennings: "If anyone is entitled to call off the Cold War, it is George Kennan, the man who invented the Western Strategy for winning it."

35 As early as 1947, Kennan criticized the Truman Doctrine and all it represented. See Kennan, Memoirs, 1925–1950, 356–367. See also: George F. Kennan. *The Nuclear Delusion: Soviet-American Relations in the Nuclear Age* (New York: Pantheon Books, 1976), 37–40 (Kennan's recognition that Khrushchev, who provided the best opportunity this country ever had to reduce tension and perhaps end the Cold War, was destroyed by Kennedy's aggressive anti-Communism); John Lewis Gaddis, *George F. Kennan* (New York: The Penguin Press, 2011), 272–275, 391, 607 (Kennan's opposition to the Truman Doctrine); 326, 329, 332–33, 335, 342, 607, 681 (Kennan's opposition to the NATO Alliance); 653, 660, 667, 669 (Kennan's opposition to Ronald Reagan's rhetoric and his anti-Soviet policies, which he believed to be the "inexcusably childish" products of "a deeply prejudiced, ill-informed, and stubborn man, not above the most shameless demagoguery").

efforts to invoke that doctrine today in situations to which it has, and can have, no proper relevance."[36] Had Kennan had his way, the chain of events that brought history's Soviet collapse in 1991 would never have occurred, which renders Talbot's analysis absurd.

For if Talbot is correct on the inevitability of history's Soviet collapse, American foreign policy from 1945-1991 was intrinsically meaningless. Why, after all, should anyone believe that containment as originally envisioned by George Kennan, a far milder policy that would not have given rise to the war in Korea, the national security state, the arms race, the Cuban Missile Crisis, the war in Southeast Asia or Reagan's arms buildup and economic warfare, would have had any effect at all? Why not just avoid opposing the Soviets entirely as Henry Wallace preferred? Indeed, with Soviet collapse in 1991 an historical inevitability, why not just demobilize America's armed forces at the end of World War II and return to the dogged pursuit of isolationism? *The uncommon foolishness of Talbot's analysis should be apparent even to a child.*

In summary, the United States drove the Soviet Union to collapse by exploiting every Soviet inadequacy and defect to maximum effect through a decades-long series of political, diplomatic, military and economic policies, the most important and effective of which were consistently ill-advised, reckless, demonstrably unlawful and driven far more by "political fears of the consequences of looking weak in the forthcoming domestic election"[37] than any semblance of "Grand Strategy" crafted by George Kennan or anyone else. To the extent that any Grand Strategy ever really existed, it had effectively run its course by 1970 and was officially repudiated by the Democrats in 1977, who initiated a new strategy based on "peaceful unilateralism" and then

---

36 Kennan, *Memoirs, 1950–1963*, 367. When the Soviet Union did collapse, Kennan found "it hard to think of any event more strange and startling, and at first glance more inexplicable, than the sudden and total disintegration and disappearance from the international scene, primarily in the years 1987 through 1991, of the great power known successively as the Russian Empire and then the Soviet Union." George Kennan, "Witness to the Fall, " *The New York Review of Books*, November 16, 1995. http://www.nybooks.com/articles/archives/1995/nov/16/witness-to-the-fall/?pagination=false, accessed May 10, 2012. This is hardly what one would expect from a man who supposedly engineered these events.

37 Halberstam, *The Best and the Brightest*, xviii.

bitterly resisted Reagan's return to anti-Communism after the anticipated benefits of "peaceful unilateralism" failed to materialize.

Yet it remained undeniable that the Democratic Party, freely led by its liberal Vital Center, had taken the lead during the Cold War's crucial early years, when long-term, anti-Communist policies central to the Cold War's outcome were initiated. Realizing the political and ideological power of America's victory in the "long twilight struggle," American liberals revised their take on the Truman Doctrine they had so recently and emphatically repudiated and, employing *blackwhite, doublethink* and the Texas sharpshooter fallacy to maximum effect, constructed a triumphal record by embracing the beginning and the ultimate outcome of America's Cold War—the "architects of victory" and the victory itself—and limiting the focus of their elaborate critiques to the Truman Doctrine's Southeast Asian campaign (which is *never* described as such). This ensures that the Vietnam War remains somehow different—a discordant note in an otherwise splendid symphony of American Exceptionalism that began with the New Deal and continued at least through the fall of the Soviet Empire, which, we are told, was a fine, well-earned victory in which all Americans should take pride. This is very seductive because America's national ideology is best served by a narrative that places the American people, whenever possible, on the right side of history. So, if America's war in Southeast Asia, alone among its Cold War conflicts, was unjust, unwinnable or unnecessary, ending the war on Hanoi's terms was not only justified, it is a tribute to America's political system and national character. Even in defeat, Americans have reason to be proud—proud of themselves, proud of their system and especially proud of those who saw the light and led them into abandoning this singularly unjust, ill-advised campaign.

No effort has been spared in impressing this "definition of the situation" upon American society, and its proponents have been successful. Any suggestion that America's war in Southeast Asia was no more right or wrong, well-advised or ill-advised, just or unjust than any other campaign during the "long twilight struggle" or that it was winnable within a reasonable definition of victory runs head-on into American society's highly developed sense of *crimestop*, "the faculty of stopping short, as though by instinct, at the threshold of any dangerous thought...of misunderstanding the simplest arguments if they are inimical to [the country], and of being bored and repelled by any train of thought which is capable of leading in a heretical direction."[38]

For the ultimate heresy is not that the war in Southeast Asia, if measured by the standards employed to legitimize the rest of this country's Cold War policies and conduct, becomes an honorable, winnable campaign mishandled by an incompetent, dishonest, corrupt political class. It is that the entire Cold War, if measured by the standards employed to condemn the war in Southeast Asia, becomes at very best a decades-long war of American aggression, directed from start to finish by an incompetent, dishonest, corrupt political class, with evil conduct, dumb luck and the law of unintended consequences providing this country with its Cold War victory.

Well I find "dangerous thought" to be often the most productive, and like Martin Luther, I believe that a little heresy now and then is good for the soul. The objective facts, figures and frames of reference needed to evaluate American conduct during the "long twilight struggle" in an honest and consistent manner—however dangerous and heretical this might be—are clear, simple and readily available, and it is time to employ them. Americans had no trouble passing judgment on Nazi Germany, Imperial Japan, Stalinist Russia and North Korea for what they were, as measured objectively by what they did. The Communists in Southeast Asia should fare no better. And neither, in the end, should Americans, Left, Right or Vital Center.

---

38 Orwell, *Nineteen Eighty-Four*, 220–221.

PART FOUR: DANGEROUS THOUGHTS

Chapter Eleven:
Jus ad Bellum

War is always judged twice, first with reference to the reasons states have adopted for fighting, secondly with reference to the means they adopt. The first kind of judgment is adjectival in character: we say that a particular war is just or unjust. The second is adverbial: we say that the war is being fought justly or unjustly.[1]

Michael Walzer

The classic "just war" analysis is two-pronged, depending upon both the justice of the cause (*jus ad bellum*) and the means employed, which must be reasonable and proportional to the ends sought (*jus in bello*). Although not overly complex in itself, the just war doctrine is rather problematic when the Truman Doctrine's campaign in Southeast Asia is examined as history rather than ideology because it forces one to judge the Truman Doctrine in its entirety, and there is no better place to start than with the analysis provided by Daniel Ellsberg in 2002. According to Ellsberg, those who critiqued what they saw as American interference in what was really a Vietnamese civil war failed to understand that what they saw in Vietnam from 1960-1975

---

1 Michael Walzer, *Just and Unjust Wars: A Moral Argument with Historical Illustrations* (New York: BasicBooks, 1977), 21. For a succinct example of the moral debate on the means employed by the Allies in World War II, see Paul Fussell, *Thank God for the Atom Bomb and Other Essays*, (New York: Summit Books, 1988), 1–52.

was not then or at any time a genuine civil war but an American war, initiated and driven entirely by and for Americans:

> In practical terms, on one side, it had been an American war almost from its beginning...[I]t was a struggle of Vietnamese—not all of them but enough to persist—against American policy and American financing, proxies, technicians, firepower, and finally, troops and pilots.

> Since at least the late 1940s there had probably never been a year when political violence in Vietnam would have reached or stayed at the scale of a "war" had not the U.S. president, Congress, and citizens fueled it with money, weapons, and ultimately manpower...funneled to wholly owned client regimes...Indeed there would have been no war after 1954 if the United States and its Vietnamese collaborators, wholly financed by the United States, had not been determined to frustrate and overturn the process of political resolution by election negotiated at Geneva.

> It was no more a "civil war" after 1955 or 1960 than it had been during the U.S.-supported French attempt at colonial re-conquest. A war in which one side was entirely equipped and paid by a foreign power—which dictated the nature of the local regime in its own interest—was not a civil war. To say that we had "interfered" in what is "really a civil war," as most American academic writers and even liberal critics of the war do to this day, simply screened a more painful reality and was as much a myth as the earlier official one of "aggression from the North." In terms of the UN Charter and of our own avowed ideals, it was a war of foreign aggression, American

aggression.[2]

In 1972, Ellsberg wrote that, after studying ten volumes of Nazi documents from the Nuremberg trials, he realized that the Pentagon Papers would easily serve to convict American officials of "crimes against peace and crimes against humanity."[3]

Now this is as clearly stated a broad, policy-based *moral* condemnation of the Truman Doctrine's Southeast Asian campaign as one can find, and Ellsberg is correct on the facts, if not on his conclusion. (This is not to say that his conclusion—"it was a war of...American aggression"—is wrong but merely to acknowledge that his conclusion does not necessarily flow from his facts.) What we call the Vietnam War was without question an *American* war, involving "American policy and American financing, proxies, technicians, firepower, and finally, troops and pilots," imposed by Americans for their purposes, through wholly owned client regimes, upon millions of people half a world away. Rhetoric like Ellsberg's, focused for some five decades with a single-minded, partisan intensity on the "Vietnam War," has helped make Americans comfortable with their decision to abandon Southeast Asia even as they continue to celebrate their victory in the "long twilight struggle" against Communism. Yet Ellsberg's analysis, fairly and consistently applied, transforms the Truman Doctrine itself into a half century of "American aggression," which is easily exemplified through even a brief review of Truman's war in Korea.

Korea, like Vietnam, was engaged in a post-colonial, revolutionary upheaval in 1945, and as in Vietnam, fiercely nationalistic Communists had assumed the leading role. Left to its own devices, Korea, like Yugoslavia, would undoubtedly have become a Communist country of its own accord in the days following World War II. But Harry Truman, with needs of his own, divided Korea with Josef Stalin, installing an authoritarian government supported by an occupying army in the American zone. The Korean people had no more say in the matter than did the Poles when Hitler and Stalin divided Poland as part of their "non-

2 Ellsberg, *Secrets*, 255.
3 Ellsberg, *Papers on the War*, 285.

aggression pact" in 1939. "Our" Koreans ("essentially demagogues bent on autocratic rule," according to a CIA analysis[4]) waged war for several years against "their" Koreans ("a cloud of terror...probably unparalleled in the world"[5]) with American encouragement and support until the Korean Communists, with Soviet encouragement and support, struck back in an effort to unite their country under their rule in June of 1950. No matter what you have heard to the contrary, this was a civil war between indigenous nationals who, although supported by outside powers, fought for nothing beyond political control of their own country. And Kim Il Sung had as much "right" to unite his country under his rule as did Ho Chi Minh. *There was no cross-border "invasion" (just what "border" would Koreans cross to invade Korea?), there were no neighboring "dominos" (Korea being a peninsula), and this war as it actually occurred was a result, not a cause, of outside intervention.*

In the first days of the Communist attack, the entire South Korean establishment, beginning with the president and his military commanders, ran away "like turpentined rats." As in Vietnam, they governed through American money and power, not democratic legitimacy, popular support or moral authority, as veteran journalist A. T. Steele noted in October 1949: "Only American money, weapons, and technical assistance enable [the Republic of Korea] to exist for more than a few hours."[6] Within weeks the war was virtually over, with American and South Korean forces driven into a tiny perimeter around the port of Pusan. But Harry Truman, who knew he could not afford to "lose" another country to Communism, introduced hundreds of thousands of foreign troops who fought, as a matter of official policy, a scorched-earth campaign that included the firebombing of densely populated urban areas and the deliberate destruction of dams and dikes in order to destroy North Korea's rice crop and starve its civilian population, some twenty percent of whom were dead by war's end. Overall, at least three million died in Korea in three short years, and

4 Halliday and Cumings, *Korea*, 23.

5 *New York Times* reporter Walter Sullivan, quoted in Halliday and Cumings, *Korea*, 45.

6 Cumings, *Korea's Place in the Sun*, 253.

South Korea would remain a military dictatorship, under American protection, for the next forty years.[7]

Viewing Truman's war in Korea through Ellsberg's lens reveals "an American war almost from its beginning...a struggle of [Koreans]—not all of them but enough to persist—against American policy and American financing, proxies, technicians, firepower, and finally, troops and pilots." There is no question that "since at least the late 1940s there had probably never been a year when political violence in [Korea] would have reached or stayed at the scale of a 'war' had not the U.S. president, Congress, and citizens fueled it with money, weapons, and ultimately manpower...funneled to wholly owned client regimes....Indeed there would have been no war after [1945] if the United States and its [Korean] collaborators, wholly financed by the United States, had not been determined to frustrate and overturn the process of political resolution...." It was no more a "civil war" after 1950 than it had been during the US-supported consolidation of power by the South Korean regime from 1945-1950 because, as Ellsberg tells us, "a war in which one side was entirely equipped and paid by a foreign power—which dictated the nature of the local regime in its own interest—was not a civil war. To say that we had 'interfered' in what is 'really a civil war,'" would be to screen "a more painful reality...as much a myth as the...official one of 'aggression from the North.' In terms of the UN Charter and of our own avowed ideals, [Truman's war in Korea] was a war of foreign aggression, American aggression."

That Ellsberg's analysis of America's war in Vietnam fits America's war in Korea like a glove is simply inescapable. America's enemies in each country were the same—Communists trained and supported by Moscow yet with undeniable nationalist credentials and widespread popular support; its indigenous allies in each country were the same—anti-Communists with a history of collaboration who could never have acquired political power on their own; and its official purpose in each country was enforcement of Truman's doctrine. Absent American intervention in Korea—which began in 1945, not 1950—there would have been no South

---

7 However difficult casualty figures are to determine, the casualties in Korea were likely higher than in Vietnam and were inflicted in a far shorter time.

Korean regime, and the Korean Communists would have consolidated their hold on Korea without a major conflict just as the Vietnamese Communists, absent French intervention in 1945, would have consolidated their power throughout Vietnam.

In summary, major conflicts in both countries—Korea (1950-1953) and Vietnam (1960-1975)—were civil wars, but absent outside intervention, they would never have occurred. Both interventions, moreover, fit the basic pattern followed by the United States from the beginning to the end of the Cold War in Greece, China, Central America, Africa and the Middle East. Korea and Vietnam were unique only because each country shared a border with China (which made for limitless Communist re-supply), and in each country, the indigenous civil and political order had been so pulverized by decades of colonial occupation that, by the end of World War II, there was *no* established governmental structure or institution to which the citizenry gave its allegiance. Each country was largely in the hands of Moscow-trained and supported leftists, who led the resistance and therefore wielded real power. Americans had to *create* governments to support in Korea and Vietnam, and most of the Koreans and Vietnamese who joined with the United States did so because they were otherwise doomed as collaborators, which made it easy for the Communists to portray Americans as foreigners who "stepped into the shoes" of their former masters. Alone among the Truman Doctrine's proxy regimes, those in Korea and Vietnam would require American troops and pilots in large numbers whereas American financing, proxies, technicians and sometimes firepower would suffice elsewhere.

So if Ellsberg is right, if America's Cold War campaign in Southeast Asia represents "a war of...American aggression," the Truman Doctrine—which was imposed upon the world from its very beginning as "American policy" and enforced throughout the Third World with American money, proxies, weapons and firepower—represented, with perhaps a brief interlude under Jimmy Carter, more than forty years of *American* aggression.

If, on the other hand, David Halberstam is right in believing that the Truman Doctrine was engineered by wise and righteous statesmen as an entirely appropriate response to *Soviet* aggression and that its incredibly ugly, brutal war in Korea was not just historically and morally defensible but a fine, proud chapter in the American experience—as orthodoxy teaches us today—the Vietnam War, by any measure, was as "good" and noble an endeavor as any undertaken by this country in the twentieth century, unless judged solely by its outcome.

Neither of these propositions is entirely dishonest or indefensible. Each finds support in the historical record and can be advanced in an intellectually honest manner. But they are fundamentally irreconcilable. *You cannot accept Ellsberg's take on Vietnam by applying legal and ethical principles like nationalism, self-determination, sovereignty, democracy and proportionality to Johnson and Nixon while ignoring Truman's conduct in Greece, China and Korea; Eisenhower's interventions in Guatemala and Iran; and Kennedy's war on Cuba.*

In fact, with the Cold War in general and the Korean War in particular having become fine chapters in American history that now bring pride to all Vital Center Americans, we have a unique opportunity to judge this country's Cold War leaders, which, like judging their wars, depends necessarily and entirely upon the frames of reference you select. Henry Kissinger noted this in the aftermath of Salvador Allende's American-supported overthrow in 1973, when he complained that he and Nixon, bitterly denounced to this very day for this affair, "would have been hailed as heroes during 'the Eisenhower period' of the mid-1950s."[8]

Based on the standards and legal norms generally cited when judging Richard Nixon and Henry Kissinger—standards and legal norms by which Christopher Hitchens accused Kissinger of "war crimes," "crimes against humanity" and "offenses against common or customary or international law, including conspiracy to commit murder, kidnap and torture"[9]—Harry Truman was an international outlaw of the first order for his flagrant violation of customary international law recognized by the Truman administration in Article 6(b) of the Nuremberg Charter. *Never has an American president shed so much blood in so tiny a country and so short a*

---

8 "Parsing the Nixon and Kissinger Pas de Deux," *New York Times*, April 17, 2007.

9 Christopher Hitchens, *The Trial of Henry Kissinger* (London: Verso, 2002), xxiii.

space of time to sustain a non-democratic government he installed against the wishes of the indigenous population. Based on these same standards, Eisenhower also behaved like an international outlaw throughout his presidency, waging proxy wars on countries with which the United States was at peace, interfering in the internal affairs of other sovereign states, overthrowing foreign governments by force and violence and installing or supporting non-democratic proxies from one end of the world to the other. And if Eisenhower, with his quick, clean, efficient and virtually bloodless interventions, "trampled on domestic and international law" as Professor Stephen Rabe wrote in 1988,[10] so did the Kennedy brothers during their terrorist campaign in Cuba, which included conspiracy to kidnap and murder among other offenses undertaken in clear violation of both international and American law.

If, on the other hand, we accept David Halberstam's view that Communism, as an ideological and political force, represented so great a threat to this country's existence that Harry Truman's war in Korea—beginning with Rhee's slaughter of leftist dissidents and continuing right through Truman's firebombing, dam-busting assault on the North's civilian population—was justified to protect this country from Moscow's evil designs, Eisenhower and his advisers can be nothing but wise and courageous leaders whose actions were beyond reproach. They secured Iran with its vast oil reserves (a genuine Cold War prize well within the doctrine of containment as envisioned by George Kennan) and acted with alacrity to keep Communism out of the Western Hemisphere. ("Guatemala will be the rotten apple that spoils the whole barrel" is how Halberstam's "brilliant" Dean Acheson would have put it.) Eisenhower's handling of Vietnam, moreover, if judged by the standards applied to hold Truman in such high esteem, was statesmanship of the highest order. Communist forces that would surely have taken all Southeast Asia (with far more resources and strategic value than Korea) were stopped through the efforts of the American-backed French. Eisenhower then stepped in to secure, through diplomacy and with Soviet and Chinese acquiescence, a

10 Rabe, *Eisenhower and Latin America*, 59.

non-Communist South Vietnam that was every bit as independent, legal and viable as South Korea without the ghastly bloodletting in which Truman engaged and without incurring military obligations to South Vietnam, where a rather low-level advisory commitment represented the extent of American *military* involvement through 1960.[11]

In summary, excepting perhaps Jimmy Carter, America's Cold War leaders were either thuggish international outlaws or statesmen of the highest order whose only real error was their failed campaign in Southeast Asia. But they cannot be both, which returns us to that crucial point that has too long been ignored: The Truman Doctrine was one long campaign that must be judged consistently and in its entirety. Where then do we start? What measure can possibly be used when sifting through all the dishonesty, the ideology and the historical and moral wreckage of the last ninety years in order to pass moral judgment on American conduct during the Cold War? Well there is one objective measure that, given the humanitarian values that increasingly dominate public discourse on international relations, speaks volumes: the body count.

The Black Book of Communism, first published in France in 1997, was compiled by European scholars with unimpeachable credentials to produce an accurate historical and moral balance sheet at the close of the twentieth century. It provides a clear definition and accounting of the crimes for which the authors hold Communist governments responsible and the casualty figures on which they rely in declaring Communist regimes "criminal enterprises in their very essence." "The total," they write, "approaches 100 million people killed."[12] Timothy Snyder, author of *Bloodlands: Europe between Hitler and Stalin,* believes after careful analysis that deaths attributable to Stalin's regime are probably closer to fifteen million, which is a twenty-five percent reduction from *The Black Book's* estimate of twenty million.[13] Yet even if we reduce all fatality estimates in *The Black Book* by twenty-

---

11 Halberstam, *The Best and the Brightest*, 156.

12 *The Black Book of Communism*, 4.

13 Timothy Snyder, "Hitler vs. Stalin: Who Killed More?" *New York Review of Books*, March 10, 2011.

five percent, we still have between sixty-three and seventy-five million people murdered by Communists during the twentieth century, making it impossible to deny that Communism, in the words of Martin Malia, represented "the most colossal case of political carnage in history."[14] "Communist regimes," he writes, "did not just commit criminal acts (all states do on occasion); they were criminal enterprises in their very essence: on principle, so to speak, they all ruled lawlessly, by violence, and without regard to human life."[15] As Bill Maher stated on *Politically Incorrect,* Communism "was more evil than we ever thought it was. It was truly beyond what Orwell even imagined as totalitarianism."

Now consider some facts and figures while analyzing this country's role in the Cold War under the "just war" paradigm: Some thirty million died during the war in Europe to destroy Nazi Germany (orthodoxy's most just of wars), which, from 1933-1945, exterminated as many as fifteen million people in the service of National Socialist ideology. *Twice as many died in the war to destroy the Nazis as were murdered by the Nazis, and virtually no one questions the sacrifice or seriously condemns Allied excesses, no matter how extravagant or unnecessary.* By comparison, some 10-12 million were killed in Cold War military conflicts (the majority in Korea and Vietnam) as part of a long, multi-faceted effort to bring down, as history actually played out, a global political order responsible for as many as 100 million deaths.[16] *Only one person died during the half-century, world-wide, American-led war on Communism for every ten who were deliberately murdered by the regimes ultimately destroyed by this country's official Cold War policies.* As compared to the defeat of Fascism, the West's American-led defeat of Communism was achieved with

---

14 *The Black Book of Communism*, x.

15 Ibid., xvii.

16 Admittedly, these casualty figures are problematic. There were conflicts throughout the world during the Cold War, many of which, although ostensibly battles between Communist and non-Communist forces, were as much driven by ethnic and historical forces that would likely have fueled wars regardless of outside support or ideological gloss, which was often just adopted to acquire the support need to sustain the conflict. I have settled on the 10–12 million figure because it appears a fair estimate of the casualties *directly* attributable to US-Soviet confrontation.

remarkable efficiency and proportionality without even considering a question that must be addressed before passing *moral* judgment on the Truman Doctrine: How many more societies would have experienced the vast tide of bloodshed and human misery wrought by Communism had Americans not stepped forward to resist as they actually did for nearly half a century?

To answer this, we must imagine a world in which American policy remained firmly within the legal and moral paradigm posited by Daniel Ellsberg, leaving Communists with a free hand to take whatever they desired throughout the Third World, directly or through proxies, and do with it whatever they pleased. (Ellsberg's ideal world can fairly be characterized as one in which, in the words of John Updike, "[W]e owe it to history to bow before a wave of the future engineered by terrorists."[17]) How then would history have unfolded? What kind of body count would the world have amassed as Frances FitzGerald's "narrow flame of revolution" "cleansed" vast areas of Asia and the Pacific Rim, Central and South America and the Middle East as it had "cleansed" first the Russian and then the Soviet Empire, China and Southeast Asia? This question demands an answer, and Indochina (Vietnam, Laos and Cambodia), which, absent Truman's doctrine and all that came with it, would have passed into Communist hands in the aftermath of World War II (and of course eventually did), provides a perfect frame of reference.

Ho Chi Minh was a doctrinaire Stalinist and, in his own words, a "professional revolutionary."[18] He led the Vietnamese resistance by 1945 because he and his followers had wiped out the non-Communist nationalists, leaving Vietnam's Washingtons, Ghandis, Havels and Mandelas buried somewhere in the jungles and rice

---

17 Updike, *Self-Consciousness*, 113. It is worth noting here that such a policy, at its most cynical and hard-nosed, might have done considerable damage to Soviet interests over the long run. In 1947, Joseph P. Kennedy urged Americans to "permit Communism to have its trial outside the Soviet Union if that be the fate or will of certain peoples. In most of these countries, a few years will demonstrate the inability of Communism to achieve its promises, while through this period the disillusioned experimenters will be observing the benefits of the American way of life, and most of them will seek to emulate it." Quoted in Schlesinger, *The Vital Center*, 31. See also Norman Mailer, *Armies of the Night* (New York: New American Library, 1968), 210–211.

18 Karnow, *Vietnam: History*, 123.

paddies, along with thousands of others whose only crime was an unwillingness to replace French rule with a Stalinist regime. And this was just the start of the Communists' handiwork. Professor R. J. Rummel[19] calculates that the Vietnamese Communists murdered some 1.1 million Vietnamese and 600,000 Cambodians and Laotians as part of land reform, social engineering, political purges and generalized repression during the twentieth century.[20] According to Professor Rummel's calculations, Vietnamese Communists murdered a greater percentage of those under their control from 1945-1987, .1 percent (1 per every 1,000 people), than did the Nazis from 1932-1945, .09 percent (9 per every 10,000 people). "Thus," he tells us, the Hanoi regime "was more deadly than the Nazis."[21] The authors of *The Black Book*, on the other hand (which, along with *Death by Government*, is *must* reading for anyone who has a serious, non-partisan interest in evaluating American conduct during the Cold War), report those killed by the Vietnamese Communists (excluding wartime casualties) at approximately one million. Even Ward Just, an icon of the antiwar Left who published his acclaimed antiwar tract *To What End* in 1968, acknowledged rather casually in his book that "Ho Chi Minh's people eventually killed half a million Vietnamese in the process of consolidating the revolution."[22]

Whichever figures you use, history reveals the Vietnamese Communists as an extraordinarily vicious group that, by any objective measure, represented *everything* this country fought during World War II and the Cold War.

This perspective is particularly important today, when, as noted by former U.N. Secretary-General Javier Perez de Cuéllar, "We are witnessing what is probably an irreversible shift in public attitudes toward the belief that the defense of the oppressed in the name of

---

19 Professor emeritus of political science at the University of Hawaii.

20 Professor Rummel's analysis of Hanoi's reign of terror is detailed in *Death by Government*, 241-296.

21 Professor Rummel, e-mail message to author, November 12, 2004.

22 Just, *To What End*, 106.

morality should prevail over frontiers and legal documents."[23] This has come about through the efforts of an entirely new generation of liberal internationalists who are "interventionist to the core,"[24] with Harvard Professor Samantha Power providing the archetype.[25]

In her acclaimed 2002 book *A Problem from Hell: America and the Age of Genocide,*[26] Power recounts what she considers to be the most appalling genocides of this century—the Ottoman slaughter of Armenians (1915-1916), Hitler's "Final Solution" (1939-1945), Pol Pot's Cambodian genocide (1975-1979), Saddam Hussein's destruction of his Kurdish minority (1987-1988), the Bosnian Serbs' "ethnic cleansing" in the former Yugoslavia (1992-1995) and the Rwandan genocide of 1994. (Note here Power's failure to include class-based Communist genocide in the Soviet Union and China, either of which dwarfs the episodes she does examine.) She roundly criticizes the American people for their failure to act when they were occurring and urges the international community to hold American leaders responsible for their failure to intervene when "genocide" occurs.[27] As charter members of today's generation of liberal internationalists, the current editors of the *New York Times* share Professor Power's worldview. They criticize "the West" (which "really means the United States"[28]) "for failing to act in time" when the victorious Communists butchered their way through Cambodia[29] and inveigh regularly against the likes of Charles

23 David Rieff, *At the Point of a Gun: Democratic Dreams and Armed Intervention* (New York: Simon & Schuster, 2005), 36.

24 Ibid., 167

25 Anna Lindh Professor of Practice of Global Leadership and Public Policy, Carr Center for Human Rights Policy, John F. Kennedy School of Government, Harvard University.

26 Samantha Power, *A Problem from Hell: America and the Age of Genocide* (New York: Basic Books, 2002).

27 Power, *A Problem from Hell*, chapter 14.

28 Rieff, *At the Point of a Gun*, 51. England, France and Germany have more than 200 million people between them and could easily, even without the rest of the European Union (population 500 million), raise sufficient armed forces to provide the security against the episodes of government terror and mass murder Power cites. Just why this duty should be imposed upon the United States, alone among the Western powers, Power never explains.

29 "The Killing Fields," *New York Times*, July 6, 2006. This is a particularly powerful example of *doublethink*. The *New York Times* was, by 1970, one of the antiwar movement's most ardent proponents, demanding American withdrawal from Southeast Asia in the belief that: 1) everyone

Taylor, Saddam Hussein and Slobodan Milosevic, thereby providing us with an excellent, contemporary frame of reference.

Taylor, a "warlord" according to the *New York Times*, was convicted in April 2012 (with *New York Times* approval) by an international tribunal of aiding and abetting war crimes and crimes against humanity by providing arms, ammunition, communications equipment and planning to rebels during the 1991-2002 civil war in Sierra Leone, in which some 300,000 people were killed.[30] (The conduct for which Taylor was convicted, it is worth noting, differed in no way from the Hanoi regime's support for the Viet Cong/NVA death squads that conducted a decades-long campaign of terror and murder in South Vietnam, in which tens of thousands of South Vietnamese lost their lives.[31]) The *New York Times* also demanded action against Saddam Hussein for his "gruesome military campaign" against Iraqi Kurds that cost 50,000 lives.[32] Slobodan Milosevic, an ardent nationalist who enjoyed wide popular support in Serbia, was also condemned for crimes against humanity by the *New York Times* after he moved aggressively to "cleanse" his territory of those he deemed ideologically unacceptable, killing some 125,000 people before his forces were

---

would be better off if only this government would let events take their course (See Sydney Schanberg, "Indochina without Americans: For Most, a Better Life." *New York Times* April 13, 1975); and 2) the war was "unwinnable," a proposition that has now moved, of course, from hypothesis to orthodoxy. Wholly apart from the dishonesty in pretending that, despite years of political, diplomatic and military intervention, this country did nothing to oppose the Khmer Rouge, the *Times* editors fail to explain how, the war in Southeast Asia being "unwinnable," American intervention in 1976 or 1977 would have differed in any way from its 1961–1973 intervention. *Based on their own historic view of the conflict, any attempt to intervene in the mid-1970s would have been a pointless, bloody exercise in futility.* Finally, the editors of the *New York Times* should explain why, as the Khmer Rouge slaughtered between 1.5 and 2 million Cambodians, the *Times* ran sixty-six articles on human rights abuses in Chile but only four on Cambodia. "The difficulty of obtaining information from Cambodia does not provide a remotely adequate explanation for this extraordinary discrepancy." Andrew and Mitrokhin, *The World was Going Our Way*, 88.

30 "The World: Legacy; A Master Plan Drawn in Blood," *New York Times*, April 2, 2006, sec. 4.

31 Lewy, *America in Vietnam*, 454. See also Rummel, Death by Government, 254-264. These casualty figures are as usual problematic, and Professor Rummel estimates Communist murders of non-combatants in South Vietnam at anywhere between 19,000 and 113,000, with the total most likely in the 60,000-70,000 range. Ibid., 264.

32 "The Saddam Hussein Trials," *New York Times*, April 10, 2006.

stopped by outside intervention led by the United States. (When sentencing one of his generals to twenty-seven years in prison, the presiding judge noted that "the crimes were committed over a long period of time, often through brutal methods, with hatred or appalling lack of concern."[33])

Clearly, Taylor, Hussein and Milosevic are nothing if not African, Middle Eastern and Balkan Ho Chi Minhs, "violent, stupid men who would be the dregs of society under normal conditions [but who] arise amid...trauma, chaos and stress and become revered leaders."[34] And since Ho Chi Minh was nothing if not a typical Communist revolutionary, today's liberal internationalists like Samantha Power, for whom "the defense of the oppressed in the name of morality should prevail over frontiers and legal documents,"[35] would naturally be expected to hold the Truman Doctrine in high regard, whatever its arguable or demonstrable shortcomings or excesses, criticizing American leaders for mishandling its Southeast Asian campaign but not for undertaking it. After all, the lives lost during the genocidal episodes recounted by Power, even if added to those killed by the Nazis, total but a fraction of the casualties inflicted by Communist regimes from 1918-1991, and absent decades of effective, decisive anti-Communist intervention by the United States (which, seeing the forest instead of the trees, can arguably be labeled "humanitarian intervention"), Frances FitzGerald's "narrow flame of revolution" would likely have "cleansed" vast areas of the world exactly as it had "cleansed" first the Russian and then the Soviet Empire, China and the former French Indochina, inevitably providing the twentieth century with far more devastation and a much higher body count. *History teaches us that non-intervention, or withdrawal as in*

---

33 "Wartime Leader of Bosnian Serbs Receives 27-Year Sentence," *New York Times,* September 28, 2006.

34 "Breaking the Clinch," *New York Times*, January 25, 2007. Indeed, when I read news reports on Charles Taylor and precisely what he did, I can think of nothing but Ho Chi Minh and the decades-long war of terror, murder and repression he and his Communists launched in Southeast Asia. See "Liberian Ex-Leader Convicted for Role in Sierra Leone War Atrocities," *New York Times*, April 27, 2012; J. Peter Pham, "An Incomplete Justice," *New York Times*, April 27, 2012.

35 Rieff, *At the Point of a Gun*, 36.

Southeast Asia, is like pacifism, which, as history reveals and George Orwell once noted, is "a tenable position provided that you are willing to take the consequences."[36]

But this puts Power and her fellow liberal internationalists on a collision course with Daniel Ellsberg, for whom the interventionist paradigm necessarily represents "American aggression," at least when the Ho Chi Minh at issue is really determined to fight and able to obtain the backing of a major power. This means that President Samantha Power would be able to send American forces to stop the Serb slaughter of Bosnian Muslims unless and until the Russians or Chinese, for reasons of their own, began aiding the Serbs, who, if sufficiently supplied, determined and brutal (like the Vietnamese Communists), would magically transform Power's humanitarian intervention into "a war of American aggression" and Power herself from human rights activist to war criminal.[37]

Although the issues are not simple, the bottom line most certainly is. If the Cold War, with the Truman Doctrine at its core, represents a just cause successfully concluded, as the orthodox Cold War narrative and contemporary standards of liberal internationalism would have us believe, embracing America's ultimate victory over Communism while condemning the campaign in Southeast Asia in the broad, policy-based manner advanced by Daniel Ellsberg is a perfect example of *doublethink*. It is like accepting World War II as this country's finest hour while denouncing MacArthur's defense of and eventual return to the Philippines because the United States, having stepped into Spanish shoes as colonial occupier at the turn of the century, had no rightful presence or interests there. In short, *jus ad bellum* provides no way

---

36 George Orwell, "As I Please 25," *Tribune*, May 19, 1944, reprinted in George Orwell, *Essays* (New York: Alfred A. Knopf, 2002), 602.

37 On August 4, 2011, the Obama administration officially began the process of turning Ms. Power's ideology into policy, declaring that "preventing mass atrocities and genocide is a core national security interest and a core moral responsibility of the United States." With that in mind, Barack Obama directed "the National Security Advisor to lead a focused interagency study to develop and recommend the membership, mandate, structure, operational protocols, authorities, and support necessary for the Atrocities Prevention Board to coordinate and develop atrocity prevention and response policy." http://www.whitehouse.gov/the-press-office/2011/08/04/presidential-study-directive-mass-atrocities, accessed August 10, 2011.

to pound the square peg of Ellsberg's "war of American aggression" into the round hole of Cold War orthodoxy, which brings us to another excellent means of highlighting the vast gulf between history and ideology, *jus in bello*.

Chapter Twelve:
Jus in Bello

I

There are other elements that make the Vietnam War different from and even worse than other wars. Even now most Americans do not realize the extent to which it was marked by arbitrary killing and the murder of civilians—out of either official policy or the casual recreational or simply half-mad behavior of individual men apparently subject to neither internal nor external constraint. It was a war in which innocents became fair game and in which our soldiers—who went to war convinced they were the saviors and guardians of freedom—found themselves perceived by the civilian population as intruders, conquerors and even murderers. It was a "Bad War" fought for all the wrong reasons and in all the wrong ways.[1]

Peter Marin

A lie can travel halfway around the world while the truth is still putting on its shoes.

Mark Twain[2]

---

[1] Peter Marin, "What the Vietnam Vets Can Teach Us," 560.

[2] Commonly attributed.

As recounted in the introduction, claims like Peter Marin's were forcefully and continuously asserted by politicians, pundits and public intellectuals like George McGovern,[3] former senator Gary Hart[4] and John Kerry (who claimed that Americans raped, tortured and murdered "on a day-to-day basis with the full awareness of the officers at every level of command"). These claims invoke frames of reference that cannot be ignored, such as the Nazis in Russia and Japan's Rape of Nanking. And as the editors of the *Chicago Tribune* noted, "Those who commit these atrocities may think that they will never answer for their crimes, but the pursuit of these Nazis tells dictators, thugs, murderers and henchmen around the world that crimes against humanity won't be overlooked or forgotten."[5] *When military personnel rape, torture and murder "on a day-to-day basis with the full awareness of the officers at every level of command," the world takes note, remembers and acts accordingly.*[6] So if the war crimes industry presents an accurate picture of American conduct during the Truman Doctrine's Southeast Asian campaign, certain judgments are unavoidable:

1. It was indeed a Bad War fought "in all the wrong

---

3 According to McGovern, this country's airmen in Southeast Asia—like me and those in my unit—engaged in "the most immoral action this nation has ever committed in its national history" and "a policy of mass murder." Podhoretz, *Why We Were in Vietnam*, 156.

4 More than twenty years after Hanoi's victory, Hart compared this country's officer corps in Southeast Asia to "demented extremists who bomb government buildings." Gary Hart, *The Patriot* (New York: The Free Press, 1996), 37, n. 1.

5 "Never forget, never stop," *Chicago Tribune*, May 31, 2008, sec. 1. See also "As Old Nazis Die Off, Pursuit Goes On," *New York Times*, August 27, 2009; "American Sues Ex-Nazi Over Killings, but Germany Doesn't See a War Criminal," *New York Times*, December 8, 2010.

6 See for example: "82 Senators Urge Reagan to Cancel His Cemetery Visit," *New York Times*, April 27, 1985; Christopher Hitchens, "The Pompous, Hypocritical Hucksterism of Günter Grass," *Slate*, August 22, 2006; "Jewish Leader Denounces Gunter Grass," *New York Times*, August 16, 2006; "Entwined at a Japanese Shrine, the Nobility and Horrific Brutality of War," *New York Times*, August 12, 2009; Edward Wong, "Japan's Gift to Shrine for Soldiers Angers China," *New York Times*, April 24, 2009; "Shrine in Japan to Its War Dead Plans to 'Soften' Section on China," *New York Times*, December 21, 2006; James Brooke, "Japan Must Show 'Deep Remorse' for Wartime Actions, Official Says," *New York Times*, December 8, 2005.

ways," even if not "for all the wrong reasons."[7]

2. Tens of thousands of those who served in Southeast Asia (at bare minimum) are war criminals, having freely chosen to "rape," "pillage" and "kill for sport"[8] on a day-to-day basis rather than resist or flee to Canada, which were options unavailable to Germans and Japanese.

3. Justice demands non-stop investigation and aggressive pursuit of the "thugs, murderers and henchmen" (like me and my comrades) who served in Vietnam, who should be hunted down and dragged from their homes and families in irons no matter how long it takes, just like Nazis. And if this country will not do it, international tribunals should assume the responsibility.

Finally, and most importantly, any war involving similar conduct by American personnel is a Bad War—an unjust war—without regard to the moral quality of either their cause or their enemies. Those involved, whatever their rank or status, military or civilian, are war criminals who should be treated accordingly, just like Nazis. This being the case, no part of this country's heroic, twentieth century narrative is safe, particularly that glittering jewel in America's crown, World War II, the Good War.

II

Our attack on marshalling yards at Bucharest was a bloody affair. . . . We killed about twelve thousand people. Six thousand of them were refugees on trains in the yards; six thousand of them were Rumanians living about the yards.[9]

General Ira Eaker

[T]he United States Air Force (in its own words) "produced more

---

7 Peter Marin, "What the Vietnam Vets Can Teach Us," 560.

8 Harris, *Our War*, 41.

9 Ronald Schaffer, *Wings of Judgment* (New York: Oxford University Press, 1985), 56.

casualties than any other military action in the history of the world" in its great fire raid on Tokyo, and Secretary of War Henry Stimson, appalled at the absence of public protest in America, thought "there was something wrong with a country where no one questioned" such acts committed in its name.[10]

Milton Mayer

No, I told him. Those people [who crashed airliners into the twin towers on 9/11] are not heroes, nor can they ever be. They deliberately took the lives of innocent men, women and children to promote their cause. No cause, even a noble cause, is worth that.[11]

Bob Schieffer

The most significant moral characteristic of a nation is its hypocrisy.[12]

Reinhold Niebuhr

In 1940, Franklin Roosevelt stridently denounced the "inhuman barbarism" of terror bombing civilians:

> The ruthless bombing from the air of civilians in unfortified centers of population during the course of the hostilities which have raged in various quarters of the earth during the past few years, which has resulted in the maiming and in the death of thousands of defenseless men, women and children, has sickened the hearts of every civilized man and woman and has profoundly shocked the conscience of humanity.
>
> If resort is to be had to this form of inhuman barbarism during the period of tragic conflagration with which the world is now confronted, hundreds of thousands of innocent human beings who have no

10 Milton Mayer, *They Thought They Were Free* (Chicago: The University of Chicago Press, 1955), xv.

11 Bob Schieffer, *Bob Schieffer's America*, (New York: G.P. Putnam's Sons, 2008), 256.

12 Reinhold Niebuhr, *Moral Man and Immoral Society* (Louisville: Westminster John Knox Press, 1932), 95.

responsibility for, and who are not even remotely participating in, the hostilities which have now broken out, will lose their lives. I am therefore addressing this urgent appeal to every Government which may be engaged in hostilities publicly to affirm its determination that its armed forces shall in no event, and under no circumstances, undertake the bombardment from the air of civilian populations or of unfortified cities, upon the understanding that these same rules of warfare will be scrupulously observed by all of their opponents. I request an immediate reply.[13]

Yet once America entered the war, Franklin Roosevelt personally ordered the "Inhuman Barbarism" to commence, telling Treasury Secretary Henry Morgenthau that "'the only way to break German morale' was to bomb every small town, to bring the war home to the ordinary German."[14] Terror bombing, which this government had considered from the outset of the war, in time became official policy.[15]

On February 3, 1945, a combined British/American assault on Berlin killed 25,000 civilians. Ten days later, a similar combined assault created a firestorm that reduced Dresden, a beautiful, medieval city packed with refugees and of virtually no military value, to a burned-out cinder, with civilian dead reliably estimated today anywhere from 35,000 to 50,000. To this day, considerable effort is made to justify the attack,[16] but there is no denying that Americans had initiated a policy of "terror bombing," as noted at the time by the *St. Louis Post Dispatch*: "Allied air bosses have made the long-awaited decision to adopt deliberate terror bombing of the great German population centers as a ruthless expedient to

---

13 Rhodes, *The Making of the Atomic Bomb*, 310.

14 Overy, *Why the Allies Won*, 109–110.

15 David M. Kennedy, *Freedom from Fear: The American people in Depression and War*, 1929–1945 (New York: Oxford University Press, 1999), 743. It should be noted that terror bombing was initiated over the objections of Roosevelt's Air Force leaders, who protested "strenuously." Schaffer, *Wings of Judgment*, 91-92.

16 See, for example, Frederick Taylor, *Dresden: Tuesday, February 13, 1945* (New York: HarperCollins, 2004).

hasten Hitler's doom."[17] In the Pacific, there were never any qualms about targeting civilians as there were in Europe. Franklin Roosevelt himself approved fire raids on Japanese cities as part of war planning in December 1940.[18] As General George C. Marshall noted in November 1941, "Flying Fortresses will be dispatched immediately to set the paper cities of Japan on fire. There won't be any hesitation about bombing civilians—it will be all out."[19] Franklin Roosevelt relentlessly pushed his commanders to bomb Japanese cities with incendiaries.[20] His son and adviser Elliot Roosevelt pressed for bombing Japan "until we have destroyed about half the Japanese civilian population."[21]

Determined to give Roosevelt what he wanted, the Army Air Force established an "Incendiary Subcommittee" under the Committee of Operations Analysts to analyze the complex problems associated with the use of firebombs against population centers, including the density of incendiaries needed to create a firestorm in a Japanese city and the appropriate percentage of delayed-action, high-explosive and anti-personnel bombs that should be included to ensure maximum casualties among firefighters and other first responders.[22] At Dugway Proving Ground in Utah, a Japanese village was "faithfully reproduced" and then burned to the ground by bombers dropping incendiaries to measure the effort required to raze Japanese population centers.[23] An optimum result of

---

17 Kennedy, *Freedom from Fear*, 744. By war's end, American and British bombing would kill 650,000 German civilians. James Bradley, *Flyboys: A True Story of Courage* (Boston: Little, Brown and Company, 2003), 259; Henry Steele Commager, *The Story of World War II* (New York: Simon & Schuster, 2001), 481. See also Randall Hansen, *Fire and Fury, The Allied Bombing of Germany, 1942–1945* (New York: New American Library, 2008).

18 Joseph E. Persico, *Roosevelt's Secret War* (New York: Random House, 2002), 60–62.

19 Michael Sherry, "The Slide to Total Air War," New Republic, December 16, 1981.

20 Stephen Ambrose, *Americans at War* (New York: Berkley Books, 1998), 126–127.

21 Bradley, *Flyboys,* 263.

22 Schaffer, *Wings of Judgment*, 112–113. In late August 2012, one of the delayed-action bombs was found during demolition of a building in Munich. See "Experts blow up 550-pound WWII bomb found in Munich." http://worldnews.nbcnews.com/_news/2012/08/28/13523220-experts-blow-up-550-pound-wwii-bomb-found-in-munich?lite.

23 Max Hastings, *Retribution: The Battle for Japan, 1944–45* (New York: Alfred A. Knopf, 2008), 283.

incendiary raids on six Japanese cities was calculated at 584,000 deaths.[24] On the night of March 9-10, 1945, Roosevelt's efforts came to fruition as 334 B-29s burned out 15.8 square miles of central Tokyo, the most densely populated city on earth, with 2,000 tons of incendiary ordnance, killing some 125,000 people by means of fire and suffocation in a raid engineered as "official policy" to kill in this manner as many as possible.[25] Captain Shigenori Kubota provided a vivid description of Roosevelt's handiwork:

> The entire river surface was black as far as the eye could see, black with burned corpses, logs and who knows what else, but uniformly black from the immense heat that had seared its way through the area...The bodies were all nude, the clothes had been burned away, and there was a dreadful sameness about them, no telling men from women or even children. All that remained were pieces of charred meat. Bodies and parts of bodies were carbonized and absolutely black...

> On some broad streets, as far as one could see, there was an even row of bodies where men, women and children, trapped by the flames, had futilely tried to escape them by laying down in the center of the paving. There were heaps of bodies in school yards, in parks, in public shelters, in vacant lots, and huddled under railroad viaducts.[26]

"CITY'S HEART GONE," headlined the *New York Times* on March 11, 1945. "NOT A BUILDING IS LEFT INTACT IN 15 SQUARE MILES PHOTOS SHOW."[27] This fire raid was just one of many in Japan, which continued until the Army Air Force ran out of incendiaries. This ferocious aerial assault was undertaken as official

---

24 Schaffer, *Wings of Judgment*, 116.

25 Rhodes, *The Making of the Atomic Bomb*, 598–599.

26 Richard B. Frank, *Downfall: The End of the Imperial Japanese Empire* (New York: Random House, 1999), 15–16.

27 Hastings, *Retribution*, 234.

policy with the full support of the American people. Journalist Henry Wolfe, writing in *Harper's*, endorsed this wholesale slaughter in the following terms: "It seems brutal to be talking about burning homes. But we are engaged in a life-and-death struggle for national survival, and we are therefore justified in taking any action that will save the lives of American soldiers and sailors. We must strike hard and with everything we have at the spot where it will do the most damage to the enemy." [28]

By 1945, Allied strategic bombing had taken the lives of some 650,000 German, 64,000 Italian and 400,000 Japanese civilians, while leaving 7.5 million German and ten million Japanese homeless. America's allies suffered terribly as well. *More than seventy thousand French civilians died under Allied bombing.* These figures are particularly impressive when one considers the fact that Americans killed and missing in combat during World War II totaled approximately 400,000. In other words, American military personnel and their allies killed, by bombing alone, at least two civilians for every member of this country's armed forces who died. However offensive, outrageous, dangerous or heretical you find this, there is no avoiding the fact that Franklin Roosevelt's official policy of targeting civilians, like Harry Truman's in Korea, was a gross violation of standards this country explicitly recognized in Article 6(b) of the Nuremberg Charter, which described the "wanton destruction of cities, towns or villages, or devastation not justified by military necessity" as "violations of the laws or customs of war" and listed such actions under the heading "WAR CRIMES."

As for the day-to-day conduct of American personnel on the field, history also provides far less purity and righteousness than ideology would have us believe.

> Earlier, there had occurred in F Company the event known as the Great Turkey Shoot. In a deep crater in a forest, someone had come upon a squad or two of Germans, perhaps fifteen or twenty in all. Their visible wish to surrender—most were in tears of terror and despair—was ignored by our men lining

---

28 Rhodes, *The Making of the Atomic Bomb*, 520.

the rim. Perhaps some of our prisoners had recently been shot by the Germans. Perhaps some Germans hadn't surrendered fast enough and with suitable signs of contrition. (We were very hard on snotty Nazi adolescents.) Whatever the reason, the Great Turkey Shoot resulted. Laughing and howling, hoo-ha-ing and cowboy and good-old-boy yelling, our men exultantly shot into the crater until every single man down there was dead. A few tried to scale the sides, but there was no escape. If a body twitched or moved at all, it was shot again. The result was deep satisfaction, and the event was transformed into amusing narrative, told and retold over campfires all that winter. If it made you sick, you were not supposed to indicate.[29]

After four days of heavy combat, Captain Ronald Spears (506th Parachute Regiment, 101st Airborne Division) passed a group of German prisoners digging a ditch under guard behind American lines. He stopped and gave them each a cigarette. As they enjoyed their first puffs, he unslung his carbine and shot all twelve of them, killing them in cold blood. "Spears walked on to complete his mission for that day, went on to become a company commander and to stay in the army, where he had a very good career."[30] Eric Sevareid witnessed the aftermath of a similar occurrence:

A young German soldier lay sprawled just inside a sagging doorway, his hobnailed boots sticking into the street. Two American soldiers were resting and smoking cigarettes a few feet away, paying the body no attention. "Oh him?" one of them said in response to a question. "Son of a bitch kept lagging behind the others when we brought them in. We got tired of hurrying him up all the time." Thus casually was

---

29 Paul Fussell, *Doing Battle: The Making of a Skeptic* (Boston: Little, Brown & Company, 1996) 123–124.

30 Ambrose, *Americans at War*, 199.

deliberate murder announced by boys who a year before had taken no lives but those of a squirrel or pheasant. I found that I was not shocked nor indignant; I was merely a little surprised. As weeks went by and this experience was repeated many times, I ceased even to be surprised—only I could never again bring myself to write or speak with indignation of the Germans' violations of the "rules of warfare."[31]

After torpedoing a Japanese transport, crewmen of the U.S.S. *Wahoo*, which had surfaced to charge batteries and continue its pursuit of a convoy, found their boat cruising in a "sea of Japanese." The water was so thick with enemy troops who had survived the sinking that the submarine pushed them aside like "driftwood." The *Wahoo's* captain ordered all guns to open fire and later reported, "After about an hour of this, we destroyed all of the boats and most of the troops."[32] Similar actions were undertaken by fighter pilots during the final sortie of the Japanese Combined Fleet in April of 1945. After the Japanese cruiser *Yahagi* was sunk, hundreds of crewmen, choking on oil in the cold water, were simply slaughtered by Navy aircraft whose pilots fired tens of thousands of .50 caliber rounds into the groups of defenseless sailors.[33]

Whether soldier, sailor or airman, Americans who served during the Good War often behaved, when on the field, just as badly as their enemies. In his memoir of the Pacific war, Professor E.B. Sledge recalled the "brutish, primitive hatred" that gripped Americans as well as Japanese. He watched as his comrades mutilated, pulled gold teeth from and urinated into the mouths of enemy dead. In one case, a marine dismissed a terrified, old Okinawan woman he cold-bloodedly killed as "an old gook woman

31 Eric Sevareid, *Not So Wild a Dream: A Personal Story of Youth and War and the American Faith* (New York: Athenuem Edition, 1976), 388–389. See also Rick Atkinson, *An Army at Dawn* (New York: Henry Holt and Company, 2002), 462–463: In North Africa, "shooting at Arabs became a sport in some units."

32 Clay Blair, Jr., *Silent Victory* (Philadelphia: J. P. Lippencott Co., 1975), 384–385.

33 Russell Spurr, *A Glorious Way to Die: The Kamikaze Mission of the Battleship Yamato, April 1945* (New York: Newmarket Press, 1981), 284–286.

who wanted me to put her out of her misery."[34]

When evaluating American behavior during the Good War, we must also consider tactical airpower and artillery, which were available in virtually limitless quantities and used accordingly. American operations razed thousands of cities, towns and villages to the ground and inflicted hundreds of thousands of civilian casualties around the world—German, Belgian, Dutch, French, Filipino and Italian. The tactical air campaign against German transportation and communication facilities that immediately preceded D-Day alone cost the lives of 12,000 Belgian and French civilians.[35] Most recent estimates reveal that by the time American forces had shot, burned and blasted their way across Okinawa, the civilian death toll had reached as high as 150,000, which equals one-third of the island's entire population.[36]

And what of the company this country kept during its heroic effort to "save the world" from Fascism? How do America's Soviet allies compare to the GVN, whose very existence was, according to antiwar dogma, an affront to common decency?

From the day Lenin arrived at the Finland Station until the outbreak of World War II, at least twenty million people (a conservative estimate) were pitilessly slaughtered—shot, bayoneted, beaten, worked or deliberately starved and frozen to death—by the Soviet government, which maintained the most extensive system of slave labor/death camps in history. In fact, Soviet state terror and mass murder proved an inspiration to the Nazis, as outlined by Auschwitz Commandant Rudolf Hess:

The Reich Security Head Office issued to the

34 John W. Dower, *War without Mercy: Race and Power in the Pacific War* (New York: Pantheon Books, 1986), 63.

35 Fussell, *Wartime,* 283; Schaffer, *Wings of Judgment,* 42–43.

36 Dower, *War without Mercy,* 298. War correspondent Edgar Jones gave Americans some hard truth in the February 1946 issue of Atlantic Monthly: "What kind of war do civilians suppose we fought anyway? We shot prisoners in cold blood, wiped out hospitals, strafed lifeboats, killed or mistreated enemy civilians, finished off enemy wounded, tossed the dying into a hole with the dead, and boiled the flesh off enemy skulls to make table ornaments for sweethearts or carved their bones into letter openers." Edgar L. Jones, "One War is Enough," Atlantic Monthly, February 1946. http://www.theatlantic.com/past/docs/unbound/bookauth/battle/jones.htm, accessed May 10, 2012.

commandants a full collection of reports concerning the Russian concentration camps. These described in great detail the conditions in and organization of the Russian camps, as supplied by former prisoners who had managed to escape. Great emphasis was placed on the fact that the Russians, by their massive employment of forced labor, had destroyed whole peoples.[37]

By the outbreak of World War II, Stalin had killed a thousand times the number of people killed by Hitler at that point in time, and his gulags held 300 inmates for each one in a German concentration camp.[38]

After annexing eastern Poland, the Soviets initiated a campaign of terror and mass murder. By 1941, the Soviets had killed about four times as many Poles as the Germans, although they controlled half as many people. More than a million were deported, and ten percent of the adult men were imprisoned and tortured.[39] In the Katyn Forest, the bodies of more than 4,000 Polish officers executed by the Soviets were uncovered in 1944 while 11,000 others taken by the Soviets in 1939-40 remain missing to this day. Indeed, excepting only the Japanese, no army in the twentieth century exceeded the record of rape, torture and murder left behind by our Soviet allies during the great crusade to "save the world" from Fascism. "For two days and two nights," German housewife Margarete Promeist recalled, "wave after wave of Russians came into my shelter plundering and raping. Women were killed if they refused. Some were shot and killed anyway. In one room alone I found the bodies of six or seven women, all lying in the position in which they were raped, their heads battered in."[40]

In Berlin alone, estimates of rape victims range from 95,000 to

37 *The Black Book of Communism*, 15.

38 Patrick Buchanan, *A Republic, Not an Empire* (Washington, D.C.: Regnery Publishing, 2002), 262–263.

39 Clive Pointing, *Armageddon: The Realty Beyond the Distortions, Myths, Lies, and Illusions of World War II* (New York: Random House, 1995), 226.

40 Cornelius Ryan, *The Last Battle* (New York: Touchstone, 1995), 488. See also 484–493.

135,000.[41] Throughout Germany, it is believed that as many as two million women were raped by the Red Army, and many of these suffered multiple rapes.[42] Thousands committed suicide.[43] Such behavior by Soviet troops was the rule, not the exception, and this was well known to Soviet commanders, who either encouraged it or simply did not care. Stalin himself reacted with cruel indifference toward the conduct of Red Army troops, even when their savagery was directed at allies. He told Milovan Djilas, who, as head of Tito's Military Mission to Moscow, had complained about Red Army atrocities in Yugoslavia, "Can't you understand if a soldier who has crossed thousands of kilometers through blood and fire has fun with a woman or takes a trifle?"[44] British historian Norman Davies said it all when he noted that "the war in Europe was dominated by two evil monsters, not by one. Each of the monsters consumed the best people in its territory before embarking on a fight to the death for supremacy. The third force in the struggle—the Western Powers— was all but eliminated in the opening stage, and took much of the war to reassert its influence."[45]

Granted, there was little anyone in this country could do about the Red Army's day-to-day criminality, but American accommodation with Stalin went much further than tolerance of behavior beyond American control, ultimately involving this country in some very shameful episodes.

Roosevelt, Churchill and Stalin met at Yalta to map out the future of the post-war world in February 1945. In addition to the territorial agreements, they agreed that all "Soviet Citizens" taken prisoner by the Western Allies would be repatriated to the Soviets, by force if necessary. Ever since the Normandy landings, increasing numbers of Russians, Ukrainians, Georgians, Latvians, Poles and others from Eastern Europe had become prisoners of the Western

41 Anthony Beevor, *The Fall of Berlin* 1945 (New York: Penguin Books, 2003), 410.

42 Ibid.

43 Ibid.

44 Djilas, *Conversations with Stalin*, 95.

45 Norman Davies, *No Simple Victory: World War II in Europe, 1939–1945* (New York: Penguin, 2006), 71. See also Timothy Snyder, *Bloodlands: Europe between Hitler and Stalin* (New York: Basic Books, 2010).

Allies. These men had originally been captured by the Germans during the early days on the Eastern Front. Some hated Bolshevism and Stalin and had volunteered to fight for the Germans. Once enlisted, they could not pick and choose their service, and they ended up on the Western Front. The majority, however, represented little more than starved, brutalized, terrified human beings who, in an effort to escape the endless misery and certain death that the Nazis inflicted on the prisoners taken in the East, agreed to don German uniforms and serve in work battalions. Often, they had been given but one choice: serve or be shot.[46]

Representing as they did a staggering indictment of the Soviet Union, these people were traitors in Stalin's mind who had to be liquidated. The United States and British governments were under no illusions regarding their fate. "I greatly regret the Cabinet's decision to send these people back to Russia. It will mean certain death for them," wrote Lord Selborne, minister for economic warfare, to British Foreign Secretary Anthony Eden in July 1944.[47] US Secretary of War Henry Stimson expressed similar misgivings: "I think we are unnecessarily running into danger by turning over German prisoners of Russian origin to the Russians. First thing you know, we will be responsible for a big killing by the Russians."[48] *The moral quality of our Soviet allies was well known to us throughout the war.*

The Western Allies had a major problem of their own, however, and it took precedence over any concerns they might have had for the fate of those whose nationality left them vulnerable to the Soviets: British and American prisoners of war. Some two-thirds of the British and Commonwealth prisoners of war in Germany were held in camps located in eastern territories that would be overrun by the Red Army.[49] American prisoners were in the same boat, as Secretary of War Henry Stimson noted: "To refuse to return those claiming Soviet citizenship to the Soviet Government, even against

---

46 Nicholas Bethell, *The Last Secret: The Delivery to Stalin of over Two Million Russians by Britain and the United States* (New York: Basic Books, 1974), 1–8.

47 Ibid., 8.

48 Ibid., 27.

49 Ibid., 19–20.

their express desires, might result in the retention of our released prisoners-of-war in Russian custody."[50]

Ultimately, this country repatriated, by whatever force was necessary, nearly two million refugees, who often reacted violently when informed of our plans for them. In Britain and the United States, prisoners rioted. Suicides were commonplace. Henry Stimson understood all too well what was happening: "[T]hese prisoners were opposed to their repatriation to Russia because of their individual fears that it would mean death for themselves and suffering for relatives and friends."[51] In fact, they rioted because they wanted the Americans to kill them all rather than return them to the Soviets.[52] In the end, nearly two million refugees were forcibly returned by the Western Allies to the Soviets, who either killed them outright or shipped them to concentration camps to die of starvation, cold and disease.[53]

Finally, no examination of the "Good War" would be complete without a review of the ethnic cleansing authorized by Article 13 of the Potsdam Agreement between the Soviet Union and the Western Allies. Under Article 13, Soviet, Polish and Czechoslovakian authorities (among others) forcibly and brutally expelled ethnic Germans from lands in Eastern Europe, where many had lived for centuries, killing some 2.1 million in the process, most of them women and children.[54] *New York Times* reporter Ann O'Hare McCormick, who was present for this man-made disaster, described it as "a crime against humanity."[55] This was done, with formal American acquiescence, despite Article 6(c) of the Nuremberg Charter, which specifically defined forced population expulsion as a crime against humanity. See also Article 49, Fourth Geneva Convention (1949): "Individual or mass forcible transfers, as well as

---

50 Ibid., 28.

51 Ibid., 167.

52 Ibid.

53 See also Nikolai Tolstoy, *The Secret Betrayal, 1944–1947* (New York: Charles Scribner's Sons, 1977). 294.

54 John Keegan, *The Second World War* (New York: Penguin Books, 1989), 592-593.

55 R.M. Douglas, *Orderly and Humane: The Expulsion of the Germans after the Second World War* (New Haven: Yale University Press, 2012), 294.

deportations of protected persons from occupied territory to the territory of the Occupying Power or to that of any other country, occupied or not, are prohibited, regardless of their motive."

>» «<

Given this country's carpet bombing of residential neighborhoods, unrestricted submarine warfare, wholesale slaughter of allied civilians to pave the way for Allied troops, executed prisoners, bombed hospitals, strafed lifeboats, forced expulsions and two million innocents returned to Stalin for slaughter during the Good War, the conduct of American troops in Southeast Asia, if uniquely evil, must have been truly horrific indeed. Yet as Daniel Ellsberg noted nearly four decades ago, this notion is "absurdly unhistorical,"[56] and this, believe it or not, is precisely why the war crimes industry has been so effective over the years. To challenge its postulates, one must prove a negative—one must provide evidence of non-events—which is nearly impossible. But there is still one very effective way to demonstrate the reality of American conduct in Southeast Asia, and this is by examining the war crimes industry itself, starting with the fact that "the Vietnam War was the most filmed, photographed and documented conflict in history..."[57] If this country's intervention in Southeast Asia was "a Bad War fought for all the wrong reasons and in all the wrong ways," one would expect to find a vast trove of records and photographs documenting it as such, much like the record amassed in connection with Hitler's Final Solution and Japan's rampage through China. Yet this is not the case. All I find when I examine the war crimes industry are "documentaries" like Dan Rather's *The Wall Within* and books like Myra MacPherson's *Long Time*

---

56 Ellsberg, *Papers on the War*, 244.

57 "The Vietnam War, as Seen in Art from the Other Side," *New York Times*, October 22, 2002. It was, its reporters tell us, "a unique war for all journalists, because there was no censorship. The U.S. military provided extraordinary access to combat operations. We could fly on bombing missions, parachute into hostile territory with an airborne unit, spend a week with Special Forces in the jungle, hitch a ride on a chopper and land amid rocket and artillery as a battle raged, or be taken prisoner like a soldier." Denby Fawcett, et al, *War Torn, Stories of War from the Women Reporters Who Covered Vietnam* (New York: Random House, 2002), vii.

Passing, which present not history but ideology in its purest form. This particular aspect of the antiwar dogma can be judged, in its entirety, through a careful examination of these highly acclaimed presentations.

The Wall Within, which aired in 1988, presented six media-classic "Vietnam veterans" who recounted their stories of torture and mass murder for a national audience. "Steve," for example, claims to have been a sixteen-year-old Navy Seal who, under direct orders, operated behind enemy lines for two years, massacring and mutilating civilians and making it look as though the Communists had done it. Driven to alcoholism and drug addiction, he came home in a straitjacket and almost strangled his own mother, having mistaken her for a Viet Cong. Terry Bradley claimed to have murdered and skinned civilians, including women and babies, at a rate of up to fifty an hour. Mikal Rice told Rather of the trauma he experienced when his friend "Sgt. Call" died in his arms after being blown in half by a grenade.[58] Dan Rather solemnly told his national audience that at least 26,000 and perhaps as many as 100,000 veterans had committed suicide since returning home.[59] This program was made part of the CBS video history series on the Vietnam War. Complete with an introduction by Walter Cronkite, it was marketed to schools and other institutions, which guarantees that the war crimes industry becomes a staple of politically correct "history" for all time.

The Wall Within writ large, *Long Time Passing* provides more than 600 pages of material that exposes the men who served in Southeast Asia as losers, outcasts, morons, drug addicts, alcoholics and criminals, with a successful or normal veteran thrown in occasionally to achieve "balance." For the full flavor of the book, one need only peruse the table of contents, where we find chapters entitled "A Different War," "Post Traumatic Stress," "The Afflicted," "The Criminals," "The Vet Centers," "The Disordered" (the subjects of the previous chapters are apparently not "disordered"), "Atrocities," "The Deserters," "Drugs, Bad Paper, Prison" and "Agent Orange," plus an epilogue entitled "Requiem for a

---

58 Burkett and Whitley, *Stolen Valor,* 87–90.
59 Ibid., 306.

Generation." In the world according to Myra MacPherson, one point is beyond question: Atrocities (rape, torture, murder, mutilation) were part of the day-to-day experience of Americans in Southeast Asia and form the common thread that runs throughout *Long Time Passing*. Atrocities lead to "Post Traumatic Stress"; atrocities are responsible for "The Afflicted," "The Disordered" and "The Criminals"; atrocities are why broken men seek solace at "The Vet Centers"; and atrocities are the indisputable cause of "Drugs, Bad Paper [and] Prison." No matter what problem these men face— unemployment, drugs, alcohol, sexual dysfunction, spousal abuse— the cause is always the same: atrocities committed in Southeast Asia.

In "A Different War," for example, we meet "James," who tells us how he spent the war high on drugs, which he never used before he went to Vietnam. MacPherson, of course, tells us that hundreds of thousands of veterans are addicts. "Where did I get hooked? Nam. Why Nam? Cheap stuff, good stuff. Why Nam? I'll give you one word: despair," says an unidentified veteran. (MacPherson's tortured heroes are consistently unidentified and unidentifiable.) In "Atrocities" we meet "Kenny," "a man of no accomplishments before or after Vietnam," according to MacPherson, whose story could have been lifted right from the Lifton/Lane playbook:

> Kenny says he was in Vietnam during Tet 1968 on reconnaissance missions, roaming the jungles with small packs of soldiers. He starts to tell in graphic detail of lifting an ax heavy with blood, after cutting off a man's head. *"That* affects me, lady."
>
> "It was just a wild, mayhem thing. We had a guy in our outfit, Davis. Didn't smoke, didn't curse, didn't go after the whores. A guy you had to respect because he had so much will power." Kenny's head is low on his chest. "Davis kicked open a door of this old French building and was cut in two. When he was found, they had cut his head off and put it at his feet. And they had his penis in his mouth. The boys come back and said, 'Oh hell, Davis is a fuckin' *mess.*' The

platoon sergeant, it really freaked him out. He just started screamin', 'Let's track 'em *down*.' We knew then he meant to kill anything—men, women, children, goddamn dogs, water buffalo. So we found 'em and killed 'em. I said to the sergeant, 'Bobo, what do we do now?' Tears was rollin' down. 'I want their goddamn heads,' he said. 'Just like they did to Davis. People in this area will *know* who we were when we get through.'"[60]

Kenny, according to MacPherson, brags that William Calley did nothing that he and his unit did not do. "We executed hundreds," he tells MacPherson.[61]

As one would expect in a chapter entitled "Atrocities," MacPherson provides all the gruesome details of My Lai, along with several little vignettes guaranteed to reinforce the image of the veterans as crazed, murderous psychotics: two children killed by a jeep being driven by an American who just did not care; a crazed G.I. who set a woman on fire; an unidentified veteran who gently strokes his dog as he tells MacPherson about an incident in which he and seven of his comrades gang-raped and murdered two North Vietnamese nurses. And finally, we meet Norman Ryman, who enjoyed killing and mutilating so much that he would "fall into a state of despair" when deprived of the pleasure for any length of time. He returned to become a multiple rapist who is now incarcerated for life. *Another typical Vietnam veteran.*

Those few veterans presented by MacPherson in the chapters entitled "Successful Veterans" and "From Losers to Winners" appear exactly as MacPherson intends them to appear, anecdotal. Even then, she makes clear that they only made it by working through their trauma from the war.

Long Time Passing closes with a chapter entitled "Requiem for a Generation." It begins at the Vietnam Memorial Wall and continues through a polemic about "the Vietnam Generation" also called "the generation of the sixties," in which MacPherson tells us

---

60 MacPherson, *Long Time Passing*, 483.
61 Ibid., 484.

what she has learned by "listening to the voices of the generation." The only heroes of the Vietnam era are found on the Left. Todd Gitlin, a former SDS leader who, of course, has *all* the answers; Bobby Muller, a paralyzed antiwar veteran and absolute darling of the Left who traveled to Hanoi to lay a wreath at Ho Chi Minh's grave. "Requiem for a Generation" ends where it began, at the Vietnam Memorial. And liberals just loved this book, which received rave reviews from the likes of Senators Tom Harkin ("powerful and relevant reading"), George McGovern ("a most perceptive and fascinating account"), Edward Kennedy ("a brilliant evocation" and "a moving story") and historian Stanley Karnow ("a portrait of America in our time").[62]

There is but one problem with the world according to Dan Rather and Myra MacPherson: It is demonstrably false in each and every particular.

"Steve," the sixteen-year-old, mass-murdering Navy Seal presented by Dan Rather, is Steven Earnest Southards. He did not enlist at sixteen, did not serve as a Navy Seal and saw no combat at all. He was an internal communications technician who served in rear areas and spent several months in the brig for going AWOL. Terry Bradley, who told Dan Rather that he murdered and skinned up to fifty civilians an hour, was also a complete fraud. Although he served in Vietnam, he was an ammunition handler in the rear, not a combat soldier at the front, and he spent 300 days either AWOL or in the stockade. (This is quite a feat when one considers that a tour of duty was only 365 days. *So many atrocities; so little time.*) He was eventually diagnosed with paranoid schizophrenia, which is an organic brain disorder unrelated to combat or trauma. Mikal Rice served as a guard assigned to a Military Police company at Cam Rahn Bay from 1969-1970. The only Sgt. Call who died in Vietnam was Sgt. Richard Joseph Call, killed when his armored vehicle was struck by rocket fire on April 4, 1968 (several months before Rice was in-country), seventy miles northwest of Saigon (more than 200 miles from Cam Ranh Bay). The truth, as B.G. Burkett outlined in *Stolen Valor: How the Vietnam Generation Was Robbed of Its*

---

62 MacPherson, *Long Time Passing*, front matter.

Heroes and Its History, was easy to uncover: "I, a rank amateur, had been able to verify with several phone calls and a FOIA request that the description Steve had given of his military service and his tales of atrocities were fraudulent." CBS, however, "made no effort to obtain Steve's record independently," although *The Wall Within* was in production for over a year.[63]

The same problems are found throughout *Long Time Passing.* Following the dishonest, deeply flawed methodology of Robert Jay Lifton, MacPherson assiduously avoided a representative sampling of veterans and focused consistently on those she finds at or through "Vet Centers." "Vet Centers" are storefront counseling centers created in response to complaints that the VA presented "Vietnam veterans" with too many hassles and too much red tape. So, the Vet Centers are hassle-free, making no attempt to verify that the "broken, wounded men" appearing with their tales of service-connected woe are who they say they are. "Don't have your DD-214, your official discharge form? No problem. There the motto was 'When in doubt, err on the side of the vet.'"[64] "At the Vet Center, each client receives a 'C-card,' a purple plastic card with a magnetic stripe that designates him an official member of the VA family. Nobody checks further. They don't even know if he's eligible....From there, it's not terribly hard to gain admittance to a VA hospital."[65] *All anyone who appears to be from the correct age group need do is show up at a Vet Center, relate his stories of combat and trauma, and he's in the system.* Now it is time to cash in through a veteran's benefits industry that provides them with tens of thousands of dollars in tax-free income annually.[66]

MacPherson attributes the Vet Center concept to Shad Meshad, whom she clearly admires. She tells us that he was a medical service officer in Vietnam who was severely injured, "scalped" as he describes it, in a helicopter crash. Years of painful operations and terrible readjustment problems turned Meshad into "a zealot for

---

63 Burkett and Whitley, *Stolen Valor,* 97–108.
64 Ibid., 153.
65 Ibid., 247.
66 Ibid., 237.

veterans."[67] Official records, however, demonstrate that Floyd Meshad was never involved in a helicopter crash, never wounded and never injured. There were no years of painful operations. He was, in fact, an antiwar agitator and a discipline problem who was court marshaled.[68] The Vet Centers were created through the efforts of a phony and liar with an antiwar, anti-government agenda.

Steven Cytryszewski is another of the poor, suffering heroes presented by MacPherson. He tells us that he awakens screaming from his nightmares and looks for snipers in the trees when he drives down the road.[69] Cytryszewski is a big fan of the Vet Centers, where they take him as seriously as MacPherson does. Cytryszewski's service record, however, reveals Cytryszewski as a supply clerk with the Ninth Infantry Division; no combat, no medals, no trauma, just an endless charade, and, in all likelihood, plenty of tax-free income.[70] MacPherson also tells the heart-breaking story of Gerald Highman, "a twice-wounded former marine" who suffered from "ten years of depression and combat flashbacks."[71] One morning, Highman called his father, informed him that he had killed his wife, hung up the phone and then killed himself. Just one more victim of Vietnam trauma. But Highman's official service record shows no Combat Action Ribbon, no Purple Heart, no wounds or hospital stays. Highman, in fact, was an office machine repairman who fixed typewriters and mimeograph machines in a rear area.

Next we have Eddie Erikson, whose wife found him dead in a closet, where he hanged himself as a result of the trauma he suffered as a door gunner with the 101st Airborne Division. Particularly devastating for Erikson were memories of the day his best friend and fellow door gunner, Michael Murphy, was killed, falling out of a gunship while still alive after having been hit by enemy fire. When he returned to base, Erikson, "sobbing" and "with trembling fingers," opened a letter to Murphy from his wife in which she wrote

---

67 MacPherson, *Long Time Passing*, 232.

68 Burkett and Whitley, *Stolen Valor*, 152–153.

69 MacPherson, *Long Time Passing*, 229.

70 Burkett and Whitley, *Stolen Valor*, 161.

71 MacPherson, *Long Time Passing*, 239.

that he had just become the father of a baby boy.[72] Heartrending indeed, but entirely false. Official United States military records reveal that four men named Michael Murphy were killed in Vietnam. Only one Michael Murphy was killed in Vietnam during Erikson's tour, and he was an infantryman in a ground unit killed by a mortar round during a firefight. He could never have received a letter from his wife regarding the birth of a son because he was single. Erikson's service record, moreover, reveals that he served as a machinist with the Headquarters Company of the 159th Aviation Battalion. He was awarded no Air Medals, which virtually everyone received for flying combat missions, no Air Crewman Badge (the equivalent of pilot's wings for non-rated crewmembers), no Combat Infantryman Badge and no Purple Hearts.[73]

It requires nothing beyond an ordinary Freedom of Information Act request to uncover the truth behind phony stories like those involving Meshad, Cytryszewski, Highman and Erikson—but that is apparently far too much effort for MacPherson. Add a little common sense and some basic math, and MacPherson's failure to meet even minimum standards of historiography becomes clear.

MacPherson cites a study in which nine percent of 350 veterans interviewed admit—and these are the ones willing to admit—to committing some type of atrocity or "violent or abusive acts" during the war while another thirty percent witnessed such acts. The study's author explicitly extrapolates his results to "the population

---

72 Ibid..

73 Burkett and Whitley, *Stolen Valor*, 302. A recent chapter in the war crimes industry was CNN's spectacular Operation Tailwind fiasco. On June 7, 1998, CNN and Time broke an incredible story, entitled "Valley of Death," about a September 1970 American raid into Laos undertaken to kill Americans who had defected to the Communists. As if a raid to kill American defectors was not sensational enough, CNN reported that sarin nerve gas was employed to kill many Communist troops, which is a war crime under international law. The story was based almost entirely on the claims of Robert Van Buskirk, a former army lieutenant who took part in the raid and claimed that he personally killed American defectors and requested the employment of sarin. As is typical of the war crimes industry, the story was exposed as a fraud shortly after it aired. In the end, *Time* apologized publicly and officially retracted the story. Producers Jack Smith and April Oliver were fired by CNN. See Jerry Lembcke, *CNN's Tailwind Tail: Inside Vietnam's Last Great Myth* (Lanham, Maryland: Rowman & Littlefield Publishers, 2003). See also "POW Benefit Claimants Exceed Recorded POWs," Associated Press, April 11, 2009.

who served," not just combat veterans.[74] Now let us pause for a moment in our national dementia and examine these figures.

Some 2.6 million men served in South Vietnam from 1960-1975, and approximately five percent of them survived wounds.[75] If the cited study is to be believed, nearly twice as many living Americans are willing to admit that they committed war crimes (nine percent or 234,000) than were wounded during the war (five percent or 130,000). If another thirty percent of those who served witnessed war crimes, nearly forty percent of the men who served, or 1.04 million men, participated in or witnessed war crimes in a military in which only fifteen percent of those who served (390,000) were assigned to line combat units![76] Where were all these atrocities taking place? On the grounds of the airbase at Da Nang or the Long Binh supply depot? This is the type of facility where eighty-five percent of the men who served in Southeast Asia were stationed, a fact that, all by itself, helps highlight the absurdity of the world according to Myra MacPherson and brings us to the real focus of MacPherson's war crimes analysis: the combat units.

We begin with the claim that nine percent of the 2.6 million veterans (234,000) committed war crimes. With only 390,000 Americans assigned to line combat units—where the war crimes recounted by MacPherson were invariably committed—MacPherson would have us believe that some sixty percent of those who served in combat units are, based on their own individual conduct, convictable war criminals. This is a staggering figure that certainly exceeds the percentage of war criminals to be found during World War II among Waffen SS units on the Eastern Front and Japanese units in China. One would necessarily expect to find support for this in an extensive, unequivocal historical record from "the most filmed, photographed and documented conflict in history." Yet (as previously noted) the wretched, ridiculous *Wall Within* and *Long Time Passing* represent the distilled essence of what we have to support the war crimes industry. We should also note that, if MacPherson is to be believed, some 28,000 (60%) of

---

74 MacPherson, *Long Time Passing*, 193.

75 Burkett and Whitley, *Stolen Valor*, 227.

76 Ibid., 223.

the 47,000 Americans killed in action in Southeast Asia are war criminals, which turns the Vietnam Memorial in Washington into America's Yasukuni Shrine.[77] *Anyone who accepts the world according to Myra MacPherson, John Kerry and David Harris, among others, should view this memorial as a national disgrace and demand its demolition.*

Consider also the kind of figures regularly cited to support the PTSD industry. MacPherson tells us that one fourth of those who served in Vietnam—between 500,000 and 700,000—are suffering from PTSD and that many more are in denial. The numbers, she tells us, are "staggering." For once, I agree with her. When analyzed rationally, they are indeed "staggering"; staggeringly false and staggeringly absurd.

We start, once again, with 2.6 million veterans. The National Institute of Mental Health reports that six percent of all adult Americans "suffer from serious mental illness." This means that some 156,000 of those who served in Southeast Asia are necessarily suffering from "serious mental illness" they would be facing had they never seen the inside of a recruiting office, including some 28,600 suffering from schizophrenia and 67,600 who are bi-polar.[78] These alone represent several times the number needed to account for every dysfunctional veteran who has ever existed, and you can rest assured that the Vet Centers are where you will find them. It would be interesting indeed to examine VA Vet Center records to determine just how many veterans who claim psychiatric disorders have been turned away because they are among those 78,000–156,000 whose disorders are *necessarily* unconnected to

---

77 Korean and Chinese leaders protest bitterly whenever Japanese leaders visit the Yasukuni shrine, which honors more than two million Japanese war dead, some of whom, as everyone writing about this long-running issue stresses, are war criminals. See "Entwined at a Japanese Shrine, the Nobility and Horrific Brutality of War," *New York Times*, August 12, 2009; "Japan's Gift To Shrine For Soldiers Angers China," *New York Times*, April 24, 2009; "Shrine in Japan to Its War Dead Plans to 'Soften' Section on China," *New York Times*, December 21, 2006; James Brooke, "Japan Must Show 'Deep Remorse' For Wartime Actions, Official Says," *New York Times*, December 8, 2005; "Chinese Outraged by Denial of Nanjing," *Wall Street Journal*, February 23, 2012.

78 See Websites: National Alliance on Mental Illness,
 http://www.nami.org/template.cfm?section=About_Mental_Illness; National Institute of Mental Health, http://www.nimh.nih.gov/health/statistics/index.shtml, accessed February 1, 2009.

their service. (It has likely never happened.)

The shortcomings of the war crimes industry are particularly impressive when you consider that, as previously noted, "The Vietnam War was the most filmed, photographed and documented conflict in history..."[79] With decades to conduct research, hundreds of journalists with first-hand knowledge, a First Amendment to ensure publication, a Freedom of Information Act for government records and hundreds of thousands of real combat veterans to interview, *Long Time Passing* and *The Wall Within* were the very best the war crimes industry had to offer until 2008, when Deborah Nelson, a Pulitzer Prize-winning journalist who has made a career of demonizing the men who fought in Vietnam, provided, ironically and inadvertently, the most powerful defense of the veterans anyone has ever written, *The War Behind Me: Vietnam Veterans Confront the Truth about U.S. War Crimes.*[80]

From the start of her book, it becomes apparent that, like Robert J. Lifton and Myra MacPherson, Nelson is not a historian but a political partisan who began work on her book because John Kerry, whom she favored in the 2004 presidential election, was damaged rather badly by attacks from veterans who took issue with Kerry's service record and his war crimes allegations. Her book is politically driven and retaliatory in nature, and her claims, based on the evidence she musters, provide as fine an example of *blackwhite* as exists in the real world.

Nelson reviewed 246 army files containing reports of violent criminal misconduct (murder, torture, battery, sexual assault) by American personnel in Southeast Asia. According to her analysis, 300 allegations within these files were "substantiated" by army investigators while another 500 were deemed "unsubstantiated/insufficient." A quarter of those were "confirmed but labeled otherwise for a variety of reasons." According to Nelson, these records constitute "an unparalleled body of evidence" comprising "nine thousand pages...implicating U.S. troops in a wide

79 "The Vietnam War, as Seen in Art from the Other Side," *New York Times*, October 22, 2002.
80 Deborah Nelson, *The War Behind Me: Vietnam Veterans Confront the Truth about U.S. War Crimes* (New York: Basic Books, 2008).

range of atrocities"—"A My Lai a Month."[81]

This is some very powerful language indeed, yet a review of the allegations Nelson cites belies her claims. In Appendix A, Nelson summarizes seventy-seven incidents classified as "founded" by army investigators, yet not one of these seventy-seven incidents even arguably approaches the kind of large-scale, widespread undertaking with command support or knowledge that would sustain her claim that "A My Lai a Month" can be found within the records she reviewed. The incidents summarized in Appendix A occurred from one end of South Vietnam to the other with no connection, no pattern and no command input. Excepting only three, all involved the conduct of enlisted men (fifty-nine) or company-grade officers (fifteen). A large number of the incidents recounted do not even involve killings, most of those that do involve only one or two deaths, and the total dead in all of the incidents listed as "founded" in Nelson's Appendix A total 196 over a period of at least five years, which assumes ninety dead in a single air attack in which the dead are listed at between thirty-nine and ninety. Best estimates indicate that between 300 and 500 people were killed at My Lai. Splitting the difference provides a figure of 400, which, if occurring as Nelson insists on a monthly basis, would provide 4,800 killed annually in large-scale massacres, with some 24,000 killed like this during the five-year period covered in Appendix A and 38,400 over the eight-year period of major American involvement. It is inconceivable that mass murder on such a scale—which would necessarily involve large numbers of troops and other witnesses—would go unnoticed and unreported for years during "the most filmed, photographed and documented conflict in history," yet no evidence of such conduct is found within the records cited by Nelson in support of her claims. In reality, the offenses she examines are nothing but the kind of common crimes committed by thousands of common criminals on a daily basis in any American city.

Moreover, with some 2.6 million Americans having been stationed in South Vietnam during roughly eight years of intense

---

81 Nelson, *The War Behind Me*, 73.

American involvement (1965-1972), it is clear that Nelson is actually dealing here with an exceedingly small number of violent offenses.[82] I exchanged a couple of e-mails with Nelson to make sure I understood her figures and then ran some calculations taking everything possible in Nelson's favor through the following assumptions: 1) I assumed that every incident she examined was an actual crime rather than an allegation; 2) I rounded her "substantiated" figure up from 300 to 500; and 3) I doubled this to 1,000 to provide her a large margin of error. My efforts yielded some interesting results.

Assuming 1,000 violent crimes committed by 2.6 million men over an eight-year period and knowing that Chicago has approximately 2.6 million residents, I reviewed the Chicago Police Department's official crime statistics over an eight-year period and found that in 2007 alone, there were 34,895 violent crimes in Chicago (ninety-five per day), which includes 442 murders, 1,599 criminal sexual assaults, 15,426 robberies and 17,428 aggravated assaults/batteries (16,834 of these involving guns, knives and other dangerous weapons). During an eight-year period (2000-2007), there were 323,787 violent crimes in Chicago, including 4,375 murders, 14,154 criminal sexual assaults, 136,801 robberies and 168,457 aggravated assaults/batteries.

Even with assumptions in Nelson's favor that are unsupported by her own evidence, there were at least thirty-five times the number of violent offenses committed by citizens of Chicago in just one year—2007—than were committed by American personnel during the five years of brutal, unconventional war covered in Nelson's Appendix A. In fact, if you round Nelson's "substantiated" figure (300) up to 500 and multiply that figure ten times for a total of 5,000, you still have only $1/7^{th}$ the number of violent crimes committed during 2007 in Chicago and $1/64^{th}$ the number committed in Chicago from 2000-2007. This leads inexorably to only one conclusion: Unless the citizens of Chicago have spent the last several years experiencing a virtual Rape of Nanking "on a day-to-day basis"—several My Lais a month—Americans who fought in

---

82 I use for my examination here the 2.6 million who were stationed in South Vietnam and as such are the focus of Nelson's attack.

Southeast Asia were remarkably decent and well-behaved despite the most difficult circumstances imaginable.

Consider Nelson's figures from another perspective. With evidence of 300 criminal offenses committed by American personnel from among 2.6 million who served in the war zone, Nelson proves that one out of every 8,666 men engaged in some form of violent or abusive criminal conduct. If we increase her figure of "substantiated" crimes by a factor of ten, providing some 3,000 criminal incidents (wildly unjustified by the evidence on which Nelson relies) we still have only one out of every 866 Americans engaged in such activity. And if the analysis is limited to the 390,000 Americans who served in combat units, 300 criminal offenses mean that one in every 1,300 Americans engaged in criminal conduct, proving once again that claims of widespread criminality by Americans in Southeast Asia remain unsustainable.

In claiming anything to the contrary based on the evidence she cites, Deborah Nelson propounds ideology masquerading as history, displaying a highly developed sense of George Orwell's *blackwhite,* which means "a loyal willingness to say that black is white when Party discipline demands this. But it also means an ability to *believe* that black is white, and more, to *know* that black is white, and to forget that one has ever believed to the contrary."

Finally, it is important to note that acclaimed journalists with unlimited access to the war zone and no censorship tell us that war crimes were neither widespread nor acceptable: "They didn't even think of it," says Peter Arnett. "Every unit I was with, [the GIs] went out of their way to be kind and decent with the people."[83] Daniel Ellsberg, a man who spent a great deal of time in the field during combat operations and eventually became a fierce opponent of the Vietnam War, tells us clearly that atrocities did not occur on a daily basis in American units: "My Lai was beyond the bounds of permissible behavior, and that is recognizable by virtually every soldier in Vietnam. They know it was wrong. . . ."[84] And remember that Neil Sheehan, author of *Bright and Shining Lie* and one of

---

83 Burkett and Whitley, *Stolen Valor,* 117.
84 Ellsberg, *Papers on the War,* 251.

those responsible for publication of *The Pentagon Papers*, described the war crimes industry as "a new McCarthyism, this time from the left. Any accusation, any innuendo, any rumor, is repeated and published as the truth."[85]

In fact, the historical record reveals that the veterans of America's war in Southeast Asia are neither haunted nor traumatized but doing better overall than almost any other identifiable group of this size in society. *Everything you have heard to the contrary is nonsense.* The men who fought in Vietnam were the best-educated group ever in service. Nearly eighty percent of those who served in Vietnam had high school diplomas, while only forty-five percent had them during World War II;[86] nearly three times as many college graduates served in Vietnam as served in World War II, and draftees were the best of the lot. "The draftees' higher level of education and intelligence, middle-class background and maturity contributed to their superior performance as soldiers."[87] This is all reflected in their post-war lives. Those who served in Vietnam have a consistently lower unemployment rate than non-veterans. In 1994, the rate for all males over the age of 18 was six percent; for those who served in Vietnam, the rate was 3.9 percent.[88] Drug use has never been higher among veterans than non-veterans.[89] Although Dan Rather told the world that as many as 100,000 veterans had committed suicide, studies undertaken by the Center for Environmental and Injury Control and the Department of Veterans' Affairs found that suicide rates among those who served in Vietnam were no higher than those of the general population. "Our estimates indicate that fewer than 9000 suicides occurred among all Vietnam veterans at a time when there were claims of at least five times as many such deaths. We found no evidence to confirm the large numbers of suicides that have been

---

85 Burkett and Whitley, *Stolen Valor*, 133.

86 Ibid, 55.

87 Ibid.

88 Ibid., 67.

89 Ibid., 60–62.

reported in the print and broadcast media."[90] As of 1985, veterans had a higher rate of homeownership than non-veterans. Eighty percent were married, ninety percent had children.

> Seventy-four percent said they "enjoyed their time in service." Eighty percent disagreed with the statement "the United States took unfair advantage of me." Fifty-six percent of Vietnam veterans said they benefited in the long run by going to Vietnam. Only 29 percent said they were set back. Ninety-one percent of those who served in Vietnam were "glad they served their country."[91]

We should also note that not one of the powerful, influential people who helped propagate the war crimes industry—George McGovern, John Kerry and David Harris among them—ever acted as though he believed anything he said. None have ever called for the apprehension and trial of America's alleged war criminals, and everyone in public life pays respects at the Vietnam Memorial without protest, here or abroad. As for the veterans—who allegedly fought in an evil manner for an evil purpose and committed untold crimes against humanity—they are warmly embraced today by absolutely *everyone*, including the Vietnamese.

Michael Blumenthal, our previously quoted draft evader, is, in his own mind, a patriotic American of high moral character who would, of course, have served in a "better" war, as he puts it, and he still claims the moral high ground, telling us that the "fear and narcissism" that drove him has now become "conviction."[92] Yet he assures us that he holds the veterans of this allegedly "criminal" war in which he would not serve in high regard: "To put it bluntly, [the veterans] have something that we haven't got. It is to be sure, somewhat vague, but nonetheless real, and can be embraced under

---

90 Ibid., 306. See also "Review of Landmark Study Finds Fewer Vietnam Veterans with Post-Traumatic Stress," *New York Times*, August 18, 2006.

91 Burkett and Whitley, *Stolen Valor*, 73. See also "Vietnam and Patriotism," National Public Radio interview with David Halberstam and James Webb, September 1, 2004. http://www.npr.org/templates/story/story.php?storyId=3883670, accessed May 10, 2012.

92 MacPherson, *Long Time Passing*, 155.

several different headings: realism, discipline, masculinity...resilience, tenacity, resourcefulness....I'm not sure that they didn't turn out to be better *men* in the best sense of the word."93 George McGovern expressed his respect for the veterans of a war so "bad" that draft evasion and disallegiance were appropriate in his mind, praising them as people "who fought bravely and courageously and sacrificed their own convenience generally, as our forces have always done representing the United States."94 John Kerry, for his part, takes every opportunity these days to assure us that this country has never produced a finer group of "citizen soldiers" than those who served in Southeast Asia: "Make no mistake. American intentions were noble, and no soldiers have ever fought with more bravery or selflessness for their country."95 "[T]he people who put on the uniform served with equal courage, equal commitment and an equal sense of contribution as anybody else in any other war and in any other time in American history."96

Even those who found America's attempt to enforce Truman's doctrine in Southeast Asia so morally offensive that they chose exile over military service have nothing bad to say about America's raping, torturing, murdering war criminals: "Above all, more than any other group of nongoers—with the exception of those who chose jail—Canada's dodgers express compassion and concern for the veterans."97 Antiwar activist David Harris, who refused induction and compared service in Vietnam to fighting for the Nazis, takes every opportunity today to assure us that "our boys" are blameless for their behavior and invokes, of all things, *obedience to orders* in their defense: "They [America's political leaders] to me are the villains of the piece and not the guys that went and did what they forced them to do. Those guys I commiserate with. And I always had

---

93 Ibid.

94 George S. McGovern, quoted in Patrick Hearden, ed., *Vietnam: Four American Perspectives* (West LaFayette: Purdue University Press, 1990), 13–14.

95 John Kerry, Speech at the World Affairs Council, Boston, Massachusetts, September 10, 2001.

96 Keynote address, Congressional Black Caucus/Veterans Braintrust, September 22, 2002.

97 MacPherson, *Long Time Passing*, 377.

a good relationship with veterans."[98]

Finally, we should note that, to this day, "the Vietnamese genuinely liked Americans, more so than they liked the Chinese (their traditional enemy), the French (who treated them like slaves in their own country), or the Soviets for that matter (the Vietnamese found them overbearing and arrogant; southern Vietnamese called them 'Americans with no money'). Despite what we did to the Vietnamese during the war, their admiration and respect of us is heartfelt and genuine."[99] "Welcome, the Vietnamese of the North seemed to say; welcome back, said the Vietnamese of the South."[100] (Now imagine, *just imagine,* the reception a group of Japanese Rape of Nanking veterans would receive if they returned to that city to mingle with the locals and reminisce.)

To accept the war crimes industry's portrayal of American conduct in Southeast Asia, we must believe that people still resentful over being treated "like slaves" by the French would admire and respect Americans who raped them, tortured them and murdered them "on a day-to-day basis" for years. We must believe that men who, according to John Kerry, "personally raped, cut off ears, cut off heads, taped wires from portable telephones to human genitals and turned up the power, cut off limbs...randomly shot at civilians, razed villages in a fashion reminiscent of Genghis Kahn, shot cattle and dogs for fun, poisoned food stocks and generally ravaged the countryside of South Vietnam in addition to the normal range of war...on a day-to-day basis," represent as fine a group of citizen soldiers as any ever produced by this country. And we must

---

98 Kim Willenson, The *Bad War: An Oral History of the Vietnam War* (New York: New American Library, 1987), 245.

99 Larry Heinemann, *Black Virgin Mountain* (New York: Doubleday, 2005), 58–59.

100 Ibid. See also William Broyles, "The Road to Hill 10," *The Atlantic*, April 1985, 90, 98; http://www.theatlantic.com/magazine/archive/1985/04/the-road-to-hill-10/6463/, accessed May 10, 2012: "The place was packed with bo doi, young Vietnamese soldiers in the uniform of my old enemies. "Lien Xo," a soldier next to me said to his friend, gesturing at me in disgust. 'Khong phai Lien Xo,' I said. 'East German?' the soldier asked in Vietnamese, suspiciously. 'No, I'm an American,' I replied in Vietnamese. At once his and his friend's eyes lit up and their faces broke out in big grins. The soldiers bought me drinks and insisted that I try on their helmets and caps with the red stars on them. Over and over they kept saying, 'America, Number One—Russia, Number Ten.' 'American, tot!' (Good!). 'Tot lam!' (Very good!). Similar scenes happened almost daily."

believe that men who, in the words of David Harris, "raped, pillaged, killed for sport"[101] are entitled to absolution because they were Americans who only obeyed orders.[102]

None of this makes any sense, of course, because, like the "phony atrocity stories of the Great War—Germans invading Belgium, children with their hands cut off, mass rapes and executions, all attested to by such authorities as Lord Bryce,"[103] the war crimes industry was contrived and propagated as a means to an end. Demonizing the enemy, after all, is a normal part of any war, and be not mistaken: To the antiwar Left, the Armed Forces of the United States were the enemy, and they were treated accordingly. Just as the Japanese were labeled "subhuman," "apes," "insects," "beasts," "vermin," "cockroaches," "treacherous" and "barbaric" (a "buck toothed, near-sighted, pint-sized monkey" according to a US Army infantry magazine) to justify turning their cities into open crematoria without scruples or remorse, Americans who served in Southeast Asia became gang-raping, torturing barbarians who "killed for sport" "on a day-to-day basis" the moment this portrayal served the interests of not only "activists," ideologues and politicians but mainstream, Vital Center Baby Boomers, who, "in claiming their moral ground on Vietnam," needed "to think that they would have been eager to fight in World War II."[104] Like those among the British upper class whose business interests and fortunes had thrived on cheap cotton produced by slave labor, antiwar partisans, whatever their individual reasons, saw what they wanted to see, believed what they wanted to believe and invented whatever they required for reasons as old as time itself:

> The coarse cruelty of [Abraham] Lincoln and his hirelings was notorious. [Thackeray] never doubted that the federals made a business of harrowing the tenderest feelings of women—particularly of

---

101 Harris, *Our War*, 41.

102 Willenson, *The Bad War, An Oral History of the Vietnam War*, 245.

103 Schlesinger, *A Life in the Twentieth Century*, 310–311.

104 David Maraniss, *First in His Class: A Biography of Bill Clinton* (New York: Touchstone, 1996), 201.

women—in order to punish their opponents. On quite insufficient evidence he burst into violent reproach. Had Adams carried in his pocket the proofs that the reproach was unjust, he would have gained nothing by showing them. At that moment Thackeray, and all London society with him, needed the nervous relief of expressing emotion; *for if Mr. Lincoln was not what they said he was—what were they?*[105]

In sum, whether viewed in terms of enemies, allies, means or ends, history provides no basis for condemning the Truman Doctrine's Southeast Asian campaign in moral terms that does not serve to demolish this country's proud, twentieth century narrative in its entirety, leaving only one perspective from which to attack the former while preserving the latter: the inevitability of American defeat.

---

105 Henry Adams, *The Education of Henry Adams* (Boston: Houghton Mifflin Company, 1918), 130–131 (emphasis added).

Chapter Thirteen:
The "Unwinnable" War

I

Johnson's problem, however, was not the incessant cries of his critics for negotiations, but rather his mistaken belief that the conflict in Vietnam could be won entirely on the battlefield. Vietnam was also a political conflict in which the hearts and minds of the people were at stake.[1]

Robert Mann

The problem, as reflective Americans were beginning to discover, was not primarily military. It was primarily political, just as the cliché had always said.[2]

Ward Just

The Vietnam War should never have been fought, since it never could have been won.[3]

Douglas Brinkley

---

1 Mann, *A Grand Delusion*, 729.

2 Just, *To What End*, 65–66.

3 Douglas Brinkley, "The Other Vietnam Generation," *New York Times Book Review*, February 28, 1999, 27.

You can convince anybody of anything if you push it at them all of the time.[4]

Charles Manson

Representing as it does the very essence of the Truman Doctrine in both ends and means (excepting only the deliberate mass slaughter of civilians as in Korea), America's war in Southeast Asia can be "different" only if it was, as orthodoxy teaches, "unwinnable." The "unwinnable war" is a complex Cold War myth that began its journey from contrivance to holy writ in October 1962, when John Paul Vann first conveyed to David Halberstam those famous words, "This is a political war."[5] Endlessly repeated and seemingly profound, the "unwinnable" "political war" is not just dishonest but uncommonly silly. All military conflicts are political in nature, as Carl von Clausewitz famously recognized, and history teaches us that success in war depends upon neither morality nor right. It depends upon might, which is itself the sum of two things and two things only: military power and the will to use it.

Military power is an objective measure of one's ability to damage an opponent. The will to use military power, on the other hand, is a measure of the moral seriousness and courage required both to face unflinchingly the reality of your conduct (Americans have remained largely unmoved to this day by their fire bombings of Dresden and Tokyo) and to suffer the consequences when your opponent strikes back. These two commodities, power and will, when in proper equilibrium even if not precisely balanced (a shortage of one can often be covered by a surplus of the other), interact to create a whole that is greater than the sum of its parts. If you lack one or both of these two commodities to the extent that the whole of your military enterprise is insufficient when compared to that of your enemy, you will be defeated, unless you are at least

4 Vincent Bugliosi, *Helter Skelter: The True Story of the Manson Murders* (New York: W.W. Norton & Company, 1994), 628.
5 Prochnau, *Once Upon a Distant War*, 162.

strong enough to force a mutually acceptable, if not entirely satisfactory, end to hostilities, and all the spirit and determination in the world will make no difference. Nothing better exemplifies this than the American Civil War, a "political problem" solved through might—military power and the will to use it.

The United States came into being when thirteen sovereign states joined together voluntarily, through representative assembly and lawful process. Secession was addressed during the Constitutional Convention in Philadelphia but dropped from consideration to ensure ratification. *New York, Rhode Island and Virginia each included a provision within its ratification ordinance reserving the right to secede if the federal government became oppressive, and all were welcomed into the Union with this reservation.* Over time, the people of the largely agrarian, slaveholding South became dissatisfied with economic and political trends that were acting against their interests as they viewed them. From banking and tariff issues to the balance of power in the Congress (which would in time move inexorably toward abolition), nothing was going in their favor, and there was little if any chance that things were going to change. So they invoked a right that had never been denied them and seceded from the Union as the original thirteen colonies had seceded from the British Empire. The "problem" Abraham Lincoln faced was clear and simple: Who would govern the South? By the spring of 1861, the "political" phase of the struggle was over, and the Confederates had won.

But Lincoln was lucky. The firebrands of Charleston, South Carolina, like all too many of their Southern brethren, were not satisfied with secession. They were itching for war with the Yankees and used Union troops in Fort Sumter as their excuse to start shooting. This was just what Lincoln needed, and he moved with alacrity to solve his "political problem" militarily. The Confederacy, however, was by any measure a viable, functioning nation-state popular among its own citizens. Its armies were as fine as any ever raised, and none were better led or backed by people more determined to secure independence. So four long years would pass and more than 750,000 would die before this country's political problems—slavery and secession—would be solved on the Union's terms, not because Lincoln won "hearts and minds" and not because he won an election but because he had the might to solve the underlying problems on his terms.[6] The attack on Fort Sumter did not change the nature of the problem Lincoln faced in any way. It merely provided the opportunity to bring military power to bear and carry on this political struggle "by other means."

Korea provides an even better example of political problems solved militarily from within the very heart of the Cold War.

The Truman administration faced the same "political problem" in Korea that later administrations would face in Vietnam: Who would govern in the South? Truman's client government—led by an expatriate and made up largely of those identified as collaborators by most Koreans—would never have survived a free election against its leftist opponents. In the "political" arena, the United States and its Korean allies would have been soundly defeated. Unwilling to accept this, Truman continued the struggle "by other means" from 1946-1950, providing whatever *military* support his authoritarian proxies needed to slaughter their domestic opponents in, it bears restatement, a "cloud of terror...probably unparalleled in the world."[7] By 1950, the South Korean regime was stable and viable, and it had achieved this through the ruthless application of military power, not through elections, political "reform" or winning "hearts and minds." There was now ample time to acquire the allegiance of citizens who would follow the victors, whichever side won. As Daniel Ellsberg noted while testifying before the United States Senate some fifty years ago, most of the people in places like Vietnam and Korea were peasants, not political theorists. They wanted peace and reasonable government (which to them meant primarily being left alone) and, absent compulsion, would typically support whichever side they felt could provide this, whether Communist or non-Communist.[8]

Kim Il Sung certainly understood this, so he swept into southern Korea with an army to solve his political problem through the use

6 Hacker, J. D. (2011). A census-based Count of the Civil War Dead. *Civil War History*, *57*(4), 307-348. https://doi.org/10.1353/cwh.2011.0061.

7 Halliday and Cumings, *Korea: The Unknown War*, 45.

8 Ellsberg, *Papers on the War*, 205–206.

of military power, not the art of persuasion, just as the North Vietnamese would sweep into southern Vietnam in the spring of 1972. Truman responded in kind, and after three years, virtually every structure from the Pusan perimeter to the Yalu River had been leveled, and several million people were dead. But Truman's creation, "South" Korea, was here to stay, which says a great deal about the "unwinnability" of the effort in Vietnam. For the United States faced the same "problem" in Vietnam as it faced in Korea and everywhere else throughout the Cold War: Who would govern? The issue would never change, but in Vietnam, its resolution would shift back and forth between political and military solutions until it became clear to the Communists that a military solution was the only solution that would work for them, thereby making it the only solution that would work for the United States.

II

What you are doing wrong is asking for peace. The North Vietnamese interpret that as weakness. . . . You must make them believe that there will be no peace until they are defeated. When they understand you are going to destroy them, then there will be peace.[9]

Ne Win, President of Burma, advising Lyndon Johnson, 1966

One point to understand about the war in Southeast Asia is both clear and simple: The only "honorable" "negotiated solution" acceptable to Washington and Saigon was defined by the armed stalemate that ended the war in Korea, which represented total defeat to Hanoi.[10] So the die was cast by 1961, and might—military power and the will to use it—would provide the deciding factor, just as it did in Korea. All claims to the contrary—such as Ted Sorensen's assertion that John Kennedy would have achieved a "negotiated" settlement ("settlement" being the key term) or the endlessly asserted claim that Richard Nixon "sabotaged" a genuine peace process in 1968—are nonsense. Of all the players involved,

9 Humphrey, *The Education of a Public Man*, 258.
10 Jones, *Death of a Generation*, 117.

Americans are the only ones who did not then and do not now understand this. The difference between "success" in Korea and failure in Vietnam was a measure of the policies formulated in Washington, not the moral quality of the intervention or the combatants, which brings us to the real question: What might this country's political leaders, beginning with John Kennedy, have done differently?

The answer requires a brief analysis of the two related factors on which the "unwinnable" "political war" paradigm is based: Saigon's lack of democratic "legitimacy" and the inefficacy of military power as a substitute.

We start by recognizing a fact that history makes rather clear: To be stable and viable, a government must have the ability to control its territorial border and enforce its will on its own citizens within its own territory, and a liberal political order is not required, as South Korea from 1945-1992, along with Vietnam and China today (not to mention *scores* of other countries around the world), amply demonstrate. There is simply no reason to believe that South Vietnam, alone among this country's Third World allies, needed a functioning, constitutionally liberal political order to survive when Taiwan got along without it just fine until the end of the Cold War, as did countries like Guatemala and the Philippines.

From another perspective, imagine how things would have gone in Korea if Kim Il Sung, rather than undertaking a conventional invasion, had begun infiltrating large numbers of military personnel into South Korea where they adopted the role of "guerilla fighters" and waged an unrelenting terrorist campaign on Rhee's regime. Imagine further that Truman, aware of what was happening but determined to avoid deployment of US forces, ceded control of South Korea's border to Kim Il Sung, allowing Kim's army into South Korea in whatever numbers Kim chose to send while conditioning aid to the South Korean regime during the late 1940s and early 1950s on "political reform" and democratic "legitimacy" and gearing American efforts toward "nation building" in the midst of Kim's assault. *Is there any doubt that South Korea would have shared South Vietnam's fate?* History did not unfold that way in Korea for one simple reason: Truman, with his party and political future at risk, was willing to provide the South Korean regime with whatever military power it required to secure its border and enforce its will on its citizens, and it wielded that power with an iron hand for several decades. *It was a matter of might, not right.* (This is not a value judgment; this is not to say that this country was *not* right— which is another issue entirely. It is merely to acknowledge that might, not right, was the deciding factor in Korea, as it always is.)

In Vietnam as in Korea, proper, effective employment of the military power that was available would have made all the difference, as no less an authority than Vo Nguyen Giap admitted. "We were not strong enough to drive out a half-million American troops..."[11] This stemmed, simply enough, from the balance of military power, best explained in terms of the classic 3:1 rule long accepted by military planners: With all other things being qualitatively equal, an attacking force requires a roughly 3:1 manpower advantage over defenders to ensure a reasonable probability of success. Even eliminating the qualitative superiority of the Armed Forces of the United States, equipped as they were with limitless artillery, armor, air mobility and tactical air support, the Communists could *never* have mustered sufficient numbers at any given time to achieve a 3:1 advantage over the forces available to secure South Vietnam's territorial border had they been so deployed. General Bruce Palmer presented the appropriate scenario (which was recommended by General Cao, the Joint Chiefs and General James Gavin during the early stages of American involvement) at the Army War College in 1977. It would have required ten divisions: five across the DMZ (two American, two South Korean and one ARVN) with three more US divisions to extend west to the Lao-Thai border and cut the Ho Chi Minh Trail. One more Army and one Marine division would be deployed to secure the Central Highlands and the coastal areas. *This is very similar to SEATO Plan 5, which McNamara recommended—and Kennedy rejected—in November 1961.*[12] The advantages of this

---

11 Record, *The Wrong War*, 53.

12 Sheehan, Smith, Kenworthy and Butterfield, *The Pentagon Papers*, document # 30, 154–156. See Blight, Lang and Welch, and Logevall *Vietnam if Kennedy Had Lived: Virtual JFK*, 127; Prados, *The Blood Road*, 33–38.

strategy "would have been enormous":

> "Moreover," [Palmer] said, "the bulk of these forces would have fought on ground of their choosing which the enemy would be forced to attack if he wanted to invade South Vietnam. [This would have provided U.S. forces with a clear and understandable objective—a peace-keeping operation to separate the belligerents.] In defending well-prepared positions, U.S. casualties would have been much fewer....[Palmer] went on to say that a much smaller U.S. logistics effort would have been required and we would have avoided much of the base development that was of no real value to the South Vietnamese. "Cut off from substantial out-of-country support, the Viet Cong was bound to wither on the vine and gradually become easier for the South Vietnamese to defeat," he concluded. This conclusion was recently reinforced by statements of former South Vietnamese leaders who believed that by providing a military shield behind which South Vietnam could work out its own political, economic and social problems, the United States could have provided a reasonable chance for South Vietnamese freedom and independence.[13]

Facing no greater *internal* threat in 1961 than the South Koreans faced from 1945-1950, the South Vietnamese would have been just as able to maintain their rule as were the South Koreans had they been afforded the opportunity to do so, free from North Vietnamese terrorism, disruption and the constant infiltration of men and supplies, as noted by former NVA Colonel Bui Tin: "If

---

13 Summers, *On Strategy*, 123–124. This option was available as late as 1969. What little indigenous insurgency ever existed had been destroyed, and North Vietnamese forces were smashed and demoralized while 500,000 US troops remained. This was the moment to move quickly and aggressively, scrapping the 1962 Geneva Accords, which the North Vietnamese had never observed, and putting the oft-discussed blocking strategy in effect. In any war being waged on the merits, or (as I will later explain) had a Democrat been elected in 1968, it would likely have happened.

Johnson had granted General Westmoreland's request to enter Laos and block the Ho Chi Minh Trail, Hanoi could not have won the war."[14]

Kennedy was convinced, however, that such a deployment on his watch would be as fatal to his presidency as the "loss of Laos." So he engineered the framework that would define this conflict for the next fifteen years and ceded control of *all* the crucial terrain in return for nothing beyond Hanoi's promise to pretend that nothing of the sort had occurred—to help him, in other words, deceive the American people. Although temporarily serving Kennedy's political needs, the 1962 Geneva Accords netted precisely *nothing* for this country while altering the balance of power in Vietnam exponentially by allowing tens of thousands of North Vietnamese into South Vietnam annually to assume the role of "guerilla fighters" whenever they chose. This transformed the role to be assumed by American forces from conventional defenders with a clear mission, defensible positions and a far better than 3:1 advantage when all factors are considered (precisely the situation they have had in Korea for several decades) into anti-guerilla forces that, as military planners generally agree, require a 10:1 advantage to ensure a reasonable probability of success. This means that 300,000 American and allied troops who could easily have secured and held South Vietnam's border in the face of a conventional assault by a million or more North Vietnamese troops (a number never available to Hanoi at one time[15]) could now be bled continuously and stalemated permanently by as few as 30,000 North Vietnamese, a figure that in time the Communists would move down the trail every few months. *This was a titanic shift in the balance of battlefield power that was accomplished with the stroke of a pen in Geneva.* This gave Hanoi exactly what it wanted by giving it the only war it could win, as Ho Chi Minh told the French in the 1940s: "You can kill ten of my men for every one I kill of yours, but even at those odds, you will lose and I will win."[16] "In

---

14 Richard H. Schultz, Jr., *The Secret War against Hanoi* (New York: HarperCollins, 1999), 205.

15 This represents the total number of troops deployed against the South by Hanoi from 1961–1975.

16 Karnow, *Vietnam: A History*, 17.

the end," he once said, "it will be you who tire of it."[17]

So the complex, nearly untenable political and military situation that forms the very heart of the "unwinnable war" paradigm was not something Americans inevitably faced in Southeast Asia but something that their political leaders, acting for their own purposes, deliberately engineered. The main-force battalions that first appeared in 1962 were not "guerilla" formations recruited from a rebellious peasantry but regular army units sent into South Vietnam through Laos with American acquiescence. They were worth more than *ten times* their actual numbers the moment they became "guerillas" in South Vietnam. "Annihilating ARVN battalions like a blast furnace consumes coke" by the summer of 1965,[18] they no more represented a "political problem" for Diem than did Lincoln's Army of the Potomac represent a "political problem" for Jefferson Davis.

Even accepting the 1962 Accords as written, John Kennedy could easily have enforced their terms through the overwhelming military power available to him, applied exactly as Truman, who learned from Roosevelt, applied it in Korea, as American leaders were told time and again by people who understood the North Vietnamese. In October 1965, Hubert Humphrey asked Laotian Prime Minister Souvanna Phouma what Johnson should do to end the war. Souvanna was clear: "Bomb the dikes in North Vietnam," he said. "That's the only thing that will be effective."[19] Similar advice was given a year later by Burma's President Ne Win: "When [the North Vietnamese] understand you are going to destroy them, then there will be peace."[20] In other words, to win like Truman, Kennedy had to play by Truman's Rules, which means almost no rules at all.

Applying Truman's Rules the moment he determined that the North Vietnamese had violated of the 1962 Geneva Accords, John Kennedy, without moving into Laos and thereby "violating" the Accords (appearances being crucial), would have dispatched B-52s to reduce Hanoi and Haiphong to ash, rubble and a hundred

---

17 Record, *The Wrong War*, 37.

18 Sheehan, *A Bright and Shining Lie*, 536.

19 Humphrey, *The Education of a Public Man*, 244.

20 Ibid., 258.

thousand charred corpses in a single night, and it would have taken but a few days to do to North Vietnam what it took months for Truman to "accomplish" in Korea. (B-29s pale next to B-52s.) After the cities and towns had been destroyed, the aerial assault could have shifted to the dikes and water control systems that produced the rice crop. With C-123s and their loads of Agent Orange, however, bombing dikes would not have been necessary. (The only reason Truman did not use Agent Orange on the rice crop in Korea was because Truman did not have it, or perhaps nobody thought to use it.) Brutality on such a scale would have provided a "satisfactory" outcome in short order just as it had in Korea, where Kim Il Sung was desperate to end the war in months, and, but for his Chinese and Soviet "allies," would have ended it on almost any terms. No matter how much nonsense and dogma you have heard to the contrary, the Communists in Vietnam were not invulnerable, invincible, immortal or magic. They were *certainly* no tougher or more determined than Japanese or North Koreans. *They could have been forced to submit, especially when the United States sought not conquest, but compromise.*

In recognizing this, I am not promoting Truman's Rules. Orthodoxy notwithstanding, I am not suggesting that it was either right or necessary for Truman to fight in this manner for some two years and ten months *after* Communist forces had been driven from South Korea and the Rhee government restored. Nor am I suggesting that Kennedy or Johnson should have attempted anything along these lines. I am merely noting that the requisite military power was available, and if any president had exercised this option, incinerating every city, town and village in North Vietnam, leveling every last structure and poisoning the entire rice crop, killing hundreds of thousands of Vietnamese men, women and children in the process, the very worst that could be said is that he behaved just like Harry Truman, who behaved just like Franklin Roosevelt.

No American president, on the other hand, was willing to apply that kind of military power on behalf of the GVN, which, having entered the 1960s under Ngo Dinh Diem every bit as legitimate and viable as South Korea, was rendered virtually indefensible by

Kennedy's agreement to host Hanoi's "insurgency" in South Vietnam and then hopelessly undermined by naïve and incredibly hostile members of the Saigon press corps, who served the Hanoi regime as conduits for the most successful disinformation campaign in history. Without control over its territory and people—which required the kind of effective, decisive military power provided to Seoul—Saigon remained not dictatorial (as orthodoxy teaches us) but weak, unstable and unable to govern.[21]

Even as badly as America's war in Southeast Asia was fought, it was winnable until the very moment this country quit.

South Vietnam was at least as viable when the Americans withdrew in 1973 as was South Korea in 1953. Its ability to defend itself with adequate American support had been established beyond question in the spring of 1972, when, in an exact replay of North Korea's "invasion" of South Korea in June 1950, the North Vietnamese attacked in conventional formations across the DMZ and through Laos. They were stopped, losing as many as 100,000 men, by a combination of South Vietnamese ground forces and US air power. *The United States government had given the South Vietnamese no more support in 1972 than it was prepared to give the South Koreans under similar circumstances, support that Americans are prepared to give the South Koreans even today.* What little indigenous insurgency had existed was long over by 1975 (it had been crushed decisively in 1968), Saigon's military forces were as strong as they were when the Easter Offensive was launched, and there had been no decline in US airpower. In other words, this country and its allies had the same power to crush a conventional attack in 1975 as in 1972, and time was no longer on Hanoi's side. Time would allow South Vietnam to gel, like South Korea, and join the world community. "One fact remained irrefutable: The North must take the country in the next few years. Le Duan made the point often and forcefully that a prolonged war would be disastrous."[22] South Vietnamese forces, which numbered more than a million men with armor and airpower, were taking

21 Daniel Pipes and Adam Garfinkle, ed., *Friendly Tyrants, an American Dilemma* (New York: MacMillan, 1991), 45–46.

22 Langguth, *Our Vietnam*, 635.

back territory while North Vietnamese units, still recovering from the 1972 Offensive, were in disarray.

> At this rate, disaster loomed for the Communists. Their spies inside the Saigon regime informed them that Thieu had developed a plan for the next two years to keep grabbing territory until he felt secure enough to authorize an election—the results of which would, of course, confirm him as South Vietnam's sole authority. He would then scrap the tattered cease-fire agreement openly and proceed to mop up the Communist remnants just as Diem had liquidated the Vietminh survivors after he consolidated his power. The clock would be turned back to the dark days of the 1950s, when the southern Communist movement was nearly extinguished.[23]

Time was what South Vietnam needed, and the military power to sustain South Vietnam over time was still available, which makes for a truly intriguing counterfactual: The Democrat in '68.

Orthodoxy holds that Richard Nixon could have acquired a settlement in 1969 on essentially the same terms as he acquired in 1973, as Christopher Hitchens maintained: "[F]our years later the Nixon administration concluded the war on the same terms that had been on offer in Paris."[24] Larry Berman (who knows better) writes in *No Peace, No Honor* that, given the "insignificant difference between the 1969 proposal and the 1973 deal, we can only conclude that many tens of thousands died for very little or simply while waiting for Thieu to give in because Nixon...feared that anyone else would not accept the American guarantee of continuous war under the guise of a paper peace."[25] A.J. Langguth also tells us that Richard Nixon "had no wish to end the war"[26] while Daniel Ellsberg writes that it was Nixon's plan to ensure that "the war

23 Karnow, *Vietnam: A History*, 658–659.
24 Hitchens, *The Trial of Henry Kissinger*, 7.
25 Berman, No Peace, No Honor, 246.
26 Langguth, *Our Vietnam*, 536.

would essentially never end."[27] (Exactly why this was Nixon's goal they never tell us.)

Democrat-in-'68 counterfactuals are many and varied. (What if Bobby Kennedy had not been assassinated?[28] What if Humphrey had broken with Johnson sooner? What if Nixon had not "interfered" with the "peace talks"?) And they all represent ideology in its purest form, as demonstrated by addressing the two questions that those who propagate these counterfactuals have assiduously avoided for several decades: 1) what exactly were the terms of the "honorable," "rational," "political solution" acceptable to both the American people *and* the North Vietnamese that any Democrat would have acquired with ease?; 2) how was a Democrat going to acquire this in 1969?

Answering these questions requires a clear understanding of certain historical facts that cannot be overstated:

As Stanley Karnow noted, Lyndon Johnson was able to hold his critics "to an apparent handful of either right- or left-wing extremists with only marginal influence"[29] until *after* the Tet Offensive. He was able to do this because domestic politics had been the deciding factor for American policy in Southeast Asia from the start, and Johnson's policies were supported by the vast majority of Americans, who, believing everything they had been told for years by liberal Democrats like Harry Truman, John Kennedy, Lyndon Johnson and Hubert Humphrey, wanted Truman's doctrine enforced in Vietnam without another "land war in Asia." Congressional Democrats, even those who deeply opposed the war in private, were not willing to lead a fight against their own president and a foreign policy created by Harry Truman, so they just followed along until, with more than 30,000 American dead and

---

27 Ellsberg, *Secrets*, 258.

28 Bobby Kennedy, for example, "could have ended the Vietnam War in 1969 rather than six years later" according to Henry Reuss, a Democratic Congressman for twenty-eight years. See Henry Reuss, *When Government Was Good* (Madison: University of Wisconsin Press, 1999), 167. As with John Kennedy, "insider" references to Bobby's (dare I say) "secret plan" to end the war "immediately" are certainly available, despite his public calls for a negotiated settlement. See Heymann, *R.F.K., A Candid Biography of Robert F. Kennedy*, 475. See also Clarke, *The Last Campaign*, 76.

29 Ibid., 558.

the war stalemated, public support shifted, just as it had on Korea, to those promising to "end the war" on rational, honorable terms acceptable to the American people, to "get out without giving up." This is just what Democrats then promised, and it is just what they would have attempted. Hubert Humphrey (who intended to invite Henry Kissinger to join his administration[30]) outlined his plan in the following terms:

> As president, I would stop the bombing of the North as an acceptable risk for peace, because I believe it could lead to success in the negotiations and thereby shorten the war. This would be the best protection for our troops. In weighing that risk—and before taking action—I would place key importance on evidence—direct or indirect, by deed or word—of Communist willingness to restore the demilitarized zone between North and South Vietnam. If the government of North Vietnam were to show bad faith, I would reserve the right to resume the bombing.
>
> Secondly, I would take the risk that the South Vietnamese would meet the responsibilities they say they are now ready to assume in their own self-defense. I would move, in other words, toward de-Americanization of the war. I would sit down with the leaders of South Vietnam to set a specific timetable by which American forces could be systematically reduced while South Vietnamese forces took over more of the burden. The schedule must be a realistic one—one that would not weaken the overall allied defense posture. I am convinced such action would be as much in South Vietnam's interest as in ours.[31]

Even cursory analysis reveals that the gap between Humphrey

---

30 Humphrey, *The Education of a Public Man*, xx.
31 Ibid., 302, n. 11.

and Hanoi was completely unbridgeable. "Communist willingness to restore the demilitarized zone between North and South Vietnam" means restoration of pre-war boundaries (which was one of the terms of Johnson's "peace initiative" in 1968[32]), and "American forces...systematically reduced while South Vietnamese forces took over more of the burden" is what Richard Nixon called "Vietnamization." In other words, Humphrey's strategy, which was actually formulated by Clark Clifford and initiated by Lyndon Johnson in the summer of 1968,[33] was identical in form and substance to Nixon's. It was designed to allow Humphrey, like Nixon, to get out without giving up—this being the next logical phase in the vicious cycle created as politicians took polls, determined what the electorate wanted and tailored their chosen policies accordingly, which is precisely how the war had developed to this point in time. A perfect appraisal of Humphrey's plan was provided, ironically, by George Ball in a 1965 memorandum to President Johnson: "For North Viet-Nam to call off the insurgency in South-Vietnam, close the border and withdraw the elements it has infiltrated into that country would mean that it had accepted unconditional surrender."[34] This being the case, it is ridiculous to suggest that the North Vietnamese would have handled a Humphrey/Kissinger attempt to get out without giving up any differently than they handled Nixon's, which is why no "honorable" "political solution" that was "fully acceptable to the American people" and available in 1969 has ever been outlined, even in theory. *One never existed.* This is not to say, however, that a Democratic president would have made no difference during a war that had always represented the "continuation of political relations" between Democrats and Republicans.

Congressional Democrats turned left at noon on January 20, 1969, and, continuing political relations with Republicans "by other means," began to undermine Nixon just as they had supported Johnson, becoming in short order the anvil to a North Vietnamese hammer. No matter what Nixon did, it was never enough. No matter

---

32 Berman, *No Peace, No Honor*, 22.

33 Prados, *Vietnam*, 261–262.

34 Goldstein, *Lessons in Disaster*, 160.

how many concessions he made, no matter how many troops he withdrew (450,000 in three years), no matter how many offensives the Communists launched during the "peace talks," no matter how many neutral countries they invaded (Laos, Cambodia), it was always, according to the Democrats, Nixon's fault. *He* was "expanding the war"; *he* was "escalating," driving them (in the country's interest, of course) to end-the-war legislation and Nixonesque, back-channel dealing, with George McGovern, for one, taking a prominent and effective role. Their cynical, partisan maneuvering was far more consequential than Nixon's, with results that speak for themselves. *It was neither the Tet Offensive nor a shift in public opinion that transformed the Party of Harry Truman into the Party of George McGovern; it was Nixon's election.*[35]

Had Humphrey (or any viable Democratic contender) won the White House, on the other hand, the war would have remained the Democrats' war. *They* would have to bear the full burden if *their* president failed to acquire the "honorable," "mutually acceptable," "political solution" that was "fully acceptable to the American people" they had promised. Which means, of course, that Nixon's congressional opponents—Mansfield, Kennedy, Muskie and Church, to name a few—would have been Humphrey's allies. Since President Humphrey would surely have kept his congressional allies apprised of the state of Henry Kissinger's "peace talks," Democrats would have known in 1969 that the North Vietnamese were demanding that a *Democratic* president backed by a *Democratic* Congress abandon not just an effort to enforce *Truman's* doctrine that *Democrats* had initiated but abandon as well, without so much as name one, hundreds of American POWs whom two preceding *Democratic* presidents had sent to fight with

---

35 This is not to say that Democrats were destined to move left after Nixon's election. No one would have attacked Nixon more stridently than congressional Democrats had he quickly thrown in the towel and abandoned Vietnam, as we are now to believe he should have, leaving Americans with, on top of everything else, a several-billion-dollar ransom to pay for return of their POWs. Democrats had promised an "honorable" "political solution" that was "fully acceptable to the American people," and a unilateral withdrawal after a few months of Hanoi's intransigence was certainly not what they would have said they had in mind.

the support of four *Democratic* Congresses in a row, leaving *Democrats* to explain to the electorate why they must now pay an enormous ransom to a third-rate Communist power in the middle of the Cold War for the return of those prisoners. They would also have been operating with the knowledge that since 1963, Richard Nixon and his party had warned the American people time and again that Democrats were mishandling the war. *Had Democrats thrown in the towel and withdrawn unconditionally after a few months of Communist intransigence, history would confirm that their opponents, not they, had been right all along.* The damage inflicted on Democrats for "losing China" would have paled in comparison, and it is ridiculous to suggest that congressional Democrats—who rationalized their way through years of conflict, oceans of blood and billions of dollars to protect their party from just this development—would have magically transformed, shortly after and wholly independent of the 1968 election, into honest, pure-hearted statesmen and humanitarians, ready and willing to fall on their swords for the good of the country. They would have remained the same venal, cynical operatives they had been up until now, which makes the strident, uncompromising tone that characterized the Democratic center within months of Nixon's inauguration unimaginable and the Humphrey-in-'68 counterfactual truly intriguing, at least when considered in light of history rather than mythology.

The only way to acquire anything close to Nixon's 1973 terms in 1969 was by applying in 1969, with congressional support, the kind of military power Nixon applied in 1972. And Hubert Humphrey, "a shallow, contemptible and hopelessly dishonest old hack"[36] who would have been furious over Communist intransigence, would have been just the man to do it. Mining the North's harbors, unleashing B-52s and launching major ground offensives against Communist forces badly weakened during Tet (with American rather than Vietnamese troops) would have been very effective in the fall of 1969. In fact, Humphrey would have been able to move into Laos and put the Joint Chiefs' blocking strategy into effect

---

36 Thompson, *Fear and Loathing on the Campaign Trail '72*, 206, 209.

while he still had more than enough American troops to do it, as congressional Democrats praised his move as "a bold stroke designed to separate the belligerents," "reduce the level of violence," "facilitate negotiation with an unreasonable enemy" and "force peaceful resolution." (I can hear it all now.) This would have radically altered the balance of power in South Vietnam, and as NVA Colonel Bui Tin noted, had American forces occupied the Ho Chi Minh Trail, "Hanoi could not have won the war."[37]

Once sufficient military power had been employed to force the kind of politically palatable settlement outlined by Humphrey in 1968, Democrats would have been as willing to defend it as they were willing to acquire it. For Democrats would have known all too well that, with tens of thousands of Americans killed enforcing Truman's doctrine on their watch with no Republican president or Congress, no way to share much less shift the blame, they and they alone would pay for any failure to defend *their* agreement ending *their* war. Humphrey and his congressional allies would have been just as unwilling to "lose" Southeast Asia in 1975 as Truman was unwilling to "lose" Korea in 1950, and he would not have hesitated to unleash the B-52s if America's ally in Southeast Asia was threatened. *However counterintuitive it seems, a Democratic victory in 1968 represented South Vietnam's only real chance.*

On the other hand, there is no plausible counterfactual by which *Richard Nixon* could have saved South Vietnam because this truly was a "political war," but not in the way that orthodoxy employs that phrase. The war in Vietnam had never been anything but an extension of political relations between Democrats and Republicans "by other means." Absent the "considerations of domestic politics, and [the] political fears of the consequences of looking weak in the forthcoming domestic election,"[38] neither Kennedy nor Johnson would have continued, much less escalated, American involvement in Vietnam. So "the paramount object" of the endeavor was never to secure Southeast Asia for the West but to acquire and maintain

---

37 Schultz, *The Secret War against Hanoi*, 205.
38 Halberstam, *The Best and the Brightest*, xviii.

405

power in Washington,[39] where the *real* enemy was to be found. The war was therefore destined to end after congressional Democrats, no longer tainted by the espionage scandals and political battles of the Truman Era, handed it off to Richard Nixon (one of the best things that ever happened to them), which allowed them in due course (now as the antiwar opposition) to stop funding the GVN they so hated without fear of the consequences. *Nothing Richard Nixon did would have altered the outcome.* Any assertion to the contrary returns us to Korea, which required Congress to appropriate *billions* of dollars every year for several decades to survive (along with tens of thousands of permanently stationed US troops who serve as a "tripwire") and *still* costs the US some $3 billion annually.[40] To suggest that opposition Democrats, who controlled both Houses of Congress until 1982 and the House of Representatives until 1994, would have continued to appropriate billions of dollars annually to support the "illegitimate," "morally bankrupt" GVN and a seemingly endless conflict ("Nixon's war," as they called it) is not just absurd; it is preposterous. *With Nixon's election, the Truman Doctrine's campaign in Southeast Asia was going to end exactly as it did, when it did, if not a short while later.*[41]

In summary, those who insist that this country failed in Vietnam because its leaders employed military power to address "political problems" are correct, but not for the reasons they advance. Kennedy, Johnson and Nixon each faced interrelated political and military problems, one domestic and one overseas, that they (along with many others) had spent years creating for themselves. Their political problem was purely domestic: Who would govern in Washington? Due to the "Legacy of the '30s," this political problem would in their minds turn on the outcome of their military problem:

---

39 The only plan advanced that was actually designed to secure South Vietnam, which was based on SEATO Plan 5, was rejected because it was politically unpalatable under Ellsberg's Rules, not because it was militarily unfeasible.

40 "Why the United States Should Not Pay for 79 percent of South Korea's National Defense." The Federalist, February 14, 2019. https://thefederalist.com/2019/02/14/united-states-not-pay-79-percent-south-koreas-national defense/.

41 This was much like World War II in the Pacific, which was destined to end with nuclear attacks on Hiroshima and Nagasaki, *regardless of anything that Japan's leaders might have done differently.*

Who would govern in South Vietnam? Just as this country's political problem in Korea (who would govern in the South?) transitioned from its political to its military phase in 1950, America's political problem in South Vietnam had so transitioned by 1960. Thereafter, Vietnam was a Cold War battlefield, not a polling place, and a successful campaign in South Vietnam required, as in South Korea, an appropriate application of power and will over a long enough period to create a viable nation-state that American leaders were willing to support for decades to come. But our presidents' political problem (who would govern in Washington?) was paramount, and Ellsberg's Rules therefore controlled. So the war would be handled, negotiated, manipulated and managed with money, political skill and a limited amount of muscle, from one election cycle to the next as our so-called leaders tried to con and glad-hand their way through a gunfight, with an outcome that was predictable if not inevitable. And this brings our first round of "heretical," "dangerous thought" to an end with several key points that matter if we are to have an honest reckoning with history:

(1) You will never understand the Vietnam War by reading about the Vietnam War. You must begin at the beginning, which, in this case, means the 1930s, when the "problem," the "virus," the "flaw in the society" entered the American body politic, providing a legacy, the "Legacy of the '30s," that would haunt American history and politics for decades. You must understand the Truman Era in all of its stupidity and folly: rampant, history-altering espionage and institutional cover-up with a toxic backlash; American armed forces stripped to the bone; a Communist attack on South Korea; Truman's order to cross the 38th parallel; China's entry into the war; and an inconclusive stalemate that haunts Americans to this very day. These were the events that "poisoned" American politics and drove this country into Southeast Asia under Ellsberg's Rules, which, in the minds of the presidents who took this country into and out of Vietnam, demanded the political commitment while limiting the military options in a manner that would preclude any chance of success. *This would all have occurred had Joseph McCarthy been killed in the Pacific during World War II.*

(2) There is no historical support whatsoever for claims of widespread, day-to-day criminality by American personnel during the Truman Doctrine's Southeast Asian campaign. Quite the contrary, in fact. And most former proponents of the war crimes industry (which, like the *Protocols of the Elders of Zion*, keeps coming back no matter how long discredited) want nothing more today than to leave it behind without serious examination, because the war crimes industry is dangerous—dangerous to American liberalism and dangerous to American Exceptionalism.[42] If American intervention in Southeast Asia truly was a Bad War for having been fought "in all the wrong ways," World War II and Korea are Bad Wars as well—and far worse at that—which transforms revered public figures like Franklin Roosevelt and Harry Truman, along with veterans of the sainted Greatest Generation, into first-rate war criminals while demolishing entirely this country's proud, orthodox, twentieth century narrative. On the other hand, if the Truman Doctrine's Southeast Asian campaign does not represent a Bad War fought "in all the wrong ways," if its veterans are not what liberal politicians, pundits, public intellectuals and anti-draft Baby Boomers said they were for decades, *what indeed are their accusers?*

(3) What Americans call the Vietnam War was a war of choice that, being policy- and politically driven, was unrelated to any *immediate* threat to American security. As such, the outcome, which was not inevitable, depended not on the availability of military power, which was always more than sufficient, but on luck when available and when not, on the courage and wisdom of this

---

42 John Kerry spurned a golden opportunity to distance himself from the war crimes industry on *Meet the Press* in May 2001. Although stating that use of terms like "war criminal" and "genocide" served no purpose, Kerry said, "I stand by the rest of what I said happened over there." "Vietnam 30 Years Later: What John Kerry Said on Meet the Press," History News Network, George Mason University, February 13, 2004. http://hnn.us/articles/3552.html, accessed May 10, 2012. Eventually, Kerry paid a heavy and well-deserved price for his embrace of the war crimes industry. As Stieg Larsson once said, "To exact revenge for yourself or your friends is not only a right, it's an absolute duty." David Carr, "Scenes from an Unmarriage," *New York Times Book Review,* July 11, 2011. "No one who is not a coward," said Professor Wilfred Reilly, "is just going to allow himself to be attacked for decades without responding." *Tucker Carlson Today,* April 7, 2021. And be not mistaken: The Swift Boat attacks, which played what was possibly a decisive role in his loss of the 2004 presidential election, were launched by veterans in retaliation for Kerry's dishonest, decades-long Vietnam veteran bashing.

country's leaders and the patience, tolerance and perception of the electorate. By this frame of reference, Korea was a "Vietnam War" that, although a conventional conflict for American forces after 1950, ended in heavily armed stalemate because: 1) American security did not require victory in a conventional sense—meaning subjugation of the enemy state; 2) American leaders did not act with either wisdom or courage; and 3) by 1953, the patience and tolerance of an electorate that demanded peace without defeat was at an end, and the political class delivered.

(4) The Truman Doctrine gave rise to a series of interventions and "Vietnam Wars"—some short, some long, some easy, some hard, some won, some lost and some still in progress—and there is no intellectually honest way to distinguish, from a moral, legal or philosophical perspective, one from another. Whether one focuses on Greece, Taiwan and El Salvador (where the United States supported existing governments); Korea, Iran and South Vietnam (where the United States installed its own); Guatemala (where the United States supported insurgents until they succeeded, then supported the government they formed); or Nicaragua (where the United States supported an existing government until it was overthrown and then supported the insurgents, who were led by former members of the overthrown regime)—this country did essentially the same things the same way for the same reasons, providing whatever "American financing, proxies, technicians, firepower and [sometimes] troops and pilots" the situation required to keep these lands out of Communist hands at almost any cost. And flagrant disregard of domestic and international law by American leaders was as much the rule as the exception. (I state this as a fact and a conclusion of law, not a moral judgment.)

(5) Daniel Ortega and the Sandinistas had the same right to seize power in Nicaragua as Castro had to seize power in Cuba, which was the same right Ho Chi Minh had to seize power in Vietnam, which was the same right Kim Il Sung had to seize power in Korea, which was the same right Mao had to seize power China, which was the same right Greek Communists had to seize power in Greece, which was the same right Lenin had to seize power in Russia. And each was equally entitled to run as hellish and vicious a dictatorship as he chose, cleansing his territory of the ideologically unacceptable in the same way Charles Taylor, Saddam Hussein and

Slobodan Milosevic "cleansed" territories they controlled. This is not to suggest that any such "rights" exist, only to note the historical and moral equivalence between all of those on the Communist side of the Cold War and others who conduct their affairs as the Communists did.

(6) Ronald Reagan had the same right to support the Contras in Nicaragua as Richard Nixon had to support the overthrow of Salvatore Allende in Chile, which was the same right Johnson and Nixon had to send troops and planes to Southeast Asia, which was the same right John Kennedy had to launch Operation Mongoose against Castro and overthrow Diem, which was the same right Eisenhower had to eliminate the Arbenz government in Guatemala and install Diem in South Vietnam, which was the same right Truman had to intervene in civil wars in Greece and Korea. This is not to say that any of these presidents had any "right" to do as they did, only to note the historical and moral equivalence of this country's Cold War campaigns.

The facts being what they are, judge America's war in Southeast Asia however you choose, but remember when so doing that it was but one chapter in a decades-long conflict we call the Cold War. If it was "fought for all the wrong reasons," so was the entire Cold War. If America's Vietnam-era leaders are guilty of "crimes against peace and crimes against humanity" as Daniel Ellsberg claims, American leaders, military and civilian, from every administration from 1945-1991, with the possible exception of the Carter years, are guilty as well, America's Cold War being one, decades-long "crime against peace" and "crime against humanity." And if this country's conduct in Southeast Asia was so brutal and disproportional that the endeavor is indefensible regardless of the overall justness of its Cold War cause, there is precious little left of America's proud twentieth century narrative as not even World War II, the Good War, can pass muster.

It is not my purpose here either to defend or condemn this country's Cold War policies and conduct but to make clear that there is no way to avoid the paradigm shift in worldview to which an honest, principled reckoning with history necessarily gives rise, which brings us to the next step in our journey from ideology to history: deconstructing the heroic myth of the antiwar movement.

III

[T]he publication of In Retrospect has led to unaccountable minions proclaiming—yet again—that since McNamara admits that we were wrong about Vietnam, those who protested the war must have been right. But the fact that two plus two doesn't equal five does not prove that two plus two must therefore equal three.[43]

Adam Garfinkle

Never homogenous, the antiwar movement, which grew exponentially over time, was built around a hard, central, Old-Left/New-Left core surrounded by concentric rings of fellow-travelers, supporters, opportunistic politicians and sympathizers of all types with little in common but a willingness to oppose the war, at least rhetorically. Its distilled essence was disingenuousness of the type described rather eloquently, if colloquially, by Princeton University Professor Harry G. Frankfurt in a little masterpiece entitled, *On Bullshit*. After describing the fundamental nature of a lie, which he defines as "deliberate falsehood," which is what a liar conveys, Professor Frankfurt explained the difference between a liar and a bullshitter, which turns essentially on "misrepresentational intent":

> [A]lthough [bullshit] is produced without concern for the truth, it need not be false. The bullshitter is faking things, but this does not mean that he necessarily gets them wrong. . . .

> What bullshit essentially misrepresents is neither the state of affairs to which it refers nor the beliefs of the speaker concerning that state of affairs. Those are what lies misrepresent, by virtue of being false. Since bullshit need not be false, it differs from lies in its misrepresentational intent. The bullshitter may not deceive us, or even intend to do so, either about the facts or about what he takes the facts to be. *What*

---

43 Garfinkle, *Telltale Hearts*, 302.

he does necessarily attempt to deceive us about is his enterprise. His only indispensably distinctive characteristic is that in a certain way he misrepresents what he is up to.[44]

The movement's Old-Left/New-Left core was made up of people whose world was devoted to lies, not phoniness or fakery, but deliberate falsehood of the kind confronted by historian Ronald Radosh during his effort to produce a definitive, historically accurate account of the Rosenberg spy case. Although he began this endeavor convinced that Julius and Ethyl Rosenberg were nothing more than "martyred innocents,"[45] he found that many who should have been sympathetic to his undertaking considered it "a betrayal of the cause."[46] One of the "principal figures" in the case told Radosh that he had no interest in "historical truth" unless it would "hurt the establishment." He explained to Radosh that he was a radical, not a liberal, and that it was best for the historical truth to remain hidden.[47] One well-known left-wing lawyer told Radosh that he was not among those who thought that the Rosenbergs were innocent but threatened to sue if Radosh published his view. It was necessary, he said, to present the Rosenbergs as victims of Cold War hysteria.[48]

Joan Baez confronted the very heart of the antiwar movement when she sought backers for "An Open Letter to the Socialist Republic of Vietnam" in 1979 to protest the murderous abuses of the Hanoi government she had supported so ardently during the war. William Kunstler, the famous radical attorney, told Baez that he did not believe "in public attacks on socialist countries, even where human rights abuses occur."[49] David Dellinger, a well-known "pacifist," responded venomously to her request for support: "You have to be naïve to believe that a Leninist revolution will allow any

44 Harry G. Frankfurt, *On Bullshit* (Princeton: Princeton University Press, 2005), 46–48, 53–54 (emphasis added).
45 Radosh and Milton, *The Rosenberg File*, ix.
46 Ibid., xii.
47 Ibid.
48 Ibid., xii–xiii.
49 Joan Baez, *And a Voice to Sing With* (New York: Summit Books, 1987), 280.

independent thought. Many Americans were totally naïve about what was coming in Vietnam if 'our side' won. I had no such illusions, although I did not oppose that criminal war any less. So don't expect me to be shocked now."[50] Kunstler, Dellinger and thousands more of their ilk were the type of "intellectual pacifists whose real though unacknowledged motive," as George Orwell once noted, "appears to be hatred of western democracy and admiration for totalitarianism."[51] For them, the war provided a priceless, heaven-sent opportunity to assault American society and culture, as Chicago Seven defendant Jerry Rubin noted: "If there had been no Vietnam War, we would have invented one. If the Vietnam War ends, we'll find another war."[52]

As for antiwar Baby Boomers, they were far from the principled, selfless patriots they would have us all believe, having been and remaining to this day almost nothing but, as Professor Frankfurt defines the term, "bullshitters," with a capacity for self-regard, self-deception and disingenuousness that is almost without limit.

When writing about the sixties, for example, Baby Boomers make every effort to ennoble themselves by claiming all the appropriate, politically correct campaigns as their own, as when political analyst Joe Klein, a typical, college-educated, liberal Baby Boomer, describes the sixties as a "decade breathless with nobility— the incredible courage of the Freedom Riders and other civil rights workers; the soaring rhetoric of the Kennedys and King."[53] History, however, shows Kennedy rhetoric to have been empty and dishonest, and where the civil rights struggles are concerned, Boomers had precious little involvement. As Democratic strategist (and Baby Boomer) Paul Begela wrote in 2000, "[T]he civil-rights movement was led by pre-Boomers like Martin Luther King Jr. (who would be seventy-one if he were alive today) and continued

50 Ibid.
51 George Orwell, *Notes on Nationalism*, May 1945.
52 Jerry Rubin, *Do It!* (New York: Simon and Schuster, 1970), 105. This brings to mind Adolph Hitler's belief that had "the Jew" not existed, "We should then have to invent him. It is essential to have a tangible enemy, not merely an abstract one." Rauschning, *Hitler Speaks:* 234.
53 Joe Klein, *Politics Lost* (New York: Doubleday, 2006), 7. See also Leonard Steinhorn, *The Greater Generation: In Defense of the Baby Boom Legacy* (New York: St. Martin's Press, 2006).

without strong support from the Boomers on college campuses."[54] One would be hard-pressed, I expect, to find one Baby Boomer in a thousand who actually did something—anything at all—in connection with the civil rights movement.

Nowhere, however, is the Baby Boomers' capacity for "bullshit" more evident than where the war in Southeast Asia is concerned. When praising the *real* heroes of the sixties, it would never occur to the likes of Klein and Begala—who cannot say enough about civil rights and antiwar activists—to say even a single decent thing about the Baby Boomers who served in Southeast Asia, not even one respectful word about the tens of thousands of them who died and thousands more who are disabled from wounds, none of whom, in the world according to Klein and Begala, are even worthy of mention, except perhaps as suckers or objects of pity. In fact, there is little if any genuine evidence that antiwar Baby Boomers believed in anything. Like Palmerston's England, they had neither "eternal allies" nor "perpetual enemies," only "interests." And their "convictions" were a product of those "interests," as draft-dodger Michael Blumenthal made clear: "What it was precisely that most of us believed, if anything, seems increasingly unclear....For most of us, the logic was hardly Aristotelian: we first decided that we wanted out, then *why*."[55] A few were perfectly frank regarding their motives: "If I lost a couple of years," said a University of Michigan student, "it would mean $16,000 to me. I know I sound selfish, but, by God, I paid $10,000 to get this education."[56] A Delaware defense worker with a job-related deferment expressed similar sentiments: "I got a steady job. I'm making good money and having a ball every weekend. Why the hell should I want to go?"[57] The vast majority, however, have always donned the requisite veneer of altruism. "[A] lot of us thought that probably the best way was not to be in jail, but to be out organizing...it wasn't an easy decision, because we realize... the moral conflict of interest that not going to jail was also

---

54 Paul Begala, "The Worst Generation," *Esquire*, April 2000, 112, 114.

55 MacPherson, *Long Time Passing*, 155 (emphasis in the original).

56 Lawrence M. Baskir and William A. Strauss, *Chance and Circumstance: The Draft, the War and the Vietnam Generation* (New York: Vintage Books 1978), 7.

57 Ibid.

very personally pleasing."[58] "[T]he overriding concerns involved organizing not the middle class but the working class, and staying out of jail to do so."[59] We are to believe from this that, in accepting their various deferments, our selfless antiwar heroes and patriots were acting in their country's interests, just like the Marines landing on Guadalcanal.

Whatever an individual's stated reason, Baby Boomers lined up by the millions for their deferments, which made them card-carrying supporters of both the selective service system and the war that could not have been waged without it, as draft dodger James Fallows later admitted:

> The children of the bright, good parents were spared the more immediate sort of suffering that our inferiors were undergoing. And because of that, when our parents were opposed to the war, they were opposed in a bloodless, theoretical fashion, as they might be opposed to political corruption or racism in South Africa. As long as the little gold stars kept going to homes in Chelsea and the backwoods of West Virginia, the mothers of Beverly Hills and Chevy Chase and Great Neck and Belmont were not on the telephones to their Congressmen screaming *you killed my boy*, they were not writing to the President that this crazy, wrong, evil war had put their boys in prison and ruined their careers. *It is clear by now that if the men of Harvard had wanted to do the very most they could to help shorten the war, they should have been drafted or imprisoned en masse.*[60]

Do not be fooled for an instant by Fallows' 1975 claim that the reality of his own conduct "was clear by now." The effect of choosing

---

58 Michael S. Foley, *Confronting the War Machine, Draft Resistance during the Vietnam War* (Chapel Hill: The University of North Carolina Press, 2003), 237.

59 Ibid.

60 James Fallows, "What Did You Do in the Class War, Daddy?" *Washington Monthly*, October 1975, 5-19, 10 (emphasis added).

compliance over resistance was no secret during the war, as *New York Times* columnist Tom Wicker wrote in 1967: "[I]f the Johnson administration had to prosecute 100,000 Americans in order to maintain its authority, its real power to pursue the Vietnamese war would be crippled if not destroyed."[61] Wicker was absolutely right. By 1969, violations of the Selective Service Act represented the fourth largest category on the federal criminal docket, although only 25,000 men out of fifteen million who registered were actually indicted under the Act during the entire Vietnam era.[62] If only ten percent of these fifteen million had actively resisted, the 25,000 prosecutions that required such an inordinate expenditure of prosecutorial resources would have turned into 1.5 million, a *sixty-fold* increase that would have made enforcement of the Selective Service Act literally impossible, and the war would have ended, no ifs, ands or buts about it.

Some of the few genuine activists, in an effort to get Baby Boomers involved, proposed "snowballing" petitions, by which signatories agreed to resist if enough signatures, anywhere from 1,000 to 15,000, could be gathered. Nothing ever worked, however, because genuine opposition to the war required genuine conviction and entailed certain risks, and few Baby Boomers were up to it. *Only one in five of the radicals who formed the very heart of the Students for a Democratic Society ("SDS") were willing to support a plan to renounce their own deferments and resist.*[63] Typical in this was Tom Hayden. One of the most prominent among the fire-breathing "revolutionary" core of the SDS, Hayden told a large crowd in 1968 that "[t]he question of draft resistance is a line you must be prepared to cross if you are to be a serious participant in opposition to the war."[64] Yet Hayden had made his own separate peace with the US government—"an outlaw institution under the control of war criminals" as he called it[65]—having long since acquired *his* deferment, which he duly maintained through years of

---

61 Baskir and Strauss, *Chance and Circumstance*, 63.

62 Ibid., 11–12 and figure 1; MacPherson, *Long Time Passing*, 380.

63 Baskir and Strauss, *Chance and Circumstance*, 64.

64 Foley, *Confronting the War Machine*, 237.

65 Garfinkle, *Telltale Hearts*, 162.

venomous anti-draft, antiwar rhetoric.[66] Mario Savio, one of the leaders of Berkeley's famous "free speech" movement, provides another fine example of antiwar leadership. Savio famously told the world that "when the operation of the machine becomes so odious, makes you so sick at heart, that you can't take part...you've got to put your bodies upon the wheels, upon the levers, upon all the apparatus and you've got to make it stop." Yet he acquired his student deferment, ensuring that whatever else happened, *his* body would remain clear of the wheels, the levers, and the apparatus no matter how long the evil machine ran or where it took the country.[67]

In their own minds, there is no reason why Tom Hayden and others like him should have gone to jail when, after all, those who served were the *real* problem, as one heroic Baby Boomer noted: "No one expected to get 100,000 men to pledge refusal on October 16, and even if they could, Resistance organizers were not so naïve as to believe that the military could not go on without those 100,000 men. Too many acquiescent conscripts prevented that."[68] *If only those who served, those "acquiescent conscripts" who fought in the Ia Drang Valley and at Khe Sanh, had the honor and courage of Tom Hayden, et al, the world would have been a much better place.*

Few moments better capture the utter vacuousness of antiwar Baby Boomers than an incident recounted by SDS member Carl Pope. Robert McNamara visited Harvard in 1967, and when a crowd of students pressed in on him demanding that he debate the war, he challenged the crowd: "Okay," he yelled back. "Let's debate the war. Who wants to debate?" What was the response from Harvard's young geniuses, young America's best and brightest? Not a word. Not one single word. "[W]e didn't have anyone to debate him," said Pope.[69]

---

66 Dorland, *Legacy of Discord*, 69. See also Tom Hayden, *Reunion: A Memoir* (New York: Random House, 1988), 177.

67 Seth Rosenfeld, "Mario Savio's FBI Odyssey: How the Man Who Challenged 'The Machine' Got Caught in the Gears and Wheels of J. Edgar Hoover's Bureau," The San Francisco Chronicle, October 10, 2004. http://www.sfgate.com/cgi-bin/article.cgi?f=/c/a/2004/10/10/CMGP08OOFI1.DTL&ao=all, accessed February 21, 2012.

68 Foley, *Confronting the War Machine*, 90.

69 Tom Brokaw, *Boom: Voices of the Sixties* (New York: Random House, 2007), 414.

In one simple paragraph—sharp and to the point—the incomparable Mike Royko cut through mountains of nonsense, hypocrisy and dishonesty surrounding America's Baby Boomers:

> [I]n an instant it was over. It was as if someone had flicked a light switch. Presto, the throbbing social conscience that had spread across America went limp. The anti-war, pro-peace signs went into the trash bins. Even if you offered free beer and marijuana, you couldn't get enough students together to hold a sit-in. That amazing transformation happened the day the President signed into law the end of the draft. At that moment, about 99.9% of those who had sobbed over napalm, Christmas bombings, and man's inhumanity to man suddenly began looking for jobs on Wall Street.[70]

For the record, dishonesty, hypocrisy and draft evasion were not at all unique to the Left. Christopher Buckley, son of William F. Buckley, was not opposed to America's war in Southeast Asia. "I was sort of quietly for the war," he tells us.[71] Yet he avoided service like millions of other bright, patriotic young Republicans: He brought a note from his doctor (the disqualifying condition was rather questionable), which leaves him today with "a spiritual sense" of having dodged the draft.[72] (Allow me this opportunity to relieve you of any "spiritual" questions you might have, Mr. Buckley. You are a draft dodger.) Although in some ways Tom Hayden's mirror image, Buckley, like Dan Quayle—whose family connections got him into a National Guard unit in Indiana after graduation from college[73]—at least had the common decency to refrain from traveling from campus to campus telling others why they should volunteer for service in Southeast Asia while he maintained his own deferment.

---

70 Garfinkle, *Telltale Hearts*, 190.

71 MacPherson, *Long Time Passing*, 157.

72 Ibid., 157.

73 "I do—I do—I do—I do what any normal person would do at that age. You call home. You call home to mother and father and say, "I'd like to get in the National Guard." Dan Quayle quoted in Paul Slansky, Steve Radlauer, "Airhead Apparent," *Esquire*, August 1992, 117, 124.

In summary, the very best that can be said of the Baby Boomers is that from 1961-1975, "they gave a war" and two identifiable groups showed up: 1) that infinitesimal number who actually resisted (this does *not* include those who deserted the Armed Forces or fled the country after failing to acquire, exhausting or losing their deferments); and 2) those few who actually served. Decades of dishonest, manipulative rhetoric notwithstanding, Joe Klein's "decade breathless with nobility" was described far more accurately by Paul Begala, in a rare moment of candor, as "a dilettante ball" for "a generation of selfish pigs."[74]

---

74 Begala, "The Worst Generation," 114.

Chapter Fourteen:
Winners and Losers

I

The twentieth century saw the developed world descend into a paroxysm of ideological violence, as liberalism contended first with the remnants of absolutism, then bolshevism and fascism, and finally an updated Marxism that threatened to lead to the ultimate apocalypse of nuclear war. But the century that began full of self-confidence in the ultimate triumph of Western liberal democracy seems at its close to be returning full circle to where it started: not to an "end of ideology" or a convergence between capitalism and socialism, as earlier predicted, but to an unabashed victory of economic and political liberalism.

The triumph of the West, of the Western idea, is evident . . . in the total exhaustion of viable systematic alternatives to Western liberalism.[1]

Francis Fukuyama

We have gained everything we would have lost had we not fought this war.

William Pitt, 1805, on England's war with France

---

1 Francis Fukuyama, "The End of History?", *The National Interest*, Summer 1989. http://www.wesjones.com/eoh.htm, accessed May 10, 2012.

It is too early to tell.

Zhou En Lai, on the consequences of the French revolution

A bsent American Cold War policies, Western Europe would almost certainly have been Finlandized, if not Communized, during the grim, cold years following World War II. The danger was not that the Red Army would invade and occupy Western Europe but rather that its demoralized, exhausted citizens might simply vote in Communist parties that would, of course, do Moscow's bidding,[2] a process aptly described as one man, one vote, one time. Once acquired in this or any other manner, the Soviets would *never* have allowed such a prize to slip from their grasp, guaranteeing a lengthy visit from the Red Army the moment any Western Europeans decided, historical determinism notwithstanding, that it was time to end their experiment with national suicide and vote Soviet proxies out of office. Western Europeans, in short, were big winners, *very big winners*. Eastern Europeans also did well. Had the Soviets avoided collapse and successfully transitioned from Marxism to a market economy, the Red Army would undoubtedly still occupy Stalin's World War II conquests with no end in sight. Most of the countries in Asia and the Pacific Rim were also big winners. As Lee Kuan Yew has noted, Thailand, Malaya, the Philippines, Indonesia and a host of other countries survived the Cold War without a domestic Stalin or Khmer Rouge due largely to American efforts, however unsuccessful some of those efforts appear at first glance.

Even the people of the former Soviet Union derived considerable benefit from American policy, whether they realize it or not. Their empire was an unworkable, ruinously expensive, dangerous geopolitical entity that might just as well have ended with a bang as a whimper, and the system on which it was based brought as much terror, murder, repression and misery to the Soviet people as it brought to anyone else. Just what Russians will do with the gift they were given remains to be seen, however, and things do not look very promising today. In fact, Americans

---

2 Gaddis, *We Now Know*, 37–38.

(however odd this might sound) seem to be the ones who gained the least from their half-century, multi-trillion-dollar, blood-soaked efforts. Even without the illusions Americans gained from their Cold War "victory"—illusions that are driving their current round of chimerical "nation building" and world saving—Americans might well have paid and might continue to pay far more than their Cold War "victory" was ever worth.

II

I beat them in every battle, but it does not get me anywhere.

Napoleon Bonaparte, Moscow

In actively fighting Communism almost everywhere instead of just protecting this country and its genuinely vital interests while allowing those outside the zone of vital interests to fend for themselves, as George Kennan proposed in 1946, Americans, whatever they accomplished, took millions of innocent lives, left millions more burned, paralyzed, blinded, maimed, widowed and orphaned, inflicted unimaginable carnage on whole societies, expended enormous amounts of American blood and treasure and, however much they want to pretend otherwise, incurred enormous moral and historical debts they cannot just write off.

Truman's "defense of democracy" in Korea has left Americans facing a rogue nuclear power run by people who, if the opportunity ever presented itself, would happily incinerate New York, Chicago or Los Angeles provided they could hide their own involvement. (Someday, when his madhouse passing for a nation-state collapses and there is, in his twisted mind, nothing left to lose, Kim Jong Un— or whoever is next in line—might just see fit to exact this vengeance himself, without regard to the consequences.) Americans, of course, feel quite aggrieved by all this, especially since, as Bill Clinton believes, "righteousness" is why they prevailed in Korea. But imagine for just a moment how Americans would feel today if this country had been divided by a foreign power that imposed an authoritarian government on half the country and then, when the other half resisted, leveled everything from sea to shining sea, leaving tens of millions of Americans shot, blasted, burned, suffocated, drowned and starved to death— most of them civilians, including millions of children. Now tell me just how forgiving and forgetful Americans would be. Face it: North Koreans hate Americans. They have hated Americans for more than half a century and will continue to hate Americans for generations to come, and no matter how deep-seated American denial, the enmity is not without cause. They hate Americans not for who they are but for what they did, and this is part of the debt Americans incurred for the destruction of the Soviet Union as history played out. (Once again, I state this as a fact, not a moral judgment.) It is well worth noting that, in all likelihood, the United States does not today face a "North Vietnam" that looks and acts just like North Korea because neither Kennedy, nor Johnson, nor Nixon was willing to play by Truman's Rules, thereby "winning" in Vietnam while leaving a wounded, dysfunctional regime in Hanoi governing millions of battered, brutalized people who view Americans as Jews view Nazis. Ironically, this government now maintains close relations with the Hanoi regime, which remains a corrupt, closed, repressive, one-party state, in the name of containing China.[3] *Nothing, it seems, ever changes.*

It is also well worth noting that this country remains locked in a dangerous confrontation with China, an emerging nuclear superpower, over Taiwan. In July 2005, Major General Zhu Chenghu of the People's Liberation Army said that "[i]f the Americans interfere into the [China-Taiwan] conflict...I think we will have to respond with nuclear weapons." When pressed, the general stated clearly that any use of force by the United States in defense of the Taiwanese, even with conventional weapons, would likely trigger a nuclear response.[4] As with North Korea, this is part of the debt Americans incurred for the destruction of the Soviet Union and its empire as history actually played out.

Then, of course, we have Iran, which the Bush administration identified on March 16, 2006, as the "single country" most threatening to the United States today.[5]

3 Joshua E. Keating, "America's Other Most Embarrassing Allies," *Foreign Policy*, January 31, 2011.
4 "General Zhu Goes Ballistic," *Wall Street Journal*, July 18, 2005.
5 "America's Iran Policy: Iraq," *New York Times*, March 17, 2006.

There is little doubt that the United States and Britain prevented Stalin from folding Iran, with its vast oil reserves, into the Soviet Empire after World War II and later acted pre-emptively to prevent any attempt at a Czech-style Communist coup by the Soviet Union's Iranian proxies. (Although this is not to say that such an occurrence was in any way certain.) Decades of Iranian complaints about the shah notwithstanding, life under the shah's regime was, to say the least, moderate compared to what would have befallen Iranians had Stalin had his way (which, ironically, might well place Iranians among those who benefited considerably from the Truman Doctrine), and there have been times when I have thought to myself, "we should have let Stalin have them." Then one day while thinking just that, I realized that this is a major reason why so many Iranians (among others) bitterly resent the United States. The very idea that someone can sit in a room halfway around the world and think "we should have let Stalin have them" is as intolerable to Iranians as it would be intolerable to Americans. Just who are "we" to let Stalin "have" anyone, and why are Americans so shocked, shocked to find that others, who spent decades as pawns in great power games, are ready and willing to defend themselves, their interests as they view them, and their countries with nuclear weapons just as Americans have for the last sixty years?

Understand here that I hold no brief for the Islamic Republic, which is run today by "violent, stupid men" like Ho Chi Minh, Fidel Castro and Slobodan Milosevic, who skillfully manipulate grievances—in this case far more imagined than real—for their own evil ends. But I recognize that the positions they hold and the power they wield represent, in no small part, the unintended consequences of American policy—a point far too few seem to notice.

And let us not forget Afghanistan, where Ronald Reagan, in his ultimately successful effort to push the Soviet Union into bankruptcy, gave the Mujahidin *everything* they needed to drive out the Soviets. This served to arm and train large numbers of Islamic radicals from all over the Middle East and ultimately brought the Taliban to power. Further radicalized by what they viewed as America's occupation forces in the land of Islam's holiest shrines (which arrived during Operation Desert Storm), the Taliban then allied itself to Osama Bin Laden and began attacks on the United States, including the World Trade Center bombing in 1993 and the attacks of 9/11, which brought American forces into a bloody, open-ended conflict in Afghanistan, where this country's Soviet enemies had been defeated during the 1980s. For all practical purposes, Americans have now stepped into Soviet shoes in attempting to subdue and remake an ancient society of Islamic tribesmen who are no more interested in American democracy than were they interested in Soviet Communism. (In stating this, I equate neither this country nor its purposes with the Soviet Union or its purposes but merely acknowledge the fact that to many Afghanis, Americans represent just another foreign occupier with designs of its own.) This chain of events arises from this country's efforts to defeat the Soviet Union, making it worth noting that Harry Truman bears exactly as much responsibility for the 9/11 attacks and the current war in Afghanistan as he shares credit for the defeat of the Soviet Union. This is not to say that he deserves either this credit or the corresponding responsibility, only to note that if he receives the former, he must bear the latter.

Most distressing, however, is the realization that, regardless of the Cold War's outcome, far less has been settled than either received wisdom or ideology would have us believe. Neither China nor Russia was occupied and "de-Communized" in the manner that Germany was de-Nazified. Not one single former Communist official from Russia or China was ever prosecuted in connection with the terror, murder and repression that cost tens of millions of lives and completely destroyed the lives of tens of millions more.[6] China's second-ranking Communist Party official issued a complete disavowal of Western-style democracy on March 9, 2009,[7] and the

---

6 Although Chinese authorities tried the so-called Gang of Four and some of their counterparts after Mao's death for various and sundry political and ideological crimes, this was an intra-party power struggle by which one faction removed another from power, not a genuine effort to recognize or right the wrongs of the past. The greatest mass murderer in history, Mao, was never implicated although he was the power behind the Cultural Revolution and crimes far more serious than those of the so-called Gang of Four.

7 "In China, No Plans to Emulate West's Way," *New York Times*, March 10, 2009.

same type of people who wielded power in Communism's name during the Cold War often wield power today, like former KGB officer Vladimir Putin, who is ensconced in the Kremlin claiming that the breakup of the Soviet Union was "the greatest geopolitical catastrophe of the century."[8] Indeed, it remains to be seen whether the Soviet Union's collapse served anyone's long-term interests or simply strengthened the enemies of Western liberalism by destroying the single greatest impediment to their expansion of power, Communism. No one understands this better than Russia's current leaders, who have opted for a "strong," "state-capitalist," "managed-democracy" model (read "Fascist") that might well come to represent a greater threat to Western liberalism than Communism ever did.[9]

Determined "to rehabilitate Russian and Soviet statehood in all epochs and in all times—for all the czars and general secretaries,"[10] the Kremlin produced a study guide for high schools that portrays Stalin as "one of the most successful leaders of the U.S.S.R."[11] According to historian Boris Trevin, today's Kremlin officials have a relatively simple, utilitarian view of history: "Russia has gotten up off its knees, and this is why [Russians] should be proud of [their] past."[12] *The less the people know about Stalin's "harsh and gloomy" repression, the better.*[13] Worst of all is the "existential void" in Russian politics that "has been filled entirely by [an] anti-Americanism" so pervasive that, according to Russian journalist Leonid Radzikhovsky, to renounce it "would be tantamount to destroying the foundations of the state ideology."[14] In a chilling throwback to the early Cold War, a film shown at a government-

---

8 "20 Years After Soviet Fall, Some Look Back Longingly," *New York Times*, August 19, 2011.

9 "The state bureaucracy," former Russian President Dmitri Medvedev warned in 2008, must not interfere with "the free individual" or "free enterprise." "A strong state and an all-powerful bureaucracy is not the same thing. The former is an instrument which society needs to develop, to maintain order and strengthen democratic institutions. The latter is extremely dangerous." "Russian President Sends Obama Warning on European Missile System," *New York Times*, November 6, 2008.

10 "Nationalism of Putin's Era Veils Sins of Stalin's," *New York Times*, November 27, 2008.

11 Ibid.

12 Ibid.

13 Ibid. See also Richard Pipes, "Pride and Power," *Wall Street Journal*, August 24, 2009.

14 "From Russia with Loathing," *New York Times*, November 21, 2008.

sanctioned anti-American rally in early November 2008 depicted a drunken George W. Bush bragging that the United States had engineered both world wars and Hitler's rise to power for America's benefit.[15] The Kremlin is tightening its grip with every passing day, now requiring scholars to submit academic work for permission before publishing it abroad.[16]

Russia also remains determined to dominate the countries of the former USSR and Eastern Europe through any means available, such as its control of oil and gas, which it has withheld over political disputes on dozens of occasions.[17] This can be difficult, however, because punishing Ukraine by closing the pipelines means cutting off the rest of Europe as well. So Russia, in cooperation with several private and government entities in Western Europe, is completing two giant gas pipelines, one bypassing Eastern Europe to the north and one to the south, making "shutoffs to Eastern Europe more likely," said Jimmy Carter's national security adviser Zbigniew Brzezinski, who called the pipelines "a grand Russian initiative to 'separate Central Europe from Western Europe insofar as dependence on Russian energy is concerned.'"[18] Poland's foreign minister compared the pipeline deal to the 1939 Molotov-Ribbentrop Pact that divided Central Europe into spheres of German and Soviet influence. He is likely more right than wrong. The French, Germans and Dutch, who anticipate billions in profits from this venture, have no interest whatsoever in fighting with Russia over Poland and Ukraine. "'Yesterday tanks, today oil,' said Zbigniew Siemiatkowski, a former head of Poland's security service."[19] As William Fulbright once noted, the means might

---

15 Ibid. See also Anne Applebaum, "Why European Leaders Can't Resist Celebrating the Sept. 1 Anniversary—Again," *Slate*, August 28, 2009: "Last weekend, Russian state television ran a long documentary essentially arguing that Stalin was justified in ordering the 1939 invasion of Poland and the Baltic states—and in doing a secret deal with Hitler—on the grounds that Poland itself was in a secret alliance with the Nazis."

16 "Some Russian Scholars Chafe at Order to Screen Scholarly Exports," *New York Times*, October 28, 2009.

17 "Eastern Europe Fears New Era of Russian Sway," *New York Times*, October 13, 2009.

18 Ibid.

19 Ibid. See "Pipeline Politics Tests Merkel's Mettle," New York Tines, September 16, 2020.

change, but the ends remain the same.[20]

Moreover, virtually nothing was done during the Cold War to alleviate the poverty, inequality, overpopulation, corruption and lawlessness, not to mention the envy, greed, stupidity and criminality that gave rise to Communism in the first place (this is a fact, not a critique), despite enormous efforts and expenditures that were initiated in 1949 by Harry Truman as part of his vaunted doctrine.[21] The West has spent $2.3 trillion in foreign aid over the last five decades while failing to get twelve-cent medicines to children (which would prevent half of all malaria deaths), failing to get four-dollar mosquito nets to poor families and failing to get to each new mother the three dollars needed to save five million infants.[22]

In June 2007, United Nations demographers determined that 3.3 billion people lived in urban areas (and more undoubtedly live in urban areas now). Nearly one billion of them (more than three times the total population of this country) live in slums without access to water, sewerage and other basic services, much less schools or health care. In sub-Saharan Africa, more than seven in ten urban residents—over 200 million people—live in slums.[23] Nearly three billion people live on less than two dollars per day. One billion adults are illiterate.[24] Corruption, which is endemic across the Third World, has absorbed hundreds of billions of dollars in Western aid over the last several decades, and nothing has changed over time. Prosecutors at The Hague believe that, from 1997-2003, when Charles Taylor was president of Liberia, more than $1 billon

---

20 "We are not fighting Communists as a political party, but we are actually fighting the Chinese and the Russians. The Russians have adopted the Communist doctrine as an instrument to be used in their effort to dominate their fellowman. They use this doctrine in the same way they might use airplanes or guns and have done so very effectively." Woods, *Fulbright: A Biography*, 165.

21 "More than half the people in the world are living in conditions approaching misery," Truman said in his second inaugural address. But "for the first time in history," he claimed, "humanity possesses the knowledge and skill to relieve the suffering of these people." It was time, therefore, to embark "on a bold new program for...the improvement and growth of underdeveloped areas." William Easterly, *The White Man's Burden* (New York: The Penguin Press, 2006), 24.

22 Ibid., 4.

23 "U.N. Predicts Urban Population Explosion," *New York Times*, June 28, 2007.

24 Easterly, *The White Man's Burden*, 8.

passed through his personal bank accounts.[25] In Angola, $30 billion in annual oil revenue, enough to provide every citizen with a king's ransom of $2,500 per year, is absorbed by a corrupt government while its people have an average life span of forty-one years. According to Michael Oren, author of *Power, Faith and Fantasy: America in the Middle East, 1776 to the Present,*[26] the Palestinian Authority, created in 1993, "has garnered more international aid than any entity in modern history—more, per capita, than the European states under the Marshall Plan," and it has disappeared into private bank accounts and semi-autonomous militias while the Palestinian people remain in squalor and lawlessness.[27]

One result of all this is a "regressive utopianism [that] is spreading...through a wave of populism" across the Third World.[28] For the Marxist dream is alive, well and firmly embedded in the minds of intellectuals and activists who passionately believe in the political future of a pure, liberal Marxism free of its criminal past. "The dream of the October revolution is still there inside me," wrote "Marxist historian" Eric Hobsbawm in 2002.[29] Radicals will undoubtedly become more numerous and powerful as pressure increases with population growth, which can be neither limited nor controlled absent draconian measures like China's "one child" policy, which no one will impose or enforce. In time, wars like the one that raged in Congo for years (some five million dead as of

---

25 "Gains Cited in Hunt for Liberia Ex-Warlord's Fortune," *New York Times*, March 9, 2008.

26 Michael Oren, *Power, Faith and Fantasy: America in the Middle East, 1776 to the Present* (New York: W.W. Norton & Company, 2007).

27 "Fatah is Not the Answer," *Wall Street Journal*, June 20, 2007. South Sudan, a newly independent state that owes its existence to American foreign policy and nation building efforts, is "a disaster by all but the lowest of standards." Government officials have stolen $4 billion intended for rebuilding this war-torn state, where three-quarters of the adults are illiterate and extreme poverty is endemic. Alan Boswell, "The Failed State Lobby," *Foreign Policy*, July 9, 2012. http://www.foreignpolicy.com/articles/2012/07/09/the_failed_state_lobby.

28 "Latin American Democrats Need U.S. Support," *Wall Street Journal*, December 12, 2008.

29 Eric Hobsbawm, *Interesting Times: A Twentieth-Century Life* (New York: Pantheon Books, 2002), 56. See also Yu Hua, *China in Ten Words* (New York: Pantheon Books, 2011), 27: "For many people in many parts of the world, I have found, what Mao did in China is not so important—what matters is that his ideas retain their vitality and, like seeds planted in receptive soil, 'strike root, flower, and bear fruit.'"

2009) will become more common as billions who live in squalor rise in rebellion (as they surely will), a scenario that will provide the developed nations with a continuing parade of "Vietnam Wars" should they choose to intervene.

Finally, we should note that America's Cold War exertions, combined with its never-ending mania for international socio-political engineering, have left Americans with a staggering national debt that does not burden their former (and perhaps future) enemies. For the end of the Cold War brought no "peace dividend." Defense budgets now exceed $800 billion annually, just as George Kennan predicted more than twenty years ago: "Were the Soviet Union to sink tomorrow under the waters of the ocean, the American military-industrial establishment would have to go on, substantially unchanged, until some other adversary could be invented."[30] By 2006, this country's annual trade imbalance was $818 billion, and its public debt now exceeds $16 trillion as Operation Iraqi Freedom continues amassing costs that might eventually exceed $2 trillion.[31] *And there is absolutely no end in sight.*

In summary, given current political, economic and population trends, foreign and domestic, it is beginning to appear as though the Cold War, far from representing some final victory of Western liberalism, represented but one phase in the rise of an illiberal, state-capitalist model that might well prove to be the last one standing in the industrialized world, as Anne Morrow Lindberg predicted some seventy-five years ago in her rather odd paean to authoritarianism entitled *The Wave of the Future: A Confession of Faith*.[32] (I fail to share her sanguinity at this prospect.) Despite all of this country's expenditures and efforts (which have been enormous) and its effect on history (equally enormous), Americans appear to be treading water in an ocean of poverty, inequality,

---

30 George Kennan, *At a Century's Ending: Reflections 1982–1995* (New York: W.W. Norton & Company, 1996), 118.

31 Andrew J. Bacevich, *The Limits of Power: The End of American Exceptionalism* (New York: Metropolitan Books, 2008), 63–65.

32 Anne Morrow Lindberg, *The Wave of the Future: A Confession of Faith* (New York: Harcourt Brace and Company, 1940).

overpopulation, corruption, lawlessness, envy, greed, stupidity and criminality, aggravated greatly by their own shortsightedness, dishonesty, delusions and political dysfunction. And treading water is the very best for which Americans can hope as they move, ignorant of history and devoid of both reason and common sense, from one Pyrrhic victory to another, which is easily demonstrated by comparing the world of the Permanent Campaign to the world that history reveals.

Chapter Fifteen:
History, Ideology and the
Tyranny of Bad Ideas

I

*Even though the truth may be readily available, the deceiver need
not give up. . . . [F]lat denial on the one hand, and the injection into
the pool of information of a corpus of positive falsehood on the
other, [are] sufficient to confuse the issue for the passively
uninstructed . . . audience, and to induce acceptance of [the
falsehood] by those actively seeking to be deceived.*[1]

Robert Conquest

avid Halberstam validated Conquest's postulate in his
keynote address at the Kennedy Presidential Library's 2006
conference entitled "Vietnam and the Presidency." After
lecturing his audience, ironically, on the dangers of "a great lying
machine," with "a dynamic all its own" and "its roots in domestic
politics"—"something that we really have to deal with anytime we
talk about Vietnam"—Halberstam launched into his *fabulous* tale of
well-meaning and intelligent men, Democrats all, struggling to
promote the national interest as best they could through a system
that had been poisoned by the phantasm of "McCarthyism," a
malevolent force injected into "the bloodstream of the society" by

---

1 Robert Conquest, *The Harvest of Sorrow: Soviet Collectivization and the Terror Famine* (New York:
Oxford University Press, 1987), 308.

right-wing conspirators in 1948.[2] Despite its tainted provenance, glaring falsehoods and manifest absurdities, this was Halberstam's story, and he stuck to it until the day he died, with unflagging support from an army of politicians, pundits and public intellectuals because—in Halberstam's own words—"the policy and the politics demand it."[3]

Democratic strategist/pundit Paul Begala, doing his best for "policy and politics," recently claimed that "the American people never really forgave the Democrats for being right about Vietnam. The left was right, of course, about Vietnam."[4] *New York Times* columnist Paul Krugman made this same assertion—"the Democrats were right about Vietnam"—on an episode of *Hardball* October 23, 2007, and on *Reliable Sources* on November 27, 2005: "Democrats and liberals have been paying the price for having been right [about Vietnam] ever since." This particular "lesson of Vietnam" is nothing less than an article of faith on the Left, and it demands answers to the following questions: Just which "Democrats" do you think Begala and Krugman have in mind when they tell us that Democrats were "right" about Vietnam? Truman? Acheson? Kennedy? Johnson? Humphrey? McGovern? The best and the brightest? And what exactly did they get "right"? Pouring some $600 million into the French effort at colonial re-conquest of Indochina? Ceding Laos to the Communists in 1962 and lying to everyone about what they had done? Consciously engineering a nasty, brutal little guerilla war in South Vietnam—a war they had no intention whatsoever of winning—with an eye toward the 1964 elections and lying to everyone about what they had done? Initiating the overthrow and murder of an ally as loyal and competent as any other in the Third World to prolong a commitment that they had grossly mishandled and, assuming that

---

2 David Halberstam, keynote speech, "Vietnam and the Presidency," Kennedy Presidential Library, March 10, 2006.

3 Ibid.

4 See Paul Begala, "Anti-War Imagery and the Iconography of Hate," TPM Café, August 17, 2005. http://tpmcafe.talkingpointsmemo.com/2005/08/17antiwar_imagery_and_the_icon/ #more, accessed fall 2005. See also James Carville and Paul Begala, *Take it Back: Our Party, Our Country, Our Future* (New York: Simon & Schuster, 2006), 89.

their apologists are to be believed, they intended to abandon within the next two years? Provoking the Gulf of Tonkin incident and then lying under oath to the Congress about what they had done? Misappropriating for non-public purposes the foreign policy, treasury and Armed Forces of the United States while sacrificing, just for good measure, tens of thousands of American lives (not to mention the lives of perhaps a million and a half others) to advance their electoral prospects and domestic agenda through 1969 while lying to everyone about what they were doing every step of the way? Undermining Nixon's every effort to negotiate an acceptable end to the war in the same manner and far more effectively than, according to Democrats, he undermined them? Shifting their attack from the war to the warriors when it served their purposes and denying to this day that they did any such thing? *"Verbally dismembering" a legless veteran for having the gall to suggest that he was proud to have served?*[5]

Moving from the absurd to the bizarre, we find George McGovern, another dishonest, manipulative, intensely partisan public figure who long served as a cog in the "great lying machine." Having reviewed transcripts released during the late 1990s of Lyndon Johnson's Oval Office conversations—transcripts that leave no doubt about the craven, partisan motives that drove Johnson's policies in Southeast Asia and the flagrant criminality of his conduct—McGovern published an editorial in the *New York Times* on December 5, 1999 that is a wonder to behold. Focusing on Johnson's domestic agenda ("the most far reaching progressive domestic program since the New Deal"), he declared Johnson "perhaps the greatest president since Abraham Lincoln" while absolving him of any responsibility for his war in Southeast Asia. "Vietnam was not of his making," wrote McGovern. "It was a war he did not begin and did not know how to stop."[6]

Having spent decades reading about the essentiality and "righteousness" of Truman's war in Korea, the fundamental decency and good faith of Stalin's American stooges and Ho Chi

---

5 Dorland, *Legacy of Discord*, xi.
6 "Discovering Greatness in Lyndon Johnson," *New York Times*, December 5, 1999, Week in Review..

Minh's humanitarianism and respect for democratic values,[7] I thought myself relatively shock proof where the "lying machine" was concerned. But I was quite astounded, I must admit, at the ease with which cowardice, pathological dishonesty, gross misappropriation of public assets for non-public purposes and homicidal abuse of power become proof of "greatness" in George McGovern's mind the moment it is clear to him that Lyndon Johnson was not a cold warrior enforcing Truman's doctrine but a loyal Democrat "wagging the dog" for his party. Anti-Communism, in McGovern's mind, was the supreme evil, and so long as Johnson avoided genuine anti-Communism, it matters not how he chose to advance the Democratic Party's political interests—no matter how much or how often he lied, no matter how many bombs he dropped, countries he destroyed or people he killed and maimed.

I was even more astounded at McGovern's attempt to convince us that Johnson "did not begin and did not know how to stop" the war, which might well be the most astonishing thing I have ever read. We are to believe, apparently, that Americans were so determined to fight in Southeast Asia that they formed a shadow government of some kind and then drafted, trained, equipped, armed and deployed themselves by the hundreds of thousands over Johnson's strenuous objection and despite his best efforts. It stands to reason, moreover, that if the war, like the "lying machine," had a life all its own and that Johnson "did not know how to stop [it]," McGovern must thank God for Richard Nixon, who somehow found a way to withdraw this country in four years, a feat, if McGovern is to be believed, that was completely beyond the abilities of "the greatest president since Abraham Lincoln." Even assuming that Nixon was so much greater a man than Johnson that he could have ended this impossible-to-end war in 1969 but chose to continue fighting to ensure *his* reelection and advance *his* party's domestic agenda, the very worst that can be said is that he acted just like John Kennedy and Lyndon Johnson. He too must be entitled to absolution within the world according to George McGovern.[8]

---

7 Stacewicz, *Winter Soldiers*, 83.

8 Equally absurd are the claims of pundit/Party Intellectual Chris Matthews, who tells us today that John Kennedy—who stoked the fires of Cold War confrontation throughout his presidency and pushed

The Right, of course, continues pummeling the electorate with its own barrage of inanities, best exemplified by remarks made by George W. Bush in Riga, Latvia, on May 7, 2005:

> The agreement at Yalta followed in the unjust tradition of Munich and the Molotov-Ribbentrop pact. Once again, when powerful governments negotiated, the freedom of small nations was somehow expendable. Yet this attempt to sacrifice freedom for the sake of stability left a continent divided and unstable. The captivity of millions in Central and Eastern Europe will be remembered as one of the greatest wrongs of history.[9]

That Soviet subjugation of Central and Eastern Europe was a great wrong is beyond question. That Yalta was *causal* in this or that heroic Republicans would have stepped forward to change any of it (the clear implication whenever Yalta is raised by the Right) is pure nonsense, much like the Left's endlessly asserted "if only JFK had lived" and "Democrat in '68" counterfactuals.

Whatever you choose to call it—"organized mass disingenuousness," "*doublethink,*" a "great lying machine"—the same polarized, ideologized, subrational thinking that drove Americans throughout the Cold War dominates their "understanding" of it today because the Cold War is still viewed through the lens of politics and ideology rather than history. So Americans have learned almost nothing beyond the fact that their "modern liberal democratic world" works as it should and that "we" (Democrats or Republicans, Left or Right, whoever happens to be thinking, speaking, or writing at the moment) had it right all along while "they" (Democrats or Republicans, Left or Right) are

---

the world to the brink of nuclear war in October 1962—"saved us from the perilous fate toward which we were heading. All those ICBMs, all those loaded warheads: The Cold War Kennedy inherited was bound for Armageddon." Chris Matthews, *John Kennedy: Elusive Hero* (New York: Simon & Schuster, 2011) 9.

9 David Greenberg, "Know Thy Allies: What Bush Got Wrong about Yalta," *Slate*, May 10, 2005. See also "60 Years After the Fact, Debating Yalta All Over Again," *New York Times*, May 16, 2005.

miserable, dishonest, manipulative demagogues who *must* be defeated at all costs, which erases a vast amount of hard-won experience and guarantees that history will repeat itself, as it repeats itself even now.[10]

II

The characteristic American adjustment to the current foreign and domestic enigmas that confound our national myths has not been to abandon the myths but to reaffirm them. Solutions are sought along traditional lines....Whatever the differences and enmities that divide advocates and opponents (and they are admittedly formidable), both sides seem predominantly unshaken in their adherence to one or another or all of the common national myths."[11]

C. Vann Woodward

As a result of the 9/11 attacks, politicians, pundits and public intellectuals Left and Right joined hands to urge Americans to sally forth and remake the world, salvaging "failed states," instilling American values and spreading free-market democracy, which, we are to believe, represent the cure for all the evils of the world and the *only* sure way to secure America's future. "The modern liberal democratic world," after all, is free of the "irrationalities," "grave defects" and "internal contradictions" that marked its ideological rivals and likely "the final form of human government," as Francis Fukuyama wrote as the Cold War neared its end.[12] (I am no more able to find American democracy free of "grave defects and irrationalities" by examining the country's Cold War "victory" than can I find "greatness" in Lyndon Johnson by reviewing his White House tapes.) Although Fukuyama has tempered his views somewhat, far too many among our chattering classes have not,

---

10 Even the ridiculous "blame America" school remains viable today. See Andrew Goldman, "His History," *New York Times Magazine*, November 25, 2012; Jon Wiener, *How We Forgot the Cold War: A Historical Journey across America* (Berkeley: University of California Press, 2012).

11 C. Vann Woodward, *The Burden of Southern History*, 3rd ed. (Baton Rouge: Louisiana State University Press, 1993), 218.

12 Fukuyama, *The End of History and the Last Man* (New York: Free Press, 2006), xi.

providing a post-9/11 Permanent Campaign that, in its apparent bi-partisanship, is eerily reminiscent of the Cold War's early years, which brings to my mind Lewis Black's observation that nothing is worse than when Democrats ("the party of no ideas") and Republicans ("the party of bad ideas") begin "working together."

The Left reminds us of "the Democratic Party's commitment to progressive internationalism—the belief that America can best defend itself by building a world safe for individual liberty and democracy,"[13] while the Right insists that "we must use this moment of opportunity to extend the benefits of freedom across the globe."[14] The Left tells us that we must stand up and oppose "repressive and corrupt governments"[15] while the Right promises to "defend the peace by fighting terrorists and tyrants."[16] Barack Obama tells Americans "that we [must] retrieve a fundamental insight of Roosevelt, Truman and Kennedy—one that is truer now than ever before: the security and well-being of each and every American depends on the security and well-being of those who live beyond our borders. The mission of the United States is to provide global leadership grounded in the understanding that the world shares a common security and a common humanity."[17] George W. Bush agreed wholeheartedly: "The survival of liberty in our land increasingly depends on the success of liberty in other lands. The best hope for peace in our world is the expansion of freedom in all the world."[18]

The Left insists on America's need to "launch a sweeping program of economic, political and social reform in the [Middle East]"[19] in order to provide "relative security against the ravages of

13 Will Marshall, ed., *With All Our Might: A Progressive Strategy for Defeating Jihadism and Defending Liberty* (Lanham, Maryland: Marshall, Rowman & Littlefield Publishers, Inc., 2006), 4.
14 George W. Bush, Introduction to the *National Security Strategy of the United States of America ("NSSUS"),* September 2002.
15 Marshall, *With All Our Might,* 7.
16 Bush, Introduction to *NSSUS.*
17 Barack Obama, "Renewing American Leadership," *Foreign Affairs,* 86, No. 4 (July–August 2007) 2-16, 4.
18 George W. Bush, Second Inaugural Address, January 20, 2005.
http://www.bartleby.com/124/pres67.html, accessed May 10, 2012.
19 Marshall, *With All Our Might,* 7.

hunger, sickness and want"[20] while the Right tells us that we must "deliver greater development assistance...to nations that govern justly, invest in their people and encourage economic freedom."[21] The Left promises to "rebuild America's strategic alliances [and] cultivate better relations with rising democratic powers"[22] as the Right promotes "strengthening alliances" and "forging new productive international relationships and redefining existing ones."[23] The Left even tells us that Americans must act to develop (I'm not kidding here) "an independent judiciary, a free press, multiple political parties and eventually, free elections" within "the world's fifty-seven Islamic countries."[24]

Crucial to meeting these needs and goals, we are told by the Left, is a return to the "tough-minded liberalism of Presidents Franklin Roosevelt, Harry Truman and John Kennedy."[25] "The liberal 'vital center,'" according to Joe Klein, "was a tough-minded, aggressively creative political movement...led by courageous politicians like Harry Truman and Hubert Humphrey, who received policy support from a remarkable generation of public servants that included George Marshall, George Kennan, Paul Nitze and Dean Acheson."[26] Will Marshall, writing for the Left in the *Wall Street Journal* shortly after Barack Obama's election, tells Americans that they need a "new internationalism" that "must recapture the spirit of tough liberalism exemplified by Presidents Harry S. Truman and John F. Kennedy."[27] This, we are told by the Progressive Policy Institute, "led to victory in the Cold War."[28] (It is interesting to note how, in their current role as Truman-loving, born-again cold warriors, our progressive internationalists always make an exception for the

---

20 Beinart, *The Good Fight*, 192 (quoting Arthur M. Schlesinger, Jr.).

21 Bush, *Introduction to NSSUS*.

22 Marshall, *With All Our Might*, 7.

23 Section III, *NSSUS*.

24 Beinart, *The Good Fight*, 193.

25 Marshall, *With All Our Might*, 15.

26 "The Truman Show," *New York Times*, June 11, 2006, sec. 7.

27 "Obama Needs a Strong Foreign Policy," *Wall Street Journal*, November 7, 2008.

28 Ronald D. Asmus et al., "Progressive Internationalism: A Democratic National Security Strategy," October 20, 2003, 6. http://www.dlc.org/documents/Progressive_Internationalism_1003.pdf, accessed May 10, 2012.

Truman Doctrine's Southeast Asian campaign, in which, according to liberal orthodoxy at its most bizarre, "conservatives," "in 1964 and 1965," "forced us into a war we shouldn't have fought," a war in which "the United States stood clearly and tragically against the cause of liberation."[29])

Former senator Gary Hart, a self-proclaimed "statesman, scholar, attorney, writer [and] Renaissance man of new ideas"[30] (you can't make this stuff up) provides his input with "a manifesto for the future...constructed of the best of our twentieth century heritage" with particular emphasis on "the legacy" of "Harry S. Truman, John F. Kennedy and Lyndon B. Johnson."[31] The first of "the three great challenges that now confront us," according to Hart, is, "Can we reinvent the world?"[32] Secretary of State Hillary Clinton agrees most emphatically with Hart: "We have it in our power to begin the world over again. . . . Today...we are called upon to use that power."[33]

To advance this internationalist/interventionist program, the Left has created two new think tanks, the Truman National Security Project and the Progressive Policy Institute. Both are based on the notion that today's "progressives," being "strong, smart [and] principled," are the true heirs of Harry Truman. "The Truman Project has a clear and simple vision: to help progressives reclaim the strong security tradition of the left. Under Franklin D. Roosevelt, Harry Truman, and John F. Kennedy, the left was widely trusted to defend our country, stand up to our enemies abroad, and to promote progressive values of freedom, democracy and human

---

29 Michael Tomasky, "Between Cheney and Chomsky: Making a Case for a New Liberal Foreign Policy," *The Fight Is for Democracy*," ed. George Packer (New York: HarperCollins, 2003), 27. 47. See also Todd Gitlin, "Varieties of Patriotic Experience." Ibid., 116–120.

30 Gary Hart's website, accessed April 2007.

31 Gary Hart, *The Courage of Our Convictions: A Manifesto for Democrats* (New York: Times Books, 2006), 3.

32 Hart, *The Courage of Our Convictions*, 80. For a near-perfect thumbnail sketch of the "liberal internationalist" worldview in all its ignorance, dishonesty and foolishness, I recommend Suzanne Nossel, "Smart Power," *Foreign Affairs* 83, No. 2 (March/April 2004), 132-142.

33 Andrew J. Bacevich, *Washington Rules: America's Path to Permanent War* (New York: Metropolitan Books, 2010), 20.

rights. It is time to reclaim this heritage."[34]

Even the Right claims membership in the "I'm just wild about Harry" club. George W. Bush admires Truman and noted that, however unpopular during his second term, "he was vindicated by history."[35] "What we sorely need now is a Harry Truman," wrote Lawrence Kudlow at Townhall.com. David Frum praises Truman and describes accusations of Communist espionage on Truman's watch as "false and demagogic."[36] (Frum apparently acquires his knowledge of history from Hollywood, public television and the *New York Times*.) David Brooks criticized Democrats' unwillingness "to reclaim the legacy of Truman and Kennedy" while Evan Thomas noted that, of this country's 2008 crop of presidential aspirants, Democrat and Republican, "all want to be Truman."[37]

It all adds up to an astonishing proposition that has become integral to the post-9/11 Permanent Campaign and is fast embedding itself in this country's national DNA: Threatened from every quarter, American democracy must conquer—benevolently if possible, by the sword if necessary—or die. In order to fully appreciate this new, bi-partisan dogma, we should note that, some five decades ago, Reinhold Niebuhr wrote that, although in Americans' minds, the "American government is regarded as the final and universally valid form of political organization, it is expected to gain its ends by moral attraction and imitation. Only occasionally does an hysterical statesman suggest that we must increase our power and use it in order to gain the ideal ends, of

---

34 http://fora.tv/partner/Truman_National_Security_Project, accessed May 10, 2012. Similar rhetoric emanates from the Progressive Policy Institute, from which we learn that it was "the Democratic Party's tradition of tough-minded liberalism" that vanquished Communism. Asmus et al., "Progressive Internationalism: A Democratic National Security Strategy," 3.

35 "Truman's Trials Resonate for Bush: President Battling Terrorism Has Shown Keen Interest in Strategies for Cold War," *Washington Post*, December 15, 2006. See also "Bush's Truman Show," *Newsweek*, February 12, 2007. (Bush clearly understands nothing about how, why and by whom the history vindicating Truman was produced.)

36 David Frum, "A Republican journalist and speechwriter wants to help revive the reputation of Harry S. Truman," *Newsweek: The 10 Best Presidents*, Special Commemorative Issue, Fall 2012, 52-54, 54.

37 Evan Thomas, "The Truman Primary," *Newsweek*, May 14, 2007, 25.

which providence has made us trustees."[38] Rhetoric deemed marginal and "hysterical" by esteemed public intellectuals but a short while ago is now at the Vital Center as Americans, with a Cold War triumph of global dimensions driving their worldview, equate the projection of power by a dysfunctional government with Grand Strategy in defense of the Republic, with predictable results.

>» «<

Transforming the Permanent Campaign against "Islamofascism" (the twenty-first century's "monolithic international Communism") into policy, George W. Bush and his cabal of "brilliant Straussian intellectuals," as Christopher Hitchens once described the "best and brightest" of the Bush administration on *Real Time with Bill Maher*, launched America's war in Iraq. Exhibiting the dispositional behavior that is typical of the professional political class and those who surround and advise it, they saw a nuclear, chemical and biological threat to the West and planned its elimination through a short war followed by a sixty to ninety-day "stabilization" phase followed by a twelve to eighteen-month "transition" phase. After this time had passed, they foresaw a stable, pro-American, representative government in place and about 5,000 US troops remaining.[39] Following John Kennedy's lead, Donald Rumsfeld sacked anyone who dissented, like General Eric Shinseki, who presciently warned that several hundred thousand troops would be required to secure Iraq.[40] In other words, like those who took this country into Korea and Southeast Asia,

---

38 Reinhold Niebuhr, *The Irony of American History* (New York: Charles Scribner's Sons, 1952), 73–74. See also J. William Fulbright, *The Arrogance of Power* (New York: Random House, 1966), 217–218; George Kennan, *Around the Cragged Hill: A Personal and Political Philosophy* (New York: W.W. Norton and Company, 1993), chapter 9, passim.
39 "A Pre-War Slide Show Cast Iraq in Rosy Hues," *New York Times,* February 15, 2007. See also "TOP SECRET POLO STEP: Iraq War Plan Assumed Only 5,000 U.S. Troops Still There by December 2006," The National Security Archive.
http://www.gwu.edu/~nsarchiv/NSAEBB/NSAEBB214/index.htm, accessed May 10, 2012.
40 "Pentagon Contradicts General on Iraq Occupation Force's Size, February 28, 2003," *New York Times*, January 12, 2007; "New Strategy Vindicates Ex-Army Chief Shinseki," *New York Times*, January 12, 2007; Thomas E. Ricks, *Fiasco: The American Military Adventure in Iraq* (New York: Penguin Books, 2007), 96–100.

America's so-called leaders saw in Iraq just what they wanted to see and led this country into a war of choice under false pretenses, with scandalous incompetence and no idea whatsoever what they were doing or how it would end. *To those who say that what this country needed post-9/11 was another Harry Truman, I say we had one. To those who want to "recapture the spirit [of] Presidents Harry S. Truman and John F. Kennedy,"[41] I say it is firmly in our grasp.*

Congressional Democrats, for their part, knew that their opposition to Operation Desert Storm, perceived as a near-flawless victory supported by the international community, added considerably to their perceived weakness and unreliability on national security issues. As Thomas Ricks noted in *Fiasco: The American Military Adventure in Iraq,* "For the next three presidential election cycles, no Democrat who had been in his party's majority opposing the 1991 war was able to make headway in presidential politics....The Democrats weren't going to make that mistake again."[42] Just like their forebears, they were driven to support the Iraq War by "considerations of domestic politics, and [the] political fears of the consequences of looking weak in the forthcoming domestic election."[43] Although few in Congress had actually read the ninety-two-page National Intelligence Estimate on Iraq, "which contained a host of doubts, caveats, and disagreements with Bush's assertions,"[44] they went right along with the Bush administration's folly, providing the authority Bush needed to govern as he campaigned just as Congress provided it to Johnson in 1964 (nothing beats Democrats and Republicans "working together," I always say), with Max Cleland providing Ricks' Democratic archetype.

Cleland, who lost three limbs to a grenade accident in Vietnam and has spent some five decades in a wheelchair, would be the last man one would ever expect to send Americans by the thousands to be killed and maimed in the name of partisan politics. But with a serious challenge to his senate seat mounted by Republican Saxby

---

41 Will Marshall, "Obama Needs a Strong Foreign Policy," *Wall Street Journal*, November 7, 2008.

42 Ricks, *Fiasco*, 62.

43 Halberstam, *The Best and the Brightest*, xviii.

44 Ibid., 61.

Chambliss, Cleland faced the same test faced by John Kennedy: his party or his country, and like Kennedy and so many others, he failed miserably. "It was obvious," he later said, "that if I had voted against the [Iraq war] resolution that I would be dead meat in the [senate] race, just handing them the victory."[45] (It's all about you, isn't it Max?) So he voted to authorize a war he found neither justified nor in the national interest, and like his liberal forebears, he now blames his opponents for his choices, freely made for his own partisan reasons: "Thirty-seven years later," he said, "and I have another president creating a Vietnam,"[46] as if he and his congressional colleagues were any less responsible for "kids dying...[and] getting blown up."[47]

The campaign in Iraq unraveled because America's political leadership, wilfully ignorant of history and devoid of reason, judgment and common sense, ignored the fact that Iraq, as Iraq-born British historian Elie Kedourie wrote in 1970, was "a make-believe kingdom built on false pretenses,"[48] "riven by obscure and malevolent factions,"[49] "full of bloodshed, treason and rapine"[50] and populated by large heterogeneous groups who share no common heritage, language, religion, ethnicity or national identity. Much like Korea in 1946, Iraq provides "no base for either a liberal or a democratic party as Americans [understand it]."[51] Yugoslavia provided a perfect example of what happens, even in the heart of Europe, when the glue of authoritarianism is removed from one of these multi-ethnic, multi-lingual, multi-cultural, make-believe states created by others while Korea, Vietnam and the Soviet experience in Afghanistan demonstrate rather clearly what you face when your chosen ground shares borders with hostile regimes guaranteed to provide both enemies to fight you and the means to

45 Ibid., 63.

46 Ibid., 63–64.

47 Ibid.

48 Elie Kedourie, *The Chatham House Version and Other Middle Eastern Studies* (Chicago: Ivan R. Dee, 2004), 278.

49 Ibid., 242.

50 Ibid., 237.

51 Cumings, *Korea's Place in the Sun*, 193.

do it. *More than seventeen years have passed since the invasion, and this country is nowhere near its goal of a stable, unified, democratic Iraq.* The Bush Administration's "surge" stabilized the situation for a short period, but the assumptions driving both the surge and the withdrawal of American personnel proved problematic at best. Barack Obama was determined to "get out without giving up" but then decided to "declare victory and go home," leaving small chance for a successful outcome. If history is any guide, this make-believe state will eventually be at Iran's mercy, and whether demolished from within or without (the former likely giving rise to the latter), the world might well face a powerful Iranian state possessing most of the world's oil reserves (and perhaps nuclear weapons), unless an American president, under enormous political pressure to reverse this "Middle Eastern Munich," sends in American forces, setting the Persian Gulf ablaze as Republicans likely blame Obama for quitting Iraq "when victory was in our grasp."[52]

In the meantime, this country's effort in Afghanistan is foundering for all the same reasons. Bush and his "brilliant Straussian intellectuals" never emplaced sufficient forces to secure the territory and population, the government this country installed is rife with corruption and its army will not fight.[53] (Does any of this ring a bell?) Lt. Col. Douglas A. Ollivant, a retired officer who has worked on Iraq for both Presidents Bush and Obama, described Afghanistan in 2009 as a conflict that might well be "several orders

---

52 As one would expect, phony veterans have come forth to garner fame and fortune with tales of torture and murder in Iraq, but having learned from John Kerry's experience that veteran bashing is bad business, none of today's politicians, pundits or public intellectuals will bite as they did during the Vietnam era. Atrocity allegations are taken seriously and investigated immediately, and no war crimes industry has arisen. See "Man Who Lied about Actions in Iraq Admits Faking Forms," *Seattle Times*, June 8, 2007. See also "New Republic Disavows Iraq Diarist's Reports," *Washington Post*, December 4, 2007.

53 "Corruption Undercuts U.S. Hopes for Improving Afghan Police," *New York Times*, April 9, 2009; "New Commander for Afghanistan," *New York Times*, May 14, 2009; "Fearing Another Quagmire," *New York Times*, January 25, 2009; "The Afghanistan Abyss," *New York Times*, September 6, 2009; "Marines Fight with Little Aid from Afghans," *New York Times*, August 29, 2009; "The Growing Gloom over Afghanistan," *The Week: The Best of the U.S. and International Media*, September 11, 2009, 4; "Afghanistan's Other Front," *New York Times*, September 16, 2009.

of magnitude" harder than the conflict in Vietnam: "Sticking it out seems to be a 10-year project and I'm not sure we have the political capital and financial capital to do that. Yet withdrawing, the cost of that seems awfully high as well. So we have the wolf by the ear."[54]

Having "the wolf by the ear," Barack Obama proclaimed Afghanistan a "war of necessity, not one of choice" and promised that he would "fully resource the war,"[55] but this was just rhetoric. Under current counterinsurgency doctrine regarding time and ratio of forces, success in Afghanistan will require hundreds of thousands of troops and several more years.[56] Yet when his hand-picked commander requested these troops, politicians, pundits and public intellectuals joined hands across the aisle to demand an end to the effort.[57]

With public support waning, Barack Obama—like John Kennedy, Lyndon Johnson and Richard Nixon rolled into one—began seeking "a middle course, a compromise,"[58] that would allow him to get out without giving up, which left an inadequate number of troops supporting an unreliable client against an enemy that is employing safe havens in Pakistan, where its fighters rest and train before returning to Afghanistan.[59] This is just how the Communists employed safe havens in Cambodia and Laos, and today's high-tech, cross-border Phoenix program—which employs drones and bombs instead of human operatives and comes complete with free-fire zones—kills innocents by the score while doing apparently little to alter the balance of power.[60] Under these circumstances, said

---

54 "L.B.J. All the Way?", *New York Times*, August 29, 2009, Week in Review.

55 "Obama's Befuddling Afghan Policy," *Wall Street Journal*, September 22, 2009.

56 Bob Woodward, *Obama's Wars* (New York: Simon & Schuster, 2010), 280.

57 Bob Herbert, "Reliving the Past," *New York Times*, September 5, 2009; George Will, "Time to Get Out of Afghanistan," *Washington Post*, September 1, 2009.

58 Evan Thomas and John Barry, "The Surprising Lessons of Vietnam," *Newsweek*, November 16, 2009, 34.

59 Woodward, *Obama's Wars*, 213, 216–217, 220, 225–226, 252, 273, 379.

60 Charli Carpenter and Lina Shaikhouni, "Don't Fear the Reaper," Foreign Policy, June 7, 2011. http://www.foreignpolicy.com/articles/2011/06/07/dont_fear_the_reaper, accessed May 10, 2012; "Death from Above, Outrage Down Below," *New York Times*, May 17, 2009, Week in Review; "Secret 'Kill List' Proves a Test of Obama's Principles and Will," *New York Times*, May 29, 2012; Tom Junod, "The Lethal Presidency of Barack Obama," *Esquire*, August 1012, 98.

General James L. Jones, "You can't win. You can't do counterinsurgency. It is a cancer in the plan."[61] General Stanley McChrystal described his position as a "painful" exercise in "selling an unsellable position."[62] Yet when the president demanded their support, his active-duty generals provided it, just as they always provided their support to Kennedy, Johnson and Nixon.[63]

As Americans prepared to declare their involvement at an end, their client in Kabul began seeking his own accommodation with the Taliban, a vicious, apocalyptic Islamic cult that was deeply involved in the 9/11 attacks, and reaching out to Iran for money and support.[64] With no hope of victory in any real sense, the Obama administration decided to "degrade" the Taliban and hope for some sort of "reconciliation" between the combatants as part of America's withdrawal, but this has now been abandoned as well.[65]

This country's failing interventions in Iraq and Afghanistan resemble nothing so much as its war in Southeast Asia, with "the modern liberal democratic world" working just as it "worked" during the Vietnam era. "It's the permanent campaign," Bob Woodward, author of *Obama's Wars,* told Larry King.[66] This proves two things as nothing else can: 1) the war in Southeast Asia was not an anomaly resulting from either "McCarthyism" or the "mistakes" of "well-meaning and intelligent men," but just one manifestation

---

61 Woodward, *Obama's Wars*, 379.

62 Ibid., 372. See also Bing West, *The Wrong War* (New York: Random House, 2011), 128: "You cannot win a war when a determined enemy has a sanctuary next door."

63 Woodward, Obama's Wars, 305-309. See also Lieutenant Colonel Daniel Davis, *Dereliction of Duty II: Senior Military Leaders' Loss of Integrity Wounds Afghan War Effort* (Draft Report, 1/27/12).

64 "Iran Cash Trail Highlights Battle for Kabul Sway," *Wall Street Journal*, October 26, 2010.

65 "Obama Sets Afghan Rollback," *Wall Street Journal*, June 23, 2011. See also Gideon Rose, "What Would Nixon Do," *New York Times*, June 26, 2011, Sunday Review. In a balanced, well-reasoned analysis, Mr. Rose outlined Nixon's strategy in Southeast Asia and noted that this is just what Obama was attempting in Afghanistan. But see "Peace Talks with the Taliban," *New York Times*, October 5, 2012: "American military commanders long ago concluded that the Afghan war could only end in a negotiated settlement with the Taliban, not a military victory. But now the generals and civilian officials say even this hope is unrealistic before 2015 -- after American and coalition troops are withdrawn. They are, instead, trying to set the stage for eventual peace talks between the Afghan Government and the insurgency sometime after their departure." With both sides now aggressively positioning themselves for the inevitable post-American civil war, this is nothing but a pipe dream.

66 *Larry King Live*, October 3, 2010.

of ignorance, ideology untempered by reason and chronic, systemic political dysfunction; and 2) today's Cold War narrative, no matter which political or ideological gloss one applies, provides frames of reference and beliefs on which Americans act that have no basis in fact, reason or common sense.

Even for those who are so steeped in orthodoxy that the first point is simply unacceptable (and if you've read this far and do not accept it, you never will), a critical analysis of "progressive internationalism's" core tenets, which come to us reaffirmed by the ideology we call history, should suffice for the second. And either one should be sufficient to induce the paradigm shift in worldview needed to arrest the insanity that has defined American foreign policy for the last several decades. So, putting aside my contempt for American politics, politicians and the pundits and public intellectuals who surround and support them (both in real time and through fabrication of the appropriate "history"), it is time to examine on their merits the beliefs, myths, ideology and dogma that have taken us from 9/11 to where we find ourselves today, keeping in mind at all times that, "It is undesirable to believe a proposition when there is no ground whatsoever for supposing it is true."[67]

III

An invented past can never be used; it cracks and crumbles under the pressures of life like clay in a season of drought.[68]

James Baldwin

Insanity: doing the same thing over and over again and expecting different results.

Albert Einstein[69]

Although "progressive internationalism" traces its roots back to

---

67 Bertrand Russell, quoted in William Easterly, *The White Man's Burden*, 37.
68 James Baldwin, *The Fire Next Time* (New York: Vintage Books, 1993), 81.
69 Commonly attributed.

Woodrow Wilson,[70] it did not come into full flower until Harry Truman embraced it as part of the Permanent Campaign for political power that, since the end of World War II, has thrived on external threats, whether real, imagined or manufactured for domestic use.[71] Progressive internationalism's primal frame of reference is still Munich, and its ultimate goal is stable, free-market, liberal democracy for all. History, reason and common sense, however, make three things painfully apparent by now: 1) the betrayal of Czechoslovakia at Munich provided a "lesson" that, although valid within narrow circumstances, was overblown and grossly misapplied in later years; 2) the Soviet Union's collapse proving largely irrelevant to "a world safe for individual liberty and democracy," Americans are no closer to that goal today than they were in 1947 despite trillions spent and millions killed; 3) campaign rhetoric aside, today's internationalists have no more idea how to build such a world than Truman and his Wise Men, Kennedy and his "best and brightest," Nixon and Kissinger or Carter and his Trilateralists, as demonstrated by their failure to grasp even the most basic facts of the world around them.

When Americans speak of "individual liberty and democracy," they invariably mean rule of law; religious, political and intellectual freedom; and protection of what they consider fundamental rights. In other words, Americans say "democracy" when they really mean Western constitutional liberalism, conflating what they consider to be the ultimate purpose of government with the means of selecting one. Few seem to understand that throughout history—the English-speaking peoples providing the prime example—constitutional liberalism, which is how "individual liberty" as Americans understand it is secured, has led to democracy, but there is very little evidence that the reverse is true. ("[I]t is not suffrage that gives life to democracy," noted Gordon S. Wood, "it is our democratic

---

70 Said Wilson, "America has a spiritual energy in her which no other nation can contribute to the liberation of mankind." Quoted in Easterly, *The White Man's Burden*, 10.

71 "If any nation would keep security for itself," said Harry Truman, "it must be ready to share security with all." "An Imperfect Institution, but Consider the Alternative," *New York Times*, August 16, 2006.

society that gives life to suffrage."[72]) George W. Bush illustrated this particular aspect of Americans' preference for ideology over history when he said on the eve of the Iraq War that, "In our desire to be safe from brutal and bullying oppression, human beings are the same. In our desire to care for our children and give them a better life, we are the same."[73] This sounds reasonable and somewhat profound until you combine a little history with some common sense and think for just a moment.

In their desire "to be safe from brutal and bullying oppression" and "to care for their children and give them a better life," Germans empowered Adolf Hitler through democratic means. (The Nuremberg laws of 1935, which provided for the systematic elimination of Jews from civil and social existence in Germany, formed a major plank in the 1932 Nazi Party platform and were among the most popular acts of the Nazi regime.) In their desire "to be safe from brutal and bullying oppression" and "to care for their children and give them a better life," Iranians embraced the Ayatollah Khomeini and are currently embarked on a program to develop nuclear weapons. In their desire "to be safe from brutal and bullying oppression" and "to care for their children and give them a better life," Palestinians empowered Hamas. In their desire "to be safe from brutal and bullying oppression" and "to care for their children and give them a better life," Venezuelans gave the world Hugo Chavez, who found unwavering support among private militias led by Marxist thugs; maintained "warm ties" to wipe-Israel-off-the-map governments in Cuba, Iran and Syria;[74] provided Iran with gasoline to help stave off citizen distress while the ruling clerics developed a nuclear arsenal;[75] and sought close military ties with Russia.[76] In their desire "to be safe from brutal and bullying

---

72 Gordon S. Wood, *The Idea of America: Reflections on the Birth of the United States* (New York: The Penguin Press, 2011), 211.

73 Francis Fukuyama, Amer*ica at the Crossroads, Democracy, Power and the Neoconservative Legacy,* (New Haven: Yale University Press, 2006), 116.

74 "Venezuelans Give Chavez a Mandate to Tighten His Grip," *New York Times*, December 5, 2006.

75 "Venezuela to Sell Gas to Iran, Which Has a Plan for Rationing," *New York Times,* July 4, 2007.

76 "Venezuela: Russian Bombers Arrive for an Exercise," *New York Times,* September 11, 2008; "Russia: North Sea Fleet Sails to Venezuela," *New York Times,* September 23, 2008; "Russia Strikes

oppression" and "to care for their children and give them a better life," Egyptians, one month after King Abdullah of Jordan said the Arab Spring would be "a disaster" for Israel,[77] gave nearly sixty-five percent of their parliamentary seats to Islamist parties—forty percent to the Muslim Brotherhood and twenty-five percent to the ultra-Islamic Salafis.[78] In their desire "to be safe from brutal and bullying oppression" and "to care for their children and give them a better life," millions of people across the Middle East already embrace radical Islam, and "soft on Zionism" might well become the kiss of death for anyone seeking public office in a genuinely democratic Middle East, making unimaginable the rise of another Anwar Sadat.[79]

The notion that capitalism and constitutional liberalism go hand in hand is another "remarkably powerful idea" that is often shared by both sides of the political divide,[80] and it is also nonsense. The Nazis, embracing capitalism, facilitated a dynamic economic recovery in Germany from 1933-1939 and, absent their propensity for military adventurism (which would have been checked had the world possessed in 1940 the nuclear weapons it possessed in 1950), the Third Reich would likely still be with us. Totalitarian states like Vietnam and China, having made seamless transitions from Marxist to state-capitalist economies, are maintaining stable one-party governments and reasonably well-running societies that bear no resemblance at all to Western constitutional democracy. *Countries embracing capitalism effectively do not necessarily carry within them the seeds of their own decay, and there is no more reason to believe that capitalism leads to democracy than to believe that democracy leads to constitutional liberalism.*

In short, history, reason and common sense teach us that: 1)

Oil Deal with Chavez and Plans Modernization of Military," *New York Times*, September 27, 2008; "Russia Is Weighing 2 Latin Bases, General Says," *New York Times*, March 15, 2009.

77 Lally Weymouth, "Everybody in Confused," *Slate*, October 24, 2011.

78 "Voting in Egypt Shows Mandate for Islamists," *New York Times*, December 1, 2011. See also "Why Islamists Are Winning," *Wall Street Journal*, November 1, 2011.

79 Consider as well the fact that, had Nikita Khrushchev been the elected leader of an illiberal democracy facing the kind of pressure from domestic opponents faced by the Kennedy brothers in October 1962, the world would likely have seen a nuclear war over Cuba.

80 "An Unexpected Odd Couple: Free Markets and Freedom," *New York Times*, June 14, 2007.

freedom, justice, morality, righteousness, "individual liberty," "democracy" and "[safety] from brutal and bullying oppression" mean very different things to different people; 2) there is no evidence whatsoever to support the notion that American values go hand in hand with either capitalism or democracy or that such values are universal, exportable or enforceable at gunpoint. Yet today's progressive internationalists, ignoring the $2 trillion expended by the West to date in the Third World to little purpose, promote even greater effort through "Marshall Plan-style proposals," as Peter Beinart describes them in *The Good Fight*,[81] designed to provide "relative security against the ravages of hunger, sickness and want" in underdeveloped societies.[82] This, we are told, is the essential prerequisite to the development of Western liberalism. *Ignorant of history and devoid of reason, judgment and common sense, our progressive internationalists believe that with sufficient effort, nothing is impossible.*

References to the Marshall Plan abound today in internationalist circles because this country's post-World War II reconstruction of Western Europe and Japan is often viewed in terms of "nation building." Yet nothing could be more inaccurate. The European states and Japan were advanced industrial powers with strong, highly developed national institutions and educated citizens—modern nation-states in every sense of the term—laid waste by war, not overpopulation, endemic poverty, internal conflict or political instability. They needed protection from Russian predation and American capital, not "nation building," and Marshall Aid was used as intended by legitimate, reform governments installed and controlled by American and Allied authorities. *The Marshall Plan had nothing to do with "nation building" in Third World territories that Americans have no intention of occupying and governing.* South Korea, on the other hand, provides the one truly successful "nation building" exercise during the Cold War, and "nation building" in South Korea meant annihilative conflict, a permanent American garrison (described to this day as a "tripwire" that will ensure American involvement in

---

81 Beinart, *The Good Fight*, 123.
82 Ibid., 192 (quoting Arthur M. Schlesinger, Jr.).

any future war on the peninsula) and nearly half a century of iron-fisted rule through authoritarian proxies. This required hundreds of thousands of troops and billions of dollars annually for decades — for one-half of one small country, mind you—which is exactly the type of commitment Americans were unwilling to make in Southeast Asia, with predictable results, and are clearly unwilling to undertake today, as evidenced by their failing campaigns in Iraq and Afghanistan.[83] Indeed, when America's interventionists discuss "Marshall Plan-style proposals" for the Third World, Iraq and Afghanistan provide some facts and figures Americans should really consider.

Iraq, with vast oil reserves, is (or at least was) a relatively advanced Third World country with a population of some twenty-eight million. Costs to complete American-led "nation-building" efforts there, which began of course with removal of the existing regime, will likely exceed $2 trillion. The United States also initiated "nation building" in Afghanistan, where, according to testimony provided to Congress by David Kilcullen, a former lieutenant colonel in the Australian Army and senior adviser to General David Petraeus in Iraq, Americans faced a ten- to fifteen-year effort at a cost of $2 billion per month if any level of genuine success was to be achieved.[84] Although today's interventionists have maintained that these commitments are essential to American security, it is clear that neither campaign will be successful. Tired of these adventures, Americans have declared victory and are leaving. And why not? History teaches us, after all, that—excepting *only* the unique British experience in Malaya—no First World power has ever defeated Third World opponents by winning their "hearts and minds" through principles of "counterinsurgency." From the Philippines (1898-1913) to South Korea (1946-1950) and South Vietnam (1954-1959), military power was the deciding factor every time a genuine, indigenous insurgency was defeated during the

83 "Counterinsurgency could ultimately work in Afghanistan if the United States were willing to stay there for generations. I'm talking 70, 80, 90 years." Colonel Gian P. Gentile, the director of West Point's military history program, quoted in "West Point Asks if a War Doctrine Was Worth It," *New York Times*, May 30, 2012.
84 Fred Kaplan, "What are We Doing in Afghanistan," *Slate*, February 5, 2009.

twentieth century. A brief review of counterinsurgency doctrine, as outlined today by our military's best and brightest, explains why.[85]

Lt. Col. John A. Nagl is a West Point graduate, Rhodes Scholar, admirer of John Paul Vann and direct descendant of those soldier-intellectuals who drafted this country's first "counterinsurgency" doctrine for John Kennedy, with the advisers, civil action programs, well digging, latrine building, hog farming, civics classes and strategic hamlets that proved such a *smashing* success in Vietnam from 1961-1963. In "Principles, Imperatives and Paradoxes of Counterinsurgency,"[86] Col. Nagl and others tell us that the "primary objective" of twenty-first century counterinsurgency is to "establish"—*establish,* mind you—a "legitimate" host government, which is defined as "a...government [that] derives its just powers from the governed," is able to ensure "free, fair and frequent selection of leaders," "a high level of popular participation in and support for the political process," "a low level of corruption," "a culturally acceptable level or rate of political, economic and social development" and "a high level of regime support from major social institutions."[87]

If this were not a serious proposition being advanced seriously by serious, highly educated people and accepted as such by large numbers of others, it would be laughable.

What Nagl *et al* describe here is nothing less than the type of government found almost exclusively among the Western democracies, and it required *centuries* for these stable, constitutionally liberal political orders to develop. Governments "legitimate" by these standards cannot be imposed by and would never need the support of a foreign army. And the very idea that a foreign army, within a few years' time, can so fundamentally rearrange another society's internal affairs, values and centuries-old culture as to create such "legitimacy" where it has not developed

---

85 For an excellent review of the brutal military campaigns undertaken by US forces in the Philippines, see James R. Arnold, *The Moro War: How America Battled a Muslim Insurgency in the Philippines* (New York: Bloomsbury Press, 2011).

86 Eliot Cohen, Conrad Crane, Jan Horvath and John Nagl, "Principles, Imperatives and Paradoxes of Counterinsurgency," *Military Review,* March–April 2006, 49.

87 Ibid.

on its own is absurd. This is so obvious that, being nowhere discussed in "Principles, Imperatives and Paradoxes of Counterinsurgency," it represents not a "paradox" of counterinsurgency (although it certainly is that) but an "elephant in the room."

From this inauspicious beginning, the "principles of counterinsurgency" descend rather quickly into a mass of intermingled platitudes, suggestions, postulates and aspirations that are devoid of comprehensible rules or guidelines that can actually be employed by troops on the ground with weapons in hand, such as:

- "Ideally, a counterinsurgent would have unity of command over all the elements of national power involved in COIN operations."
- "Connecting with joint, interagency, coalition, and indigenous organizations is important to ensuring that objectives are shared and that actions and messages are synchronized. The resulting synergy is essential for effective counterinsurgency."
- "Soldiers and Marines must understand demographics, history, and the causes, ideologies, aims, organizations, capabilities, approaches, and supporting entities for every player in the conflict. The interconnected politico-military nature of insurgency requires the counterinsurgent to immerse himself in the lives of the people in order to achieve victory. Successful U.S. COIN operations require Soldiers and Marines to possess a clear, nuanced, empathetic appreciation of the essential nature of the conflict, particularly the motivation, strengths, and weaknesses of insurgents and indigenous actors."
- "With good intelligence, a counterinsurgent is like a surgeon cutting out the cancers while keeping the vital organs intact."
- "Soldiers...must also help establish indigenous institutions (police forces, court systems, and penal

facilities) that will sustain that legal regime."[88]

This nonsense goes on for several paragraphs, culminating in the authors' lament that after Vietnam, "the hard won experience of a generation of officers was deliberately ignored," which fails to recognize that: 1) the "hard won experience" they reference was gained by losing, through politically inspired "principles of counterinsurgency," a Vietnam War that this generation of officers could have won through appropriate application of available military power while sustaining a fraction of the losses ultimately incurred; and 2) it was this very generation of officers—best exemplified by General Colin Powell—not some unseen "establishment," who decided that the Army should waste no more time on "counterinsurgency" and "nation building."[89] Col. Nagl *et al* also fail to note that in later years, history would vindicate the Army's rejection of "counterinsurgency" time and again. The Soviets were defeated in Afghanistan by insurgents supported by its enemy through Afghanistan's unsecured border with Pakistan (a classic "Vietnam War" for the Soviets) while decades-long insurgencies in Central and South America ended not when "principles of counterinsurgency" carried the day but when the Soviet Union's collapse ended outside support for the insurgents, forcing them to accept negotiated solutions when faced with the inevitability of *military* defeat. From an entirely different perspective, we should note that Yugoslavia collapsed the instant the glue of authoritarianism and military power was removed. Anyone who imagines that Yugoslavia's central government, supported by trained American specialists, could have acquired the "legitimacy" needed to hold this multi-ethnic, multi-lingual, multi-cultural, make-believe state invented by others together through "principles of counterinsurgency" is delusional. And does anyone actually believe that a foreign army could enter *our* country and in 5-10 years, through kind, gentle principles of "nation building," erase several hundred years of our history, society and culture and

---

88 Cohen, Crane, Horvath and Nagl, "Principles, Imperatives and Paradoxes of Counterinsurgency," 50-51.
89 Bacevich, *Washington Rules*, 155–156, 158–159.

transform 300 million Americans into devout Muslims happy to live under a theocracy installed by the Islamic Republic of Iran?

Finally, we should always be mindful of the greatest "nation building" experiment in history: Communism, the "elephant in the room" that proves as nothing else can that, as George Orwell once noted, "To see what is in front of one's nose needs a constant struggle."[90]

Following the Bolshevik Revolution and the Russian Civil War, Communists in Moscow initiated history's most determined, ruthless and total attempt to, in Gary Hart's words, "reinvent the world."[91] Yet despite seven decades of social engineering managed and enforced by a regime wielding virtually absolute power, the effort failed *completely*. Cold War or no Cold War, the failure of Communism (not to be confused with either the Soviet Union or its empire) was inevitable. The "new Soviet Man" was never created within Communism's orbit, and the Soviet state descended rather quickly to a level of corruption, dysfunction and poverty almost inconceivable in the Western democracies. None of the people in occupied republics such as Georgia, Ukraine and the Baltic States ever acquired any taste for Mother Russia or her socialist embrace, and the moment they were able, they seceded and never looked back while Russia reverted to its pre-Communist form of government, that being a decidedly illiberal regime with a rather poorly functioning market-based economy. The Chinese, for their part, neither built their utopian experiment around an empire that required enormous armed forces to maintain nor engaged in the economic suicide of an arms race against the West. (Conditions in China never really allowed this.) Yet Communism failed in China just as totally as it failed in Russia, proving beyond question that social engineering at this level is simply not possible. Human beings are not automatons to be reprogrammed at will, and ancient nations cannot be remade on a whim, as exemplified by the history of the English-speaking peoples, who required centuries of unique historical experience to reach their current state of social liberalism and political stability, proving beyond all doubt that evolutionary

90 George Orwell, "In Front of Your Nose," *Facing Unpleasant Facts: Narrative Essays,* 213.
91 Hart, *The Courage of Our Convictions*, 80.

change requires evolution, not "principles of counterinsurgency" and "nation building."

This being what history teaches us, why would anyone imagine that Americans, who represent less than five percent of the world's population and have so far proven unable to alleviate poverty within their own country or secure their own borders, can sally forth with money they do not have, armed forces that are constitutionally unsuited to "nation building," grand ideas that defy both historical experience and common sense and moral authority that exists only in American minds to secure, secularize, westernize, govern and police a planet of seven billion people, expecting evolutionary change in ancient societies without evolution? *Just how, I ask myself, can so many believe such nonsense, when, in the words of Bertrand Russell, "there is no ground whatsoever for supposing it is true"?*[92]

Granted, I do not offer figures and calculations of peer review caliber (although they are accurate enough to demonstrate the folly of this country's present course) and I do not insist that, in any given instance, "nation building" is factually impossible. There is after all South Korea, and at $2 billion per month for several more decades, there *might* be a stable, functioning if not genuinely democratic Afghanistan, with several times the money, effort and time required to produce a stable and functional, if not genuinely democratic, Iraq. What I am saying is that there is no evidence, historical or otherwise, to support the interventionist belief that this country has the money, power or wisdom to create a world of self-governing, free-market liberal democracies where they have not existed before. The historical evidence available, combined with but a little common sense, suggests rather strongly that this country will bankrupt itself in the quest just as the Soviets bankrupted themselves chasing their Marxist chimera. As for the wars and intrigues into which this mania for interventionism and social engineering has already launched this country, I cite Norman Mailer, who noted in 1968 the "divisions, schisms, and sects," the "endless number of collisions between primitive custom and

---

92 Quoted in Easterly, *The White Man's Burden* 37.

[modern] dogma," the "thousand daily pullulations of intrigue [and the] heritage of cruelty, atrocity, and betrayal"[93] that fall upon those who seek to remake the Third Word into some image of themselves, whether capitalist or Communist, democrat or dictator. *How many "Vietnam Wars" will it take?*

Americans should also take note that, contrary to the delusions of their interventionists, they will travel the interventionist road alone as virtually nothing remains of the extraordinary political, economic and historical dynamic that gave rise to the Cold War's Atlantic Alliance. Western Europeans entering adulthood today have no personal experience with or memory of the Soviet Empire and are increasingly unwilling to fund their own NATO infrastructure despite Russian revanchism.[94] Like their parents and grandparents—who largely refused to participate in America's anti-Communist adventures around the globe—Western Europeans today have no intention of participating in messianic campaigns to, in Gary Hart's words, "reinvent the world" and do not seem to care what they do or whose interests they serve as long as they benefit in the short term. The French, for example, recently agreed to sell the Russians four *Mistral*-class amphibious assault ships. Two of these vessels, which represent to the Russian armed forces a quantum leap in technology and capability, were to be built in Russian shipyards, ensuring maximum transfer of knowledge and technology. Even one such vessel in Russian hands would have reduced the time required for the Russians to launch their 2008 war with Georgia from twenty-six hours to some forty minutes.[95] All things considered, Western Europeans seem determined to consign Eastern Europe back to the Russians while ensuring their own dependence on Russian oil and gas supplies (which in time will serve as a noose around their necks), and, just for good measure,

---

93 Mailer, *Armies of the Night*, 210–211.

94 "Gates Sees Danger in Europe's Anti-Military Views," *New York Times*, February 24, 2010; "The Demilitarization of Europe," *Wall Street Journal*, October 6, 2010; "Gates Delivers a Blunt Warning on NATO Future," *New York Times*, June 11, 2011.

95 "France, Turning to a New Partner, Dismays an Old One over a Ship," *New York Times*, December 7, 2010; "France Sells Assault Ships to Russia," *New York Times*, January 26, 2011. Under enormous pressure from the US and UK, the French ultimately cancelled the *Mistral* deal with Russia.

providing the Russians with military technology and power they cannot develop on their own. One could not design a better way to effectively reverse, over time and without a shot fired, the Cold War's outcome in Europe.

And anyone who believes that some "renaissance" in American leadership—defined by a "return" to the "tough-minded liberalism" of Harry Truman and John Kennedy—is what the world really wants should keep in mind that the "tough-minded liberalism" of Harry Truman and John Kennedy gave history brutal, ugly wars in Korea and Vietnam and a nuclear crisis over Cuba. This "tough-minded liberalism" also involved such habitual violation of law that, under myriad treaties, conventions and long-standing international norms, every single Cold War president excepting perhaps Jimmy Carter, along with nearly every senior member, military and civilian, of every Cold War administration, would be judged outlaws and war criminals by today's international community—none more prominently than Harry Truman and John Kennedy. (I state this as a fact, not a moral judgment.) Liberal intellectuals in the United States and in Western Europe have repeatedly invoked notions of "universal jurisdiction" in an effort to investigate various aspects of the "long twilight struggle." They have mounted an obsessive campaign against Henry Kissinger, whose conduct differed in no meaningful way from Truman's, Kennedy's or Johnson's, and produced a considerable number of law review and other articles highlighting the alleged criminality of American foreign policy on Kissinger's watch,[96] the most notable being Christopher Hitchens' polemic entitled *The Trial of Henry Kissinger,* in which Hitchens advocated Kissinger's imprisonment for war crimes and crimes against humanity.

More recently, liberal intellectuals here and abroad campaigned

---

96 See, for example: "The World Reaches out for Justice, *Chicago Tribune,* August 12, 2001, sec. 2; Nicole Barrett, "Note: Holding Individual Leaders Responsible for Violations of Customary International Law: The U.S. Bombardment of Cambodia and Laos." 32 Colum. Human Rights L. Rev. 429, Spring 2001; Steven Feldstein, Comment: "Applying the Rome Statute of the International Criminal Court: A Case Study of Henry Kissinger." 92 Calif. L. Rev. 1663, December 2004; Brandon Mark, "Acknowledging Our International Criminals: Henry Kissinger and East Timor," 32 Denv. J. Int'l L. & Pol'y, 1 Winter 2003.

against American officials involved with this country's intervention in Iraq.[97] Scott Horton, who chaired the International Law Committee of the Association of the Bar of the City of New York, wrote that "no prior administration has been so systematically or brazenly lawless" as the George W. Bush administration.[98] (Truly Mr. Horton, you should make at least *some* attempt to study history before making ridiculous pronouncements like this.[99]) And the recently established International Criminal Court now assumes jurisdiction over government officials the world over, like Slobodan Milosevic, who was not an arms-bearing officer or non-com but a European head of state who, like American presidents, formulated policy and issued orders. The Court also issued a warrant for Libyan leader Muammar Qaddafi, whose country, like the United States, has never ratified the Rome Treaty by which the Court was established.[100]

The bottom line here should be clear to any thinking person: American leadership is not trusted, American leadership is not desired, and American leadership will not be accepted by today's "international community." The rest of the world is simply not anxiously awaiting the kind of leadership that did more damage to Korea than Hitler did to Russia and took the world to the brink of nuclear war in 1962 over fears that "the next House of

---

97 Jeremy Brecher, Jill Cutler and Brendan Smith, eds., *In the Name of Democracy: American War Crimes in Iraq and Beyond* (New York: Metropolitan Books, 2005); Philippe Sands, "The Green Light," *Vanity Fair*, May 2008, 218. See also Scott Horton, "Justice after Bush," *Harper's*, December 2008, 49; Editorial, "A Tale of Two Farces," *Wall Street Journal*, April 2, 2009; "Spanish Court Weighs Criminal Inquiry on Torture for 6 Bush-Era Officials," *New York Times*, March 26, 2009; Bruce W. Nelan and Barry Hillenbrand, "The Pinochet Problem," *Time*, December 14, 1998; Lisa Abend, "Will a Spanish Judge Bring Bush-Era Figures to Justice?", *Time*, March 31, 2009. http://www.time.com/time/world/article/0,8599,1888572,00.html, accessed October 16, 2009.

98 Scott Horton, "Justice after Bush," *Harper's,* December 2008, 49.

99 See also Fred Branfman, "If Henry Kissinger Isn't Guilty of War Crimes, No One Is: A Vietnam War Whistleblower on Christopher Hitchens' Case against the Former Secretary of State." *Slate*, May 18, 2001. Branfman describes the 1970–71 bombing campaign in Laos as "the most brutal and sustained bombing campaign against a civilian population in history," which is another perfect example of an ideologue who needs to acquaint himself with history before anyone should take him seriously.

100 "Court Issues Gadhafi Warrant," *Wall Street Journal*, June 28, 2011.

Representatives is likely to have a Republican majority."[101]

By recognizing the shortcomings and manifest absurdities of the interventionist paradigm currently in vogue, I do not imply that "isolationism" is an appropriate foreign policy, nor am I suggesting that the Western democracies cannot assist the Third World with the enormous problems its people confront. What I am saying is that the fantasies of "counterinsurgency" and "nation building" are based on ideology rather than history, which provides no support for today's "progressive interventionist" paradigm.

Americans must also accept the fact that they no more support today's mania for global engineering than did they ever *really* support the Truman Doctrine, which becomes clear with an understanding of the term "Chickenhawk." However offensive Americans might find what I have to say, "Chickenhawk" describes a core aspect of contemporary American character that crosses all social and political lines and speaks volumes on the relationship between the American people and "progressive internationalism."

Former President George W. Bush—an archetypal Chickenhawk whose family connections helped him secure a safe, coveted slot in an Air National Guard unit during the Vietnam War—told us that we currently face a fight to the death between good and evil as he exhorted Americans to stand fast in Iraq. Yet *his* military-age daughters were no-shows. Former Vice-President Dick Cheney employed several different deferments to avoid service during the Vietnam era, saying that he had "other priorities." Like Cheney, Mitt Romney, who came of age during the Vietnam War, never served, acquiring draft deferments through the Mormon Church to serve as a missionary in France.[102] He assures us, however, that he "longed in many respects to actually be in Vietnam and be representing our country there..."[103] (Of course, he did not "long" to be in Vietnam enough to walk down to his local recruiter's office.) Romney urged Americans to view the "war on terror" as a Manichean battle for

---

101 Alterman, *When Presidents Lie*, 127.

102 "The Making of Mitt Romney," Part 1, *Boston Globe*, June 24, 2007.

http://www.boston.com/news/politics/2008/specials/romney/articles/part1_side_2/, accessed June 1, 2010.

103 Ibid.

survival, but not one of his five sons has ever served a day in the Armed Forces. (According to Romney, they were serving the country in 2007 by helping to elect him president.[104])

On the Left we find the late Christopher Hitchens, who worshiped at the altar of Ho Chi Minh until the end of his life and never let pass an opportunity to criminalize American intervention in Southeast Asia yet stood firmly behind the war in Iraq because "[t]he government and people of these United States are now at war with the forces of reaction."[105] *Three times in two consecutive paragraphs he made this point.* Paul Berman, a former SDS man and life-long man of the Left, defends the Bush Administration's war in Iraq in similar terms: "Mass graves, three hundred thousand missing Iraqis, a population crushed by thirty-five years of Baathist boots stomping on their faces—that is what fascism means."[106] (Hundreds of thousands of dead and decades of Communist boots stomping on Vietnamese faces bother him not one bit.) Where Comrade Hitchens and his "progressive" ilk are concerned, the mere fact that "forces of reaction" exist is enough to justify hundreds of thousands of killed and wounded as part of, in his own words, the "noble anti-fascist tradition."[107] Yet like millions of others, Hitchens never served in the military, would never have served in the military, and had children, you can rest assured, who will never see the inside of a recruiting office.

You see, like Vietnam-era draft avoiders, Chickenhawks, along with the hypocrisy and self-deceit that go hand in hand with the type, are everywhere. They come in all shapes and sizes and belong to every political group imaginable, Left and Right. In fact, it is my firm belief that the overwhelming majority of Americans today, both Left and Right, can fairly be labeled "Chickenhawks," who

---

104 "It's All about Them," *New York Times*, August 13, 2007; "Question of Sons' Choices Dogs Romney Campaign," *New York Times*, August 15, 2007.

105 Christopher Hitchens, *A Long Short War: The Postponed Liberation of Iraq* (New York: The Penguin Group, 2003), 53. See also Hitchens, "The Hell of War: Why Haditha Isn't My Lai," *Slate,* June 5, 2006, and "Beating a Dead Parrot," *Slate,* January 31, 2005.

106 Paul Berman, "A Friendly Drink in a Time of War," *A Matter of Principle, Humanitarian Arguments for War in Iraq*, ed. Thomas Cushman (Berkeley: University of California Press, 2005), 151.

107 Christopher Hitchens, "A Kinder, Gentler Tory Party," *Slate,* February 27, 2007.

provide their taxes and go about their business while others, in a so-called volunteer military, pay the price and bear the burden of interventionism. This is the one and only reason why tens of millions of people acquiesce so easily in imperial adventures of questionable utility, as Lyndon Johnson recognized in May 1964, when McGeorge Bundy suggested that, instead of sending conscripts to Vietnam, Johnson should limit service in Southeast Asia to volunteers.

> Bundy: "I suspect the Joint Chiefs won't agree to that. But I'd like to know what would happen if we really dramatized this as 'Americans Against Terror' and 'Americans Keeping Their Commitment' and 'Americans Who Have Only Peace as Their Object' and 'Only Americans Who Want to Go Have to Go.' You might change the temper of it some."

> Johnson: "You wouldn't have a corporals' guard, would you?"

> Bundy: *"I just don't know. If that's true, then I'm not sure we're the country to do this job."*[108]

Studying historical orthodoxy, one would never grasp the significance of this conversation since it has nothing to do with "McCarthyism." For those of us who take their history non-fiction, however, this single conversation tells us a great deal about the last several decades of the American experience.

When the citizenry believed that the American Republic was genuinely threatened, as it was during World War II, Chickenhawks were few and far between. Americans not only sent their children to fight by the millions, but the overwhelming majority would have been ashamed beyond belief to find that a son had dodged the draft. Once this country's "progressive internationalist" empire began taking shape in the aftermath of World War II, however, Chickenhawks multiplied exponentially until now, they form an

---

108 Beschloss, *Taking Charge*, 372 (emphasis added).

overwhelming majority.[109] This is the best measure of the citizenry's real beliefs, and by this measure, precious few Americans ever actually believed in the Truman Doctrine ("for the affluent [of 1948, 1949, and 1950] the draft was not difficult to evade"[110]) or anything that came with it, as precious few really ever supported the Bush administration's war in Iraq. On this count, "progressive internationalism" is much like Fascism, which, as Francis Fukuyama noted, "was highly appealing not only to Germans but to many people around the world when it was mainly a matter of torchlight parades and bloodless victories, but made much less sense when its inherent militarism was carried to its logical conclusion."[111]

So it is with this "highly appealing" program of "progressive internationalism" that, in order to succeed, demands the unflagging support of the electorate, which can best be measured by one magic word: conscription.

Imagine for the sake of discussion a world in which the regular US military was a relatively small professional force buttressed by a large reserve force that included every single young American, who provide one year of active duty for training at age eighteen followed by five more years of reserve status, with rigorous annual training and virtually no deferments of any kind. While such a system would certainly not add in any way to the quality of this country's armed forces, it would alter the social and political landscape dramatically.

First, it would end the near monopoly on military service held by what we call today "Red Staters," who are far more prone to

---

109 Americans are so unwilling to serve in their own armed forces that Max Boot (a classic Chickenhawk), writing in the *Los Angeles Times*, suggests opening recruiting offices all over the world for the creation of a "Freedom Legion" made up of foreigners whose reward at the end of their service will be US citizenship. Making no claim that such a force is needed to defend this country, Boot outlines its usefulness as a tool of the American Empire, a means to allow "U.S. politicians, so wary (and rightly so) of casualties among U.S. citizens," to "take a more lenient attitude toward the employment of a force not made up of their constituents." Max Boot, "Uncle Sam Wants Tu," *Los Angeles Times*, February 24, 2005. How anyone can recommend anything that allows this country's political class to indulge its imperial aspirations while taking a more lenient attitude toward war is beyond me.

110 Blair, *The Forgotten War*, 28.

111 Fukuyama, *The End of History*, 17.

support the government when the president says it is time for war. (A friend of mine who was both an Air Force pilot and a "Blue Stater" told me he was, to his knowledge, the only officer in his entire squadron to vote for George McGovern in 1972.) Second, to launch his imperial adventure in Iraq, George W. Bush would have required several hundred thousand conscripted reservists, who would have been taken from their homes, families, schools and careers for at least eighteen to twenty-four months of service regardless of who they were or what they did (and this just for the assault and initial occupation; several hundred thousand more would have to be called over the next several years). This would mean that, in addition to perhaps 300,000 citizens of both major political persuasions being pressed from civilian life into service, all of whom are eligible to vote, some 600,000 parents of both major political persuasions who vote, along with millions of grandparents, aunts, uncles, brothers, sisters and neighbors of both major political persuasions who vote—at least half of whom are prone to object no matter whom George Bush was sending—would have faced the immediate prospect of watching loved ones pressed into active service for a war of choice, a "Vietnam War" if ever there was one. Millions of Americans predisposed to object bitterly would have been in this war up to their eyeballs the moment it was proposed, making it ludicrous to suggest that exponentially more scrutiny would not have been applied to this venture by the Congress and inconceivable that this war would have occurred as it did, assuming that it occurred at all.

Yet it did occur, and it occurred as part of yet another round of democracy spreading and world saving that, if history provides any guide, will bring Americans and others a great deal of destruction and bloodshed along with an enormous reservoir of resentment while costing trillions of dollars better spent elsewhere and ultimately changing the world in which they live very little. History teaches no better way to "contain" and ultimately destroy American democracy—and Americans, of all people, should know this. For it is not, as so many seem to believe, the Roman or British Empires that provide a blueprint for American overreach and decline but Soviet Russia, whose leaders, like all too many of our own, were convinced that they had reached the "end point of mankind's ideological evolution," having created a state that was free of the "grave defects and irrationalities" that characterized all preceding states and, in their minds, represented "the final form of human government" toward which history was leading all of humankind. Knowing that they "[could] best defend themselves by building a world safe for [Marxism]," which provided the only means to secure "individual liberty and democracy,"[112] they raised enormous armed forces and sallied forth to fulfill their manifest destiny by bringing their social and governmental order to the world, one way or another, along with food, clothing, shelter, employment and health care for all, with no regard for history, reason, common sense or the most basic concepts of finance, bookkeeping or cost accounting. The results, needless to say, speak for themselves.

Soviet citizens, however, had no real say in their world. They did not choose Communism, they did not choose the leaders who repressed and enslaved them, and they did not choose the policies, foreign or domestic, that helped bring their once-powerful state to its ignoble, pathetic end. Americans, on the other hand, are, by and large, the masters of their fate, as their experience in Southeast Asia amply demonstrates. From Truman's disaster in Korea to the slow, steady decent into Southeast Asia under Kennedy and Johnson, through Nixon's plan to get out without giving up and the congressional decision to abandon the effort in 1975, "the system" delivered exactly what the people wanted, when they wanted it, as Leslie Gelb noted in *The Irony of Vietnam: The System Worked*.[113] And therein lies our ultimate problem.

---

112 Marshall, *With All Our Might*, 4.
113 Gelb, *The Irony of Vietnam*, 1-26

Chapter Sixteen;
"We Have Met the Enemy, and He is Us"[1]

As the means of defining national identity, history becomes a means of shaping history. The writing of history then turns from a meditation into a weapon. "Who controls the past controls the future," runs the Party slogan in George Orwell's 1984; "who controls the present controls the past."[2]

Arthur M. Schlesinger, Jr.

We are all drowning in filth. When I talk to anyone or read the writings of anyone who has any axe to grind, I feel that intellectual honesty and balanced judgment have simply disappeared from the face of the earth.[3]

George Orwell

I know that what is contained herein will be bitterly denied. I am prepared for this. In my boyhood I witnessed the savagery of the

---

1 Pogo, Earth Day Poster, 1970, by Walt Kelly. The full quote is, "There is no need to sally forth, for it remains true that those things that make us human are, curiously enough, always close at hand. Resolve then, that on this very ground, with small flags waving, and tinny blasts on tiny trumpets, we shall meet the enemy, and not only may he be ours, he may be us."

2 Arthur M. Schlesinger, Jr., *The Disuniting of America*, (New York: W.W. Norton & Co., 1992), 45-46.

3 Quoted in Christopher Hitchens, "The Importance of Being Orwell," *Vanity Fair,* August 2012.

WE HAVE MET THE ENEMY, AND HE IS US

Slavery agitation – in my youth I felt the fierceness of the hatred directed against all those who stood by the Nation. I know that hell hath no fury like the vindictiveness of those who are hurt by the truth being told to them.[4]

John McElroy

I

Over the past four years, virtually every media outlet, every public intellectual and every member of the commentariat—those "who control the present"—have hammered Americans with a withering barrage of claims that Donald Trump was the most horrible, terrible, abominable criminal who ever held public office and that he has done incalculable damage to this country. James Fallows recommends establishment of a "Crimes Commission" to investigate Trump's "corrupt and possibly criminal" conduct and tells us that, "President-elect Joe Biden faces a decision rare in American history: what to do about the man who has just left office, whose personal corruption, disdain for the Constitution, and destructive mismanagement of the federal government are without precedent." He goes on to advise us that, "The disproportion between Trump offenses and past political scandals may seem like a tired point, but it has been 'normalized' enough by its fire-hose nature that the sense of outrage inevitably fades."[5] Timothy Naftali writes that "Trump is the first president since America became a superpower to subordinate national-security interests to his political needs" and tells us further that "[t]he methodical destruction of the government's competence and integrity has been nearly invisible but is one of Trump's most consequential legacies.[6] Andrew Sullivan sums it all up when he accuses Trump of a "relentless assault on the institutions, norms, and practices of

---

4 John McElroy, *Andersonville, A Story of Rebel Military Prisons, Fifteen Months a Guest of the So-called Southern Confederacy: A Private Soldier's experience in Richmond, Andersonville, Savannah, Millen, Blackshear and Florence* (Toledo: D.R. Locke, 1879).

5 James Fallows, "How Biden Should Investigate Trump," *The Atlantic,* January/February, 2021.

6 Timothy Naftali, "The Worst President in History," *The Atlantic,* January 19, 2021.

America's liberal democracy" and labels him "the most lawless president in our history."[7]

If these were not serious assertions being advanced seriously by serious people and accepted as such by tens of millions of others, they would be laughable (as I will demonstrate below), which brings us to a recent matter in which the law and standards of conduct advanced by those "who control the present" are not laughable: Donald Trump's impeachment for abuse of power.

In the summer of 2019, Donald Trump asked Ukrainian President Volodymyr Zelensky to initiate an investigation of his political rival Joe Biden, whom he would eventually face in the 2020 presidential election. When this became public, howls of outrage and demands for Trump's impeachment were quickly forthcoming, with the *New York Times* outlining the basis rather succinctly:

> A president's use of his power for his own political gain, at the expense of the public interest, is the quintessence of an impeachable offense. It was, in fact, one of the examples the Constitution's framers deployed to explain what would constitute "high crimes and misdemeanors," the standard for impeachment.[8]

Stated Congressman Adam Schiff: "The Ukraine call was one piece of a larger operation to redirect US foreign policy to benefit Trump's personal interests, not the national interest."[9] "It is a core premise of our liberal democracy," wrote Andrew Sullivan, "that the powers of the presidency are merely on loan, and that using them to advance a personal interest is a definition of an abuse of power."[10]

A president's use of official power to advance his interests at the country's expense is without question an impeachable offense, as is

7 "This is no ordinary impeachment." *New York Magazine,* November 9, 2019.
8 "Why the Trump Impeachment Inquiry Is the Only Option," *New York Times,* September 29, 2019.
9 "Trump betrayed America. Soon the public will hear from patriots who defended it." *USA Today,* November 5, 2019.
10 "This is no ordinary impeachment." *New York Magazine,* November 9, 2019.

a president's violation, in his official capacity, of criminal statutes.[11] That being the case, a brief review of John Kennedy's administration easily reveals why assertions that "[t]he methodical destruction of the government's competence and integrity"[12] began with Donald Trump and that he is "the most lawless president in our history"[13] are demonstrably false.

Operation Mongoose, John Kennedy's two-year war on Castro's Cuba, involved violations of the UN Charter, the OAS Charter and, most importantly, felony violations of 18 USC 641 (embezzlement of public money, property or records) and 18 USC 956 (conspiracy to kill, kidnap, maim, or injure persons or damage property in a foreign country). Moreover, as recounted in numerous historical works, John and Bobby Kennedy, using the FBI and the CIA, regularly conducted warrantless eavesdropping on members of congress, congressional staff, reporters, private attorneys, lobbyists and anyone else who interested them.[14] More than 1,300 warrantless wiretaps and bugs were installed by the Kennedy administration.[15] With certain narrow exceptions, warrantless eavesdropping is a criminal violation of 47 USC §605, and a burglary—a felony in any jurisdiction—is generally required for access to telephonic lines and devices. *And for the record, planting bugs (among other things) is exactly what the Watergate burglars were doing for Richard Nixon, leaving John Kennedy with any number of Watergates during his famous "Thousand Days."*

As for Southeast Asia, there is not a shred of evidence that John Kennedy ever believed that this country could prevail there, having stated in the House of Representatives in January 1952 that "I am frankly of the belief that no amount of American military assistance in Indochina can conquer an enemy which is everywhere and at the same time nowhere. . . . The forces of nationalism are rewriting the

---

11 In contrast, Bill Clinton was impeached for conduct that, although illegal (perjury), arose from matters that were personal in nature and unconnected to his official duties.

12 Timothy Naftali, "The Worst President in History," *The Atlantic,* January 19, 2021.

13 "This is no ordinary impeachment." *New York Magazine,* November 9, 2019.

14 Beschloss, *The Crisis Years,* 346–347.

15 Weiner, *Enemies,* 224, 230–233. Many of these were aimed at Soviet and Eastern Block personnel and lawful as national security eavesdropping. But just as many were likely not.

geopolitical map of the world."[16] Yet he publicly declared Vietnam "the finger in the dike" of American security in 1956 and, as president, escalated the war in Southeast Asia, increasing the commitment from some 500 troops to 16,000 while killing, on his watch and as a direct consequence of his policies, 120 American and more than 14,000 South Vietnamese troops.[17]

Determined to defend Kennedy, his apologists have insisted for decades that his escalation of the commitment was all part of a (dare I say) "secret plan" to terminate this country's involvement in Vietnam after the 1964 election, as Kenny O'Donnell wrote in *Johnny, We Hardly Knew Ye*: "The President told [Senator Mike] Mansfield that he had been having serious second thoughts about Mansfield's argument and that he now agreed with the Senator's thinking on the need for a complete military withdrawal from Vietnam. 'But I can't do it until 1965—after I'm re-elected.'" Kennedy voiced similar views to newspaperman Charles Bartlett in April 1963: "We don't have a prayer of staying in Vietnam. Those people hate us. They are going to throw our asses out of there at almost any point. But I can't give up a piece of territory like that to the Communists and get the American people to re-elect me."[18] The best way to facilitate his designs, he told his top advisers in early 1963, would be to "put a government in there that would ask us to leave."[19] Yet when Ambassador Lodge informed Kennedy in the summer of 1963 that "the government the United States was officially supporting and financing and fighting for might be dealing secretly with the Communists—and might ask the Americans to leave,"[20] Kennedy authorized the coup that would cost Diem his life,

16 Reeves, *President Kennedy: Profile of Power*, 254. See also Dallek, *An Unfinished Life*, 185–187.
17 South Vietnamese military dead from 1961-1963 totaled 14,123, or 14 per day, and these figures do not include civilian casualties. South Vietnamese military wounded totalled 24,132. Clarke, Jeffrey J., *United States Army in Vietnam: Advice and Support: The Final Years, 1965-1973* (Washington D.C., Center of Military History, United States Army, 1988), 275.
18 Logevall, *Choosing War*, 38–39. See also Geoffrey C. Ward and Ken Burns, *The Vietnam War: An Intimate History* [E-book] (New York, Alfred A. Knopf, 2017): "'There are just so many concessions that we can make in one year and survive politically' he told a friend in the spring of 1961. 'We just can't have another defeat this year in Vietnam.'" *It's all about you, isn't it, Jack!*
19 Goldstein, *Lessons in Disaster*, 238.
20 Reeves, *President Kennedy: Profile of Power*, 577

which gives rise to an unavoidable conclusion: Diem was overthrown and murdered for one purpose: to keep the war going, and it continued thereafter as a reelection campaign that was to wind down in 1965 after serving Kennedy's personal and political interests while costing thousands of lives and expending vast sums from the public treasury.

Without question, assertions such as those by Fallows, Naftali and Sullivan, who focus exclusively on Donald Trump, provide the best standards and frames of reference needed to judge John Kennedy's conduct and policies. And it cannot be overstated: this exercise serves in no way as a defense of Donald Trump.

First, John Kennedy consistently "subordinate[d] national-security interests to his political needs," and he did so knowingly (as would Lyndon Johnson), at the cost of thousands of lives.

Second, "the disproportion between Trump offenses and past political scandals" is a chimera that appears only because those who rule our dominant institutions decided decades ago that John Kennedy's habitual criminality and political scandals were to be shielded from the public, exactly as outlined by George Orwell:

> Unpopular ideas can be silenced, and inconvenient facts kept dark, without the need for any official ban. Anyone who has lived long in a foreign country will know of instances of sensational items of news— things which on their own merits would get the big headlines—being kept right out of the . . . press, not because the Government intervened but because of a general tacit agreement that "it wouldn't do" to mention that particular fact.[21]

Third, James Fallows recently argued that Donald Trump is guilty of negligent homicide for his handling of the coronavirus

---

21 George Orwell, "The Freedom of the Press," Proposed Introduction to *Animal Farm.* http://theorwellprize.co.uk/george-orwell/by-orwell/essays-and-other-works/the-freedom-of-the-press, accessed May 10, 2012.

pandemic.[22] If this is so, then John Kennedy was guilty of cold-blooded murder in Southeast Asia, *and it is worth noting that, with South Vietnamese troops killed in action totaling 7,457 during 1964, Kennedy fully intended several thousand more deaths as part of his reelection campaign.*[23]

I cannot help but wonder, how many Watergates can John and Bobby order, how often must they violate federal criminal laws, before their conduct is deemed, and reported widely as, a political scandal? How many people must John Kennedy kill and maim in support of his reelection before his conduct is recognized for, and reported widely as, the homicidal abuse of power that it clearly was?

Whatever can be said of Donald Trump's policies and his Ukraine phone call (and it bears restatement that I am *not* defending him), John Kennedy's presidency was a day-to-day criminal enterprise if ever there was one. In fact, if Kennedy's conduct is within Andrew Sullivan's "norms and practices of America's liberal democracy," these "norms and practices" mean nothing, which would seem to be the case given that Kennedy's unlawful and incompetent conduct was the rule and not the exception throughout the Cold War.

Consider Harry Truman's illegal eavesdropping; his years-long obstruction of Congress and obstruction of justice; his ruthless purge of the Federal Civil Service; his fecklessness on internal security, which provided the Communists with everything they needed to launch the war in Korea—a certifiable disaster due largely to incompetence and espionage that led directly into Vietnam. As General S.L.A. Marshall noted in *The Atlantic* (September 1953): "Korea is a strategically profitless area for the United States, of no use as a defensive base, a springboard to nowhere, a sinkhole of our military power. We don't belong there." Yet there we remain, and Truman is consistently ranked among the top ten presidents.

---

22 James Fallows, "Trump's Indifference Amounts to Negligent Homicide," *The Atlantic,* November 20, 2020.
23 Clarke, Jeffrey J., *United States Army in Vietnam: Advice and Support: The Final Years, 1965-1973* (Washington D.C., Center of Military History, United States Army, 1988), 275.

Consider Eisenhower's illegal overthrows of legitimately elected foreign governments by force and violence; his attempted murder of Patrice Lumumba; his installation of Jupiter missiles in Turkey, which he knew was a dangerous provocation of no strategic value that was driven entirely by domestic politics. Consider Lyndon Johnson's illegal eavesdropping; his lifelong personal corruption; his endless lies about Southeast Asia. Like John Kennedy, he deliberately "subordinate[d] national-security interests to his political needs," leaving millions killed and maimed on his watch in the name of domestic politics. Consider Richard Nixon, who, like John Kennedy and Lyndon Johnson before him, subordinated foreign policy to his political interests and allowed his opponents to control his actions; whose minions, just like Kennedy's and Johnson's, illegally burglarized and eavesdropped on political opponents; who falsified official records to conceal illegal bombing in Cambodia and Laos. Like it or not, his conduct and policies were pretty much standard fare for the Cold War era, and our march of folly did not end in 1991.

Consider George W. Bush, who, along with his "brilliant Straussian intellectuals" (his "best and brightest"), gave us our current debacle in Iraq, with some 4,400 American dead and more than 32,000 wounded to date, not to mention more than $2 trillion expended.[24] Based on what? Ginned-up intelligence and delusions of grandeur that were devoid of reason, judgment and common sense. (You can always count on our fabulous intelligence agencies and bureaucracy to provide our presidents with anything they need to justify whatever harebrained scheme they are hatching.) Consider Bush's failure to occupy and secure Iraqi military bases and facilities while disbanding the entire Iraqi government and

---

23 American War and Military Operations Casualties: Lists and Statistics, Congressional Research Service, Updated July 29, 2020; Neta C. Crawford, "The Iraq War has cost the US nearly $2 trillion," *Military Times*, militarytimes.com/opinion/commentary/2020/02/06/the-iraq-war-has-cost-the-us-nearly-2-trillion/.

army, leaving the country in the hands of heavily armed, unemployed young men, who meandered into various militia bands that exist to wage war on American personnel and each other. Consider Iraqi casualties, which although estimates vary widely, total at least several hundred thousand dead and millions wounded as of 2021. Without question, our war on and in Iraq has been nothing short of catastrophic, and our march of folly continues unabated.

In summary, from the New Deal through the end of the Cold War and after, the presidency was held more often by partisan criminals and incompetents than by honest, capable men, and Donald Trump is, by no measure, "the most lawless president in our history." Yet our national ideology is best served by an agreed-upon, orthodox narrative in which this country's path thorough the Cold War was charted by honorable, competent public officials operating within a political system that "worked" as intended. Now "I know that what [follows] herein will be bitterly denied" by "those who are hurt by the truth being told to them," but this orthodox narrative is a delusion, as even a brief, closing analysis reveals.

II

The central conclusion of this book is that people were rational and the system worked. Vietnam was not the product of evil intent or massive stupidity. It was the logical consequence of a set of assumptions and concepts adopted by every president from World War II on, endorsed enthusiastically by Congress, and supported by the majority of the American people. Once those concepts were accepted, the American decisionmaking system worked as it was designed, forcing policy toward middle-of-the-road solutions.[25]

Fareed Zakaria

---

25 Fareed Zakaria, Foreword to Leslie Gelb, *The Irony of Vietnam: The System Worked* (Washington D.C.: The Brookings Institution, 2016), xvi-xvii.

WE HAVE MET THE ENEMY, AND HE IS US

One has to belong to the intelligentsia to believe things like that; no ordinary man could be such a fool.[26]

George Orwell

As noted in the Introduction, those who rule the dominant institutions, both Left and Right, have arrived today at the following two-part consensus: 1) this country was led to defeat in Southeast Asia by competent, "well-meaning and intelligent men"[27] through an almost endless cascade of mistakes, miscommunications, miscalculations and misjudgments, all undertaken, honestly and in good faith, with the best interests of this country in mind;[28] 2) "the system" was a "well-functioning democracy"[29] throughout, and it "worked."

These are not just preposterous; they are the two most pernicious falsehoods in American history.

For the well-meaning and intelligent men paradigm requires one to ignore plain facts, such as declarations by John Kennedy and Lyndon Johnson that South Vietnam was of no strategic value to this country and that, but for Republicans in Washington—but for "considerations of domestic politics, and [the] political fears of the consequences of looking weak in the forthcoming domestic election"[30]—they would have ended American involvement, leaving alive and unharmed millions of people subsequently killed and maimed. *How many times do American leaders, their advisers and their loyalists have to admit plainly that they are killing thousands of people to enhance their prospects in an upcoming election before we believe them? How many are they allowed to kill and maim before they are no longer "well-meaning and intelligent men"?*

Moreover, the well-meaning and intelligent men paradigm requires one to undertake a massive suspension of disbelief to

---

26 George Orwell, *The Sayings of George Orwell*, ed. Robert Pierce (London: Gerald Duckworth & Company, Ltd., 1994), 27.

26 Summers, *On Strategy*, 181–182.

28 Mann, *A Grand Delusion*, 3-4.

29 Leslie Gelb, Preface to *The Irony of Vietnam*, xxi-xxii

30 Halberstam, *The Best and the Brightest*, xviii.

accept the notion that highly intelligent, sophisticated men, educated at the finest universities and service academies in the world, made consistent and inexcusable but *honest* mistakes over a period of years, although the basic principles and truths applicable to the endeavor had been known throughout the world for centuries. It requires one to believe, for example, that this country's best and brightest analyzed the world in 1962 and, acting honestly, in good faith and in the national interest, determined that this country would best be served by quietly ceding Laos and several hundred miles of South Vietnam's border to the North Vietnamese and then committing American forces to the resulting guerilla war—a war that they had no intention of winning—under the worst conditions imaginable. It also requires one to believe that well-meaning and intelligent men, acting in good faith and in this country's interest, initiated the overthrow and murder of an allied head of state to ensure the continuation of a war that they did not believe this country could win and knew would soon end if they just let events take their course. *How can anyone suggest that well-meaning and intelligent men, while acting in good faith in the national interest, would ever do such things?*

Finally, it requires one to believe that well-meaning and intelligent men, doing honestly and in good faith what they thought best in the national interest, found it necessary and appropriate to lie, year after year, to everyone about everything. John Kennedy, who never believed that the US could prevail in Vietnam, lied to everyone about his policies in Southeast Asia from 1961-1963. Lyndon Johnson lied to congressional leaders about US activities during the Gulf of Tonkin Incident and lied to them, year after year, about the troop requirements, reserve mobilization, costs and time required to prevail after being briefed honestly on these issues by the Joint Chiefs. The Joint Chiefs then lied to Congress about the troop requirements, reserve mobilization, costs and time required to prevail after briefing Johnson honestly. And let us not forget Johnson's congressional and other enablers—Fulbright, McGovern, Church, Mansfield, Humphrey *et al.*, "nuts and bolts politician[s] to whom party and personal loyalty took precedence over immediate issues."[31] They never believed for an instant that the US belonged in Vietnam, yet they lied daily to support their president, year after year, until millions had been killed and maimed.[32] The list goes on and on, and the deceit alone reveals both the "evil intent" and the "massive stupidity" behind the decision making.

In summary, from 1960-1975, this country's political leaders could not have inflicted more pointless cruelty and harm on both this country and Southeast Asia if that had been their intended purpose. When viewed in terms of common sense, reason and the "truths and principles of war,"[33] their decisions make no sense and cannot possibly be deemed the rational conduct of well-meaning and intelligent men. Yet when viewed as the conduct of power-obsessed politicians working within the Permanent Campaign— "don't look past the next election, or you might not get past the next election"[34]—it all makes perfect sense, all of it, including the torrent of falsehoods from those who made the decisions, those who surrounded and advised them, those who supported them and those who have chronicled the era. And this brings us to "the system," the supposedly "well-functioning democracy"[35] that gave rise to it all.

III

"Liberal democracy" is "arguably free from the internal contradictions," "enormous weaknesses" and "grave defects and irrationalities," that marked its ideological rivals and likely "the final form of human government."[36]

Francis Fukuyama

---

31 McGovern, *Grassroots*, 231.

32 Calls for retribution against Donald Trump's "enablers" are ubiquitous these days. See for example, Anne Applebaum, "History Will Judge the Complicit," *The Atlantic,* July/August 2020; "Trump had Plenty of Corporate Enablers. Don't Give Them a Free Pass" *Boston Globe,* January 7, 2021; "It's Inevitable: Donald Trump's Enablers Will Get Rolled by History," *Los Angeles Times,* July 3, 2020.

33 Summers, *On Strategy,* 181.

34 Wolf Blitzer, interview with Bill Clinton, August 11, 2005.

35 Leslie Gelb, Preface to *The Irony of Vietnam,* xxi-xxii.

36 Fukuyama, *The End of History,* Introduction.

When the gap between ideal and real becomes too wide, the system breaks down.[37]

Barbara Tuchman

History reveals rather clearly that this country's debacle in Southeast Asia resulted from a breakdown of its liberal, democratic government. Yet many people insist, as John Kerry does, that this shameful episode really represents a "triumph of the system."[38] This notion is perfectly tailored to fit America's national ideology and guaranteed to bring the greatest comfort to the greatest number. But no one with a modicum of historical knowledge and an ounce of moral sense should buy into this given the "grave defects and irrationalities" that brought the world to the brink of nuclear war in 1962 before taking this country into, through and out of Southeast Asia with several million dead in its wake.

For there is something frightfully wrong with a political system in which major decisions—decisions that generate years of conflict and millions of dead and wounded around the world—are made in secret based on "considerations of domestic politics, and [the] political fears of the consequences of looking weak in the forthcoming domestic election."[39] There is also something wrong with a nation of people who, like George McGovern, Leslie Gelb and John Kerry, accept as a given their right to conduct their affairs in this manner, as if Southeast Asia was created to provide Republicans and Democrats with a place to work out their political differences "by other means." Likewise with a system in which lies and deceit are the leadership's stock in trade; in which everyone at the top, both military and civilian, knows that the American people and their representatives are being conned, yet say nothing, year after year, as the bodies are stacked by the hundreds of thousands. While it is true that American voters got what they wanted, when they wanted it, every step of the way, their consensus was built almost entirely on lies, and a democracy is neither well-running nor

---

37 Barbara Tuchman, *A Distant Mirror: The Calamitous 14th Century* (New York: Ballentine Books, 1978), xix-xx.

38 Dorland, *Legacy of Discord,* 115.

39 Halberstam, *The Best and the Brightest,* xviii.

functional when being operated in this manner. Contrary to Mr. Naftali's claim, "the methodical destruction of the government's competence and integrity"[40] was in full swing decades before Donald Trump's appearance on the scene.

I wonder, moreover, how the Vietnamese, Laotians and Cambodians (especially Cambodians) must feel knowing that prominent Americans who influence millions view the catastrophe that befell them as proof of America's greatness and the functionality of its liberal democratic system. And I might be wrong here, but I cannot believe that James Madison, after studying this country's path through Southeast Asia, would tell us proudly that this is exactly what he had in mind when drafting the Constitution of the United States.

In summary, this country's path through Southeast Asia does not represent a triumph of any kind. It was neither the product of good-faith decisions made by well-meaning and intelligent men, nor was it the "logical consequence" of a well-running, functional democracy that worked as it should have. *Had it been a well-running and functional democracy, the war in Vietnam would never have occurred.* The system, however, is not what failed. The "enormous weaknesses," "grave defects" and "irrationalities" to which so much is attributable are found primarily within a dishonest, largely incompetent political class whose members will do anything to acquire or hold office—no matter what it costs or where it takes us—because those who populate each side know that they and they alone are fit to wield power. *Just think about it. Democrats escalated, year after year, a war that would have ended had they just left well enough alone because they believed that if they failed to do so, "militant Republicans" might acquire power, "and then we'll end up with half a million men in Vietnam!"*

The political class is aided and abetted in this lunacy by equally dishonest, intensely partisan media figures, academics and public intellectuals who produce the news, analysis and history required to justify most everything the political class does. And until we do

---

40 Timothy Naftali, "The Worst President in History," *The Atlantic*, January 19, 2021.

something to change this, our several-decade downward trajectory will continue.

IV

"When this nightmare is over, we need a Truth and Reconciliation Commission. It would erase Trump's lies, comfort those who have been harmed by his hatefulness, and name every official, politician, executive, and media mogul whose greed and cowardice enabled this catastrophe."[41]

Robert Reich

Calls for a "Truth and Reconciliation Commission" are all the rage these days, coming from a host of politicians, pundits and public intellectuals along with all the usual suspects like *The Atlantic, The New Republic, The Nation,* and the *New York Times.* And for once, I agree with them. A genuine process of "Truth and Reconciliation," a reckoning as I call it, is long overdue and would be immensely beneficial. The first thing necessary to such an undertaking, however, is truth; an accurate, agreed set of facts that everyone *must* accept. Without this, it is all a waste of time, and today's omnipresent cant about our recent "nightmare" and "catastrophe" exemplifies the vast gap between perception and reality that, if not overcome, will preclude any semblance of "Truth and Reconciliation." I will therefore advance a point on which all reasonable people should agree: 2016 is not year zero. Several decades of history brought us to our current state, so our agreed set of facts must begin with the Legacy of the 1930s, when, using David Halberstam's words, the "problem," the "virus," the "flaw" entered "the bloodstream of [American] society." Starting there, Americans must face honestly and acknowledge decades of incompetence, criminality and homicidal abuse of power by president after president, Republican and Democrat alike, regardless of the effect this has on our belief in "American Exceptionalism" and its "well-functioning democracy."

---

41 "Robert Reich Calls For 'Truth and Reconciliation Commission' To 'Erase Trump's Lies,' Expose Enablers," *The Daily Wire,* October 18, 2020.

Secondly, "Truth and Reconciliation" requires consistent standards—factual, legal and moral—consistently applied. Without this, "Truth and Reconciliation" becomes nothing but a partisan charade. In criminal law, statutes and jury instructions provide the standards by which judgments must be made based on the evidence presented. For "Truth and Reconciliation" with history, on the other hand, we have law in statutes and treaties but no fixed jury instructions, so ultimate judgment rests entirely on the open mindedness and intellectual honesty of the citizenry, and therein lies our major roadblock, as outlined below.

Sticking my toes into the water of today's state of play, I recently posted, almost word for word (complete with citations), the comparison between John Kennedy's conduct and Donald Trump's outlined above, in a place where I knew people who identify with the Left would read it. History provided the facts and evidence while treaties, federal criminal law and the principles advanced in support of the Trump impeachment provided the standards to which Kennedy should be held, and I sought an answer to the following question:

> Do you agree that, based on JFK's consistent violations of federal law (felonies committed on a day-to-day basis through the use of official power throughout his presidency) and, more importantly, his misappropriation of foreign policy and lives, not to mention vast sums from the treasury for his personal benefit at the country's expense, he should have been impeached and removed from office? After all, "It is a core premise of our liberal democracy that the powers of the presidency are merely on loan, and that using them to advance a personal interest is a definition of an abuse of power."

The responses were more childish, abusive, sarcastic and irrational than anything I expected, and they could not have been more perfectly designed to exemplify the pointlessness of attempting "Truth and Reconciliation" had they been so intended.[42] Virtually every response was an attack on me, and not one addressed Kennedy's conduct except to offer mild excuses while displaying a spectacular lack of historical knowledge and intellectual honesty. Kennedy "acted within the template of his times," said one of my interlocutors. What do you think that means exactly? And if that is a defense to Kennedy's clearly illegal and impeachable conduct, when did the "template of the times" change such that similar conduct became criminal and impeachable when undertaken by Richard Nixon? The same individual praised John Kennedy for having "surrounded himself with recognized scholars and professionals and [seeking] strong debate on matters of both foreign and domestic policy." This ignores the plain fact that these "recognized scholars and professionals," who went on to serve and advise Lyndon Johnson, were intimately involved in the decision making that brought the world to the brink of nuclear war in 1962 and left this country with a conflict raging in Southeast Asia, with no coherent strategy, no plan to win and more than 1.5 million dead by 1969. As Doris Kearns Goodwin noted, "[Johnson's] every self-deception was repeatedly confirmed in the men around him."[43] Comparing the world that these scholars and professionals inherited in 1961 to the world they left behind in 1969, it is no exaggeration to describe them as likely the most dishonest group of political hacks, fools and incompetents who ever served in a presidential administration. But no matter. Having served Kennedy and Johnson, they were well-meaning and intelligent men who were "right on Vietnam," as most anyone who identifies with the Left will tell you.[44]

---

42 The responses to my post are found in the Appendix.

43 Doris Kearns Goodwin, *Lyndon Johnson and the American Dream* (New York, St. Matin's Press, 1976), 317.

44 Similarly, James Fallows, writing in *The Atlantic,* recounted 1968, "the most traumatic year in modern American history": "The assassinations. The foreign warfare. [Fifty US troops killed *every day,* he notes.] The domestic carnage and bloodshed. The political chaos and division." After discussing each of these issues in some detail, Fallows, in an Orwellian display of cognitive dissonance, declares that "everyone contending for power in American politics in those days

My rather mild attempt at Truth and Reconciliation through reasonable, fact-based discourse accomplished nothing, and I was ultimately dismissed as a "half-assed pseudo-intellectual historian." That is where I let it drop, having found time and again that this kind of treatment is the rule rather than the exception and knowing that, when you argue with fools, you look like one. *So much for "Truth and Reconciliation."*

The entire exchange reminded me of the public service commercial in which a man holds and egg and says, "This is your brain." He then points to a hot frying pan and says, "This is drugs." He cracks the egg into the pan, and as it sizzles inside, he says, "This is your brain on drugs." Replace "drugs" with "politics" and you understand exactly why my interlocutors responded as they did, and why smart, educated people like Timothy Naftali, Andrew Sullivan and James Fallows make the absurd, demonstrably false statements quoted above. *Their brains are sizzling in the frying pan of politics.*

What we have today is not so much a broken system as a broken electorate, comprised, on both sides of the aisle, of bitter, partisan, absentee landlords who angrily refuse to learn what they do not want to know. Spectacularly ignorant of history and devoid of judgment and common sense, they live their lives secure in the knowledge that, whatever has happened: 1) officeholders from their side of the aisle were and remain honest, competent and beyond reproach; 2) those on the other side of the aisle are corrupt, malevolent and responsible for all our ills; and 3) anyone who takes issue with their worldview or attempts to teach them anything they

---

was *competent.*" Citing "Nixon, Johnson and Humphrey . . . Kennedy, McCarthy, and even Wallace," he assures us that, "The American choice in the turmoil of 1968 was among competent exponents of different outlooks." "Is this the Worst Year in Modern American History?", *The Atlantic,* May 31, 2020. How anyone can review this era as Fallows does and then declare, with a straight face, that those who brought this country to 1968 were competent is simply incomprehensible. *"War is Peace; Freedom is Slavery; Ignorance is Strength."* Orwell, *Nineteen Eighty-Four, passim.*

do not want to know is not just stupid but dishonest and irredeemably evil. H.L. Mencken once wrote that, "Democracy is a pathetic belief in the collective wisdom of individual ignorance,"[45] and the American electorate validates this with every passing day.

I would love to end this effort with some hopeful prediction that Americans will work through their current state and find common ground. But with Americans intensely partisan and unwilling to learn what they do not want to know, this will never happen, and they will continue stumbling forward in ignorance, as outlined by Arthur Schlesinger, Jr.:

> [H]istory is more than an academic discipline up there in the stratosphere. It also has its own role in the future of nations. For history is to the nation rather as memory is to the individual. As an individual deprived of memory becomes disoriented and lost, not knowing where he has been or where he is going, so a nation denied a conception of its past will be disabled in dealing with its present and its future. [46]

For "there is no means," as George Kennan once noted, "other than the cultivation and dissemination of historical knowledge, by which a society can measure its own performance and correct its own mistakes."[47] And Americans must make choices and formulate policies today that, just as in 1945, will affect them for decades in a dangerous world where, ideology aside, their vaunted democracy is deeply dysfunctional, their leaders consistently inept and corrupt, their power to control world events *very* limited and the law of unintended consequences, which worked remarkably well for this country throughout the Cold War, a more powerful and unpredictable force than anyone imagines.

---

45 H. L. Mencken Quotes. BrainyQuote.com, BrainyMedia Inc, 2021.
https://www.brainyquote.com/quotes/h_l_mencken_129257, accessed February 3, 2021.
46 Schlesinger, Jr., *The Disuniting of America*, 45-46.
47 Thompson, *The Hawk and the Dove*, 166.

Abraham Lincoln questioned whether this democracy, "or any nation so conceived and so dedicated, can long endure." John Kennedy returned to this theme in 1961: "Before my term has ended, we shall have to test anew whether a nation organized and governed such as ours can long endure. The outcome is by no means certain."[48] Economist Herbert Stein was blunt and even more to the point: "If something cannot go on forever, it will stop." And as run for the last ninety or so years, this country cannot go on forever. Just what will stop, how and when, remains to be seen. But sooner or later, there will be a reckoning. Either we will reckon with the reality of our history, learning what we should learn, experiencing a paradigm shift in world view and changing our ways accordingly, or reality will surely reckon with us.

---

48 Reeves, *A Question of Character*, 253.

APPENDIX

Bxxxxx: A great review of the early 60s, the then ongoing Cold War, and the strange machinations of American Policy, inherited from Eisenhower and continued by JFK. Unlike Trump, a man of no consistent foreign policy, just whimsical acts based more on emotion than logic. Kennedy acted within the template of his times.

Equally opposite to Trump, Kennedy surrounded himself with recognized scholars and professionals, and sought strong debate on matters of both foreign and domestic policy. He couldn't stand for sycophant "yes men," unlike out current POTUS who demands praise at – it must be a primary requirement to participate or maintain a cabinet position.

As well, Kennedy never got, nor accepted, the political endorsement of the Ku Klux Klan, something your hero has obviously been pleased to accept. Kennedy reluctantly engaged in protecting the civil rights movement from Klansmen something Trump would likely not undertake. It's telling, indeed. I guess in the end the only thing JFK and DJT have in common is a strong attraction to women outside of marriage. Of course, there is no record of JFK having to pay for the experiences, nor that he was interested in unprotected sex with porn stars.

Once again, thank you for the history lesson of 60 years ago. Times have changed indeed.

Neal Thompson: Bxxxxx   The question is, do you agree that, based on JFK's consistent violations of federal law (felonies committed on a day-to-day basis through the use of official power throughout his presidency) and, more importantly, his misappropriation of foreign policy and lives, not to mention vast sums from the treasury for his personal benefit at the country's expense, he should have been impeached and removed from office? After all, "It is a core premise of our liberal democracy that the powers of the presidency are merely on loan, and that using them to advance a personal interest is a definition of an abuse of power." [Andrew Sullivan, NY Magazine 11/8/19]

Understand here that I am not defending Donald Trump. Far from it. I am using him as a frame of reference. And if use of foreign policy for personal benefit at the country's expense is wrong and impeachable when undertaken by Trump, is it not equally wrong when Undertaken by JFK? Or do you claim a Kennedy-family exception to the application of federal criminal law?

Mxxxxx: What's next? A comparison of past presidents and the Indian Wars?

Neal Thompson: Mxxxxx It is interesting that you put it that way. Our friends on the left have been revisiting history for years now to condemn in vitriolic terms figures such as Andrew Jackson and George Washington for their demonstrably bad conduct (ethnic cleansing by Jackson; slave owning by Washington). This is all well and good, but let's not stop at the bad and/or criminal conduct by those on only one side of the aisle. And let's not offer rhetorical questions to avoid the one I posed.

Mxxxxx: Why not? Maybe if fact denying doesn't work for you currently then you can run to the comparison issues to defend and deflect Trump behavior, policies; or lack of in his quest to divide and conquer. Your Stephen Miller attitude is telling.

Bxxxxx: You take a great deal of liberty with your statement "JFK's consistent violations of federal law (felonies committed on a day-to-day basis through

489

the use of official power throughout his presidency..." Not to mention, other questionable conclusion from almost 60 years ago.

Is this your best defense of Donal Trump? Really? I don't recall JFK ever claiming to be, among other things, "...a very stable genius.." This example is among so many other characteristics the Republicans intentionally overlooked about this astonishingly incompetent individual who threw away any conservative values in his quest to be king.

You willingly chose to embrace this non-conservative, perhaps due to the delusion he was somehow different than all his bluster and horrific track record; you chose an indecent man—not a traditional Republican—who seeks wealth and love at all costs, the constitution be damned. You apparently aren't conservative at all, so what are you?

Neal Thompson: Bxxxxx I just cannot understand why you interpret my statements as "a defense of Donald trump" and accuse me of embracing him. I am NOT defending him; I have not embraced him; I am using him as a frame of reference. If I were to note that Nixon was a criminal (and he was) for wiretapping political opponents (violations of the Communications Act and the purpose of the Watergate break-in) and further note that JFK was involved in the same conduct, would you accuse me of "embracing" Richard Nixon or would you understand that I am judging JFK by the same standards?

Please tell me what is questionable about JFK's violations of the UN Charter, the OAS Charter and, most importantly, felony violations of 18 USC 956 (conspiracy to kill, kidnap, maim, or injure persons or damage property in a foreign country) and 18 USC 640 (public money, property or records)?

Do you actually deny that Operation Mongoose was launched by the Kennedy brothers, or do you deny that the statutes I cite apply? Without any deep research, just search Operation Mongoose on Wikipedia, note what they did and tell me why it was not unlawful.

Let's try to have an intelligent discussion rather than hurling a mass of partisan talking points. Tell me where my facts are wrong or my analysis flawed.

Mxxxxx: No one here has denied possible or probable past presidential wrongdoing. However your comparison defense of Trump is way too obvious. Don't piss down my neck and tell me it's raining. I'll call you on it.

Neal Thompson: Mxxxxx Wrong.   From wiretaps and undeclared private wars to use of this country's foreign policy, armed forces and lives to enhance his reelection prospects, JFK committed impeachable acts on a daily basis. I recount long-documented historical facts that represent Elephants in the Room that no one wants to acknowledge. This angers you considerably, so you read everything I say backwards and attack me as someone I am not, engaged in conduct in which I am not engaged.

Stop changing the subject and tell me where I am factually or analytically inaccurate on JFK.

Gxxxxx: So you're more concerned about a president who's been dead almost 60 years than the "clear and present danger to our American way of life" (Adm. William McRaven, in charge of the Osama bin Laden operation). What would you have done during WW II-attempt to smear Teddy Roosevelt? That's an interesting narrative about JFK. I will try to research more about his presidency-after we are out of this dark and threatening time in our history. It's all hands on deck right now.

491

Neal Thompson: B<u>xxxxx</u> The bottom line (as I expected) is that you are not going to answer my question: "Do you agree that, based on JFK's consistent violations of federal law (felonies committed on a day-to-day basis through the use of official power throughout his presidency) and, more importantly, his misappropriation of foreign policy and lives, not to mention vast sums from the treasury for his personal benefit at the country's expense, he should have been impeached and removed from office?

Or, as I always ask, tell me where I am factually or analytically inaccurate.

M<u>xxxxx</u>:   Just curious, do you call yourself an independent voter? And if so, how many times have you voted for a Democrat. Be honest.

M<u>xxxxx</u>:   You may well be a half-assed pseudo-intellectual historian but it appears you made an effort to deflect and use comparisons to defend Trump. Your comments and points are moot.

INDEX

NOTE: Definite articles (A, An, The) are ignored in alphabetization of book and film titles, which are in italic. Footnotes are indicated by n following the page number, e.g., 323_n52.

360; "Vietnam and the Presidency," 432; on Vietnam as political war, xviii; on Vietnam as vital to American interests, 167–168

Haldeman, H. R., 254

Halperin, Maurice, 25

Halifax, Lord, 10

Halliday, Jon, 91n4

Halpern, Sam, 124

Hannah, Norman, xix, 137

Harbert, Michael, 260

Harkin, Tom, xvii, 304, 371

Harkins, Paul, 158-159, 164, 167

Harriman, Averell: on neutralization of Laos, 144; on Nhu's role in pagoda raids, 180; on overthrow of Diem, 189–190; pressuring Diem for concessions toward Buddhists, 180; on relations with Soviet Union, 32-33

Harris, David, viii; on Vietnam veterans as blameless for bad behavior, 383-384; war crimes industry and, 382

Harris, Lou, 207, 210 219

Hart, Gary, 353, 353_n4, 440, 416-417, 418, 459

Hayden, Tom, 416–417, 418

Haynes, John Earl, 13

Hell to Eternity (film), x

Helms, Richard, 123, 124, 124_n41

Herrick, John, 208

Herring, George, 221

Hess, Rudolf, 363

Higgins, Marguerite, 177, 178, 189n324

Hilsman, Roger: on Geneva Accords (1962) as temporary postponement of Laos problem, 145-146; on Ngo's role in the pagoda raids, 180; on Nhu's call for US withdrawal from South Vietnam, 174; on vulnerability of Kennedy administration on Cuba, 131

Hiss, Alger: denial to HUAC of Communist activities, 43-44; heading Office of Special Political Affairs, 29; perjury of, 43-44; as Soviet agent, xxxiii, 9-10, 24, 42, 53, 243; Truman on guilt of, 53, 53_n173

Hiss, Donald, 9, 10, 29-30, 42

Hitchcock, Robert, 20–21

Hitchens, Christopher: on Bush administration, 442; as Chickenhawk, 463; on guilt of Alger Hiss, 53; on Kennedy, 133; on Kennedy hagiographers, 190; on Khrushchev, 198; on Kissinger, 341, 460; on Nixon's delay in ending war, 300; on totality of US Cold War victory, 317

Hitler, Adolph, 344, 366

Ho Chi Minh: annihilating non-Communist Vietnamese, 84, 345–346; avoiding another Korean War in Vietnam, 146-147; birth and early life, 83; as Communist organizer in Southeast Asia, 83-84, 345–346; compared with George Washington by McGovern, x; on Diem's

Mao Tse-tung: not implicated in Gang of Four trial, 425_n6; refusing compromise in Korea, 76; support for invasion of South Korea, 65, 66

Maoist Revolutionary Union, 259

Marin, Peter, viii, 352

Markey, Edward, 306

Marshall, George C.: authorizing MacArthur to cross 38th Parallel, 69; on incendiary bombings of Japanese cities, 357; on military intervention in Southeast Asia, 150

Marshall, S.L.A., 474

Marshall, Will, 439

Marshall Plan, 268, 452–453

Martin, Joseph, 72

Marxism, liberal, 429

Masaryk, Jan, 40

Maslow, Abraham Harold, 147

Matak, Sirik, 281

Matthews, Chris, xvii, 435_n8

Mayer, Milton, 355

Mazowiecki, Tadeusz, 311

McCain, John S., III (senator), 250

McCain, John S., Jr. (Admiral), 250

McCarthy, Eugene, 226, 231, 237

McCarthy, Joseph: accuracy of charges about Communist infiltration, xxxii-xxxiii, 8; Ellsberg on Vietnam War and, xxv; alleged failure to expose genuine Soviet agents, 29; Kennedy avoiding vote to censure, 118; orthodox view of, xxx

McCarthy, Mary, ix-x

McCarthy Era: Democratic Party's late 1940s rejection of Communism launching, 28;

McCarthyism: demonology of, xxxi–xxxviii, 31; *doublethink* and, xxxi; Halberstam on, xxv, xxviii, 432-433; McCarthy era predating, xxviii, xxviii_n74, 12; McCarthy right about Communist infiltration of government, xxxii–xxxiii; toxic political environment of 1950s attributable to Truman, 81-82, 82-n295. *See also* anti-Communist rhetoric; House Un-American Activities Committee (HUAC)

McChrystal, Stanley, 447

McCloy, John J., 136

McCormick, John, 94, 95

McCone, John, 127, 182

McConnell, John P., 214, 215

McDonald, Admiral, 215

McElroy, John, 468

McGovern, George
anti-Communist rhetoric, 269-270, 435
as antiwar senator, 236, 272, 382
as "Bomber pilot," 277, 277_n135
as Democratic Party man, 269, 434-435
as one of LBJ's enablers, 477
on LBJ's presidency, 434-435
leftist philosophy, 268
passionate supporter of Henry Wallace, 268-269

praise for *Long Time Passing,* 371

as Presidential candidate: campaign proposal for ending war, 277-273; extreme positions of, 273; seeking Johnson's support, 274; selection of Eagleton as running mate, 274

support for Carter's proposed withdrawal from Korea, 293

Vietnam War and: calling for withdrawal of troops, 231, 272-273; early criticism of Vietnam interventions, 270-271; embracing defeat in Southeast Asia, xix, 467, 480; endorsing North Vietnam demands for US withdrawal, 246; expressing admiration for Vietnam veterans, 383; on immorality of war, ix, 353, 353_n3; meeting with Hanoi negotiators, 246, 264-265; proposal for resolution of war, 270-271; support for Gulf of Tonkin Resolution, 209-210, 270; unwillingness to bargain for American POWS, 273; votes against military appropriations, 246

McGranery, James, 22

McInerney, James, 21-22

McNamara, Robert
Johnson administration, 211; advice on call-up of reservists, 213; lying to Congressional leaders about Westmoreland's

troop requests, 215-216; lying to Senator Morse about attack on *USS Maddox,* 209; proposing Vietnamization strategy, 245; on seeking negotiations with North Vietnam, 222; on Vietnam status at beginning of Johnson administration, 206-207

Kennedy administration: denying missile gap, 119; as Executive Committee member, 128; on forces needed to secure South Vietnam border, 142; lying about Cuba-for-Turkey missile trade, 132; ordering preparations for naval blockade of Cuba, 127; reaction to unauthorized support for Diem coup, 187; on Castro's perception of US Cuba policy, 134; on Soviet missiles as political problem, 130

on Reagan's deployment of Pershing II missiles in Europe, 294-295

unaccepted offer to debate war with antiwar protesters, 417

McNaughton, John, 211

Means employed *(jus in bello),* 335, 352-386

Medvedev, Dmitri, 426_n9

Memoirs 1925–1950 (Kennan), 31

Mencken, H.L., 484

Mendes-France, Pierre, 106

Mental illness: in Vietnam veterans, 376-377

INDEX

Meshad, Shad, 372–373
Middle East: radicalization as Cold War outcome, 424-425
Military honor, 218, 218_n77
Military power: commodities of, 388; successful manpower advantage, 393
Miller, Arthur, 13
Milosevic, Slobodan, 347, 349, 409, 424, 461. 469
Missile gap, 118-119, 199. *See also* arms race
Mitchell, James McCormick, 21
Mitchell, Kate, 14, 15, 20, 21
Mitchell v. Forsyth, 18
Mitterand, Francois, 302
Mobutu, Joseph, 197-98
Moffit, Ronni, 100
Mondale, Walter, 290-291
Moorer, Thomas, 277
Morality and law, 102, 102_n57
Morris, Robert, 22
Morse, Wayne, 209, 236, 238, 205_n10
Moscow show trials, 6
Mossadegh, Mohamed, 93
Moynihan, Daniel Patrick, xxxiii, 9, 43, 103
Mundt, Karl, 43, 44
Munich, lesson of, 36, 449
Murillo, Marino, 327
Muskie, Edmund, 237, 403
My Lai massacre, 370, 380-381

N
Naftali, Timothy, 469, 472, 479
Nagl, John A., 454-456
Napalm, 40, 73, 74, 172
Nardone v. United States, 17
Nation building: failure of Communism as, 457; fiscal impact on US

economy, 458; as ideology, 462; in Iraq and Afghanistan, 453; "Marshall Plan-style proposals," 452; in South Korea, 452
National ideology: American Exceptionalism as, xx; definition, xxvi_n57; fallacies of, xx–xxii; how best served, 332
National Intelligence Estimate on Iraq, 443
National Liberation Committee (Vietnam), 83
National Salvation Committee (Lithuania), 313
National Security Act of 1947 (NSA): covert operations authorized by, 101; as enabling legislation for NSC Directive 10/2, 98; Fifth Function authorizing CIA intelligence actions only, 99; Iran-Contra funding violating, 309; unlawfulness of overthrow of another country's government, 99
National Security Council (U.S.), 58, 65, 85, 97, 99, 142, 229
NATO (North Atlantic Treaty Organization), 65, 294
Nazi regime: murders committed by, xiii
Ne Win (President of Burma), 391, 396
Negroponte, John, 277
Nelson, Deborah: providing inadvertent defense of veterans, 377; *The War Behind Me,* 377–380

519

Communists, 153-155, 155_n174; Buddhist uprising in Hue, 175-179; changes in peace agreement demanded by, 276; collapse of, 280-281; Communist murders of non-combatants, 223, 346, 348_n31; Congress cutting funding for combat operations, 279-280; military support recommended for South Vietnam, 214-215, 393-394; Ngo Dinh Diem as Prime Minister, 108-110; Nixon urging Thieu to boycott Paris peace talks, 233-234; non-Communist, American support for as of 1968, 235-236; resettlement of North Vietnamese before Communist consolidation in power in North, 107; Revolutionary Development Program, 221-222; seizure of Phouc Long province, 280

Vietnamese Communists: American praise for, ix-x

Vietnamization, 191, 245, 247, 259, 250, 256, 402

Vital Center Democrats, xiv, 28, 51

The Vital Center: The Politics of Freedom (Schlesinger), xiv_n32

Vo Bam, 111

Vo Nguyen Giap, 167, 393

Von Hoffman, Nicholas, xxxii, 33_n91

W

Wadleigh, Julian, 57_n190

The Wall Within (TV documentary), 368, 371-372

Wallace, Henry: changing attitudes toward, xii; Communist sympathies of, 46, 324_n23, 341n23; McGovern's admiration for, 269; newspaper attacks on, 47-48; third-party presidential campaign (1948), 46

The War Behind Me (Nelson), 377-381; blackwhite thinking in statistical analyses, 377-379; ideology masked as history, 380; as inadvertent defense of veterans, 377

War crimes: forced population expulsion under Potsdam Agreement as crime against humanity, 366-367; Iraq War atrocity allegations, 445_n52; military actions targeting cities as, 359. *See also* World War II, war crimes

War crimes industry (Vietnam era), 257-264; advanced by prominent figures, 353, Americans killed in action as war criminals, 376; *Conversations with Americans* (Lane), 257-259; current attitudes toward Vietnam veterans, 382-384; as dangerous to American liberalism, 407-408; documentation of war and, 367, 367_n57; exaggerated estimates of war crimes prevalence, 374-377; false claims in narratives, 371-374; flawed methodologies of veteran studies, 324-377; Kerry's statement on, 261-263, 353, 382, 408_n32; lack of evidence of widespread war crimes, 407-408; prominent figures never acting on war crimes beliefs 383-384; Lifton and, 257; *Long Time Passing* (MacPherson), 368-377; as means to an end, 385; narratives as ideology, 367-368; PTSD prevalence among veterans, 376-377; shortcomings of, 377–397; successful veterans, anecdotal recognition of, 370-371; US armed forces viewed as enemy by antiwar activists, 385, *The Wall Within* (TV documentary), 368, 371-372; *The War Behind Me* (Nelson), 377-381

War Powers Act (1974), 279

War Production Board, 6

Ward, Harry, 6

Warfare, modern: as dirty business, 102-103

Warnke, Paul, 292-293

Warsaw Pact countries, 311-312

Warshow, Robert, xxix-xxxiii

Watergate burglary, 20, 55, 129, 279

Wattenberg, Ben, 292

The Wave of the Future (Lindberg), 4300

We Were Soldiers Once, and

Young (film), xvi-xvii

Webb, James, 259

Weinberger, Casper, 299

Weisband, William, 57

Well-Meaning and Intelligent Men Paradigm: 475-479

West, Rebecca, 71

Westmoreland, William: inadequate responses to deteriorating situation in South Vietnam, 217; rejecting troop recommendations for Vietnam as politically unacceptable, 241_n57; troop requests for Vietnam, 221

Wheeler, Donald, 25

Wheeler, Earl: estimates of resources needed to win Vietnam War, 214; on Joint Chiefs' concerns about handling of war, 217-218; not contradicting McNamara's lies to Congress, 209

Where Men Win Glory (Krakauer), 218

White, Henry Dexter (Harry): Roosevelt ignoring espionage allegations, 10; as Soviet agent, 11, 25, 27, 30, 42, 91, 268-269

Whiting, Allen, 184

Wicker, Tom, 285, 415-416

Wiley, Alexander, 95

Willoughby, Charles, 70

Wills, Gary, viii, 131, 133

Winchell, Walter, 9

Wiretapping: of *Amerasia* offices, 14; Executive Orders permitting warrantless

eavesdropping, 17-18, 18_n25; foreign intelligence exception, 18-19; Johnson administration, 234; Kennedy administration, 129; outlawed by Communications Act of 1934, 17; Roosevelt administration, 17; Truman administration, 14, 18, 19-20
Wise Men: Johnson advisory group, 222-223, 227; Truman advisory group, 80, 88, 177, 449
Wood, Gordon S., 449-450
Woodward, Bob, 447
Woodward, C. Vann, 437
World Trade Center bombing (1993), 425
World War II
  as Bad War, 354-367
  casualties, 344-345, 362, 362_n36
  film depictions, x
  as Good War, 354
  Hitler's "Final Solution" as genocide, 347
  lesson of Munich and Truman Doctrine, 36-37
  Soviet penetration of U.S. government, 7-11, 8_n31, 10_n41
  war crimes, American: civilian casualties of incendiary bombings, 359; civilian casualties of military actions, 362; murder of German POWs, 359-360; mutilation of enemy dead, 361-362; slaughter of Japanese survivors of sunken

vessels, 361; terror bombing of cities, 356-359
  war crimes, Soviet: atrocities in Yugoslavia, 364; rape victims of Red Army, 363-364; terror and mass murder in Poland, 364; treatment of ethnic Germans in Soviet zones, 366-367; treatment of refugees forcibly returned by Allies to Soviets, 364-366
  Yalta Conference and POW exchange, 364-366

Y
Yalta Conference (1945), 364
Yalu River, 69, 391
Yasukuni Shrine, 376, 376n77
Yeltsin, Boris, 314-315
Young, Kenneth, 322-323
Yugoslavia, xii, 40, 60, 337, 347, 364, 444, 456

Z
Zackaria, Fareed, 476
Zelensky, Volodymyr, 469
Zho Chenghu, 423
Zhou Enlai, 69, 106, 421
Ziegler, Ron, 242
Zinoviev, Grigory, 3
Zweibon v. Mitchell, 17_n21, n22, 18_n24, 25